THE BOOK OF TOFU

THE BOOK OF
TOFU

PROTEIN SOURCE OF THE FUTURE...NOW!

VOLUME I

WILLIAM SHURTLEFF & AKIKO AOYAGI

Illustrated by Akiko Aoyagi

Ten Speed Press
A Soyfoods Center Book

BY THE SAME AUTHORS

Tofu & Soymilk Production (Soyfoods Center)
The Book of Miso (Ten Speed Press; Ballantine Books)
Miso Production (Soyfoods Center)
The Book of Tempeh (Harper & Row)
Tempeh Production (Soyfoods Center)
Soyfoods Industry and Market: Directory & Databook (Soyfoods Center)
History of Soybeans and Soyfoods (Soyfoods Center)
The Book of Kudzu (Soyfoods Center)

Cover Illustration: A traditional tofu shop based on Kyoto's Yuba Han, by Akiko Aoyagi.

TEN SPEED PRESS
P.O. Box 7123
Berkeley, California 94707

You may order single copies prepaid direct from the publisher for $11.95 (paperbound) or $16.95 (clothbound) plus $1.00 for postage and handling (California residents add 6% state sales tax; Bay Area residents add 6½%).

Library of Congress Catalog Number: 83-070113
ISBN: 0-89815-095-7 (paperbound)
       0-89815-096-5 (clothbound)

Book Design and Typography by Beverly Stiskin

Printed in the United States of America

10   9   8   7   6   5   4   3   2   1

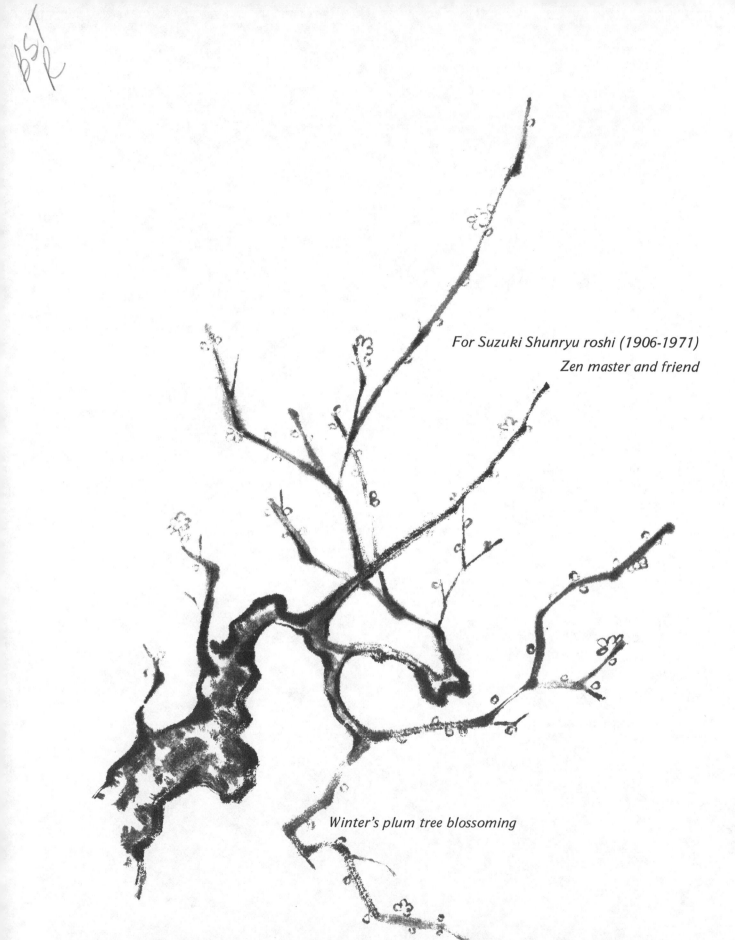

For Suzuki Shunryu roshi (1906-1971)
Zen master and friend

Winter's plum tree blossoming

gaté gaté pāragaté parasamgaté bodhi svāhā

Contents

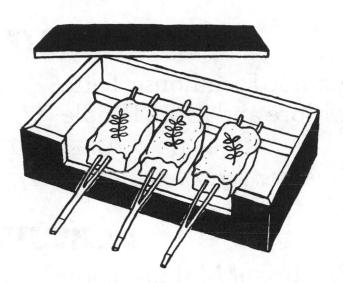

PART III

Japanese Farmhouse Tofu: Making Tofu for More and More People

PART IV

The Practice of Making Tofu: The Traditional Tofu Shop

Preface

AFTER RETURNING to America from my first visit to Japan, a summer practicing Zen meditation, I had the good fortune to meet Shunryu Suzuki *roshi*, head abbot of the Tassajara Zen Mountain Center. Moved by his example, I joined the Tassajara community, nestled in the wild beauty of the Santa Lucia mountains near Big Sur, California. Working as a cook in the Center's fine kitchens, I grew to appreciate the value of our natural food diet and soon came to feel that the utterly simple way of life and practice that this man brought to the West was the most wonderful gift I had ever received.

After two and a half years at Tassajara, I spoke to Suzuki roshi about returning to Japan to continue practicing meditation, study the culture and language from which his teaching emerged, and learn more of the art of Buddhist vegetarian cookery. He encouraged me in my desire to help bring more of the East to the West, and I soon found myself a penniless student in Kyoto. It was thus out of necessity that I first made tofu—also known in the West as soybean curd—a part of my daily diet, grateful that it was both nutritious and inexpensive.

Akiko and I met not long thereafter and quickly found that we shared an interest in the traditional life-styles and arts of the Far East. She was working as a designer and was also a good cook. Knowing that I was intrigued by tofu, she prepared me many of her favorite recipes using each of Japan's seven different types of tofu. One evening, through a mutual friend who considers himself a tofu connoisseur, we received our first introduction to the world of tofu haute cuisine at one of Japan's oldest and most re-nowned tofu restaurants. The dinner was composed of twelve small dishes, each artistically presented and each featuring tofu in one of its many forms. Here, indeed, was tofu like we had never tasted it before: that evening *The Book of Tofu* was born.

We soon began to explore the realm of tofu cookery in earnest. Each morning we walked to our neighborhood tofu shop—one of the 38,000 scattered throughout Japan—and bought our supply for the day, always freshly prepared. I had never imagined that tofu could be coaxed into such a range of forms and textures, nor that it could combine harmoniously with so many different foods and flavors. Our low-calorie meals grew richer in protein and more deliciously varied, while our food bill remained as low as ever.

At first our repertoire was largely Japanese. We began to visit tofu restaurants throughout Japan, enjoying what seemed like an endless variety of tofu dishes served in elegant but simple settings: next to a garden in autumn colors, by a pond with its symphony of cicadas, or in a quiet temple overlooking a garden of white sand raked into wavelike eddies. Whenever possible, we met with the head cook at these restaurants and stood at his elbow watching, taking notes, trying to absorb the subtleties of his art as he prepared each of his specialties. Later, we tried each of these recipes at home—sometimes over and over again—until we were satisfied with the results. We then grew bolder and began experimenting with tofu in traditional Western-style dishes. Akiko's creative touch yielded delicious tofu dips and puréed dressings, egg dishes and casseroles, salads and soups, barbequed tofu, and deep-fried tofu burgers.

As word of our special interest spread throughout the neighborhood, the master of our local tofu shop invited us to visit him early one morning to watch the tofu-making process first hand. We were deeply impressed with the feeling of alertness and care in his work. His movements were precise and graceful, joined in an effortless rhythm that, at times, flowed like a dance. A true master, he held in highest esteem the traditional, natural way and the spirit of fine craftsmanship. Working in an attractive, compact shop attached to his home, he used only natural ingredients to prepare the tofu he sold from his shop window and throughout the neighborhood. Like the traditional swordmaker or potter, his daily life was a practice, a spiritual path or, as the Japanese say, a Way. It was obvious that his work was more than a means of economic livelihood. For him, the joy of fine craftsmanship was its own fulfillment and reward.

I returned again and again to watch this master at work. Finally I asked to become his disciple and apprentice. Over a period of more than a year, he gradually taught me the techniques of making tofu in the traditional way.

This man urged us to record the methodology and, if possible, the spirit of his art both for Westerners seeking meaningful work and for future generations of Japanese who might someday wish to rediscover the rewards of fine craftsmanship presently obscured by modern industrial values and the "economic miracle." Throughout my apprenticeship, Akiko and I were encouraged to scour Japan to seek out every traditional tofu master we could find. To do so, we spent the warm months travelling up and down the islands, carrying backpacks and the tools necessary for our study. Often spending the night in temples, we met many Zen masters and practiced meditation with their students. And on many mornings, under a sky full of stars, Akiko and I wound our way to the one lighted shop on the sleeping streets of Japan's towns or cities to join a tofu master at his work.

Traditional tofu makers had often spoken to us with nostalgia and praise of the fine tofu once made in farmhouses throughout the country. To locate this legendary tofu and learn the secrets of its preparation, we backpacked early one spring into the remotest parts of Japan. We learned the traditional art from grandmothers in the mountainous back country while, to our surprise, the members of Banyan Ashram—a farming and meditation community on tiny Suwanose Island—taught us a remarkably simple way of making tofu unknown to even the more professional craftsmen with whom we studied.

As we continued our work, several simple facts came together to broaden our prespective. The writings of nutritionists, ecologists, and experts studying world food and population problems convinced us that a meat-centered diet makes very inefficient use of the earth's ability to provide mankind with protein. It soon seemed to us imperative that the West learn to use soybeans directly as a source of inexpensive, high-quality protein, as people in East Asia have been doing for thousands of years. Here, where density of population has long posed serious problems, tofu is the most important and most popular way of transforming soybeans into a delicious food. Yet how unfortunate it seemed that there were fewer tofu shops in the combined countries and continents of India, Africa, South America, Russia, Canada, Europe, and America, than within the space of one-half square mile in Tokyo, Taipei, Seoul, or Peking.

We also came to feel that the tofu shop, requiring a minimum of energy resources, technology, and capital, could serve as a model for decentralized home or cottage industries throughout many parts of the developing and developed worlds. With this thought in mind, we took to studying shops in Japan and Taiwan which, we felt, combined the best of both traditional and modern techniques, making possible the large-scale production of good-quality tofu at relatively low cost. We also visited Japan's largest and most modern tofu factories to study their production-line methods in detail.

Traditional tofu masters have a saying that there are two things they will not show another person: how to make babies and how to make tofu. But to our continual surprise, these men invited us in—sometimes hesitatingly at first—to observe them at work and ultimately opened their hearts and homes to us in a way that was a continual source of inspiration to our research. We returned again and again to our favorite shops, each time with new questions, each time able to understand things we had not noticed or grasped before. Perceiving the sincerity of our intention to transmit the fundamentals of their craft to the West, they ended up sharing secrets with us that they would never have dreamed of revealing to their compatriots. We only hope that our efforts here do justice to their kindness, and to the care and patience they showed us in making sure that we *really* understood.

A rhythm emerged between our research in the field, writing, art work, and daily meditation which nurtured our growing book. Over a period of almost three years, we prepared and enjoyed more than 1,200 tofu dishes. This book contains only the 500 recipes which seem to us best suited to Western tastes. Each recipe uses only natural foods and none requires the inclusion of meat.

As our work neared its completion, both Akiko and I realized that perhaps our finest teacher had been tofu itself. Like water that flows through the worlds, serving as it moves along, tofu joyfully surrenders itself to the endless play of transformation. Pierced with a skewer, it sizzles and broils above a bed of live coals; placed in a bubbling, earthenware pot over an open fire, it settles down next to the mushrooms and makes friends; deep-fried in crackling oil, it emerges crisp and handsome in robes of golden brown; frozen all night in the snow under vast mountain skies, it emerges glistening with frost and utterly changed. All as if it knew there was no death to die, no fixed or separate self to cling to, no other home than here.

A true democrat in spirit, tofu presents the same face to rich and poor alike. Placed before nobility in East Asia's finest haute cuisine, it is humble and unpretentious. Served up as peasant fare in rustic farmhouses, it is equally at home. Though unassertive, it is indispensable in the diet of more than 900 million people. Holding to simplicity, it remains in harmony with all things, and people never tire of its presence. Through understatement and nuance, it reveals its finest qualities.

Since earliest times, the people of East Asia have honored tofu in poem and proverb. Known as "meat of the fields" and "meat without a bone," tofu has provided them with abundant sustenance. In yielding and offering itself up, it seems to find its perfect balance in the greater dance. In the coming decades and centuries, tofu could nurture people around the world. To this end, we wish to send it on its way in the four directions.

Tokyo, Japan
March 1975

Acknowledgments

WE WOULD like to thank the following people for their help in making this book: Mr. Toshio Arai, who gave us hundreds of hours of his time, taught us the traditional art and practice of making tofu, and prepared the tofu we ate and enjoyed each day; Mr. Shinji Morii, master of Morika, one of Japan's oldest and most famous tofu shops; Mr. Koryu Abe, Japan's foremost tofu historian; Mr. Hiroyoshi Masuda and his father, masters of one of Kamakura's finest traditional tofu shops; Ms. Kisa Asano and Mr. Mankichi Nagai, head craftspeople at two of Kyoto's oldest and finest yuba shops; Mr. Kiyoichi Oya, vice president of the Japanese National Tofu Union and president of the Tokyo Tofu Union; Mr. Tokuji Watanabe, director of the National Food Research Institute in Tokyo and one of the world's foremost authorities on tofu; Mr. Takichi Okumura, owner of Tokyo's renowned Sasa-no-yuki restaurant, and his head chefs, Mr. Sugita and Mr. Fushimi; Mr. Shigemitsu Tsuji, master and chief chef at Kyoto's Nakamura-ro restaurant, famous throughout Japan as a lecturer and writer on Japanese cuisine and tofu, and author of a recent book on tofu cookery; Mr. Toshio Yanaihara, author of many works on tofu and head of a large Japanese cooking school; Messrs. Scott Sawyers, Lloyd Reid, and Jack Yamashita of the American Soybean Association in Japan; Dr. Harry W. Miller, the West's foremost authority on soymilk and pioneer in the field of using soybeans as foods; Mr. Teisuke Yabuki, president of the Luppy Soymilk Company; Mmes. Ito Kidoguchi, Kazuko Ozawa, and Minoru Watanabe, all in their seventies, who first taught us how to make farmhouse tofu; the members of Banyan Ashram who taught us how to make tofu solidified with sea water and introduced us to the riches of their simple way of life; Mr. Kyo Ko, owner of Fukyo-dofu, Tokyo's largest manufacturer of Chinese-style tofu; Mr. Tadashi Honma, director of research for Japan's largest manufacturer of dried-frozen tofu; Messrs. Itaro Hayashi, Ei Tamura, Daisaburo Noma and Kinjiro Sugai, each masters of fine traditional tofu shops at which we studied; Messrs. Shotaro Yoshikawa and Minoru Narahara, two leaders of Japan's movement to return to the use of natural nigari solidifier; Mr. Kiyoshi Takato, manager of one of Japan's largest and most modern tofu factories; and tofu makers throughout Taiwan, Korea, and America who gave generously of their time and experience.

Finally, we would like to give special thanks to our parents for their aid and encouragement, to Mr. Tyler Smith for his editorial suggestions, and to our publisher, Nahum Stiskin, whose faith and support were with us from the first conception of this book until its completion.

PART I

Tofu:
Food for Mankind

Protein East and West

1

FOR OVER TWO millenia in China and 1,000 years in Japan, soybeans have served as one of the most important sources of protein. In countries such as these, where people have long had to live with the problem of overpopulation, soybeans have been prized for their remarkable ability to produce over 33 percent more protein from an acre of land than any other known crop and *twenty* times as much usable protein as could be raised on an acre given over to grazing beef cattle or growing their fodder (fig. 1). It is thus easy to understand why meat protein is a great deal more expensive than soy protein and why, as population pressure on the land increases, it seems inevitable that more and more farmers all over the world will be planting soybeans. Their "protein efficiency" is the first and, perhaps, primary reason why soybean foods have played such a key role in the daily diet of the people of East Asia.

Not only is the protein yield of soybeans high in terms of quantity—soybeans contain about 35 percent protein, more than any other unprocessed plant or animal food—it is also excellent in terms of quality. Soy protein includes all of the eight essential amino acids in a configuration readily usable by the human body. It is now becoming common knowledge that there is no essential difference between plant and animal proteins. From the body's point of view, the amount of usable protein contained in ½ cup of soybeans is no different from that contained in 5 ounces of steak. And inexpensive soybean foods contain no cholesterol, almost none of the relatively indigestible saturated fats found in most animal foods, and an extremely low ratio of calories to protein. These basic facts, now scientifically well documented, have been understood intuitively throughout East Asia since earliest times.

But just as Westerners prefer to transform whole kernels of wheat into breads, pasta, and other foods made from flour, so have the people of East Asia preferred to transform whole soybeans into other forms. Since long before the Christian era, men and women throughout Asia have participated in a

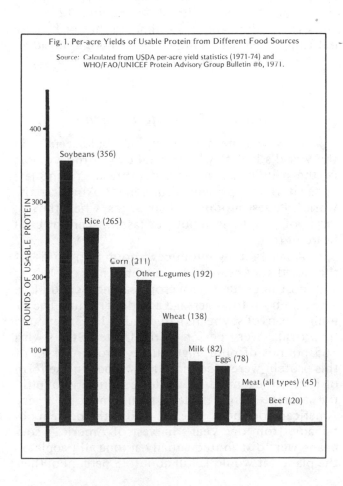

Fig. 1. Per-acre Yields of Usable Protein from Different Food Sources

Source: Calculated from USDA per-acre yield statistics (1971-74) and WHO/FAO/UNICEF Protein Advisory Group Bulletin #6, 1971.

POUNDS OF USABLE PROTEIN

400

300

200

100

Soybeans (356)
Rice (265)
Corn (211)
Other Legumes (192)
Wheat (138)
Milk (82)
Eggs (78)
Meat (all types) (45)
Beef (20)

15

vast experiment to find simple yet effective ways of creating soybean foods that are versatile, easily digestible, and, above all, delicious. Centuries of creative endeavor have yielded three great products which now serve as the cornerstones of East Asian nutrition and cuisine: *tofu, miso* (fermented soybean paste), and *shoyu* (soy sauce). Whereas miso and shoyu are essentially high-protein seasonings, tofu is a food that can serve as the backbone of a diet in much the same way that meat and dairy products are now used in the dietary pattern of the West. The development of traditional technologies and methods for transforming soybeans directly into these foods may someday be regarded as one of East Asia's greatest contributions to mankind, and a major step in the direct utilization by man of the earth's bounty of protein.

Today, throughout much of Asia, tofu is by far the most important way of using soybeans as a daily food. Indeed tofu is as much a part of Oriental culture, language, and cookery as is bread in the West. In America, a country with twice the population of Japan, there are 19,000 bakeries and the average annual consumption of bread is 73 loaves per person. The tofu made in Japan's 38,000 tofu shops provides the average Japanese with about seventy 12-ounce cakes each year. And it is estimated that in Taiwan and China, the per capita consumption is considerably higher than it is in Japan.

America's Soy Protein Tragedy

Now imagine how strange it would seem if, in the world's largest wheat producing country, most of the people had never tasted bread. Yet no less unusual is the present situation in America, the world's largest producer of soybeans, where the majority of people have not yet tasted, seen, or even heard of tofu.

America now produces about two-thirds of the world's soybeans. They are presently our largest and most important farm crop, leading second-place wheat in both total acreage and dollar value. The 47 million tons of soybeans harvested in 1973 is enough to provide every person in the United States with 165 pounds of pure, high-quality protein. If all of this protein were used directly as food—in the form of tofu, for example—it would be sufficient to fulfill the average adult protein requirement of every American for about 3 years! And if the protein obtainable from one year's harvest of America's soybeans were distributed equally among all people on the planet, it would fulfill about 25 percent of their

yearly protein requirements, according to even the most conservative Western standards.

But the tragedy of our present situation is that less than 15 percent of America's non-exported soy protein ever reaches human beings: 1½ percent directly in soybean foods and about 13 percent indirectly in the form of meat and dairy products.

What happens to all the rest? To understand the answer to this question we must first recognize that, while in East Asia soybeans have traditionally been used to make tofu and other soybean foods, in the West they have been viewed primarily as an oilseed. Almost all of America's non-exported soybeans are shipped to huge modern factories where their oil is extracted in a continuous, automated process. The largest and most important piece of machinery employed is a counter-current hexane solvent extractor, capable of handling over 4 million pounds of soybeans per day. Soy oil, which contains no protein, is degummed, refined, bleached, deodorized, and winterized by industro-chemical processes and then sold as cooking or salad oil. Some of the oil is hydrogenated to produce margarine and vegetable shortenings. The defatted soybean meal, a byproduct of the oil extraction process, contains about 2½ times as much protein by weight as steak.

Now, *where* does this protein go? In America, about 95 percent of all non-exported soy protein ends up as feed for livestock, and of this, 77 to 95 percent is irretrievably lost in the process of animal metabolism. In addition, we feed livestock 78 percent of all our grain, most of which could be used directly as food. American farmers use more of their soybeans and grain as fodder than farmers in any other country. These losses, creating the appearance of scarcity in the midst of actual plenty, are a direct result of our failure to understand and make use of the soybean's great potential as a food. For if the total protein available from these crops were utilized directly by human beings, it could make up an estimated 90 percent of the world's protein deficiency.

The process described above, inherent in the Western meat-centered diet, is the cause of our immense protein waste. In *Diet for a Small Planet*, Frances Moore Lappé shows how we use the cow as a protein factory in reverse: we feed it from 14 to 21 pounds of protein from sources that could be used directly as food, and we obtain only 1 pound of protein from the meat. In this highly inefficient process, only 5 to 7 percent of the total protein consumed by a feedlot steer or cow is returned for human consumption as meat. Likewise only 12 percent is returned by a hog as pork, 15 percent by a chicken as meat and 22 percent as eggs, and 23 percent by a cow as milk. In her appeal for a more rational use of the earth's bounty, Ms. Lappé urges Westerners to get off the "top" of the food chain and begin to utilize sources of high-quality, non-meat protein.

Although Americans make up only 6 percent of the world's population, they account for 30 percent of its total meat consumption. The per capita American consumption of beef, pork, and poultry presently runs about 254 pounds per year, or 316 grams per day. This is about 5 times the world average and 15 times the average intake for people in East Asia. In order to produce this much meat, American farmers plant an astounding 50 percent of their total acreage in feed crops, and U.S. livestock are fed 120 million tons of feed-grains each year. Consequently, the average American now consumes the equivalent of 2,000 pounds of grain and soybeans annually, roughly 90 percent of which is in the form of meat, poultry, and eggs. But in developing countries—where most grains and soybeans are used directly as food—the average person consumes only about 400 pounds of grain per year. Hence the birth of one meat-eating American has the same effect on world food resources as the birth of *five* children in India, Africa, or South America. On the other hand, a reduction in American meat consumption of only 10 percent could free 12 million tons of soybeans, corn, wheat, and other grains, enough to meet the annual grain requirements of 60 million people in less developed countries.

Worldwide Protein Crisis

It is now generally conceded that the world is facing a serious food crisis. More precisely, it is a protein crisis, and not one that is likely to go away or even become less critical during the coming decades. We have watched regional famines spread and become more frequent, and experts are no longer as optimistic as they once were about the "green revolution," with its climatically sensitive "miracle" seeds, its petroleum-based chemical fertilizers and toxic pesticides which steadily deplete the soil, and its heavy dependence on expensive and complex Western technology.

It is now estimated that more than one-fourth of the world's four billion people (including 450 million children equalling more than twice the population of the United States!) confront hunger or famine during at least some part of each year. In developing countries, according to United Nations statistics, 25 percent to 30 percent of all children never see their fourth birthday, largely due to malnutrition.

And many who do survive are permanently damaged physically and mentally because of the lack of sufficient protein in their diet. These facts so boggle the mind that most of us are simply unable or unwilling to face them. But this crucial problem of our age *must* be faced and understood *now*, for each of us can begin *today* to contribute directly to its solution.

The food crisis is continually aggravated by two basic trends that all experts agree must be reversed as rapidly as possible. The first trend, understood since the time of Malthus, is that linear increases in food production fall farther and farther behind exponential increases in population. In the less developed countries, the amount of food available to each person is steadily decreasing. With the world's population doubling every 35 years and expanding onto what is now farmland, and with most of the earth's good-quality land already under intensive cultivation, the cost of farming previously unused land on mountain sides or in deserts and jungles grows increasingly expensive. And hungry people are the least able to pay these costs.

The second trend, which is just now beginning to be recognized, concerns the relationship between affluence and the consumption of basic foods. As people develop a higher standard of living, they generally desire a larger proportion of meat and other animal protein in their diet (fig. 2). During the past 12 years, cattle herds have increased 30 percent in the United States and 28 percent throughout the rest of the world. During the same period per-capita livestock meat consumption has increased 22 percent in the United States, 26 percent in France and Canada, 30 percent in Russia, 33 percent in West Germany, 94 percent in Italy, and an astonishing 364 percent in Japan. (Japan, however, still has the lowest annual per capita meat consumption of any of the above countries; its 51 pounds per year is only 20 percent of top-ranking America's 254 pounds.) Since more than 14 pounds of fodder protein are needed to produce 1 pound of protein from beef, a small increase in demand for meat leads to enormous increases in the indirect consumption of soy and grain proteins. This results in a sharp decrease in the amounts of these foods available for human consumption, especially in poorer countries. In addition, rising demand for soybean and grain fodders pushes up their prices, creating a vicious cycle that further aggravates the shortages in poorer countries.

To reverse the first trend, every effort must be made to reduce population growth and raise agricultural productivity by increasing per-acre yields, bringing more land under cultivation, and using this

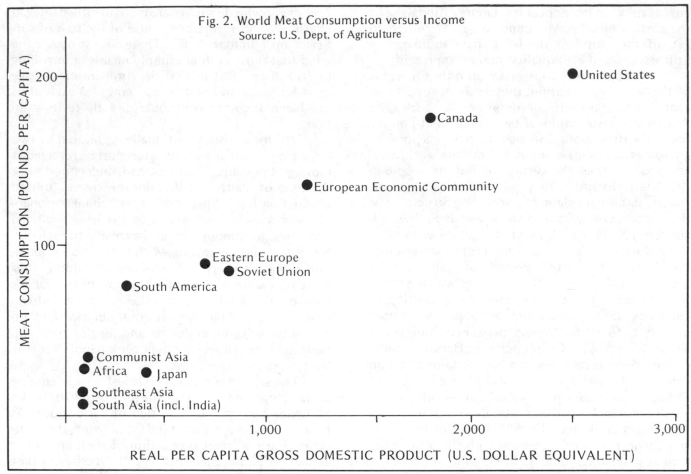

Fig. 2. World Meat Consumption versus Income
Source: U.S. Dept. of Agriculture

land for essential high-protein food crops (rather than cash crops such as coffee, tobacco, cocoa, and tea, which have little or no nutritional value). One hope for the coming decades is that developing countries with suitable topography and climate will follow the lead of Brazil in realizing the tremendous economic and nutritional potential of soybeans. From a mere 650,000 tons in 1968, Brazil's soybean production soared to 10.5 million tons in 1974, a *sixteenfold* increase in only 6 years. Having recently surpassed China to become the world's second largest soybean producer, Brazil is now working to boost production to 15 million tons by 1980 and hopes eventually to overtake first-place America. With exports totaling almost 1 billion dollars annually, soybeans have now surpassed coffee as Brazil's chief export crop, and the government is actively encouraging farmers to turn their coffee plantations into soybean farms.

(At the same time, however, industrialized nations are now becoming increasingly aware of the limits and dangers of conventional agricultural methods to create an ever-expanding food supply. Intensive use of pesticides and chemical fertilizers, the two main factors responsible for the great postwar

jump in agricultural output, and attempts to clear more and more land for agricultural use are beginning to place such heavy stresses on the planet's basic ecosystems that they could easily create environmental problems of a greater magnitude than the food problems they are now intended to solve.)

While most Westerners—and particularly those not involved in agriculture—can participate directly in the reversal of the first trend only through family planning, every Westerner can participate in a very vital and immediate way to reverse the second trend, and thereby actively help to relieve the suffering that afflicts millions of our fellow human beings around the world. We can and must make more efficient use of the food presently available on the planet. And we must understand clearly the fact, often overlooked in discussing world food shortages, that there is presently more than enough food and protein for all the people in the world. The extremely complex problem of distributing this food in a just and compassionate way, avoiding large-scale misuse of its great nutritional potential, demands our fullest attention. Not the earth's natural limitations but the wisdom with which we use the earth's bounty will determine whether or not there is sufficient food for all human beings during the coming decades.

Most experts agree that to make fullest use of the protein we now have, the citizens of the world's affluent, industrialized nations will have to make basic changes in their eating habits. Most important, they will have to start eating less meat—especially beef. All of man's food comes initially from plant sources and, in fact, 70 percent of the world's protein is still consumed directly from plants. By rediscovering the wisdom inherent in traditional dietary patterns that make use of non-meat protein sources, we can free millions of tons of high-quality soy and grain protein to be used directly as food. (Since, according to various government estimates, the average American now receives from 12 to 45 percent more protein than his body can even use, Americans can perhaps most easily reduce their consumption of expensive protein foods.) In a world where the affluent nations appear to many as islands of plenty in a sea of hunger, each of us must make a personal effort to rectify this dangerous imbalance. We can begin by working to make best use of our ample protein supplies.

Hopefully, more and more people, recognizing that a meat-centered diet squanders the earth's food resources, will turn to nutritionally and ecologically viable alternatives—such as tofu. Many have already found that a meatless diet, low in saturated fats and cholesterol, makes sense in terms of good health, mental alertness, and a general feeling of physical well being. For many more people, the determining forces may well be primarily economic: skyrocketing meat prices. The basic inefficiencies of land use inherent in meat production have led food experts and economists to predict that in the coming decades, the prices of most meats could rise to the point where only the very rich could afford them. Yet whether we are moved by economic, ecological, religious or health considerations, or by a feeling of identification with the millions of hungry people around the world, each of us can help solve the world food problem by starting now to change the way we eat.

The Growing Importance of Soy Protein

One thing is virtually certain: Over the coming years, we can expect soy protein to play an increasingly important role in our daily lives. Although scientists continue to explore futuristic protein sources (such as cottonseeds, algae, petroleum, microbes, tree leaves, and synthetics), most experts now consider soybeans to be the most realistic and promising source of low-cost, high-quality protein available in large enough quantities to meet human needs on a worldwide scale. Hence, throughout the world, there is great interest in finding ways of using soybeans directly as a source of protein. In the United States, where 70 percent of all food protein presently comes from animal sources and only 30 percent from plants, major food research firms estimate that within 10 to 20 years these figures will be reversed. And the most rapid increase is, of course, seen in the use of soy protein. Whereas an estimated 150,000 tons of the latter were used in U.S. foods in 1972, it is predicted that more than *twelve* times this amount will be used by 1980.

Although these figures sound promising, an examination of their actual relevance to the world food crisis seems to suggest several problems. We must remember that the total amount of soy protein now used directly as food in the U.S. is still extremely small—only about 1½ percent of the total available from the domestic crop. Most of this protein is used in the form of plain or defatted soy flour (containing 40 to 52 percent protein), which is purchased primarily by the food industry and used in small amounts as a conditioner, extender, emulsifier, or moisture retainer in canned foods, baked goods, and processed meats. The presence of this soy additive is usually acknowledged only in small print on the label, and the word "soy" is often carefully omitted. Some soy flour is sent to developing countries in food supplements as part of America's worldwide nutritional aid program. Yet it is not expected that these ways of using soy protein will be of major importance during the coming decades.

Rather, experts in the food industry foresee the use of advanced Western technology to create a wide range of new, synthetic soybean foods. Many of these are already available: protein concentrates, isolates, spun proteins and, most important, textured vegetable proteins. The latter, extruded from defatted soybean meal (or whole soy flour) in highly sophisticated factories, are generally added as extenders to ground or processed meat products in order to lower their cost (and levels of saturated fats) while raising their protein content and improving their cooking qualities. Spun proteins, composed of tiny fibers or monofilaments of almost pure protein, are used to make imitation livestock products and meat analogs. By compressing the protein fibers to simulate the fibrous texture of meat, and adding the appropriate flavorings and colorings, food technologists are able to create imitation bacon, ham, sausages, beef, chicken, and a wide variety of new high-protein snacks. Many of these fabricated products are now available in Western supermakets. For relatively affluent Westerners, such foods can provide protein which is somewhat less expensive than that found in meat, while also helping to make more efficient use of domestic soy protein. Yet it is now clearly understood that the technology for producing these foods is far too complex and costly to be of use in developing countries where hunger is most acute. And to the growing number of Westerners interested in natural foods, these highly refined products are bound to be of limited appeal.

As a clear and practical alternative, we must turn our attention to traditional East Asian methods for transforming soybeans into foods; methods that recognize food to be man's most direct link with the nurturing earth and which bind season and soil, man and food into a holistic, organic cycle. Each of the seven basic types of tofu can be made in any Western kitchen, or in small, decentralized enterprises using technology on a human scale and employing a minimum of energy. The tofu shop can be adopted as easily in Bangladesh, Brazil, and Nigeria as in the industrialized or "post industrial" societies of the West.

In tofu shops now located throughout America, craftsmen have already begun making tofu available at reasonable prices. We believe these shops are situated at an historic crossroads, and that they can and will make an invaluable contribution to the betterment of life on our planet during the years ahead.

2
Tofu as a Food

NUTRITIONALLY, the various types of tofu—there are seven in Japan and even more in China—have much the same importance for the people of East Asia that dairy products, eggs, and meat have for us in the West. (In figures 3 and 4, tofu products are listed and illustrated in the approximate order of their availability in the U.S.) When looking for alternate sources of protein and when considering the benefits of a meatless way of eating, many people ask: "What will we use to replace meat?" Some experiment with eggs and dairy products, or with soybeans and grains. The traditional answer throughout East Asia has been tofu.

Before replacing all or part of the meat in our diet with less expensive protein from another source, most nutrition-conscious people will want to have enough sound, factual information to make this important decision with complete confidence. We feel that the following facts show tofu to be a truly remarkable food. And tofu's excellent nutritional record, extending over a period of thousands of years in China and Japan, gives practical substantiation to the findings of modern research.

Rich in High Quality Protein

The value of any food as a protein source depends on two factors: the *quantity* of protein in the food and the *quality* of that protein. Quantity is usually expressed as a simple percentage of total weight. By comparing the following figures, it can be seen that the highest percentages of protein are found in plant rather than animal foods:

Food	Percent Protein by Weight
Dried-frozen tofu	53
Yuba, dried	52
Soy flour (defatted)	51
Soy flour (natural)	40
Soybeans (whole, dry)	35
Cheeses	30
Fish	22
Chicken	21
Beef (steak)	20
Cottage cheese	20
Agé (Tofu Pouches)	19
Ganmo (Tofu Burgers)	15
Whole-wheat flour	13
Hamburger	13
Eggs	13
Doufu (Chinese-style Tofu)	11
Thick agé (Tofu Cutlets)	10
Tofu	8
Brown rice (uncooked)	6
Milk (whole)	3

(Source: *Standard Tables of Food Composition* [Japan] and *Diet For a Small Planet*)

Furthermore, we notice that dried-frozen tofu and *yuba* (a close relative of tofu) contain the highest percentages of protein found in any natural foods in existence. Moreover, the top five protein sources are all derived from soybeans. The data presented in figure 5 shows the percentages of protein and other nutrients in the various types of tofu now available

21

Fig. 3. Tofu Products Available in the West

Name Used in This Book	Other Names	Description	Where Sold*	How Sold
Tofu	Soybean Curd	Regular, Medium-firm Japanese-style tofu	N,J,C,S,T	12- to 21-ounce cakes water-packed in plastic tubs or cartons; also canned
Chinese-style Tofu	Doufu, Dow-foo, Bean Cake	Chinese-style firm tofu	N,J,C,S,T	Two or more 6-ounce cakes water-packed in plastic tubs
Silken Tofu	Kinugoshi, Soft, or Custard Tofu, Shui Dow-foo, Sui-doufu	Soft Japanese-style tofu	N,J,C,S,T	12- to 20-ounce cakes water-packed in plastic tubs or cartons
Deep-fried Tofu Cutlets	Thick Agé, Nama-agé, Atsu-agé, Raw-fried Tofu	Deep-fried tofu cakes	N,J,C,S,T	Cakes or slices of 5 ounces or less, dry-packed in plastic cartons or tubs; also sold in small triangles and cubes
Deep-fried Tofu Pouches or Puffs	Aburagé, Agé or Agé Puffs	A hollow pouch or puff of deep-fried tofu	N,J,C,S,T	Three ½- to 1-ounce pieces dry-packed in a a cellophane bag
Hollow Deep-fried Tofu Cubes	Hollow Agé Puffs, Dow-foo Bok, Yudoufu	Chinese-style, hollow 1½-inch cubes of deep-fried tofu	N,J,C,S,T	15 cubes, each ⅓ ounce, dry-packed in a cellophane bag
Soymilk	Dou-jiang, Tonyu, Soyalac	Regular or flavored with honey or carob	N,J,C,S,T	1-pint glass, paper, or plastic containers
Tofu Pudding	Fresh Soybean Pudding, Soft Tofu Curds	Soft curds of soymilk	N,J,C,S,T	1-pound portions in plastic tubs
Wine-fermented Tofu	Doufu-ru, Fuyu, Chinese Cheese, Bean Curd Cheese	Chinese-style soft cubes of fermented tofu in brining liquor	C	White varieties in 1-pint bottles; red varieties in small cans
Deep-fried Tofu Burgers	Ganmo, Ganmodoki	Deep-fried tofu patties or balls containing minced vegetables	J	3½-ounce patties or 2-ounce balls dry-packed in plastic bags; or canned
Grilled Tofu	Yaki-dofu	A cake of firm regular tofu which has been grilled or broiled	J	10-ounce cakes water-packed in plastic tubs; or canned
Dried-Frozen Tofu	Koya-dofu, Kori-dofu	Very lightweight cakes of tofu which have been frozen and then dried	J,S	Five to ten 1-ounce cakes in an airtight carton
Instant Powdered Tofu	Dehydrated Instant Tofu	Do-it-yourself, instant home-made tofu	J,S	A foil-wrapped package of powdered soymilk accompanied by a small package of solidifier
Okara	Soy Pulp, Tofu Lees, Unohana	Insoluble portions of the soybean remaining after filtering off soymilk	J,T	8- to 16-ounce portions in plastic bags, balls, or mounds
Dried Yuba	Bean Curd Sheets	A high-protein film made from soymilk	J,C	4- to 8-ounce portions in paper or cellophane bags
Soymilk Curds	Oboro	Unpressed soft curds of coagulated soymilk	T	Available directly from tofu shops by special order
Pressed Tofu	Doufu-kan, Dow-foo Gar	Chinese-style small cakes of very firmly pressed tofu	C	Three 4-ounce cakes sealed in a plastic pouch
Savory Pressed Tofu	Wu-hsiang Kan, Flavored Soybean Cake	Pressed tofu seasoned with soy sauce and spices	C	Three 4-ounce cakes sealed in a plastic pouch

*N Natural and health food stores   J Japanese food markets   C Chinese food markets
 S Supermarkets, especially co-op markets   T Available at most tofu shops by special request

Fig. 5. Tofu products available in the West

Tofu

Chinese-style Tofu
(Doufu)

Silken Tofu
(Kinugoshi)

Deep-fried Tofu Cutlets
(Thick Agè)

triangles

cubes

cakes

Deep-fried Tofu Pouches &Puffs
(Agè)

Hollow Deep-fried Tofu Cubes

Soymilk

Tofu Pudding

Wine-fermented Tofu
(Doufu-ru; white and red)

Deep-fried Tofu Burgers
(Ganmo; patties, balls,
and treasure balls)

Grilled Tofu

Dried-frozen Tofu

Instant Powdered Tofu

Okara

Dried Yuba

Soymilk Curds

Pressed Tofu

Savory Pressed Tofu

Fig. 5. Composition of Nutrients in 100 grams of Tofu

Sources: *Standard Tables of Food Composition* (Japan), *FAO Food Composition Tables*, and *USDA Composition of Foods* (Wash., D.C.)

Type of Tofu	Food Energy (Calories)	Moisture (Percent)	Protein (Percent)	Fat (Percent)	Sugars (Percent)	Fiber (Percent)	Ash (Percent)	Calcium (Mg)	Sodium (Mg)	Phosphorus (Mg)	Iron (Mg)	Vit. B_1 (Thiamine) (Mg)	Vit. B_2 (Riboflavin) (Mg)	Vit. B_3 (Niacin) (Mg)
Tofu	72	84.9	7.8	4.3	2.3	0	0.7	146	6	105	1.7	0.02	0.02	0.5
Chinese-Style Tofu (Doufu)	87	79.3	10.6	5.3	2.9	0	0.9	159	7	109	2.5	0.02	0.02	0.6
Silken Tofu (Kinugoshi)	53	88.4	5.5	3.2	1.7	0	1.2	94	23	71	1.2	0.02	0.02	0.3
Deep-fried Tofu Cutlets (Thick Agé)	105	79.0	10.1	7.0	2.8	0	1.1	240	15	150	2.6	0.02	0.02	0.5
Deep-fried Tofu Pouches (Agé)	346	44.0	18.6	31.4	4.5	0.1	1.4	300	20	230	4.2	0.02	0.02	0.5
Soymilk	42	90.8	3.6	2.0	2.9	0.02	0.5	15	2	49	1.2	0.03	0.02	0.5
Wine-fermented Tofu (Doufu-ru)	175	52.0	13.5	8.4	13.6	1.2	11.6	165	458	182	5.7	0.04	0.18	0.6
Deep-fried Tofu Burgers (Ganmo)	192	64.0	15.4	14.0	5.1	0.1	1.4	270	17	200	3.6	0.01	0.03	1.0
Grilled Tofu	82	83.0	8.8	5.1	2.1	0	1.0	180	15	120	1.9	0.02	0.02	0.4
Dried-Frozen Tofu	436	10.4	53.4	26.4	7.0	0.2	2.6	590	18	710	9.4	0.05	0.04	0.6
Okara	65	84.5	3.5	1.9	6.9	2.3	0.9	76	4	43	1.4	0.05	0.02	0.3
Dried Yuba	432	8.7	52.3	24.1	11.9	0	3.0	270	80	590	11.0	0.20	0.08	2.0
Pressed Tofu and Savory Pressed Tofu	182	61.6	22.0	11.0	6.0	0.1	1.9	377	16	270	4.4	0.05	0.05	0.6
Dry Soybeans	392	12.0	34.3	17.5	26.7	4.5	5.0	190	3	470	7.0	0.50	0.20	2.0
Defatted Soybean Meal	322	8.0	49.0	0.4	33.6	3.0	6.0	220	4	550	8.4	0.45	0.15	2.0
Kinako & Roasted Soybeans	426	5.0	38.4	19.2	29.5	2.9	5.0	190	4	500	9.0	0.40	0.15	2.0

Note: Regular Japanese tofu varies in protein content from 6 to 8.4, and in water content form 87.9 to 83.9 percent; the mineral data above refer to tofu (and kinugoshi) solidified with calcium sulfate. Kinugoshi and the rich soymilk prepared at tofu shops vary in protein from 4.9 to 6.3, and in water content for 89.7 to 87.4 percent. Commercially-distributed soymilk varies in protein from 3.6 to 5.8, and in water content from 90.8 to 88.2 percent. Thick agé prepared with nigari often contains up to 17.7 percent protein and only 58.7 percent water. Differences in composition depend primarily on the method of preparation, the type of solidifier, and the grade and protein content of the soybeans used.

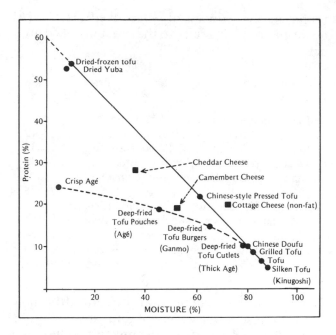

Fig. 6. Tofu Protein versus Moisture Content
*For Non-deep-fried Tofu:
 Protein (%) = 59.6 − .61 × Moisture (%)

Food	NPU (Percent)
Wheat germ	67
Beef and hamburger	67
Oatmeal	66
Tofu	65
Chicken	65
Soybeans and soy flour	61
Peanuts	43
Lentils	30

(Source: *Diet for a Small Planet*)

From the body's point of view, the protein in tofu is identical to the protein in chicken. Note that tofu has the fourth highest NPU of any plant food. It also has the highest NPU rating of all soybean products and all members of the protein-rich legume family. The soybean is the only legume which is a "complete protein," that is, one containing all of the eight essential amino acids. And the amino acid analysis of tofu is remarkably similar to that of most animal protein (including casein milk protein).

By combining the two sets of figures given above we can compare the true value of various protein sources. Regular tofu, for example, contains 7.8 percent protein, 65 percent of which is actually usable by the body. Thus, a typical 8-ounce (227 gram) serving of tofu can supply us with 227 x .65 x .078 or 11.5 grams of *usable* protein. This is a full 27 percent of the daily adult male protein requirement of 43.1 grams. The same amount of usable protein could be supplied by 3¼ ounces of steak (at a much higher cost) or 5½ ounces of hamburger.

in the West; figure 6 illustrates the relationship between protein and moisture content in the different types of tofu.

Protein quality refers to the percentage of protein in a food that can be utilized by the body; it is usually expressed in terms of NPU (Net Protein Utilization), "biological value," or "protein score." The NPU of a food depends largely on the food's digestibility and on the degree to which the configuration of the eight essential amino acids making up the protein matches the pattern required by the body.

It is a common misconception that the protein found in animal foods is somehow basically different from (and superior to) plant protein. In fact, there is no basic difference. It is simply a question of degree. The higher the NPU of any food, the more completely the body is able to utilize that food's protein. The following figures show that, although animal foods tend to have the highest NPU ratings, a number of plant foods—including tofu—rank quite high on the scale:

Food	NPU (Percent)
Eggs	94
Fish	80
Cottage cheese	75
Brown rice	70
Cheeses	70

High Protein Complementarity

Tofu is an excellent food to use in combining proteins since it contains an abundance of lysine, an essential amino acid that is deficient in many grain products. Most grains, on the other hand, are well endowed with the sulfur-containing amino acids methionine and cystine, the limiting amino acids in soybeans (fig. 7). Thus soy and grain proteins, having exactly the opposite strengths and weaknesses, complement each other. By serving foods such as tofu and whole-grain bread or rice at the same meal and combining them in the correct ratios, we are able, in effect, to "create" new protein at no extra cost. The NPU of the resultant combination is considerably higher than that of either of the individual foods and, therefore, the total usable protein is much greater than if the foods were served at separate meals. Applying this principle of protein complementarity in planning our daily meals allows us

Fig. 7. Amounts of Essential Amino Acids and their Percentages with Minimum Daily Requirements in 100 gram portion of Tofu (Source: Japanese Scientific Research Council)

Amino Acids	MDR (gm)	Tofu (gm)	MDR (%)
(Methionine-Cystine)	1.10	0.20	17
Tryptophan	0.25	0.12	47
Methionine	0.20	0.10	52
Leucine	1.10	0.59	52
Valine	0.80	0.43	53
Isoleucine	0.70	0.41	59
(Phenylalanine-tyrosine)	1.10	0.75	67
Lysine	0.80	0.57	71
Threonine	0.50	0.37	72
Phenylalanine	0.30	0.48	160
Protein, usable (gm)	43.10	5.06	12

Note: Amino acids in shortest supply are listed first. Those in parentheses are important combinations of essential and non-essential amino acids with common properties. Thus 100 grams of regular Japanese tofu (7.8% protein) contains 0.20 grams of the sulfur-containing amino acids (methionine-cystine), or 17 percent of the minimum adult daily requirement of 1.10 grams.

to make fullest use of the earth's abundant protein supplies. For example, by serving only 3½ ounces of tofu together with 1¼ cups brown rice, we obtain 32 percent more protein than if we served these foods separately. Thus, tofu's unique amino-acid composition makes it not only a basic protein *source*, but also a truly remarkable protein *booster*. As the figures below show, the use of even small amounts of tofu combined with grains and other basic foods (in the ratios indicated) can produce large increases in usable protein. Herein lies the key to tofu's value as an essential daily accompaniment to the grain-centered diet, the way of eating characteristic of virtually all traditional societies since earliest times. Furthermore, the use of whole grains together with soy products creates a "protein-sparing effect": the body uses the grain carbohydrates as its source of fuel or energy and allows the protein to fulfill its basic function of tissue growth and repair.

Each of the following combinations provides exactly 50 percent of the daily adult male requirement of usable protein, or the equivalent of that found in 4½ ounces of (uncooked) steak. (All quantities of grains refer to the raw, uncooked product.)

Combination	Percent Increase
1 cup whole-wheat flour, 1½ tablespoons sesame butter, 3 ounces tofu	42
1 cup whole-wheat flour, 4½ ounces tofu	32
1¼ cups brown rice, 3½ ounces tofu	32
3 tablespoons each peanut and sesame butter, 4 ounces tofu	25
3/8 cup each whole-wheat flour and brown rice, 1¼ tablespoons peanut butter, 6¾ ounces tofu	24
¾ cup cornmeal, 1 cup milk, 5 ounces tofu	13

(Adapted from: *Diet for a Small Planet*)

The protein-rich combinations of tofu with whole-wheat flour suggest a variety of tofu (and nut butter) sandwiches or deep-fried tofu burgers, noodle or bulgur wheat dishes, and even *chapati, taco,* or pizza preparations. The traditional East Asian combination has, of course, been with rice.

Easy to Digest

While many high-protein foods, such as meats, dairy products, and beans, are quite difficult for some people to digest, tofu, prepared by a process that carefully removes the crude fiber and water-soluble carbohydrates from soybeans, is soft and highly digestible. Indeed, with a digestion rate of 95 percent, it is by far the most digestible of all natural soybean foods, and is much more digestible than cooked whole soybeans (68%). Thus, tofu can be an excellent food for babies, elderly adults, and people with digestive problems. The Chinese say that sages, yogis, and monks, who rely for sustenance on nothing but the mists of heaven and the fresh morning dew, are particularly fond of tofu as their third choice.

An Ideal Diet Food

Tofu is also the ideal diet food. A typical 8-ounce serving contains only 147 calories. An equal weight of eggs contains about 3 times as many calories, and an equal weight of beef about 4 to 5 times as many. Perhaps more important, next to mung- and soybean sprouts, tofu has the lowest ratio of calories to protein found in any known plant food. One gram of total protein costs you only 9 calories, and 1 gram of usable protein only 12 calories. The only animal foods which have a lower ratio are some types of fish and seafoods. Because of its low carbohydrate content, tofu is widely recommended for starch-restricted diets by doctors throughout East Asia. While providing 27 percent of your daily protein requirements, an 8-ounce serving of tofu costs you only 5 grams of carbohydrate and less than 7½ percent of the recommended daily adult requirement of 2,200 calories.

Low in Saturated Fats and Cholesterol

Tofu is unique among high protein foods in being low in calories and saturated fats and entirely free of cholesterol. And in this fact may be its greatest potential importance as a key to good health and long life. There is now a near consensus among doctors on the contributive role of animal fats and cholesterol to heart disease, the number-one health problem in the United States. It is well known that most doctors recommend a reduction in the consumption of animal foods as the first step in the treatment of heart disease, high blood pressure, arteriosclerosis, and atherosclerosis. Yet the standard American diet contains one of the world's highest proportions of saturated fats and cholesterol, since Americans presently obtain about 70 percent of all their protein from animal foods. And many low-carbohydrate reducing diets, because they depend on a large intake of meat, eggs, dairy products, and fish, result in an even larger intake of saturated fats and cholesterol. (The latter, present in all animal foods, is never found in tofu or other plant foods.) Moreover, the problem is becoming increasingly more serious as the proportion of saturated fats in the diet continues to rise: during the past 20 years, per capita American consumption of beef has more than doubled, while poultry consumption has increased by 150 percent. It is largely for these reasons that the American Heart Association now recommends that Americans cut their per capita meat consumption by one third while further reducing their intake of beef and pork in favor of poultry, which is lower in saturated fats.

Cross-cultural studies seem to indicate a clear relationship between low intake of animal fats and freedom from the heart and circulatory diseases mentioned above. The Japanese, for example, blessed with one of the world's lowest rates of these diseases, obtain only 39 percent of their protein from animal sources—primarily fish which are relatively low in saturated fats—and have about one-eighth the intake of saturated fats of most Americans. In China, where only 10 percent of the protein comes from animal sources, the cholesterol level is less than half that of most Americans. And observers have reported that the healthy, long-lived Hunzas rely on animal foods for only 1½ percent of their protein intake.

There is also a clear correlation between problems of overweight and the intake of animal foods high in saturated fats. Large-scale studies among Americans show that people practicing a meatless way of eating are 20 pounds below the national average weight, and that people following a standard meat-centered diet are 12 to 15 pounds above their ideal weight. Tests taken throughout the world likewise show that in societies with relatively low meat consumption (such as Japan), the people more closely approach their ideal weight.

Using tofu in place of livestock products as a basic protein source is an easy way to greatly reduce total intake of saturated fats and cholesterol. Regular tofu contains only 4.3 percent vegetable-quality fats. These are very low in saturated fats (15%), high in unsaturated fats (80%), and remarkably high in linoleic acid, one of the most important polyunsaturated fatty acids. By comparison, beef fat is high in saturated fats (48%), low in unsaturated fats (47%), and contains only 9 percent linoleic acid. An essential fatty acid, linoleic cannot be synthesized by the body and must therefore be obtained directly from sources such as soy products. Like natural lecithin, which is also found in abundance in tofu's unrefined oils, linoleic acid performs the vital functions of metabolizing, dispersing, and eliminating deposits of cholesterol and other fatty acids which have accumulated in the vital organs and blood stream. Soybeans, the best known source of lecithin and linoleic acid, are used for the extraction of these products now so popular in tablet form at Western health food stores.

Rich in Minerals and Vitamins

Tofu is an excellent source of calcium, an essential mineral for building and maintaining sound teeth and bones, and one which is often deficient in the diets of people who cannot afford dairy products. When solidified with calcium chloride nigari or calcium sulfate—as is most of the tofu presently made in America—regular tofu contains 23 percent, and *kinugoshi* 50 percent, more calcium by weight than dairy milk. A standard 8-ounce serving of tofu, therefore, provides 38 percent of the average daily calcium requirement. As shown in figure 5, tofu is also a good source of other minerals such as iron, phosphororus, potassium, and sodium, of essential B vitamins, and of choline and fat-soluble vitamin E.

A Health-giving Natural Food

Tofu is a traditional, natural food, prepared in essentially the same way today that it was more than one thousand years ago. Unlike so many high-protein foods, it has an alkaline composition which promotes long life and good health. In America, as in Japan, tofu is now a popular item in many natural- and health food stores, and Japanese doctors regularly prescribe it (and soymilk) in curative diets for diabetes, heart disease, hardening of the arteries, and a variety of other circulatory problems. Except for the loss of crude soybean fiber, tofu is a whole food made from simple, natural ingredients. Whereas cow's milk is curdled or solidified with an acid (rennet) to make cheese or curds, soymilk is generally solidified with either *nigari* or calcium sulfate to make tofu. Nigari—also called bittern—is the mineral-rich mother liquor that remains after natural sea salt is extracted from sea water. Calcium sulfate, now generally used in its refined form, was traditionally prepared from ground, lightly roasted gypsum, which is found in abundance in the mountains of East Asia.

Backbone of the Meatless Diet

For the rapidly increasing number of Westerners who find that a meatless or vegetarian diet makes good sense, tofu can serve as a key source of protein just as it has since ancient times for the millions of people throught East Asia practicing similar ways of eating.

Free of Chemical Toxins

Tofu—like other soybean products—is unique among high-protein, high-calcium foods in being relatively free of chemical toxins. It is well known that heavy metals, herbicides, and pesticides tend to concentrate in the fatty tissues of animals at the tops of food chains. Meat, fish, and poultry contain about 20 times more pesticide residues than legumes. Dairy foods, the next most contaminated group, contain 4½ times more. Since soybeans are an important legume feed crop at the base of the beef and dairy food chains, their spraying is carefully monitored by the Food and Drug Administration to keep the level of contamination at an absolute minimum.

Low in Cost

In addition to tofu's many fine qualities as a source of protein and basic nutrients, another endearing feature is its low cost. At the time of this writing, a typical 8-ounce serving of American-made tofu costs only 19½ cents. If the tofu is purchased directly from a tofu shop, the cost may be as low as 14 cents, and if the tofu is prepared at home, only 6½ cents! Storebought tofu costs only 56 percent of the price of an equivalent weight of hamburger, 34 percent of chicken, and 15 percent of lamb rib chop. Furthermore, unlike most meats, a pound of tofu is a pound of tofu: no fat or bones. As the following figures show, the cost of one day's supply of usable protein (43.1 grams for an adult male) derived from or purchased in the form of tofu is relatively low compared with other common protein sources:

Food	Cost
Whole dry soybeans ($0.35/lb)	$0.16
Tofu, homemade (.13/lb)	.24
Whole eggs, medium (.66/doz)	.35
Tofu, Packaged Lactone Kinugoshi (in Japan; 5.5% protein [.15/lb])	.38
Tofu, dried-frozen (in Japan) (1.72/lb)	.47
Tofu, regular (in Japan) (.26/lb)	.49
Tofu, regular, at U.S. tofu shops (.28/lb)	.52
Hamburger, regular grind (.69/lb)	.56
Whole milk, nonfat (.35/qt)	.59
Cottage cheese, from skim milk (.60/lb)	.60
Tuna, canned in oil (1.30/lb)	.65
Tofu, regular, at U.S. supermarkets (.39/lb)	.74
Spaghetti (.51/lb)	.75
Swiss cheese, domestic (1.64/lb)	.83
Peanuts (1.02/lb)	.84
Cheddar cheese (1.70/lb)	.93
Whole-wheat bread (.59/lb)	1.02
Chicken, breast with bone (1.16/lb)	1.04
Pork loin chop, med. (1.29/lb)	1.36
Yogurt (.43/lb)	1.75
Porterhouse steak, choice grade w. bone (1.99/lb)	2.10
Lamb rib chop (2.59/lb)	3.14

(Source: Prices sampled at California and Tokyo supermarkets and tofu shops, Feb. 1975. Figures calculated from data in *Diet for a Small Planet*.)

Note that in Tokyo, where the cost of living is now higher than in the United States, the retail price of tofu is relatively low. As tofu becomes more popular in the West and the number of shops making it increases, we can expect similar price reductions due to greater competition, elimination of middlemen, and the economies of large-scale production and distribution.

Because tofu is inexpensive, it is a truly democratic food that can be enjoyed by people throughout the world, especially those whose nutritional needs are the greatest. In Taiwan, for example, a pound of tofu presently retails for about one-fourth the cost of tofu in America.

Easily Made at Home

Each of the different varieties of tofu can be prepared at home using utensils found in most kitchens and ingredients which are readily available. Homemade tofu will be ready in an hour, and the cost drops to about one-third the retail price. Like fresh bread warm from the oven, fresh tofu prepared at home has a richness and delicacy of flavor that is rarely matched by storebought varieties.

Quick & Easy to Use

Like yogurt, cottage cheese, or cheese, each of the different types of tofu are ready to eat and re-quire no further cooking. We find that most of our favorite ways of serving tofu are the simplest, sometimes taking less than a minute to prepare. For people who are often in a hurry and like their food ready instantly, this ease of use will, no doubt, add to tofu's appeal.

Versatile

Finally, tofu is so versatile that it can serve as an ingredient in almost the entire range of your favorite dishes and be used in the national cuisine of countries around the world. Perhaps no other food has such a wide range of interesting forms, textures, and flavors; each variety invites experimentation, ingenuity, and inventiveness. We have found again and again that tofu can transform even the simplest dishes into something completely new. Among the most adaptive of foods, it may be used in both virtuoso and supporting roles. Like the taste of water from a mountain stream or a breath of crisp autumn air, simple flavors are often the most satisfying. And because its simplicity is inexhaustible, tofu, in its many forms, can be enjoyed day after day, adding body and richness of flavor—as well as protein—to your daily meals.

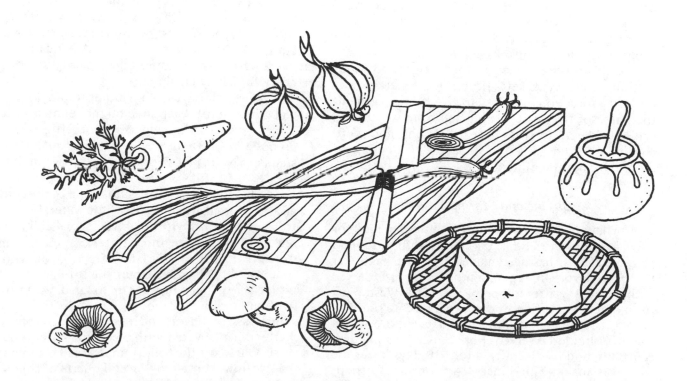

3
Getting Started

THERE ARE presently more than 180 tofu shops in the United States (see Appendix B). Since these are often small Japanese or Chinese family-run operations, tofu products and their names vary slightly from shop to shop. Each shop prepares a number of varieties of fresh tofu each day and retails them through a rapidly growing number of food stores in its area. Larger shops often distribute their tofu up to 200 miles away. In many cases, tofu is available at reductions of 25 percent if purchased directly from the tofu shop or if ordered unpackaged in bulk.

Look for fresh tofu in the refrigerated foods section of most markets. If your local market does not carry tofu, you may wish to give its management the name of the nearest tofu shop from which tofu can be ordered. In cities near tofu shops, good tofu cuisine is often served at Japanese, Chinese, and natural food restaurants.

Buying and Storing Tofu

What are the most important things to look for when buying tofu? First, try to buy tofu as soon as possible after it has been made; fresh tofu has by far the best flavor. In Japan, almost all tofu is served within one day after it is prepared. In the West, most fresh, packaged tofu now comes with a date stamped on the container indicating the date before which the tofu should be served. For regular tofu this date is 7 days, and for deep-fried tofu 10 days, after the tofu was made. Since many American tofu shops start work at 2 o'clock in the morning, their fresh

tofu is often available in local food stores early the same day.

Next, look for the name of the tofu solidifier, which will be printed in small letters on the package. Traditional-style tofu will be made with a nigari-type solidifier (natural nigari, calcium chloride nigari, or magnesium chloride nigari). Similarly, try to find tofu advertized as being cooked in an iron cauldron over a (wood) fire, rather than with steam. If the tofu is prepared with organically grown (Japanese-variety) soybeans and/or well water, so much the better. Almost all tofu made in America is free of preservatives and other chemical additives, but check the label to make sure.

When storing tofu (including doufu, kinugoshi, and grilled tofu), keep in mind the following points:

* Keep tofu under constant refrigeration but do not allow it to freeze. See that it is not allowed to stand in a warm place before being refrigerated.

* If tofu was purchased water-packed and is not to be used right away, slit the top of the container along one edge and drain off the water. If you plan to serve the tofu within 24 hours, seal and refrigerate (without adding more water). If you are unable to serve the tofu until a later date, re-cover with cold water and refrigerate. Drain the tofu and add fresh water *daily*. It can be kept up to ten days in this way without spoiling, although naturally there will be some loss of flavor and texture. Since tofu keeps better when covered with plenty of water, you may wish to transfer the tofu from its small container to a pan or bowl containing several quarts of cold water; cover or seal the container before refrigerating.

* Always drain water-packed tofu briefly before use. For slightly firmer tofu, drain for several hours or overnight. Effective draining procedures are described on page 96.

* Tofu that is several days old can be refreshed by parboiling (p. 96).

* Regular or deep-fried tofu can be stored indefinitely as homemade frozen tofu (p. 230).

When storing deep-fried tofu, simply refrigerate in an airtight container. Do not store under water.

Basic Ingredients

We recommend the use of whole, natural foods. Since cans and bottles tend to contribute to environmental clutter, the recipes in this book call for ingredients which can be purchased free of non-biodegradable packaging. The rarer ingredients used in Japanese-style recipes are defined in the glossary at the the end of this book. Many basic Oriental foods are now widely available at natural food stores and supermarkets, as well as at Japanese and Chinese markets. Or contact the Japan Food Corporation with offices in San Francisco, Los Angeles, New York, Chicago, Houston, Columbia (Md.), and Sacramento (Calif.). The following ingredients, listed alphabetically, are those we consider basic to tofu cookery:

Flour: Since all-purpose white flour contains only about 75 percent of the protein, 36 percent of the minerals, and 25 percent of the vitamins found in natural whole-wheat flour, we generally prefer to use the latter for baked goods, sauces, and the like. However, in tempura batters and pie crusts where lightness is essential, we recommend the use of unbleached white flour or a mixture of equal parts whole-wheat and white flours.

Miso: Also known as fermented soybean paste, miso is one of the basic staples and seasonings in every Japanese and Chinese kitchen. Its range of flavors and colors, textures and aromas is at least as rich and varied as that of the world's fine cheeses or wines. Miso has a consistency slightly softer than peanut butter and comes in both smooth and chunky textures. It contains an average of 14 percent high-quality soy protein and is very low in calories. Traditionally sold out of handsome cedar kegs, it is now also widely available in the West in polyethylene bags (fig. 8). Miso can be substituted for salt or shoyu (soy sauce) in almost all recipes in this book; for ¼ teaspoon salt or 1 teaspoon shoyu, use 1½ teaspoons salty miso or 1 tablespoon sweet miso. Although most miso may be stored indefinitely at room temperature, sweet varieties should be refrigerated.

Fig. 8. Miso

ated. (For additional information, see *The Book of Miso*, by the authors of the present work, listed in the bibliography.) The basic types of miso are:

Rice miso: Made from rice, soybeans, and salt. Basic varieties include red, light-yellow, semi-sweet beige, sweet red, and sweet white miso.

Barley miso: Made from barley, soybeans, and salt. Basic varieties are (regular) barley miso and sweet barley miso.

Soybean miso: Made from soybeans and salt. Basic varieties include Hatcho miso and one-year soybean miso.

Special Japanese miso: Finger Lickin' Miso has a relatively sweet flavor and chunky texture and is fermented together with chopped vegetables. The most popular varieties are *Kinzanji* miso, *moromi* miso, *hishio*, and *namémiso*. Sweet Simmered Miso (p. 41) and *akadashi* miso (p. 45) are other varieties used as tofu toppings.

Chinese chiang: The Chinese equivalent of miso, its main varieties are sweet wheat-flour chiang (*tien-m'ien chiang*), chunky chiang (*tou-pan chiang*), and red-pepper chiang (*la-chiao chiang*).

Oil: For best flavor, use cold-pressed, natural vegetable oils. For sautéing and salad dressings, we prefer soy, corn, or "salad" oil—often mixed with small amounts of sesame oil; for deep-frying, rapeseed or soy oil. Olive oil works well in Western-style dressings. Sesame oil, especially popular in Chinese dishes, is now widely available in the West. No recipes require the use of hydrogenated oils or animal fats.

Rice: Polished or white rice contains an average of only 84 percent of the protein, 53 percent of the minerals, and 38 percent of the vitamins found in natural brown rice. We prefer the flavor, texture, and nutritional superiority of the natural food.

Salt: Natural, unrefined sea salt contains an abundance of essential minerals which are lost during the refining process. Its flavor is richer and more concentrated than that of pure-white, refined table salt.

Shoyu: The skillful use of authentic shoyu (and miso) is the key to most tofu cookery. An all-purpose seasoning as important to Oriental cuisine as salt is to Western cookery, shoyu is called for in a majority of the recipes in this book. Containing 6.9 percent protein and 18 percent salt, natural shoyu has been a mainstay of Japanese cooking for more than 500 years. We use the Japanese name to distinguish this fine product from the modern, synthetic soy sauces now widely used in the West. In most recipes in this book, 1 teaspoon of shoyu may be substituted for ¼ teaspoon of salt. Sold traditionally in re-usable cedar kegs and returnable bottles, shoyu is now also widely sold in cans (fig. 9). The four basic types of shoyu and soy sauce available in the United States are:

Natural Shoyu: This traditional product is always brewed using a natural (rather than temperature-controlled) fermentation process, generally for 12 to 18 months. The finest varieties are prepared from whole soybeans, natural salt, and well water fermented together in huge cedar vats. All types also contain *koji* spores and roasted cracked wheat. All natural shoyu presently available in the West—some of which is sold as *Tamari* shoyu—is imported from Japan. Actually, Japanese *tamari*, the progenitor of shoyu, is a different product prepared without the use of wheat; it has a distinctive, slightly stronger flavor and aroma.

Shoyu: At present, this is the standard shoyu sold in Japan. A high quality product now produced on a large scale in the U.S., its flavor, aroma, and color are quite similar to those of the finest natural shoyu, and its price is considerably lower. Using techniques based on the traditional method but first developed during the 1950s, it is generally prepared from defatted soybean meal and brewed in large tanks for about 4 to 6 months under conditions of strictly controlled temperature and humidity.

Chinese Soy Sauce: This traditional Chinese product, which has a stronger and saltier flavor than shoyu, is also made by natural or temperature-controlled fermentation. Although some varieties are excellent, they are not widely available in the West. Our Chinese recipes call for this product. If unavailable, substitute shoyu.

Synthetic or Chemical Soy Sauce: This domestic product, sold under various Chinese brand names, is what most Westerners mean when they speak of soy sauce. It is not brewed or fermented but is prepared from hydrolyzed vegetable protein (HVP) by the reaction of defatted soybeans with hydrochloric acid. Its flavor and coloring come from additives such as corn syrup and caramel. Since it takes only a few days to prepare, the production costs are quite low. Some varieties may contain sodium benzoate or alcohol preservatives.

Sugar: Most recipes in this book call for natural or brown sugar, generally used together and balanced with shoyu or miso in the minimum amounts we consider necessary to create the desired flavor. In most recipes, 1¼ teaspoons of honey can be used to impart the same sweetening as 1 teaspoon of natural sugar. (We feel it is important that decreases of meat in the diet be accompanied by proportional decreases of sugar usage.)

Fig. 9. Shoyu

Vinegar: Use either Western-style cider or white wine vinegar, or the milder, subtly-sweet Japanese rice vinegar (*su*). The latter is especially tasty in salad dressings, sweet-sour sauces, and sushi rice. For 1 teaspoon rice vinegar, substitute ¾ teaspoon cider or mild white vinegar.

NOTE: Monosodium glutamate—also known as MSG or *ajinomoto*—is a crystalline, pure-white powder widely used as a chemical flavor-enhancing agent in contemporary Japanese and Chinese cooking. Because of the growing awareness that excessive use of this product may cause burning sensations, headaches, a feeling of pressure in the chest, and other discomforting symptoms, and because it is a highly refined substance prepared by the hydrolosis of petroleum, cane molasses, or starch with hydrochloric acid, it does not appear in any recipes in this book.

Japanese vegetable knife: One of the finest knives ever designed for cutting vegetables, the *hocho* makes the art of cutting and slicing a true joy. Most varieties are quite inexpensive. The finest of these knives are handmade and bear the stamp of the craftsman on the blade near the knife's wooden handle.

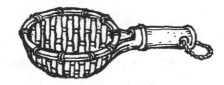

Japanese Kitchen Tools

The Japanese chef (like most Japanese craftsmen) uses only a small number of relatively simple tools in his work. While the recipes in this book can be prepared using only the utensils found in most Western kitchens, the following tools may make cooking with tofu somewhat easier and more enjoyable. Most of these tools are inexpensive and are available at many Japanese and Chinese hardware stores, as well as at some large Japanese markets.

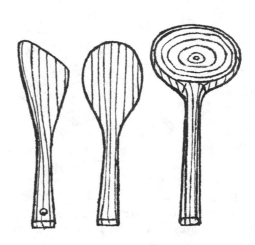

Wooden spatulas, rice paddles, and spoons: These utensils make the work of sautéing, stirring, and serving easier and more enjoyable.

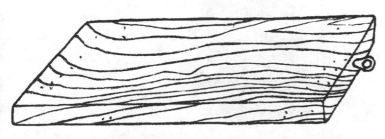

Cutting board: A board about 19 by 9 by 1 to 2 inches thick, the *manaita* is designed to be set across the kitchen sink and hung on the wall when not in use. Excellent for pressing tofu.

Bamboo colander: Usually round and slightly concave, a typical *zaru*, made of thin strips of woven bamboo, is about 12 inches in diameter. It is used for draining and straining foods, for separating curds from whey when preparing homemade tofu, and as a serving tray for such foods as tempura and parboiled green soybeans.

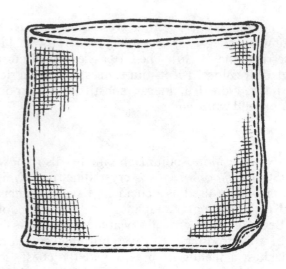

Suribachi: An earthenware grinding bowl or mortar with a serrated interior surface, the usual *suribachi* is 10 inches in diameter and 3½ inches deep, and is accompanied by a wooden pestle (*suri-kogi*).

Japanese grater: A metal tray about 9 inches long, the *oroshi-gane* has many sharp teeth protruding from its upper surface. Since there are no holes in the grater, the grated foods collect in the trough at one end.

Sudare: A bamboo mat about 10 inches square used for rolling sushi and other foods. A small bamboo table mat makes a good substitute. One special variety, called the devil's sudare (*oni-sudare*), is made of triangular bamboo slats designed to leave a distinct corrugated impression in the rolled foods.

Pressing sack: A simple cloth sack about 15 inches wide and 15 inches deep made of coarsely woven cloth is very helpful in squeezing, crumbling, or reshaping tofu, as well as in preparing all varieties of homemade tofu and soymilk.

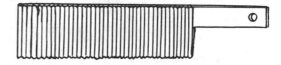

Serrated tofu-slicing knife: A small, all-metal knife with a vertically serrated blade, this is used in fine tofu restaurants and shops to create a fluted surface when cutting kinugoshi tofu.

Tawashi scrub brush: Made of natural palm fiber, the *tawashi* is the perfect utensil for scrubbing root vegetables or washing pots. It is inexpensive and outlasts most synthetic brushes.

Wok set: Popular now in the West, the wok is the Orient's standard utensil for deep-frying, stir-frying, steaming, and sautéing.

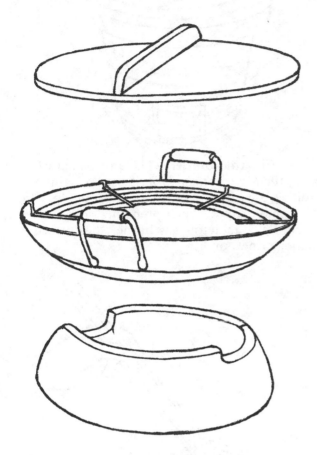

1. *The wok:* The wok itself is a metal pan about 13 inches in diameter and 3½ inches deep. Always used over a gas or charcoal burner, it is not suitable for use with electric ranges. Surprisingly low in cost and now widely available in the West, its design has numerous advantages over that of a regular flat-bottomed skillet, especially when deep-frying: a) It provides the maximum oil surface and depth with the minimum necessary oil volume (3 to 5 cups); b) Each piece of food can be slid gently down the wok's sides rather than dropped with a splash into the oil; c) Freshly-fried foods can be drained into the pan on an inobtrusive rack which saves oil and allows more thorough draining when the foods are later placed on absorbent paper; d) The wok's rounded bottom and thin metal sides allow for quick heating and oil temperature adjustment; e) During stir-frying and sautéing, the wok's large surface area allows each piece of food to have maximum contact with the bottom of the pan, yielding crisp-textured foods in minimum cooking time; f) Cooked foods can be scooped out easily and thoroughly and, when all is done, the wok is easier to clean or wipe free of oil than angular, flat-bottomed pots. After sautéing or stir-frying, wash the hot wok immediately with water and a scrub brush. Do not use soap.

Wooden lid: Used when simmering foods, the lid fits inside the wok's rim.

Draining rack: A semi-circular rack, the *hangetsu* is attached to the wok during deep-frying so that excess oil from the draining foods drips back into the wok.

Wok support: Used in most Chinese kitchens to give the wok stability and focus the strong fire at its base.

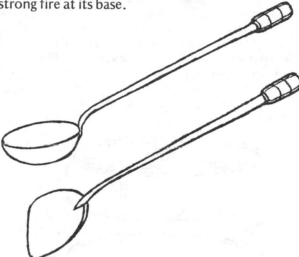

Stir-frying ladle and spatula: In Chinese kitchens, these large, sturdy tools are used during stir-frying. The ladle is employed to measure (by eye) and add all liquids and seasonings to foods cooking in the wok.

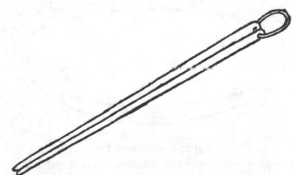

Long cooking-chopsticks: Shaped like regular Japanese wooden chopsticks but about 10 to 14 inches long and often joined with a string at one end, these *saibashi* are used mostly during deep-frying for turning foods in the hot oil or transferring cooked foods to the draining rack. Substitute a pair of long cooking tongs.

Mesh skimmer: Used for skimming debris from the surface of the hot oil during deep-frying and for removing very small deep-fried foods.

Deep-frying thermometer: Use a regular Western-style deep-fat thermometer that measures temperatures up to 380°.

Charcoal brazier: Made of baked earthenware, the *konro* or *shichirin* is used for grilling and broiling, as well as for heating *nabe* dishes (p. 143) or the family teapot. When preparing *nabe*, you may substitute a tabletop gas burner, heating coil, or chafing-dish warmer.

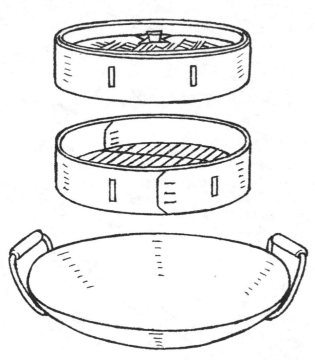

Chinese bamboo steamer: Although most varieties of *seiro* are round and are set into a *wok* during steaming, some types are rectangular. They are made of slatted or woven bamboo with ¼-inch gaps between the bottom slats. This design allows steam to rise through the steamer's lid and prevents it from collecting and dripping on the steaming foods. Two to four steaming compartments may be stacked in layers during steaming.

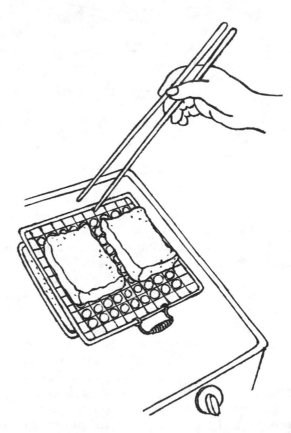

Broiling screen: This double-layer, 8-inch-square screen rests atop a stove burner and is used for broiling. Both layers are made of thin metal sheets, the bottom one perforated with 1/8-inch, and the top with 3/8-inch holes. The top layer slides out for easy cleaning. Broils foods faster and with less fuel than a Western oven broiler.

Basic Preparatory Techniques

The following preparatory techniques will be referred to in many of the recipes in this book. We list them all here for easy reference.

Salt-rubbing

This process softens and seasons vegetables (and *konnyaku*) without cooking.

Place thinly sliced vegetables into a bowl and sprinkle with salt. Rub the salt into the vegetables with your fingertips until the vegetables are fairly soft, then let stand for 15 to 20 minutes. Fill the bowl with water and rinse away the salt. Empty vegetables into a strainer or colander and drain briefly. Wrap vegetables in a clean cloth and squeeze gently to expel excess moisture.

Rinsing and Pressing Leeks or Onions

This is a quick and easy method for neutralizing the harsh and evoking the mild, sweet flavors of these vegetables.

Slice leeks or onions into thin rounds or slivers. Combine with several cups water in a small bowl and soak for 2 or 3 minutes. Pour into a cloth-lined strainer, gather the cloth's corners to form a sack, and press vegetables gently between your palms. Use immediately or refrigerate in a covered container.

Soaking Burdock Root

Burdock root has a slightly harsh, alkaline flavor that is easily removed by proper cutting and soaking. If unsoaked, burdock will lose its white color and turn a dark reddish brown soon after it is cut and exposed to the air.

Holding the root under running cold water, scrape off its dark peel with a knife or scrub it off with a scrub brush (*tawashi*). Cut the root into 2-inch lengths and submerge the lengths in cold water. Cut one section at a time into matchsticks and return these immediately to the water. Soak for about 10 minutes, then change the water and soak for 20 to 40 minutes more. Soaking time can be decreased by using warm or hot water, but some of the burdock's flavor will be lost. Drain quickly before sautéing.

Reconstituting Dried Sea Vegetables, Wheat Gluten, and Kampyo

Dried Hijiki: Immerse in several cups (warm) water and allow to soak for 20 to 30 minutes. Stir gently, then lift *hijiki* carefully out of water so that any grit stays at bottom of bowl. Place *hijiki* in a colander or strainer and press lightly to rid it of excess moisture. Note: ¼ cup (27 gm) dry *hijiki* yields 1 cup (200 gm) reconstituted.

Dried Wakame: Rinse *wakame* once, then soak for 15 to 30 minutes. Strain, reserving the nutritious liquid for use in stocks. Remove the midrib of each leaf only if it is unusually large. Squeeze *wakame* firmly, place in a compact mound on a cutting board, and cut at ½-inch intervals. (Place fresh *wakame* in several quarts of water, rinsing and squeezing 2 or 3 times to rid it of excess surface salt.) Note: 25 gm dried *wakame* yields 1 cup (125 gm) reconstituted.

Agar *(Kanten):* Tear agar stick crosswise into halves and soak in 1 quart water for several minutes. Lift out agar and squeeze firmly. Change water and resoak briefly. Squeeze again, then tear into small (1-inch) pieces.

Dried Wheat Gluten: Soak for several minutes in water. Press lightly with fingertips to expel excess moisture before use.

Kampyo: Soak for 15 minutes in water to cover seasoned with a pinch of salt. Drain briefly, then rub lightly with salt.

Parboiling

To parboil vegetables, drop them into more than enough boiling water to cover, and cook until just tender. When parboiling green vegetables, add about ¼ teaspoon salt for each 2 cups water to help the vegetables retain their color. Vegetables that are easily overcooked may be plunged into cold water as soon as they are done. Length of cooking depends both on how finely the ingredients have been cut and on whether they will be cooked again. Shredded or slivered vegetables, or leaves that will be simmered again in a seasoned liquid, may be parboiled for 30 to 60 seconds; boil for 30 to 60 seconds more if they will not be recooked. Small rectangles of *konnyaku* and root vegetables should be parboiled for 1 to 2 minutes. Larger pieces may be boiled for as much as 3 to 4 minutes.

Cutting Tofu and Vegetables

Most of the cutting techniques used in the recipes presented in this book are familiar to any Western cook. A few, however, deserve special mention. The Japanese pay great attention to the way in which each ingredient is cut, because careful cutting not only lends beauty to the preparation when it is served but also assures that each uniform piece will be cooked to precisely the desired degree of tenderness.

Cutting tofu into small rectangles: Cut the cake of tofu lengthwise into halves, then cut crosswise into slices about ½ inch thick.

Cutting vegetables into small rectangles: Cut thick vegetables (carrots, *daikon*, etc.) into 1½-inch lengths, then cut each section vertically into thirds. Now place each piece on its largest surface and cut lengthwise into small rectangles about 1/8 inch thick.

Cutting into matchsticks: This technique is used with long, thin root vegetables. Cut crosswise into 2-inch lengths; then stand each piece on end and cut vertically into 1/8-inch-thick pieces. Stack these on top of one another and cut lengthwise into 1/8-inch-wide strips the size of wooden matchsticks. Slivering or cutting *julienne* are variations on this basic technique.

Cutting into half moons: Use with long, thick roots or tubers. Cut lengthwise into halves, then cut each half crosswise into pieces about ¼ to ½ inch thick.

Cutting into ginkgo leaves: Cut lengthwise into quarters, then cut crosswise into thin pieces.

Using Sesame Seeds

When roasted and ground, sesame seeds have a wonderful nutty flavor and aroma, and almost every Japanese kitchen is equipped with a *suribachi* and *surikogi* (a serrated earthenware bowl and wooden pestle, p. 34), used for grinding them. Small quantities of seeds can also be ground in a pepper grinder, a spice or coffee mill, or a special grinder that fits over the mouth of a jar of sesame seeds and is sold at Japanese hardware stores. If you are using ½ cup or more of seeds, you can grind them in a hand mill or meat grinder, or, in some cases, purée them in a blender with a dash of oil or shoyu. You may wish to make enough to last for several days or to use in Sesame Salt (p. 51). Grind the seeds with a firm but light touch until they are well crushed but not oily.

Two parts of ground roasted seeds impart about the same flavoring as 1 part pre-packaged sesame butter or *tahini*.

(Proper care of the *suribachi* is very important. Before use, scrub the *suribachi* with hot water and douse with boiling water. Dry with a dishcloth, then turn the bowl upside down and dry thoroughly with one edge raised to allow air to circulate. After use, fill the *suribachi* with hot water and soak for 1 hour; then scrub and dry as above.)

Heat a heavy skillet until a drop of water flicked across its surface evaporates instantly. Add seeds and reduce heat to low. Shaking the pan and stirring seeds constantly, roast for about 3 minutes or until seeds are fragrant and light brown and just begin to pop. (A seed pressed between the thumb and little finger should crush easily.) Transfer about ½ cup seeds at a time to the *suribachi* and grind with the pestle until no more than 10 to 15 percent of the seeds remain whole. For best flavor and aroma, use seeds immediately. To store, allow leftover seeds to cool, then seal in an airtight container in a cool, dry place. Prepare just enough for a week.

Toasting Nori

Wave a sheet of *nori* over medium heat for about 30 seconds or until crisp and slightly green.

Preparing a Steamer

Chinese Bamboo Steamer: Set the steamer over a wok filled with water to a depth of about 1½-inches. Bring water to a boil over high heat, then reduce heat to medium. Place the food in the steamer, cover with the bamboo lid, and steam for the required length of time. The woven bamboo lid prevents dripping by allowing steam to pass out. With this tool, several layers of food can be steamed at one time.

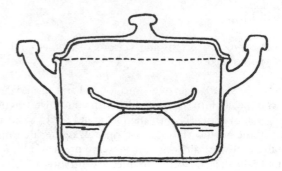

Covered Pot Steamer: Fill a 10- to 12-inch-diameter pot with water to a depth of about 1 inch. Bring to a boil over high heat, then reduce heat to low. Into the pot place a collapsible French steamer, a colander, or a plate set on top of an inverted bowl (above). Now put in the food to be steamed. (In many cases, tofu will be wrapped in a *sudare* bamboo mat before insertion.) Place a single layer of absorbent toweling or paper over the mouth of the pot to prevent moisture from dripping onto the food, then cover the pot. Steam as directed.

Chawan-mushi Steamer: Prepare as for a covered pot steamer, but place the cups directly in the water (above). If the cups do not have individual lids, cover with a sheet of absorbent paper topped with a plate to hold the paper in place. (Omit the toweling over the mouth of the pot.) Cover pot and steam for the required length of time. Good for custards and the like.

Basic Recipes

The following stocks, sauces, toppings, dressings, rice and noodle dishes, and other basic preparations are often served with tofu. They play important supporting roles in tofu cookery, so we have grouped them all together here. They will be called for frequently in later recipes.

SOUP STOCKS AND BROTHS

The different varieties of fresh *dashi* (Japanese soup stock) serve as the basis for a wide variety of tofu preparations and are easily made from natural ingredients. An instant dried dashi (dashi-no-moto) is now available in the West. Refrigerated in a sealed container, fresh dashi will last for 2 to 3 days without appreciable loss of flavor. Western-style vegetable or vegetable bullion stocks make satisfactory substitutes.

Number 1 Dashi *(Ichiban Dashi)*   MAKES 3 CUPS

This preparation is a cornerstone of Japanese cooking. The amount and variety of bonita flakes used varies slightly from chef to chef, as does the (often highly secret) method of preparation. For best flavor use flakes which have been shaved just before use.

3 cups water, Kombu Dashi, or Niboshi Dashi
¼ to 1 cup bonita flakes (15 to 30 grams)

Heat the water until quite hot in a small saucepan. Add bonita flakes and bring to a boil. Turn off heat and allow to stand for 3 minutes, or until flakes settle; skim off foam. Filter the dashi through a (clothlined) strainer placed over a saucepan. Press flakes with the back of a spoon to extract remaining dashi, then reserve flakes. (Some cooks add fine-textured flakes to simmered broths, *nabe* dishes, and miso soups together with the dashi, or simply omit straining.)

For a richer flavor, use a relatively large amount of flakes, simmer flakes for 2 or 3 minutes, and allow the dashi to stand (covered) for 15 to 30 minutes before straining.

Number 2 Dashi *(Niban Dashi)*   MAKES 2½ CUPS

The basic dashi ingredients are generally reused at least once to make a milder-flavored "Number 2" dashi. Thereafter the kombu may be slivered and simmered in shoyu and *mirin* to make *tsukudani* (a garnish for rice), pressure cooked with brown rice (p. 50), or cut into strips, each of which are tied into a simple loop and simmered in Oden (p. 175) or Nishime (p. 178); whole pieces are sometimes used to prepare vinegar- or *nukamiso* pickles (p. 326).

Whereas Number 1 Dashi is featured primarily in Clear Soups, this stock is generally used when simmering vegetables, with miso soups, or in noodle broths.

2½ cups water
Bonita flakes and *kombu* reserved from Number 1 Dashi

Combine all ingredients in a small saucepan and bring just to a boil. Remove *kombu* immediately, then simmer for 1 more minute. Strain and allow to cool.

Two tablespoons of fresh bonita flakes may be added to the boiling water after removing the *kombu*; reduce heat to lowest point and simmer for 5 minutes before straining. Leftovers may be reboiled in 1¼ cups water to make Number 3 Dashi.

Kombu Dashi *(Kombu Stock)*   MAKES 3 CUPS

Used in many homes as the basis for Number 1 Dashi (see above), this stock is featured in its own right in Zen Temple Cookery. *Kombu's* flavoring components (such as glutamic acid) reside mostly on its surface; be careful not to remove them by washing. Since they and the *kombu's* nutrients pass quickly into the stock, lengthy cooking is unnecessary, and actually leads to a decline in flavor.

1 strip of *kombu*, about 3 by 7 inches, wiped lightly with a damp cloth
3 cups water

Combine *kombu* and water in a saucepan and bring just to a boil. Turn off heat, remove *kombu*, and reserve for use in other cooking. Use dashi as required or, if preparing Number 1 (or *Niboshi*) Dashi proceed to add bonita flakes (or *niboshi*) immediately.

For a more pronounced flavor but somewhat more viscous consistency, score *kombu* surface across grain at ½-inch intervals; simmer for 3 to 5 minutes before removing; double the amount of *kombu* if desired.

VARIATIONS
*Cold Water Method: Combine water and *kombu* and allow to stand for at least to six hours, preferably overnight. Remove *kombu* and use dashi as required. (Some cooks bring the stock just to a boil before removing the *kombu*.) The lengthy soaking is often said to make best use of the *kombu's* nutrients and give the finest flavor.
*Shiitake & Kombu Dashi: Select 2 or 3 *shiitake* mushrooms, preferably ones having thick, partially opened caps and whitish (rather than darkish or yellowish) gills. (Or use ¼ cup dried stems or broken pieces.) Rinse briefly under running water, then soak either in cold water with the *kombu* or for 30 minutes in hot, freshly prepared Kombu Dashi. Strain dashi before use; do not squeeze *shiitake* to extract absorbed dashi lest stock turn a dark brown.

Soybean Stock   MAKES 1 QUART

Prepare Pressure Cooked or Boiled Soybeans (p. 50) doubling the amount of water used. (At the end of cooking, about 1 quart cooking liquid should remain for each cup soybeans.) Strain stock before serving beans.

Shiitake Dashi *(Mushroom Stock)*

The preparation of Shiitake Dashi as an integral part of the process for making miso soup is described on page 219. In Chinese Buddhist vegetarian restaurants and temples, a soybean & *shiitake* stock is prepared by adding 1 to 2 cups washed and drained *shiitake* stems or pieces to the ingredients for Soybean Stock (see above). The *shiitake* are usually removed before serving the beans.

Niboshi Dashi *(Sardine Dashi)*   MAKES 3 CUPS

3 cups water or Kombu Dashi (p. 39).
¼ to ½ cup tiny (2-inch-long) dried sardines

Combine ingredients and bring to a boil over medium heat. Reduce heat to low and simmer for 3 to 5 minutes, skimming off any foam that rises to the surface. Strain through a (cloth-lined) sieve, reserving fish for use in other cookery. Use dashi as required or, if preparing Number 1 Dashi, proceed to add bonita flakes immediately.

Clear Broth *(Sumashi)*   MAKES 1½ CUPS

1½ cups Number 1 Dashi (p. 39) or Kombu Dashi (p. 39)
1 teaspoon shoyu
½ teaspoon salt
½ teaspoon sake or *mirin* (optional)

Bring the dashi just to a boil over moderate heat. Reduce heat to low and stir in the shoyu, salt, and, if used, the sake or *mirin*. Proceed immediately to add the ingredients called for in the particular recipe in which the broth is used.

Noodle Broth   MAKES 2½ CUPS
(Mentsuyu or Sobatsuyu)

2 cups dashi (p. 39), stock, or water
4 tablespoons shoyu
1 tablespoon natural sugar
2 tablespoons sake or *mirin* (optional)
¼ teaspoon salt

Combine all ingredients in a saucepan and bring to a boil. Serve hot or cold over cooked noodles.

Sweetened Shoyu Broth   MAKES ½ TO ¾ CUP

In Japan, this preparation is widely used to season thinly sliced vegetables before using them in other recipes. If a large quantity of vegetables is being prepared, double or triple the recipe.

¼ to ½ cup dashi (p. 39), stock, or water
2 tablespoons shoyu
2 tablespoons natural sugar
1 tablespoon sake or *mirin* (optional)

Bring all ingredients to a boil in a small saucepan. Add thinly sliced vegetables and return to the boil. Reduce heat to low, cover, and simmer, stirring until all liquid is absorbed or evaporated. If crispier vegetable pieces are desired, simmer for only 2 to 3 minutes. Drain off broth, reserving it for later use.

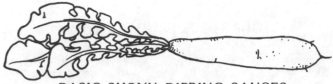

BASIC SHOYU DIPPING SAUCES
(TSUKE-JIRU)

The following preparations are widely used with Chilled Tofu (p. 105), Crisp Deep-fried Tofu (p. 156), and Simmering Tofu (p. 142). Mirin-Shoyu is also used with Agédashi-dofu (p. 133), while *Nihaizu* and *Sambaizu* are favorite dressings for the many Vinegared Salads *(Sunomono)* which feature tofu.

Shoyu Dipping Sauces   SERVES 1

Pour 1½ teaspoons shoyu into a small (3-inch-diameter) dish. Stir in any of the following:

½ teaspoon grated gingerroot or juice pressed from grated gingerroot
¼ teaspoon grated *wasabi* or *wasabi* paste
¼ teaspoon crushed or minced garlic
½ teaspoon slivered *yuzu*, lemon, or orange peel
¼ teaspoon hot mustard
½ teaspoon sesame butter, *tahini*, or ground roasted sesame seeds (p. 38)
½ teaspoon nut butter (peanut, almond, cashew, etc.)
½ to 1 teaspoon orange, lemon, lime, or *yuzu* juice
1 to 3 tablespoons grated *daikon*

Vinegar-Shoyu   MAKES 2½ TABLESPOONS
(Nihaizu or Sujoyu)

2 teaspoons shoyu
2 tablespoons (rice) vinegar

Combine ingredients, mixing well.

Lemon-Shoyu *(Ponzu-Joyu)*   MAKES ¼ CUP

2 tablespoons shoyu
2 tablespoons lemon, lime, or *yuzu* juice

Combine ingredients, mixing well. Vary their proportions to taste. Tangy.

Mirin-Shoyu *(Wari-shita)*   MAKES 2/3 CUP

5 tablespoons dashi (p. 39) or soup stock
3 tablespoons shoyu
2 tablespoons *mirin*
2 teaspoons grated gingerroot

Combine ingredients in a small saucepan and bring just to a boil. Serve hot or cold, garnished with grated gingerroot.

Grated Daikon & Shoyu Dipping Sauce   SERVES 1

½ cup grated *daikon* (from top of fat daikon for best sweetness)
2 teaspoons shoyu
3 green beefsteak leaves, slivered; or ½ teaspoon grated gingerroot or carrot (optional)

Combine all ingredients in a small bowl; mix well. Serve with deep-fried tofu or tempura.

Sweetened Vinegar-Shoyu   MAKES ¼ CUP
(Sambaizu)

2½ tablespoons vinegar
2 teaspoons shoyu
4 teaspoons sugar
½ teaspoon sake or white wine (optional)
Dash of salt

Combine ingredients in a small saucepan and bring just to a boil. Remove from heat and allow to cool to room temperature. To use as a dressing, add 6 tablespoons dashi, stock, or water.

Tangy Shoyu Dipping Sauce   MAKES 1 CUP
(Chirizu)

¼ cup shoyu
¼ cup lemon, *yuzu*, or lime juice
2 tablespoons *mirin* or sake
1/3 cup grated *daikon*
½ leek or 2 scallions, sliced into thin rounds (1/3 cup)
Dash of 7-spice red pepper

Combine all ingredients, mixing well. Serve cold.

Chinese-style Soy Dipping Sauce   MAKES ¼ CUP

3 tablespoons soy sauce
½ teaspoon hot mustard
1 teaspoon sesame oil
2 teaspoons vinegar

Combine ingredients; mix well.

Korean-style Soy Dipping Sauce   SERVES 1

1 tablespoon soy sauce
¼ teaspoon sesame oil
Pinch of minced red peppers, or dash of tabasco or 7-spice red pepper
¼ teaspoon crushed or minced garlic

Combine ingredients on a small dish; mix lightly.

Tosa-joyu   MAKES 1 CUP
(Shoyu Dipping Sauce for Simmering Tofu)

¾ cup shoyu
3 tablespoons *mirin*

Combine ingredients in a small saucepan and bring just to a boil.

For variety, add ¼ to ½ cup bonita flakes to the ingredients and proceed as above. Strain before serving. Increase the proportion of *mirin* (up to 5 tablespoons), or substitute sake or pale dry sherry.

MISO TOPPINGS

Five basic types of miso toppings are widely used in tofu cookery: Sweet Simmered Miso, Miso Sauté, Special Miso Toppings, Finger Lickin' Miso, and regular miso. All varieties make excellent toppings for Crisp Deep-fried Tofu, Chilled Tofu, and many grain and vegetable dishes.

Sweet Simmered Miso
(Nerimiso)

Nerimiso derives its name from the verb *neru* which means "to simmer, stirring constantly, until smooth and thick." These tasty toppings are prepared by combining miso with sugar, water or dashi, seasonings and, in some cases, nuts, vegetables, or seafoods. Some varieties of Sweet Simmered Miso such as peanut, walnut, *tekka* and *yuzu* miso— are sold commercially in Japan. Most varieties are made at home and in traditional or Zen-temple restaurants, where this type of preparation is said to have originated. Nerimiso is generally prepared as a preserved food meant to be served over a period of several weeks. One or 2 cups are usually prepared at a time and are kept in a small attractive container, often an earthenware crock. Nerimiso is served as a convenient topping or seasoning for cooked grains and fresh or cooked vegetables and salads, as well as for tofu. The sweeter varieties also make delicious spreads for toast or sandwiches, waffles, crêpes and pancakes, potatoes, sweet potatoes, and steamed vegetables (such as cauliflower or broccoli). Unused portions will keep their peak of flavor for 2 to 4 weeks if refrigerated in a sealed container.

Vary the amount of sugar to taste. If *mirin* is unavailable, use a mixture of honey and sake (or white wine) as described on page 322.

Red Nerimiso

MAKES ½ CUP

This is the simplest and most basic form of Sweet Simmered Miso; all other recipes may be thought of as variations or elaborations on this fundamental theme. By adding different ingredients and seasonings (sesame, gingerroot, grated lemon rind, etc.) to those listed below, you can create a wide array of delicious toppings.

5 tablespoons red or barley miso
2 to 4 tablespoons natural sugar
1 tablespoon water
1½ teaspoons sake, white wine, or *mirin* (optional)

Combine all ingredients in a small saucepan or skillet. Simmer for 2 to 3 minutes over low heat, stirring constantly with a wooden spoon or spatula, until mixture has a slightly firmer consistency than that of regular miso. Remove from heat and allow to cool to room temperature before serving. Cover and refrigerate unused portions.

VARIATIONS
*Rich Red Nerimiso:

    6 tablespoons red or barley miso
    3½ to 4 tablespoons natural sugar
    ¼ cup *mirin*
    2 tablespoons sake
Prepare as above. A favorite for use in Miso Oden.

*Hatcho Nerimiso: Use Hatcho miso and reduce the amount of sugar used above by about one-third. This preparation has a deep, chocolate-brown color and savory aroma.
*Crunchy Granola Miso: Prepare ½ cup Red Nerimiso (using a relatively small amount of sugar) and allow to cool to room temperature. Combine with ½ to 2/3 cup crunchy granola, mixing well.
*For use in Tofu Dengaku (p. 139), divide prepared Red Nerimiso into two equal portions. To one portion add ½ to 1 teaspoon hot mustard or ½ teaspoon *sansho* pepper.

White Nerimiso

MAKES 1¼ CUPS

1 cup sweet white miso
3 tablespoons *mirin*
1½ tablespoons sake
1 egg yolk
3 tablespoons ground roasted sesame seeds (p. 38), or 1½ tablespoons sesame butter or *tahini*

Prepare as for Red Nerimiso (see above).
For use in Tofu Dengaku (p. 139), divide the prepared miso into two equal portions. To one add any of the following: ½ to 1 teaspoon grated gingerroot; 2 to 3 tablespoons thinly sliced leeks or green onions; 3 to 4 tablespoons ground

roasted sesame seeds (p. 38) or sesame butter; 1 to 2 tablespoons bonita flakes and 1½ teaspoons water.

Sesame Miso

MAKES ¾ CUP

¼ cup sesame butter, *tahini*, or ground roasted sesame seeds (p. 38)
1/3 cup red, barley, or Hatcho miso
2 to 3 tablespoons natural sugar
1 tablespoon sake or white wine
1 tablespoon water
1 to 2 teaspoons grated orange or lemon rind (optional)

Prepare as for Red Nerimiso (see above).
For the sweet, chocolate-like flavor of Chinese Tien M'ien Chiang, use akadashi miso (p. 45) instead of red miso.

Peanut Miso

MAKES ½ CUP

½ cup whole (roasted) peanuts or ¼ cup peanut butter
¼ cup red, barley, or Hatcho miso
2 to 3 tablespoons natural sugar, honey, or *mizuame*
2 tablespoons water; or 1 tablespoon each water and sake, white wine, or *mirin*

Prepare as for Red Nerimiso (see above).

VARIATIONS

*Peanut & Raisin Miso: Use ¼ cup each peanuts and raisins, and 1½ to 2 tablespoons sugar. Add 1 to 2 tablespoons whole or ground roasted sesame seeds if desired.
*Substitute whole cashews, almonds, or sunflower seeds for the peanuts.
*Use akadashi miso and reduce the sugar to 1½ tablespoons.

Walnut Miso

MAKES ¾ CUP

1½ tablespoons oil
½ to 1 cup walnut meats, whole or sliced
1/3 cup red, barley, Hatcho, or akadashi miso
3 to 4 tablespoons natural sugar
1½ teaspoons water
1 tablespoon sake (optional)

Heat a skillet or wok and coat with the oil. Add **walnut** meats and sauté for about 1 minute. Stir in remaining ingredients and proceed as for Red Nerimiso (above).
For variety, pre-roast walnuts until fragrant in a dry pan and/or add ¼ cup sesame butter to the ingredients listed above.

Yuzu Miso

MAKES 1 CUP

½ teaspoon grated *yuzu* peel, or substitute 1 to 2 teaspoons grated lime, lemon, or orange peel.
½ cup red, barley, or Hatcho miso
5 to 6½ tablespoons natural sugar
6 tablespoons water

Prepare as for Red Nerimiso (above).

Lemon Miso

MAKES ¼ CUP

¼ cup red, barley, or Hatcho miso
1 to 2 tablespoons natural sugar
1 tablespoon water
1 teaspoon lemon juice
1 teaspoon grated lemon rind

Combine the first three ingredients in a skillet and proceed as for Red Nerimiso (p. 42). After removing from heat, stir in lemon juice and rind; allow to cool to room temperature.

Garlic Miso

MAKES ¼ CUP

3 cloves of garlic, thinly sliced or crushed
¼ cup red, barley, or Hatcho miso
1½ to 2½ tablespoons natural sugar
2 teaspoons sake, white wine, or water (optional)

Prepare as for Red Nerimiso (p. 42), but simmer over very low heat for 8 to 10 minutes, or until quite firm.

Gingerroot Miso

MAKES ½ CUP

2 to 3 teaspoons grated gingerroot
5 tablespoons red, barley, or Hatcho miso
2 to 3 tablespoons natural sugar
2 teaspoons sake, white wine, or water

Prepare as for Red Nerimiso (p. 42).

Kinome Miso
(Miso with Fresh Sansho Leaves)

MAKES ½ CUP

60 kinome leaves (not sprigs) (about ¼ cup)
5 tablespoons sweet white miso
1 tablespoon natural sugar
2½ tablespoons water
1 teaspoon shoyu (optional)
1½ teaspoons mirin or sake (optional)
Dash of sansho pepper (optional)

Place leaves in a strainer, douse with boiling water, and drain well. Grind leaves thoroughly in a suribachi (or mortar), or mince with a knife. Combine the next five ingredients in a small saucepan and prepare as for Red Nerimiso (p. 42). Add contents of saucepan and pepper, if desired, to ground kinome in suribachi; mix well.

VARIATIONS

*Jade-Green Miso: Collect 4 ounces of the tender tips of (horenso) spinach and/or daikon leaves. Mince thoroughly, then grind almost to a paste in a suribachi or mortar. Pour in 1 cup water and, using your fingertips, free the ground leaves from the grooves in the bowl. Now pour the contents of the suribachi into a fine sieve set over a small saucepan and rub the leaves through the sieve with the back of a large spoon. Heat contents of saucepan over high heat until puréed leaves float to the surface, then reduce heat to low and simmer for 1 minute. Pour contents of pan into a cloth-lined strainer; drain well. Using a small spoon, carefully remove green purée (called aoyose) from cloth. Add 1 teaspoon aoyose to Kinome Miso, stirring well, until the miso has turned a delicate green.

Egg Yolk Miso

MAKES 1 CUP

6 tablespoons sweet white miso
2 egg yolks
2 tablespoons natural sugar
6 tablespoons dashi (p. 39), stock, or water
Dash of sansho pepper (optional)

Prepare as for Red Nerimiso (p. 42).
For use in Tofu Dengaku (p. 139), divide the prepared miso into 2 equal portions. To one add 1 teaspoon aoyose (see preceeding recipe) and 60 kinome leaves prepared as for Kinome Miso. Stir in these ingredients just after removing miso from the heat.

Miso Sauté
(Abura Miso)

Each of these distinctly different toppings is prepared following the same basic pattern. Experiment with other vegetables and nuts, or even with fruits. Serve with chilled or deep-fried tofu, brown rice, rice porridge, or fresh vegetable slices. Refrigerated, unused portions will keep for up to 1 week.

Plain Miso Sauté

MAKES ¼ CUP

1½ tablespoons (sesame) oil
4½ tablespoons red, barley, or Hatcho miso

Heat a skillet and coat with the oil. Add miso and sauté over low heat for about 1 minute, or until miso just begins to stick to skillet. Allow to cool before serving.

Mushroom Miso Sauté

MAKES ⅓ CUP

2 tablespoons oil
10 mushrooms, thinly sliced
1 tablespoon, red, barley, or Hatcho miso
1½ to 2 teaspoons natural sugar

Heat a skillet or wok and coat with the oil. Add mushrooms and sauté over medium heat for about 1 minute or until tender. Reduce heat to low, add miso and sugar, and cook, stirring constantly, for about 1 minute more, or until mushrooms are evenly coated with miso. Allow to cool to room temperature before serving.
Or, substitute butter for one-half of the oil, and sauté over low heat, adding ¼ cup chopped walnut meats.

Each of the following recipes is prepared in basically the same way as Mushroom Miso Sauté. Use 1½ to 2 tablespoons oil, 1 to 1½ tablespoons miso, and 1½ to 3 teaspoons natural sugar.

*Lotus root: Sauté 1½ cups ginkgo leaves of lotus root over low heat for about 5 minutes, or until tender but still crisp. Proceed as above.

*Kabocha: Use ¼ onion cut into thin wedges and 1½ cups thinly sliced pieces of *kabocha*, squash, or pumpkin. Sauté over medium-high heat for 4 to 5 minutes, or until softened. Add 1 tablespoon sesame butter, *tahini*, or ground roasted sesame seeds (p. 38) together with the miso and sugar.

*Eggplant: Use 1 diced onion and 1½ cups 2-inch matchsticks of eggplant. Sauté just until all oil is absorbed, then add miso and sugar.

*Sweet potato: Use 1¼ cups of sweet potato, yam, or Irish potato cubes. Sauté over high heat for 3 to 5 minutes until softened. If desired, sauté ½ diced onion and ½ thinly sliced carrot for 3 to 4 minutes before adding potatoes.

*Burdock root: Use 1½ to 2 cups matchsticks of burdock root, soaked (p. 37), and 1 carrot cut into matchsticks or grated. Sauté burdock root over high heat for 8 to 10 minutes, or until softened. Add carrot and sauté for 5 minutes more, or until both vegetables are tender. If desired, add 1 to 2 tablespoons roasted sesame seeds together with the miso and sugar.

*Onion: Use 2 onions, cut into thin wedges, and 1 carrot, thinly sliced, slivered, or grated. Sauté both vegetables together over medium heat for 5 to 6 minutes, or until carrot is tender. Proceed as for Mushroom Miso Sauté.

Lemon-Walnut-Mushroom Miso Sauté

MAKES ¾ CUP

1½ teaspoons oil or butter
4 (*shiitake*) mushrooms, thinly sliced (about 1/3 cup)
1 tablespoon minced lemon, lime, or *yuzu* rind
¼ to ½ cup chopped walnut meats
1/3 cup red, barley, or Hatcho miso
2½ to 4 tablespoons natural sugar
¼ cup water

Prepare as for Mushroom Miso Sauté (p. 43) but sauté mushrooms for 2 minutes, then add lemon rind and walnuts, and sauté for 1 minute more.

Crumbly Tekka Miso

MAKES ¾ CUP

The word *tekka* is composed of the Chinese characters "metal" and "fire," since this all-purpose condiment was traditionally simmered for a long time on a metal griddle or in a heavy iron pot. It is a favorite topping for brown rice as well as all types of tofu.

2 tablespoons sesame oil
¼ cup minced burdock root
3 tablespoons minced carrot
2 tablespoons minced lotus root
½ teaspoon grated gingerroot
½ cup Hatcho, barley, or red miso
2 to 4 tablespoons roasted soybeans (optional)
Dash of 7-spice or minced red pepper (optional)

Heat a wok or skillet and coat with the oil. Add the burdock and sauté over high heat for about 1 minute. Reduce heat to medium, add carrots and lotus root, and sauté for 2 or 3 minutes. Mix in gingerroot, miso, and, if used, soybeans and red pepper; sauté for 2 minutes more. Reduce heat to low and cook, stirring constantly with a wooden spatula, for 20 to 30 minutes, or until miso is crumbly and fairly dry. Allow to cool. Store unused portions in an airtight container.

Sweetened Tekka Miso

MAKES 1¼ CUPS

1 tablespoon oil
2/3 cup thin rounds of burdock root, soaked (p. 37)
½ carrot, cut into matchsticks
½ cup diced lotus root (optional)
1/3 cup Hatcho, red, or akadashi miso
¼ cup natural sugar
1 tablespoon sake or white wine
2 tablespoons ground roasted sesame seeds (p. 38), sesame butter, or *tahini*.
¼ cup roasted soybeans (p. 63) or soynuts

Heat a wok or skillet and coat with the oil. Add burdock and carrot and sauté over medium-high heat for 3 or 4 minutes. Reduce heat to low, then stir in next four ingredients and sauté for 3 or 4 minutes more. Stir in soybeans and remove from heat. Transfer to a bowl and allow to cool. Use as an all-purpose condiment.

Carrot & Red Pepper Miso Sauté

MAKES ¾ CUP

Many delicious varieties of Miso Sauté may be prepared without the use of sugar using the basic techniques given in the following two recipes.

3 tablespoons sesame oil
¼ teaspoon minced red peppers, Chinese red-pepper *chiang*, or tabasco sauce
1 carrot, grated fine
1 tablespoon grated gingerroot
¼ cup red, barley, or Hatcho miso

Heat a wok or skillet and coat with the oil. Add the red pepper and sauté for 15 seconds. Add grated carrot and gingerroot and sauté for 1 minute more. Stir in miso and sauté for 6 more minutes. Remove from heat and allow to cool before serving.

Onion-Sesame Miso Sauté
MAKES ½ CUP

1 tablespoon sesame oil
½ cup minced wild onions, scallions, leeks, or onions
3 to 4 tablespoons sweet red miso
Dash of 7-spice red pepper, tabasco sauce, or paprika

Heat the oil over high heat in a wok or skillet. Add onions and sauté for about 1 minute. Stir in the miso and red pepper, reduce heat to low, and sauté for 2 or 3 minutes more.

Garlic & Green Pepper Miso Sauté
MAKES ½ CUP

1 tablespoon oil
½ clove garlic, crushed or minced
1 or 2 green peppers, thinly sliced
2 tablespoons barley, red, or Hatcho miso
1 tablespoon natural sugar
3 tablespoons water

Heat a wok or skillet and coat with the oil. Add garlic and sauté over high heat for about 15 seconds. Add green peppers and sauté for 1 minute more. Reduce heat to medium, stir in remaining ingredients and cook, stirring constantly, for 2 more minutes. Allow to cool before serving.

Spicy Korean Miso Sauté
MAKES ¾ CUP

2 tablespoons sesame oil
1 clove of garlic, crushed
1 tablespoon grated gingerroot
2 green peppers, minced
½ small onion, diced
Dash of minced red pepper, tabasco sauce, or 7-spice red pepper
3 tablespoons red, barley, or Hatcho miso
2 teaspoons soy sauce
1 tablespoon sake or white wine

Heat a wok or skillet and coat with the oil. Add the next five ingredients and sauté for 2 minutes. Stir in the miso, soy sauce, and sake, return just to the boil, and remove from heat. Allow to cool before serving.

Vinegar Miso Sauté (Abura-su Miso)
MAKES ½ CUP

The addition of vinegar to many varieties of Miso Sauté gives a tangy flavor which is particularly well suited to deep-fried tofu.

1 tablespoon oil
1 small onion or leek, thinly sliced
1 clove of garlic, crushed or minced
1½ tablespoons red, barley, or Hatcho miso
1½ to 3 teaspoons natural sugar
1 tablespoon vinegar

Heat a wok or skillet and coat with the oil. Add onion and garlic and sauté over high heat for 2 minutes. Reduce heat to low, mix in miso and sugar, and simmer for 1 minute more. Remove from heat, mix in vinegar, and allow to cool.

For variety, substitute for the onions an equal volume of thinly sliced green peppers, mushrooms, or bamboo shoots.

Special Miso Toppings and Dipping Sauces

These preparations are delicious with chilled or deep-fried tofu. Or they may be used in many of the same ways as Shoyu Dipping Sauces.

Mixed Miso Toppings
MAKES ABOUT ¼ CUP

¼ cup red, barley, or Hatcho miso
Seasonings: Choose one of the following:
    2 cloves of garlic, grated
    4 teaspoons minced *umeboshi* (about 10) and, if desired, 2 tablespoons bonita flakes.
    1 teaspoon freshly grated *wasabi* or *wasabi* paste and, if desired, 2½ teaspoons natural sugar
    ¼ cup bonita flakes
    1 tablespoon each sesame butter and bonita flakes (or grated cheese) and ¼ teaspoon grated lemon rind. Serve in a hollowed half-lemon rind.
    ½ to 1 teaspoon hot mustard and 2 tablespoons *mirin*, sake, or white wine.

Combine miso and seasoning(s); mix well.

Peking Duck Dipping Sauce
(Homemade Tien M'ien Chiang)
MAKES ½ CUP

¼ cup Hatcho miso
1½ teaspoons sesame oil
½ teaspoon vegetable oil
¾ teaspoon sake or white wine
1 teaspoon shoyu
2¾ tablespoons natural sugar
¼ cup water

Combine the first five ingredients, mixing well. Dissolve sugar in water, then stir into the miso mixture until smooth. Refrigerate unused portions in a sealed container.

Akadashi Miso
MAKES ¼ CUP

2 tablespoons Hatcho miso
2 tablespoons red or light-yellow miso
2 tablespoons natural sugar
½ to 1 teaspoon shoyu

Combine all ingredients, mixing well.

Broiled Miso (Yakimiso)

Spread 1 to 2 teaspoons, red, barley, or Sweet Simmered Miso in a thin layer on the underside of a lid to an earthenware bowl, on a thin cedar plank the size of a large matchbox, in a clam or scallop shell, or on the concave surface of a large spoon. Holding the miso just above an open fire, move it slowly back and forth and broil for about 15 seconds, or until fragrant. (If broiling the miso on a lid, place the lid immediately on an empty bowl to minimize loss of aroma.) Serve miso as soon as possible (in container in which it was broiled) as an accompaniment for Crisp Deep-fried Tofu (p. 156) or Chilled Tofu (p. 105).

Gingerroot-Miso Barbeque or Dipping Sauce
MAKES ½ CUP

1½ teaspoons oil
½ teaspoon minced gingerroot
3½ tablespoons red, barley, or Hatcho miso
¼ cup water, stock, or dashi (p. 39)
1½ tablespoons natural sugar
1½ tablespoons *mirin*, dry sherry, or white wine
Dash of 7-spice red pepper or *sansho* pepper (optional)

Heat a wok or skillet and coat with the oil. Add gingerroot and sauté for 1 minute, or until just fragrant. Add the next four ingredients and cook, stirring constantly, for 3 minutes, or until mixture has the consistency of a thick sauce. Stir in the red or *sansho* pepper and remove from heat. Allow to cool before serving. Delicious with deep-fried tofu, barbequed foods, tempura, or fresh vegetable slices.

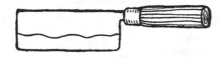

Vinegar Miso Dressings
(Sumiso)

These tangy preparations are widely used in Japanese-style tofu salads *(Aemono)* or as toppings for deep-fried tofu. Try adding small amounts of your favorite herbs and use with Western-style salads containing regular or deep-fried tofu and fresh vegetables.

Vinegar Miso Dressing
MAKES ¼ CUP

2 tablespoons red, barley, or Hatcho miso
1 tablespoon vinegar or 5 teaspoons lemon juice
4 teaspoons natural sugar
½ teaspoon *mirin*

Combine all ingredients, mixing well.

Mustard-Vinegar Miso Dressing
(Karashi Sumiso)
MAKES ½ CUP

3 tablespoons sweet white miso
3 tablespoons vinegar
1 tablespoon natural sugar
1 teaspoon *mirin* (optional)
¼ teaspoon hot mustard

Combine all ingredients, mixing well.

Sesame-Vinegar Miso Dressing
MAKES ¼ CUP

1 tablespoon red, barley, or Hatcho miso
1 tablespoon vinegar
1 tablespoon ground roasted sesame seeds (p. 38), sesame butter, or *tahini*
1 to 1½ tablespoons natural sugar

Combine all ingredients; mix well.

MISO SALAD DRESSINGS

When used with salads containing regular or deep-fried tofu, these Western-style dressings serve as delicious seasonings able to evoke tofu's subtle, delicate flavors.

Floating-Cloud Miso Dressing
MAKES ½ CUP

6 tablespoons oil
2 tablespoons (rice) vinegar or lemon juice
2 tablespoons red, barley, or Hatcho miso
¼ teaspoon sesame oil
½ clove garlic, crushed
Dash of powdered ginger
Dash of dry mustard

Combine all ingredients; whisk or shake well.

Miso-Sour Cream Dressing
MAKES ¾ CUP

3 tablespoons sour cream
1 tablespoon red, barley, or Hatcho miso
1½ tablespoons cream cheese or Roquefort cheese, softened
4 tablespoons oil
2 tablespoons lemon juice
1 tablespoon minced onions or chives

Combine all ingredients, mixing well.

Miso-Cream Cheese-Mayonnaise Dressing

MAKES ½ CUP

4 tablespoons mayonnaise
2 tablespoons lemon juice
1 tablespoon red, barley, or Hatcho miso
1½ tablespoons cream cheese, softened
1 tablespoon sesame or peanut butter
1½ teaspoons grated onion and juice

Combine all ingredients, mixing well.

NUT AND SEED BUTTER TOPPINGS, SPREADS, AND DRESSINGS

These uncooked Western-style preparations, seasoned with a little salt, miso, or shoyu, can be used in much the same way as miso toppings and dressings. Delicious with deep-fried tofu or Dengaku (p. 139) as well as on sandwiches and toast.

Miso-Walnut Butter

1 cup walnut meats, lightly roasted and ground to a paste
¼ cup red, barley, or Hatcho miso
3 to 4 tablespoons water or stock

Combine all ingredients, mixing well.

Cinnamon-Sesame Butter

MAKES ¼ CUP

2 tablespoons sesame butter or *tahini*
1 tablespoon honey or natural sugar
1 tablespoon water
Dash of cinnamon
Dash of salt or ½ teaspoon red miso

Combine all ingredients, mixing well.

Lemon-Sesame Butter

MAKES ¾ CUP

5 tablespoons sesame butter or *tahini*
½ teaspoon grated lemon, lime, or *yuzu* rind (or 2 teaspoons of their juice)
2 tablespoons red, barley, or Hatcho miso; or 4 teaspoons shoyu
1½ tablespoons water or stock
1 tablespoon honey or natural sugar (optional)

Combine all ingredients, mixing well.
To make a sauce or dressing, use 1 tablespoon miso and 3 to 4 tablespoons water.

Spicy Sesame Butter

MAKES ¼ CUP

3½ tablespoons sesame butter
2 teaspoons shoyu
1 tablespoon natural sugar or honey
2 tablespoons water
Dash of 7-spice red pepper or tabasco sauce

Combine all ingredients; mix well.

Vinegar-Peanut Butter

MAKES ¼ CUP

2 tablespoons peanut butter
2 tablespoons oil
4 teaspoons vinegar
1 tablespoon natural sugar
½ teaspoon salt or 1 tablespoon red miso

Combine all ingredients, mixing well.

Miso-Peanut Butter

MAKES ¼ CUP

3 tablespoons peanut butter
1 tablespoon red, barley, or Hatcho miso
1 tablespoon honey
2 tablespoons water

Combine all ingredients, mixing well.
For variety, use 1 tablespoon each sweet white miso and peanut butter, 2 teaspoons each honey and vinegar, and a dash of shoyu.

White Sesame-Vinegar Miso Dressing

MAKES ¼ CUP

3 tablespoons sweet white miso
1½ tablespoons vinegar
1 tablespoon sesame butter or *tahini*, or 1½ tablespoons ground roasted sesame seeds (p. 38)
½ teaspoon natural sugar

Combine all ingredients; mix well.

Peanut-Vinegar Miso Dressing

MAKES ¼ CUP

1 tablespoon sweet white miso
2 teaspoons vinegar or lemon juice
20 peanuts, minced
2 teaspoons honey
½ teaspoon shoyu

Combine all ingredients, mixing well.

BASIC SAUCES

Each of these sauces may be served with a wide variety of different tofu preparations. They will all be called for in recipes throughout this book.

Onion Sauce

MAKES 3½ CUPS

This naturally sweet, rich brown sauce is prepared slowly like the basis for a French onion soup. Its basic form and many variations go well with a number of different types of tofu. For best results, make a large quantity at one time since the flavor improves after several days and re-warmings. It may be served hot or cold to equal advantage.

2 tablespoons oil
6 onions, thinly sliced
2 tablespoons shoyu; or 3 tablespoons red miso creamed in ¼
    cup water
1 tablespoon butter

Heat a large casserole or heavy pot and coat with the oil. Add onions, cover, and simmer over low heat for about 2 to 3 hours, stirring thoroughly once every 10 minutes. When onions are a rich brown and very soft, mix in the butter and shoyu and simmer for 10 to 15 more minutes. (If using miso, return just to the boil, then remove from heat.) Serve hot or, for best flavor, allow to cool overnight and serve reheated or chilled the next day.

VARIATIONS:

*To ½ cup chilled Onion Sauce add 1 to 2 tablespoons shoyu or miso. Serve as a topping for chilled or deep-fried tofu. For variety garnish with diced or grated cheese or thinly sliced onions.

*Seasoned Onion Sauce with Nut Butters: Thin your favorite nut butter with a small amount of water or stock and, if desired, some lemon or orange juice, and add to 2 parts Onion Sauce. Season with herbs, 7-spice red pepper, shoyu, or miso. Garnish with thinly sliced green onions or parsley. For variety add large chunks of nuts, diced cheese, or sprouts. Serve with Chilled Tofu or as a topping for any variety of deep-fried tofu.

Mushroom Sauce

FOR 2 TO 3 SERVINGS

1½ tablespoons butter
½ teaspoon minced garlic
1 tablespoon minced onion
½ teaspoon grated gingerroot
4 to 5 small mushrooms, thinly sliced
1/3 cup ketchup
1 tablespoon red miso (optional)
Dash of pepper

Melt butter in a skillet. Add garlic, onion, and gingerroot and sauté for about 1 minute. Add mushrooms and sauté for 2 more minutes. Add ketchup, miso, and pepper and sauté for 1 minute more. Serve with Tofu Burgers (p. 127), Okara Chapati (p. 83), Crisp Tortillas (p. 170), or as a topping for Chilled Tofu (p. 105).

White Sauce

MAKES 1 CUP

Also known as Cream- or Béchamel Sauce, this traditional Western favorite acquires a distinctive flavor and creaminess when seasoned with miso. Season lightly for use with vegetables (such as cauliflower or potatoes) and more prominently for use with tofu dishes. Numerous variations prepared with soymilk and containing tofu are given on page 207.

2 tablespoons butter or oil
2 tablespoons (whole-wheat) flour
1 cup milk (soy or dairy); or stock
3 to 4 teaspoons red miso; 2 to 2½ teaspoons shoyu; or ½ to
    2/3 teaspoon salt
Dash of pepper, paprika, or cayenne
1 tablespoon minced parsley (optional)

Melt the butter (or heat the oil) in a skillet. Add flour and, stirring constantly, cook over low heat for 1 to 2 minutes, or until flour is well blended and its raw taste has vanished. Add ½ cup milk (or stock) a little at a time, continuing to stir, then mix in the miso and slowly add the remainder of the milk. Increase heat to medium and cook, whisking or stirring, for 3 to 4 minutes more, or until sauce develops a smooth, nicely thickened consistency. Stir in pepper and parsley and remove from heat.

Note: Many cooks prefer to heat the milk to just scalding before it is added. In this case, after sautéing flour, remove skillet from heat until flour stops bubbling. Then pour in the near-boiling milk. When it stops steaming, stir briskly until smooth and proceed as above.

Brown Sauce

Prepare as for a white sauce except cook the flour until it is lightly browned and fragrant.

Teriyaki Sauce

MAKES 2/3 CUP

Generally used in Japan to baste broiled fish, this savory sauce is now used by many Westerners with shish kebab and other barbequed preparations. Also good as a dip for fresh vegetables or a topping for deep-fried tofu.

¼ cup shoyu or 6 tablespoons red miso
3 tablespoons sake or white wine
3 tablespoons brown sugar
1 teaspoon grated gingerroot or 1½ teaspoons powdered ginger
2 cloves of garlic, crushed
1 tablespoon sesame or vegetable oil
¼ teaspoon dry mustard

Combine all ingredients, mixing well. Marinate foods (deep-fried tofu, green peppers, onions, tomatoes, etc.) for at least 1 hour before skewering and broiling. Use remaining sauce to baste.

Gingerroot Sauce

MAKES 1¾ CUPS

1 cup dashi (p. 39), stock, or water
¼ cup shoyu
2 to 2½ tablespoons natural sugar
1 tablespoon cornstarch or arrowroot, dissolved in 4 table-
　　spoons water
1 tablespoon grated gingerroot
Dash of 7-spice red pepper

Combine the dashi, shoyu, and sugar in a small saucepan and
bring to a boil. Stir in the dissolved cornstarch to thicken. Mix
in the grated gingerroot and season with the pepper. Delicious
with deep-fried tofu dishes.

Ankake Sauce

MAKES 1¼ CUPS

1 cup dashi (p. 39), stock, or water
5 teaspoons shoyu
1 tablespoon natural sugar
2 teaspoons cornstarch, arrowroot, or *kuzu*, dissolved in 1½
　　tablespoons water
½ teaspoon grated lemon rind or gingerroot (optional)

Combine dashi, shoyu, and sugar in a small saucepan and
bring to a boil. Stir in dissolved cornstarch and, if used, the
lemon rind, and cook for about 1 minute more until thick.

　　For a Mild Ankake Sauce use 3½ teaspoons shoyu, 1
teaspoon sugar, and 1½ teaspoons cornstarch. Omit lemon
rind.

Rich Gingerroot-Ankake Sauce

MAKES 1 CUP

2/3 cup dashi (p. 39), stock, or water
3 tablespoons shoyu
2 tablespoons natural sugar
2 teaspoons arrowroot or cornstarch, dissolved in 2 table-
　　spoons water
2 teaspoons freshly grated gingerroot or gingerroot juice

Prepare as for Ankake Sauce, above.

Korean Barbeque Sauce

MAKES ¼ CUP

2 tablespoons shoyu
2 teaspoons natural sugar
2 teaspoons sesame oil
1 tablespoon ground roasted sesame seeds (p. 38) or 1 tea-
　　spoon sesame butter or *tahini*
1 tablespoon diced leeks or onions
1 clove garlic, crushed
¼ teaspoon 7-spice red pepper or tabasco sauce
Dash of pepper

Combine all ingredients, mixing well. Serve with Grilled
Thick Agé (p. 174), Grilled Tofu (p. 223), or any variety of
deep-fried tofu.

Sweet & Sour Sauce

MAKES 1¼ CUPS

1 tablespoon oil
½ onion, thinly sliced
½ small carrot, cut into irregular pieces
1 green pepper, cut into irregular pieces
¾ cup water or stock
2 tablespoons shoyu
2½ tablespoons natural sugar
2 teaspoons rice vinegar
1½ teaspoons cornstarch dissolved in 1½ tablespoons water

Heat a skillet or wok and coat with the oil. Add onion, carrot,
and green pepper, and sauté for 3 to 4 minutes, or until onion
is transparent. Add the next four ingredients, bring to a boil,
and simmer for 3 minutes. Stir in dissolved cornstarch and
cook for 30 more seconds or until thick.

　　For variety, omit the oil and vegetables, and add 1
teaspoon grated gingerroot and 1 tablespoon sake or white
wine to the remaining ingredients.

Tomato & Cheese Sauce

MAKES 1¼ CUPS

2 tablespoons butter
1¼ cups chopped tomatoes
½ onion, minced
¾ cup grated cheese
½ teaspoon salt, 1 tablespoon shoyu, or 1½ tablespoons red
　　miso
¼ teaspoon paprika
¼ teaspoon oregano or basil
Dash of pepper

Melt butter in a skillet. Add tomatoes and onions and sauté
for 2 minutes. Cover, reduce heat to low, and simmer for 3
minutes. Uncover and continue simmering, stirring occasionally, for 15 minutes more, or until sauce is thick. Stir in
remaining ingredients and remove from heat. Delicious served
over deep-fried tofu.

Ketchup-Worcestershire Sauce

MAKES 6 TABLESPOONS

¼ cup ketchup
2 tablespoons Worcestershire sauce

Combine ingredients, mixing well. Serve with deep-fried tofu.

Tangy Ketchup & Lemon Sauce

MAKES ¾ CUP

1/3 cup ketchup
5 teaspoons lemon juice
1 teaspoon shoyu
1 teaspoon minced onions

Combine all ingredients, mixing well.

　　For variety add ¼ to ½ teaspoon hot mustard, 1
teaspoon horseradish, ½ teaspoon crushed anise or ground
roasted sesame seeds, or 1 tablespoon minced parsley.

RICE, NOODLES, AND
OTHER BASIC PREPARATIONS

Brown Rice

The Japanese say that when cooked, both regular and *sushi* rice are at their peak of flavor when the rice at the bottom of the pot is golden brown and slightly crisp. And even moderns prize the aroma of rice cooked in a heavy iron pot over a wood fire.

2 cups brown rice, rinsed and soaked overnight in 2 2/3 cups water

In a heavy covered pot, bring water and rice to a boil over high heat. Reduce heat to low and simmer for 45 to 50 minutes or until all water is absorbed or evaporated. Uncover pot, remove from heat, and stir rice thoroughly with a wooden spoon. (If a slightly drier consistency is desired, transfer rice to a wooden bowl before stirring). Allow to cool for several minutes, then cover pot (or bowl) with a double layer of cloth until you are ready to serve.

To pressure cook: Rinse and drain 1 cup rice. Without soaking, combine in a pressure cooker with 1 cup water. Bring to pressure (15 pounds), reduce heat to low, and simmer for 25 minutes. Allow pressure to come down naturally for 10 to 15 minutes. Open pot and mix rice well. Allow to stand uncovered for 3 to 5 minutes, then cover with a cloth as above.

Brown Rice Porridge
SERVES 2 OR 3

Called *Congee* in China and *Okayu* in Japan, this is a popular main course at breakfast in many homes and temples. Easy to digest, rice porridge is considered the ideal food for sick people, and nursing mothers sometimes skim the creamy liquid from the porridge's surface to feed their babies as a breast milk supplement. In China, rice porridge is often served garnished or seasoned with doufu-ru (p. 264), as are the hundreds of varieties of rice gruel. The latter, a close relative of Japan's *Zosui* (p. 138), is prepared by cooking vegetables (often leftovers) with rice porridge and seasoning the mixture with miso or soy sauce.

½ cup brown rice, soaked overnight in 4½ cups water

Prepare as for brown rice, setting lid slightly ajar and simmering for about 90 minutes, or until rice develops a porridge-like consistency. Serve immediately, seasoned with Sesame Salt (p. 00) or salt- or miso-pickled vegetables. If desired, add crumbled *nori* and minced leeks.

Or combine 1¼ cups (leftover) cooked rice with 3½ cups water and, without soaking, proceed as above.

To pressure cook: Rinse and drain ½ cup rice. Without soaking, combine in a pressure cooker with 2½ cups water. Bring to pressure (15 pounds), reduce heat to low, and simmer for 45 minutes. Allow pressure to come down naturally for 10 to 15 minutes. Open pot and mix porridge well. Allow to stand uncovered for 3 to 5 minutes before serving.

Sushi Rice
(Rice in Vinegar Dressing)
MAKES 2½ CUPS

1 cup (brown) rice, soaked in 11/3 cups water overnight in a heavy 2- to 4- quart pot
Vinegar Dressing:
2 1/3 tablespoons (rice) vinegar
1 tablespoon natural sugar
2 teaspoons *mirin* (optional)
½ teaspoon salt

Bring soaked rice to a boil in a covered pot. Reduce heat to low and simmer for 40 to 50 minutes or until all water has been absorbed and rice is quite light and dry. (If using white rice, simmer for only 15 to 20 minutes). Remove rice from heat and allow to stand for 5 minutes. Transfer hot rice to a large wooden bowl, platter, or other non-metallic container and immediately sprinkle on the dressing. With a wooden spoon, chopsticks, or a wide fork in one hand, and a fan or flat pot lid in the other, mix the rice vigorously while fanning to cool it as quickly as possible. Fan and stir for about 3 minutes, then allow rice to cool to room temperature.

For variety, prepare Unsweetened Sushi Rice by omitting the sugar and *mirin* in the dressing, and by increasing the vinegar to 4 tablespoons and the salt to 1½ teaspoons.

Noodles
SERVES 2 OR 3

4½ to 5 ounces dry buckwheat or whole-wheat noodles (*soba* or *udon*)

Bring 2 to 3 quarts of water to a rolling boil over high heat. Scatter noodles slowly over surface of water and return to the boil. Lower heat until water is boiling actively but does not overflow. Cook uncovered for about 5 minutes, or until noodles are tender but not soft. Pour noodles into a colander placed in the sink and drain briefly, then transfer to a large container filled with circulating cold water. Stir noodles with chopsticks for several minutes until they cool to temperature of water, then transfer noodles back into colander; drain well and serve.

To serve hot: Bring about 1 quart of fresh water to a boil in a saucepan. Place 1 individual portion of noodles into a small strainer, dip noodle-filled strainer into boiling water for about 5 seconds, then shake strainer above saucepan to rid noodles of excess moisture. Transfer noodles to individual serving bowls, pour on Noodle Broth (p. 40), and top with garnishes. Serve immediately.

In many fine Japanese soba restaurants, a portion of the nutritious hot water in which the noodles were initially cooked is poured into a small teapot and served after the meal. Each guest seasons his portion to taste with leftover Noodle Broth.

Sesame Salt *(Gomashio)*   MAKES ABOUT ½ CUP

A delicious all-purpose seasoning for grains, salads, beans, eggs, cereals, and sautéed vegetables, Sesame Salt is generally made with about 7 parts whole sesame seeds to 1 part salt. Please begin by studying instructions for preparing ground roasted sesame seeds (p. 38).

2 teaspoons sea salt
5 tablespoons white or black sesame seeds

Heat a heavy skillet. Pour in the salt and roast, stirring constantly, for about 1 minute. Add the sesame seeds and roast until done. Grind the salt-sesame mixture in a *suribachi* or hand mill as for Ground Roasted Sesame Seeds (p. 38). Store in an airtight container.

Sweet Vinegared Gingerroot *(Gari)*

3 tablespoons vinegar
2 tablespoons natural sugar
Dash of salt
1 piece of gingerroot, sliced into paper-thin rounds (¼ cup), parboiled, drained, and patted dry with a towel

Combine the first three ingredients in a small saucepan and heat, stirring constantly, until the sugar just dissolves. Now combine with the sliced gingerroot in a small bowl so that the gingerroot is fully immersed in the liquid. Cover and refrigerate overnight or for at least several hours. Serve with Inari-zushi, Sushi Rice, or other rice dishes.

Paper-thin Omelets   MAKES ABOUT 8

These omelets may be made into an envelope or purse *(chakin)* used to contain Sushi Rice or Sushi Okara, or they may be cut into thin strips called "threads of gold" and scattered over the top of Sushi Rice.

4 eggs
¼ teaspoon salt
1 teaspoon ground roasted sesame seeds (p. 38) (optional)
1 to 2 teaspoons oil

In a small bowl, combine eggs, ¼ teaspoon salt and sesame; mix well. Heat a small skillet and coat lightly with oil, pouring off any excess. Pour about one-eighth of the egg mixture into the skillet, swishing it around quickly so that it just covers the bottom of the pan. Cook over high heat for about 20 to 30 seconds on one side only to form a thin omelet. Transfer omelet to a plate and allow to cool. Prepare 8 omelets, oiling the pan lightly after every 3 or 4. Sliver to use as a garnish.

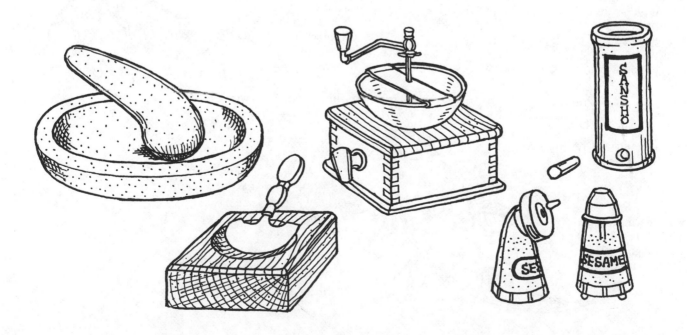

Our Favorite Tofu Recipes

Among the more than 500 dishes in this book, there are certain ones we enjoy again and again, and like to serve to guests as an introduction to tofu cookery. Most take very little time to prepare and use readily available Western ingredients. We have starred those we **suggest** you make your very first dishes. In later chapters we list our favorites first.

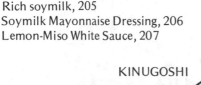

PART II

Cooking with Tofu:

Recipes from East and West

4

Soybeans

WHOLE DRY soybeans are the essential ingredient in the tofu maker's art. Each evening, he concludes his daily cycle of work by measuring out 15 to 20 gallons of beans in a special wooden box made with precisely mitered corners and a brand of the gods of good fortune burned into one of its sides (fig. 10). One of the gods is *Ebisu*, the deity of craftsmen, tradesmen, and fishermen; he symbolizes the hard worker who earns his living by honest toil. The other is *Daikoku*, the happy god whose wealth is so vast that he does not mind the rats nibbling at his bales of grain. The tofu maker washes the measured beans in a large cedar barrel bound together with hoops of brightly-polished brass, then sets them aside to soak overnight. He and the beans sleep under the same roof.

The story of tofu must begin with the story of soybeans. Officially known as *Glycine max* and botanically a member of the family *Leguminosae* (legumes), the soybean plant stands about 2 feet tall, has a slightly woody stem, and sprouts its leaves in groups of three. The leaves, stems, and pods are covered with soft brownish-green hairs, and the plant's seeds—soybeans—are borne in the pods which grow near the stalk in clusters of three to five (fig. 11). Each pod usually contains two to three seeds. Fresh soybeans are similar in color and size to green peas. The mature, dried beans are usually tan, beige, or yellow, but some varieties are also black, brown, green, or bi-colored. American beans are slightly smaller and yellower than most Japanese varieties. They grow from Louisiana in the south to Minnesota in the north, and from Texas in the west to the Carolinas in the east. Planted from May to June in rows about 40 inches apart, the fresh green beans are ready to eat by mid-July; the mature beans are harvested in September or October, after the leaves have fallen and the seeds have dried on the vine.

Soybeans are pulses, a term which refers to the seeds of leguminous plants such as peas, lentils, and beans. These plants have a symbiotic relationship with bacteria called *rhizobia,* which form nodules in the plants' roots. *Rhizobia* capture nitrogen (the essential element in all protein) from the air and fix it in the soil, thereby greatly enhancing the soil's fertility. Hence, many of the first soybean plants grown in the United States were used simply as cover crops or "green manure"; even today, all farmers, after harvesting the beans, plow under the remainder of the plant to create nitrogen-rich humus soil. Easy to grow in small vegetable gardens or window boxes, the soybean plant is a favorite with organic and biodynamic gardeners, too, for much the same reason.

Where did the word "soybean" come from? The present-day Chinese call soybeans *ta tou*, or "great beans." The Japanese pronounce the same written characters as *daizu*. It is obvious that neither of these words resembles the word "soy." But in a Chinese dictionary dating from about the beginning of the Christian era, soybeans are called *sou*. In addition, the Japanese pronounce the word for soy sauce (*chiang-yu*) as *shoyu*. The etymology of the English word may therefore be traced either to the Japanese word for soy sauce or to the ancient Chinese word for soybean.

The origins of the soybean plant are obscured by legend and the Oriental urge to endow all things worthy of respect with ancient ancestry. It is said

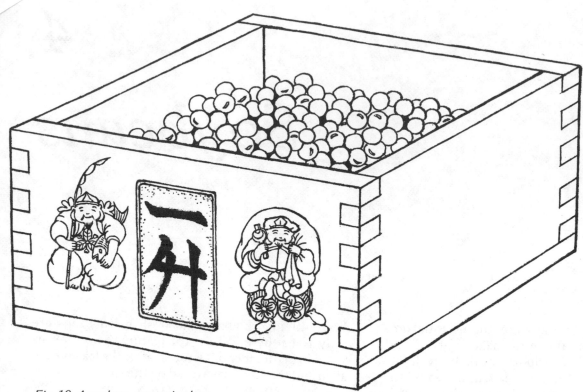

Fig. 10. A soybean measuring box

that long ago, sages and wise rulers bestowed the bounty of soybeans upon the generations of mankind. The numerous myths, legends, and historical accounts of its ancestry all reflect a common wish to honor the soybean for the service it has given to humanity.

From evidence based on distribution, it seems likely that soybeans originated in Eastern Asia, probably either in northern China or Mongolia. Legend has it that soybeans are one of the oldest crops grown by man, extensively cultivated and highly valued as a food for centuries before written records were kept.

In an eighteenth-century Chinese encyclopedia, the discovery of the soybean was attributed to two legendary characters, *Yu-hsiung* and *Kung-kung shih*, who were said to have lived more than five thousand years ago. But it is not clear whether they discovered beans in general or soybeans in particular. A more widely known theory states that in 2838 B.C., a Chinese emperor named *Sheng-nung* wrote a *Materia Medica* which describes the plants of China and includes a description of the soybean together with a long discourse on its medical properties. And in writings reported to be published as early as 2207 B.C., Chinese agricultural experts give detailed tech-

nical advice concerning soybean planting and soil preferences.

It is known from reliable historical sources that soybeans were cultivated in China before the Han Dynasty (206 B.C.-220 A.D.) and that they were used in processed form as food by the second century B.C., when the ruler Liu An of Huai-nan is said to have discovered the process for making tofu. According to the ten-volume *Chi'min Yaushu*, mankind's oldest encyclopedia of agriculture, compiled in the sixth century, soybeans were initially brought to China by the great Chinese explorer *Choken*, who was the first to make contact with Greece, Rome, and India, and to open the Silk Road.

The transmission of soybeans from northern China or Manchuria to Japan, probably via Korea, may have taken place sometime between the sixth and eighth centuries, concurrent with the spread of Buddhism. (The discovery of charred soybeans together with husked rice in neolithic dwellings in Japan suggests that soybeans may actually have arrived in Japan long before the existence of written records.) Mention is made of soybeans in Japan's earliest existing documents, the famous *Kojiki* of 712 A.D. and the *Nihonshoki* of 720 A.D.. Records from the Nara period (710-794) show that soybean foods (such as miso and the progenitor of shoyu) were taxed by the government, and thus were an important part of the Japanese way of life even then.

Along with rice, wheat, barley, and millet, soybeans were included among China's venerated *mu-ku,* or Five Sacred Grains, as early as the beginning of the Christian era. Since soybeans are not technically a grain, some scholars believe that it was beans in general rather than the soybean that were given this lofty title. Nevertheless, living close to the earth, the people of East Asia grasped the dependence of human life upon these basic crops. Their sense of the sacred grew out of a feeling of interrelationship—and gratitude—and determined their way of relating to soybeans and other essential foods.

The sense of the sacredness of soybean foods is still alive in Japan today; here the words tofu, miso, and shoyu are commonly preceeded in everyday speech by the honorific prefix *o.* Rather than saying *tofu,* most people say *o-tofu,* meaning "honorable tofu." And on the last day of winter, as determined by Japan's traditional lunar calendar, roasted soybeans play a key role in one of the country's most ancient and widely observed celebrations of ritual purification. In homes and temples throughout Japan, these *fuku-mame* or "beans of good fortune" are scattered by the handful in each room, then tossed through an open window into the cold night air with everyone chanting "Out with all evils; in with good fortune."

Today, the soybean has become the king of the Japanese kitchen. Indeed, the arrival of tofu, miso, and shoyu in Japan initiated a revolution in the national cuisine. Now when Japanese connoisseurs speak of these foods, they use many of the same terms we employ when evaluating cheeses or wines; traditional tofu masters often say that the consummation of their art is but to evoke the fine flavors latent in the soybean. Again and again we have heard them declare that "only *nigari* can unfold the delicate nuances of sweetness and the fine, subtle bouquet in the best domestic beans." And when the new crop of soybeans arrives at tofu shops late each fall, ardent devotees sample the first tofu with the discrimination and relish of French vintners.

Many Japanese grow soybeans in their vegetable gardens and they are cultivated extensively along the paths which separate one rice paddy from another. Varieties considered to have the finest flavors have been known for centuries by such names as "child of the white cranes" or "waving sleeves."

Except for Manchuria, the countries of East Asia have not traditionally pressed or crushed soybeans on a large scale to extract their oil. Nor have they generally baked, boiled, or ground the beans into flour. Using simple tools and processes, countless generations have discovered other ways of trans-

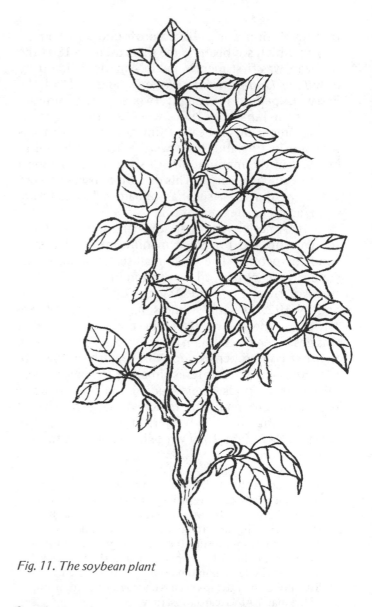

Fig. 11. The soybean plant

forming soybeans into delicious foods. After almost 1,000 years of use in China, the soybean was transmitted to Japan. Over the period of another millenium, the Japanese modified each of the basic Chinese soybean foods and created a number of new ones. Finally, at the beginning of the present century, the Japanese made the first major commercial shipment of soybeans to the Western world. In its contact with the West's unique patterns of cooking, farming, and food-processing, the soybean entered a new phase in its long history.

A German botanist, Englebert Kaempfer, spent 3 years in Japan from 1690 to 1693 and was the first Westerner to study and write about Japanese soybean foods. The first small samples of seed soybeans arrived in the West as early as 1790 and were planted in England's Botanical Gardens. The fact that their arrival corresponded with the beginning of the industrial revolution was to have a profound effect on the way in which soybeans came to be used. In 1804 the soybean was first mentioned in American literature in *Willic's Domestic Encyclopedia*, and in 1854, the Perry Expedition brought two soybean varieties back from Japan. In 1908, when the first commercial shipment of soybeans from Asia to the West was received in England, they were processed for oil to be used in the manufacture of soap, while the meal was fed to dairy cattle. This pattern of use, so different from that in Asia, has remained basically unchanged up to the present time.

In America, the first soybeans were used as a forage crop and for green manure rather than as a food for people. The first small-scale processing of soybeans to obtain oil was begun in 1911. In 1920 the American Soybean Association was organized and by 1922 Decatur, Illinois, had become the center of soybean processing in the U.S. In 1923, Charles Piper and William Morse wrote *The Soybean*, the first comprehensive book in English on this subject. Showing great interest in all of the basic Oriental soybean foods, they studied their methods of preparation in detail and included a large number of recipes using them in Western-style cookery. With remarkable insight, they wrote in the preface to their classical study:

> The importance of the soybean lies largely in the fact that the seeds can be produced more cheaply than those of any other leguminous crop. This is due to both its high yielding capacity and to the ease of harvesting. These facts alone insure the increasing importance of the crop in the future when the land shall be called upon to yield its maximum crop of food. There can be little doubt that the soybean is destined to become one of the major American crops. (p. v).

When Piper and Morse wrote these words, soybeans were still a relatively unknown commodity. It was not until 1935 that the acreage of beans used for oil extraction equalled that used for forage. Blessed with expanses of territory well suited by climate and soil quality for soybean production, and equipped with a technology that has made it possible to produce a bushel of beans with less than 8 minutes labor, the U.S. farmer was able by the 1950s to grow soybeans competetive price- and quality-wise with those originating in the Orient. By 1973, the U.S. soybean crop had reached the phenomenal figure of 1½ billion bushels (47 million tons), a *twentyfold* increase in size since 1940 and a 24 percent increase over the previous year. Over the same period, the yield per acre increased 68 percent to a high of 27 bushels. Recent tests plots have yielded as much as 60 to 100 bushels per acre, and experts feel that in the near future a nationwide average of 40 bushels may be possible. It is not likely that such large increases in production and yield will ever again be duplicated by soybeans or any other crop.

In the short space of two generations, America has become the world's largest producer of soybeans, supplying over 65 percent of the planet's total output. The number-two producer, Brazil, supplys about 18 percent, and China about 13 percent. Canada, Australia, Russia, and Indonesia also produce fairly large crops. Soybeans are now the number one U.S. farm export, and foreign demand is ever on the rise. Worth an astounding 5 *billion* dollars in 1974 and accounting for more than 8 percent of our total exports, soybean sales abroad generate a large proportion of the foreign currency used to import oil and other basic raw materials.

Thus, a nutritional cornerstone of East Asian cuisine has emerged as the most important American cash crop. Called "meat of the fields" in Asia, soybeans are now known among American farmers as "gold from the soil." Nevertheless, as late as September 1973, the then president of the United States could make a statement—that made headlines throughout Japan—to the effect that he had never seen a soybean. A majority of adult Americans are reported to have first heard the word "soybean" less than ten years ago and many have never seen a soybean plant, nor tasted fresh (green) or whole dry soybeans, or soybean sprouts. Yet, having become so well established in our agriculture and economy, soybeans are now gradually becoming part of our language and culture. At least one relatively large-scale American farming enterprise, a Tennessee-based new-age community called *The Farm*, has taken the historic step of cultivating them for use primarily as a food staple in the vegetarian diet of its members. *The Farm* is bound to be only the first of many as, over the coming years, the soybean becomes an ever-more integral part of our national cuisine.

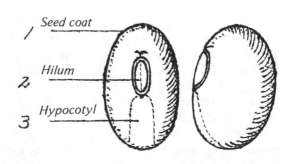

1 Seed coat
2 Hilum
3 Hypocotyl

COOKING WITH WHOLE DRY SOYBEANS

In Japan, soybeans are only occasionally cooked at home. To save time and the cost of lengthy cooking, most people purchase ready-made soybean dishes, usually at the local delicatessen. Many of these store-bought preparations contain large amounts of shoyu and/or sugar to serve as natural preservatives. Whole (tan) soybeans are also available commercially deep-fried in a sweetened batter and sold as Soy Brittle (p. 62), while black soybeans are often used in confectionery treats.

But when most of us in the West set out to use soybeans, we usually start with those available in their whole, dry form at natural food stores and supermarkets. Presently the least expensive known source of usable protein, whole soybeans are also rich in iron, and vitamins B_1 and B_2. A truly remarkable food, they contain 1½ times as much protein as any other legume (34% to 38%), and are low in carbohydrates. Many recent cookbooks, especially those emphasizing natural foods, have begun to include a wide variety of recipes using boiled or baked soybeans in Western-style salads, soups, casseroles, and spreads.

Fresh, new-crop soybeans—the tastiest type—are generally available from the beginning of November. When storing large quantities, always use cloth rather than plastic sacks. When soybeans are kept over long periods, a small harmless moth and its eggs may appear among the beans. These can be easily removed by sifting and then exposing the beans to direct sunlight for one day.

Once you decide to make soybeans, tofu, and soymilk a basic part of your diet, buy a 60- to 100-pound sack of food- or seed-grade beans at greatly reduced prices from a wholesaler or farmer's supply store; avoid the little packages retailed at inflated prices.

To ensure best flavor, digestibility, and deactivation of trypsin inhibitor (see p. 70), soybeans must be cooked—preferably pressure cooked—until they are very soft; a single bean should be easily crushed between the thumb and ring finger or between the tongue and roof of the mouth. The beans should also be throughly soaked in plenty of water (see graph, p. 289), the water discarded, and new water used for cooking; this helps remove the oligosaccharides believed to cause flatulence. When pressure cooking, some cooks add 1½ teaspoons oil for each cup of beans in order to prevent the seed coats from clogging the steam escape valve; some also prefer to add salt and seasonings before pressure cooking. If cooking the beans at only 10 pounds pressure, double the cooking times given in the following recipes.

Pressure Cooked Soybeans Plus   MAKES 2¼ CUPS

1 cup dry soybeans, rinsed and soaked for 2 or 3 hours in 2 quarts water
2 cups water
A thin wedge of lemon or lime (optional)

Drain and rinse soaked beans; combine with 2 cups water in a pressure cooker. Bring to full pressure (15 pounds) over high heat, then reduce heat to low and simmer for 25 minutes. (If soaked overnight, simmer beans for only 20 minutes). Remove from heat and allow to stand for 10 to 15 minutes as pressure returns to normal. Cool lid under running cold water and open.

Return cooker to stove, stir in any of the ingredients listed below, and simmer uncovered over low heat for 10 to 15 minutes, or until flavors are nicely married. If necessary, add ¼ cup water during simmering. Stir from time to time. Serve hot or cold.

*2 tablespoons red, barley, or Hatcho miso (creamed with a little of the cooking liquid), or 4 teaspoons shoyu, or 1 teaspoon salt. If desired, add 1 teaspoon lemon juice or 1 tablespoon butter. For a deliciously rich flavor, add 1 (sautéed) minced onion together with the miso and stir in ½ cup grated or ¼ cup Parmesan cheese just before removing from heat.

*2 to 4 tablespoons molasses (honey or natural sugar) and 1 to 1½ tablespoons miso or shoyu.

*¼ cup sesame butter, *tahini*, ground roasted sesame seeds, or peanut butter, and 1 tablespoon miso or shoyu.

*3 to 4 tablespoons dry *hijiki* or slivered *kombu* (reconstituted, p. 37), 1 tablespoon shoyu or 1½ tablespoons red miso, 3 tablespoons sesame butter, and 1 onion or ¾ cup grated carrot (pre-sautéed in 1 tablespoon oil, if desired). For extra sweetness, add 1½ teaspoons honey or sugar.

*½ to 1 cup diced tomatoes, onions, carrots, celery, mushrooms, lotus root, burdock root, sprouts, fresh or dried *daikon*, or *kombu*. Add vegetables alone or in combination. Season with ½ teaspoon salt or 2 tablespoons shoyu (or miso). Add ½ teaspoon curry powder and 1 clove of crushed garlic with the onions or carrots.

*In any of the above recipes, after the beans and seasonings have finished cooking, try sautéing the mixture for a few minutes in a little (sesame) oil.

Boiled Soybeans   MAKES 2¼ CUPS

This recipe is for those who don't own a pressure cooker. You may wish to prepare 2 or 3 times the amounts given and refrigerate the unused portions.

1 cup dry soybeans, rinsed and soaked overnight in 2 quarts water
6½ to 7 cups water
½ to 1 teaspoon lemon juice (optional)

Drain soaked beans and combine with 4 cups water in a heavy pot. Bring to a boil over high heat, then reduce heat to low. Cover pot, leaving lid slightly ajar, and simmer for 2 hours. Add 1 cup water and simmer for 1 hour more. Again add 1 cup water and simmer for 1 hour. Add ½ to 1 cup water and simmer for 1 to 1½ more hours, or until beans are soft enough to be easily crushed between the thumb and ring finger. Add seasonings and/or vegetables and proceed as in the previous recipe.

Combine cooked soybeans and rice, mixing well. Serve hot or chilled, topping each portion with a large dollop of the mayonnaise and, if desired, a sprinkling of parsley.

Soybeans in Tortillas
SERVES 4

2 tablespoons oil
3 onions, minced
1 cup soybeans, pressure cooked (p. 59), drained, and mashed
¼ cup soybean cooking liquid
2 tablespoons shoyu or 3 tablespoons red miso
Dash of tabasco sauce or ½ teaspoon cumin (optional)
12 tortillas, warmed and buttered
1½ cups grated cheese
1 tomato, chopped
1 cup shredded lettuce or ½ cup thinly-sliced leeks

Heat a skillet and coat with the oil. Add onions and sauté for 6 minutes, then remove from heat and mix with the next four ingredients. Spoon into a bowl and serve together with the tortillas and remaining condiments, each in separate bowls. Invite guests to spoon soybean-onion mixture in a line across the center of a tortilla and top with a little of the cheese, tomato, and lettuce. Roll up tortilla and eat like a taco.

Soybean Spreads and Dips
MAKES ABOUT 2 CUPS

1 cup cooked soybeans (p. 59), mashed or pureéd
¼ to ½ cup diced onions, raw or sautéed; or 1 clove garlic, crushed
¼ to ½ cup nut butters, sesame butter, sunflower seeds, cheese, yogurt, diced apple, or raisins
1 to 2 tablespoons lemon juice, shoyu, or honey
Dash of pepper, cardamon, coriander, chili powder, or grated orange peel

Combine all ingredients in a bowl and mix together to make a thick spread.

Tangy Sesame-Soybean Spread
MAKES 2½ CUPS

1 cup cooked soybeans (p. 59), mashed or puréed
1/3 cup sesame butter
2 tablespoons lemon juice
1/3 cup diced raw onion
1 clove of garlic, crushed or minced
1 tablespoon honey
1 tablespoon shoyu or 1½ tablespoons red miso
Dash of pepper

Combine all ingredients and mash together until smooth.

Soybeans Pressure Cooked with Brown Rice
SERVES 4 TO 6

This simple preparation is our favorite for using whole soybeans and is also popular in many Zen temples. The combination of rice and beans increases the total available protein by over 30 percent.

2 cups brown rice
½ cup soybeans
2½ cups water

Combine rice and beans in a pressure cooker, rinse well, and drain. Add the 2½ cups water, cover, and bring to full pressure (15 pounds) over high heat. Reduce heat to low and simmer for 25 minutes. Set aside and allow to stand for 10 minutes as pressure returns to normal. Cool pot under running cold water and open. Mix gently with a wooden spoon to distribute soybeans evenly. Cover cooker with a dish towel until ready to serve. Delicious with Sesame Salt (p. 51), Tekka Miso (p. 44), Finger Lickin' Miso (p. 31), or Sweet Simmered Miso (p. 41).

VARIATION

*Soybeans with Brown Rice Porridge: To the ingredients for Brown Rice Porridge (p. 50) add ¼ cup water and ¼ cup dry soybeans soaked for at least 3 hours in water to cover and drained. Proceed as for porridge. If desired, stir in any or all of the following just before serving: 1 tablespoon shoyu, 1½ tablespoons red miso, 1 tablespoon butter, 1 tablespoon minced parsley.

Soybeans & Brown Rice Stroganoff
SERVES 4 TO 6

2¼ cups Pressure Cooked Soybeans Plus (p. 59; season with miso or shoyu)
1 cup brown rice, cooked (p. 50)
2 cups Tofu Mayonnaise (with garlic; p. 107)
2 to 3 tablespoons minced parsley (optional)

Soybean Salads

SERVES 6

Cooked, chilled soybeans make a nice addition to a wide variety of salads. Experiment with your favorites or try the following:

1 cup soybeans, pressure cooked (p. 59)
1 small apple, diced
6 tablespoons raisins
1 carrot, grated
1/3 onion, minced, rinsed, and pressed (p. 37)
¾ cucumber, cut into thin rounds
1 green pepper diced
5 tablespoons (tofu) mayonnaise (p. 107)
¼ teaspoon salt
Dash of pepper

Combine all ingredients in a salad bowl; mix lightly.

Soybean Soups

Cook 1 part soybeans with 3½ to 4 parts water as for Pressure Cooked Soybeans (p. 59). Add diced, sautéed vegetables and salt, shoyu, or miso. Simmer uncovered for 30 to 40 minutes. Season with a favorite spice.

For a tasty summertime dish, add cheese or yogurt to the cooked soup. Purée the mixture in a blender and serve chilled, topped with dollops of yogurt.

Soybean Casserole with Corn and Tomatoes

SERVES 4

1 cup cooked soybeans
1 cup cooked corn
1 cup cubed tomatoes
¼ teaspoon paprika
¾ teaspoon salt
½ teaspoon natural sugar
1 teaspoon minced onion
2 ounces grated cheese
¼ cup chopped peanuts

Preheat oven to 350°. Place the first seven ingredients in a lightly oiled casserole. Top with the cheese and peanuts, and bake for 45 minutes.

Soybeans and Sautéed Vegetables with Noodles

SERVES 4

2¼ cups Pressure Cooked Soybeans (p. 59; unseasoned), drained
3½ tablespoons shoyu
2 tablespoons oil
1 clove of garlic, minced or crushed
1½ cups shredded cabbage
1 cup thinly sliced leeks or onions
½ cup grated carrot
6½ ounces (buckwheat or Chinese) noodles, cooked (p. 50)
    Dash of pepper

Combine cooked soybeans and 2 tablespoons shoyu. Mix well, mash one-half of the beans, and set aside. Heat a wok or large skillet and coat with the oil. Add garlic and sauté for 30 seconds. Add cabbage, onions, and carrot, sauté for 4 minutes more, and turn off heat. Add soybeans, mixing until evenly distributed. Stir in noodles, sprinkle with the remaining 1½ tablespoons of shoyu, and season with pepper; mix lightly. Delicious hot or chilled.

Soyburgers

MAKES 8

Now increasingly available at natural food stores, soyburgers are also easily prepared at home; we like to make a large batch and freeze the leftovers. The addition of brown rice boosts the protein content. We find that deep-frying gives the finest flavor and texture, although slow broiling or pan-frying also give good results.

2¼ cups Pressure Cooked Soybeans (p. 59; unseasoned), drained and mashed
1¼ cups cooked Brown Rice (p. 50)
½ onion, diced
½ cup grated carrot
2 cups bread crumbs or bread crumb flakes; or substitute up to ½ cup (toasted) wheat germ or pre-cooked rolled oats
1 egg, lightly beaten
1 clove of garlic, minced or crushed
2 tablespoons minced parsley
2½ tablespoons shoyu or 3½ tablespoons red miso
¾ teaspoon curry powder or ¼ teaspoon ground dill seeds
Dash of pepper
Oil for deep-frying

Combine all ingredients, mixing well until mixture has the consistency of hamburger; shape into patties. Heat the oil to 350° in a wok, skillet, or deep-fryer. Drop in patties and deep-fry until golden brown (p. 130); drain well. Serve hot or cold as for Ganmo Burgers (p. 188). Also delicious topped with Tofu Mayonnaise (p. 107), fried with eggs and grated cheese, crumbled and used as a *taco* filling, or added to casseroles.

VARIATION:

*Soy "Meatballs": Shape mixture into 1-inch balls and deep-fry. Use in place of tofu in Stir-fried Noodles (p. 138) or Tofu Italian Meatballs (p. 123).

Deep-fried Soybeans

MAKES 4 CUPS

2 cups soybeans, soaked overnight in water and drained
Oil for deep-frying
Salt, onion salt, or garlic salt

Spread the beans out on a baking sheet and place in a 200° oven for 5 to 10 minutes until beans are dry. Heat oil to 350° in a wok, skillet, or deep-fryer. Deep-fry beans ½ cup at a time for 6 to 8 minutes, or until crisp and golden brown (p. 130). Drain beans on absorbent paper, season with salt, and serve immediately. Stored in an airtight jar, deep-fried soybeans keep quite well.

Curried Soy Fritters
SERVES 6

1 cup soybeans, cooked (p. 59) and drained
¾ cup soybean cooking liquid
1 clove of garlic, crushed or minced
1 onion, minced
1 cup (whole-wheat) flour
1½ teaspoons salt or 3 tablespoons red miso
1½ teaspoons curry powder
2 eggs, lightly beaten; or 2 teaspoons baking powder
Dash of pepper
Oil for deep-frying
Tofu Mayonnaise (with onion or curry; p. 107), Tofu Tartare
   Sauce (p. 109), Pineapple Sweet & Sour Sauce (p. 166), or
   Ketchup-Worcestershire Sauce (p. 49)

Mash three-fourths of the soybeans, leaving the remainder
whole. Combine with the next eight ingredients, mixing well,
to form a very thick batter. Heat oil to 350° in a wok, skillet,
or deep-fryer. Drop in batter by large spoonfuls and deep-fry
until golden brown (p. 130). Drain well on absorbent paper;
serve immediately, accompanined by the mayonnaise or
sauce.

Deep-fried Soy Brittle
SERVES 3 OR 4

¼ cup dry soybeans, soaked in water to cover for 1 hour,
   drained in a colander and allowed to stand overnight
Batter: Prepare as for Tempura Batter (p. 134)
   2 tablespoons (whole-wheat) flour
   4 teaspoons arrowroot, cornstarch, or kuzu
   2 teaspoons natural sugar
   3 tablespoons water
   1/8 teaspoon salt
   Dash of cinnamon (optional)
Oil for deep-frying

Combine drained beans and batter in a large bowl; mix lightly. Heat oil to 350° in a wok, skillet, or deep-fryer. Spoon
several tablespoons of the bean-batter mixture onto a (wood-
en) spatula, then smooth to form a thin layer. Using chopsticks or a second spatula, slide the beans-and-batter mixture
into the hot oil so that it forms a thin patty in the oil. Deep-
fry for about 8 minutes until golden brown (p. 130). Drain
well. Serve as hors d'oeuvre.

Soybean & Miso Garnish
MAKES 1 CUP

2 tablespoons sesame oil
1 cup cooked soybeans (p. 59), well drained
2 tablespoons red, barley, or Hatcho miso
½ teaspoon grated gingerroot
Dash of 7-spice red pepper (optional)

Heat a skillet or wok and coat with the oil. Add soybeans and
sauté for 2 or 3 minutes. Reduce heat to low, add remaining
ingredients, and sauté for 2 minutes more. Allow to cool to
room temperature. Serve as a garnish or seasoning for Brown
Rice or Rice Porridge.

Deep-fried Soybean Croquettes

Prepare Pressure Cooked Soybeans Plus (p. 59). Mash
together with sautéed onion and carrot (diced), and shape the
mixture into patties. Dust patties with flour, dip into beaten
egg, and roll in bread crumbs. Deep-fry until golden brown.

Budomame (Sweet Soybeans)
12 SERVINGS

This and the following preparations are often sold in
Japanese delicatessens and served in very small portions as
desserts or hors d'oeuvre. Budomame means literally "grape
soybeans," perhaps because of the rich, sweet flavor.

1 cup soybeans, rinsed and drained
7 cups water
4 to 6 tablespoons natural sugar
2 teaspoons shoyu or ½ teaspoon salt

Combine soybeans, 5 cups water, and two-thirds of the
sugar; soak overnight. Bring to a boil, reduce heat to low, and
simmer covered for 2 hours. Add 1½ cups water and simmer
for 1 hour more. Add ½ cup water, the remaining sugar
and the shoyu, and simmer for 50 minutes more, or until
most of the liquid has been absorbed or evaporated. Cool
before serving as a dessert or side dish.

OTHER SOYBEAN DELICATESSEN PREPARATIONS

*Kombu Mame: Add 2 tablespoons dried kombu (cut into
strips 2½ inches long and ¼ inch wide) together with the
shoyu.
*Kuro Mame: Soak black soybeans overnight in lightly salted
water. Simmer (without draining) as above. Add one-half of
sugar and simmer for 10 minutes. Add remaining sugar (omitting shoyu), season with salt and finish cooking as above. A
favorite New Year's preparation.
*Gomoku Mame: Simmer soybeans in water seasoned with
equal parts shoyu and sugar until beans are tender. Add small
amounts of diced carrots, burdock root, lotus root, kombu,
and konnyaku, and simmer for 30 minutes more.

Roasted Soy Grits

Prepare either Roasted or Deep-fried Soybeans. Place in a blender and chop at low speed for about 30 seconds until chunky. (Do not grind to a meal or powder.) Use like nuts in casseroles, salads, soups, granola, cooked vegetables, or grain dishes.

ROASTED SOYBEANS
(Iri-mame)

Many delicious varieties of roasted soybeans or soy nuts are now available in the West in natural food and health food stores. Dry-roasted varieties contain a remarkable 47 percent protein. (By comparison peanuts contain only 27 percent protein and almonds and cashews only 19 percent.) They are usually lightly salted and have a nut-like flavor and crunchy crisp texture. Oil-roasted varieties are available salted or unsalted with plain, garlic, or barbeque flavors, and contain 37 percent protein.

Roasted soybeans can be eaten like peanuts as a snack, or used to add a crunchy texture and nutlike flavor to a wide variety of salads, sauces, casseroles, and miso preparations. In the West roasted soybeans are also used in health food "candy" such as soy honey- or nut bars. In their ground form, they are used in commercial soy spreads.

In Japan, these are the "beans of good fortune" enjoyed on the first day of the lunar spring. Roasted beans covered with multiple coatings of sugar, starch, and *nori* are sold commercially as *Mishima Mame* and served as a sweet snack. Green soybeans, roasted with salt until they have a crunchy texture and greenish-beige color, are sold as *Irori Mame*.

Homemade Roasted Soybeans	MAKES 3 CUPS

3 cups whole dry soybeans, rinsed and soaked for 5 to 6 hours

Drain beans well, then spread between layers of dry towelling for 1 hour. Transfer to large unoiled cookie tins or baking pans and spread 1 layer thick over the surface of pans. Place in an unheated oven and roast at 200° to 250° for 2 to 2½ hours, or until beans are light brown. Shake pans once every 15 minutes for the first hour, then every 30 minutes thereafter. Do not allow beans—which are inside tan hulls—to turn dark brown. While beans are still slightly soft, remove from oven, salt lightly, and set aside to cool until crunchy. Serve as is, like nuts, or use to make Roasted Soy Grits (see below).

For a salty variety, soak the beans in a mixture of 4 cups water and 2 tablespoons salt before roasting.

In Japan, roasted soybeans are prepared on a community scale in a large screen basket held over a strong flame and shaken like popcorn for about 40 minutes. The flame is then reduced to low and the beans cooked without shaking for 5 to 7 minutes until golden brown.

FRESH GREEN SOYBEANS
(Edamame)

Many Westerners who have lived or traveled in East Asia find it remarkable that fresh green soybeans have not yet become a favorite summertime vegetable in the West—as they are in Japan. The green beans, simmered in the pod until tender, lightly salted, and then cooled are served as a delicious hors d'oeuvre—often with sake or beer—or as part of a meal. From mid-June until October, the beans' brilliant emerald color graces the dining tables of restaurants and private homes throughout Japan.

Immediately after soybean plants are uprooted, the dirt is shaken from the roots, most of the leaves are removed, and about 15 pod-bearing plants, each approximately 2½ feet long, are tied into bundles. About 10 to 12 soybean pods are clustered along the stalk of each plant, and a single 3-inch pod usually contains 3 green soybeans. The plants are taken to markets where they are sold by the bunch. After boiling the beans in the pods, the housewife may use the stems as fuel.

Highly digestible and containing over 12 percent protein, a typical 3½ ounce serving of green soybeans supplies more than 40 percent of an adult's daily protein requirement. They also contain as much vitamin C as oranges, and are rich in vitamin B_1. Although best served fresh and in season, green soybeans may also be frozen or canned like green peas; in the West they are generally available in the latter form. In Japan, cooked green soybeans (*hitashi mame*) are now available packaged in a sausage-shaped plastic container together with a little of the cooking liquid.

Green Soybean Hors D'oeuvre

SERVES 2

Like potato chips, these little devils are positively addicting.

2 cups green soybeans (in pods)
4 cups water
½ teaspoon salt

Combine soybeans and 4 cups water in a large pot and bring to a boil over high heat. Reduce heat to low and simmer for 15 to 20 minutes, or until pods just begin to open. Drain, sprinkle beans with salt, and allow to cool. Serve in the pods.

Or, after draining, combine beans in a small saucepan with ¼ cup water and 2 tablespoons each shoyu and natural sugar. Simmer for about 20 minutes, stirring occasionally. Drain and allow to cool. If desired, serve Japanese-style in a small (bamboo) basket or colander accompanied by cold drinks or hot tea.

Hot Buttered Soybeans

SERVES 3 TO 4

1 pound fresh green soybeans (in pods)
½ teaspoon salt
Butter

To shell beans, cover with boiling water and allow to stand for 5 minutes. Drain and cool briefly. Break pods crosswise and squeeze out beans (yielding about 1½ cups).

Bring 1 cup water to a boil in a small saucepan. Add beans and salt and return to the boil, then cover and simmer for 15 to 20 minutes. Drain well and serve hot (like lima beans or green peas) topped with butter. Salt lightly if desired.

Prepared this way, green soybeans also make an excellent addition to salads.

Green Soybeans with Brown Rice

Substitute 1 to 1½ cups fresh, shelled green soybeans for the dry soybeans in Soybeans Pressure Cooked with Brown Rice (p. 60). Serve as in the basic recipe or use as a filling for Agé Pouches (p. 192) or Inari-zushi Pouches (p. 194).

To prepare Aomame Meshi, combine in a heavy pot the above shelled green soybeans and rice plus 3½ cups water, a 4-inch square of kombu, and ½ teaspoon salt. Allow to stand overnight, then bring water to a boil and remove kombu. Cook as for Brown Rice (p. 50). For best flavor, allow to stand for several hours before serving.

Green Soybean Tempura

Shell, then parboil the beans until just tender. Stir into tempura batter (p. 134); deep-fry and serve as for Kaki-agé (p. 136).

Sweet Emerald Bean Paste (Jinda)

Shell and parboil green soybeans, then grind in a suribachi or purée in a blender. Combine 2 parts beans with 1 part sugar or honey. Use like an—a sweetened paste usually made with adzuki beans—as a filling for various mochi treats or cupcakes.

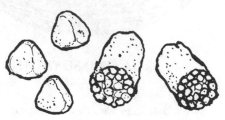

KINAKO
(Roasted Full-Fat Soy Flour)

Kinako is a tan or beige flour made by grinding whole roasted soybeans. It has a nutty flavor and fragrance and contains over 38 percent protein. Many of Japan's most popular confections are dusted with a light coating of sweetened kinako. These confections usually consist of a grain such as mochi (pounded glutinous rice), or steamed, pounded millet filled with an (sweetened adzuki bean paste). In the Kyoto area alone more than twelve popular confections are prepared with a covering of sweetened kinako. In a number of Japanese health-food treats (such as kinako amé, gokabo, kokusen, and kankanbo) kinako serves at the main ingredient; it is mixed with mizuame to give a chewy taffy-like texture and rich sweetness. We feel that kinako itself and a number of the following preparations—especially Kinako Butter, Kinako Candy, and Kinako Coffee—could be produced in cottage industries and sold commercially with excellent results.

A delicious and inexpensive source of high-quality protein, kinako is generally sold in ¼-pound bags and used in small quantities.

Homemade Kinako

MAKES ½ CUP

¾ cup whole dry soybeans

Place the beans in a large heavy skillet and roast over low heat, stirring constantly, for about 20 minutes, or until beans are light brown and slightly fragrant. Grind to a fine powder using a blender or hand mill. Sift through a fine mesh strainer to remove particles of the soybean hulls. The resulting kinako should be light yellowish beige and have a subtly sweet, fragrant aroma.

For commercial kinako, 5 to 10 gallons of unsoaked, whole soybeans are turned in a large (4-foot-long, 18-inch-diameter) rotating screen drum over an open fire for 30 to 40 minutes. When browned, and while still warm, they are ground to a flour or powder between slowly-turning stone wheels.

Kinako Butter

MAKES ½ CUP

This preparation tastes like a cross between sesame and peanut butter but is less expensive and higher in protein than both.

2½ tablespoons oil or butter
½ cup kinako
1 teaspoon red miso or shoyu; or ¼ teaspoon salt
2 to 3 teaspoons honey
1½ to 2 tablespoons water

Heat the oil in a skillet, then turn off heat. Add remaining ingredients, mixing until smooth. Delicious on crackers, canapés, or fresh vegetable slices. Covered and refrigerated, unused portions will last indefinitely.

Creamy Kinako Butter

MAKES ½ CUP

This tasty, high-protein preparation is now sold in natural food stores in Japan.

½ cup kinako
¼ cup butter or soybean margarine
1 to 2 teaspoons honey
Dash of cinnamon

Combine all ingredients, mixing well. Serve as a spread on toast or sandwiches.

Kinako-Peanut-Sesame Spread

MAKES 1 CUP

¼ cup kinako
2½ tablespoons peanut butter
¼ cup sesame butter
¼ cup water
1 tablespoon oil
1 tablespoon red miso or ½ teaspoon salt
½ clove garlic, crushed (optional)
1 tablespoon minced onion

Combine all ingredients in a small bowl; mix well. For best flavor, cover and refrigerate overnight. Use like any nut butter. Try it as a sandwich spread with tomatoes, cucumbers, and thinly sliced tofu (regular or deep-fried).

Apple-Cucumber Salad with Kinako Dressing

SERVES 2

½ apple, cut into thin wedges
½ cucumber, sliced into thin rounds
Dressing:
    1 tablespoon Kinako Butter (above)
    1½ tablespoons lemon juice
    2½ teaspoons honey

Combine all ingredients in a bowl and mix gently.

Kinako in Brown Sauces and Roux

Add 1 to 2 tablespoons (lightly roasted) kinako for every 2 tablespoons (whole-wheat) flour. While contributing a nut-like toasted flavor and complementary soy protein, kinako does not further thicken sauces since it contains almost no gluten.

Kinako in Breads and Muffins

Use kinako like soy flour, adding 10 to 15 percent to your favorite baked goods in order to boost the protein content by up to 32 percent, and to give a richness of flavor. Kinako Butter (above) works well as a filling for rolled loaves and pastries.

Sweetened Kinako

MAKES ¼ CUP

This preparation is used as a coating for many Japanese treats.

3 tablespoons kinako
1½ to 2 tablespoons natural sugar
Dash of salt

Combine all ingredients, mixing thoroughly. Place in a shallow bowl in which the treats may be rolled or dusted.

Abekawa Mochi

SERVES 3

This preparation is the most popular way of serving kinako in Japan.

6 cakes of *mochi* (each about 3 by 2 by ½ inch thick)
¼ cup Sweetened Kinako (see above)

Broil or bake *mochi* in a medium oven (or on a grill over a fire) until each cake swells to twice its original size and is crisp and nicely browned. Dip cakes immediately into very hot water, then roll in the kinako. Serve hot or cold as a dessert.

For a richer flavor, reduce the amount of sugar in the kinako mixture and omit the salt. Dip hot *mochi* into shoyu rather than water before rolling in kinako.

Chinese-style Kinako & Peanut Butter Balls

MAKES 12

These sweet, almost crumbly delicacies are a favorite in China where they are sold commercially.

½ cup kinako
2 tablespoons peanut butter
2 to 3 teaspoons natural sugar
1 teaspoon honey
Dash of salt

Combine all ingredients and shape into small balls.

Kinako Candy
(Kinako Amé or Genkotsu Amé)

MAKES 16

This rich, chewy treat is a favorite throughout Japan. Watch out!

1 cup kinako, approximately
2 tablespoons water
3 tablespoons *mizuame* (millet or barley malt), or substitute honey and reduce the amount of water above by ½ tablespoon
1 tablespoon natural sugar

Place ¾ cup kinako in a heatproof bowl. Combine remaining ingredients in a small saucepan and simmer over low heat, stirring constantly, for about 7 minutes, or until thick. Pour contents of pan into kinako, mix well and knead until firm, adding more kinako if necessary. Roll out onto a breadboard dusted with 2 tablespoons of kinako and continue kneading until dough is very stiff. Roll out into a long cylinder ¾ inch in diameter, and cut into ¾-inch lengths. For best flavor and a chewier texture, chill overnight.

For variety, try adding 2 tablespoons ground roasted sesame seeds (or carob) and a pinch of salt to the dough just before kneading.

VARIATIONS

Kokusen and Kankanbo: Prepare as above, but use slightly less water and more sugar, and add ground sesame seeds for *kokusen:* Roll out and cut to form small cylinders the size of cigarettes. Dry or bake in a slow oven until brittle.

Gokabo: Prepare dough as for Kinako Candy using *mizuame* but add 1 tablespoon water. Allow to cool, then roll out on a bread board (well-floured with kinako) to form a thin 6- by 8-inch rectangular sheet. Combine 2/3 cup puffed rice, rice crispies, or minced popcorn with 2 tablespoons softened *mizuame* or honey, mix well, then sprinkle in an even layer over kinako sheet. Roll up sheet from one side to form a compact cylinder, then gently roll back and forth under palms of hands on bread board until cylinder doubles in length and is reduced to 1 inch diameter. Cut crosswise into 1½-inch lengths, dust pieces liberally with kinako, and chill briefly before serving.

Kinako Coffee

SERVES 4

Caffeine-free, easy to prepare, and rich in protein, this hearty brew, with its roasted nutlike aroma, will surprise and delight even the staunchest coffee lover.

½ cup kinako, or substitute full-fat soy flour
3 cups (hot) water

Roast kinako over low heat in a heavy, dry skillet, stirring constantly for 3 to 4 minutes, or until dark brown and fragrant. Mix in water, bring to a boil, and simmer for 2 minutes. Filter through a fine-mesh strainer, cloth, or coffee filter. Serve hot or chilled, adding rich soymilk (or cream) and sugar (or a pinch of salt) to taste. Also delicious with malt or carob.

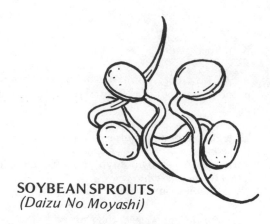

SOYBEAN SPROUTS
(Daizu No Moyashi)

One of the world's finest diet foods, soybean sprouts contain less calories per gram of protein than any other known vegetable food. Although mung bean sprouts are the most popular both in the West and in East Asia, soybean sprouts are inexpensive, tasty, and easy to prepare at home. Most contain both the bright yellow soybean and the sprout root which will grow to a length of 3 to 5 inches in 5 to 7 days. Soybean sprouts may be served as a green vegetable throughout the year either parboiled in fresh salads (where they serve as a good source of vitamin C) or in soups, sautéed, or baked dishes.

Homemade Soybean Sprouts

MAKES 3 TO 6 CUPS

1 to 1½ cups dry soybeans

Prepare a sprouter by making small holes in the bottom of a 10- to 12-inch-deep plastic container, milk carton, or coffee can. Pour in soybeans to a depth of at least 2 inches, then place sprouter in a slightly larger pot and fill with water to more than cover beans. Cover pot and allow beans to soak for 4 hours (no longer). Lift out sprouter and drain beans being careful not to mix or agitate them. Cover sprouter and place in a dark place at 72°F. Rinse beans 3 to 4 times daily by sprinkling with water, again taking care not to mix them. Repeat for 5 days or until sprouts are about 4 inches long. Transfer sprouts to a large pot and rinse with plenty of water; pour off loose hulls and remove unsprouted beans. Refrigerate unused sprouts in a sealed container.

Soybean Sprout Salad with Tofu

SERVES 3

2 cups soybeans sprouts, parboiled for 6 to 8 minutes and well drained
½ cup grated carrot
1 cucumber, thinly sliced
5 ounces deep-fried tofu (or 12 ounces regular tofu, pressed; p. 96), cut into bite-sized cubes
Dressing:
    2 tablespoons vinegar
    2 tablespoons sesame oil
    1½ tablespoons shoyu
    Dash of 7-spice red pepper or tabasco sauce

Combine the first four ingredients in a salad bowl. Add dressing and toss lightly. Also tasty with French dressing.

Egg Foo Yung with Soybean Sprouts and Tofu

SERVES 4

2 cups soybean sprouts, parboiled for 4 to 6 minutes and drained
6 eggs, lightly beaten
5 ounces deep-fried tofu (or 12 ounces regular tofu, pressed; p. 96) cut into small cubes
1 green pepper or 2 mushrooms, thinly sliced
½ cup minced onion
½ teaspoon salt or 2 teaspoons soy sauce
8 teaspoons oil
Pepper

Combine the first six ingredients, mixing well. Heat 2 teaspoons oil in a heavy skillet or wok. Pour in one-fourth of the egg-tofu mixture to form a thin omelet. Cook for about 2½ minutes on each side until nicely browned. Repeat until all ingredients have been used. Serve hot, topped with a sprinkling of soy sauce and pepper. Or top with Ankake or Gingerroot Sauce (p. 49). A delicious accompaniment for brown rice.

For variety, substitute ½ cup firmly packed okara for the tofu.

Chop Suey or Chow Mein with Soybean Sprouts and Tofu

SERVES 2 OR 3

8 teaspoons butter
12 ounces tofu, diced
1 cup thinly sliced celery pieces
1 small onion, thinly sliced
2/3 cup water or stock
2/3 teaspoon cornstarch, dissolved in 2 teaspoons water
1 cup soybean sprouts
2 tablespoons soy sauce

Melt 4 teaspoons butter in a skillet. Add tofu and fry, stirring occasionally, for 5 minutes, or until tofu is nicely browned, then transfer tofu to a separate container.

Melt remaining 4 teaspoons butter in the skillet. Add celery and onion and sauté for 2 to 3 minutes. Add cooked tofu and water, bring to a boil, and simmer for 5 minutes. Stir in the dissolved cornstarch, sprouts, and soy sauce. Return to the boil and simmer for 2 to 3 minutes. Serve hot as is, or over steamed rice. For *Chow Mein*, serve over fried Chinese noodles.

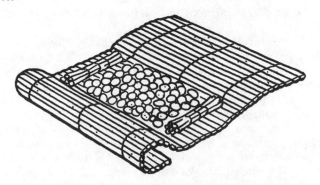

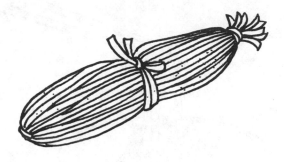

Fig. 12. Natto wrapped in rice straw

NATTO
(Sticky Fermented Whole Soybeans)

Natto are prepared (commercially or at home) by steaming soaked soybeans until they are soft, innoculating the warm (104°) beans with the bacteria *Bacillus natto*, and then allowing them to ferment for 15 to 24 hours in a humid environment at about 104°. The dark-brown beans have a fairly strong and unusual aroma and flavor, and a sticky, slightly slippery surface texture. When lifted from the bowl with chopsticks (fig. 13), like some varieties of melted cheese, they form gossamer-like threads. Although most whole soybeans are somewhat difficult to digest, natto are highly digestible because the beans' complex protein molecules have been broken down by the bacteria during fermentation. A whole, natural food, natto contain 16.5 percent protein and are rich in vitamins B_2, B_{12}, and iron. In Japan and in Japanese grocery stores in the West, natto are sold in small (3 to 4 ounce) packages wrapped in straw, from which they traditionally received bacteria for fermentation. Generally served as a topping for rice, natto are also used in miso soups and *Aemono*-dressings or sautéed with vegetables. In the provinces, they are mixed with a little sugar and served as an hors d'oeuvre. About 50,000 tons of soybeans are made into natto each year in Japan, about one-fourth the amount used to make either miso or shoyu.

Natto Topping For Brown Rice

SERVES 2

½ cup natto (1 package)
1½ tablespoons thinly-sliced leeks; or minced onions or *daikon* leaves
1½ tablespoons bonita flakes
¼ to ½ teaspoon hot mustard
1½ tablespoons powdered green *nori*, or crumbled toasted *nori* (optional)
1½ tablespoons shoyu or 7 teaspoons red miso

Combine the first five ingredients, mixing with chopsticks for about 1 minute until cohesiveness develops. Stir in shoyu and serve as a topping for hot rice, rice gruel, or crackers.

Natto are often mixed with only shoyu or with sugar and powdered green *nori* when served over rice.

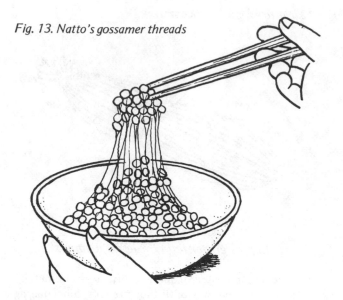

Fig. 13. Natto's gossamer threads

Natto Miso Soup

SERVES 2 OR 3

1¼ cups dashi (p. 39), stock, or water
2 (Chinese) cabbage leaves, cut lengthwise into halves, then
    crosswise into 1½-inch-wide strips
1 tablespoon red, barley, or Hatcho miso
2 tablespoons sweet white miso
½ cup natto
¼ cup thin rounds of leek or scallion
Dash of 7-spice red pepper

Bring dashi to a boil in a saucepan. Add Chinese cabbage, cover, and simmer for 2 to 3 minutes. Add miso creamed in a little of the hot broth. Add natto and return just to the boil. Sprinkle on leeks and remove from heat. Serve seasoned with a sprinkling of the red pepper.

TEMPEH
(Fermented Soybean Cakes)

These cakes of cooked soybeans, bound together by a fragrant, white mycelium of *Rhizopus* mold, have a delectable flavor: fried or deep-fried, they taste remarkably like fried chicken or veal cutlets. Rich in protein (18.3% fresh or 48.7% dried), tempeh is also highly digestible, and *Rhizopus* serves as an effective deactivator of trypsin inhibitor (p. 70). Like other fermented soy products (miso, shoyu, natto) and sea vegetables, tempeh is one of only a few non-meat sources of vitamin B_{12}.

For centuries prepared daily on a cottage scale throughout Indonesia (where it is a basic food for millions of people and makes use of more than 50 percent of the country's soybean crop), tempeh is also an important staple in New Guinea and Surinam, and is eaten on a small scale in Malaysia and Holland. Its adaptability to household industries and its low cost should make it, like tofu, a food of worldwide commercial interest during the coming decades.

Before you begin, you will need to obtain tempeh starter, which is available from Farm Foods, 156 Drakes Lane, Summertown, TN 38483 or from USDA/NRRC, 1815 North University Street, Peoria, Il 61604.

For a more detailed, illustrated description of making tempeh at home and hundreds of delicious recipes, see *The Book of Tempeh*, available from The Soyfoods Center.

Homemade Soy Tempeh

MAKES 30 OUNCES

2½ cups whole dry soybeans, washed and drained
18 to 20 cups water
1½ tablespoons (distilled white) vinegar
1 teaspoon tempeh starter

1. **Precook Soybeans:** Combine soybeans and 7½ cups water in a large cooking pot, cover, and bring just to a boil. Remove from heat and allow to stand, covered, at room temperature, for 8 to 16 hours. (Or simmer for 20 minutes and allow to stand for 1 hour.)

2. **Dehull Soybeans:** Carefully pour off water from pot and discard. Now rub or squeeze beans vigorously with hands for 3 to 4 minutes to remove hulls. Fill pot with water, stir gently in a circle to cause hulls to rise, then pour off water and hulls. Repeat until hulls are removed.

3. **Cook Soybeans:** Add 10 cups (hot) water and the vinegar to the drained beans in the cooking pot. Bring to a boil and cook, uncovered, at an active boil for 45 minutes.

4. **Dry and Inoculate Cooked Soybeans:** Drain beans in a colander or strainer for several minutes, then shake well to expel moisture. Line beans over toweling in an even layer, and allow to cool for 20 to 30 minutes, to body temperature. Transfer beans to a clean, large mixing bowl, sprinkle on tempeh starter, and mix well, for 2 minutes.

5. **Put Soybeans in Incubation Container:** Perforate two 7-by-8-inch plastic Ziploc bags with an ice pick over their entire surface at ½-inch intervals. Spoon half the inoculated soybeans into each bag, seal mouth, place on a flat surface, and press upper surface of bag with palm of hand to distribute beans in a uniform layer about ¾ inch thick.

6. **Incubate:** Place tempeh containers on a rack in a warm place (such as an oven with the door ajar or over a hot water heater) at about 86 to 88° F for 22 to 26 hours. Check temperature occasionally, especially toward the end of the fermentation, when it may rise rapidly. Tempeh is done when the beans are bound into a firm, compact cake by a dense, uniform, white mycelium, which has a pleasant, clean, mushroomy aroma. Gray or black spots, indicating sporulation, are not harmful if the smell is fresh and clean.

The tempeh is now ready to cook.

*Deep-fried or Fried: Deep-fry cakes (or pan-fry on both sides) until crisp and golden brown. Serve topped with shoyu, ketchup, Worcestershire, or any of the following Basic Sauces (pp. 48 to 49): Onion, Mushroom, Sweet & Sour, Ketchup-Worcestershire, or Tomato & Cheese. Also delicious in sandwiches and soups.

*Tempeh Goreng (*Savory Cutlets*): Score both surfaces of 3 fresh tempeh cakes to a depth of 1/8 inch. Combine 3 tablespoons water, ½ teaspoon salt, ½ clove of crushed garlic, and ¼ teaspoon coriander. Add tempeh, marinate for 5 minutes, and drain well. Deep-fry in (coconut) oil (p. 130). Serve as an accompaniment for rice dishes, topped with red-pepper sauce (*sambal*) if desired.

*Tempeh Kemul *(Crisp Chips):* Cut 3 tempeh cakes horizontally into paper-thin slices; sun-dry for 5 minutes if desired. Combine 6 tablespoons (rice) flour, 1 clove of crushed garlic, ¾ teaspoon salt, and ¼ teaspoon coriander. Mix in enough (coconut) milk to form a fairly thin batter, then add tempeh slices and allow to stand briefly. Deep-fry until crisp, and serve like potato chips. For variety use a well-salted tempura batter.

*Tempeh Bacham (*Rich Fillets*): Combine in a skillet ¼ grated onion, ¾ teaspoon salt, 3 to 4 tablespoons brown sugar, and 1¼ cups water. Add 3 tempeh cakes (cut crosswise into fourths), bring to a boil, and simmer until all liquid has evaporated. Deep-fry cakes and serve as for Tempeh Goreng.

*In Soups: Add diced fresh tempeh to soups and simmer for 30 minutes. Season with salt, miso, or shoyu.

*Baked or Roasted: Bake at 350° for about 20 minutes, or until nicely browned and fragrant. If desired, use as the basis for a pizza-type preparation, or serve topped with any of the sauces mentioned above.

HAMANATTO AND DAITOKUJINATTO
(Raisin-like Natto)

Hamanatto is a unique variety of natto soybeans which looks like raisins except that its surface has a grayish black tinge and is smooth and soft. Hamanatto beans have a pleasant, somewhat salty flavor resembling that of mellow Hatcho miso. Sprinkled over rice or rice gruel, served as an hors d'oeuvre with green tea, or cooked with vegetables as a seasoning, they add zest to bland dishes. A similar type of natto, called *Daitokuji natto*, is prepared in Daitokuji temple in Kyoto. Hamanatto are also widely enjoyed in China where they are known as *toushih*.

MODERN WESTERN SOYBEAN FOODS

This section would be incomplete without a brief description of the following foods. Of particular importance is soy flour which now appears in a large number of recipes for baked goods in Western-style cookbooks. The contrast between the character of most of these highly refined foods and the traditional East Asian products described above serves to emphasize the strikingly different roles that soybean foods play in the East as compared with the West.

Natural Soy Flour: This full-fat product, containing 35 to 40 percent protein and 20 percent natural oils, makes an excellent addition to breads, pasta, and pastries. It is used in amounts of about 10 to 15 percent of the total flour content.

Soy Granules: Containing 50 percent protein, this newly developed product is available at most health food stores. Easy to use, granules can be added to soups, stews, casseroles, or even puréed beverages.

Defatted Soy Flour and Grits: Containing about 50 to 52 percent protein, these foods are left over after the oil is extracted from whole crushed soybeans using hexane solvent. The least expensive source of soy protein in the West, they are now widely used in bakery products, processed and simulated meats, breakfast cereals, dietary and infant foods, and confections.

Soy Protein Concentrates: Containing 70 percent protein (on a moisture-free basis), these refined products cost only about 10 percent more than flour and grits and are used in processed meats, breakfast cereals, and infant foods.

Soy Protein Isolates: Containing 90 to 98 percent protein (on a moisture free basis), these products are prepared like concentrates from defatted flakes and flours. Resembling a white powder with a bland flavor, they cost about twice as much as flour or grits. First widely used in meat analogs, sausages, and canned meats as binding agents, they are now also employed to make simulated dairy products such as coffee creams, whipped toppings, and frozen desserts (imitation ice cream). Now sold as Natural Soy Protein in 1-pound bags at many health food stores.

Spun Protein Fibers: These are made by dissolving or suspending protein isolates in alkalai, then extruding them through spinnerettes into an acid-salt bath to form tiny monofilaments. Combined with ingredients such as wheat gluten, egg albumen, fats, flavoring, and coloring agents, they are formed into simulated meat items.

Textured Vegetable Protein: TVP is made from low-cost soy flour continually extruded under heat and pressure to form small chunks. When hydrated, these have a chewy texture and are capable of carrying a variety of colors and flavors. Considerably less expensive than both isolates and spun protein fibers, TVP is now becoming widely used as an extender in ground or simulated meats, and in infant foods.

Soy Oil Products: Although it contains no protein, refined soy oil is rich in polyunsaturates and linoleic acid, and low in cost. In the U.S. over 2½ billion pounds are produced yearly and used as cooking or salad oils, or in salad dressings. Another 4 billion pounds are hydrogenated to make margarine and vegetable shortenings.

5
Gô (Fresh Soy Puree)

Gô is a thick white purée of well-soaked uncooked soybeans. It is more full-bodied in texture than whipped cream, but not as thick as cream cheese. It is interesting to note that the Japanese character for gô is also used to represent the verb *kureru* meaning "to give." This is appropriate, since gô is the source of each of the various tofu products (fig. 14); it is the first transformation of whole soybeans in the alchemy of tofu-making. As in an archetypal image from the Chinese *Book of Changes,* the soft beans, heaped high, pass downward between heavy granite millstones. Turning slowly, the whispering stones merge the many bright-yellow soybeans into cream-white, smooth gô, which flows over the sides of the lower, stationary stone and is caught in a large cedar tub (as shown on the cover illustration of this book). Nearby, in a massive black cauldron, boiling water awaits with the benediction of fire.

Gô is the only stage in the tofu making process where the entire soybean is still together; in the next step, the gô will be separated into *okara* and soymilk. Thus by using gô in cooking, we can enjoy the full range of the soybean's nutrients in their natural balance and completeness.

By soaking and grinding the soybean into gô, we greatly reduce the amount of time and fuel required for its thorough cooking, just as it is quicker and more economical to cook rolled- rather than whole-grain oats. Moreover, unlike most other grains and pulses, soybeans contain a substance called "trypsin inhibitor" (TI), which obstructs the func-

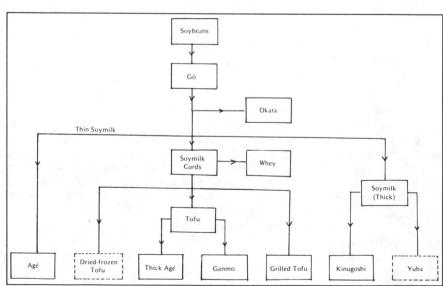

Fig. 14.
Gò as the Source of all Tofu Products

Fig. 15. Hand-turned grinding stones

Fig. 16. Push-pull grinding stones

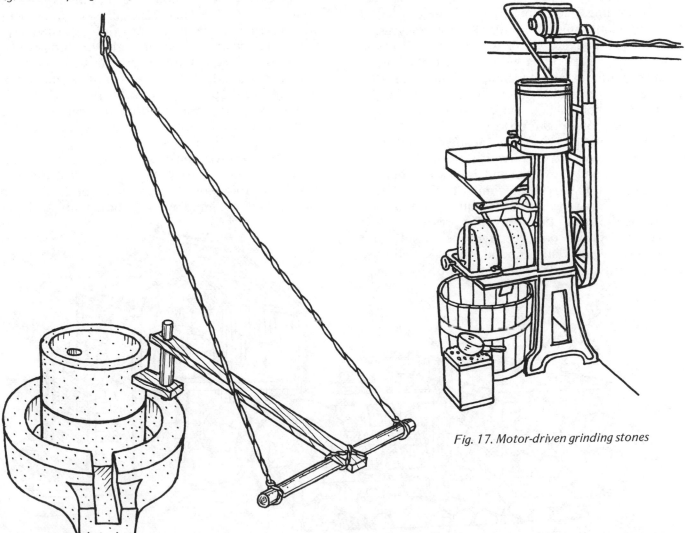

Fig. 17. Motor-driven grinding stones

tioning of the pancreas-secreted trypsin enzyme essential for the digestion of protein and the maintenance of proper growth. TI can—and must—be inactivated by cooking. Laboratory tests show that 70 to 80 percent of all TI present in the soybean must be destroyed if the body is to make use of the full array of nutrients in the bean. They also show that soaking and grinding whole soybeans greatly reduces the cooking time to attain this level of inactivation. Nutritionists recommend that well-soaked whole soybeans be simmered for four to six hours or pressure cooked (at 15 pounds) for 20 to 30 minutes. Gô, however, need be simmered for only 15 minutes or pressure-cooked for 10 if it is to be used directly as a food (or be further processed into soymilk); it requires as few as 10 to 15 minutes of simmering if it is to be made into tofu, since TI is contained in the soluble carbohydrates that dissolve in the whey during the curding process.

To prepare gô with the best flavor and nutritional value, soak your soybeans for the correct length of time (see graph, p. 289). Purée or grind them to a fine, smooth-textured consistency using an electric blender, a Corona- or Quaker City-type hand mill, a meat grinder with a fine attachment, an electric grain mill, a coffee mill, a mortar and pestle, a *suribachi*, or a juicer. Most important, cook the fresh gô without delay, and do not overcook, lest some of the protein value be lost.

The word "gô" is used by Japanese tofu makers in three different ways. First, it refers to the white purée mentioned above. Second, it is used to refer to a property of dry soybeans, similar to the gluten in wheat, which is a measure of the quantity and quality of the protein in the beans. The presence of this property depends on the soybeans' variety and grade, the region, climate, and soil in which they were grown, and their particular year of "vintage."

It is important in determining the amount of tofu that can be made from a given quantity of beans, and it determines the cohesiveness and delicate resilience of both the purée and the tofu made from it.

Finally, "gô" may refer to an elusive essence of the purée which determines the amount of tofu it will yield. Improper treatment of the purée can cause a decrease in this vital essence; tofu makers assert that this gô can "fall" or "drop out." Combining the three usages into a single sentence, a tofu maker might say: "To make fine tofu, use soybeans containing good gô, grind them between slowly-turning stones to make smooth, fine-textured gô, and cook immediately, to prevent any of the essential gô from escaping"!

Since ancient times and until really quite recently, most Japanese kitchens were equipped with a pair of 10-inch-diameter, hand-turned grinding stones (fig. 15). These were used to grind soybeans into gô during the preparation of farmhouse tofu or Gôjiru soup (p. 74). On special occasions, they were used to grind whole grains into flour, roasted soybeans into *kinako*, or tender tea leaves into *matcha* used in the tea ceremony. In farmhouses where tofu was made regularly or in large quantities, and in traditional tofu shops throughout Japan and China, an interesting design was developed whereby large, heavy stones were turned using a push-pull system (fig. 16). While one person worked the push-pull handle that revolved the upper stone, another ladled soaked soybeans into the stone's upper surface. Working in this way, it often took 1 or 2 hours for tofu makers to grind enough beans for a single

Fig. 18. Water-powered millstones

cauldronful of tofu yielding 120 cakes. Work usually started as early as 2 o'clock in the morning and, during the summer, the beans were often ground and cooked in two separate batches each day to ensure freshness. In several of Kyoto's elegant old tofu and yuba shops where granite stones are still used, the stone floor near the base of the grinding platform is distinctly indented and worn smooth in the spots where many generations of fathers and sons pivoted their feet as they turned the great stones by hand.

While all of the gô made in Japanese tofu shops is still ground between stone wheels, the great majority of the shops presently use relatively small, lightweight wheels that revolve more rapidly than the traditional, heavy stones. Some shops, however, have carefully preserved their beautiful heirloom millstones, mounting them vertically and driving them with a fanbelt and electric motor (fig. 17). The tofu master must chisel the cutting grooves of both stones every three months to keep them sharp. Like the finest Western stone-burr mills used for making stone-ground flours, these heavy stones yield gó, and hence tofu, of the finest quality.

It is interesting to note that although grinding stones have been used for more than 2,000 years in East Asia, the power to revolve them was traditionally provided entirely by man. It apparently never occurred to these craftsmen that natural forces—such as wind and water—could be used as energy sources. Less than a century ago, most of the flour prepared in the West was freshly ground each morning in stone mills powered by either water wheels (fig. 18) or windmills (fig. 19). The large stones were 3 to 4 feet in diameter and 12 inches thick, whereas in Japan and China, we have never seen a stone larger than 17 inches in diameter and 5 inches thick.

The same basic principles used in making high-quality whole-grain flours are also applied in preparing gô. Each morning the tofu maker drains and rinses his well-soaked soybeans, then places them in a hopper above the grinder. He runs a slow trickle of water—often drawn from the shop's deep well—over the beans, down through the hopper and in between the stones to give his gô the desired thickness. The stone wheels revolve slowly and at medium pressure to ensure that the germ, skin, and body of the beans are smoothly blended, and to avoid overheating, which would cause the essential gô to escape. This way of grinding yields gô with a very fine grain; the latter, in turn, increases the tofu yield. It also helps to develop the natural cohesiveness or glutinous quality found in soybeans in much the same way that kneading develops gluten in bread.

Lest the essential gô escape, the purée should be used as soon as possible after it has been ground. Thus, in tofu shops it is scooped immediately into a cauldron of boiling water. Gô loses its potency the longer it sits unused and the tofu yield consequently declines.

In modern Japan, most of the gô made in tofu shops is used directly in the tofu-making process. Only occasionally do the more tradition-minded order it from the tofu shop for use in home cooking. Since most homes are now equipped with a blender, cooks can make their own.

Gô can be added to soups or breads, or it can be sautéed with vegetables, mixed with diced foods and deep-fried, or used as a protein rich base for casseroles and other baked dishes. Try using it in place of pre-packaged soy flour, meal, or grits in your favorite recipes; in most cases, cooking time will be reduced by 50 percent or more. This creamy-white, smooth purée invites imaginitive experimentation to find new uses for a food that is rarely, if ever, mentioned in Western cookbooks.

Fig. 19. Wind-powered millstones

The most popular way of using gô in Japanese cookery, this famous wintertime soup is said to have originated in Japan's snowy northeast provinces. It can be prepared using a wide range of vegetables, seasonings, or garnishes. Experiment with whatever is available, in season, or simply appealing. Some cooks like to make Gôjiru as thick as porridge; others prefer to use more water and fewer vegetables and beans to create a texture resembling that of typical miso soup.

2 tablespoons oil
1 onion, thinly sliced; or 1 leek cut into 2-inch lengths
½ carrot, cut into thin half moons
2 ounces agé, cut into thin strips
3 mushrooms, thinly sliced
2 inches *daikon*, cut into half moons; or ½ cup chopped
   celery
1 potato, sweet potato, yam, or taro, diced
2 cups Homemade Gô Purée
3½ to 4 cups water, stock, or dashi (p. 39)
5 to 6 tablespoons red miso or 3½ tablespoons shoyu

Heat a heavy pot and coat with the oil. Add the next six ingredients and sauté over medium heat for 5 to 10 minutes, or until potatoes are softened. Add gô and water, bring to a boil, and simmer uncovered for 10 to 15 minutes, stirring occasionally. Add miso thinned in a few tablespoons of the hot broth and simmer for 1 minute more. Serve immediately or, for a richer, sweeter flavor, allow to cool for about 6 hours. Use leftovers in Gô Cracker Dip (see above) or in a casserole *au gratin* as described as a variation under Thick Onion Soup with Gô (see above).

VARIATIONS

*Any of the following garnishes or seasonings may be added to the soup with the miso or sprinkled on top of individual servings: 7-spice red pepper, powdered green *nori*, *sansho* pepper; minced trefoil, sake lees, slivered *yuzu* or lemon rind; pepper, crushed garlic, croutons, sage, or thyme.
*Experiment using other vegetables such as green beans, celery (including leaves), snow peas, *kombu*, or shelled green soybeans. Substitute an equal quantity of green soybeans for the dry soybeans when preparing the Homemade Gô Purée. When preparing a thin soup, add several lightly beaten eggs together with the miso.
*Seasoned Gôjiru with Deep-fried Potatoes: Sauté the vegetables and agé given in the recipe above, omitting the potatoes. Add 3 tablespoons each shoyu and natural sugar, cover pan, and simmer for 5 minutes. Cut 2 potatoes into thin rounds, deep-fry until golden brown, and add to the soup with the gô.
*Suritate and Hikitate: These are two country-style variations on the Gôjiru theme. In *Suritate*, which contains no vegetables, the gô is seasoned only with shoyu and simmered in water or dashi. *Hikitate* is made by parboiling, then thoroughly grinding soybeans and adding them to regular miso soup just before adding the miso.

Homemade Gô Purée

MAKES 2 CUPS

Gô purée has the consistency of a thick milkshake. Ground gô (below) is a thick paste. The two types may be used interchangeably in most recipes. To make 2 cups of gô purée from ground gô, simply mix the latter thoroughly with 7/8 cup water. (Note: 1 cup dry soybeans expands to about 2½ cups when soaked overnight.)

½ cup dry soybeans, soaked for 8 to 10 hours in 1 quart water
7/8 cup water

Rinse, then drain the beans in a colander. Combine beans and water in a blender and purée at high speed for about 3 minutes, or until smooth. Or, if a crunchier texture is desired, purée for only 1 minute.

Homemade Ground Gô

MAKES 1¼ CUPS

This variety of gô is slightly thicker than that made in most tofu shops, but resembles that made traditionally in Japanese farmhouses using either hand-turned grinding stones or a *suribachi*.

½ cup dry soybeans, soaked for 8 to 10 hours in 1 quart water

Rinse, then drain the beans in a colander. Using a hand mill or meat grinder with a fine-blade attachment, grind beans to a smooth paste.

Gô Cracker Dip or Spread

MAKES 1½ CUPS

1 tablespoon butter
½ cup minced onion
1 clove of garlic, crushed
1 cup Gôjiru (below)
¼ cup (tofu) mayonnaise (p. 107)
¼ teaspoon salt
Dash of pepper

Melt the butter in a skillet. Add onion and garlic and sauté until onion is nicely browned. Combine in a blender with remaining ingredients and purée until smooth. Serve as a dip for potato chips, crackers, or fresh vegetable sticks, or use as a sandwich spread.

Thick Onion Soup with Gô

SERVES 6

Use gô in place of *roux* or cream sauces to give body, flavor, and a rich infusion of protein to your favorite soups. The following two recipes work well as patterns for experimentation.

2 tablespoons oil
4 onions, thinly sliced
2 cups Homemade Gô Purée (p. 74)
3¼ cups water
3½ tablespoons shoyu or 5 tablespoons red miso
2/3 cup grated cheese
2 tablespoons butter
Dash of pepper
1 cup croutons (sautéed lightly in butter, if desired)
¼ cup minced parsley (optional)

Heat a heavy pot or large casserole and coat with the oil. Add onions and sauté for 5 minutes. Mix in purée and water and bring to a boil. Reduce heat to low and simmer for 10 minutes, stirring occasionally. Stir in the shoyu, cheese, butter, and pepper, and return to the boil. For best flavor, allow to stand for at least 6 hours. Serve as is or reheated, garnished with croutons and parsley.

VARIATIONS

*Add 5 to 10 ounces diced thick agé or ganmo together with the purée. Increase shoyu to 4 (or miso to) 6 tablespoons.
*Use leftovers to make a delicious casserole as follows: To each cup of leftover soup add 1 lightly beaten egg and, if desired, ¼ to ½ cup leftover vegetables or grains. Mix well, place into a baking pan or casserole and sprinkle lightly with cheese. Bake at 350° for 20 minutes, or until nicely browned.

Scrambled Eggs with Gô

SERVES 3 OR 4

2 tablespoons butter
¼ cup diced onion
¼ cup diced mushrooms
1 cup Homemade Gô Purée (p. 74)
2 eggs, lightly beaten
½ teaspoon salt
Dash of pepper
¼ cup grated cheese (optional)

Melt the butter in a skillet. Add onion and mushroom and sauté until onion is just transparent. Add gô and, stirring constantly, cook for 5 to 7 minutes, or until purée has a subtly sweet fragrance. Mix in remaining ingredients and cook for a few more minutes until eggs have set.

Go in Oven Cookery

When used in place of, or together with, eggs as a basis for casseroles, baked grain or egg dishes, or even for cheesecake-like desserts, gô lends body and flavor to each dish while providing the tasty richness and high protein usually supplied by dairy milk.

Whole-wheat Bread with Gô

MAKES 6 LOAVES

This high protein bread has a delightfully moist texture and rich flavor. By properly combining soy and wheat proteins, we increase the total amount of usable protein by about 30 percent.

2 cups soybeans, soaked overnight in water, drained and rinsed
4 cups lukewarm water
2 tablespoons dried yeast
½ cup honey or natural sugar
22 cups whole-wheat flour, approximately
¼ cup oil
2½ tablespoons salt

Combine half the beans and 2 cups water in a blender; purée for about 3 minutes, or until smooth. Pour the purée into a large mixing bowl. Purée the remaining beans in the same way and add to the bowl together with honey, yeast, and 4 cups flour. Using a large wooden spoon, mix for about 5 minutes to form a smooth sponge. Cover bowl with a moist towel, and allow to stand for about 40 minutes in a warm place until sponge doubles in volume.

Add the oil and salt. Fold in about 2 cups flour at a time to form a smooth, firm dough. Turn dough out onto a well-floured bread board and incorporate the remaining flour while kneading. When dough has been kneaded 200 to 300 times and is fairly light and smooth-textured, place in a large, lightly oiled bowl, cover, and allow to double in volume. Punch down and allow to rise once again.

Preheat oven to 350°. Turn dough out onto a lightly floured bread board and divide into 6 equal portions. Knead each portion about 20 times, shape into a loaf, and place into a lightly oiled bread pan. When the last loaf is in its pan, allow all loaves to rise for 5 to 10 minutes more. Bake for 40 to 50 minutes, or until nicely browned. Serve warm with butter.

Corn Bread with Gô

MAKES 1 LOAF

½ cup soybeans, soaked overnight in water and drained
2 tablespoons oil
1 tablespoon honey or natural sugar
2 tablespoons sesame butter, *tahini,* or ground roasted sesame seeds (p. 38)
1½ teaspoons salt
2 cups water
1½ cups cornmeal
Oil

Preheat oven to 375°. Combine the first five ingredients in a blender, adding 1½ cups water; purée for 3 minutes or until smooth. Pour into a mixing bowl and add remaining ½ cup water and cornmeal; mix well. Bake in a lightly oiled square pan for about 45 minutes. Serve with butter, molasses, or sesame butter—or try cottage cheese.

Gô Casserole

SERVES 2 OR 3

2 cups Homemade Gô Purée (p. 74)
½ cup milk (soy or dairy)
2 tablespoons melted butter
2 tablespoons ground roasted sesame seeds (p. 38), sesame butter, or *tahini*
½ teaspoon salt
Dash of pepper
2 tablespoons bread crumbs

Preheat oven to 350°. Combine the first six ingredients in a bowl; mix well. Pour into a lightly oiled casserole or bread pan and top with a sprinkling of bread crumbs. Bake for 30 to 40 minutes, or until nicely browned.

Egg Casserole with Cheese and Gô

SERVES 2 OR 3

2 cups Homemade Gô Purée (p. 74)
5 eggs, lightly beaten
¾ teaspoon salt, 1 tablespoon shoyu, or 1½ tablespoons red miso
Dash of pepper
1½ tablespoons butter
2 ounces sliced or grated cheese
Ketchup or Ketchup-Worcestershire Sauce (p. 49)

Preheat oven to 350°. Combine the first five ingredients in a large bowl; mix well. Pour the mixture into a lightly oiled bread pan or casserole, dot with butter and top with cheese. Bake for 40 to 50 minutes, or until nicely browned. Serve hot or cold with ketchup or the sauce.

Deep-fried Gô Patties *(Bakudan Agé)* SERVES 3 OR 4

2 cups Homemade Gô Purée (p. 74)
2 cups bread crumbs or bread crumb flakes
½ carrot, diced or slivered
1 small onion, diced
½ teaspoon salt
1 tablespoon ground roasted sesame seeds (p. 38), sesame butter, or *tahini* (optional)
Oil for deep-frying

Combine the first six ingredients in a large bowl, mixing well. Shape the mixture into 2½-inch patties or 1¼-inch balls. Heat oil to 350° in a wok, skillet, or deep-fryer. Slide in patties or balls and deep-fry for about 2 minutes, or until golden brown (p. 130). Serve topped with ketchup, Ketchup-Worcestershire Sauce (p. 49) or Tofu Tartare Sauce (p. 49).

VARIATION
*Gô Croquettes: Into 1 cup Homemade Ground Gô (p. 74) mix ¼ cup minced and steamed sweet potatoes or yams and ¼ cup minced onions. Add just enough bread crumbs to hold the mixture together, season lightly with salt, and shape into 2-inch patties. Dust each pattie with flour, dip in lightly beaten egg, and roll in bread crumbs. Deep-fry and serve as above.

Or, substitute grated lemon or *yuzu* rind for the potatoes. Use grated glutinous yam as a binding agent, adding flour only if necessary.

Rice Pudding with Gô and Apple

SERVES 4 TO 6

¾ cup gô (made from ¼ cup dry soybeans soaked overnight, drained, and blended with 6 tablespoons water)
2 cups cooked Brown Rice (p. 50)
1½ tablespoons dark brown sugar
½ cup raisins
2 cups milk (soy or dairy)
1 apple, diced
1 tablespoon butter
¼ teaspoon salt
¼ teaspoon cinnamon

Combine the first six ingredients and, stirring constantly, bring just to a boil. Reduce heat to low and, continuing to stir, simmer for 10 minutes. Mix in remaining ingredients and remove from heat. Allow to cool uncovered for about 2 hours before serving.

Or, combine all ingredients and bake for 1 hour at 350°.

Rich and Spongy Loaf with Gô

SERVES 2 OR 3

2 cups Homemade Gô Purée (p. 74)
½ cup milk
¼ cup raisins
1 tablespoon butter
1 tablespoon honey
2 tablespoons natural sugar
1 egg, lightly beaten
Butter
¼ cup thinly sliced or grated cheese

Preheat oven to 350°. Combine the first seven ingredients in a bowl; mix well. Pour the mixture into a bread pan coated lightly with butter, and top with the cheese. Bake for about 30 minutes, or until nicely browned. Serve hot or cold.

Okara or Unohana

6

U NOHANA *(Deutzia scabra)* is a tiny white flower that grows in thick clusters on briar bushes and blossoms in the spring (fig. 20). In 1869, the *haiku* poet Basho, on his last long trek to the back country of northern Japan, wrote of unohana in his journal:

> *Mounting towards the Shirakawa barrier*
> *"Autumnal winds" hummed in my ears,*
> *"The maple" stood imagined,*
> *But leaf-green branches haunting too.*
> *Against unohana white white briars,*
> *As if pushing through snow.*
> > *(CID CORMAN translation)*

The word "unohana" is also used in connection with tofu. After gô is ladled into a cauldron of boiling water and simmered, it is transferred to a heavy cloth sack set on a rack on top of a wooden curding barrel. The sack's mouth is twisted closed and the sack is pressed. In farmhouses a grinding stone is set atop the sack; in tofu shops the sack is pressed either with a traditional lever (fig. 21) or with more modern equipment. In each case liquid soymilk filters through the sack into the curding barrel. The soybean pulp—called *okara* or unohana—remains in the sack. The soymilk is eventually made into tofu; the okara has its own special uses.

Okara is beige in color and has a crumbly, fine-grained texture. Some Westerners have remarked—only half in jest—that its appearance reminds them of moist sawdust. But the Japanese, in line with their ancient tradition of honoring even the simplest and most humble of foods, place the honorific prefix

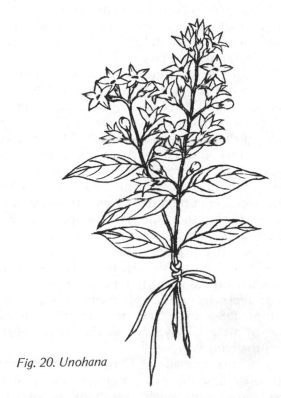

Fig. 20. Unohana

o before the word *kara*, which means "shell, hull, or husk." Thus *o-kara* means "honorable shell." In Chinese it is called "child of tofu lees" (*doufu chatsu*), "soy lees" (*doucha*), or "tofu's head" (*douto*) in contrast with the soft curds which are called the "tofu's brain." Trying to translate any of these words into descriptive English is almost impossible; terms such as "soybean lees, grounds, mash, pulp, fines, residue, dregs," or the like hardly do justice to this fine food.

When Japanese refer to okara as an ingredient in cooking, they call it *unohana*, in honor of Basho's tiny white blossoms. And, indeed, it deserves this

77

high evaluation for, when properly prepared, it is a tasty and nutritious food which serves as an important ingredient in traditional Japanese cuisine. Okara dishes are available in most delicatessens and at many fine restaurants. Light and almost fluffy, okara absorbs flavors well and gives body to sautéed vegetable dishes, soups, casseroles, breads, and salads.

The most important constitutent of okara is what nutritionists and doctors call "dietary plant fiber" and now consider to be an essential part of every well-balanced diet. Fiber, by definition, is indigestible. Composed of carbohydrates found in the outer bran layers of whole grains and the cell walls of natural vegetables and pulses, it passes unchanged through the human digestive tract performing two key functions: it provides the "bulk" or "roughage" necessary for regular bowel movements and the prevention of constipation; and it absorbs toxins (including environmental pollutants) and speeds their passage out of the body.

The recent re-evaluation of the importance of fiber-rich foods such as okara has resulted from the recognition of three dangerous trends in the dietary patterns of most industrialized nations: 1) our intake of dietary fiber is now only 20 percent of what it was one hundred years ago due both to the rapid rise in the consumption of sugar, meat, fats, and dairy products (all of which contain *no* fiber) and the decrease in the use of grains and vegetables; 2) a large proportion of the grains we do consume are in their refined, processed forms (such as white bread, rice, or pasta) which have been stripped of their fiber-rich (and nutritious) outer layers; 3) the average person has a steadily increasing intake of toxic substances from both food additives and the environment. Serving okara, therefore, allows us to make use of natural soybeans in the most holistic and health-giving way.

Containing about 17 percent of the protein in the original soybeans, okara itself consists of 3.5 percent protein by weight, or about the same proportion found in whole milk or cooked brown rice. While it is perhaps unfortunate that all of this protein is not transferred to tofu, its presence in okara is just that much more reason for utilizing this byproduct of the tofu-making process.

The tastiest and most nutritious okara is that removed in the process of making kinugoshi tofu, a variety made from very thick soymilk. Since this okara is pressed only once, it retains a great deal of the soymilk's flavor and nutrients, and has an obviously moist, cohesive texture. In the process of making regular tofu in tofu shops, soymilk is filtered through first a coarsely woven and then a finely woven sack. The small quantity of very fine-grained okara that collects in the second sack is usually pressed by hand (rather than with a press) so that it, too, retains a large portion of the soymilk taste and food value. During the winter months when the cold air ensures their freshness, both varieties are shaped into 4½-inch-diameter balls or sealed in small plastic bags to be sold for a few pennies per pound. Some tofu makers present okara to their customers free of charge as a token of appreciation for their patronage.

Before World War II, most tofu-shop okara was sold for use in cooking. Young apprentices at the shop were often allowed to cook the day's okara any way they wished and then sell their creations from door to door. At New Year's, okara croquettes and other tasty dishes, made and sold in this way, earned an impoverished apprentice a little pocket money.

In some parts of China, okara is pressed into cakes about 6 inches in diameter and 1 inch thick, and allowed to ferment for 10 to 15 days until each is covered with a mycelium of white mold. The cakes are dried for a few hours in the sun, then deep-fried or cooked with vegetables and sold as a nutritious flavoring agent called *meitauza*. In Indonesia, a similar product called *ontjom* is said to be well liked for its tasty almond-like flavor.

In Japan, a typical tofu shop produces about 15 gallons of okara daily, or roughly 1 gallon for each gallon of dry soybeans used. But at most, only one gallon or so of this is retailed. The remainder is picked up daily at the shop by local dairymen who feed it to their cows to stimulate milk production and enrich the milk's nutrient content. In China, many tofu makers run small hog farms and use okara as their principal source of fodder. Okara also works well as an organic mulch and fertilizer, or as a free, high-protein pet food. (In Japan it is now used commercially in dried dog- and cat foods.)

Nursing mothers have used okara for centuries to enrich their milk and stimulate its flow. It also serves as a traditional cure for diarrhea. Wrapped in a cloth and used to rub down the household woodwork, okara's natural oils coat and darken the wood, thus serving as a wax and polish.

At present in the United States, okara is available at some Japanese and Chinese groceries and, of course, at all tofu shops. But the easiest way to obtain okara is to prepare Homemade Tofu (p. 99) or Soymilk (p. 204). If you prepare enough tofu for two people, you will have as a byproduct about 1 cup of okara, or enough for two to four servings.

Fig. 21. A traditional lever press

Roasting or Parching Okara

The dry-roasting or parching called for in some recipes is meant to reduce okara's water content and give it a light, almost fluffy texture. When added to breads, muffins, cookies, or croquettes, roasted okara not only saves on flour but also gives much lighter results.

To roast using a skillet or wok, heat but do not oil the pan. Put in the okara and roast over low heat, stirring constantly with a wooden spoon or spatula, for about 3 minutes or until okara is light and dry but not browned.

When parching okara in an oven, spread the okara out on a large baking tin. Place in an unheated oven set at 350° and heat for 5 to 10 minutes.

Homemade Okara

The 1 cup of okara which results as a byproduct left over from the preparation of homemade tofu, soymilk, or kinugoshi is superior in taste, texture, and nutritional elements to that which is available from commercial tofu shops. It is also free. Since the soybeans are ground in a blender rather than between heavy stones, the okara has a slightly crunchy texture like that of finely chopped nuts. And since okara is pressed by hand rather than mechanically, it retains the flavor and nutrition of the unpressed soymilk. The okara that remains after making soymilk or kinugoshi is the tastiest and most nutritious, since some of the thick soymilk always remains in it. Since the okara from homemade tofu is generally separated from the soymilk before the milk is thoroughly cooked however, it is important that the okara be cooked slightly longer than commercial okara, hence the cooking times in the recipes that follow.

To prepare homemade okara, refer to the recipes for Homemade Tofu (p. 99), Soymilk (p. 204), or Kinugoshi (p. 215).

OKARA IN SALADS

Okara Salad with Noodles and Greens SERVES 4

3 tablespoons oil
7 chrysanthemum, Chinese cabbage, chard, cabbage, or spinach leaves, cut into 1-inch-wide strips
2/3 cup okara, firmly packed
2/3 cup cooked noodles (rice flour or buckwheat)
1 tablespoon ground roasted sesame seeds (p. 38)
1 teaspoon grated gingerroot
½ teaspoon salt
Dash of pepper

Heat a skillet or wok and coat with the oil. Add the green leaves and sauté briskly over high heat. Reduce heat to medium, add okara and cooked noodles, and sauté for 5 to 10 minutes more, or until okara is light and fluffy. Stir in gingerroot, add salt and pepper, and remove from heat. Allow to cool to room temperature before serving.

For variety, mix in 1 diced apple and 1 teaspoon lemon juice after the salad has cooled. Serve topped with Tofu Mayonnaise (p. 107) and a sprinkling of roasted sesame seeds.

OKARA IN SOUPS

Okara may be added to most vegetable and miso soups. To prepare a thick soup, use about 4½ parts liquid to 1 part firmly packed okara. For a thin soup, use a ratio of 8 or 9 to 1. In Japanese okara soups, the vegetables are either sautéed in the pot until tender and then simmered briefly in the stock, or uncooked vegetables are added to the stock and simmered slowly until tender. The okara is generally added after the vegetables have been sautéed or partially simmered. In miso soups, use 6 tablespoons (3½ ounces) of okara to serve 4.

Chilled Okara Soup (Unohana-jiru) SERVES 4

2 tablespoons oil
2 onions, diced
8 small mushrooms, thinly sliced through crown and stem
2/3 cup okara, firmly packed
3 cups water or stock
1 teaspoon salt
Dash of pepper
2 tablespoons butter
6 or 7 tablespoons red or barley miso; or 4 tablespoons shoyu
2 tablespoons sake or white wine (optional)
Minced parsley or chives

Heat a skillet or wok and coat with the oil. Add the onions and mushrooms and sauté over medium heat for 2 or 3 minutes. Add okara and water and bring to a boil; reduce heat to low. Add salt, pepper, butter, miso, and, if used, the sake, and simmer for 10 to 15 minutes more. Allow to cool, then chill overnight or for at least several hours. Serve garnished with parsley or chives.

OKARA IN SAUCES

Use small amounts (about 10% by volume) of okara (roasted or unroasted) as a thickener in mushroom, onion, curry, or spaghetti sauces.

OKARA WITH EGGS

Okara Scrambled Eggs

SERVES 3 OR 4

3 eggs
½ cup milk
¼ teaspoon salt
Dash of pepper
½ cup okara, firmly packed
1½ tablespoons butter

Combine the first four ingredients in a mixing bowl; whisk or mix with a fork. Now stir in the okara. Melt the butter in a skillet, add the egg-and-okara mixture, and scramble over high heat for about 3 minutes or until firm but not dry. Serve hot or cold.

Okara & Egg Patties with Raisins

SERVES 4

2 cups okara, firmly packed
2 eggs, lightly beaten
¼ cup raisins
1 tablespoon natural sugar
¼ teaspoon salt
1 teaspoon baking powder
1 to 2 teaspoons oil
2 tablespoons butter

Combine the first six ingredients in a large bowl; mix well. Heat a skillet and coat lightly with part of the oil. Shape the okara mixture into 2½-inch patties. Pan-fry patties on both sides until golden brown. Serve hot, each pattie topped with a dab of butter.

Or, bake the patties on a lightly oiled cookie sheet in a medium oven for about 20 minutes until nicely browned.

Okara Eggs with Sweet Potatoes and Raisins

SERVES 2 OR 3

1½ tablespoons butter
½ cup okara, firmly packed
1 sweet potato or yam (5 inches long), steamed and diced
¼ cup raisins
½ cup water or stock
1 egg, lightly beaten
¼ teaspoon salt
Dash of pepper

Melt butter in a skillet. Add the next four ingredients. Stirring constantly, simmer until water is absorbed. Mix in the egg, season with salt and pepper, and cook, stirring constantly, for about 2 minutes until egg is firm and slightly fluffy. Allow to cool before serving.

OKARA BAKED

Okara may be used in your favorite recipes for stuffed, baked vegetables. Okara & Vegetable Sauté (below) can serve as a delicious filling for green peppers, mushrooms, potatoes, or eggplants. Use small amounts (about 10%) of okara in casseroles or breads, adding the okara to your ingredients either as is, lightly roasted (p. 79), or simmered in Sweetened Shoyu Broth (p. 40). Okara is also delicious in baked desserts (p. 84).

Scalloped Okara & Mushrooms

SERVES 4 TO 6

3 tablespoons butter
3 tablespoons whole-wheat flour
1½ cups milk (soy or dairy)
Dash of pepper
1½ tablespoons oil
12 mushrooms, thinly sliced
1½ onions, thinly sliced
1½ cups okara, lightly packed
2½ tablespoons shoyu
½ cup grated cheese
2 tablespoons bread crumbs
2 tablespoons Parmesan cheese

Preheat oven to 350°. Use the first four ingredients to prepare a White Sauce (p. 48). Heat a skillet and coat with the oil. Add mushrooms and onions, sauté for 4 to 5 minutes, and remove from heat. Combine with the sauce, okara, shoyu, and cheese; mix well, then spoon into a lightly oiled loaf pan or casserole. Top with a sprinkling of bread crumbs and Parmesan; bake for 30 minutes.

Okara-Onion-Cheese Soufflé

SERVES 2

Use ingredients for Okara Dessert Soufflé (p. 84) except omit the honey and vanilla. Add to the okara: ½ onion, minced and sautéed until transparent, ¼ cup grated cheese, 2 tablespoons grated carrot, salt and pepper to taste. Proceed as for the dessert.

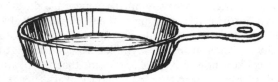

**OKARA STIR-FRIED, SAUTÉED,
AND DEEP-FRIED**

Okara Burgers

MAKES 4 TO 5

1 cup okara
½ cup whole-wheat flour
1 egg, lightly beaten
¼ cup minced onion
¼ cup grated carrot
1 clove of garlic, minced or crushed
1 tablespoon shoyu
¼ teaspoon curry powder
Dash of pepper
Oil for deep-frying

Combine the first nine ingredients, mixing well, and shape into patties. Heat the oil to 350° in a wok, skillet, or deep-fryer. Drop in patties and deep-fry until crisp and golden brown (p. 130). Serve as for Ganmo Burgers (p. 188).

If deep-frying is inconvenient, patties may be fried or broiled.

VARIATIONS

*Okara Fritters: Add 6 tablespoons (soy) milk and 1 egg to the above ingredients. Drop by spoonfuls into the hot oil to deep-fry. Mix skimmings from oil back into batter after each batch has been deep-fried. Delicious topped with Tofu Mayonnaise (p. 107). Makes 12 to 14.

Okara Tempeh

SERVES 3 TO 4

This delicious preparation, developed at *The Farm* in Tennessee (p. 316), is a variation on the traditional Indonesian *tempeh* recipe (p. 68). It is important to use okara which has been well cooked during the preparation of the soymilk. Coarse-textured okara seems to allow the best air circulation during fermentation; it must be pressed as firmly as possible to expel soymilk, thereby giving a light, high-quality product. For best results, prepare a shallow incubation tray having a bottom made of rustproof aluminum screen.

2½ cups well-pressed okara, cooled to room temperature
2 teaspoons vinegar
½ teaspoon tempeh starter or ¼ to ½ cup minced tempeh from a previous fermentation

Combine all ingredients, mixing well. Spread to a depth of ½ to ¾ inch in a shallow tray or pan and cover with a sheet of perforated plastic wrap as for Homemade Tempeh (p. 68). Proceed to incubate, cook and serve as directed in the basic recipe.

Okara-Potato Pancakes

MAKES 5 TO 6

1 cup coarsely-grated mature potatoes
2/3 cup okara
3 eggs, lightly beaten
1 teaspoon salt
1½ tablespoons minced onion
1½ tablespoons whole-wheat flour
Oil for frying
Applesauce or butter

Place potato gratings in a cloth towel and wring towel to extract as much moisture from potatoes as possible. Combine in a bowl with the next five ingredients; mix well. Shape into ¼-inch-thick patties and fry in a well-oiled skillet on both sides until golden brown. Serve hot, topped with either applesauce or butter.

Okara Croquettes

MAKES 10

1 cup White Sauce (p. 48; use 1 teaspoon salt for seasoning)
2 teaspoons oil
½ onion, minced
2 tablespoons grated carrot
1 cup okara
¼ cup whole-wheat flour
1 egg, lightly beaten
2/3 cup bread crumbs or bread crumb flakes
Oil for deep-frying

Prepare White Sauce and set aside to cool. Heat a skillet and coat with the oil. Add onion and carrots, and sauté for 4 to 5 minutes, then add to the sauce together with the okara; mix well. Shape into (soft) cylinders 1 inch in diameter and 2½ inches long. Dust with flour, gently dip into egg, and roll in bread crumbs; set aside briefly to dry.

Heat oil to 350° in a wok, skillet, or deep-fryer. Drop in croquettes and deep-fry until golden brown (p. 130). Serve hot or cold, as is or topped with Tofu Tartare Sauce (p. 109) or Tofu Mayonnaise (p. 107; with onion).

Okara & Vegetable Sauté
(Unohana no iri-ni)

SERVES 3 OR 4

This dish, sold ready-made in Japanese markets and delicatessens and prepared at fine restaurants, is the most popular way of serving okara in Japan. Most recipes call for carrots, *konnyaku*, *shiitake* mushrooms, leeks, and agé as the basic ingredients, but almost any other vegetables may be added or substituted. The flavor of this dish is substantially improved by allowing it to cool to room temperature. It is served as a side dish.

2 tablespoons oil (up to half of which may be sesame)
½ carrot, cut into matchsticks
2 onions or leeks, thinly sliced
1 cup okara, firmly packed
1½ cups water, stock, or dashi (p. 39)
2 to 3 tablespoons natural sugar or honey
3 tablespoons shoyu
1 tablespoon sake or white wine

Heat a skillet or wok and coat with the oil. Add carrot slivers and sauté for about 2 minutes, then add onion slices and sauté until transparent. Mix in remaining ingredients and bring just to a boil. Reduce heat to low and simmer, stirring occasionally, for 10 to 15 minutes, or until most of the liquid has evaporated. Remove from heat and allow to cool to room temperature. Do not reheat to serve. For best flavor, refrigerate overnight or for at least 5 hours.

VARIATIONS

*To the ingredients listed above, add 2 thinly sliced mushrooms (fresh, or dry *shiitake*), ¼ cake of *konnyaku* cut into small rectangles, and 2 ounces of agé cut into thin strips; sauté together with the onions. (Some cooks prefer to parboil carrot slivers, mushroom slices, and *konnyaku* chunks before sautéing them, and add them to the leeks about 30 seconds before the okara has finished cooking.) Other vegetables commonly sautéed with the okara include lotus root, bamboo shoots, burdock root, *udo*, snow or green peas, green beans, sweet potatoes, yams, or cabbage. Serve garnished with slivers of gingerroot.

*Use Okara & Vegetable Sauté as a filling for stuffed peppers, eggplants, or tomatoes, or in Agé or Inari-zushi Pouches (p. 192 and 194).

Deep-fried Okara Balls in Thickened Sauce: Prepare Okara & Vegetable Sauté and allow to cool. Combine in a small bowl with 1 egg and mix well. Sauté mixture in a lightly oiled pan until egg is firm, then allow to cool for 5 to 10 minutes. Shape into 1¼-inch balls, roll in cornstarch, and deep-fry until golden brown. Cut some of the balls into halves and top with Ankake Sauce, Gingerroot Sauce, or Sweet & Sour Sauce (p. 49). Allow to cool before serving.

Unsweetened Fried Okara
(Unohana-iri)

SERVES 4 TO 6

---

2 tablespoons oil (up to ¼ of which may be sesame)
1 small onion, diced
4 mushrooms, thinly sliced
½ carrot, cut into matchsticks
½ cup diced lotus root
2 or 3 ounces agé, ganmo, or thick agé, diced (optional)
1 cup okara, firmly packed
1 cup water or stock
1 tablespoon shoyu
½ teaspoon salt

Heat a wok or skillet and coat with the oil. Add onion and sauté over high heat for 30 seconds. Reduce heat to medium, add mushroom, carrot, lotus root, and, if used, deep-fried tofu, and sauté for 2 to 3 minutes. Add remaining ingredients and bring just to a boil, then simmer for 3 minutes more. Allow to cool to room temperature (at least 3 to 4 hours) or refrigerate before serving.

If desired, use with any of the variations listed in the previous recipe.

Fried Okara Patties
(Unohana Dango)

SERVES 2 OR 3

½ cup okara
¾ to 1 cup arrowroot or cornstarch
½ teaspoon salt
Water or milk
Oil
Worcestershire sauce or shoyu

Combine okara, arrowroot, and salt, mixing well. Add just enough water or milk to form a stiff dough and knead briefly. Shape dough into 1-inch balls, then press into 2-inch patties. Oil a skillet very lightly and fry patties on both sides until golden brown. Serve hot (like *mochi*) topped with a sprinkling of the sauce or shoyu.

Deep-fried Okara Balls in Sweet & Sour Sauce

SERVES 4

---

1 cup okara, firmly packed
1 clove of garlic, crushed or minced
1 leek or onion, minced
1 teaspoon grated gingerroot
¼ cup ground roasted sesame seeds (p. 38)
2 tablespoons red or barley miso
¼ cup cornstarch or arrowroot
Oil for deep-frying
2½ cups Sweet & Sour Sauce (p. 49) or Pineapple Sweet & Sour Sauce (p. 166).

Combine the first six ingredients in a large bowl, mixing well. Form the mixture into 16 balls and roll the balls in the cornstarch. Heat the oil to 350° in a wok, skillet, or deep-fryer. Slide in the balls and deep-fry until golden brown (p. 130). Prepare the sauce. Just after it thickens, add the okara balls and simmer, stirring constantly, for 1 minute. Cut 8 of the balls into halves and allow all to cool to room temperature before serving.

Ankake or Gingerroot Sauce (p. 49) may be substituted for the Sweet & Sour Sauce. If desired, lightly roast the okara (p. 79) and add lightly beaten egg to aid in binding the mixture.

OKARA WITH GRAINS AND SUSHI

Okara has been used for centuries in Japan as a substitute for rice in sushi preparations. And in times when rice was scarce (due to war or famine), okara was cooked with or even served in place of rice as a staple food. By combining soy protein with that of grains, the okara boosted the total protein content by as much as 32 percent.

Okara also may be used in waffles, cornmeal muffins, spoonbread, and all yeasted breads. Use 2 parts flour to 1 part packed okara.

Okara Chapaties

MAKES 8

1¼ cups whole-wheat flour
½ cup okara, firmly packed
½ teaspoon salt
2 tablespoons water
1 tablespoon oil (optional)

Preheat oven to 350°. Combine 1 cup flour with remaining ingredients in a large bowl, mixing well. Knead for about 5 minutes to form a smooth dough. Divide dough into 8 parts and roll out each one on a floured board into a very thin 6-inch round. Place rounds on large baking trays and bake for 5 to 10 minutes, or until nicely browned. Allow to cool for at least 5 minutes, or until crisp. Serve topped with Mushroom Sauce (p. 48), butter, or a tofu spread (p. 109), or mounded with a salad or grain preparation.

The make *puri*, roll *chapati* dough into 4-inch rounds and deep-fry in 350° oil. Turn after about 30 seconds and continue deep-frying until *puri* have puffed up and are golden brown.

Okara Whole-wheat Pancakes

MAKES 10

1¼ cups whole-wheat flour
1 tablespoon baking powder
1 teaspoon salt
1 1/3 cups milk
¼ cup oil
2 tablespoons honey
½ teaspoon vanilla extract
3 eggs, separated into yolks and whites
¾ cup okara, lightly packed

Combine and sift the first three ingredients. In a separate container, combine the milk, oil, honey, vanilla, and egg yolks; mix well, then stir in okara. Beat egg whites until stiff. Lightly mix dry ingredients into wet ingredients, then fold in egg whites; avoid overmixing. Spoon batter in 6-inch rounds into a lightly oiled skillet and fry on both sides until golden brown. Serve with butter and either honey or maple syrup.

Wonderful Okara & Barley Flour Muffins

MAKES 12

1¼ cups barley flour
2 teaspoons baking powder
¼ teaspoon salt
1¼ cups milk
¼ cup honey or natural sugar
¼ cup oil
¼ teaspoon vanilla extract
¾ cup okara, lightly packed

Preheat oven to 400°. Roast barley flour in a heavy skillet, stirring constantly, until well browned and fragrant. Cool briefly, then combine with baking powder and salt, mixing well. Combine the next four ingredients in a separate bowl, mix thoroughly, then stir in okara. Fold dry ingredients lightly into wet. Spoon batter to a depth of about ¾ inch into a lightly oiled muffin tin and bake for about 35 minutes or until well browned. Invert on a rack and cool thoroughly before serving.

For variety, omit roasting; use Japanese-style pre-roasted barley flour *(mugi-kogashi)* or the regular Western variety.

Okara Rice

SERVES 4

1½ tablespoons oil
¼ cup diced carrot
2 onions or leeks, thinly sliced or diced
½ cup diced lotus root (optional)
2/3 cup okara, lightly roasted (p. 79)
2 cups cooked Brown Rice (p. 50)
2 tablespoons shoyu
2/3 teaspoon salt
Minced parsley and/or crumbled toasted *nori*

Heat a skillet or wok and coat with the oil. Add the carrot and onions and sauté for 3 or 4 minutes, or until onions are transparent. Add lotus root and sauté for 1 minute more. Add okara, rice, shoyu, and salt, mixing thoroughly. Cook for 2 or 3 minutes more, stirring constantly, until rice is well heated. Serve hot or cold, garnished with the parsley and/or *nori*.

For variety, cool the mixture, then shape into small patties. Dip patties in lightly beaten egg and roll in bread crumbs. Deep-fry until golden brown (p. 130) or pan-fry in butter. Serve with ketchup.

Sushi Okara *(Vinegared Okara)*

MAKES ¾ CUP

½ cup okara, firmly packed
1½ to 2 tablespoons rice vinegar
1 tablespoon natural sugar
1½ teaspoons sake or white wine (optional)
¼ teaspoon salt or 1½ teaspoons Sesame Salt (p. 51)

Roast okara for about 3 minutes until light and dry (p. 79). Transfer to a large bowl and allow to cool for 1 minute. Meanwhile, combine the remaining ingredients in a small bowl, mixing well. Stir mixture into okara as when preparing Sushi Rice (p. 50). Serve in any of the following ways:

*Garnished with slivered gingerroot as a topping for rice. (This may also be prepared as follows: In a skillet or wok, combine all the ingredients in the above recipe except the vinegar. Add 1 lightly beaten egg, 1 tablespoon hemp- or sesame seeds, and 2 tablespoons water or dashi. Simmer together until okara is light and dry, then remove from heat and stir in the vinegar.)

*Prepare 4 Inari-zushi pouches (p. 194) or plain Agé Pouches (p. 192) and serve filled with Sushi Okara. (Or, to make this filling, combine 1 part Sushi Okara with 1 part

Sushi Rice (p. 50) or plain Brown Rice (p. 50). If desired, add to the mixture any of the following diced or slivered vegetables simmered until tender in Sweetened Shoyu Broth (p. 40): carrots, lotus root, mushrooms, *kampyo*, or snow peas. The addition of whole or ground roasted sesame seeds (p. 38) or slivered Paper-thin Omelet (p. 51) to the mixture further enhances its flavor.)

*Substitute Sushi Okara for Sushi Rice in Nori-wrapped Sushi (p. 170).

Okara-Omelet Pouches
(Sushi Okara Chakin)

MAKES 8

These little pouches filled with vinegared okara are close relatives of Inari-zushi. Here, thin omelets take the place of agé pouches and Sushi Okara replaces Sushi Rice.

½ carrot, diced
1 tablespoon shoyu
1 tablespoon natural sugar
1 ounce agé, ganmo, or thick agé, diced (optional)
¾ cup Sushi Okara (p. 83)
8 Paper-thin Omelets (p. 51)

Bring 1½ cups water to a boil in a small saucepan. Drop in the carrot and simmer for 2 minutes; drain, reserving ¼ cup of the cooking water. In the same saucepan, now combine reserved water, cooked carrots, shoyu, sugar, and, if used, the agé. Simmer uncovered for 4 to 5 minutes until liquid is absorbed or evaporated, then set aside to cool.

In a large bowl, combine the carrot-agé mixture with the Sushi Okara, mixing lightly. Spoon equal portions of this filling onto the center of each of the omelets, then fold over each omelet to form an envelope (fig. 22). Serve as hors d'oeuvre or as part of a meal.

VARIATIONS

*Okara Chirashi-zushi: Prepare 2 Paper-thin Omelets (p. 51). Arrange the Sushi Okara—and—carrot mixture in a large (wooden) bowl and top with the slivered omelets.
*Five-Color Okara Sushi (Okara Gomoku-zushi): Double the amount of shoyu, sugar, and cooking water used in the seasoned broth. Simmer together with the carrot at least three of the following vegetables: snow peas, lotus root half-moons, green beans, *kombu* slivers, *(shiitake)* mushroom slivers, *kampyo* strips, or leek pieces. Mix the cooked vegetables with Sushi Okara and serve on a large platter garnished with a sprinkling of crumbled toasted *nori*.

OKARA DESSERTS

Okara Granola

MAKES 1½ CUPS

This is our favorite okara recipe. Golden brown, crumbly, and slightly sweet, it has much the same nutty aroma as toasted wheat germ, for which it makes an excellent substitute. You may wish to prepare a large quantity and store it in sealed jars.

2 cups okara
4 to 5 tablespoons natural sugar or honey
2 tablespoons oil
1 tablespoon vanilla
1/8 teaspoon salt

Preheat oven to 350°. Combine all ingredients, mixing well. Spread in a large, shallow pan and roast, stirring occasionally, for 50 to 60 minutes, or until nicely browned, crumbly, and fragrant. Serve with milk (try using the soymilk from which the okara was extracted) and top with raisins or fresh fruit. Also delicious as a topping for (soymilk) yogurt, a lightweight mix to take on hiking trips, or a substitute for bread crumbs in casserole toppings. Serve small portions; it expands!

For a crunchier texture and richer flavor, add ¼ cup any or all of the following: raisins, shredded coconut, toasted sunflower seeds or pine nuts, chopped almonds or walnuts, minced dates or apricots, toasted sesame seeds or wheat germ. Mix in these ingredients 5 minutes before the end of toasting. Use in any of the recipes in this book calling for crunchy granola.

Okara Dessert Soufflé

SERVES 4

3 eggs, separated into yolks and whites
½ cup okara
2 tablespoons honey
¼ teaspoon vanilla
1 tablespoon oil
Dash of salt
2 tablespoons raisins (optional)

Preheat oven to 400°. Beat egg yolks, then combine with the next five (or six) ingredients; mix well. Beat egg whites until stiff, then fold into okara-egg yolk mixture. Spoon into a lightly oiled loaf pan and bake for about 30 minutes, or until nicely browned.

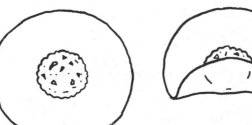

Fig. 22. Okara Omelet Pouches

Okara Sponge Cake

SERVES 4

Use ingredients for Okara Dessert Soufflé, but double amounts of honey and vanilla; omit salt, oil, and raisins. Sift together ½ cup whole-wheat flour, 1 teaspoon baking powder, and ¼ teaspoon salt; stir into okara-egg yolk mixture before folding in egg whites. Proceed as for soufflé. Delicious topped with Tofu Icing (p. 149).

Baked Okara-Apple Dessert

SERVES 4

1 cup okara, firmly packed
2 small apples, cut into thin wedges
¼ cup raisins
2 eggs, lightly beaten (optional)
3 tablespoons natural sugar
¾ cup milk
Dash of salt
2 tablespoons bread crumbs
2 tablespoons butter
¼ teaspoon cinnamon
2 ounces grated cheese (optional)

Preheat oven to 350°. Combine the first seven ingredients in a bowl, mixing well. Spoon mixture into a lightly oiled casserole. Top with bread crumbs, dot with butter, and sprinkle with cinnamon and, if used, grated cheese. Bake for about 30 minutes, or until nicely browned.

Okara Doughnuts

MAKES ABOUT 10

2/3 cup okara, firmly packed
2/3 cup flour
1 egg, lightly beaten
1½ teaspoons baking powder
½ teaspoon salt
¼ cup raisins
3 to 6 tablespoons natural sugar
½ teaspoon cinnamon
Oil for deep-frying

Combine the first eight ingredients in a bowl; mix well to form a dough. Roll out on a floured board and cut as for doughnuts. Heat the oil to 370° in a wok, skillet, or deep-fryer. Slide in the doughnuts and deep-fry until golden brown (p. 130).

To make lighter doughnuts, roast the okara lightly (p. 79) before combining with ½ cup flour and 1 or 2 eggs.

Okara Peanut Butter Cookies

MAKES 20

¼ cup butter
¼ cup sifted natural sugar
1 egg, lightly beaten
½ cup peanut butter
¼ teaspoon salt
¼ teaspoon baking soda
¾ cup okara, lightly roasted (p. 79) if desired
¼ teaspoon vanilla

Preheat oven to 375°. Beat butter until soft. Blend in sugar, then mix in the remaining ingredients. Form this mixture into small patties and place on a lightly oiled baking tin. Bake for about 15 minutes or until nicely browned.

VARIATIONS

*Substitute ½ cup Kinako Butter (p. 65) for the peanut butter and add ½ cup grated coconut to the ingredients listed above.
*Omit the salt and vanilla. Substitute 1 cup sweet white miso for the peanut butter and add 6 tablespoons raisins to the ingredients listed above.

7

Curds and Whey

THE ART OF preparing homemade butter and cheese, and the vocabulary that went with it, are slowly disappearing from Western culture. But it was once commonly understood that when a solution of rennet—an enzyme extracted from the membrane of the fourth stomach of unweaned calves, lambs, or kids—was added to cow's milk, or when the milk was left uncovered for several days in a warm place, it curdled, separating into a thin, watery liquid (whey) and soft white semi-solids (curds). The curds, primarily coagulated milk protein called "casein," could then be fermented and aged to make cheese, or churned to make butter.

Although many Westerners today have never seen or tasted curds, they were widely enjoyed by our forefathers and are still a common delicacy in countries such as India where they are served in curries and puddings with sliced bananas and oranges. When Yogananda, one of the first great Yoga masters to teach in the West, was considering a life of blissful meditation in solitude rather than one of working for the spiritual benefit of others, he was asked critically by his master: "Do you want the whole divine *channa* (curds) for yourself alone?" And the Indian saint, Ramakrishna, indicating how people tend to chit-chat aimlessly until something vital appears in their lives, once said: "When the curds, the last course, appear, one only hears the sound 'soop-soop' as the guests eat the curds with their fingers."

The process of making tofu curds from soymilk resembles that for making dairy curds from cow's or goat's milk. Soymilk can be curdled or solidified with either a "salt" (such as nigari or magnesium

chloride) or an acid (such as lemon juice or vinegar). When solidifier is stirred into hot soymilk and the soymilk is allowed to stand undisturbed for several minutes, the milk separates into delicate, white curds and pale yellow whey.

Soymilk Curds

After stirring nigari into the soymilk in his large, cedar curding barrel, the tofu craftsman covers the barrel with a wooden lid and allows the nigari to begin its work. Slowly it solidifies the soybean protein, which forms into curds and separates from the whey. After 15 or 20 minutes, the tofu maker rinses off a large, handsome bamboo colander and wraps its underside with cloth (fig. 23). He sets this on the surface of the mixture in the barrel and it slowly fills with whey. (The cloth keeps out the finer particles of curd.) The whey in the colander is ladled off and reserved for later use, and the colander is then weighted with a brick and replaced until it is again full (fig. 24). This whey, too, is ladled off into a large wooden bucket where it forms a billowy head of

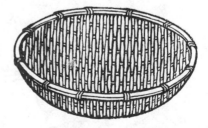

Fig. 23. A bamboo colander

86

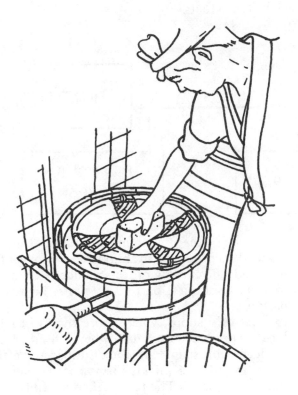

Fig. 24. Weighting the colander

Fig. 25. Ladling whey from curds

foam (fig. 25). When all the whey has been removed, only white curds remain in the barrel.

The Japanese refer to curds as *oboro,* meaning "clouded over, hazy, or misty." The same word is used in the translation of the Biblical passage "through a glass darkly," and for describing a moon half hidden in clouds. The term "oboro" is particularly appropriate when used in reference to the tofu-making process, for a container of curding soymilk looks like a translucent, amber sky filled with soft white clouds. Curds made with nigari generally resemble cirrus clouds—long, thin, and wispy. If stirred or handled too roughly, they vanish. Curds made with calcium sulfate are more substantial and billowing, like cumulonimbus.

Like the clouds it resembles in so many other ways, *oboro* is transient; in a few moments it will be gone, only to reappear as tofu. But before it vanishes or changes form, it may be tasted. As soft as the most delicate custard, warm fresh curds have the richness of cream and a wonderful subtle sweetness.

When inviting guests to sample his *oboro,* the tofu maker scoops up a small dipperful of curds,

which he empties carefully onto a bamboo pressing mat, allowing the curds to drain briefly. He then slides the curds gently into a lacquerware bowl, seasons them with a few drops of shoyu, and asks his guests to partake of them while they are still warm. Many traditional masters have treated us to fresh curds in this way as we watched them making tofu.

When curds are ladled into cloth-lined settling boxes and pressed to make tofu, their fragile, almost insubstantial nature is given body and firmness. In most shops the finished curds are then soaked in water for several hours to firm and cool them, and thereby ensure maximum freshness. During the soaking, however, some of the rich and subtly sweet flavor of the curds is inevitably lost. Hence there are two simple ways to make their full goodness available commercially: one can either sell curds before they are pressed, or one can refrain from soaking finished tofu in water. In Taiwan and China, the warm curds themselves, called "flowers of tofu," are sold from pushcarts by street venders (fig. 104, p. 253). And many Chinese take a small pot or bowl to the neighborhood tofu shop each morning to

Fig. 26. Percentage of Original Soybean Protein Contained in Byproducts of the Tofu-making Process

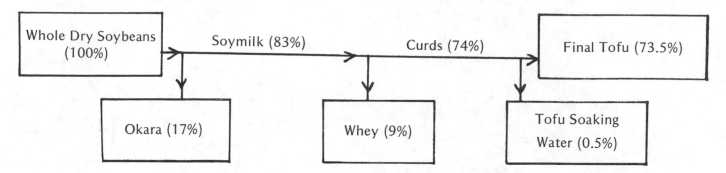

purchase these "flowers" for the family breakfast.

Almost all Japanese farmhouse tofu, and most commercial tofu in China and Taiwan, is allowed to cool either in the settling box or on a wooden pallet. Since these varieties of tofu are never soaked in water, their flavor remains closest to that of fresh curds. Homemade tofu can also be easily prepared in this way to keep it at its peak of flavor.

In Japan during the New Year's season, some tofu makers deliver warm curds from door to door. These are generally added to miso soups or seasoned with a little shoyu and any of the garnishes used for Chilled Tofu(p. 105). Curds are much more widely used in daily cookery in China than in Japan, being added there to noodle dishes, soups, and even sautéed vegetable dishes.

Many people may wonder why soymilk curds have never been fermented and aged in order to make Western-style cheeses. Research begun in the 1960s in California and Japan indicates that, in fact, tasty mild-flavored cheeses can be prepared inexpensively using bacteria from a dairy cheese starter and allowing well-pressed soymilk curds to ripen naturally for 3 to 9 weeks. These will soon be available commercially in flavors such as Cheddar.

In some parts of the United States, soymilk curds are now sold as Fresh Tofu Pudding, available in sealed polyethylene containers.

Whey

In the process of making tofu, whether at home or in a tofu shop, there are two inevitable byproducts: okara and whey. Containing valuable nutrients, both can be used in cooking. Whey is composed of 1 percent solids, 59 percent of which are proteins that were not solidified during the curding process. As shown in figure 26, whey contains 9 percent of the protein originally found in the dry soybeans,

plus much of the B vitamins and some of the natural sugars. It is produced in abundance whenever tofu is prepared; the curding process reduces 10 volumes of soymilk to about 1 part firmly-pressed curds and 9 parts whey.

At tofu shops, where more than 15 to 20 gallons are produced each day, whey is used as a gentle biodegradable soap. Hot whey is especially effective in cutting oils and quickly forms a head of suds when poured or stirred. The tofu maker carefully reserves the whey produced in his shop and uses it at the end of work each day to wash his tools. Both the deep-frying utensils and the barrels and dippers used for handling soymilk—which latter contains the natural oils found in soybeans—quickly become sparkling clean. On cold winter mornings, hot whey is also used to wash and warm the hands.

Some women use whey as a facial wash to remove oils and treat the complexion; others use it as a shampoo. It is also excellent for washing dishes, work clothes, or even fine silks. In Taiwan we noticed that many people come to tofu shops with a large pail to take home enough free "soap" to last for the day. In many homes it is used for washing and polishing wooden floors or woodwork, and for helping to give new woodwork a natural, seasoned look. Whey can also be used at home as a plant nutrient.

Like okara, warm whey is used to fatten livestock. Cows and horses are said to be able to gulp down a 3-gallon bucketful without taking a single breath. A tofu master in Kyoto told us how he offered a dray horse a pailful of whey one morning outside his shop (fig. 27). It seems that for years afterwards, whenever the horse passed, he stopped and refused to move until he was given his morning refresher.

Whey is collected in two different ways at tofu shops. First, as described above, it is ladled out of the curding barrel and reserved in a separate barrel or bucket. In addition, as it is pressed out of the tofu it is collected in the large wooden whey catch-box positioned underneath the settling boxes (see figure, p. 304). If soymilk has been solidified with just the right amount of nigari, its whey will have a transparent amber color and subtly sweet flavor. If too little solidifier is used, the whey will be cloudy due to the presence in it of unsolidified soymilk proteins. If too much is used, the whey will be bitter. To preview the flavor of the tofu, many craftsmen therefore take a sip of whey as they begin to ladle it out of the curding barrel.

About 70 percent of the solidifier added to soymilk dissolves in and is separated off with the whey. Sometimes, therefore, when a little uncurdled soymilk remains in the bottom of the curding barrel, the tofu maker will solidify it by stirring in some warm whey.

The 6 or 7 cups of whey resulting from the preparation of Homemade Tofu (p. 99) can be used place of water or milk when making bread, in cooking as a broth or soup stock, or as a soap for washing your tofu-making (or other) utensils. At last, a soap so mild and delicious you can drink it!

Fig. 27. A morning refresher

For each dumpling, moisten a 4- to 6-inch square of cheese-cloth (or a thin cotton cloth) and place it over the mouth of a cup. Push the cloth about 1/3 of the way into the cup to form a concave surface, and slip a rubber band around the rim of the cup to hold the cloth in place. Place 1 ladleful of warm curds onto the cloth (fig. 28), heaping the curds above the rim of the cup to give an evenly rounded upper surface. Allow curds to stand for 10 minutes, then immerse cloth and attached dumpling in cold water. After several minutes, carefully peel away the cloth; slip a small dish under each dumpling, lift out, and drain.

Warm Soymilk Curds *(Oboro-dofu)*

Proceed as for Homemade Tofu (p. 99). Just after ladling the whey out of the cooking pot (i.e. before ladling the curds into the settling container), scoop curds by the ladleful from the firm upper layer in the pot. Carefully place each ladleful of curds into a soup bowl and allow to stand for 1 minute. Holding the curds with your fingertips, pour off any excess whey that may have accumulated in the bowl. Serve immediately as is or:

*Top warm curds with a few drops of shoyu, some whole or ground roasted sesame seeds, and/or a dash of *sansho* pepper. Or serve with any of the dipping sauces, garnishes, or miso toppings used with Chilled Tofu (p. 105).

*Serve ¼ to ½ cup fresh curds in each cup of your favorite miso soup (p. 118).

*Add curds to individual servings of tomato, onion, split pea or your favorite Western-style soups, then try seasoning lightly with shoyu or miso.

*Place individual servings of curds in deep bowls and top with Ankake Sauce (p. 49). Season each portion lightly with a dab of grated gingerroot or a few drops of lemon juice, or serve with Gingerroot Sauce (p. 49) or the sauce for Takigawa-dofu (p. 210).

*Mix curds with lightly beaten eggs and stir into Chinese egg-flower soups.

*Gently stir curds into curry sauces or noodle dishes just before serving.

*Serve curds Chinese-style seasoned with soy sauce, minced garlic, red pepper, and sesame oil, or topped with Spicy Korean Miso Sauté (p. 45).

Awayuki *(Homemade Curd Dumplings)*

Awayuki, meaning "light snow," is an excellent description of the texture and color of these soft and delicate dumplings. Traditional tofu shops prepare and sell them for use in various soup and *nabe* dishes.

Karashi-dofu
(Curd Dumplings with Mustard)   MAKES 4

Prepared in many traditional tofu shops, these dumplings are sometimes filled with ginkgo nuts or some of the other ingredients used in ganmo.

Mix 1 teaspoon powdered hot mustard with just enough water to form a very thick paste. Cut a sheet of *nori* into 4 rectangles, each 1 by ½ inch. Form the mustard paste into 4 small cylinders about ½ inch long, then roll up each cylinder in one of the *nori* rectangles.

Prepare 4 cups, each 2½ inches in diameter, with cheesecloth squares set over their mouths as for Awayuki (see recipe above). Indent the cheesecloth to a depth of about 1½ inches below the rim of each cup and slip a rubber band around the rim of the cup to hold the cloth in place. Sprinkle the concave surface of each cloth with ¼ teaspoon powdered green *nori*, then using a small dipper or ladle (fig. 28), place a single scoop of curds in the cloth, filling it just to the rim. Place 1 *nori*-mustard roll in the center of the curds in each cup, then top with an additional half scoop of curds so that the upper surface of the curds in each cup is slightly rounded. Fill each of the cups in this way, then place the 4 cups close together, cover the curds with a moistened cloth and top with a cutting board. Place a 2-pound weight on the board and press the tofu for 20 to 30 minutes. Carefully remove the cloths from the curds and serve in any of the following ways:

*Deep-fry the dumplings (without batter) in moderately-hot oil until golden brown; drain. Dip dumplings briefly into boiling water to remove excess surface oil, then simmer for 20 minutes in a mixture of 1 cup water or dashi, 3 tablespoons sugar, and 1½ tablespoons shoyu. Serve with a little of the cooking broth and garnish with thinly sliced leek or scallion rounds.

*Serve in iced water as for Chilled Tofu (p. 105). Accompany individual servings with a small dish of shoyu, a garnish of grated gingerroot, and a topping of thinly sliced leek or scallion rounds.

*Serve dumplings (chilled, warm, or deep-fried) topped with Ankake Sauce (p. 49) or Gingerroot Sauce (p. 49).

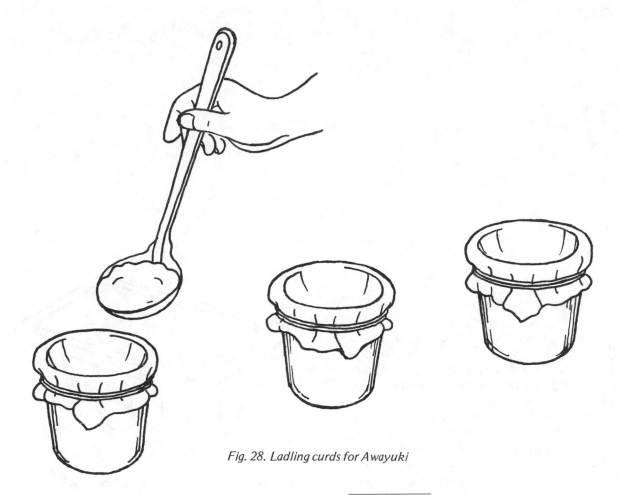

Fig. 28. Ladling curds for Awayuki

Kinugoshi Curds

SERVES 4

Prepare Homemade Kinugoshi (p. 215) or Soft Tofu (p. 216). After stirring in solidifier, allow tofu to stand for only 8 to 10 minutes, or until it is firm but still warm. Fill serving bowls with ¾ cup curds and serve topped with a few drops of shoyu or with the following sauce, popular in Taiwan and China.

> **Sweet Peanut Sauce**
> ¾ cup water
> 3 to 4 tablespoons unsalted peanuts
> 1½ tablespoons natural sugar or honey
> ½ teaspoon shoyu

Combine all ingredients in a small saucepan and bring to a boil. Reduce heat to low, cover pan, and simmer for 5 to 10 minutes. Serve hot. For a thicker preparation: after sauce has finished cooking, stir in ¼ teaspoon cornstarch dissolved in 1 tablespoon water and simmer for 30 seconds more.

Chilled Curds

When chilled, soymilk curds lose a bit of their subtle sweetness and fragile texture but make a refreshing summertime treat or dessert. Any type of tofu curds can be used. Place several scoops of the chilled curds into small bowls and serve topped with fruit cocktail, orange sections, honey, maple syrup, or fruit syrup. Or serve in iced water as for Chilled Tofu (p. 105). (In the western United States, Tofu Pudding or Fresh Soybean Pudding, made from chilled soft tofu, is now available commercially.)

Homemade Whey

Reserve the 6 to 7 cups of whey which separate from the curds in the process of preparing Homemade Tofu (p. 99) for use as stock with soups or stews, in breads, or in simmered vegetable dishes. Or serve hot, like tea, as is. The most delicious whey comes from tofu that has been solidified with natural (clean) seawater which evokes the whey's subtly sweet flavors.

8

Tofu

JUST AS the word "bread" is used in reference to a wide variety of baked goods, the word "tofu" in its broad sense refers to a number of different soybean foods. Each of the seven basic types of Japanese tofu will be discussed in the following chapters; the many varieties of Chinese tofu will be treated in Chapter 15.

The word "tofu" is also used in a more limited sense to refer to "regular tofu," the simplest, least expensive variety and the one most widely known in the West (fig. 29). This tofu has no exact equivalent in Western cuisine and does not quite fit the English terms "soybean curd" and "soybean cheese" often used to describe it. Tofu is made *from* soybean curds just as cheese is made *from* dairy curds: after ladling off whey from the soymilk curds in his curding barrel, the tofu maker scoops the curds into two cloth-lined wooden settling boxes and tops them with a pressing lid and heavy weight for about thirty minutes (fig. 30). During this time the curds are firmed and made *into* tofu. Similarly, although the finished tofu, stored under water in deep sinks, has the color and shape of a light cheese, it is not fermented, aged, or ripened; hence the name "soybean cheese" is also inappropriate. (For a more detailed description of the tofu-making process, see Part IV.)

Of East Asia's three great soybean foods—tofu, miso, and shoyu—only tofu has a theory associated with its historical origin. According to ancient Chinese and Japanese references, as well as to popular tradition, the method for preparing both soymilk and tofu was discovered by Lord Liu An of Huai-nan in about 164 B.C. A famous scholar and philosopher, ruler and politician, Liu An is said to have been inter-

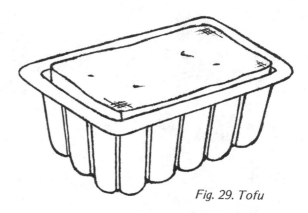

Fig. 29. Tofu

ested in alchemy and Taoist meditation. A close friend of many Taoist students, he may have undertaken his experiments with tofu as a way of introducing nutritious variety into their simple meatless diet. Historians believe that Liu An's tofu was probably solidified with either nigari or seawater and had a firm texture similar to most of the tofu made in China today.

There are two basic theories which try to account for the discovery of tofu. Lord Liu An or earlier Chinese may have discovered the method for curding soymilk quite by accident. Since soybeans were considered one of the Five Sacred Grains, they were probably dried like other grains before being cooked. If later boiled, they would either be added to water whole, or first ground or mashed into a purée. If used in purée form, the result would be a thick "soup" that would have to be seasoned. If the cook added natural salt—which contains bittern (nigari)—curds would soon form: the salt, intended as a seasoning, would have worked as a solidifying agent. The cook may later have decided to remove the fibrous okara from the purée to give the resulting

Fig. 30. Pressing tofu in settling boxes

curds a finer, more delicate texture. The next step, pressing, would have helped the food stay fresh longer and would have given it a texture firm enough to keep its form after being cut. The final result would then have been very similar to present-day tofu.

The second theory proposes that, since they did not generally raise cows or goats for milk, the Chinese were probably not familiar initially with the curding process; they may have learned it from the Indians in the south or the Mongols in the north, both of whom made curds and cheese. Advocates of the "importation theory" also note that the three other mild-flavored foods most favored by the Chinese—shark fins, swallow's nest, and trepang (sea slugs)—were also imported.

Tofu next appears in Chinese history about 800 years later. It is said that Bodhidharma, who lived in China from about 520 to 528 and founded the Chinese *Ch'an* (Zen) school, engaged tofu in "Dharma combat" to probe tofu's understanding of the Buddha's way. Bodhidharma later praised tofu for its simplicity, its honest, straightforward nature, and its "lovely white robes."

The earliest existing document containing mention of tofu is the *Seiiroku*, written during the Sung Dynasty (960-1127), more than 1,000 years after the food's discovery. Numerous other books of this period refer to a work written about 60 to 100 B.C. (but no longer in existence) which contained the story of Lord Liu An and the earliest tofu. In a work of the late Sung Dynasty, there is a description of the menu served by a king to a prince, and tofu is included.

Tofu reached Japan during the eighth century and was probably brought from China by the numerous Buddhist monks and priests who were going back and forth between the two countries. Tofu is thought to have entered Japanese society through the upper classes, those who were connected with Chinese cultural and economic interchange, the court nobility, and the priesthood. Buddhist monks probably used tofu as a daily food in Japanese temples at a very early date. Emphasizing the value of a meatless diet, they were certainly a major factor in the early spread of tofu as a popular food. Some scholars believe that all of Japan's (and China's) earliest tofu shops were located within large temples or monasteries and were run by Buddhist priests and temple cooks.

During the Kamakura period (1185—1333), there was a large-scale movement to make Japanese Buddhism available to the common people. The five major Kamakura Zen temples each opened Buddhist vegetarian restaurants within their temple compounds, and existing records show that tofu was included on the menus. Laymen, having tasted tofu there for the first time, apparently learned from the monks how to prepare it, then opened their own shops in the capital cities of Kamakura and Kyoto. It was only later that tofu-making spread from the cities to the countryside.

During the Kamakura period, the new *samurai*

Transferring tofu-filled settling box to sink

Cutting tofu into cakes under water

ruling class practiced a simple, frugal, and down-to-earth way of life. These warriors greatly simplified the national cuisine by their example. It is said that tofu and miso replaced fresh river fish as the ruling shogun's prized delicacies, and that the samurai came to cherish agé and tofu, particularly as ingredients in their breakfast miso soup. It was also at this time that farmers started growing soybeans on a large scale in Japan's cold, dry provinces.

During the Muromachi period (1336-1568) tofu spread throughout Japan and became a popular daily food at all levels of society. Many of the great tea masters of the period used tofu extensively in their Tea Ceremony Cookery, which helped to bring tofu into the world of Japanese haute cuisine and to introduce it to famous chefs and restauranteurs. Since most Japanese followed the Buddhist practice of refraining from eating the meat of "four legged animals," tofu was welcomed as a source of inexpensive and tasty protein. The Japanese went on to invent several new forms of the food, including dried-frozen tofu, agé, ganmo, grilled tofu, and nigari kinugoshi.

As tofu became widely used in Japan, its basic character was gradually changed. In the hands of native craftsmen, tofu became softer, whiter, and more delicate in flavor. Farmhouse tofu alone retained some of the firmness and rich flavor of its Chinese predecessor.

When the Chinese Zen master, Ingen, came to Japan in 1661 he was surprised to find tofu unlike any he had known in China. In praise of this new food he composed an intricate yet simple proverb which is well known to this day. It described both the character of Japanese tofu and that of a man who wishes to pass freely and peacefully through this fleeting, illusory world. The proverb went:

> *Mame de*
> *Shikaku de*
> *Yawaraka de*

Each line had a double meaning, allowing the poem to be read either:

Made of soybeans, *or*	Practicing diligence,
Square, cleanly cut,	Being proper and honest
And soft.	And having a kind heart.

The word "tofu" first appears in a Japanese written document (the diary of Nakatomino Sukeshige) in 1183, where it is mentioned that tofu was used as a food offering at an altar. Mention is again made of it in a letter of thanks from the famous Buddhist priest Nichiren Shonin, written in 1239. The word "tofu" written with the present characters did not appear in Japan until the 1500s. The first Japanese "Book of Tofu" (*Tofu Hyaku Chin*) was written in 1782 and contained 100 tofu recipes culled from throughout Japan. A famous book in its day, it is still widely quoted.

Throughout its long history in Japan, tofu has appeared in numerous forms, some of which no longer exist. For example, when the Zen master Ingen, mentioned above, established the well-known

Mampuku-ji temple south of Kyoto, he taught the monks and local tofu masters how to prepare Chinese-style Pressed Tofu (see p. 251). Although this very firm variety became popular during the next century, it is now prepared by only one shop in Japan and is featured in Zen Temple Cuisine only in restaurants near Mampuku-ji. A closely related type of firm tofu called *rokujo-dofu* was prepared by tying 5 pieces of pressed tofu together with rice straw (fig. 90, p. 228), then drying them in direct sunlight until they were dark brown and quite hard. Finely shaved, rokujo-dofu was used like bonita flakes; it is presently prepared only in Fukushima prefecture. A third variety of virtually extinct tofu was walnut tofu, prepared by mixing chunks of walnuts into soybean curds just before they were pressed. Chinese fermented tofu (called *nyufu* in Japan and *doufu-ru* in China) was transmitted to Japan in early times and became popular among the aristocracy, in temples, and in a few rural areas. Its strong flavor, however, led to its gradual decline; today it is rarely if ever seen.

As tofu became a part of the language and culture in both Japan and China, it came to be used in proverbs and sayings. In China, finding fault with a person is compared to "finding a bone in your tofu." When a Japanese wants to tell a person to "get lost," he may say "Go bump your head against the corner of a cake of tofu and drop dead." Or when speaking of something as being hopeless he might say "It's as futile as trying to clamp two pieces of tofu together."

Tofu became a part of the culture in other ways too. For example, in the Women's Mass for Needles, started 1600 years ago by the Emperor Nintoku and still practiced in Japan, a cake of tofu is placed on the household altar and all the needles that have been bent or broken during the year are thrust into it. Each needle is thought of as a living being whose body has been sacrificed in service, and the woman of the house, as an expression of her gratitude, gives it this soft resting place as a reward for its hard work.

Up until the start of World War II, virtually all Japanese tofu was prepared in small household shops from gô cooked over a wood fire in an iron cauldron and soymilk solidified with natural nigari. Only after World War II did new solidifiers (such as calcium sulfate) and ways of cooking (such as with pressurized steam) come into vogue. In recent years, large shops and factories have begun to mass-produce tofu; each 10½ ounce cake is water-packed in a polyethylene container, thermally sealed with a sheet of transparent film, and pasteurized by immersion for one hour in hot water to give a shelf life of up to 1 week. Distributed over an area of several hundred miles in refrigerated trucks, this tofu is sold in supermarkets and neighborhood grocery stores at a price slightly below that of the tofu sold in most neighborhood shops.

About 900 years passed from the time of the discovery of tofu in China until its arrival in Japan. Another 1200 years passed before it made the leap westward across the Pacific Ocean to America where there are now more than 50 tofu shops, the oldest of which has been making tofu since the turn of the century. The history of tofu in the West, therefore, has only just begun.

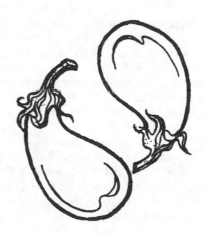

PREPARATORY TECHNIQUES

The following procedures are used regularly in cooking with tofu. Try to master them from the outset, since each gives the tofu a unique consistency and texture. The eight techniques listed below are in order of the amount of water each allows to remain in the tofu. Thus parboiling, the first technique, expels very little water, while crumbling rids the tofu of more than 65 percent of its moisture, leaving it very firm and containing more than 20 percent protein. Figure 31 shows the effect of each technique on the weight, protein, and moisture content of a 12 ounce cake of tofu originally containing 7.8 percent protein and 84.9 percent water. For a graphic description of the relationship between protein and moisture content in different types of tofu, see figure 6 on page 25.

When fresh tofu is mashed or blended, 9 ounces yield 1 cup, and 12 ounces yield approximately 1½ cups.

Fig. 31. Effects of Preparatory Techniques on 1 Cake of Tofu

Preparatory Technique	Final Weight of 12 oz of Tofu (oz)	Percent Protein in Final Tofu (%)	Percent Reduction in Weight from Loss of Water (%)
Parboiling	11.5	8.0	3.5
Draining	10.0	8.5	17.0
Pressing	8.5	10.0	30.0
Squeezing	6.5	13.0	47.0
Scrambling	6.3	13.5	48.0
Reshaping	4.5	19.0	63.0
Crumbling	4.0	20.5	66.0
Grinding	4.0	21.0	67.0

Parboiling

This technique is used with both regular and kinugoshi tofu for at least four different purposes: 1) To warm the tofu before serving it topped with hot sauces; 2) To freshen stored tofu that shows signs of spoiling; 3) To make the tofu slightly firmer so that when simmered in seasoned broths it absorbs flavors without diluting the cooking medium; 4) To impart to the tofu a slight cohesiveness desired when preparing *aemono* (Japanese-style tofu salads).

The addition of a small amount of salt to the water seasons the tofu slightly, imparts to it a somewhat firmer texture, and makes possible longer parboiling without the tofu developing an undesirably porous structure. (It is for these reasons that *kombu* or salt are generally added to the broth of Simmering Tofu [p. 142] and other *nabe* preparations.)

Because parboiling causes a slight loss in some of the tofu's delicate flavors, it should be used only when necessary.

*Regular Parboiling: Bring 1 quart water to a boil in a saucepan. Reduce heat to low and drop in tofu. Cover and heat for

2 to 3 minutes, or until tofu is well warmed. (For a firmer texture, cut tofu into 4 equal pieces before parboiling.) Lift out finished pieces with a slotted spoon.

*Salted Water Method: Bring 2 cups water to a boil in a saucepan. Add ½ teaspoon salt, drop in (uncut) 12-ounce cake of tofu, and return to the boil. Remove pan from heat and allow to stand for 2 to 3 minutes. Remove tofu, discarding water.

Draining

Draining or storing tofu out of water (for no more than 12 hours) gives it a fairly firm texture and also helps preserve its flavor, since its subtle natural sweetness is lost quite easily in water. A 12-ounce cake of tofu drained for 8 hours will lose moisture equal to about 17 percent of its weight. The protein content of the final 10-ounce cake thereby increases from 7.8 to about 8.5 percent.

Place the tofu in a 1- or 2-quart flat-bottomed container. Cover well and refrigerate for 1 to 2 hours or, for a firmer texture, overnight.

If set on a small colander or folded towel placed into the container beforehand, the tofu will drain even more thoroughly.

If two cakes are stacked one on top of the other, the one on the bottom will be almost as firm as if it were pressed (see below).

If the tofu was purchased in a sealed plastic tub, prick a tiny hole in bottom of tub, drain out any water, and place tofu and tub in container as described above.

Pressing

When pressing tofu, it is important to preserve the form and structure of the cake so that it may later be cut into thin slices. Tofu is fully pressed when it can be picked up and held vertically in the air without crumbling. Pressing time may be varied to suit the dish being prepared: light pressing preserves the tofu's softness for use in tossed salads, while lengthy pressing gives firmer, stronger tofu for use in deep-frying.

Because of its delicate texture and unique structure (which holds water in millions of tiny "cells"), kinugoshi is almost never pressed. Doufu (Chinese-style firm tofu) has a cohesive structure and low water content and may be used without further pressing in any recipe calling for pressed tofu. Pat its surface dry with a cloth before use.

*Towel and Fridge Method: Wrap the tofu firmly in a small terry-cloth or cotton towel folded into fourths (facing), and set on a plate in a refrigerator for 1½ to 2 hours or overnight. To decrease the pressing time, drain the tofu beforehand, place a 2- or 3-pound weight on top of the tofu, and replace the damp towel with a dry one after about 30 minutes. Or cut the cake horizontally into halves before pressing and place in the towel as illustrated.

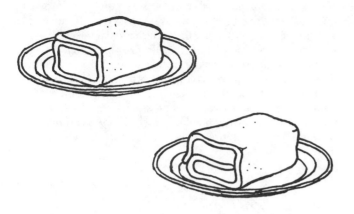

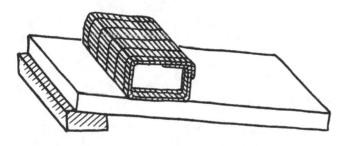

*Slanting Press Method: Wrap the tofu in a towel or bamboo mat *(sudare)* (or sandwich the tofu between bamboo mats) and place on a cutting board, tray, or large plate next to the sink; raise the far end of the board several inches. Set a 2- to 4-pound weight on the tofu and let stand for 30 to 60 minutes (below).

*Sliced Tofu Method: Cut the tofu crosswise into ½- to ¾-inch-thick slices and arrange on two towels placed on a raised cutting board (below). Cover the slices with a double layer of towels and pat lightly to ensure even contact. Allow to stand for 30 to 60 minutes. This method is commonly used when preparing tofu for deep-frying. For faster results, top with a cutting board and 5-pound weight and change the towels after 10 minute intervals.

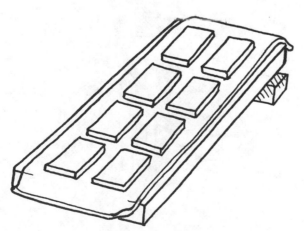

Squeezing

This process results in a mashed tofu that is slightly cohesive and has a texture resembling that of cottage cheese.

Place drained, parboiled, or pressed tofu (or doufu) at the center of a large dry dishtowel and gather its corners to form a sack. (Or use a tofu pressing sack [p. 34] if available.) Twist sack closed, then squeeze tofu firmly, kneading it for 2 or 3 minutes to expel as much water as possible (below). Squeeze lightly enough so that no tofu penetrates the sack. Empty the squeezed tofu into a mixing bowl.

Scrambling

This technique causes a further separation of tofu curds and liquid whey resulting in a texture similar to that produced by squeezing, but one which is slightly firmer and more crumbly.

Place tofu in an unheated skillet. Using a (wooden) spatula, break tofu into small pieces. Now cook over medium heat for 4 to 5 minutes, stirring constantly and breaking tofu into smaller and smaller pieces until whey separates from curds. Pour contents of skillet into a fine-mesh strainer; allow curds to drain for about 15 seconds if a soft consistency is desired, or for about 3 minutes for a firmer consistency. Spread curds on a large plate and allow to cool to room temperature.

Reshaping

This process yields a tofu cake having a very firm and cohesive consistency similar to that of natural cheese, Chinese doufu-kan (p. 251), or processed ham. Called *oshi-dofu*, or "Pressed Tofu," in Japan, it is used in recipes calling for pieces the size of French-fried potatoes which hold their shape during cooking or tossing.

The first method given below takes about twice as long as the second, but yields a tofu that retains more of its natural flavor and texture. The addition of salt that it calls for prevents the tofu from developing a somewhat elastic, web-like structure while also seasoning it. The second method yields a firmer structure that holds together better during sautéing. The tofu undergoes a slight loss in flavor that is not very noticeable if served with a well-seasoned sauce in the typical Chinese style.

*Firm Seasoned Tofu: Combine 24 ounces tofu and 1 teaspoon salt in a saucepan; mix well. Stirring constantly, cook over medium heat for about 4 minutes or until tofu begins to boil vigorously. Pour the tofu into a cloth-lined colander in the sink and allow to drain for several minutes. Transfer the cloth onto a cutting board and carefully fold the edges of the cloth over the tofu; shape the tofu into a cake about 5 inches square and 1 inch thick. Place a pan filled with 3 or 4 quarts of water on top of the cloth (below) and press for 1 to 2 hours in a cool place. Unwrap and cut as directed; or re-wrap in a dry towel and refrigerate for later use.

*Very Firm Tofu: Boil the tofu in unsalted water as when crumbling (see below). Drain tofu, then proceed as above, pressing the tofu for 30 to 60 minutes.

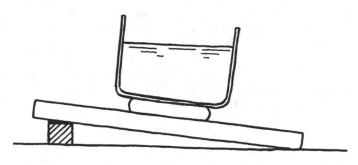

Crumbling

By reducing its water content to a minimum, we can obtain tofu with much the same texture as lightly sautéed, crumbly hamburger. Yet the tofu is slightly firmer, lighter, and fluffier, which makes it ideal for use in tossed salads, egg and grain dishes, spaghetti or curry sauces, and casseroles. (Kinugoshi, too, can be crumbled, either by the method described below or by scrambling [p. 97] and then pressing as follows.)

Combine 12 ounces tofu and 1 cup water in a saucepan. With a wooden spoon or spatula, break the tofu into very small pieces while bringing the water to a boil. Reduce heat and simmer for 1 to 2 minutes. Place a colander in the sink and line with a large cloth (or a tofu pressing sack). Pour the contents of the pan onto the cloth, gather its corners to form a sack, then twist closed. Using the bottom of a jar or a potato masher, press the tofu firmly against the bottom of the colander to expel as much water as possible. Empty the pressed tofu into a large bowl and allow to cool for several minutes. Now break the tofu into very small pieces, using your fingertips or a spoon.

Grinding

This process yields tofu having much the same light, dry consistency as crumbled tofu, but with a texture that is finer and more uniform.

Using either regular tofu or kinugoshi, prepare reshaped or crumbled tofu (p. 98). Refrigerate tofu in a covered container until well chilled. Then, cutting into chunks if necessary, run through a meat grinder with a medium-fine attachment.

HOMEMADE TOFU

If you find that fresh tofu is not available at a nearby store, try preparing your own at home using either whole soybeans or powdered soymilk. It's as enjoyable as baking bread—and considerably faster.

Homemade Tofu
MAKES 33 TO 39 OUNCES

We have found the following recipe, based on the traditional Japanese farmhouse method, to be easy to follow and virtually foolproof. The tofu will be ready 50 to 60 minutes after you start. One pound of soybeans yields about 3½ to 4 pounds of tofu at a cost about one-third to one-fourth that of commercial tofu and less than one-half the cost (on a usable protein basis) of hamburger. Solidified with nigari, made from soymilk simmered over an open fire (rather than steamed), and served at its peak of freshness, homemade tofu contains a fullness of flavor and subtle sweetness seldom found in even the finest storebought varieties.

Utensils

To make fine homemade tofu, you will need the following common kitchen tools (fig. 32):

An electric blender, food- or grain mill, or meat grinder
A "cooking pot" with a capacity of 2½ to 3 gallons
A "pressing pot" with a capacity of 1½ to 2 gallons, or a basin of comparable size
A 2-quart saucepan
A wooden spatula, rice paddle, or wooden spoon with a long handle
A shallow ladle or dipper about 1 inch deep and 3 or 4 inches in diameter, or a large spoon
A rubber spatula
A sturdy 1-quart jar or a potato masher
A 1-cup measuring cup
A set of measuring spoons
A large, round-bottomed colander (that will fit into the "pressing pot")
A flat-bottomed colander ("settling container") preferably square or rectangular
A shallow fine-mesh strainer or bamboo colander (zaru)
A coarsely-woven cotton dishcloth, 2 feet square, or a "pressing sack"
A 2-foot square of cheesecloth, or a light cotton dishtowel of comparable dimensions.

Fig. 32. Utensils for making tofu

Two special pieces of equipment, both easy to assemble, will make the work even easier:

*Make a "pressing sack" of the coarsely-woven cotton dishtowel mentioned above, or use a piece of sturdy linen cloth with about the same coarseness of weave as cheesecloth.. Fold the towel or cloth end to end and sew up the sides to form a sack about 15 inches wide and 15 inches deep. Or use a small flour sack with a fairly coarse weave.

*The flat-bottomed colander listed above is for use as a "settling container" which gives its shape to the finished tofu. If a 1-quart strainer or small, round-bottomed colander is used in its place, the tofu will naturally be rounded.

The three settling containers in figure 33 can easily be made at home. Container (a) is prepared from a 1½-quart wooden, tupperware, or plastic box with an open top and non-removable bottom. In containers (b) and (c) the bottom is removable, allowing for easy removal of the tofu without immersing the container in water. Good dimensions for the container are 4½ inches square by 4½ inches deep, or 6½ by 3½ by 4½ inches deep. Use a drill or heated icepick to bore 3/8-inch-diameter holes about 1½ inches apart in the bottom and sides of the container. Fashion a flat wooden or plastic pressing lid (with or without holes) to fit down inside the rim of the box. Good woods to use are Philippine mahogany, vertical-grain Douglas fir, pine, maple, cedar, or cherry. An easy-to-use, high-quality TOFU KIT containing everything you need (including Philippine mahogany box, nigari solidifier, muslin pressing sack, and cloths, but *not* soybeans) can be ordered from The Soyfoods Center, P.O. Box 234, Lafayette, CA 94549.

Ingredients

You will need only the following readily available ingredients:

Soybeans

The soybeans now sold at almost all natural- and health food stores, most co-op stores, and many supermarkets will make good tofu. However, to obtain the highest yield, try buying soybeans directly from a tofu shop in your area (see Appendix B), for they have been carefully chosen by the tofu maker.

Solidifier

The solidifiers most readily available in the West are Epsom salts, lemon or lime juice, and vinegar. All make delicious tofu, although they are not used in Japanese tofu shops. Japanese-style solidifiers are available from many natural food stores, local tofu shops, Japanese food markets, chemical supply houses (check your phone directory), or your local school chemistry lab. Usable seawater can be retrieved from clean stretches of ocean. Natural nigari comes in the TOFU KIT described on this page and is sold at some natural food stores, or it can be prepared at home using natural salt (p. 283). We recommend the use of refined nigari unless the natural nigari is certified to have come from a clean source of sea water. While we believe the nigari-type solidifiers are the easiest to use and result in the best tasting tofu, Epsom salts and calcium sulfate seem to give somewhat higher bulk yields and a softer end product by incorporating more water into the tofu. The yield of tofu solids or nutrients is about the same regardless of the type of solidifier used, except that lemon juice and vinegar give rather small yields. (Note: Calcium sulfate, a fine white powder, is sometimes mislabeled in the West and sold as nigari. The latter usually has a coarse, granular or crystaline texture; natural nigari is beige and refined nigari is white.)

The recipe below calls only for "solidifier." Your choice of solidifier depends upon the type of tofu you want.

For subtly sweet, nigari tofu use: 2 teaspoons magnesium chloride or calcium chloride (refined nigari); or 1½ to 2¼ teaspoons granular or powdered natural nigari; or 1½ to 2½ teaspoons homemade liquid nigari; or 2 to 4½ teaspoons commercially prepared liquid nigari; or 1½ cups seawater (freshly collected; p. 282).

For mild, soft tofu use: 2 teaspoons Epsom salts (magnesium sulfate) or calcium sulfate; or 1½ tablespoons each calcium lactate and lemon juice (the latter being stirred into the soymilk just after the last of the calcium lactate has been added).

For subtly tart or sour tofu use: 4 tablespoons lemon or lime juice (freshly squeezed); or 3 tablespoons (apple cider) vinegar.

Fig. 33. Three designs for a homemade settling container

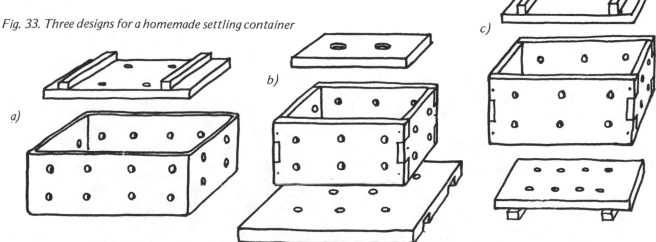

Method

1½ cups soybeans, washed, soaked in 6 cups water for 10
   hours (see graph, p. 289), rinsed and drained
16 cups water, approximately
Solidifer

Prepare in advance:

Place pressing pot in sink and set colander into pot.
Moisten pressing sack lightly and line colander with sack, fitting mouth of sack around rim of colander. Or line colander
with a moistened 2-foot-square dish towel (fig. 34a).

Moisten cheesecloth or thin cotton dishtowel and use
to line bottom and sides of settling container. Place container
on rim of large bowl or pan placed in sink.

After making the above preparations, proceed as follows:

Fig. 34. Preparing homemade tofu

1) Heat 7½ cups water over high heat in cooking pot.
While water is heating, divide beans into two equal portions.
Combine one portion with 2 cups water in a blender and
purée at high speed for about 3 minutes, or until very smooth.
Add purée (gô) to water heating (or boiling) in cooking pot,
then purée the remaining soybeans with 2 cups water in the
same way and add to the pot. (If using a food mill or meat
grinder, grind beans without adding water and add 4 cups
more water to cooking pot.) Rinse out blender with a little
water to retrieve any purée that may cling to blender's walls.

2) Taking care that pot does not boil over, continue
heating on high heat, stirring bottom of pot frequently with a
wooden spatula or spoon to prevent sticking (fig. b). When
foam suddenly rises in pot, quickly turn off heat and pour
contents of cooking pot into pressing sack (fig. c). Using a
rubber spatula, retrieve any soybean purée that may still
cling to the sides of the cooking pot and transfer to pressing
sack. Quickly rinse out cooking pot and replace on top of
stove.

3) Twist hot pressing sack closed. Using a glass jar or
potato masher, press sack against colander, expressing as
much soymilk as possible (fig. d). Open sack, shake okara it
contains into one of its corners, close and press again. Now
empty okara into the saucepan (or a large bowl) and add 3
cups water; stir well, then return moist okara to pressing

sack set in the colander. Close sack and press well as before; squeeze by hand to express the last of the soymilk (fig. e). Empty okara into the 2-quart saucepan and set aside.

4) Measure solidifier into dry 1-cup measuring cup and set aside.

5) Pour soymilk into cooking pot and bring to a boil over high heat, stirring frequently to prevent sticking. Reduce heat to medium and cook for 5 to 7 minutes; turn off heat and remove pot from burner.

6) Add 1 cup water to solidifier in measuring cup (unless using seawater) and stir until dissolved. With a to-and-fro movement, stir soymilk vigorously 5 or 6 times and, while stirring, pour in 1/3 cup solidifier solution. Stir 5 or 6 times more, making sure to reach bottom and sides of pot. Bring spoon to a halt upright in soymilk and wait until all turbulence ceases; lift out spoon (fig. f). Sprinkle 1/3 cup solidifier over surface of soymilk, cover pot, and wait 3 minutes while curds form. Using a measuring spoon, stir remaining 1/3 cup solidifier solution, uncover pot, and sprinkle solution over surface of soymilk.

7) Very slowly stir upper 1/2-inch-thick layer of curdling soymilk for 15 to 20 seconds, then cover pot and wait 3 minutes. (Wait 6 minutes if using Epsom salts or calcium sulfate). Uncover and stir surface layer again for 20 to 30 seconds, or until all milky liquid curdles.

(White "clouds" of delicate curds should now be floating in a clear, pale-yellow liquid, the whey. If any milky, uncurdled liquid remains suspended in whey, wait 1 minute, then stir gently until curdled. If milky liquid persists, dissolve a small amount of additional solidifier [about 1/4 of the original amount] in 1/3 cup water and pour directly into uncurdled portions; stir gently until curdled.)

8) Place cooking pot next to settling container in sink. Gently press fine-mesh strainer into pot and allow several cups whey to collect in it. Ladle all of this whey into settling container to re-moisten lining cloths (fig. g). Set strainer aside.

9) Now ladle curds—and any remaining whey—into settling container one layer at a time. Ladle gently so as not to break curds' fragile structure (fig. h). Fold edges of cloth neatly over curds (fig. i), place a lid on top of cloth (a small board or flat plate will do), and set a 1/2- to 1 1/2-pound weight on top of lid for 10 to 15 minutes, or until whey no longer drips from settling container (fig. j).

10) Fill pressing pot, a large basin, or sink with cold water. Remove weight and lid from atop tofu, then place container holding tofu into basin of water (fig. k). Slowly invert container, leaving cloth-wrapped tofu in water; lift out container. While it is still under water, carefully unwrap and cut tofu crosswise into halves. Allow tofu to remain under water for 3 to 5 minutes, until firm. To lift out, slip a small plate under each piece of tofu; drain briefly (fig. l).

For best flavor, serve immediately as Chilled Tofu (p. 105) or Simmering Tofu (p. 142). Store tofu in a cool place until ready to serve. (If not to be served for 8 or 10 hours, store under cold water.) Use the remaining 6 to 7 ounces (1 firmly packed cup) okara in the recipes given in Chapter 6, or refrigerate in an airtight container. Use the 6 to 7 cups whey in stocks and/or for washing your utensils.

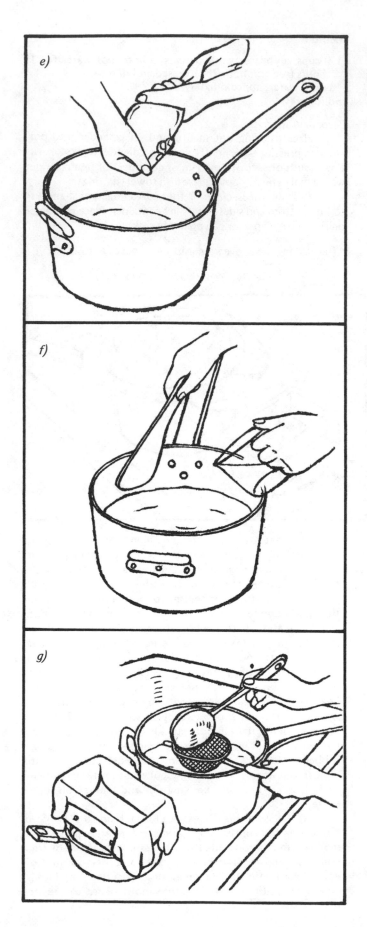

e)

f)

g)

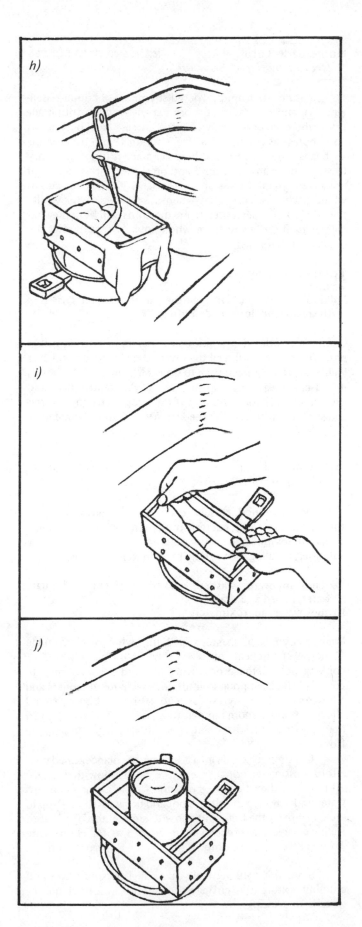

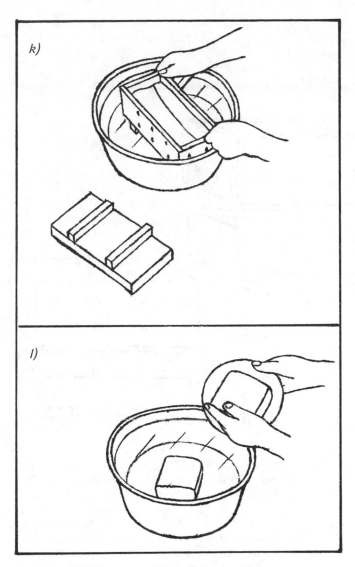

VARIATIONS

*Firm Farmhouse- or Chinese-style Tofu: We find this tofu to have the finest flavor, texture, and aroma. The apparent drop in bulk yield is due only to a loss of water, not of protein or other nutrients.

Cook the puréed soybeans in a heavy iron pot over an open wood fire. Use a nigari-type solidifier and, if possible, new-crop, organically grown (Japanese) soybeans. Ladle the curds quickly and not too carefully into the settling container, and press for 30 to 40 minutes with a 2-pound weight. Then invert the container leaving the tofu resting on the lid. (Or lift off the sides of a farmhouse-style container [fig. 35].) Remove the cloths and serve the tofu without immersing it in water.

*Omit Rinsing and Re-pressing Okara: This simplifies the basic method but gives a slightly lower yield. Begin by heating 7 rather than 5 cups water in cooking pot. After first pressing okara, open pressing sack in colander and allow okara to cool for 3 to 5 minutes. While okara is cooling, reheat soymilk. Holding pressing sack over cooking pot, squeeze by hand to expel any soymilk remaining in okara.

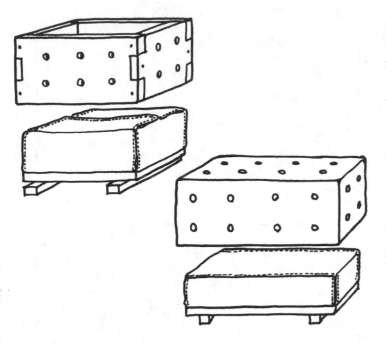

Fig. 35. Removing tofu from a farmhouse-style settling container

Homemade Tofu
(from Powdered Soymilk)
MAKES 20 TO 23 OUNCES

Tofu made from powdered soymilk is not quite as delicious as, and is somewhat more expensive than, tofu made from whole soybeans. However the process takes only about 35 minutes—as compared with 50 minutes when using whole soybeans—and is considerably easier since it is not necessary to grind the beans or remove and press the okara. One cup of powdered soymilk gives about the same yield as one cup of whole soybeans. Note that when using powdered soymilk, the whey which separates from the curds will be somewhat milkier than the whey from whole soybeans, even after the curds are well formed.

1 cup powdered soymilk
9 cups water
Solidifier: Use any of the solidifiers in the amounts listed in the recipe for Homemade Tofu (p. 99)

Combine powdered soymilk and water in a 1- to 1½-gallon pot. Whisk milk until well dissolved, then bring to a boil over high heat, stirring from time to time. Measure solidifier into a dry, 1-cup measuring cup and set aside. Reduce heat and simmer soymilk for 3 minutes. Add 1 cup water to solidifier and stir until dissolved. Proceed from step 6 as for Homemade Tofu.

Homemade Tofu
(Fermentation Method)
MAKES 18 TO 22 OUNCES

In this method, closely related to that for making Soymilk Yogurt (p. 205), bacteria present in the kitchen air enter the warm soymilk and produce lactic acid. The latter serves as solidifier, curdling the soymilk protein to form curds.

1½ cups soybeans, washed, soaked overnight in 1 quart water, rinsed and drained
10 cups water, approximately

Prepare soymilk as in steps in 1 through 5 of Homemade Tofu (p.99), but heat only 2¼ (rather than 7½) cups water in cooking pot. Remove pot from heat and allow soymilk to cool slightly, then pour soymilk into wide-mouthed jars and allow to stand uncovered for 8 to 10 hours. Cover jars and allow to stand at room temperature (at least 70°) for 18 to 36 hours, or until curds have solidified and just begun to separate from whey.

Gently pour curds into a strainer or colander lined with a tofu pressing sack or coarse-weave cloth; allow to drain for 20 minutes, then tie closed mouth of sack. Combine 4 cups water and 1 teaspoon salt in a pot and bring to a boil. Drop in sack, return to the boil, and allow to simmer for 20 minutes. Remove sack and proceed from Step 8 as for Homemade Tofu (p. 99) or press tofu in sack as for Reshaped Tofu (p. 98).

Since this tofu generally has a slightly sour flavor and crumbly texture (like cottage cheese), it is best used in dips, spreads, or dressings.

*Cook Soymilk Completely Before Pressing Okara: This method is similar to that used in most tofu shops, however here water rather than oil and limestone is used as bubble extinguisher (see p. 287). Unless a heavy-bottomed pot is used, the soymilk will overflow. Using a 2½- to 3-gallon pot, cook soybean purée in 9 cups water. When foam begins to rise, reduce heat to low and immediately sprinkle ¼ cup water over surface of foam while stirring with a wooden spoon. Stirring constantly, allow foam to rise 3 more times, adding water and stirring down each time. (Total simmering time should be about 15 minutes.) Empty contents of pot into pressing sack as in basic method and press okara thoroughly. (Omit rinsing and re-pressing of okara.) When all soymilk has been squeezed from okara, dissolve solidifier in 1 cup warm water and add to soymilk in pressing pot. Amount of solidifier used may have to be increased slightly due to lower temperature of soymilk.

*Soft High-yielding Tofu: Allow soymilk to cool to 170° before stirring in magnesium sulfate or calcium solidifier. Wait for 15 minutes before ladling curds very gently into settling container. Press curds with a 3-ounce weight for 15 minutes, then immerse tofu in cold water and allow to stand for 10 minutes before unwrapping cloths. For a milder flavor, allow to soak for 1 hour more.

*Lightly Seasoned Tofu: Combine 2 cups water and 1 to 1½ teaspoons salt in a bowl or large-mouth jar; mix well. Cut cooled tofu into 1½-inch cubes, place into brine, and cover jar. Refrigerate for at least 8 hours. For a more subtle seasoning, bring brine just to a boil before removing and serving tofu.

Five-Color Tofu (Gomoku-dofu) MAKES 21 OUNCES

Although no longer widely available in Japan, this delicious tofu used to be prepared in traditional tofu shops on festive occasions or on special order. It was then usually deep-fried like thick agé (p. 180). The deep-fried variety is still available in the food section of several of Japan's finer department stores.

Ingredients for Homemade Tofu (p. 99)
¼ cup grated carrot
¼ cup grated burdock root or minced lotus root
¼ cup minced mushrooms or cloud-ear mushrooms
¼ cup green beans, fresh corn, or ginkgo nuts, parboiled in lightly salted water

Prepare soymilk as in steps 1 through 5 of Homemade Tofu. After cooking soymilk for 5 minutes, stir in vegetables. Now proceed as for homemade tofu, steps 6 through 10. Serve as Chilled Tofu (p. 105) or, for best flavor, deep-fry and serve as Homemade Thick Agé (p. 182).

VARIATIONS: (Use 2 to 4 tablespoons of each finely cut ingredient.)

*Seashore Gomoku: *Hijiki,* powdered green *nori,* bamboo shoots, sesame seeds, burdock root, and leeks.
*Wild Mountain Vegetable Gomoku: Osmund fern, cloud-ear mushroom, butterbur, and bamboo shoots.
*Gohoji-dofu: Use ¾ cup parboiled green soybeans.

Fig. 36. Chilled Tofu

TOFU QUICK AND EASY

In Japan, the quickest and easiest ways of serving tofu are also generally considered the most delicious. Here, in the preparation of food as in all the arts, simplicity is honored as the foundation of fine taste and beauty. The following dishes can be served at any meal and require no cooking at all.

Chilled Tofu (Hiya-yakko) SERVES 1

Many connoisseurs maintain that this is the only recipe you need to know when using tofu. They are quick to add, however, that a creative cook can serve Chilled Tofu in a different way each day of the year if full use is made of seasonal garnishes, subtly flavored dipping sauces, and richly seasoned toppings.

Chilled Tofu is at its best, though, on hot summer afternoons and balmy summer evenings. Both regular tofu and kinugoshi (p. 211) may be used in preparing it: kinugoshi is preferred for its smooth, custard-like texture, and regular tofu for what many consider to be its more full-bodied flavor. Most important is the quality and freshness of the tofu itself.

It is said that this simple way of enjoying tofu first appealed to Japan's *yakko,* or lowest ranking samurai, about 300 years ago. A combination feudal retainer-servant-valet-and-footman, the yakko was not allowed to carry a sword, but was well known to the common folk because he marched at the very front of the procession whenever his lord made a public appearance. His prescribed uniform was a navy blue, waist-length coat with large square sleeves resembling heraldic banners. A distinctive 6- to 8-inch white square, the yakko's "crest" or "coat of arms," was dyed on the center of each sleeve. Since the color and shape of this square resembled the cubes of chilled tofu the yakko loved to eat, the new dish came to be known as "chilled yakko." And to this day, Japanese recipes call for cutting a 12-ounce cake of tofu into *yakko,* meaning 6 cubes. Chilled tofu is best cut and eaten with chopsticks since the cut surface is then better able to hold or absorb dipping sauces and garnishes.

6 to 8 ounces tofu (regular or kinugoshi), chilled
1½ to 2 teaspoons shoyu, Shoyu Dipping Sauces (p. 40), Sweet Simmered Miso (p. 41), Finger Lickin' Miso (p. 31), or regular miso (p. 31)
Garnishes and Condiments (see below)

Place the tofu on a small plate or in a shallow bowl. If desired, cut tofu into 1-inch cubes.

If using shoyu or a shoyu dipping sauce, sprinkle it over the tofu and top with your choice of garnishes and/or condiments. Or serve the shoyu separately in a small dish and arrange the garnishes on a platter nearby (fig. 36). Invite each person to add garnishes to the shoyu to taste.

If using miso or a miso topping, place a dab of the miso on top of the tofu and serve without garnishes.

Garnishes and Condiments (in order of popularity):
  Thinly sliced leeks or onions, rinsed and pressed (p. 37)
  Grated or slivered gingerroot
  Crushed or minced garlic
  Bonita flakes
  Thin strips of *nori*
  7-spice red pepper
  Slivered *yuzu* peel
  Grated fresh *wasabi* or *wasabi* paste
  Wasabi pickled in sake lees

Grated *daikon*
Diced green beefsteak leaves
Slivered or diced *myoga*
Minced red pickled gingerroot
Hot mustard
Diced *asatsuki*, chives, or wild onions
Ground roasted sesame seeds
A mixture of equal parts grated *daikon* and carrot
Beefsteak plant blossoms or buds
Tiny dried *oboro* shrimp
Benitade or *akame*
Kinome sprigs
Powdered green *nori*
Grated cucumber, or a mixture of equal parts grated
    carrot and grated cucumber
Slivered *kombu tsukudani*
Nori tsukudani
Chopped hard-boiled eggs
Diced cheese
Sesame butter

Popular Combinations:
    Gingerroot and leeks
    Bonita flakes, gingerroot, and leeks
    Nori and bonita flakes
    Hot mustard and bonita flakes
    Gingerroot, leeks, 7-spice red pepper, and bonita
        flakes
Other Sauces and Toppings:
    Mirin-shoyu (p. 40)
    Chinese oyster sauce
    All basic sauces (p. 48)
    Worcestershire or Worcestershire-Ketchup Sauce (p.
        49)
    Special Miso Toppings (p. 45)
    All varieties of Miso Sauté (p. 43)
    Nut and Seed Butter Toppings (p. 47)

VARIATIONS

*Menoha-dofu: Serve chilled tofu uncut, set in a glass bowl on several pieces of *wakame*. Top with thinly sliced green peppers and cucumbers, and diced *myoga* and green beefsteak leaves. Surround with chunks of ice and serve with a dipping sauce made of equal parts shoyu and vinegar (or lemon juice).
*Nameko-dofu: Mix *nameko* mushrooms with grated *daikon*. Season with shoyu, vinegar, and sugar, then whip with chopsticks until bubbles form. Serve over Chilled Tofu and top with grated *wasabi* and thin strips of toasted *nori*.

Iceberg Chilled Tofu

SERVES 1

6 to 8 ounces tofu, cut into 1-inch cubes
Shoyu or Shoyu Dipping Sauces (p. 40)
Garnishes and Condiments for Chilled Tofu (p. 105)

Place the tofu cubes in a small serving bowl. Arrange 4 to 6 ice cubes around tofu, then add enough cold water to just cover tofu. Serve the shoyu or dipping sauce in a separate small dish accompanied by a variety of garnishes. Serve immediately to prevent tofu's subtle sweetness from being lost to the water.

SERVING HINTS

*When serving a group, float the cubed tofu in a large salad bowl at the center of the table. Provide guests with slotted spoons, or let each person remove the tofu with chopsticks. Float thin slices of radish, cucumber or lemon, or parsley sprigs in the iced water as both decoration and garnish.
*Place tofu cubes in attractive natural wooden boxes—about 6 by 8 by 2 inches deep—each box coated with red or black lacquerware, or in large sections of bamboo cut lengthwise into halves. Surround tofu with several large chunks of ice, but do not add water. Place a thinly sliced crescent of watermelon next to the tofu.

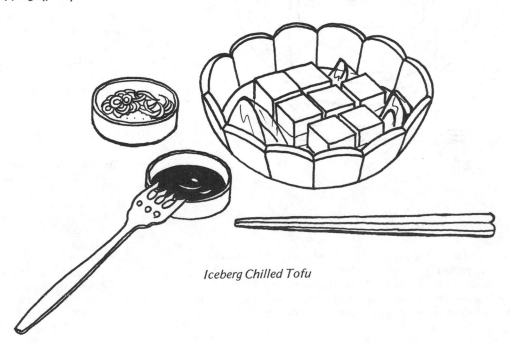

Iceberg Chilled Tofu

Chinese-style Chilled Tofu
(Ryanban-doufu)   SERVES 1

6 to 8 ounces doufu or tofu, chilled
1½ teaspoons minced leeks or onions
1½ teaspoons minced *cha-tsai* or *takuan* pickle
1 teaspoon tiny dried shrimp or bonita flakes
Dash of red-pepper *chiang* (p. 31), tabasco sauce, or minced
    pepper
½ teaspoon sesame oil
1½ teaspoons soy sauce

Place the doufu in a shallow bowl. Arrange the next four
ingredients on top of the doufu, then sprinkle with the sesame oil and soy sauce.
    Or, omit the pickles and red-pepper *chiang* and use 1
tablespoon each minced leeks and soy sauce, 1½ teaspoons
sesame oil, and ¼ cup dried shrimp or bonita flakes.

Sweet-and-Crunchy Chilled Tofu   SERVES 1

6 to 8 ounces tofu, chilled
1 to 1½ teaspoons honey
1½ tablespoons (toasted) slivered almonds or walnut meats
½ banana, sliced into thin rounds
1½ tablespoons raisins
Dash of nutmeg

Place the tofu in a bowl and top with the remaining ingredients.

Chilled Tofu with Applesauce & Granola   SERVES 2

6 ounces tofu, drained (p. 94) and chilled
¼ teaspoon salt
1 cup applesauce, chilled
½ cup raisins
Dash of cinnamon
¼ cup crunchy granola or nuts

Mash tofu together with salt. Mix in applesauce and raisins.
Serve topped with cinnamon and granola.

Chilled Tofu with Glutinous Yam and Egg   SERVES 1
(Imokake-dofu)

½ cup grated glutinous yam
6 to 8 ounces tofu
1 egg, uncooked
½ teaspoon grated *wasabi*
1 to 2 teaspoons shoyu
¼ sheet *nori*, cut into thin strips
½ teaspoon powdered green *nori*

Place grated yam in a serving bowl and place uncut tofu on
top of yam. Hollow out 1 spoonful of tofu from the center of
the upper surface of tofu and break the egg into this hollow.
Serve together with remaining ingredients, inviting each guest
to chose the seasonings and condiments he prefers. Each per-

son cuts the tofu into bite-sized pieces and mixes the ingredients together in the serving bowl.

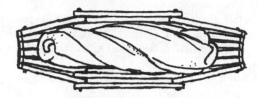

TOFU DRESSINGS, SPREADS, DIPS,
AND HORS D'OEUVRE

Using an electric blender, you can make a wide variety
of Western-style tofu preparations in less than a minute.
When blended or mashed, a 12-ounce cake of tofu makes
about 1½ cups. Fresh or dried herbs make excellent additions to many of these recipes.
    A word to dieters: although most salads are excellent
slenderizers, many conventional dressings definitely are not.
Use tofu to create rich-and-creamy dressings which work together with your favorite salads to save you calories and reduce saturated fats.
    Most of the following dressings plus Tofu Sour Cream
can also be used with excellent results as sauces: spoon them
over cooked vegetables just before serving. To prevent separation, do not reheat.

Tofu Mayonnaise Dressing   MAKES ABOUT 1 CUP

These delicious mayonnaise dressings, dips, and spreads
take only 30 seconds to prepare. Whereas commercial mayonnaise must, by law, consist of at least 65 percent fat (most
homemade varieties contain even more), the following tofu-
based preparations contain no eggs and very little oil, making
them ideal for use in low-calorie, low-fat diets. Refrigerated
in a covered container, they will stay fresh for 1 or 2 days. A
similar mayonnaise can be prepared by substituting soymilk
for the tofu (p. 206).

6 ounces tofu, drained or pressed (p. 96) if desired
1½ to 2 tablespoons lemon juice or vinegar
2 tablespoons oil
½ teaspoon salt, or 2 teaspoons shoyu, or 1 tablespoon red
    miso
Dash of pepper

Combine all ingredients in a blender and purée for about 30
seconds, or until smooth. Or mash all ingredients and allow to
stand for 15 to 30 minutes before serving.
    For variety, add 1 tablespoon finely chopped parsley,
or use equal parts lemon juice and vinegar.

VARIATIONS: Add any of the following ingredients to those
listed above before puréing:
*Onion: ¼ cup diced onion. Excellent on all types of deep-
fried tofu and with many vegetable dishes.
*Curry: ½ teaspoon curry powder and 2 tablespoons minced
onion. Top with a sprinkling of 1 tablespoon minced parsley.

*Cheese & Garlic: ¼ cup Parmesan or grated cheese and ½ clove of garlic or ¼ onion, minced. Serve topped with a sprinkling of minced parsley.

*Gingerroot: 1 teaspoon grated or 1½ teaspoons powdered gingerroot and a dash of (7-spice) red pepper or tabasco sauce. Try over a tomato & cucumber salad. Top with 1 tablespoon minced parsley.

*Dill & Garlic: ¼ teaspoon dill and 1 clove minced garlic. Omit the pepper.

*Pickle: 2 small Western-style cucumber pickles, minced. Try over tomato wedges.

*Celery & Onion: 3 tablespoons each diced celery and onion. Serve with Tofu Cutlets (p. 134) or with squash dishes.

*Sweetened: 2 tablespoons each natural sugar and minced parsley. Use only a dash of salt and omit the pepper. Serve with Apple-Raisin Salad (p. 113) or melon balls.

*Sesame: 2 tablespoons sesame butter or *tahini* and 3 tablespoons minced celery.

*Walnut: ¼ cup each walnut meats and ketchup. Try over a salad of hard-boiled eggs, asparagus, and tomato wedges.

*Spicy Onion: 2 tablespoons diced onion, ¼ teaspoon paprika, and a dash of 7-spice red pepper, tabasco sauce, or cayenne.

*Ketchup: 5 tablespoons ketchup. Top with 2 tablespoons minced parsley.

*Sweetened Miso: 1 tablespoon red, barley or Hatcho miso and 1 or 2 tablespoons natural sugar. Omit the salt. Try over tomato wedges.

*Sweet White Miso: 2 tablespoons sweet white miso and ¼ cup chopped leeks, scallions, or onions.

*Miso & Peanut: 1 tablespoon red or akadashi miso, and 2 tablespoons each peanuts and minced parsley. Omit the salt.

*Egg Yolk: 1 egg yolk (or press the tofu and use 1 whole egg). If desired, add 1 teaspoon sugar, ½ teaspoon hot mustard, and a dash of red pepper.

*Mustard: 1 teaspoon hot mustard. Delicious with fresh tomatoes, steamed broccoli, or deep-fried tofu.

*Garlic: 1 to 1½ teaspoons minced or pressed garlic. Serve over tomato salads. If desired, add 3 tablespoons minced onion and top with chopped parsley.

*Raisin: 2/3 cup raisins. Use only ¼ teaspoon salt. Serve as a dessert topping over apples or on Waldorf salads.

*Green Beefsteak: 2 green beefsteak leaves.

*Umeboshi: 1/3 onion (minced), 1 tablespoon ground roasted sesame seeds or sesame butter, and 4 pitted *umeboshi*. Omit the salt.

*Herb: ½ teaspoon fresh or dried herbs (oregano, marjoram, sorrel, caraway).

*Substitute for part of the lemon juice or vinegar: sake or white wine, 1 teaspoon beet juice, or 1½ tablespoons orange juice.

Creamy Tofu Dressings and Dips   MAKES 1¼ CUPS

These preparations resemble tofu mayonnaise but contain no oil and are often slightly sweet. If a blender is not available, simply mash the ingredients together with a fork.

6 ounces tofu
1 tablespoon grated gingerroot
2½ teaspoons shoyu
1 tablespoon ground roasted sesame seeds (p. 38), sesame butter, or *tahini*
1 tablespoon natural sugar

Combine all ingredients in a blender and purée until smooth. Delicious with Green Bean Salad (p. 115), parboiled bean-sprouts, or over cucumbers mixed with thin slices of deep-fried tofu.

VARIATIONS: Proceeding as above, use the following ingredients:

*Tofu-Peanut Butter Dressing
      6 ounces tofu
      3 tablespoons peanut butter
      1 tablespoon vinegar or lemon juice
      1 to 2 tablespoons natural sugar

Try with cucumber salads

*Tofu-Sesame-Miso Dressing
      6 ounces tofu
      1½ tablespoons sweet white miso
      1 tablespoon ground roasted sesame seeds (p. 38), sesame butter, or *tahini*
      2 teaspoons natural sugar
      ½ teaspoon *mirin*

Serve over fresh vegetables, or a combination of carrots, *konnyaku*, and *(shiitake)* mushrooms simmered in Sweetened Shoyu Broth (p. 40).

*Tofu-Garlic-Shoyu Dressing
      6 ounces tofu
      1 clove garlic, minced
      1½ tablespoons shoyu
      Juice of ½ lemon
      ¼ teaspoon oregano
      ¼ teaspoon marjoram

*Tofu-Sour Cream Dip
      6 ounces tofu
      2½ to 3 tablespoons sour cream
      2½ teaspoons red, barley, or Hatcho miso
      ½ teaspoon lemon juice or vinegar
      1½ teaspoon minced parsley
      Dash of pepper

Chinese-style Tofu-Sesame-Shoyu Dressing   MAKES 1½ CUPS

12 ounces tofu
2 tablespoons shoyu
2 teaspoons sesame oil
¾ teaspoon natural sugar
1 to 2 tablespoons minced leek, scallion, onion, or parsley (optional)

Combine all ingredients, mashing well. Serve over tomato and cucumber slices.

Tofu Tartare Sauce   MAKES 2½ CUPS

1 cup minced Western-style cucumber pickles
8 ounces tofu
4 tablespoons oil
5 tablespoons lemon juice
1 teaspoon salt
½ teaspoon hot mustard
2 hard-boiled eggs
2 tablespoons diced onions
2 tablespoons minced parsley
2 tablespoons chopped green olives (optional)

Combine ¼ cup minced pickles with the next five ingredients and purée in a blender until smooth. Combine with the remaining pickles and other ingredients and mix well. Serve with deep-fried tofu and tofu croquettes. If desired, top with a sprinkling of parsley.

Tofu Cream Cheese   MAKES 1 CUP

Easily prepared at home, tofu cream cheese contains no animal fats and costs about one-fourth as much as its dairy counterpart. Use as you would dairy cream cheese but do not reheat.

12 ounces tofu, squeezed (p. 97)
2 tablespoons oil
3/8 teaspoon salt
Dash of white pepper
1 teaspoon lemon juice (optional)

Combine all ingredients in a blender and purée until smooth and thick.

Tofu Sour Cream   MAKES 1½ CUPS

12 ounces tofu, parboiled (salted water method, p. 96) and
    squeezed (p. 97)
2 tablespoons lemon juice
¼ teaspoon salt

Combine all ingredients in a blender and purée until smooth.

Tofu Cottage Cheese   MAKES 1 CUP

12 ounces tofu, pressed (p. 96) if desired
½ teaspoon salt
Dash of pepper

Combine all ingredients and mash together; stir well to develop texture. Serve as cottage cheese.

VARIATION

*Sweetened Tofu Cottage Cheese: Use the ingredients for Tofu Whipped Cream (p. 148) and prepare as above. Try adding a few drops of vanilla. Serve with fresh fruit salads topped with raisins, slivered almonds, or sunflower seeds.

Tangy Tofu Cottage Cheese   SERVES 2

12 ounces tofu, drained (p. 96) if desired
2 tablespoons oil or ¼ cup mayonnaise
3 tablespoons lemon juice or vinegar
1 teaspoon salt or 4 teaspoons shoyu
1 clove minced garlic
Dash of pepper

Mash together all ingredients. Allow to stand for 30 minutes. Serve as a dressing for fresh vegetable salads.

For a deliciously rich flavor, omit the garlic and salt; add 3 tablespoons red miso and 2 tablespoons each natural sugar and minced parsley. If desired, top with a sprinkling of ground roasted sesame seeds.

Or try using any of the variations listed at Tofu Mayonnaise (p. 107).

VARIATIONS: Proceed as above:
*Deviled Tofu
        12 ounces tofu
        ¼ cup mayonnaise
        ½ teaspoon dill
        1 clove garlic, minced
        1 tablespoon shoyu or 1½ tablespoons red miso
        2 tablespoons oil
        2 tablespoons vinegar or lemon juice
        Dash of pepper

Tofu-Egg Spread   MAKES 1½ CUPS

12 ounces tofu, squeezed (p. 97)
2 hard-boiled eggs, diced
2 tablespoons oil
1 to 2 tablespoons lemon juice
½ teaspoon salt or 1 tablespoon red miso
2 tablespoons minced onion (optional)
1 tablespoon minced parsley

Combine the first six ingredients in a blender and purée for 30 seconds. Garnish with the parsley and serve as a sandwich spread.

Tofu-Nut Butter Spread or Topping   MAKES 2 CUPS

Serve as is on whole-grain bread or crackers, together with sprouts and fresh vegetables in sandwiches, or as a topping for fresh or cooked vegetables and vegetable salads.

12 ounces tofu, drained (p. 96)
6 tablespoons peanut or sesame butter
1 tablespoon honey
2 teaspoons lemon juice
2 tablespoons red or barley miso; or ½ teaspoon salt

Combine ingredients and mash together with a fork.

For a crunchier texture, add ¼ cup each raisins and peanuts (or sunflower seeds).

Tofu Guacamole

MAKES 2 CUPS

12 ounces tofu, squeezed (p. 97)
1 avacado, peeled and seeded
2 tablespoons red miso, or 4 teaspoons shoyu, or 1 teaspoon salt
2 tablespoons sesame butter or *tahini*
2 tablespoons minced onion
¼ tomato, diced
2 or 3 teaspoons lemon juice
1 clove garlic, crushed
Dash of paprika and/or pepper
2 tablespoons minced parsley or ¼ cup alfalfa sprouts

Combine the first nine ingredients and mash together with a fork until smooth. Serve as a dip, spread, or dressing, garnished with the parsley.

Tofu Pickled in Miso
(Tofu no Misożuke)

MAKES 6 OUNCES

This preparation, salty and richly fragrant, has a soft, cheeselike consistency resembling that of Chinese fermented tofu (doufu-ru). The many commercial varieties of Chinese firm tofu pickled in miso—called *chiang-doufu* or *chiang-doufu chin*—are generally served cut into small cubes as a seasoning for rice or rice porridge. Kept in a cool place, the tofu gradually grows saltier and will last indefinitely.

12 ounces tofu, well pressed (p. 96)
Miso Bed:
  ½ cup red, barley, or Hatcho miso
  ½ teaspoon grated gingerroot
  ½ teaspoon sesame oil
  1 teaspoon sake or white wine
  Dash of 7-spice red pepper or tabasco sauce

Cut pressed tofu crosswise into ½-inch-thick slices and parboil for 3 minutes (p. 96); drain and allow to cool to room temperature. Combine all ingredients to make miso bed, mixing well. Place one-half the mixture into a shallow 1-quart container and smooth to form an even layer. On this arrange the tofu slices, cover with remaining miso mixture, and then with a layer of plastic wrap spread over miso surface to keep out air; allow to stand for 12 to 15 hours. Remove tofu carefully from container and wipe off miso on tofu surface with a damp cloth. Cut into ½-inch cubes and serve with rice or, for best flavor and aroma, broil on both sides until well browned before serving. Also delicious as hors d'oeuvre.

VARIATIONS

*Dry very well-pressed tofu in a slow oven for about 1 hour. Cut each cake crosswise into thirds and embed in miso for one year. Sold commercially in Japan, the flavor, texture, and appearance of this product resemble those of a very firm cheese. Scme varieties are wrapped with *kombu* and beefsteak leaves before pickling in semi-sweet barley miso.

*Embed miso for 24 hours or more in plain red miso. Mash and serve as a cracker spread topped with a slice of tomato or cucumber, or combine with equal parts Tofu Cream Cheese (p. 109), a little diced onions, and your choice of herbs to use as a dip.
*Combine 3 tablespoons mashed miso-pickled tofu with 2 tablespoons sesame or peanut butter, 1 tablespoon honey, and ½ teaspoon lemon juice; mix well. Serve as a sandwich spread or cracker dip.
*Sprinkle parboiled tofu slices with ¼ teaspoon salt and embed for 2 days in a mixture of 1½ cups sweet white miso and 2 teaspoons sake (or white wine). Broil and serve as above.
*Tofu Pickled in Shoyu: Press and cut tofu as above, then soak overnight in shoyu rather than miso.

Four-Color Tofu Hors D'oeuvre

MAKES 30 TO 40

1 cucumber, cut diagonally into thin ovals
1 carrot, cut into ovals
3 ounces cheese, cut into thin slices each 1½ inches square
1 sweet potato or yam, steamed and cut into thin rounds
¼ cup red miso, Sesame Miso (p. 42), or Sweet Simmered Miso (p. 41)
16 ounces tofu, pressed (p. 96) and cut into small rectangles

Arrange the first four ingredients on serving platters. Spread the surface of each vegetable piece and cheese slice with a thin coating of miso, then top with a slice of tofu. If desired, pierce with foodpicks. If miso is unavailable, dip each slice of tofu in shoyu.

Tofu Canapés

MAKES 16

16 slices of buttered bread or toast, each 1 by 3 inches
1½ tablespoons red miso or Walnut Miso (p. 42)
3 tablespoons sweet white, red, or Sweet Simmered Miso (p. 41)
12 ounces tofu, pressed (p. 96) and cut crosswise into 16 slices
Canapé Toppings: Your choice of the following, thinly sliced:
  Hard-boiled eggs
  Cucumbers
  Tomatoes
  Green peppers
  Cheese
  Snow peas or green beans, parboiled
  Potatoes or sweet potatoes, steamed
  Carrots

Spread half of the bread pieces with red miso and half with white miso. Cover each piece with a slice of tofu, and top with one slice of any of the canapé toppings. Pierce with foodpicks if desired.

If miso is unavailable, sprinkle the tofu and topping with a few drops of shoyu. Substitute crackers for the bread.

TOFU IN SALADS

Tofu is a wonderful addition to almost any salad. Its soft texture complements the crisp crunchiness of fresh vegetables. And because tofu has so few calories per gram of protein, tofu salads can be enjoyed by weight-watchers.

Tofu can take at least 6 different forms when served in salads. Mashed or squeezed and lightly seasoned, it resembles cottage or ricota cheese. Lightly drained and cubed, it can be used with or in place of croutons. Well-pressed and diced, it has the texture of soft cheese and goes well in marinated salads. Parboiled and crumbled, it may be used to keep a salad light. Reshaped and cut into thin strips, it has the consistency of firm cheese or ham. Finally, blended and seasoned, tofu can be turned into a variety of rich and creamy salad dressings.

Western-style Salads

We have divided the following tofu salads into Western and Japanese varieties depending on the type of dressing used and the method of preparation. Thus, a number of the Western salads—characterized by the use of a dressing containing oil and/or dairy products generally served over fresh, crisp greens and vegetable slices—also may contain typically Japanese ingredients.

Cauliflower Salad with Mashed Tofu   SERVES 4

1 small cauliflower
12 ounces tofu, mashed
2 ounces cheese, diced (optional)
¼ cup sunflower seeds (optional)
Caesar or Miso-Cream Cheese Dressing (p. 47)

Steam cauliflower for 10 minutes or until tender. Allow to cool, then separate into flowerets. Combine in a large bowl with remaining ingredients; toss lightly.

Or, marinate flowerets overnight in a well-seasoned oil and vinegar dressing.

Carrot, Raisin & Walnut Salad   SERVES 4
with Tofu

6 ounces tofu, pressed (p. 96) and mashed
1 cup grated carrots, or diced apple or celery
½ cup raisins
½ cup (roasted) walnut meats, diced
1½ tablespoons red, barley, or Hatcho miso
2 teaspoons natural sugar
1 teaspoon sake or white wine
2 tablespoons sesame butter
4 lettuce leaves (optional)

Combine all ingredients, mixing well. If desired, serve mounded on lettuce leaves. Also delicious in sandwiches and on toast.

Curried Rice Salad with Tofu   SERVES 6

18 ounces tofu, pressed (p. 96) and broken into very small pieces
2½ cups cooked Brown Rice (p. 50), chilled
3 tablespoons minced green onion or leek
2 tablespoons minced parsley
2 green peppers; one slivered and one cut into rings
Dressing:
    6 tablespoons oil
    1/3 cup (rice) vinegar
    1 tablespoon lemon juice
    1 teaspoon curry powder
    ¼ teaspoon (7-spice) red pepper
    1 clove of garlic, crushed
    ¾ teaspoon salt
    Dash of pepper
4 lettuce leaves
1 tomato, cut into wedges

Combine the first four ingredients with the slivered green pepper. Add dressing, mix lightly and, for best flavor, allow to stand for several hours. Serve mounded on lettuce leaves in a large bowl; garnish with tomato wedges and green pepper rings.

Tofu Cottage Cheese Salad with   SERVES 3
Tomatoes and Walnut-Miso

1½ tablespoons Lemon-Walnut Miso Sauté (p. 44) or Sesame Miso (p. 42)
3 tablespoons mayonnaise
12 ounces tofu, scrambled (p. 97)
3 tablespoons minced parsley
1 tomato, cut into thin wedges
¼ cup chopped walnut meats (optional)
Dash of pepper

Combine miso and mayonnaise, mixing well. Place tofu in a serving bowl and lightly mix in the miso-mayonnaise, parsley, tomato and, if used, the chopped nutmeats. Season with a sprinkling of pepper. Chill before serving.

Sweet Potato & Cucumber Salad with Mashed Tofu

SERVES 2

1 cucumber, cut into matchsticks
1 sweet potato, steamed and cut into ¼-inch-thick half moons

3 Chinese cabbage or lettuce leaves, cut into thin strips
6 ounces tofu, mashed
½ cup Caesar or Miso Sour Cream Dressing (p. 46)

Combine all ingredients; toss lightly.

Lettuce and Tomato Salad with Mashed Tofu

SERVES 4

12 ounces tofu, mashed
Caesar, bleu cheese, or Floating Cloud Miso Dressing (p.46)
4 lettuce leaves
3 tomatoes, cut into wedges
2 cucumbers, cut into ovals
¼ cup sunflower seeds (optional)

Combine tofu and dressing in a bowl; mix well. Divide lettuce leaves among 4 serving dishes. Place tomato wedges and cucumber slices on top of lettuce, then top with tofu-dressing mixture and a sprinkling of sunflower seeds.

Western-style Vinegared Shira-ae (Shirozu-ae)

SERVES 2

6 ounces tofu, pressed (p. 96) and mashed
1 tablespoon sesame butter or *tahini*
1 tablespoon lemon juice
1½ tablespoons vinegar
½ teaspoon salt or 1 tablespoon red miso
1 teaspoon sake or white wine
1 cucumber or small carrot, sliced into thin rounds
2 hard-boiled eggs, chopped
¼ cup walnut meats
¼ cup raisins
2 tablespoons minced cucumber pickles (optional)

Combine the first six ingredients, mixing until smooth. Gently stir in the remaining ingredients and serve immediately.

Western-style Shira-ae

SERVES 2 OR 3

1 cucumber, cut into thin ovals
3 celery stalks, diced
6 ounces tofu, pressed (p. 96) and mashed
4 teaspoons sugar
½ teaspoon salt
4 teaspoons peanut butter or sesame butter
4 teaspoons rice vinegar

Combine the first five ingredients in a large mixing bowl. Cream the peanut butter and vinegar in a separate cup and pour over the tofu mixture. Mix all ingredients together lightly. For best flavor, chill before serving.

Tossed Green Salad with Soft Tofu Cubes

SERVES 4

6 to 8 lettuce or Chinese cabbage leaves
1 tomato, cut into thin wedges
2 fresh mushrooms, thinly sliced
1 large cucumber, cut into thin ovals
1 green pepper, thinly sliced
1 hard-boiled egg, diced
¼ cup French or Floating Cloud Miso Dressing (p. 46)
6 ounces tofu, drained (p. 96) and cut into ½-inch cubes
½ teaspoon salt
¼ cup sunflower seeds (optional)

Tear lettuce into salad-sized pieces and combine with the next five ingredients. Add the dressing and toss lightly. Now add the tofu cubes and season with salt; toss again. Serve topped with a sprinkling of sunflower seeds.

Marinated Salad with Diced Tofu

SERVES 4

12 ounces tofu, pressed very firm (p. 96) and cut into ½-inch cubes
1 cucumber, diced
1 small carrot, diced
1 tomato, chopped fine
10 green beans, parboiled (p. 37) and chopped fine
Dressing:
    2 tablespoons shoyu
    3 tablespoons (sesame) oil
    1 tablespoon (rice) vinegar
    ½ teaspoon natural sugar

Combine tofu and vegetables in a large bowl. Add dressing, cover bowl, and marinate for 8 to 10 hours in a cool place. Drain vegetables lightly before serving.

If desired, season the dressing with oregano or 7-spice red pepper. Or drain the salad well and use as a filling for Agé Pouches (p. 192).

Mushroom Tomato Salad with Crumbled Tofu

SERVES 4

4 lettuce leaves
4 small tomatoes, thinly sliced
4 large fresh mushrooms, thinly sliced
12 ounces tofu, crumbled (p. 98)
1 tablespoon minced parsley
Dressing:
    1 tablespoon shoyu
    ½ cup salad oil
    ¼ cup lemon juice
    ½ clove of garlic, crushed or minced
    Dash of pepper

Arrange lettuce leaves on serving dishes and distribute tomato slices around edges of leaves. Combine mushrooms and tofu and divide among the 4 lettuce leaves. Top with a sprinkling of parsley, then the dressing.

Hard-Boiled Egg Salad with Soft Tofu Cubes

SERVES 4

3 hard-boiled eggs, diced
5 Chinese cabbage or lettuce leaves, cut into thin strips
1 green pepper, thinly sliced
12 ounces tofu, drained (p. 96) and cut into ½-inch cubes
3 mushrooms, thinly sliced
Garlic dressing or Tofu Mayonnaise Dressing (p. 107)

Combine the first five ingredients in a salad bowl and top with the dressing; toss lightly.

Tofu Potato Salad

SERVES 5 OR 6

8 ounces tofu, cut into 1-inch cubes
2 cups cubed boiled potatoes
1 large cucumber, thinly sliced
½ cup celery, thinly sliced
Dressing:
    6 tablespoons (tofu) mayonnaise (p. 107)
    2 teaspoons shoyu
    Dash of pepper
6 lettuce leaves
Radish roses (optional)

Combine the first four ingredients with the dressing and toss lightly. Serve on the lettuce leaves, garnished with radish roses.

Tossed Green Salad with Reshaped Tofu

SERVES 3 OR 4

24 ounces tofu, reshaped (p. 98) and cut into matchsticks or pieces 3 inches long and ½-inch square
4 Chinese cabbage or lettuce leaves, torn into small pieces
3 small mushrooms, thinly sliced
1 tomato, cut into wedges
1 small cucumber, cut into thin ovals.
½ cup garlic dressing or Tofu Mayonnaise Dressing (p. 107)
¼ cup roasted peanuts or sunflower seeds

Combine tofu and vegetables in a salad bowl; dress and toss lightly. Serve topped with a sprinkling of peanuts.

Squash or Pumpkin Salad with Tofu Mayonnaise Dressing

SERVES 3 OR 4

2 cups 1-inch cubes of boiled or steamed *kabocha*, squash, or pumpkin
1 tomato, diced
¼ onion, diced
½ cucumber, slivered
2 tablespoons minced parsley
2 to 4 ounces deep-fried tofu, cut into thin strips (optional)
¾ cup Tofu Mayonnaise Dressing (p. 000)

Combine all ingredients in a large bowl; toss.

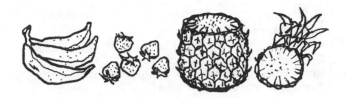

Fresh Fruit Salads with Tofu Dressings

*Tofu Whipped Cream** (p. 148): Serve over any or all of the following: strawberries, thinly sliced apples, bananas, pears, peaches, or melon balls.
*Tofu Cottage Cheese** (p. 109): Especially tasty as a filling for pear halves.
*Sweetened Tofu Cottage Cheese** (p. 109): Serve in the same way as for Tofu Whipped Cream. Add a few drops of vanilla if desired. If using apples as the basis of the salad, top with raisins, slivered almonds or walnuts, sunflower seeds, and a sprinkling of toasted wheat germ and cinnamon. If using bananas, try the same toppings but substitute nutmeg for cinnamon.

Tofu-Banana Salad

SERVES 4

6 ounces tofu, mashed
3 bananas, cut into thin rounds
1 tablespoon honey
4 large lettuce leaves
¾ cup Tofu Whipped Cream (p. 148)
3 tablespoons toasted wheat germ

Combine tofu, bananas, and honey in a large bowl; mix gently. Spoon the mixture onto lettuce leaves, top with whipped cream, and sprinkle with wheat germ. Serve chilled.

Apple-Raisin Salad with Tofu Dressing

SERVES 4

2 apples, diced
½ cup raisins
½ cup peanuts or walnut meats
1 celery stalk, diced (optional)
½ teaspoon salt
1 cup Tofu-Peanut Butter Dressing (p. 108)

Combine all ingredients in a large bowl; mix well.

Tofu Fruit Salad

SERVES 2 OR 3

6 ounces tofu, cut into 1-inch cubes
1 cup orange sections or ½ cup pineapple chunks
2 tablespoons peanuts
¼ cup walnut meats
French dressing
1 cup alfalfa or bean sprouts

Combine the first four ingredients, add the dressing, and toss lightly. Serve mounded on the sprouts.

Mushroom Salad with Tofu Mayonnaise

SERVES 2 OR 3

8 white mushrooms, thinly sliced
4 large Chinese cabbage leaves, thinly sliced
½ cup Tofu Mayonnaise Dressing (p. 107)

Combine all ingredients in a salad bowl; toss lightly.

Tofu & Tomato Aspic or Molded Salad

SERVES 3 TO 4

½ stick of agar (4 gm), reconstituted and torn into small
   pieces (p. 37)
1 cup tomato juice
1 tomato, chopped
6 ounces tofu, rubbed through a sieve, puréed in a blender, or
   diced
4 teaspoons vinegar
2 tablespoons ketchup
1 tablespoon shoyu or ¾ teaspoon salt
1 teaspoon natural sugar
¼ teaspoon basil or oregano
Dash of black pepper
¼ cup chopped green pepper
½ cup chopped celery
Lemon wedges or Tofu Mayonnaise Dressing (p. 107)

Combine agar and tomato juice in a saucepan and bring to a
boil. Simmer, stirring constantly, for 2 to 3 minutes, or until
agar dissolves. Stir in the next eight ingredients, remove from
heat, and allow to cool until partially thickened. Mix in green
pepper and celery, pour into a mold, and refrigerate until set.
Serve chilled, topped with freshly-squeezed lemon juice or
dollops of the mayonnaise dressing.

Jelled Tofu (Kanten-dofu)

MAKES 2½ CUPS

Diced cubes of jelled tofu make an excellent addition
to tossed green salads and fruit cocktail mixtures. Or try
serving them accompanied by a dipping sauce of Vinegar-
Shoyu (p. 40), or the sauce used with their close relative
Takigawa-dofu (p. 210).

1 stick of agar (8 gm), reconstituted and torn into small
   pieces (p. 37)
1¼ cups water
12 ounces tofu, rubbed through a sieve or puréed in a blender
¼ teaspoon salt

Combine agar and water in a saucepan and bring to a boil.
Simmer, stirring constantly, for 2 to 3 minutes, or until agar
dissolves, then pour through a (warmed) strainer into a second pan. Add tofu and salt, mixing well, then pour tofu-agar
mixture into a (moistened) mold and allow to cool to room
temperature. Cover and refrigerate for several hours, or until
set. Cut into cubes, drain briefly if necessary, and serve as
for Tofu & Tomato Aspic.

Japanese-style Salads

In Japan, mixed foods served with a seasoned dressing
are called *aemono*. Unlike most Western salads, which are
made with vegetables in their raw state, these *aemono* salads
are generally prepared with lightly cooked vegetables and
served in tiny portions as an accompaniment to a main dish,
which they are meant to complement in color, texture, and
taste. Most *aemono* contain little or no oil, mayonnaise, or
dairy products. The dressing, generally prepared with vinegar
(or lemon juice) and shoyu or miso, is often quite sweet.
Aemono are generally named after the dominant seasonings
in the dressing: Sesame Miso-ae, Mustard-Vinegar Miso-ae,
Walnut Miso-ae, etc.

Shira-ae with Miso and Kinome

SERVES 4

Shira-ae, or "white salad," is one of Japan's most popular—and, in our opinion, most delicious—tofu dishes. All
varieties are at their best when chilled for 4 to 6 hours before
serving. They are delicious used as fillings for agé pouches or
as spreads for buttered toast or sandwiches. Any of the following recipes may be prepared without sugar, or with less
than half the amount ordinarily used. To make tangy *Shiro-
zu-ae* (p. 112), add several tablespoons of vinegar or lemon
juice to your favorite variety of Shira-ae, and reduce the
amount of sugar slighty.

1 cake of *konnyaku*, cut into small rectangles (p. 37) and
   parboiled (p. 37)
1 carrot, cut into small rectangles
½ cup dashi (p. 39), stock, or water
½ teaspoon shoyu
½ teaspoon salt
3 tablespoons natural sugar
4 tablespoons ground roasted sesame seeds (p. 38); or 2½
   tablespoons sesame butter, or *tahini*
4 ounces tofu, parboiled and pressed (p. 97).
2 tablespoons sweet white miso or 1 tablespoon red miso
4 sprigs *kinome*, or substitute minced mint leaves

Combine the first five ingredients with 1 tablespoon sugar in a small saucepan. Simmer until all liquid is absorbed or evaporated, then allow vegetables to cool to room temperature. To the sesame seeds in the *suribachi* add tofu, miso, and 2 tablespoons sugar; grind together with a wooden pestle, then mix in the vegetables. Serve individual portions garnished with a sprig of *kinome*.

Shira-ae with Mushrooms and Sweet White Miso

SERVES 4 OR 5

4 ounces *daikon*, cut into small rectangles (p. 37)
¼ carrot, cut into matchsticks
½ cake of *konnyaku*, cut into small rectangles
1¼ teaspoons salt
3 mushrooms (fresh or dried), thinly sliced
2 teaspoons shoyu
4 teaspoons *mirin*
1 tablespoon ground roasted sesame seeds (p. 38), sesame butter, or *tahini*
8 ounces tofu, pressed (p. 96)
3 tablespoons sweet white miso or 1½ tablespoons red miso
1 teaspoon natural sugar

Combine the first three ingredients in a small bowl; rub vegetables with 1 teaspoon salt, then rinse and press (p. 37). Heat a dry skillet or wok. Add *konnyaku* and fry for several minutes, stirring constantly, until *konnyaku* is dry and begins to shrink; transfer to a bowl and allow to cool.

Combine mushrooms, shoyu, and 1 teaspoon *mirin* in a small saucepan. Simmer until most of the liquid is absorbed or evaporated, then drain and allow mushrooms to cool.

To the sesame seeds in the *suribachi* add ¼ teaspoon salt, the tofu, miso, sugar, and remaining 1 tablespoon *mirin*; grind together thoroughly. Mix in the *daikon*, carrot, *konnyaku*, and mushrooms. Serve chilled.

Shira-ae with Sweet Potatoes and Konnyaku

SERVES 4 TO 6

½ small carrot, cut into matchsticks and parboiled (p. 37)
1 cake of *konnyaku*, cut into matchsticks and parboiled
3 tablespoons dried (cloud-ear) mushroom, reconstituted (p. 37), drained, and cut into thin strips
3 tablespoons sugar
2 tablespoons shoyu
6 tablespoons ground roasted sesame seeds (p. 38); or 3 tablespoons sesame butter, or *tahini*
¼ teaspoon salt
12 ounces tofu, well pressed (p. 96)
1 small sweet potato, steamed and cut into ½-inch cubes

Combine the first four ingredients with 2 tablespoons sugar in a small saucepan. Simmer until most of the liquid has been absorbed or evaporated. Cool to room temperature, then drain. To the ground sesame seeds in the *suribachi* add salt, tofu, and 1 tablespoon sugar. Grind or mash together well. Mix in the potatoes and vegetables.

Or, omit the sesame and garnish with thin strips of toasted *nori* (p. 38).

Lotus Root Salad with Tofu Dressing

SERVES 2 OR 3

6 lettuce leaves
1 tomato, cut into thin wedges
Tofu-Garlic Dressing:
    6 ounces tofu, mashed
    ½ clove garlic, crushed
    1½ tablespoons lemon juice
    3 tablespoons oil
    ¼ teaspoon salt
    Dash of pepper
½ cup thin half-moons of lotus root, parboiled (p. 37)

Spread lettuce leaves in individual salad bowls and arrange tomato wedges around the leaves. Combine dressing ingredients in a small bowl and mix with a whisk or chopsticks until smooth. Stir in the lotus root and mound the mixture on the lettuce leaves.

Burdock and Green Beans with Tofu Sauce

SERVES 4

2 cups matchsticks of burdock root, soaked (p. 37) and parboiled (p. 37)
½ cup dashi (p. 39), stock, or water
1 tablespoon sugar
½ teaspoon salt
16 to 20 green beans, parboiled
¾ cup Quick Tofu-Sesame Sauce (p. 121)

Combine the first four ingredients in a small saucepan and simmer until most of the liquid has been absorbed or evaporated. Allow to cool to room temperature, then drain. Serve garnished with green beans and topped with the sauce.

Hailstones Salad
(Arare-dofu no Aemono)

SERVES 3 or 4

24 ounces tofu, reshaped (p. 98) and cut into ½-inch cubes or 2-inch matchsticks
1¾ ounces *narazuke* pickles, or substitute 2 small carrots, cut into matchsticks
1 tablespoon diced leeks or onions
1 tablespoon diced pickled red gingerroot (beni shoga), or substitute Western-style cucumber pickles
Dressing:
    1 tablespoon Sesame Miso (p. 42) or red miso
    2 tablespoons water (or tea)
    ½ teaspoon salt
    1 teaspoon shoyu
    ¼ teaspoon vinegar

Combine the first four ingredients in a bowl; dress and toss lightly.

Shira-ae Stuffed Vegetables

SERVES 2

4 large mushrooms, with stems removed
2 green peppers, with seeds removed
1 cup Shira-ae (any variety; pp. 114 to 115)
2 tablespoons whole roasted sesame seeds
6 sprigs of *kinome* (optional)

Broil the mushrooms and peppers until lightly browned and fragrant. Use half the Shira-ae to stuff the peppers, and mound the remainder on the mushrooms. Sprinkle with sesame seeds and top with *kinome*.

TOFU WITH SANDWICHES AND TOAST

Tofu sandwiches may be used as the main course for a high-protein, low-calorie lunch. Thin slices of pressed tofu contribute to sandwiches much the same texture as a soft, mild cheese. The firm crunchiness of whole-grain toast and the softness of tofu make a particularly nice combination. The use of miso or shoyu is the key to seasoning. Due to protein complementary (p. 25), serving tofu and whole-wheat bread together can yield up to 42 percent more protein.

Tofu-Grilled Cheese Sandwich

SERVES 4

4 slices of whole-wheat bread, buttered
2 teaspoons mustard
¼ cup (tofu) mayonnaise (p. 107)
4 thin slices of tomato
12 ounces tofu, pressed (p. 96) and cut crosswise into eighths

Shoyu or 2 teaspoons red miso
4 slices of cheese

Spread each piece of bread with mustard and mayonnaise, and top with a slice of tomato and 2 slices of tofu. Season tofu with a few drops of shoyu or a thin layer of miso, then cover with the cheese. Broil until cheese melts.

Or place tofu on top of cheese and broil until tofu is lightly browned.

Open-faced Vegetable Sandwiches with Sliced Tofu

SERVES 4

If the sandwich is to be served immediately after it is prepared, little or no pressing of the tofu is required. However, if the sandwiches are to be used in a box lunch, press thoroughly to rid the tofu of excess moisture.

4 slices of whole-grain bread or toast, buttered
4 teaspoons red miso, Miso Toppings (p. 41), or Finger Lickin' Miso (p. 31); or 4 tablespoons Nut Butter Spreads (p. 47) or Kinako Butter (p. 65)
12 ounces tofu, well drained or pressed (p. 96) and cut crosswise into eighths
Your choice of the following, thinly sliced or minced:
    Lettuce
    Cucumber
    Tomatoes
    Onions or grated gingerroot
    Cheese, grated or sliced
    Hard-boiled eggs
    Parsley or alfalfa sprouts
Shoyu and/or Sesame Salt (p. 51)
Pepper (optional)

Spread each piece of bread or toast with the miso and top with 2 slices of tofu. (If desired, mash tofu with a fork to give a cottage cheese-like texture.) Cover with several varieties of vegetables and season to taste with a few drops of shoyu and a dash of pepper.

Sliced Tofu on Toast with Onion Sauce

SERVES 4

4 slices of whole-grain toast, buttered
1 cup Onion Sauce (p. 48), cooled
1¾ teaspoons shoyu
2 ounces cheese, grated
12 ounces tofu, pressed (p. 96) and cut crosswise into eighths

Shoyu

Arrange the toast on individual serving plates. Combine onion sauce and shoyu in a bowl; mix well. Spoon the mixture over the toast, sprinkle on cheese, and top with 2 slices of tofu. Season with a few drops of shoyu.

Additional Suggestions for Serving Tofu with Sandwiches

*Use Tofu-Nut Butter Spreads (p. 47), Tangy Tofu Cottage Cheese (p. 109), or Tofu Cream Cheese (p. 109). Serve on buttered bread or toast, as is, or with fresh vegetable slices.
*The many varieties of Tofu Mayonnaise (p. 107) may be combined in sandwiches with ingredients ranging from diced hard-boiled eggs to lettuce, tomatoes, and cucumbers.
*Western-type salads made with mashed tofu (p. 112) and Japanese cooked salads such as Shira-ae (p. 114) go deliciously on buttered toast.

TOFU IN SOUPS

Fresh tofu adds flavor, protein, and a delightful texture to almost any soup. Cut into small cubes, crumbled, thinly sliced, or made into dumplings, it should be added to the soup 1 or 2 minutes before you have finished cooking. (If cooked over high heat or for too long, tofu loses some of its softness and delicate texture.) Use about 2½ to 3 ounces of tofu per serving. In each of the following recipes, kinugoshi, deep-fried tofu, grilled tofu, frozen tofu, or yuba may be substituted for the regular tofu.

Western-style Soups

Some of the Western-style soups we believe go best with tofu include onion, tomato, mushroom, cabbage, squash or pumpkin, bean, split pea, and lentil. The addition of a small amount of miso or shoyu, and perhaps an egg or some grated cheese, to a soup containing tofu often enhances its overall taste and texture.

Cream of Tomato Soup with Tofu   SERVES 3 OR 4

1 tablespoon oil
1 onion, diced
1 tomato, diced
1 cup milk (soy or dairy)
3 tablespoons red miso or 2 tablespoons shoyu
Dash of pepper and/or tabasco sauce
¼ teaspoon oregano or marjoram
12 ounces tofu or 6 ounces deep-fried tofu, diced
2 tablespoons minced parsley

Heat a pot and coat with the oil. Add onion and sauté over medium heat until transparent. Add tomato and sauté for 2 or 3 more minutes. Add the next five ingredients and cook, stirring constantly, for 1 minute. Remove from heat and allow to cool briefly, then transfer to a blender and purée until smooth. Return to heat and bring just to a boil. Add tofu, return to the boil, and remove from heat. Chill for 4 to 5 hours. Serve garnished with parsley.

Creamy Tomato-Rice Soup   SERVES 5 OR 6
with Tofu

1 cup cooked Brown Rice (p. 50)
1¼ cups milk (soy or dairy)
¾ cup water
½ onion, diced
2 large tomatoes, diced
4 teaspoons shoyu or 1 teaspoon salt
Dash of pepper
1 teaspoon natural sugar (optional)
Dash of basil or oregano
¾ cup grated cheese
12 ounces tofu or 6 ounces deep-fried tofu, diced

Combine the first nine ingredients in a blender and purée until smooth. Transfer to a heavy-bottomed pot and bring just to a boil. Cover and simmer for 15 minutes, stirring occasionally. Mix in the cheese and tofu, return just to the boil, and remove from heat. Serve hot or, for a richer, sweeter flavor, chill for 4 to 6 hours.

Gazpacho Guadalahara   SERVES 8
with Diced Tofu

This Latin American favorite is at its best chilled on hot summer afternoons. Many varieties of *gazpacho* are also prepared without cooking.

6 cups tomato juice
1 teaspoon Worcestershire sauce
2 teaspoons lemon juice
½ teaspoon (seasoned) salt or 2 teaspoons shoyu
1 small clove of garlic, crushed; or 2 tablespoons minced mint leaves
1 small bay leaf
4 green onions, sliced into thin rounds
2 tablespoons finely chopped parsley
1 avocado, cut into bite-sized pieces
4 to 6 ounces tofu, cut into small cubes
1 small cucumber, thinly sliced
½ cup thinly sliced celery
¼ cup chopped green pepper

Combine the first six ingredients in a pot and simmer for 15 minutes. Cool to room temperature and add remaining ingredients. Chill for several hours and remove bay leaf before serving.

Thick Pumpkin or Squash Soup   SERVES 4 OR 5
with Tofu

1½ tablespoons oil
1 pound seeded *(kabocha)* pumpkin or squash, cut into ½-inch squares
2 onions, thinly sliced
2 cups water or stock
¼ teaspoon nutmeg or cinnamon
1 clove garlic, minced
4 tablespoons red, barley, or Hatcho miso; or 3 tablespoons shoyu
12 ounces tofu, cut into ½-inch cubes
3 tablespoons parsley, minced
½ cup croutons or dry bread pieces
2 tablespoons ground roasted sesame seeds (p. 38) (optional)

Heat the oil in a casserole or large pot. Add pumpkin, onion, and water, cover, and bring to a boil. Reduce heat to low and simmer for 25 minutes. Stir in nutmeg, garlic, and miso thinned in a little of the hot soup. Add tofu, return just to the boil and remove from heat. For best flavor, allow to cool to room temperature. Serve cold or reheated, topped with parsley, croutons and, if used, the sesame seeds.

Tofu-Onion Soup

One of the most delicious of all Western-style soups with tofu. Simply substitute 12 ounces tofu for the deep-fried tofu in the recipe on page 162.

Japanese-style Soups

Savory miso soups and delicately flavored clear soups almost always feature tofu and are among the most popular of all home and restaurant preparations.

About Miso Soup

In Japan, more tofu is used in miso soup than in any other type of cookery. Of the three most popular ways of serving tofu—chilled, simmering, and in miso soup—only the latter is enjoyed throughout the year and at any of the day's three meals. And since miso soup is an indispensable part of the traditional Japanese breakfast—together with rice and *tsukemono* (salt-pickled vegetables)—tofu makers generally start work long before sunrise to be sure that fresh tofu is ready for early morning shoppers.

In Japan, entire cookbooks are devoted to the preparation of miso soup. By using fresh seasonal vegetables, sprigs and even flowers, the sensitive cook is able to reflect in a dark lacquerware soup bowl the great rhythms of the four seasons. And by combining various types of miso with the proper choice of seasonings and seasonal garnishes, it is quite easy to prepare a unique type of miso soup each day of the year. In fact some Japanese cookbooks contain detailed and elaborate charts suggesting different ways of preparing miso soup each day of the week at both breakfast and dinner throughout the year.

Yet of all the many ingredients used in miso soups, tofu is the most essential and widely used. The most popular forms are small cubes of regular tofu and thin slices of agé, although each of the other types of tofu and yuba are also used on occasion.

For the Japanese, miso soup is much more than just a food; it is a cherished and traditional cultural possession which can inspire poetry and touch the heartstrings while warming the body and soul. For some, miso soup is one of the keystones of good health and family harmony, the hallmark of a good wife who expresses her love and judgment through cooking. A well-known Japanese proverb even goes so far as to say that only when a young woman has mastered the art of making fine miso soup is she ready to become a bride!

Miso Soup with Tofu and Onions   SERVES 2

2 cups dashi (p. 39), stock, or water
1 small onion, thinly sliced
2½ to 3 tablespoons red, barley, or Hatcho miso
4 to 6 ounces tofu, cut into 3/8-inch cubes
Dash of 7-spice red pepper

Combine dashi and onion in a small covered saucepan and bring to a boil. Reduce heat to medium and cook for 4 to 5 minutes. Place miso in a small cup, cream with about ½ cup cooking broth, and add to the soup. (Or, place miso in a small strainer or sieve, partially immerse strainer into broth in saucepan, and rub miso through strainer with the back of a wooden spoon. If desired, add to soup any kernels of grain or soybeans left in strainer.) Stir soup lightly, add tofu cubes and return just to the boil; remove from heat. Season with red pepper and serve immediately, Japanese-style if you wish, in covered lacquerware bowls.

Or use 1 piece of broiled agé cut into thin strips or 6 tofu dumplings (p. 127) instead of the diced tofu.

VARIATION

*Picnic Miso Soup: Combine 3 tablespoons miso with 2 tablespoons bonita flakes in a small bowl. Mix well, then shape into 2 balls. Skewer and roast each ball over a burner until its surface is well browned. Place miso balls, sliced onion, tofu, and seasoning into a picnic container. To serve, divide ingredients among 2 soup bowls, cream the miso in the bowls with a little hot water, then stir in remaining hot water.

Creamy Miso Soup   SERVES 4

1 tablespoon oil
1 onion, thinly sliced
1½ to 2 cups half-moons of eggplant or cauliflowerets
2 tablespoons butter
2 tablespoons (whole-wheat) flour
1 cup milk (soy or dairy)
½ cup water
2 ounces cheese, grated or minced
12 ounces tofu or 5 ounces deep-fried tofu, cut into small rectangles
2 tablespoons light-yellow or red miso
Dash of pepper

Heat the oil in a casserole. Add onions and sauté for 3 minutes, or until lightly browned. Add eggplants and sauté briefly or until all oil is absorbed; turn off heat.

Using the butter, flour, and milk, prepare a white sauce (p. 48). Add the sauce and ½ cup water to the casserole, cover, and simmer over low heat for 5 minutes. Add cheese and tofu, increase heat to medium, and cook for 3 minutes. Stir in miso thinned in a little of the cooking broth, and season with pepper. Stirring constantly, simmer for 1 minute more. Serve hot or cold.

Miso Soup with Tofu, Leeks, and Wakame

SERVES 2

2 cups dashi (p. 39), stock, or water
¼ large leek, or ½ onion, cut into thin rounds
3 to 4 ounces tofu, cut into 3/8-inch cubes
¼ to 1/3 cup fresh or refreshed *wakame* (p. 37), cut into 1-inch lengths
2 tablespoons red or light-yellow miso
Dash of 7-spice red pepper or 1 tablespoon thinly-sliced leeks

Bring dashi to a boil in a saucepan. Add leek or onion and return to the boil. Add tofu and *wakame*, and simmer for 1 minute. Stir in miso creamed with a little of the hot broth and return just to the boil. Serve immediately, garnished with the red pepper or leek slivers.

Serving Tofu in Miso Soups Throughout the Year

Many Japanese cookbooks contain charts suggesting different ways of serving tofu in miso soups with seasonal vegetables and garnishes. The following suggestions are examplary:

*Spring, Sunday dinner: egg tofu, *junsai* (water shield), red miso, *sansho* pepper
*Fall, Tuesday breakfast: tofu, *nameko* mushrooms, Hatcho miso, hot mustard
*Fall, Wednesday dinner: *shimeji* mushrooms, tofu, chrysanthemum leaves, white and red miso, *yuzu* peel
*Winter, Monday morning: tofu, milk, chives or *asatsuki*, light-yellow miso, pepper
*Winter, Friday morning: tofu, bean sprouts, red miso, thinly sliced leeks
*Winter, Friday evening: tofu, salmon roe, sweet white miso, grated Mandarin orange peel
*Winter, Saturday dinner: tofu, oysters, leeks, red miso, *sansho* pepper
*Summer, Tuesday dinner: tofu, onion, egg, barley miso, parsley

OTHER SUGGESTIONS FOR SERVING MISO SOUPS

*Garnishes and Seasonings: In addition to those mentioned above, the following are also used to add the crowning touch: grated gingerroot or its juice; all wild, springtime sprouts, sprigs, and buds; *kinome*, *myoga*, slivered cucumber, ground roasted sesame seeds, minced parsley, *shiso* leaves, buds and seeds, *daikon* leaf tips, *wasabi*, trefoil, powdered green *nori*, crumbled toasted *nori*, butter, and sake.
*Other Common Basic Ingredients: *Daikon*, turnips, pota-
toes, sweet potatoes and taro, burdock root, wild vegetables, cooked soybeans, *konnyaku*, carrots, lotus root, dried or fresh wheat gluten, *mochi*, (*kabocha*) pumpkin and squash, noodles, ginkgo nuts, cottage cheese, and fresh peas and beans.
*For a description of the large-scale preparation of miso soup, combining the preparation of Number 1 and Number 2 Dashi, see page 219.
*Substitute 12 ounces of tofu for 5 ounces of deep-fried tofu or 2 ounces of dried-frozen tofu in miso soup recipes in those sections.

About Clear Soup
(Suimono)

The dewlike freshness and utter simplicity of Japanese clear soups are a subtle delight to the senses. Within the dark hollow of a lacquerware bowl, the chef creates a miniature floating world in which textures, colors, and shapes are as mindfully balanced as flavors. For as the Japanese say, "A man eats with his eyes as well as his mouth." A tiny crescent of *yuzu* or lemon peel, a brilliant green sprig of *kinome*, or as few as two slender white mushrooms and a small cube of tofu can form a still life in the fragrant, steaming broth.

When used in clear soups, tofu may be cut into a variety of attractive shapes: chrysanthemum leaves, circles, half moons, cherry blossoms, triangles, tiny cubes called "hailstones" and larger cubes called "yakko," cylinders (which are then sometimes broiled), maple or ginkgo leaves, or little loops and bows. Some of these shapes are also used in miso soups.

Clear soups are usually served at the beginning of the meal. The ingredients are generally limited to about three, and each must be fresh and attractive. They are used either fresh or parboiled, then carefully arranged in the bottom of a lacquerware bowl. To avoid disturbing the decorative arrangement, the broth is then poured very gently down the sides of the bowl.

Clear Soup with Citrus Fragrance

SERVES 2

1½ cups Clear Broth (p. 40)
6 ounces tofu, drained (p. 96) and cut into 1½-inch cubes
½ leek or 2 scallions, cut into thin rounds
4 slivers of lemon or *yuzu* peel

Bring broth to a boil in a small saucepan. Add tofu and simmer for 2 minutes, until heated through. Remove tofu carefully with a slotted spoon and divide among two soup bowls. Garnish with sliced leeks and lemon peel, then carefully pour in the simmering broth. Serve immediately.

VARIATION

*Clear Soup with Tofu Bow *(Musubi-dofu):* Prepare reshaped firm tofu (p. 98). Cut into long strips the shape of thin French-fried potatoes. Carefully tie each of 4 strips into a simple overhand loop. Add to the broth in place of the tofu cubes.

Egg Flower Soup with Onions and Tofu

SERVES 2

1½ cups Clear Broth (p. 40)
¼ small onion, thinly sliced
1 egg, lightly beaten
3 ounces tofu, cut into 3/8-inch cubes

Bring broth to a boil in a small saucepan. Add onion and simmer for 3 minutes. Now bring broth to a rolling boil and pour in beaten egg while stirring briskly in a circle. Reduce heat to medium, add tofu, and cook for 1 minute more. Serve hot in covered bowls.

Clear Soup with Chrysanthemum Tofu (Kikka-dofu)

SERVES 2

6 ounces tofu, cut into 2 equal pieces
Dash of salt
A 4-inch square of kombu (optional)
1½ cups Clear Broth (p. 40)
24 *nameko* mushrooms or 4 to 6 white mushrooms
2 cakes of dried wheat gluten
4 slivers of *yuzu* or lemon peel

Hold one of the pieces of tofu in the palm of one hand immersed in a bowl of water. Using a sharp knife, cut the large surface of the tofu into ¼-inch squares, cutting half way down through the piece of tofu (fig. 37). Set the cut piece of tofu under water on the bottom of the bowl and repeat with the second piece.

Bring 3 cups water to a boil. Add salt, *kombu*, and water, then carefully add the tofu. Return to the boil and simmer for 30 seconds. Using a slotted spoon or mesh skimmer, transfer tofu to empty soup bowls.

Bring clear soup broth to a boil in a small saucepan, add mushrooms and return just to the boil. Pour broth and mushrooms into bowls containing tofu. Garnish each serving with wheat gluten and *yuzu* peel.

Kenchin-jiru

SERVES 5

This popular dish derives its name from an unusual anecdote. It is said that several centuries ago in the Kamakura Zen temple Kenchin-ji, a young monk carelessly dropped a cake of fresh tofu on the kitchen floor. Since the floor was always kept immaculately clean, the head cook unhesitatingly gathered up the scattered curds and used them in the evening soup. In honor of this spirit of using each thing fully, the tofu was thereafter crushed or broken into small pieces before being added to the soup.

According to another tradition, this soup, with its distinctive sesame flavor, has its origins in Chinese-style *shippoku* cookery. The word *kenchin* derives from the Chinese *kenchen* and means "rolled slivers of food" or "rolled parched food." In one famous version of this dish, the sautéed tofu and vegetables are served rolled in yuba and deep-fried rather than as part of a soup.

1½ tablespoons sesame oil
18 ounces tofu, pressed (p. 96) and broken into small pieces
½ cup shaved burdock root
1 cup half-moons of *daikon*
5 *shiitake* or cloud-ear mushrooms, thinly sliced
1 to 1¼ cups large irregular chunks of sweet potato, yam, or taro
½ cup gingko-leaf pieces of carrot (p. 37)
½ cake of *konnyaku*, broken into small pieces and lightly salted
2¼ cups dashi (p. 39), stock, or water
3½ tablespoons shoyu or 5 tablespoons red miso
¼ teaspoon salt
2 teaspoons sake or *mirin*
Garnishes: 7-spice red pepper, slivered leeks, crumbled *nori*, and/or grated lemon or *yuzu* rind

Heat the oil in a heavy-bottomed saucepan. Add consecutively: tofu, burdock root, *daikon*, mushrooms, sweet potato, carrot, and *konnyaku*, sautéing each over medium heat for about 1 minute. Reduce heat to low, and add broth, shoyu, salt, and sake. Cover pan and simmer for 30 to 40 minutes, or until *daikon* is transparent. For best flavor, allow to stand for 6 to 8 hours, then serve individual portions topped with a sprinkling of the garnishes.

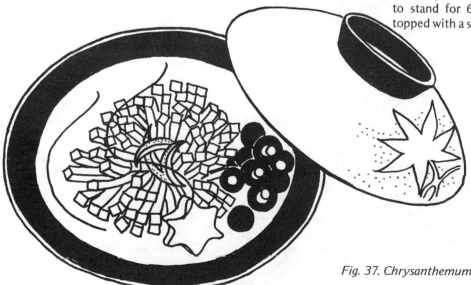

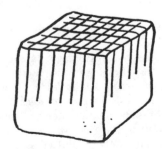

Fig. 37. Chrysanthemum Tofu

TOFU IN SAUCES

Friends or extra guests arriving just before mealtime? The spaghetti or curry sauce will only feed 6 but there will be 12 for dinner? Mash 2 or 3 cakes of fresh tofu, season with shoyu or miso, and stir into the sauce, thereby adding body, flavor, and plenty of protein. Seasoned this way, tofu also makes an excellent and inexpensive replacement for meat in many sauces. Most sauces become even more delicious if reheated or served cold after the flavors are given time to marry. Tofu may also be used with good results in most Basic Sauces (p. 48), Soymilk Sauces (p. 207), and Deep-fried Tofu Sauces (p. 165). The various types of Tofu Mayonnaise, Tofu Tartare Sauce, Creamy Tofu Dressings, and Tofu Sour Cream (pp. 107 to 109) also work well as sauces when served over cooked vegetables.

Quick Tofu-Sesame Sauce   MAKES 1¾ CUPS

12 ounces tofu
¼ cup sesame butter, *tahini*, or ground roasted sesame seeds (p. 38)
1 tablespoon shoyu
½ teaspoon salt
2 tablespoons natural sugar or honey

Combine all ingredients in a blender and purée until smooth. (Or mash ingredients together with a fork.) Serve over cooked vegetables or deep-fried tofu. If desired, substitute nut butters for the sesame.

Tofu Spaghetti Sauce   SERVES 4 TO 6

Regular or deep-fried tofu makes an excellent addition to any spaghetti sauce and may be used to replace meat. Use it in your favorite recipes or try the following:

2 tablespoons oil
1 clove garlic, crushed
2 onions, diced
2 large tomatoes, diced
2 green peppers, diced
3 mushrooms, thinly sliced
½ carrot, grated or diced; or 2 leaves of Chinese cabbage, thinly sliced
6 green beans, thinly sliced (optional)
2 cups water
1 bay leaf
24 ounces tofu, crumbled (p. 98); or 10 ounces thick agé, diced
7 cakes of dried wheat gluten (optional)
½ cup ketchup
3 tablespoons butter
¾ teaspoon salt or 2½ tablespoons shoyu
Dash of pepper
1/3 cup grated or Parmesan cheese

Heat a large heavy pot and coat with the oil. Add garlic and onions and sauté for 3 to 4 minutes. Add the next five ingredients and sauté for 3 to 4 minutes more. Add water, drop in bay leaf, and bring to a boil; cover pot and simmer for 15 minutes. Add the next six ingredients and re-cover; simmer, stirring occasionally, for about 1 hour. Remove from heat and cool to room temperature. Remove bay leaf and serve, either reheated or cold, over spaghetti or buckwheat noodles. Top with cheese.

For variety, season with grated gingerroot, green beefsteak leaves, oregano, or basil.

Tofu-Apple-Onion Curry Sauce   SERVES 3 OR 4

Substitute 18 ounces tofu (pressed; p. 96) for the deep-fried tofu in the recipe on page 166. Sauté the tofu in a little oil until tofu is firm and crumbly; add apples, potato, and water, and proceed as directed. For best flavor, allow sauce to stand for 6 to 8 hours before serving.

TOFU IN BREAKFAST EGG DISHES

One of the easiest and most delicious ways to incorporate tofu into your breakfast menu is by serving it in traditional Western-style egg preparations. Tofu goes well with cheese and all those vegetables which lend variety and zest to egg dishes. The Japanese often season their tofu-egg preparations with shoyu or Sesame Salt (p. 51) and a little sugar.

Butter-fried Tofu with Fried Eggs   SERVES 2

6 ounces tofu, pressed (p. 96)
1 tablespoon butter
2 eggs
Salt and pepper, or shoyu

Cut tofu lengthwise into halves, then crosswise into ¾-inch-thick pieces. Place pieces between cloth towels for several minutes until pieces are firm.

Melt the butter in a large skillet. Add tofu and sauté over medium heat for about 1 minute until golden brown. Turn tofu pieces with a spatula and cook second side. Use spatula to clear a small space at center of pan between the tofu pieces. Break the eggs into this space, cover skillet, and cook until eggs are firm. Season with salt and pepper, or shoyu. Try in place of bacon-and-eggs.

VARIATIONS

*Break the tofu into small pieces and sauté together with your choice of vegetables. Top the eggs with cheese and minced parsley just before covering the skillet.
*Poached Egg on Toast with Butter-fried Tofu: Cut the tofu as above and fry in butter. Cover several pieces of buttered whole-grain toast with the tofu slices, sprinkle lightly with shoyu, and top with poached eggs.

Tofu Sautéed in Butter with Scrambled Eggs

SERVES 2

1 tablespoon butter
6 ounces tofu
2 eggs, lightly beaten
Salt and pepper

Melt the butter in a skillet. Add tofu and mash, then sauté over medium heat until lightly browned. Add eggs and scramble until firm. Season with salt and pepper.

If desired, sauté any of the following together with the tofu: chives, bean or alfalfa sprouts, crushed garlic, mushrooms, scallions or onions, green peppers or lotus root (each diced or thinly sliced). Season with ½ to 1 teaspoon shoyu.

Scrambled Eggs with Tofu and Gingerroot

SERVES 2

3 eggs, lightly beaten
3 tablespoons shoyu
1½ to 2 tablespoons natural sugar
1 tablespoon grated gingerroot
12 ounces tofu

Combine eggs, shoyu, sugar, and gingerroot in a bowl; mix well. Place tofu in a skillet over medium heat and, using a spatula, cut tofu into small pieces. Stirring constantly, cook tofu for about 2 minutes until it is no longer moist. Pour in egg-shoyu mixture and scramble until firm. Serve hot or cold.

Scrambled Eggs with Tofu and Mushrooms

SERVES 4

12 ounces tofu, pressed (p. 96) and mashed
3 eggs, lightly beaten
2 tablespoons butter
1 cup diced fresh mushrooms
¼ teaspoon salt
Dash of pepper

Combine tofu and eggs in a bowl; mix well. Melt the butter in a skillet. Add mushrooms and sauté for several minutes until fragrant and tender. Pour in tofu-egg mixture and scramble until firm. Season with salt and pepper. Serve hot or cold.

Japanese-style Tofu, Eggs & Onions (Tamago-toji)

SERVES 2

1 tablespoon oil
1 small onion, thinly sliced
1 egg, lightly beaten
6 ounces tofu, thinly sliced
2 teaspoons shoyu
2 teaspoons natural sugar

Heat the oil in a skillet. Add onion and sauté for 3 to 4 minutes, or until transparent. Stir in remaining ingredients, cover, and cook for 2 or 3 minutes until egg is firm.

If desired, serve seasoned with sansho pepper or topped with grated cheese. Or serve as a topping for buckwheat noodles and garnish with crumbled, toasted nori (p. 38).

Tofu Poached Egg

SERVES 1

6 to 8 ounces tofu, pressed (p. 96) or well-drained

½ teaspoon shoyu or 1 teaspoon red miso
½ teaspoon lemon juice
1 egg

Scoop a deep hollow out of the upper surface of the tofu. Pour shoyu and lemon juice, then break the egg into this hollow.

Bring 1 inch of water to a boil over high heat in a saucepan. Carefully slide in tofu and return to the boil (fig. 38). Reduce heat to low, cover, and simmer for 3 minutes, or until egg is just firm. Scoop out tofu with a large slotted spoon and serve hot.

To distribute shoyu-lemon seasoning more evenly, mix tofu and egg together just before serving.

Fig. 38. Tofu Poached Egg

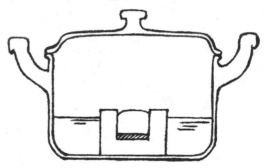

Tofu-Egg Omelet with Mushrooms

SERVES 2 OR 3

6 ounces tofu, pressed (p. 96) and diced
3 eggs, lightly beaten
1 tablespoon shoyu
½ teaspoon natural sugar
2 tablespoons ground roasted sesame seeds (p. 38), sesame butter, or tahini
1 tablespoon butter or oil
3 large fresh mushrooms, cut into thin strips
2 leeks or onions, cut into thin rounds

Combine the first five ingredients in a large bowl; mix well. Melt the butter in a skillet. Add leeks and mushrooms, and sauté for 2 or 3 minutes until fragrant and tender. Pour in tofu-egg mixture and cook over low heat. When omelet has an even consistency, fold and serve.

If desired, fill with grated cheese, cream cheese, or tomato wedges and minced parsley. Japanese chefs often cover omelets with several sheets of nori before rolling, then season the omelets with sansho pepper, powdered green nori, or Worcestershire sauce.

Tofu-Eggs a là Caracas

SERVES 3

2 tablespoons butter
8 ounces tofu, diced
2 tomatoes, minced or puréed
½ teaspoon salt or 1½ teaspoons shoyu
1 tablespoon minced onion
3 eggs, lightly beaten
¼ cup grated cheese
Dash of cinnamon

Melt the butter in a skillet. Add the next four ingredients, cover, and simmer over low heat for 20 to 30 minutes, or until tomatoes form a thick sauce. Add eggs, cheese, and cinnamon and cook, stirring constantly, for 2 or 3 minutes until eggs develop a creamy consistency. Serve hot or cold.

Chinese-style Egg Tofu
(Nanjen-dofu or Iritsuke-dofu)

SERVES 2 OR 3

1 tablespoon oil
12 ounces tofu, drained (p. 96) and cut crosswise into ¾-inch-thick pieces
2 eggs, lightly beaten
Sauce:
    ½ cup water
    1 tablespoon soy sauce
    ¼ teaspoon salt
    ¼ teaspoon sesame oil
    Dash of (7-spice) red pepper
    1 teaspoon cornstarch or arrowroot
¼ cup slivered leeks, scallions, or onions

Heat the oil in a wok or skillet. Add tofu and stir-fry for 2 or 3 minutes, being careful not to break individual pieces. Add eggs and stir-fry for 30 to 60 seconds more. Add the sauce and cook, stirring constantly, until thickened. Remove from heat and stir in leeks. Serve hot.

Okonomi-yaki *(Tofu-Egg Pancakes)*

SERVES 4

In Japan's many tiny restaurants specializing in O-konomi-yaki, each guest cooks his own pancakes on a small tabletop grill, then chooses seasonings and garnishes from the wide assortment available.

2/3 cup whole-wheat flour
2/3 cup milk (soy or dairy) or water
3 eggs
¼ teaspoon salt or 1 teaspoon shoyu
12 ounces tofu, pressed (p. 96)
½ carrot, grated
¼ onion, diced
3 mushrooms, thinly sliced
2 tablespoons corn kernels, parboiled (p. 37)
2 tablespoons green peas, parboiled
1 cup shredded cabbage
4 teaspoons oil
Worcestershire sauce, shoyu, or any Miso Topping (p. 41)
Powdered green *nori* or grated cheese

Combine the first four ingredients and mix well to make a batter. Stir in the tofu and vegetables. Heat 1 teaspoon oil in a large skillet. Spoon in one-fourth of the batter to form several pancakes and cook over low heat on both sides until golden brown. Repeat with remaining batter. Serve piping hot topped with a sprinkling of Worcestershire sauce and *nori*.

TOFU BAKED

Tofu may be used with excellent results in the baked dishes of countries throughout the world. It goes particularly well with all dairy products and with grains. The Japanese often sauté and season their vegetables with a little shoyu or miso (and sugar) before adding them to tofu baked dishes in order to give a richer and more distinctive flavor. Always use pressed tofu or doufu in casseroles where a firm or slightly dry consistency is desired. Experiment freely using tofu in your favorite recipes for oven cookery. Since baking—which uses a relatively large amount of fuel or energy—has never been a traditional Japanese way of cooking foods, most of the following recipes are typically Western. For baked desserts, see page 150.

Tofu Italian Meatballs

SERVES 2 OR 3

A remarkably good facsimile of its namesake, this preparation is one of the many creative and delicious tofu recipes served as part of the vegetarian cuisine at Tokyo's Seventh-day Adventist Hospital.

12 ounces tofu, well pressed (p. 96) or squeezed
¼ cup chopped walnut meats
½ onion, minced
¼ to 1/3 cup bread crumbs
1 egg, lightly beaten
3 tablespoons minced parsley
Dash of pepper
4 teaspoons red miso or ½ teaspoon salt
Oil for deep-frying
¼ cup tomato juice or tomato soup
¼ cup ketchup
Dash of oregano
3 tablespoons Parmesan or grated cheese

Combine the first seven ingredients and 1 tablespoon miso. Mix well and shape into 1½-inch balls. Heat oil to 350° in a wok, skillet, or deep-fryer. Drop in balls and deep-fry until cooked through and well browned (p. 130). Drain balls, then arrange in a loaf pan. Preheat oven to 350°. Combine remaining 1 teaspoon miso with tomato juice and ketchup, mixing to form a sauce, and pour over tofu balls. Top with a sprinkling of cheese and bake for 15 minutes, or until nicely browned. For best flavor, allow to stand for 6 to 8 hours. Serve hot or cold, as is or as a topping for spaghetti. Also delicious in Tofu Spaghetti Sauce (p. 121).

For variety, bake topped with Mushroom Sauce (p. 48) or Soymilk Cheese Sauce (p. 207).

Tofu & Brown Rice Casserole   SERVES 4

4½ teaspoons oil
1½ tablespoons butter
1½ onions, thinly sliced
1 cup cooked Brown Rice (p. 50)
12 ounces tofu, pressed (p. 96); or 9 ounces doufu
1 teaspoon salt
Dash of pepper
1 cup milk (soy or dairy)
¼ to ½ cup bread crumbs
2 ounces cheese, grated

Preheat oven to 350°. Heat a large skillet or wok and coat with 2 teaspoons oil and the butter. Add onion and sauté until lightly browned. Add brown rice, then tofu, sautéing each for 2 minutes. Season with salt and pepper. Place tofu-onion mixture in a casserole or bread pan coated with remaining oil. Pour in the milk, then sprinkle with bread crumbs and cheese. Bake for about 15 to 20 minutes, or until cheese is nicely browned.

Mushroom & Onion Casserole with Tofu   SERVES 3

2 onions, diced
8 mushrooms, thinly sliced
1 tomato, cut into thin wedges
1 teaspoon oil
1 pint yogurt
2 ounces dried onion soup or mushroom soup
24 ounces tofu, cut into ½-inch cubes
2 tablespoons roasted sesame seeds

Preheat oven to 350°. Combine the first three ingredients in a bowl; mix lightly. Layer one-half of mixture at the bottom of a lightly oiled casserole. Combine yogurt and dried onion soup in a bowl, mixing well. Pour one-fourth of yogurt-soup mixture over vegetables in casserole, and top with a layer of one-half of the tofu and 1 tablespoon sesame seeds. Then pour another one-fourth of the yogurt mixture over the tofu. Use the remaining ingredients to form an identical series of layers. Bake for 30 minutes.

Tofu-Cheese Soufflé   SERVES 4

3 slices of whole-wheat bread
2 tablespoons butter
6 ounces tofu, cut into ½-inch-thick slices
6 ounces (sharp cheddar) cheese, grated
1 tablespoon chopped onion or ¼ teaspoon onion powder
1¼ cups milk (soy or dairy)
2 eggs, lightly beaten
½ teaspoon salt or 2 tablespoons red miso
Dash of pepper

Butter the bread and tear each slice into 4 or 5 pieces. Coat a casserole lightly with butter, then layer bread, tofu, cheese, and onion, repeating the layers until all ingredients are used. Combine milk, eggs, salt or miso, and pepper, and pour into the casserole; allow to stand for 1 to 2 hours. Bake casserole in a pan of water for 45 minutes in a preheated 350° oven.

Mushroom & Tofu Soufflé   SERVES 6

2 ounces butter
1 pound fresh mushrooms
¼ cup diced onions
½ teaspoon salt and dash of pepper
½ cup (tofu) mayonnaise (p. 107)
6 slices of (whole wheat) bread, buttered and broken into
      ½-inch squares
8 ounces tofu, cut into ½-inch cubes
2 eggs, lightly beaten
1½ cups milk (soy or dairy)
2 cups white sauce (p. 48)

Melt butter in a skillet. Add mushrooms and sauté until tender. Add onions and sauté for 1 minute more, then remove from heat. Add salt, pepper, and mayonnaise; mix well.

In a lightly buttered casserole, layer the bread, tofu, and mushrooms, repeating until all ingredients are used. Combine eggs and milk and pour into the casserole. Allow to stand for at least 2 hours, preferably overnight. Pour white sauce evenly over casserole, then bake for 1 hour in a preheated 325° oven.

Tofu Loaf with Onions and Cheese   SERVES 4

4 tablespoons butter
2 tablespoons whole-wheat flour
1 cup milk (soy or dairy)
¾ teaspoon salt
1 onion, minced
4 ounces cheese, diced
12 ounces tofu, pressed (p. 96) and mashed
¼ cup bread or cracker crumbs

Melt 2 tablespoons butter in a skillet. Add flour and sauté until fragrant and lightly browned. Gradually add 1½ cups milk, stirring constantly, to form a smooth brown sauce. Season with the salt, then simmer until sauce is thick. Stir in onion, cheese, and tofu and remove from heat.

Coat a pie tin with 1 tablespoon butter and fill with tofu-sauce mixture. Sprinkle on bread crumbs and dot with remaining 1 tablespoon butter. Bake in a 350° oven for about 15 minutes, or until set.

Delectable Tofu & Onion Gratin   SERVES 4 OR 5

18 ounces tofu, diced
3½ cups Onion Sauce (p. 48)
2 cups dry bread pieces or croutons
2 teaspoon shoyu or 1 tablespoon red miso, dissolved in ½
      cup water
¼ cup Parmesan or grated cheese

Combine the first four ingredients, mixing well, and pour into an oiled or buttered casserole or large bread pan; allow to stand for 1 to 2 hours. Preheat oven to 350°. Sprinkle casserole with cheese and bake for 20 to 30 minutes, or until nicely browned. Serve hot or cold.

For variety, press 4 to 6 hard-boiled egg halves into the tofu-onion mixture. Top with cheese and bread crumbs, and dot with butter before baking.

Tofu-Cheese Patties

MAKES 6

2 tablespoons oil
½ onion, minced
1 green pepper, diced
12 ounces tofu, pressed (p. 96)
1/3 cup mashed baked potatoes
½ cup bread crumbs
2 ounces cheese, grated or diced
½ teaspoon salt
Dash of pepper

Preheat oven to 350°. Heat a small skillet or wok and coat with 1 tablespoon oil. Add onions and peppers and sauté until onions are lightly browned. Combine tofu, potatoes, bread crumbs, cheese, and onion-green pepper mixture in a mixing bowl. Season with salt and pepper, mash together with a fork, and shape into 6 patties. Arrange patties on a baking tin lightly oiled with remaining oil, and bake for 40 minutes or until nicely browned. Serve topped with ketchup, Ketchup-Worcestershire Sauce (p. 49), or Onion Sauce (p. 48).

Savory Tofu-Pumpkin Delight

SERVES 4

2 tablespoons oil
½ onion, thinly sliced
3 cups boiled and mashed *kabocha* or pumpkin
12 ounces tofu, pressed (p. 96) and diced
1 egg, lightly beaten
3 tablespoons shoyu
3 tablespoons natural sugar
Dash of salt
Dash of cinnamon or *sansho* pepper (optional)

Preheat oven to 350°. Heat a large skillet or wok and coat with 1 tablespoon oil. Sauté onion until lightly browned, then turn off heat. Add pumpkin, tofu, egg, shoyu, sugar, and salt, mixing well. Coat a pie tin with 1 tablespoon oil and spoon in the tofu mixture; sprinkle with cinnamon or *sansho*. Bake for about 15 minutes, or until set.

Tofu & Pumpkin Patties

MAKES 8

2 cups boiled and mashed *kabocha* or pumpkin
24 ounces tofu, pressed (p. 96) and mashed
1 tablespoon salt
Dash of pepper
1 teaspoon oil
1/3 cup raisins
2 ounces cheese, grated or diced
2 tablespoons butter

Preheat oven to 350°. Combine pumpkin and tofu in a large bowl, mixing well, and season with salt and pepper. Shape the mixture into 4-inch patties and place on a baking pan coated with the oil. Dot the top of each pattie with raisins, cheese and butter. Bake for 20 to 30 minutes, or until lightly browned. Or bake in a pie shell as for pumpkin pie.

Buckwheat Noodle Gratin with Tofu

SERVES 5

3 tablespoons oil
1 onion, cut into thin wedges
½ carrot, cut into thin half moons
6 ounces tofu, pressed (p. 96) and mashed
1¼ teaspoons salt
2 tablespoons whole-wheat flour
½ cup milk (soy or dairy) or water
10 ounces *(soba)* buckwheat noodles, cooked (p. 50)
¼ cup minced parsley
5 slivers of *yuzu* or lemon peel

Preheat oven to 350°. Heat a skillet and coat with 1 tablespoon oil. Add the onion and sauté until transparent. Add the carrot and tofu and sauté for 4 to 5 minutes more. Transfer to a large bowl and season with ½ teaspoon salt.

Reheat skillet and coat with 1 tablespoon oil. Add flour and sauté until fragrant and lightly browned. Gradually add the milk, stirring constantly, to form a smooth brown sauce. Simmer until sauce is thick, then season with ¾ teaspoon salt.

Place noodles in a lightly oiled gratin dish. Add sautéed vegetable-tofu mixture, then pour on the sauce. Sprinkle with 1½ teaspoons oil and bake for about 20 minutes, or until slightly crisp and nicely browned. Serve hot or cold, topped with parsley and garnished with slivered *yuzu*.

Or, sauté ¼ cup yuba with the vegetables, and add 1 tablespoon sesame butter to the sauce just after stirring in the milk. Substitute rice flour noodles for buckwheat, and top with grated or Parmesan cheese before baking.

Tofu-Stuffed Green Peppers

SERVES 4

2 tablespoons oil
1 onion, minced
½ cup cooked Brown Rice (p. 50) or mashed potatoes
12 ounces tofu, pressed (p. 96); or 9 ounces doufu
2 tablespoons ketchup
½ teaspoon salt
4 large green peppers, cut vertically into halves and seeded

Preheat oven to 350°. Heat the oil in a skillet or wok and sauté onion until nicely browned. Add rice and sauté for 1 minute more. Add tofu, mash it in the pan, and sauté for about 2 more minutes; season with ketchup and salt. Use the mixture as a stuffing for the green peppers. Coat the outside of each pepper lightly with oil, arrange stuffed peppers on a lightly oiled pan, and bake for 20 minutes.

Baked Potatoes with Tofu Stuffing

SERVES 6 TO 8

4 potatoes, baked and cut lengthwise into halves
12 ounces tofu, pressed (p. 96); or 9 ounces doufu
2 ounces cheese, grated or diced
½ teaspoon salt
Dash of pepper
1½ tablespoons butter
1 onion, minced
1 tablespoon oil

Preheat oven to 350°. Scoop potato out of shells, then spoon 1 cup of potato into a mixing bowl and reserve the remainder. Mash tofu and cheese with potato in bowl; season with salt and pepper. Melt butter in a skillet and sauté onions until nicely browned. Mix onions into potato-tofu mixture, then divide the mixture among the potato shells. Coat a cookie tin with the oil and bake stuffed potatoes on tin for about 30 minutes, or until nicely browned. Delicious served topped with butter (or sour cream) and minced chives (or parsley).

Additional Suggestions for Serving Tofu in Baked Dishes

*Tofu makes a very nutritious addition to vegetable pies and quiches, tamale casseroles, and ravioli dishes. Use thin strips of pressed tofu as one of the ingredients in pizza toppings. In *enchiladas*, *tostadas*, *tacos*, or *quesarillas*, well-pressed, diced tofu may be used with or in place of beans, mixed with shredded lettuce, tomatoes, cheese, or other fillings.
*Kenchin-yaki: Sauté ¼ cup each slivered mushrooms, carrot, onion, and 3 tablespoons green peas. Combine with 12 ounces pressed tofu, 1 egg, 1½ tablespoons shoyu, and 2 teaspoons each sake and sugar. Mix well and bake in a loaf pan for 15 to 20 minutes.

TOFU SAUTÉED, STIR-FRIED, OR TOPPED WITH SAUCES

There are many ways of using tofu with cooked vegetables. Mastery of the Chinese technique for stir-frying will add a new dimension to your cooking repertoire. Sautéing with oil previously used for deep-frying (p. 130) will add flavor and savory aroma to even the simplest preparations.

Butter-fried Tofu Teriyaki

SERVES 2

1/3 cup Teriyaki Sauce (p. 48)
12 ounces tofu, pressed (p. 96) and cut into 12 small rectangles about ½ inch thick
1½ tablespoons butter

Place sauce and tofu in a shallow pan. Marinate for 1 hour, turning tofu rectangles over after 30 minutes. Melt the butter in a skillet. Add tofu and fry for 2 to 3 minutes on each side until golden brown. Serve any remaining marinade as a dipping sauce.

Tofu with Onion Sauce and Cheese

SERVES 4

3 tablespoons oil
6 onions, thinly sliced
5 tablespoons shoyu
24 ounces tofu, pressed (p. 96) and cut into 1-inch cubes
2½ teaspoons natural sugar (optional)
1 tablespoon sake or white wine
1 egg, lightly beaten
2 ounces cheese, thinly sliced
4 slices of whole-wheat toast (optional)

Using the oil, onions, and 3 tablespoons shoyu, prepare an Onion Sauce (p. 48). Add tofu cubes, sugar, sake, and the remaining 2 tablespoons shoyu, and simmer over low heat for 10 to 15 minutes. Turn off heat, then pour egg over surface of sauce; top with a layer of cheese. Cover and allow to stand until cheese melts. Serve as is or over toast.

Fried Tofu Patties with Eggs and Vegetables

MAKES 8

24 ounces tofu, squeezed (p. 97)
Thin tips and leaves of 1 celery stalk, minced
1 small onion, minced
¼ cup green peas or thinly sliced green peppers or leeks (optional)
4 eggs, lightly beaten
2 tablespoons ground roasted sesame seeds (p. 38), sesame butter or *tahini*
½ teaspoon salt
1 tablespoon shoyu
4 teaspoons oil
½ cup ketchup or Ketchup-Worcestershire (p. 49); or 4 teaspoons shoyu

In a large mixing bowl, combine the first eight ingredients; mix well to form a batter. Heat a skillet and coat with ½ teaspoon oil. Spoon about one-eighth of the batter into the pan and press lightly with a spatula to form a patty about 3/8 inch thick. Fry until nicely browned, then flip with the spatula and press again until patty is about ¼ inch thick. Fry until second side is golden brown. Repeat with remaining oil and batter until all are used. Serve patties hot or cold, topped with ketchup.

VARIATIONS

*Egg Patties with Oatmeal: Use 20 ounces tofu, ¾ cup quick-cooking oatmeal, ½ cup minced green onion, 2 eggs, ½ cup shredded carrot, and ½ cup diced green pepper. Use the batter to make ½-inch-thick patties and fry in butter for about 2 minutes on each side. Top with a sprinkling of shoyu, or pass sour cream or yogurt to spoon on top.
*Tofu-Yam Patties with Sweet Simmered Miso: Mix 12 ounces well-pressed tofu (p. 96) with ¼ cup grated glutinous yam and ¼ teaspoon salt. Shape into thin patties and fry in oil until golden brown. Serve topped with Sweet Simmered Miso (p. 41) and seasoned with *sansho* papper. Or serve topped with melted butter.

Tofu Burgers with Mushroom Sauce   SERVES 3

3 tablespoons oil
1 small onion, minced
24 ounces tofu, crumbled (p. 98) and allowed to cool
3 eggs, lightly beaten
½ cup bread crumbs or bread crumb flakes
¾ teaspoon salt
Dash of pepper
Mushroom Sauce (p. 48) or ketchup

Heat a skillet and coat with 1 tablespoon oil. Add onion and sauté for 3 minutes, then allow to cool. Combine onion with tofu, eggs, bread crumbs, salt, and pepper in a large bowl, and use the mixture to make 8 patties. Heat the skillet and re-coat with 1 tablespoon oil. Add 4 patties, cover, and cook over low heat for about 5 minutes on each side. Repeat with remaining 4 patties. Serve hot or cold, topped with the sauce.

Tofu Dumplings with Mushroom Sauce   SERVES 3 OR 4

24 ounces tofu, squeezed (p. 97)
1 egg, lightly beaten
1 tablespoon cornstarch or arrowroot
½ teaspoon salt or 3 tablespoons red, barley, or Hatcho miso
1 clove garlic, crushed
3 tablespoons parboiled minced vegetables (green peas, mushrooms, etc.)
¼ cup ground roasted sesame seeds (p. 38) (optional)
Mushroom (p. 48), Spaghetti (p. 121), or Sweet & Sour Sauce (p. 49)

Combine the first six ingredients, mixing well, and shape into 1-inch balls. Bring 1 quart water to a boil over high heat in a large pot. Drop in the balls and return to the boil. Reduce heat to medium and cook until dumplings float to surface. Scoop out dumplings with a slotted spoon, drain, and allow to cool briefly.

Prepare the sauce of your choice, adding balls about 10 minutes before sauce has finished cooking. For best flavor, allow to cool for 4 to 6 hours, then reheat or serve cold.

This dish also makes an excellent topping for spaghetti, noodles, or brown rice. Try using the dumplings in your favorite soups or in place of tofu in any of the soup recipes in this book. Or use in Oden (p. 175) or *nabe* dishes.

Butter-fried Tofu   SERVES 4

24 ounces tofu, pressed (p. 96)
3 to 4 tablespoons butter
½ onion, sliced very thin, rinsed and pressed (p. 37)
1 tablespoon minced parsley
2 ounces cheese (grated or Parmesan)
1 tablespoon slivered lemon peel
Dash of salt

Cut tofu lengthwise into halves, then crosswise into ½-inch-thick pieces. Melt the butter in a skillet. Add the tofu and fry on both sides until golden brown. Arrange pressed onions, parsley, cheese, and lemon peel in separate condiment dishes. Serve tofu hot, sprinkled with your choice of condiments and a little salt.

For variety, serve with any of the shoyu dipping sauces and garnishes used with Chilled Tofu (p. 105), or top with Sesame Miso (p. 42).

Chinese-style Bean Sauce with Tofu   SERVES 3

Although this popular type of preparation is called a "sauce," it is generally served as an entrèe in its own right.

2 tablespoons oil
1 teaspoon grated gingerroot
1 teaspoon crushed or minced garlic
2 small *(togarashi)* red peppers, minced
5 mushrooms, thinly sliced
3 green onions, whites thinly sliced and greens cut into 2-inch lengths
16 ounces tofu, pressed (p. 96) and cut into ½-inch cubes; or 12 ounces doufu
2 tablespoons red miso creamed with ½ cup water
1 tablespoon soy sauce
1 tablespoon honey
1 tablespoon cashew or sesame butter
½ teaspoon vinegar
1 teaspoon arrowroot or cornstarch, dissolved in 2 tablespoons water

Heat the oil in a wok or skillet. Add gingerroot, garlic, and red peppers, and sauté for 2 or 3 minutes. Add mushrooms and onion whites, and sauté for 2 or 3 minutes more. Add onion greens and tofu cubes and sauté for 1 minute. Combine miso, soy sauce, honey, cashew butter, and vinegar; mix well. Stir into tofu-mushroom mixture and simmer for 1 minute. Stir in dissolved arrowroot and simmer for about 30 seconds more, or until thick.

Tofu Sautéed with Bean Sprouts *(Okinawa-style)*   SERVES 4 TO 6

1¼ tablespoons oil
24 ounces tofu, well pressed (p. 96) and broken into ¾-inch pieces
8 to 10 ounces bean sprouts
3 to 4 scallions, cut into 2-inch lengths
1 tablespoon sake or white wine
1¼ teaspoons salt
1 teaspoon shoyu

Heat a wok or skillet and coat with the oil. Add tofu and stir-fry over high heat until golden brown. Add bean sprouts and scallions and stir-fry for about 2 minutes more, or until scallions are tender. Mix in sake, salt, and shoyu, and cook for 30 seconds more. Serve steaming hot.

If desired, add slivered *daikon*, Chinese cabbage, leeks, onions, or *hijiki* to the ingredients listed above.

Sautéed Tofu with Lotus Root & Carrot

SERVES 4

1½ tablespoons oil
1 small lotus root, diced
1 small carrot, diced
12 ounces tofu, pressed (p. 96) and diced
2 tablespoons shoyu
1½ tablespoons natural sugar

Heat a skillet or wok and coat with the oil. Sauté the lotus root and carrot over low heat for 2 or 3 minutes. Add enough water to cover the vegetables, cover pan, and simmer for 10 to 15 minutes, or until soft. Add tofu, shoyu, and sugar, mixing well. Re-cover pan and simmer for 5 minutes more.

Chinese-style Tofu Sauté

SERVES 2 OR 3

2 tablespoons oil (up to one-half of which may be sesame oil)
½ carrot, cut into half moons
3 small green peppers, thinly sliced
1 small onion, cut into very thin wedges
12 ounces tofu, pressed (p. 96); or 9 ounces doufu
2 tablespoons soy sauce
3 tablespoons natural sugar
1 tablespoon vinegar
1½ tablespoons arrowroot or cornstarch, dissolved in ¼ cup water

Heat the oil in a wok or skillet. Add consecutively: carrot, green peppers, onion, and tofu, sautéing each for about 2 minutes, or until just tender. Add soy sauce, sugar, and vinegar, and simmer for 3 minutes more. Stir in dissolved arrowroot and cook for 30 seconds more, or until thick.

Iridofu *(Crumbly Scrambled Tofu)*

SERVES 3 OR 4

One of Japan's most popular tofu dishes, *Iridofu* has a light, dry texture and is remarkably similar to Western-style scrambled eggs in both flavor and appearance. This dish may be prepared with or without eggs, sweetened or unsweetened, and with or without the addition of any of the diced or slivered vegetables that are generally used in scrambled eggs.

1 tablespoon oil
1 small onion, diced
1 small carrot, diced
24 ounces tofu, crumbled into very small pieces (p. 98)
2 tablespoons ground roasted sesame seeds (p. 38) (optional)
½ teaspoon salt
2 teaspoons shoyu
Dash of pepper

Heat a skillet or wok and coat with the oil. Add onion and carrot and sauté for 3 to 4 minutes until onion is lightly browned. Add crumbled tofu and the remaining ingredients. Stirring constantly, sauté over medium-low heat for about 5 minutes, or until tofu is light, dry, and almost fluffy. Serve hot or cold.

VARIATIONS

*Add ¼ cup of any of the following with the tofu: parboiled green peas, diced (*shiitake* or cloud-ear) mushrooms, diced bamboo shoots, dried yuba flakes. Or add 1 to 2 pieces of diced agé or 1 teaspoon grated gingerroot. Try sautéing the vegetables in sesame oil.
*Add 1 or 2 eggs, 2 to 3 tablespoons natural sugar, and 1 tablespoon sake. Use only 2 tablespoons shoyu and a dash of salt, adding these together with the tofu. Add the lightly beaten egg after tofu has been sautéed for about 2 minutes.

Mabo-dofu
(Chinese-style Tofu with Red Pepper Sauce)

SERVES 2

The most popular Chinese-style tofu dish in Japan, *Mabo-dofu* usually contains a small amount of ground beef. It is representative of the many Chinese tofu dishes sautéed with pork, shrimp, chicken, or beef.

1 tablespoon corn or soy oil
1½ teaspoons sesame oil
1 clove garlic, crushed
¼ cup minced leeks, scallions, or onions
½ teaspoon minced red peppers
4 mushrooms, diced
½ cup water, stock, or dashi (p. 39)
1½ teaspoons sake
2½ teaspoons soy sauce
½ teaspoon salt
Dash of *sansho* or 7-spice red pepper
1½ teaspoons ketchup
24 ounces tofu or kinugoshi, cut into pieces 1¼ inches square by ½ inch thick
2 teaspoons cornstarch, dissolved in 2 tablespoons water
1 tablespoon minced leek or scallion greens

Heat a wok or skillet and coat with both types of oil. Add the garlic, leeks, and red peppers, and stir-fry over high heat for 15 seconds. Reduce heat to medium, add mushrooms, and sauté for 1 minute. Add water and next five ingredients, bring to a boil, and cook for 30 seconds. Add tofu and return to the boil. Stir in dissolved cornstarch and simmer until thick. Serve hot, garnished with the greens.

Chinese-style Oyster Sauce & Tofu
(Hao-yu Doufu)
SERVES 1 OR 2

3½ tablespoons oil
3 tablespoons leeks, cut into ½-inch lengths
2 tablespoons gingerroot, cut into ½- by ½- by 1/8-inch pieces
½ cup mushrooms, thinly sliced through the caps
¼ cup water
12 counces tofu or 9 ounces doufu, cut into 1½- by ½-inch pieces
¼ cup green peas
3 tablespoons sake
3 tablespoons oyster sauce (available at Chinese food markets)
2 tablespoons soy sauce
½ teaspoon salt
2 tablespoons cornstarch, dissolved in 3 tablespoons water

Heat the oil in a wok over high heat. Add the leeks and gingerroot and stir-fry for 30 seconds. Add the mushrooms and stir-fry for 30 seconds more. Add the next four ingredients and cook for 1 minute, stirring occasionally. Add the oyster sauce and cook for 1 minute. Add the soy sauce and salt and cook for 1 minute more. Mix in the dissolved cornstarch and cook for about 2 more minutes, lifting the wok occasionally and swishing its contents around the hot sides to aid evaporation of the cooking liquids. Serve hot on a large oval plate or platter.

Chinese-style Sautéed Firm Tofu
SERVES 4

24 ounces tofu, reshaped (p. 98)
2 tablespoons oil
½ teaspoon salt
1 small onion, thinly sliced
6 mushrooms or 1 large cooked bamboo shoot, thinly sliced
1 small carrot, cut into matchsticks
2 green peppers, cut into thin strips
1 tablespoon sake or white wine
1½ tablespoons soy sauce
1 teaspoon grated gingerroot
1 tablespoon natural sugar
1 tablespoon water
1 teaspoon cornstarch, dissolved in 3 tablespoons water

Cut tofu crosswise into pieces the shape of French-fried potatoes. Heat a wok or skillet, coat with the oil and sprinkle on the salt. Add onion, then the mushrooms, stir-frying each over high heat for about 30 seconds. Reduce heat to medium-low and add carrot, green pepper, and tofu, in that order, sautéing each for about 1 minute. Reduce heat to low and add sake, soy sauce, gingerroot, sugar, and water; simmer for 3 to 4 minutes. Stir in dissolved cornstarch and simmer for 30 seconds more.

For extra tang, add 2 teaspoons vinegar together with the sake.

Fanchie-dofu
(Chinese-style Tofu & Tomatoes)
SERVES 4

24 ounces tofu
5 tablespoons oil
1 teaspoon salt
2 tomatoes, each cut into 8 wedges
1 clove of garlic, crushed or minced
1 teaspoon sake or rice wine
3 tablespoons stock or water
½ leek or onion, diced
1 tablespoon cornstarch or arrowroot, dissolved in 3 tablespoons water
1 cup green soybeans or green peas, parboiled (p. 37)

Cut tofu lengthwise into halves, then crosswise into ½-inch-thick pieces. In a small saucepan bring 3 cups water to a boil. Drop in the tofu and return to the boil, then quickly empty tofu into a colander to drain.

Heat a wok or skillet and coat with 4 tablespoons oil and the salt. Add tomatoes and sauté until soft. Add tofu, garlic, and sake and sauté for 2 or 3 minutes. Add stock (or water) and leek, reduce heat and simmer for 4 to 5 minutes. Stir in dissolved cornstarch and remaining 1 tablespoon oil and simmer for 1 minute more until thick. Add green soybeans just before serving.

Braised Tofu
SERVES 4

¼ cup flour
2 eggs, lightly beaten
1½ teaspoons salt
9 tablespoons oil
24 ounces tofu, pressed (p. 96) and cut crosswise into 8 pieces; or 18 ounces doufu
2 tablespoons minced leeks
1½ cups dashi (p. 39), stock, or water
2 teaspoons shoyu
1½ tablespoons sake, mirin, or white wine
1½ teaspoons cornstarch, dissolved in 3 tablespoons water

Combine flour, eggs, and salt in a bowl, mixing lightly to form a batter. Heat 6 tablespoons oil in a skillet. Use the batter to coat each piece of tofu, then fry on both sides until golden brown. Drain and set aside, reserving excess oil.

Heat remaining 3 tablespoons oil in a skillet. Add leeks and brown lightly. Add fried tofu pieces, dashi, shoyu, and sake, mixing gently. Stir in dissolved cornstarch and simmer for about 30 seconds more, or until thick. Serve immediately.

Crispy Fried Tofu

SERVES 2

12 ounces tofu, well-pressed (p. 96); or 9 ounces doufu
1 teaspoon salt
5 tablespoons (whole-wheat) flour
5 tablespoons oil
2 tablespoons shoyu

Cut tofu lengthwise into halves, then crosswise into thirds. Pat each piece lightly with a cloth towel to remove surface moisture, then sprinkle with salt and roll in flour. Heat the oil in a skillet until it is quite hot but does not smoke. Add tofu and fry on both sides until golden brown and fairly crisp. Drain on absorbent paper and serve immediately to be seasoned with shoyu to taste.

For variety, sprinkle powdered green *nori* on the fried tofu and top with grated *daikon* or gingerroot before sprinkling with shoyu. Or omit salt and roll tofu in cornstarch or arrowroot instead of flour.

Additional Suggestions for Serving Tofu Sautéed or Stir-fried

*Tofu in Fried Mexican Dishes: Try tofu (pressed, then mashed or crumbled) in any of the following: *tostadas, enchiladas* with cheese, *chili rellenos,* or refried beans. Fry tofu in oil and season with shoyu and red peppers.
*Tofu with Fried Potatoes: Combine well-pressed, mashed tofu with potatoes when preparing hashed browns, potato pancakes, or thinly-sliced browned potatoes.
*Fried Tofu Topped with Sauces: Fry thin slices of well-pressed tofu in butter or oil until golden brown. Serve topped with any of the following sauces: Mushroom (p. 48), Sweet & Sour (p. 49), Tomato & Cheese (p. 49), or Lemon-Miso White Sauce (p. 207).

Fig. 39. Filling a wok with oil

TOFU DEEP-FRIED

Although three varieties of deep-fried tofu are available at most tofu shops (p. 154), tofu can also be deep-fried at home. One of the culinary arts raised to great heights by the Japanese, the technique of deep-frying comprises a world of its own, yielding light, crisp textures and delicate, delicious flavors. Learning to prepare fine, deep-fried foods is quite easy once you master the basic principles. This section contains recipes using nine different closely related methods for deep-frying tofu, listed here in order of ease of preparation: 1) without coating or batter; 2) rolled in *kuzu,* arrowroot, or cornstarch; 3) rolled in bread crumbs, bread crumb flakes, flour, or cornmeal; 4) dipped in lightly-beaten eggs and rolled in bread crumbs, *kuzu,* cornstarch, or flour; 5) rolled in flour or *kuzu* and dipped in eggs; 6) dipped into a thick batter of *kuzu* (or cornstarch) and egg whites; 7) dipped into a moderately thick batter of *kuzu* (or cornstarch) and water; 8) dusted with flour, dipped in lightly-beaten eggs, and rolled in bread crumbs to form a bound breading; and 9) coated with tempura batter.

About Deep-frying

Although deep-fat frying has long been a part of Western cookery, it has never attained the degree of popularity or artistry that it enjoys throughout the Orient, and particularly in Japan. Deep-frying is as common in the typical Japanese kitchen as baking is in the West, while it is faster and uses much less fuel. In only a few minutes, it transforms the simplest fresh vegetables, pieces of tofu, and even leftovers into prize creations. The art of deep-frying is a joy to practice and, fortunately, one of the easiest ways to begin learning is by making your own deep-fried tofu.

In Japanese, the verb *ageru* means "to deep-fry," and *agé-mono* or "deep-fried things" are the many foods that make up this vast world. The simplest form of deep-frying is called *kara-agé* or "deep-frying without a coating or batter." The three basic types of deep-fried tofu—thick agé, ganmo, and agé—are each prepared in this way. After mastering this technique, you should find no difficulty in preparing fine, crisp tempura.

If you wish to make deep-frying a permanent part of your repertoire of cooking techniques, it is best to start with the proper tools. Most important is the deep-frying pot. While many Westerners use a heavy 3- to 4-quart kettle, or an electric deep-fryer, most Japanese use either a wok (see p 35) or a heavy-bottomed skillet 2½ to 3 inches deep and 10 to 12 inches in diameter.

For best results use a simple vegetable oil. Japanese tofu masters prefer rapeseed oil, but many Western tofu shops also use soybean or cottonseed oil. Some chefs specializing in vegetable tempura prefer a combination of oils. If 10 to 30 percent sesame oil is added to any of the above basic oils, it will give the foods a delicious, nutty flavor. Other popular combinations are: peanut or corn (70%) and sesame (30%); peanut (75%), sesame (20%), and olive (5%); cottonseed (85%), olive (10%), and sesame (5%). For a light, crisp texture, avoid the use of animal fats in deep-frying.

Used deep-frying oil should be kept in a sealed jar and stored in a cool, dark place. When sautéing vegetables or frying eggs, you may use some of this oil to impart added flavor to the foods and help use up the oil. When deep-frying, try to use about one part fresh oil and one part used. Dark or thick used oil has a low smoking point and imparts a poor flavor. Foods deep-fried in used oil only are not as light and crisp as they could be. Pour oil from the storage jar into the deep-fryer carefully so that any sediment remains at the bottom of the jar. Then add fresh oil to fill the wok or skillet to a depth of 1½ to 2 inches (fig. 39).

Maintaining the oil at the proper temperature (about 350°) is the most important part of deep-frying. At first it may be easiest to measure the temperature with a deep-frying thermometer. More experienced chefs or tofu makers judge the oil's temperature by its appearance, aroma, and subtle crackling sound. If the oil begins to smoke, it is too hot. Overheating shortens the life of the oil Japanese say it "tires" the oil— and imparts a bad flavor to the foods cooked in it. Tempura chefs drop a little batter into hot oil to test its temperature. If the batter submerges slightly, then rises quickly to the surface where it browns within about 45 seconds, the temperature is just right (fig. 40). If the batter sinks to the bottom and rises only slowly to the surface, the oil is not hot enough; if it remains on the surface and dances furiously, the oil is too hot. Oil which is too hot will smoke—and burn the batter—whereas that which is too cold will not give the desired crispness.

Keeping the oil clean is another secret of successful deep-frying. This is especially important when using the batter or bound-breading methods. Use a mesh skimmer, or a perforated metal spatula or spoon, to remove all particles of food and batter from the oil's surface. Most cooks skim after every two or three batches of ingredients have been cooked. Place the small particles of deep-fried batter skimmed from the oil into a large colander or bowl lined with absorbent

paper, and allow to drain thoroughly. These may be used later as tasty additions to soups, salads, sautéed vegetables, noodles-in-broth, or other grain dishes.

To ensure that tofu and other deep-fried foods are served at their peak of texture and flavor, do your deep-frying just before you are ready to serve the meal, preferably after your guests have been seated at the table. If you have a large quantity of ingredients to deep-fry and wish to serve them simultaneously, keep freshly cooked pieces warm in a 250° oven.

After all foods have been deep-fried, allow the oil to cool in the wok or skillet, then pour it through a mesh skimmer or fine-weave strainer held over a funnel into your used-oil container. Seal the jar and discard any residue in the skimmer. Wipe all utensils with absorbent paper (washing is unnecessary) and store in a sealed plastic bag.

Crisp Agé Slices *(Tofu no Kara-agé)*   SERVES 2

The following technique is the basis of all types of deep-frying; 12 ounces of tofu yield 5 ounces of Crisp Agé Slices. Please begin by studying illustrations of the closely-related tempura process given on page 134.

Oil for deep-frying
12 ounces tofu, pressed (p. 97; sliced tofu method)

Use the oil to fill a wok, heavy skillet, pot, or deep-fryer to a depth of 1½ to 2 inches. Heat over high heat until temperature registers 350° on a deep-frying thermometer. Reduce heat to medium and slide half the tofu pieces down the side of the wok into the oil. Deep-fry for 1½ to 2 minutes, or until tofu is light golden-brown and floating near surface of oil. Turn each piece with long chopsticks or tongs and continue deep-frying for 1 to 3 minutes more until each piece is golden brown. Using chopsticks, transfer freshly cooked pieces onto the draining rack and allow to drain for several minutes. Skim surface of oil, check oil temperature, and slide in remaining tofu. Transfer well-drained tofu onto pieces of absorbent paper placed on a large tray or platter and allow to drain for several minutes more. Arrange tofu on plates, or serve Japanese style in a basket, bamboo colander, or serving bowl lined with neatly folded white paper. Serve immediately as for Crisp Deep-Fried Tofu (p. 156), or use in any of the recipes in Chapter 9. For variety, marinate for 1 hour in Teriyaki Sauce (p. 48) before serving.

Tofu French Fries   SERVES 2

12 ounces tofu, pressed (p. 97; sliced tofu method); or 9 ounces doufu
Oil for deep-frying
½ teaspoon salt

Cut tofu crosswise into pieces about the size of French-fried potatoes. Heat oil in a wok, skillet, or deep-fryer. Drop in tofu and deep-fry until golden brown (p. 130). Drain, then sprinkle with salt. Serve hot and crisp. Delicious with Ganmo Burgers (p. 188) and Tofu-Banana Milkshake (p. 149).

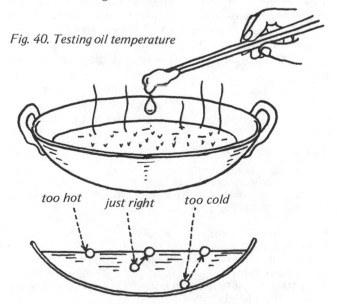

Fig. 40. Testing oil temperature

too hot   just right   too cold

Tofu Mock Eels (Unagi-dofu)

MAKES 16

12 ounces tofu, pressed (p. 96) and mashed
¼ cup whole-wheat flour
1½ to 2 tablespoons red, barley, or Hatcho miso
2 teaspoons natural sugar
1 tablespoon sesame butter
½ teaspoon grated gingerroot
2 sheets of *nori*, each cut into 8 equal squares
Oil for deep-frying

Combine the first six ingredients, mixing for 2 to 3 minutes, then spread in a thin layer on the upper surface of each *nori* square. Heat the oil to 350° in a wok, skillet, or deep-fryer. Drop in the squares and deep-fry until golden brown. Drain well on absorbent paper and serve as a topping for brown rice or as an hors d'oeuvre.

Crispy Deep-fried Tofu

SERVES 2

The key to obtaining a crisp, delicately crunchy crust lies in using powdered *kuzu* (Japanese arrowroot), although other coatings also work well.

12 ounces tofu, well pressed (p. 96); or 9 ounces doufu
3 to 5 tablespoons *kuzu*, cornstarch, arrowroot, or whole-wheat (pastry) flour
Oil for deep-frying
Shoyu

Cut tofu into 6 rectangular pieces and roll each piece in the *kuzu*. Heat oil to 350° in a wok, skillet, or deep-fryer. Drop in tofu and deep-fry until golden brown (p. 130); allow to drain. Invite each person to season his or her tofu to taste with shoyu and garnishes such as grated gingerroot, *daikon*, *wasabi*, or thinly sliced leeks. Also delicious served with lemon wedges and a little salt, or with Tempura Dipping Sauce (p. 134).

VARIATIONS

*Iso Agé (Deep-fried Nori-wrapped Tofu): Cut well pressed tofu crosswise into sixths, then wrap a 1- by 5-inch piece of *nori* around the center of each piece, moistening end of *nori* in water to seal. Roll *nori*-wrapped tofu in *kuzu* and deep-fry as above. Accompany each portion with a small bowl containing a mixture of 1/3 cup grated *daikon*, 1½ teaspoons shoyu and, if desired, a sprinkling of minced parsley. Or serve with Tempura Dipping Sauce.

*Shinano Agé (Tofu Deep-fried in Buckwheat Flour): Roll tofu slices in buckwheat flour and deep-fry as above. For the dipping sauce, mix 1/3 cup dashi (p. 39), 1 tablespoon shoyu, and 2 tablespoons minced leeks. Or serve as for Thunderbolt Tofu, below.

Thunderbolt Tofu (Kaminari Agé)

SERVES 2

This popular recipe derives its name from the crackling sound made when the soft tofu is dropped into the hot oil.

12 ounces tofu, cut crosswise into halves and drained (p. 96)
¼ cup *kuzu*, cornstarch, or arrowroot
Oil for deep-frying
¾ cup dashi (p. 39), stock, or water
3 tablespoons shoyu
3 tablespoons *mirin* or sake
2 tablespoons grated *daikon*
2 tablespoons thinly sliced leeks or scallions
1 sheet of *nori*, cut into 1/8-inch-wide strips

Pat the tofu pieces with a dry cloth to remove surface moisture and roll them in *kuzu* powder. Heat oil to 350° in a wok, skillet, or deep-fryer. Drop in tofu and deep-fry until golden brown (p. 130); allow to drain, then place into deep serving bowls. Combine dashi, shoyu, and *mirin* in a small saucepan and bring almost to the boil. Pour this sauce over the tofu and top each portion with grated *daikon*, leek slices, and *nori*.

Tofu-Brown Rice Croquettes

MAKES 10

Oil for deep-frying
½ onion, diced
12 ounces tofu, pressed (p. 96); or 9 ounces doufu, cut crosswise into 1-inch-thick slices
1 cup cooked Brown Rice (p. 50)
1 tablespoon shoyu
2 teaspoons Sesame Salt (p. 51)
½ cup bread crumbs or bread crumb flakes
¾ cup Tofu Tartare Sauce (p. 109) or ketchup

Heat a skillet and coat with 1 tablespoon deep-frying oil. Add onion and sauté for 3 or 4 minutes until transparent. Add tofu and sauté until onion is lightly browned. Now add brown rice, season with shoyu and Sesame Salt, and cook for several minutes until rice is well heated. Transfer mixture to a separate bowl and shape into ten 2-inch patties; roll in bread crumbs.

Heat the oil to 350° in a wok, skillet, or deep-fryer. Drop in the patties and deep-fry until golden brown (p. 130). Drain, then serve topped with Tofu Tartare Sauce.

Tofu-Sweet Potato Croquettes

SERVES 4

24 ounces tofu, squeezed (p. 97)
2 cups cooked sweet or Irish potatoes, mashed
¼ cup chopped onions, scallions, or leeks
½ teaspoon salt
½ teaspoon curry powder (optional)
Dash of pepper
1 cup bread crumbs or bread crumb flakes
Oil for deep-frying
Tofu Mayonnaise (with onion; p. 107), Tofu Tartare Sauce (p. 109), or ketchup

Combine the first six ingredients in a large bowl; mix well. Shape into 2½-inch patties, roll in bread crumbs, and tap lightly to remove excess crumbs. Set aside to dry for 5 to 10 minutes.

Heat the oil to 350° in a wok, skillet, or deep-fryer. Slide in the croquettes and deep-fry until golden brown (p. 130); drain briefly. Serve with the Mayonnaise or Tartare Sauce.

For variety, substitute 1 cup parboiled corn kernels for 1 cup sweet potato. Dust patties with flour and dip in lightly-beaten egg before rolling in bread crumbs.

VARIATION

*Tofu Croquettes with Leftovers: Mash drained tofu together with leftover grains, diced fresh or cooked vegetables, thick soups, beans, or bread pieces. Season lightly with miso or curry powder. If necessary, add bread crumbs or bread crumb flakes to create a croquette consistency. Shape into patties, dip in beaten egg, and roll in bread crumbs or bread crumb flakes. Deep-fry as above. Serve topped with ketchup, Ketchup-Worcestershire (p. 49), or your favorite sauce. Extra croquettes may be refrigerated or frozen for later use. To reheat, fry lightly in butter.

Agédashi-dofu
(Deep-Fried Tofu in Dipping Sauce)

SERVES 4

Agédashi is one of Japan's favorite deep-fried tofu dishes. Its name is composed of two Chinese characters meaning "to deep-fry" and "to serve." What could be quicker or easier? The key to the texture lies in the use of *kuzu* and in serving the tofu immediately after it is deep-fried. The key to the flavor lies in the use of sesame oil and in cutting the tofu with chopsticks (rather than with a knife) after placing it in the dipping sauce. The roughly cut surface helps the sauce's flavor permeate the tofu. Agédashi is prepared with or without batter and is served in any number of different dipping sauces.

2 cakes of tofu (each 12 ounces), pressed (p. 96); or 18 ounces doufu
Oil for deep-frying (3 parts vegetable and 1 part sesame, if available)
1 egg, lightly beaten
¼ to ½ cup *kuzu*, arrowroot, or cornstarch
Mirin-Shoyu, Lemon-Shoyu, or Vinegar-Shoyu (p. 40)
2 teaspoons grated gingerroot or a mixture of 1 teaspoon each grated *daikon* and grated carrot.
2 tablespoons minced leeks

Cut each cake of tofu lengthwise into halves, then crosswise into thirds. Pat each piece with a dry cloth. Heat oil to 350° in a wok, skillet, or deep-fryer. Dip tofu into egg, then roll in *kuzu*. Deep-fry until golden brown. Serve accompanied by a dipping sauce and garnishes.

VARIATION

*Agédashi-dofu (without coating): Cut tofu as above but deep-fry without using eggs or *kuzu* coating. Serve with Mirin-Shoyu, garnished with either grated *daikon* or a mixture of 6 parts grated *daikon*, 2 parts grated gingerroot, and 1 part bonita flakes.

Deep-fried Tofu with Rice and Broth
(Tendon)

SERVES 2

¾ teaspoon sesame oil
5 teaspoons shoyu
1½ teaspoons natural sugar
½ teaspoon salt
1 tablespoon sake or white wine
1 teaspoon grated or minced gingerroot
2 teaspoons minced leeks, scallions, or onions
12 ounces tofu, drained (p. 96) and cut into 16 small rectangles (p. 37)
3 to 4 tablespoons (whole-wheat) flour
1 egg, lightly beaten
Oil for deep-frying
2/3 cup water
2 mushrooms, minced
2 cups cooked Brown Rice (p. 50)
¼ cup minced leek or scallion greens
Dash of 7-spice red pepper

In a flat-bottomed container, combine ¼ teaspoon sesame oil, 1 tablespoon shoyu, 1 teaspoon sugar, and the salt, sake, gingerroot, and leeks; mix well. Add tofu and marinate for 10 minutes on each side. Remove tofu, reserving the marinade, dust each piece with flour, and dip in the egg. Heat the oil to 350° in a wok, skillet, or deep-fryer. Slide in the tofu and deep-fry until golden brown (p. 130).

In a saucepan, combine the water and mushrooms with the remaining marinade, ½ teaspoon sesame oil, 2 teaspoons shoyu, and ½ teaspoon sugar. Bring to a boil over high heat, then add the deep-fried tofu. Return to the boil, reduce heat to medium, and cook uncovered for about 3 minutes.

Divide the rice among 2 large serving bowls. Top with the tofu and a sprinkling of scallions and red pepper. Now pour on the broth and serve steaming hot.

VARIATION

*Chinese-style Seasoned Deep-fried Tofu (Goda-dofu): Prepare the marinade using ¼ teaspoon each sesame oil and salt, ½ teaspoon each sugar and minced gingerroot, 1 teaspoon minced leeks, and 1½ teaspoons each soy sauce and sake. Marinate, then deep-fry the tofu as above. In a saucepan combine 1/3 cup soup stock or water, 1 diced mushroom, ¼ teaspoon sesame oil, and the remaining marinade. Bring to a boil, add the tofu, and simmer uncovered until all liquid is absorbed or evaporated. Sprinkle with 2 tablespoons diced leek greens and serve immediately, as is, or over rice as for Tendon.

Sizzling Tofu with Gingerroot-Ankake Sauce

SERVES 4

Deep-frying with a *kuzu* & egg white batter gives each piece of tofu a crisp and billowy coating, light and delicate as spindrift.

¼ cup *kuzu*, arrowroot, or cornstarch
2 egg whites
24 ounces tofu, pressed (p. 96); or 18 ounces doufu
Oil for deep-frying
1 cup Rich Gingerroot-Ankake Sauce (p. 49)

Combine *kuzu* and egg whites in a small bowl; mix until smooth. Cut tofu into 12 equal cubes (or thin rectangles; p. 37), dip into the batter, and deep-fry as for Crisp Agé Slices (p. 131). Serve immediately, topped with the hot sauce.

For variety, substitute 2/3 cup water for the egg whites. Or use the cornstarch & egg white batter described at Crispy Thick Agé (p. 168).

Breaded Tofu Cutlets *(Tofu Furai)*

SERVES 2

12 ounces tofu, pressed (p. 96); or 9 ounces doufu
1/3 cup flour or cornstarch
1 egg, lightly beaten (with 2 or 3 teaspoons of water or
    milk, if desired)
¾ cup sifted bread crumbs or bread crumb flakes
Oil for deep-frying
Salt
Tofu Mayonnaise (with onion; p. 107) or Tofu Tartare Sauce
    (p. 109)

Cut tofu lengthwise into halves then crosswise into ½-inch-thick pieces. Place between absorbent towels and allow to dry for several minutes. Gently dust tofu, one piece at a time, with the flour, then dip in the egg and roll in the bread crumbs. Place on a rack and allow to dry for 10 to 15 minutes; tap off any excess crumbs.

Heat the oil to 350° in a wok, skillet, or deep-fryer. Drop in the tofu and deep-fry until golden brown (p. 130). Add a piece of tofu to the oil about once every 15 seconds. No more than 6 pieces should be in the oil at one time. Drain briefly, then serve, inviting each guest to season the tofu with salt to taste, and top with the Mayonnaise or Tartare Sauce.

VARIATION

*After rolling each piece of tofu in flour, dip it in lightly beaten egg whites and roll in a dish of ¼- to ½-inch-long strips of transparent noodles. Deep-fry, then serve with salt and lemon juice, Tempura Dipping Sauce (p. 134), or thickened Gingerroot Sauce (p. 49). Or substitute *(somen)* thin noodles, cracker crumbs, cereal flakes, or minced carrots for the transparent noodles.

About Tofu Tempura

Tempura stands as one of Japan's great contributions to the art of fine cooking. Described by various foreign writers as "the pride of Japanese cuisine," "delicately flavored, light as air and wonderfully crisp," and "light and dry as spindrift," tempura's fine flavors and textures epitomize the beauty and subtlety of Japanese cuisine.

Nevertheless, tempura was originally "imported" from the West. It was probably brought to Japan by Portuguese sailors or Spanish missionaries during the 16th century, and is said to have been Japan's first contact with the art of deep-frying with batter. Good Catholics, the Portugese did not eat meat on Ember days, which occur four times each year. Instead, they asked for deep-fried shrimp. The word *tempura* is a corruption of the ancient Latin term *Quator Tempora*, meaning "four times." The Japanese now write the word using Chinese characters, the first of which, pronounced *ten*, means "heaven," perhaps in honor of the flavor.

Restaurants specializing in tempura are among Japan's most popular. The chef does his deep-frying behind a clean, natural-wood counter right in front of his customers. At its peak of crispness and flavor, each delicacy is quickly and artfully placed on a carefully-folded piece of white paper set on a bamboo tray that is then whisked across the counter to the waiting patron.

Tempura Batter

FOR 4 TO 6 SERVINGS

1 cup ice-cold water
1 egg yolk or whole egg
1¼ to 1½ cups (coarsely ground) unbleached white flour
½ teaspoon salt (optional)

In a mixing bowl, combine the water and egg yolk and beat well with a wire whisk or chopsticks. Sprinkle the flour and, if used, the salt evenly over the mixture. With a few quick strokes of the whisk (or a wooden spoon) lightly stir in the flour until all flour is moistened and large lumps disappear. (The presence of small lumps is alright.) Do not stir batter again after the initial mixing. Use as soon as possible and do not place too near the heat.

For variety, use your favorite fritter batter. Or omit the egg in the recipe above and add sesame seeds; decrease the amount of white flour used and compensate for the difference with several teaspoons of arrowroot or cornstarch.

Tempura Dipping Sauce *(Ten-tsuyu)*

FOR 4 TO 6 SERVINGS

1 cup dashi (p. 39), stock, or water
3 to 4 tablespoons *mirin*, sake, or pale dry sherry
¼ cup shoyu
4 to 6 tablespoons grated *daikon*
4 to 6 teaspoons grated gingerroot

Combine the dashi, *mirin*, and shoyu in a small pan. Bring just to a boil over high heat, then set aside to cool. Divide the dipping sauce, grated *daikon*, and grated gingerroot among 4 to 6 small serving bowls and serve with the tempura (fig. 42).

Each guest holds the container of dipping sauce in one hand, then transfers a piece of tempura from his place into the sauce, and cuts the food with chopsticks. The roughly cut surface helps the sauce's flavor to penetrate the tofu thereby giving the finest flavor.

The use of *daikon*, which is rich in the enzyme diastase, aids in the digestion of oils in the tempura. Each of the following accompaniments is also widely used in place of the dipping sauce and garnishes described above:

*Shoyu with Grated Daikon: A small dispenser of shoyu and some *daikon* are placed on the table. Each guest combines about 1½ teaspoons shoyu with 2½ tablespoons *daikon* in a small dish. In some cases 1 part grated gingerroot is mixed with 3 parts grated *daikon*. Or a few drops of lemon juice may be added to the shoyu-*daikon* mixture.

*Lemon Juice and Salt: Serve each portion of tempura garnished with several lemon wedges. Each guest squeezes a little lemon juice over the tempura, then sprinkles each piece with salt or dip it in salt served in a separate tiny dish.

*Salt or Shoyu: Tofu tempura is delicious sprinkled with either of these.

Fig. 41. Deep-frying tofu tempura

Tofu and Vegetable Tempura SERVES 4 TO 6

12 ounces todu, well pressed (p. 96); or 9 ounces doufu
Vegetables:
      6 mushrooms
      24 green beans
      ½ sweet potato or yam
      1 onion
      2 green peppers
      2 inches of lotus root
Oil for deep-frying
Tempura Batter (see above)
Tempura Dipping Sauce and garnishes (see above)

Cut tofu crosswise into sixths and press for several minutes more using the sliced tofu method (p. 97). Cut sweet potatoes, onion, and lotus root into ½-inch-thick rounds, and cut pepper lengthwise into quarters. To rid vegetables of excess moisture, pat the cut surfaces lightly with a dry cloth.

Pour the oil into a wok, skillet, or deep-fryer and heat over low heat. Meanwhile quickly prepare tempura batter. When the oil temperature reaches 350° (test with a few drops of batter), dip tofu pieces into batter and slide them into oil. Deep-fry on both side until golden brown, drain briefly on a wire rack, then transfer onto absorbent paper. Dip vegetable slices into the batter and deep fry 6 to 8 at a time until golden brown. Arrange tofu and vegetable tempura in individual portions (atop fresh sheets of white paper) on serving plates or small bamboo colanders *(zaru)*. Serve accompanied by the dipping sauce and garnishes (fig. 42).

If any batter is left over, add this in spoonfuls to the oil and deep-fry. Combine these deep-fried batter balls with the pieces skimmed from the oil during deep-frying and use in (miso) soups or salad dressings, or with sautéed vegetables or Japanese-style noodle dishes.

VARIATIONS

*Other ingredients which make excellent tempura are tender eggplants, carrots (and green tops), *(kabocha)* pumpkin, all squashes, snow peas, cauliflower, apple, pear, banana, bamboo shoots, chrysanthemum leaves, green beefsteak leaves, *nori*, burdock root, ginkgo nuts, and yuba.

*Flower Tofu (Hana-dofu): Cut the pressed tofu horizontally into two ½-inch-thick slices. Use milk instead of water to make a slightly thick batter. Serve the tofu tempura topped with mild Red Nerimiso (p. 42). Garnish with leek slivers which have been soaked in water for 15 minutes and then drained.

*After dipping tofu or vegetables in tempura batter, roll in bread crumbs, bread crumb flakes, cereal flakes, finely diced carrots, ¼- to ½-inch long pieces of transparent noodles, or thin noodles *(somen)*. During deep-frying, the noodles puff up and become light and crisp.

Fig. 42. Serving Tofu and Vegetable Tempura

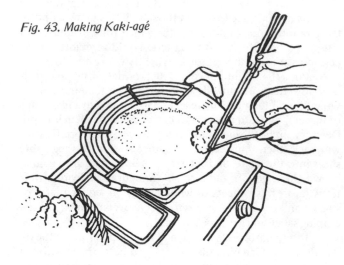

Fig. 43. Making Kaki-agé

*Kaki-agé: Cut the pressed tofu and other vegetables into 3/8-inch cubes or matchsticks. Mix these in a bowl with batter that has been thickened slightly with flour. Place about 2 tablespoons of the batter-and-vegetable mixture on a (wooden) spatula. Using chopsticks, flatten the mixture to form a 2½-inch round, then carefully slide round into hot oil (fig. 43) and deep-fry as above.

*Skewered Tabletop Tempura: Heat the oil over a tabletop burner. Have each guest skewer three or four ingredients on a 12-inch bamboo or metal skewer. The skewer is dipped into batter and immersed in hot oil while being held at one end. Ginkgo nuts and green beans skewered on foodpicks are often prepared in this way: they are placed into the oil using chopsticks.

*Floured Tempura Retouched with Batter: This technique gives a very light, whispy coating to the tempura. Roll each ingredient lightly in flour before dipping it into batter. Deep-fry at 340°. When the ingredients float to the surface, dip both chopsticks (or two fingers) into the batter, then touch the batter quickly to the top of each piece of tempura bobbing in the oil. Repeat several times with each piece of food. Turn each piece with chopsticks and retouch the second side. Turn again and cook until crisp and golden brown.

Deep-fried Onions with Tofu Mayonnaise

SERVES 4

Oil for Deep Frying
2/3 cup flour
2 eggs, lightly beaten
1½ cups bread crumbs
4 onions, cut into ¼-inch-thick rounds; or ½ *kabocha* cut into thin wedges
¾ cup Tofu Mayonnaise (p. 107) or Tofu Tartare Sauce (p. 109)

Heat the oil to 350° in a wok, skillet, or deep-fryer. Quickly dust a slice of onion with flour, dip in egg, then roll in bread crumbs. Deep-fry until crisp and golden brown (p. 130); drain briefly. Serve with Tofu Mayonnaise for dipping.

Additional Suggestions for Serving Tofu Deep-fried

*Deep-fried Walnut Tofu: Mix 3 parts well-pressed tofu with 2 parts coarsely chopped walnuts. Season with salt and, if desired, add a small amount of egg white as a binder. Shape into patties (or roll out into a 1-inch-diameter cylinder, wrap in a sheet of *nori* and dip into tempura batter). Deep-fry and serve with a Shoyu Dipping Sauce (p. 40).

*Deep-fried Tofu-Miso Patties: Mix 2 to 4 tablespoons Hatcho, red, or barley miso, or Sweet Simmered Miso (p. 41) with 12 ounces tofu (well pressed). Shape into patties, roll in *kuzu*, flour, or cornstarch, and deep-fry. Serve with shoyu or a Shoyu Dipping Sauce (p. 40).

*Stuffed Deep-fried Tofu: Cut a 12-ounce cake of tofu diagonally into halves and deep-fry. Slit each half open along its long side, scoop out soft tofu and fill with fried rice and vegetables seasoned with a little shoyu.

*Deep-fried Tofu with Umeboshi *(Bainiku):* Mash well-pressed tofu, season lightly with salt, and shape into patties. Place a seeded *umeboshi* in the center of each pattie. Dip in tempura batter, press a green beefsteak leaf against one side of pattie, and deep-fry. Serve with salt and lemon juice.

*Deep-fried Rolled Tofu *(Isobe-maki):* Mash well-pressed tofu and mix with slivered carrots, green peas, and mushrooms. Season with salt and mix in sesame seeds. Any of the other ingredients used in Homemade Ganmo (p. 186) may also be added. Place a sheet of *nori*, yuba, or agé on a bamboo rolling mat. Spread the tofu mixture on the *nori* and roll the *nori* to form a 1½-inch-diameter cylinder. Dip into tempura batter and deep-fry. Cut into 1½-inch lengths and serve with shoyu or a Shoyu Dipping Sauce (p. 40).

*Tofu Bourguignon: This dish, originally made with beef, is now often served at fondue restaurants using bread instead of tofu. Fill a small metal pot half full of peanut oil and heat to 350° over a tabletop burner. Cut pressed tofu into 1-inch cubes and skewer on long (fondue) forks. Invite each guest to deep-fry the tofu in the oil until golden brown. Dip in shoyu or a Shoyu Dipping Sauce (p. 40). Or top with Sweet Simmered Miso (p. 41) or Tofu Tartare Sauce (p. 109).

*Deep-fried Bananas with Tofu Toppings: Deep-fry thin banana ovals covered with tempura batter (p. 134) or egg-and-bread crumbs. Serve immediately, topped with Banana-Lemon Whip (p. 148) or Tofu Whipped Cream (p. 148) seasoned with a little nutmeg and a few drops of lemon juice.

*Deep-fried Tofu Dumplings Filled with Mustard: Prepare Karashi-dofu (p. 90), dust each piece lightly with wheat-or rice flour, and deep-fry at 350° until golden brown. Serve in deep bowls topped with Simmering Tofu Dipping Sauce (p. 142) and garnished with thinly sliced leeks or beefsteak leaves.

*Deep-fried Chinese-style Tofu: This dish is a specialty of the Hakuun-an restaurant near Mampukuji temple. Simmer a 3-inch square of reshaped tofu (p. 98), or well-pressed regular tofu, for 2 hours in shoyu to cover. Allow to dry, dust with *kuzu* or arrowroot, and deep-fry. Serve with a dip of shoyu mixed with grated gingerroot or *wasabi*.

TOFU WITH GRAINS

Serving tofu with grains can increase the availability of their combined protein content by as much as 30 to 40 percent. A number of the best combinations and proportions are given on page 26. Tofu may be used in grain salads; fried, stir-fried or baked grain and noodle dishes; or sauce toppings. Use tofu with leftover grains in gruel (p. 170).

Tofu-filled Enchiladas   SERVES 2 OR 3

4 teaspoons oil
1 clove of garlic, minced or crushed
1 onion, minced
1 tablespoon whole-wheat flour
1½ tablespoons red miso or 1 tablespoon shoyu
1 cup water
Dash of 7-spice red pepper or tabasco sauce
Dash of white or black pepper
¼ teaspoon oregano
2 tablespoons tomato ketchup
6 tablespoons Parmesan cheese
8 ounces tofu
1 green pepper, minced
5 tortillas, each 5 inches in diameter

Heat a skillet and coat with 1 tablespoon oil. Add garlic and sauté for 30 seconds. Add one half the onion and sauté for 3 to 4 minutes. Mix in flour and sauté for 30 seconds, then add 1 tablespoon miso and sauté for 15 seconds more. Add water a little at a time, stirring constantly until smooth. Mix in the next four ingredients and 2 tablespoons Parmesan, cover, and simmer for 15 minutes. Remove sauce from heat and allow to cool, then mix in 2 tablespoons minced raw onion.

While sauce is cooling, heat a wok or skillet and coat with 1 teaspoon oil. Add green pepper and the remaining onion, and sauté for 3 minutes. Stir in the remaining 1½ teaspoons miso, season with white pepper, and remove from heat. Combine with tofu and 2 tablespoons Parmesan; mash well.

Preheat oven to 350°. Pour one half the sauce into a loaf pan or casserole. Dip one surface of a tortilla into remaining sauce, then holding this side upward, spread with one fifth of the tofu mixture. Roll tortilla loosely and place into loaf pan. Repeat with remaining tortillas and tofu until all are used. Pour remaining sauce over tortillas in pan and top with a sprinkling of 2 tablespoons Parmesan. Bake for 15 to 20 minutes, or until nicely browned. Serve hot or cold.

Brown Rice Porridge with   SERVES 3
Tofu and Vegetables

½ cup brown rice
1 tablespoon (sesame) oil
½ small carrot, slivered or diced
2 onions, thinly sliced
½ cup diced celery, cabbage, or vegetable leftovers
12 ounces tofu
2½ tablespoons shoyu or 3½ tablespoons red miso
Dash of pepper

Use the rice to prepare Brown Rice Porridge (p. 50). About 15 minutes before porridge is ready, heat a wok or skillet and coat with the oil. Add carrot and sauté for 3 minutes. Mix in onion and celery and sauté for 5 minutes more. Add tofu, mash well, and sauté for 3 minutes. Stir in shoyu and pepper and remove from heat. Add sautéed tofu-vegetable mixture to the finished porridge, mix well, and allow to stand for 5 to 10 minutes before serving.

If desired, substitute 5 to 10 ounces diced deep-fried tofu for the regular tofu. Top with crumbled *nori* and diced leeks.

Bulgur Pilaf with Tofu   SERVES 4

3 tablespoons butter or oil
1 cup bulgur wheat
1 small onion, minced
2 cups water or stock
¼ teaspoon oregano
Dash of (freshly ground) pepper
9 ounces tofu
2 teaspoons shoyu or 1 tablespoon red miso
Sesame Salt (p. 51) or salt

Melt butter in a heavy skillet. Add bulgur and onion and sauté for 4 to 5 minutes. Add stock, oregano, and pepper, cover pan, and bring to a boil. Reduce heat and simmer for 15 minutes, or until all liquid is absorbed. Combine tofu and shoyu in a small bowl and mash together, then stir into the cooked grain. Serve hot seasoned with sesame salt.

For variety stir in 2 tablespoons minced parsley or 1/3 cup grated cheese just before serving.

Tofu & Eggs Domburi   SERVES 4

1 tablespoon oil
1 cup minced leek, scallion, or onion
1 cup grated carrot
2 ounces agé or ganmo (or 4 mushrooms), diced
12 ounces tofu, pressed (p. 96) and mashed; or 5 ounces thick agé, minced
¼ cup cooked, chopped spinach (optional)
2 tablespoons shoyu
1½ tablespoons natural sugar
¼ teaspoon salt
2 eggs, lightly beaten
1½ cups brown rice, cooked (p. 50)

Heat a skillet or wok and coat with the oil. Add the next four ingredients and sauté for 4 minutes. Add tofu and sauté for 2 minutes more. Mix in spinach, shoyu, sugar, and salt; cook for 1 minute. Stir in eggs, cover, and remove from heat.

Spoon hot rice into 3 large *(domburi)* bowls and top with tofu-and-eggs; serve immediately or allow to cool to room temperature. In Japan, the latter version is widely used in box lunches.

VARIATION

*Use Crumbly Agé Soboro (p. 169) or Iridofu (p. 128) as the topping.

Tofu with Fried Grains and Vegetables
SERVES 4

2 tablespoons oil
1 clove garlic, crushed
2 onions, thinly sliced
1 cup diced mushrooms, lotus root, celery, or eggplant
1 small carrot, grated or slivered
2 cups cooked (buckwheat) Noodles (p. 50) or Brown Rice (p. 50)
24 ounces tofu, crumbled (p. 98); or 12 ounces tofu, pressed (p. 96) and diced
1 to 1½ tablespoons shoyu
4 to 5 tablespoons ketchup
2 tablespoons Sesame Salt (p. 51) or ½ teaspoon salt
½ cup crumbled *nori* (optional)

Heat a skillet or wok and coat with the oil. Add consecutively: garlic, onions, mushrooms, carrot, and noodles (or rice), sautéing each for about 1 to 2 minutes. Add the next four ingredients and cook. stirring constantly, for about 3 minutes more. For best flavor, allow to cool for 4 to 6 hours. Serve topped with *nori*.

Italian-style Spaghetti with Tofu Meatballs
SERVES 4 OR 6

4½ to 5 ounces (whole-wheat) spaghetti or *(soba)* buckwheat noodles, cooked (p. 50)
Tofu Italian Meatballs (p. 123)
Tofu Spaghetti Sauce (p. 121)
Parmesan cheese and/or tabasco sauce

Divide the hot spaghetti among individual bowls and top with the meatballs and spaghetti sauce. Pass the cheese and tabasco.

Zosui or Ojiya *(Rice Gruel)*
SERVES 1 OR 2

Zosui (known colloquially as *Ojiya*) is a popular way of using rice or rice porridge and either miso- or clear soup, foods served daily in most Japanese homes. During the winter, thick Zosui served piping hot is prized for its ability to warm body and soul. The amounts of rice and soup can be varied considerably depending on the amounts of leftovers available.

1½ cups Tofu-Miso soup (p. 118) or Clear Soup with Tofu (p. 119)
1 cup cooked Brown Rice (p. 50) or Rice Porridge (p. 50)
4 to 6 ounces tofu, diced (optional)
1 to 2 eggs, lightly beaten (optional)
7-spice red pepper or grated gingerroot (optional)
Crumbled toasted *nori*, powdered green *nori*, slivered leeks or citrus rind, or minced parsley

Bring miso soup just to a boil in a saucepan. Mix in rice and return to the boil. Cover and simmer for 15 to 30 minutes, or until rice is soft. Just before removing from heat, stir in tofu and eggs. Season with the red pepper, garnish with *nori*, and serve immediately.

Tofu-Oatmeal
SERVES 2

1½ cups water
½ cup rolled oats or oatmeal
¼ teaspoon salt
1 tablespoon Sesame Salt (p. 50)
2 tablespoons butter
1/3 cup raisins
½ cup milk
1 tablespoon honey
12 ounces tofu, diced or mashed

Bring the water to a boil in a saucepan. Gradually stir in the rolled oats, add salt, and cook for 15 minutes or until softened. Stir in the remaining ingredients and cook, stirring constantly, for several minutes more. Serve hot or cold.

Tofu With Tacos
MAKES 6

12 ounces tofu
2/3 cup brown rice or bulgur wheat, cooked (p. 50)
¼ cup peanuts
½ green pepper, diced
2 cloves of garlic, crushed
¼ teaspoon chili powder
¼ cup ketchup
½ teaspoon salt or 1 tablespoon red miso
2 to 3 tablespoons oil
6 *tortillas*
Garnishes:
    Chopped tomato
    Minced onion
    Shredded lettuce
    Grated cheese
Tabasco or taco sauce

Combine the first eight ingredients in a large bowl; mash thoroughly. Heat the oil in a skillet and fry the *tortillas*. Top each *tortilla* with your choice of garnishes, spoon on the tofu mixture, and season with tabasco sauce.

Additional Suggestions for Serving Tofu with Grains:

*Grains with Tofu Sauces: Serve cooked brown rice or (buckwheat) noodles topped with any of the basic Tofu Sauces (p. 121), or with Japanese-Style Tofu, Eggs & Onions (p. 122).
*Gomoku-dofu: Substitute crumbled tofu (p. 98) for the okara or rice in Sushi Okara (p. 83) or Okara-Omelet Pouches (p. 84).
*Tofu in Chop Suey or Chow Mein: See p. 67.

TOFU BROILED

Since grilled tofu is one of the basic types of tofu prepared at tofu shops, regular tofu is not ordinarily grilled, broiled, or barbequed in the home. With one important exception: *Tofu Dengaku*. There are also many broiled dishes made from tofu that has already been deep-fried, since these acquire a particularly delicious flavor from direct contact with fire and lend themselves to basting and marinating.

Tofu Dengaku   SERVES 4

In *dengaku*, one of Japan's most popular treatments of tofu, firm pieces the size of small match boxes are pierced with bamboo skewers and lightly broiled. A topping of Sweet Simmered Miso is then spread on one of the tofu's surfaces, and the tofu is rebroiled until lightly speckled.

The two Chinese characters which form the word *dengaku* mean "rice paddy" and "music." It is said that the name originated about 600 years ago, when an ancient form of folk drama consisting of music and dance was popular in Japan's rural villages. In one famous play using a rice paddy as its stage setting, a Buddhist priest mounted a single stilt (resembling a pogo stick) called a "heron's leg." Precariously balanced, this character was called Dengaku Hoshi (fig. 44), and he did a dance known as the *dengaku*, or "music in the rice paddy." The newly conceived broiled tofu dish, with its distinctive, individual bamboo skewers, apparently reminded many people of the dengaku dancer, and the tasty preparation soon became known as Dengaku.

About 400 years ago, Nakamura-ro (p. 307) in the Gion geisha section of Kyoto became the first restaurant to serve dengaku. Attractively dressed women kneeling at small tables in front of the restaurant near the famous Yasaka shrine cut the tofu in a swift staccato rhythm to the accompaniment of shamisen music, and the new dish soon became known locally as Gion-dofu. Today the dengaku at Nakamura-ro is famous throughout Japan, especially its springtime variety which is topped with fresh bright-green sprigs of *kinome* and served with thick sweet sake *(amazake)*. It is prepared over a bed of live coals and served in lacquerware boxes (fig. 45).

From the early 1600s until the late 1900s many tofu shops prepared and delivered dengaku to order, and by about 1775 it had become very fashionable for Tokyo tea shops, way stations, and inns to serve this delicacy.

According to ancient chronicles, some of Japan's earliest types of dengaku were prepared in country farmhouses, especially during the winter. We have enjoyed sizzling-hot dengaku prepared from homemade tofu and homemade miso in several mountain villages. The well-pressed tofu is cut into pieces about 4 by 3 by 1 inch, or into ¾-inch-thick rounds. Each piece is pierced with a flat skewer 12 inches long made of green bamboo which has been soaked overnight in lightly salted water to prevent it from burning. The butt end of each skewer is poked into the sand or ashes around an open-hearth fireplace so that the tofu leans a few inches above and over a bed of live coals (p. 221). The savory broiled tofu is spread

Fig. 44. Dengaku Hoshi
(from the "Tofu Hyaku Chin")

田楽法師高足曲

with plain miso on both sides, quickly rebroiled until the miso is fragrant, and served as a light wintertime snack with tea. This traditional method of broiling, which imparts a savory fragrance of woodsmoke to the tofu, is practiced at the Dengaku restaurant in Kamakura (p. 309). Gifu Prefecture is especially famous for the dengaku served as a special treat during nighttime displays of fireworks. And in some villages, a special offering of dengaku—said to be the favorite food of the local gods—is made each year on November 14 at all *Ichi-fusha* shrines.

A unique type of dengaku called "quick dengaku" is prepared in some tofu shops after the master finishes making the day's supply of grilled tofu. He broils both sides of an entire 12-ounce cake of tofu, spreads one surface with sweet white miso, broils the miso until it is fragrant, then sits down to enjoy a hefty treat.

There are a great many varieties of dengaku in Japan. Although the most popular are generally prepared using regular tofu, others are made with grilled tofu, thick agé, ganmo, or agé. Occasionally, tofu is even replaced by skewered pieces of eggplant, *konnyaku*, *mochi*, *shiitake* mushrooms, green peppers, fresh or deep-fried wheat gluten, sweet or Irish potatoes, bamboo shoots, *daikon*, or boiled quail eggs.

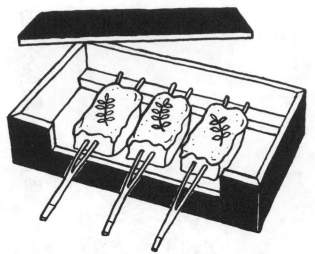

Fig. 45. Skewered Tofu Dengaku

Miso Topping: Use a total of ¼ to ½ cup of one or more of the following types of Sweet Simmered Miso
- Red- or White Nerimiso
- Yuzu- or Lemon Miso
- Kinome- or Egg Yolk Miso
- Sesame- or Walnut Miso; or a Nut Butter Topping (p. 47)

12 to 24 ounces tofu, pressed (p. 96)

Garnishes (optional):
- *Kinome* sprigs
- Slivered *yuzu* or lemon rind
- Poppy or roasted sesame seeds
- Hot mustard

Prepare the miso toppings in advance and allow to cool. In a large skillet or pan, heat water to about the temperature of a hot bath. Drop in the tofu, then cut into pieces as large as 2½ by 1 by ¾ inch or as small as 1¼ by ¾ by ½ inch. Pierce each of these under water using either 2 round bamboo skewers or 1 flat skewer as shown in figure 46. Cover a cutting board or flat tray with a dry dishtowel and raise one end of the board. Carefully place the pieces of skewered tofu on the cloth and allow to stand for about 15 minutes, or until tofu is firm.

Preparing Dengaku in old Japan (from Hokusai's sketchbooks)

Holding 3 to 4 pieces of skewered tofu at a time side by side over a gas burner, broil for about 30 seconds or until tofu is lightly speckled; or broil tofu on one side over a charcoal brazier or barbeque. Turn tofu over and coat broiled side with a 1/8-inch-thick layer of topping, then broil second side. Turn tofu again and broil miso topping until it too is speckled, then arrange garnishes, if used, atop miso. Repeat with remaining ingredients; if desired, use a different miso topping with each set of tofu pieces. Serve Dengaku hot with the meal or as an hors d'oeuvre.

VARIATIONS

*Deep-fried Dengaku: Cut well-pressed tofu into Dengaku-sized pieces and pierce each piece with 10-inch-long bamboo skewers. Deep-fry with or without batter until golden brown. Spread on the topping and serve hot. When deep-fried in a bound breading, this dish has an excellent crunchy texture.

*Butter-fried Dengaku: Prepare Butter-fried Tofu (p. 128). Skewer each piece and coat one surface with Sweet Simmered Miso or Miso-Sesame Butter Topping (p. 41) sprinkled with toasted wheat germ. Serve as an hors d'oeuvre.

*Oven-broiled Dengaku: Preheat oven broiler to its highest temperature. Place unskewered tofu pieces into a baking dish in one snug layer, then pour in water to a depth of ¼ inch. Broil tofu as near the flame as possible until speckled. Turn tofu over with a spatula and broil the second side. Spread with miso topping about 1/8 inch thick, and broil once again until topping is lightly speckled. Insert skewers or small forks into the end of each tofu piece before serving.

*Oven-baked Dengaku: Spread the pieces of tofu with topping and bake on a cookie sheet at 350° until lightly browned.

*Skewered, Charcoal-broiled Dengaku: In this method used at the Nakamura-ro restaurant, the tofu is broiled over a bed of live coals in a rectangular brazier about 24 by 3½ by 4 inches deep. Cut tofu into Dengaku-sized pieces and pierce with small bamboo skewers so that the skewer tips extend about ½ inch out the front of each piece. Lay skewered tofu across mouth of brazier and broil as in the basic recipe above. Spread with Kinome Miso (p. 43) and serve each piece topped with a sprig of *kinome*.

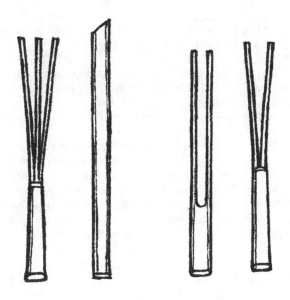

Fig. 46. A variety of skewers

*Simmered Dengaku: Prepare Simmering Tofu (p. 142). Remove tofu from the hot water, cut into dengaku-sized pieces, and insert skewers. Spread on topping and serve. Or the tofu may be skewered before it is simmered; invite each guest to hold one end of skewer as tofu cooks.

*Unheated, Unskewered Dengaku: Drain tofu well, then cut into Dengaku-sized pieces. Arrange on a platter and top each piece with a dollop of Sweet Simmered Miso.

Tofu Teriyaki   SERVES 4

24 ounces regular or grilled tofu, drained and pressed (p. 96;
    sliced tofu method)
2/3 cup Teriyaki Sauce (p. 48)

Combine tofu and sauce in a shallow pan; marinate tofu pieces for 30 minutes on each side. Grill tofu over a barbeque or broil in an oven (or on a Japanese-style broiling screen; see p. 36), basting with the sauce from time to time. Serve hot, accompanied by the remaining sauce for dipping, or by a mixture of 1/3 cup grated *daikon* and 1½ teaspoons shoyu. Also delicious served topped with a sprinkling of *sansho* pepper.

For variety, roll the pressed tofu in *kuzu* or arrowroot and deep-fry before marinating.

Additional Suggestions for Serving Tofu Broiled

*Barbequed Tofu: Press whole 12-ounce cakes of tofu until quite firm (p. 96). Barbeque until both sides are lightly speckled. Cut tofu horizontally into halves and barbeque the uncooked surfaces. Serve topped with a few drops of shoyu, a Shoyu Dipping Sauce (p. 40), or Sweet Simmered Miso (p. 41).

*Broiled Tofu Patties: Prepare Tofu-Brown Rice Croquettes (without bread crumbs) (p. 132), Tofu Burgers (p. 127), or Homemade Ganmo (p. 186). Broil like hamburger patties until richly browned. Serve topped with your favorite sauce.

TOFU SIMMERED IN ONE-POT COOKERY AND SEASONED BROTHS

In *nabe* (pronounced nah-bay) "one-pot" cookery, the food is prepared right at the table in a large earthenware casserole or tureen placed on top of a charcoal brazier, table-top burner, electric coil, or alcohol burner. An electric skillet can also be used, or the food may be prepared in the kitchen and brought steaming hot to the table. The *nabe* contains the entire meal, and each guest serves himself from the bounty of its many delicacies. Usually served during the cold months, *nabe* dishes almost always contain tofu together with a wide range of vegetables. The tofu is cooked for only a few minutes, since overcooking gives it an undesirably firm and porous structure.

The tradition of Japanese *nabe* cookery probably had its origins in the various Chinese "firepots" or "chafing pots," of which there are two main types. The Mongolian firepot *(huo kuo)*, typical of northern China, consists of a large brass or pewter bowl 9 to 12 inches in diameter. Through its center rises a hollow, vertical funnel containing a grating set at the same level as the bottom of the pot. Live coals lowered onto the grating from the mouth of the chimney-funnel heat the water or broth in the surrounding bowl (fig. 47). The second type of pot resembles a traditional American chafing dish. A large, shallow basin resting on a brass stand is heated by a small alcohol burner. As the flames from the burner dance up through the latticework in the collar of the stand, they take on a greenish hue from the copper in the brass. Placed at the center of the large round dining table found in most Chinese homes, the firepot itself becomes a warm and friendly centerpiece for the communal dinner on chilly evenings from about November to March. Each person cooks his own ingredients in the pot's simmering broth.

As in most Japanese *nabe* dishes, tofu is one of the key ingredients in Chinese firepots. The Sandy Pot of Chekiang, for example, is a close relative of Japan's famous Simmering Tofu, with tofu serving as the main ingredient. Prepared in the kitchen rather than at the table, the tofu is cooked in a chicken-base stock together with long rice noodles, Chinese cabbage, black mushrooms, bean sprouts, water chestnuts, various seafoods, and thin slices of meat. Deep-fried tofu is used in the *Huichou* Pot, the Ten Varieties Pot, and the Chrysanthemum Pot. In the latter preparation, the ingredients simmer in a light fish broth in a large chafing dish and receive a topping of white chrysanthemum petals just before being served. In the Porcelan Pot of Yunan, the food is steamed in the covered bowl by means of a perforated funnel rising through the bowl's center. Like *nabe* dishes, each of these dishes is served accompanied by a dipping sauce (see p. 263).

Fig. 47. Chinese firepots

Simmering Tofu
(*Yudofu or Tofu no Mizutaki*)

SERVES 4 TO 6

One of Japan's three or four most popular tofu dishes, Simmering Tofu is the simplest of the many *nabe* dishes. The wintertime counterpart of Chilled Tofu, it brings out the delicate flavors of fine tofu and allows them to be enjoyed to their utmost.

The early history of Simmering Tofu centers in two Zen temples in the ancient capital of Kyoto. According to one tradition, this dish was first served in Japan about 500 years ago at Tenryu-ji temple. At that time, the abbot of Myochi-in, a subtemple of Tenryu-ji, was invited by a Chinese high prince to the Imperial Court at Peking to study Ming dynasty culture. The abbot was apparently well received at the capital, where he was introduced to the finest of Chinese cuisine, including the tradition of firepot cookery. Upon his return to Japan, he is said to have introduced Simmering Tofu to the monks at his temple. Several centuries later, the temple became the well-known restaurant Nishiyama Sōdo (p. 312), where to this day Simmering Tofu remains the specialty of the house.

According to another tradition, Simmering Tofu was invented by the monks at Nanzen-ji temple in the eastern part of Kyoto. It is said that since "ancient times" the dish has been served each year on the evening of December 8, at the end of the intensive one-week meditation period held annually to commemorate the enlightenment of Shakyamuni Buddha. Nanzenji's Simmering Tofu is now famous throughout Japan. It is served within the temple compound at the Okutan *Shojin-ryori* restaurant (p. 308) and at a number of other restaurants in the vicinity. Each restaurant has its own type of heating and serving container (fig. 48).

Fig. 48. A Simmering Tofu serving container
heated by coals from within

Thus, Japan's finest Simmering Tofu is still to be found in Kyoto where it is typical of the simple, delicate flavors characterizing Kyoto cuisine. Since the tofu—like the melted cheese in fondue—retains a remarkable amount of heat, it is often served outdoors on chilly winter nights; the bright fire, bubbling pot, and feeling of warm conviviality that accompany it all lend a special magic to this do-it-yourself delicacy.

Tosa-joyu Dipping Sauce (p. 41)
2 leeks or 4 scallions, sliced into very thin rounds
1 teaspoon 7-spice red pepper
1 tablespoon grated gingerroot
1 sheet of *nori*, toasted and cut into thin strips (or crumbled)
A 5- to 6-inch square of *kombu*, wiped clean; or substitute ½ teaspoon salt
6 cups boiling water
3 pounds tofu, cut into 1¼-inch cubes or 2-inch squares ¾-inch thick

Bring the sauce to a boil and pour into a heat-resistant cup. Arrange the leeks, red pepper, gingerroot, and *nori* on a platter and place on the table. Set a charcoal brazier or gas burner at the center of the dining table. Atop heat source place a large casserole, tureen, chafing dish, or copper pot. Place *kombu* at the bottom of casserole and set the cup of dipping sauce atop the *kombu*. Now fill the casserole with boiling water, return to the boil, and drop in tofu.

Invite each guest to ladle some of the dipping sauce into a small dish provided for this purpose and add to it his choice of garnishes and seasonings. After 2 or 3 minutes, or as soon as the tofu begins to sway in the simmering water or float to the surface, each guest uses a slotted spoon or pair of chopsticks to lift out the tofu. Dip tofu into sauce-and-garnish mixture before eating.

VARIATIONS
*Chinese-style Dipping Sauce:
    1 egg yolk
    2 tablespoons shoyu
    2 tablespoons sake or white wine
    1 tablespoon minced leek greens
    1 tablespoon bonita flakes

Place all ingredients in the heat resistant cup, and heat in the *nabe*. Stir occasionally until mixture is quite thick, then remove from *nabe* and serve as above.
*Use Mirin-Shoyu, Lemon-Shoyu or Shoyu Dipping Sauces (p. 40) in place of Tosa-joyu.
*Any of the following garnishes may also be used: Grated *wasabi*, bonita flakes, grated *daikon*, grated *yuzu* or lemon peel, *sansho* pepper, finely minced garlic, or lemon juice. The combination of leeks, gingerroot, and lemon juice is a tangy favorite. Western-style garnishes which may be mixed with shoyu include diced hard-boiled egg, diced or grated cheese, chives, garlic, or sesame butter.
*Add 2 to 4 tablespoons of sake or white wine to the water in the casserole.
*Use kinugoshi or grilled tofu.
*Add any of the following to the simmering broth several minutes before adding the tofu:
    8 to 10 mushrooms (Western-style, *shiitake*, cloud-ear, or *enokidake*)
    8 ounces chrysanthemum leaves
    4 leaves of Chinese cabbage cut into 3-inch-wide strips
    2 celery stalks, cut into matchsticks

Four Nabe Dishes Containing Tofu

Each of the following popular *nabe* dishes is prepared in basically the same way as Simmering Tofu. After the broth is brought to a boil in the *nabe* pot, however, each guest adds to it his choice of ingredients which are arranged on large platters. After the foods have been cooked for 2 or 3 minutes or until tender, they are removed from the simmering broth one piece at a time and dipped into the garnished dipping sauce. *Nabeyaki Udon* features whole-wheat or buckwheat noodles, often freshly prepared by the head cook just before mealtime. *Yosenabe* means "a gathering of everything." In the countryside, Chinese cabbage and leeks are its basic ingredients, while in the cities and particularly along the seacoasts, this dish generally includes lobster, fish, clams, prawns, and sometimes chicken and pork. *Mizutaki* means "cooked in water." The main ingredient here is usually chicken and the broth is a chicken stock. *Chirinabe* is very similar to *Mizutaki* except that it usually contains chunks of white fish rather than chicken. Each of these *nabe* dishes serves 6.

Nabeyaki-udon, Nabeyaki-soba, and Udon-tsuki

Basic Ingredients:
   1 pound *(udon)* whole-wheat noodles or *(soba)* buck-
      wheat noodles, cooked (p. 50)
   6 eggs, poached in the broth
   6 mushrooms and ½ pound sliced bamboo shoots pre-
      simmered in Sweetened Shoyu Broth (p. 40)
   1 pound Chinese cabbage leaves, cut into 3-inch-wide
      strips
   ½ pound spinach leaves
   24 ounces tofu, cut into 1-inch cubes
   6 cakes of dried wheat gluten
   6 pieces of vegetable tempura (optional)
   6 small ganmo balls (optional)
Broth:
   9 cups dashi (p. 39), stock, or water
   ¾ cup shoyu
   ¼ cup *mirin* or natural sugar
Garnishes:
   Thinly sliced leeks
   Grated *yuzu* or lemon peel
   Crumbled, toasted *nori*
   7-spice red pepper

Sprinkle garnishes over broth in casserole just before serving.
Since dipping sauce is not ordinarily used, invite each guest to
ladle garnished broth into individual serving bowls to be used
for the purpose.

Yosenabe

Basic Ingredients:
   4 Chinese cabbage leaves, cut into 3-inch-wide strips
   2 leeks (including green stems), cut into 2-inch lengths
   6 chrysanthemum or spinach leaves
   1 carrot, cut diagonally into thin ovals and parboiled
   2 ounces dry transparent noodles
   12 small mushrooms
   4 ounces dry noodles
   24 ounces tofu, cut into 1-inch cubes
   6 cakes of dried wheat gluten
   3 small ganmo balls (optional)
   3 eggs, poached in the broth
Dipping Sauce:
   Tangy Shoyu Dipping Sauce (p. 41)
Broth:
   6 cups dashi (p. 39), stock, or water
   2 teaspoons shoyu
   2 teaspoons sake
   ¾ teaspoon salt

Mizutaki

Basic Ingredients:
   4 carrots, cut diagonally into thin ovals
   2 leeks, cut into 4-inch-long matchsticks
   ½ pound bamboo shoots, cut into thin half moons
   12 mushrooms

   1½ pounds Chinese cabbage (if desired, parboil leaves,
      roll into tight cylinders, and cut into 1-inch lengths)
   12 sprigs of watercress
   24 ounces tofu, cut into 1-inch cubes
   9 ounces ganmo cut into thin strips, used as a substitute
      for the chicken
Broth:
   4 cups dashi (p. 39), stock, or water, seasoned with a
      5-inch square of *kombu*
Dipping Sauce:
   ¾ cup Lemon-Shoyu (p. 40); or 6 tablespoons each
      lemon juice and vinegar, and ½ cup shoyu
Garnishes:
   Grated *daikon*
   Sliced leeks or scallions
   7-spice red pepper

Chirinabe

Prepare as for *Mizutaki* but use Vinegar-Shoyu (p. 40), Sweetened Vinegar-Shoyu (p. 41), or Tangy Shoyu Dipping Sauce
(p. 41) instead of Lemon-Shoyu. Additional ingredients include transparent noodles and trefoil.

Chinese-style Firepots with Tofu

   Although generally more elaborate and complex than
Japanese *nabe* dishes, and containing a number of distinctly
Chinese ingredients, Chinese-style firepots are prepared in
basically the same manner as their Japanese counterparts.
Dipping sauces, which often contain red doufuru, may be
either a mixture of up to ten spicy ingredients (p. 263), or a
raw egg mixed with a little soy sauce and some of the cooking
broth (p. 143). Detailed recipes for the Chrysanthemum
Chafing Pot, Ten Varieties Pot, *Huichou* Pot, and Sandy Pot
are given in Buwei Yang Chao's delightful *How to Cook and
Eat in Chinese* (see Bibliography).

Miso Oden
SERVES 3

Gingerroot-Miso Dipping Sauce (p. 46), Rich Red Nerimiso
   (p. 42), or Yuzu Miso (p. 42)
12 ounces tofu or grilled tofu, cut into 1- by 3- by ½-inch
   strips
1 cake of *konnyaku*
4 inches large *daikon*, cut into ½-inch-thick half moons
A 5-inch square of *kombu*, wiped clean; or substitute ½ teaspoon salt

Place the miso sauce into a small heat-resistant cup. Spear
each tofu strip with two (6-inch bamboo) skewers or a fork.
Rub *konnyaku* well with salt, rinse, cut crosswise into ½-
inch-wide strips, and skewer each piece. Parboil *daikon*, then
skewer each piece.

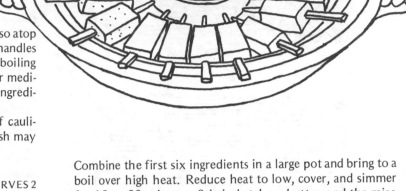

Fig. 49. Miso Oden

Place *kombu* in a casserole and set the cup of miso atop it. Arrange skewered ingredients around the cup with handles of skewers resting on rim of casserole (fig. 49). Add boiling water to just cover ingredients, return to the boil over medium heat, then simmer for 3 minutes. Dip skewered ingredients into miso sauce before eating.

For variety, add parboiled skewered pieces of cauliflower, potato, sweet potato, yam, or turnip. This dish may also be prepared at the table as for Simmering Tofu.

Yukinabe *(The Snow Pot)*   SERVES 2

This dish derives its name from the fact that the grated *daikon* turns snow white after it has been thoroughly cooked.

¼ cup shoyu
½ cup grated *daikon*
1 cup boiling water
12 ounces tofu, cut into 1¼-inch cubes
½ leek, cut into thin rounds, rinsed and pressed (p. 37)
1 tablespoon bonita flakes or crumbled, toasted *nori*

Pour the shoyu into a small heat-resistant cup and place in the center of a casserole set atop a tabletop brazier. Surround the cup with the grated *daikon* mixed with the boiling water, and return to the boil over high heat. Reduce heat to low and simmer for 3 minutes, or until *daikon* starts to become transparent. Place tofu on surface of *daikon*, return to the boil, and serve. Invite each guest to ladle a little hot shoyu and *daikon* into his or her individual serving dish, and garnish with leeks and bonita flakes; use as a dipping sauce.

Other possible garnishes include grated gingerroot, 7-spice red pepper, and grated *yuzu* peel.

Tofu & Miso Stew   SERVES 4

1½ onions, cut into thin rounds or wedges
4 mushrooms, cut into halves
1½ cups cubed sweet potatoes, yams, or potatoes
½ small carrot, cut into thin rounds
¼ cup green peas or thinly sliced green peppers
2 cups water or stock
¼ cup ketchup
1½ tablespoons butter
¼ cup red, barley, or Hatcho miso
12 ounces tofu, cut into 14 small rectangles (p. 37)
¼ cup grated cheese (optional)

Combine the first six ingredients in a large pot and bring to a boil over high heat. Reduce heat to low, cover, and simmer for 15 to 20 minutes. Stir in ketchup, butter, and the miso thinned in a few tablespoons of the hot broth. Cover and simmer for 15 minutes more. Add tofu and simmer, covered, for 5 more minutes. Stir in the cheese, if used. Serve hot or cold.

If desired, add chunks of deep-fried tofu, *daikon*, burdock root, cabbage, or broccoli; season with curry powder.

VARIATION

Jibu-ni (Country-style Tofu & Miso Stew): In a heavy pot combine 2 cups water or dashi, ¼ cup each barley miso and bonita flakes, and 12 ounces thinly-sliced, parboiled tofu. Cover and bring to a boil, then reduce heat and simmer for about 1 hour. Serve steaming hot. Nothing better for chilly winter nights!

Niyakko   SERVES 2

This popular dish is the simmered counterpart of *Hiyayakko* or Chilled Tofu. In both preparations the tofu is cut into large cubes called *yakko* (see p. 105).

2/3 cup dashi (p. 39) or stock
1½ tablespoons shoyu
2 teaspoons *mirin*
12 ounces tofu, cut into 6 cubes
¼ cup sliced leeks (very thin rounds)
3 tablespoons bonita flakes
Dash of *sansho* pepper (optional)

Combine the first three ingredients in a small saucepan and bring to a boil. Add tofu, return to the boil, and simmer for 3 minutes, or until tofu is just warmed through. Add sliced leek and remove from heat. Divide among serving bowls and serve immediately, topped with a sprinkling of bonita flakes and *sansho* pepper.

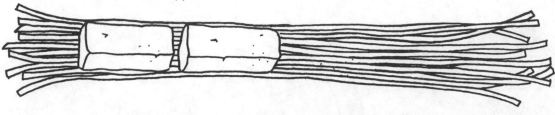

Fig. 50. Tofu wrapped in rice straw

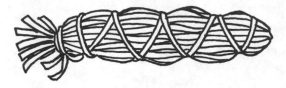

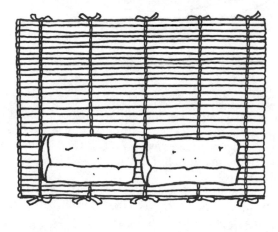

Simmered Tofu Wrapped in Rice Straw
(Tsuto-dofu or Komo-dofu)

A *tsuto* is a wrapper made of rice straw; a *komo* is a piece of straw or rush matting. Traditionally, both were used throughout Japan for wrapping foods. This tofu preparation is a favorite in the countryside, especially on Japan's southern island of Kyushu. Fresh rice straw imparts its tasty aroma and subtle flavor to the tofu, and lengthy simmering expels excess water from the tofu and gives it the porous texture that makes it more absorbent when simmered in seasoned broths. In urban areas, where fresh rice straw is not available, the tofu is often wrapped in a *(sudare)* bamboo mat while being simmered.

Cut a 12-ounce cake of tofu lengthwise into halves. Place 16 to 20 strands of fresh rice straw, each 20 inches long, side by side on a cutting board. Lay the tofu pieces end to end on top of the straw near one end (fig. 50). Fold the other end of straw over top of tofu, and tie with a single strand. Now bind straw around tofu from end to end, wrapping tofu 8 to 10

times with a long strand of rice straw to form a cylindrical bundle about 1½ inches in diameter. (If using a bamboo mat, lay the tofu pieces end to end across one end of the mat, roll up the mat to form a cylinder, and tie in several places with string.)

Combine the wrapped tofu and 1 to 2 quarts water in a large pot. Bring to a boil and simmer for 20 minutes. Unwrap and serve with your choice of Shoyu Dipping Sauces (p. 40) and garnishes, or simmer for 20 to 30 minutes more with vegetables in a broth of dashi or stock seasoned with shoyu. Also delicious in Clear Soups (p. 119) or Oden (p. 175).

For a more elaborate variety of *tsuto-dofu*, mash the tofu and mix with chopped vegetables, ground sesame, and slivered mushrooms. Shape mixture into cylinders and wrap in rice straw.

TOFU STEAMED

Any Japanese or Chinese family kitchen can get along fine without an oven—but not without a good steamer. In the few Chinese homes which have ovens, they are used for baking pastries only. In Japan, foods are usually steamed in a bamboo steamer *(seiro)* set over a wok (p. 35). But a collapsible French steamer or a plate set on top of a bowl in a lidded pot or pressure cooker are both satisfactory substitutes. For instructions on preparing a steamer see page 38.

Tofu Steamed in Chinese Lotus Spoons

SERVES 2 OR 3

12 ounces tofu, pressed (p. 96) and mashed
3 1/3 tablespoons milk
1 egg white
½ teaspoon natural sugar
½ teaspoon salt
¾ cup Gingerroot Sauce (p. 49)

Combine the first five ingredients, mixing well. Press the mixture into 8 Chinese porcelan "lotus spoons" (the kind with the flat bottom used for serving Chinese soups), or into large Western-style serving spoons. Steam tofu in the spoons for 10 minutes in a preheated steamer (p. 38). Remove firm tofu from spoons, invert, and arrange on a large serving plate. Serve topped with the hot sauce and accompanied by the spoons, which are now used to eat the tofu.

Tofu Chawan-mushi
(Steamed Egg-Vegetable Custard)

6 ounces tofu, cut into ½-inch cubes
4 small mushrooms, cut into thin strips
¼ onion, thinly sliced
4 slivers of lemon peel
4 ginkgo nuts (optional)
4 lilly bulb sections (optional)
4 small cakes of dried wheat gluten (optional)
2 cups dashi (p. 39) or stock, cooled to room temperature
1 tablespoon shoyu
2 teaspoons *mirin*
3 eggs, lightly beaten
½ teaspoon salt
4 trefoil or spinach leaves

Divide the first seven ingredients among 4 custard cups with lids or 4 *chawan-mushi* cups. Combine the dashi, shoyu, *mirin*, eggs, and salt, and pour through a strainer into the four cups. Set a trefoil leaf on surface of liquid in each cup. Place cups into a large pot and pour water into pot until water comes halfway up the sides of the cups. Cover cups with individual lids, aluminum foil, or a large sheet of paper (figure, p. 38). Now cover pot and bring to a boil over high heat. Reduce heat and simmer for about 13 minutes, or until custard is firm but not porous. Serve hot or cold.

VARIATIONS

*Simmer the mushrooms in Sweetened Shoyu Broth (p. 40) before placing them in the custard cups.
*Substitute soymilk for all or part of the dashi.
*Add to or substitute for the vegetables used one or more of the following: snow peas, fresh corn, parboiled cubes of sweet potato, yam or potato, chestnuts, small rolls of fresh or dried yuba, green peas, or turnip cubes.

Nanzen-ji Wrapped Tofu

24 ounces tofu
¼ to ½ cup Yuzu Miso (p. 42) or any Sweet Simmered Miso (p. 41)

Cut tofu into four pieces. With the sharp point of a knife, cut a section 2 inches square and 1 inch deep from the surface of each piece, and lift out carefully (fig. 51). Fill the well that remains with 1 to 2 tablespoons of the miso, then replace the small piece of tofu atop the miso. Wrap each piece of tofu in strong, absorbent paper (the Japanese use *washi* for this purpose) or in aluminum foil.

Bring water to a boil in a steamer (p. 38). Place wrapped tofu in steamer and steam for 5 to 10 minutes, or until miso is well heated. Serve hot, inviting each guest to unwrap his portion just before eating.

Other Ways of Serving Tofu in Steamed Dishes

*Yuzu Treasure Pot *(Yuzu-gama):* Cut a large *yuzu* horizontally into halves and hollow out the insides. Place 1 or 2 teaspoons Yuzu Miso (p. 42) in the bottom of each half, then pack firmly with squeezed tofu (p. 97). Spread a thin layer of the miso on top of tofu and rejoin the *yuzu* halves. Place in a heated steamer and steam for about 13 minutes. Serve hot or cold.
*Tofu Spiral in Butterbur Leaves *(Naruto-dofu):* Soak 2 small butterbur leaves overnight in a mixture of 5 cups water and 1 tablespoon baking soda. Parboil drained leaves, then drain again. Mix 2 parts squeezed tofu (p. 97) with 1 part grated glutinous yam and season lightly with salt. Spread this mixture in an even layer on each of the leaves, then roll up. Steam until firm. Cut into ½-inch sections to serve.
*Use tofu in Shinoda-maki (p. 195).

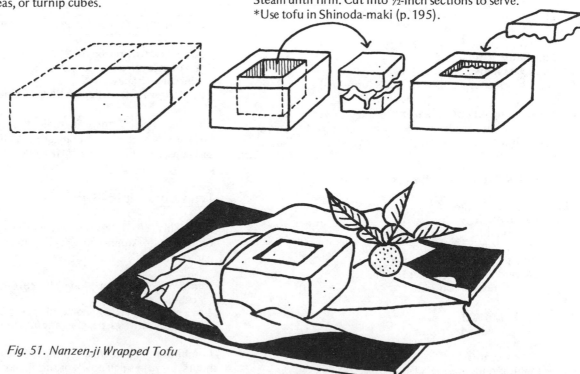

Fig. 51. Nanzen-ji Wrapped Tofu

TOFU DESSERTS

Tofu can be adapted to fresh fruit purées, whipped cream toppings, puddings, dessert soufflés, Japanese-style confections—even cheese cake.

Uncooked Desserts

In each of these preparations, nigari tofu gives by far the best flavor and consistency. Most take only a few minutes to prepare and, containing little sweetening, can also be used as side dishes at any meal.

Tofu Whipped Cream or Yogurt   MAKES 1½ CUPS

This delicious dish can be used like whipped cream or, as the basis of desserts, like yogurt.

12 ounces tofu
2 tablespoons honey or natural sugar
Dash of salt (optional)
½ teaspoon vanilla extract (optional)

Combine all ingredients in a blender and purée until smooth. To serve as yogurt, top with a sprinkling of slivered almonds or walnut meats, shredded coconut, and raisins. Or reduce the sweetening by one-half and top with Okara Granola (p. 84).

Tofu-Fruit Whips   SERVES 2 OR 3

These refreshing summertime desserts can be transformed into high-protein breakfast dishes by reducing or eliminating the sweetening.

½ pound fresh strawberries or peaches
12 ounces tofu, chilled
2 tablespoons honey or natural sugar
Chopped nutmeats or sunflower seeds (optional)

Combine all ingredients in a blender and purée until smooth. If desired, top with nutmeats. Serve immediately in small dessert dishes or use as a topping for pancakes, crêpes, or waffles.

VARIATIONS: Prepare as in the basic recipe:

*Banana-Lemon Whip
    2 small bananas
    6 ounces tofu
    Juice of ½ lemon
    1 to 2 tablespoons honey
    ½ teaspoon sesame butter (optional)
    Dash of nutmeg (optional)

*Coconut-Raisin Whip
    ½ cup shredded coconut
    ¼ cup raisins
    12 ounces tofu
    3 tablespoons marmalade

*Banana-Raisin Whip
    2 bananas
    ¼ cup raisins
    6 ounces tofu
    1 teaspoon honey
    ¼ cup toasted wheat germ
    Dash of nutmeg (optional)
*Honey-Lemon Whip
    1 tablespoon lemon juice
    ¼ to ½ teaspoon grated lemon rind (optional)
    1 tablespoon honey
    6 ounces tofu

Chunky Tofu-Pineapple Purée   SERVES 3

1½ cups pineapple chunks, drained
12 ounces tofu, drained (p. 96)
1½ teaspoons honey (optional)

Combine 1 cup pineapple chunks with the tofu and honey in a blender and purée until smooth. Served topped with remaining pineapple chunks.

Tangy Tofu-Prune Purée   SERVES 2

1½ cups stewed prunes
8 ounces tofu
3 tablespoons lemon juice

Combine all ingredients in a blender and purée until smooth. For best flavor, chill for several hours before serving. Delicious also as a breakfast fruit dish or topping for buttered toast.

Tofu-Orange Juice Purée with Tangerines   SERVES 4

12 ounces tofu, pressed (p. 96)
1 cup orange juice
1 tablespoon honey
1 cup tangerine or orange sections, drained

Combine the first three ingredients in a blender and purée until smooth. Stir in the tangerine sections, spoon into dessert cups, and chill for several hours.

Fruit Cocktail Chilled Tofu   SERVES 2

This refreshing summertime dish is a close relative of Chinese-style Annin-dofu (p. 268) in which mock tofu is prepared from milk jelled with agar.

6 to 8 ounces tofu or kinugoshi, chilled and cut into ½-inch
    cubes
1 to 2 cups canned fruit cocktail or sections of fresh mandarin
    oranges, cherries, peaches and/or chunks of pineapple

Combine all ingredients, mixing lightly, and chill for about 6 hours. Serve in small bowls or shrimp cocktail dishes.

Banana-Sesame Cream

SERVES 4

12 ounces tofu
2 tablespoons honey
2 bananas
¾ cup milk (soy or dairy)
1 to 1½ tablespoons sesame butter, *tahini*, or ground roasted
    sesame seeds (p. 38)

Combine all ingredients in a blender and purée until smooth.
Serve chilled as a dessert, or use as a topping for pancakes,
waffles, crêpes, or Nut Crunch (see below).

Banana Dessert with Tofu Whipped Cream

SERVES 4 TO 6

4 bananas, cut into long ovals
½ cup peanut or sesame butter
2 tablespoons honey
½ cup raisins
1½ cups Tofu Whipped Cream (p. 148)
¼ to ½ cup toasted wheat germ or Okara Granola (p. 84)

Arrange banana slices on a large platter. Combine peanut
butter and honey and mix until smooth. Spread mixture over
each banana slice, dot with raisins, and top with a spoonful of
the whipped cream. Serve sprinkled with wheat germ.

Banana-Tofu Milkshake

SERVES 3 TO 4

6 ounces (nigari) tofu
3 small frozen bananas, or fresh bananas and 3 ice cubes
1 tablespoon honey
¼ cup toasted wheat germ
¼ teaspoon nutmeg
¼ cup cold milk (soy or dairy)

Combine all ingredients in a blender and purée until smooth.
Serve immediately. When milk is omitted, this preparation
has the texture of banana ice cream.

Nut Crunch with Tofu Whipped Cream

SERVES 6

2 bananas, cut into thin rounds; or 2 apples, cut into wedges
¼ cup chopped almond meats
¼ cup chopped walnut meats
¼ cup sunflower seeds
¼ cup raisins
¼ cup chopped pitted dates
¼ cup shredded coconut
1½ cups Tofu Whipped Cream (p. 148) or Banana-Sesame
    Cream (p. 149)
3 tablespoons toasted wheat germ (optional)

Combine the first seven ingredients in a large bowl; mix well.
Serve in individual bowls topped with the whipped cream and
a sprinkling of wheat germ.

Tofu-Strawberry Dessert

SERVES 4 TO 6

24 ounces tofu, chilled and mashed
4½ tablespoons honey
2 teaspoons vanilla extract
12 to 15 strawberries, cut vertically into halves
¼ cup sliced hazel or almond nutmeats

Combine the tofu, honey, and vanilla in a large serving bowl;
mix well with a fork. Dot the surface with strawberries, then
sprinkle with sliced nutmeats.

Tofu Cream Cheese Dessert Balls

MAKES 6 TO 8

1 cup Tofu Cream Cheese (p. 109)
2 tablespoons shredded coconut
2 tablespoons chopped dates or raisins
¼ teaspoon cinnamon
½ teaspoon grated lemon or orange rind
½ teaspoon vanilla extract
½ cup chopped almonds

Combine the first six ingredients and 2 tablespoons chopped
almonds in a large bowl. Mix well, shape into 1½-inch balls,
and roll in remaining almonds. Serve chilled.

Tofu Icing

MAKES 1 CUP

12 ounces tofu, squeezed (p. 97); or 1 cup Tofu Cream
    Cheese (p. 109)
2 or 3 tablespoons sugar; or 2 tablespoons honey
½ teaspoon vanilla
Dash of salt
2 tablespoons powdered milk (optional)
1½ teaspoons grated lemon or orange rind (optional)

Combine all ingredients in a blender and purée for 30 seconds; refrigerate until just before serving on cake or cupcakes.

Tofu Ice Cream

SERVES 3 OR 4

18 ounces tofu, well chilled
3 tablespoons honey
¼ teaspoon vanilla extract
1/8 teaspoon salt

Combine 12 ounces tofu, honey, vanilla, and salt in a blender
and purée for about 1 minute. Transfer to a covered container
and place in the freezer overnight.

    Purée remaining 6 ounces tofu in the blender until
smooth. Cut the frozen tofu into small chunks. While purée-
ing at high speed, add a few chunks at a time to the tofu in the
blender until all has been added and the mixture is smooth
and thick. Serve immediately.

    For variety, add toward the end of puréeing: 1 egg
yolk, 2 to 4 tablespoons each chopped almonds or shredded
coconut, and your choice of fresh or frozen fruits. Serve
topped with chopped nutmeats. Or add 1 teaspoon powdered
green tea *(matcha)* and 1 additional tablespoon honey; omit
vanilla.

Cooked and Baked Desserts

Tofu can be used like dairy products to add plenty of protein and a rich, creamy texture to your favorite desserts. Apples, raisins, and small amounts of honey make delicious natural sweeteners.

Tofu Cheesecake

SERVES 6 TO 8

Filling:

    24 ounces tofu, well drained or pressed (p. 96)
    1½ tablespoons natural sugar or honey
    ¼ cup raisins, minced
    1 tablespoon lemon juice
    ½ teaspoon grated lemon rind
    1 tablespoon *tahini* or sesame butter
    ½ teaspoon vanilla
    1/8 teaspoon salt
    1 or 2 eggs (optional)
    1 teaspoon white wine or sake (optional)
    ¼ cup walnut meats, minced (optional)
2 teaspoons butter
Crust:
    1 cup crunchy granola
    2 teaspoons honey
    2 teaspoons lemon juice

Preheat oven to 350°. Combine all filling ingredients in a blender and purée until smooth. Coat an 8-inch pie tin with the butter. Combine ¾ cup granola with the honey and lemon juice, mix well, and press into the tin to form a crust. Spoon filling over crust, smooth filling surface, and sprinkle with remaining ¼ cup granola. Bake for about 25 minutes or until surface is lightly browned. Allow to cool for at least 6 to 8 hours before serving.

This filling also works well with conventional cheesecake crusts. If desired, served topped with applesauce or Tofu Whipped Cream (p. 148).

Tofu-Rice Pudding

SERVES 4

12 ounces tofu, mashed
1 cup cooked Brown Rice (p. 50)
1 cup milk (soy or dairy)
3 tablespoons honey
¼ teaspoon salt
¼ teaspoon cinnamon
¼ cup raisins
1 teaspoon oil
3 tablespoons crushed corn flakes or cracker crumbs
2 tablespoons butter

Preheat oven to 350°. Combine the first seven ingredients in a large bowl; mix well. Coat a casserole or bread pan with the oil, spoon in the tofu-rice mixture, sprinkle with corn flakes, and dot with butter. Bake for 25 minutes, or until set. Or omit the corn flakes and simmer all ingredients in a large saucepan over low heat for 10 to 15 minutes, or until firm.

Apple-Raisin Dessert with Tofu Whipped Cream

SERVES 4

¼ cup water
3 apples, cut into thin wedges
¼ to ½ cup raisins
4 teaspoons lemon juice (optional)
1 tablespoon butter (optional)
¼ teaspoon cinnamon
Tofu Whipped Cream (p. 148)

Combine water and apple in a small saucepan. Simmer, covered, stirring occasionally, for 10 to 15 minutes until apples are tender and the water has mostly evaporated. Stir in remaining ingredients and cook for several minutes more. Spoon into serving bowls, sprinkle with cinnamon, and serve hot or cold topped with whipped cream.

For variety, core the apples and fill with raisins, brown sugar, and cinnamon. Wrap in aluminum foil and bake in a 350° oven for about 20 minutes. Cut vertically into halves and serve topped with the whipped cream.

Crêpes with Apple-Whipped Cream Filling

MAKES 12 TO 15

1½ cups (whole-wheat) flour, sifted
1 cup milk (soy or dairy)
2 eggs, lightly beaten
¼ teaspoon salt
2 tablespoons oil or butter
Apple-Raisin Dessert with Tofu Whipped Cream (above)

Combine the first four ingredients in a large bowl; mix just until smooth. Heat a skillet and coat very lightly with oil. Add just enough batter to cover bottom of skillet in a very thin layer. Cook over medium-high heat on both sides until golden brown. Repeat until all batter is used. Top each crêpe with the apple-raisin dessert.

Tofu Dessert Soufflé

SERVES 4

2 tablespoons oil
2½ tablespoons whole-wheat flour
¾ cup milk (soy or dairy)
6 ounces tofu, mashed
½ cup chopped roasted soybeans or chopped peanuts
¼ teaspoon salt
3 tablespoons honey
½ cup raisins
4 egg yolks
4 egg whites, beaten until stiff
½ teaspoon butter

Preheat oven to 350°. Heat a skillet and coat with the oil. Add 2 tablespoons flour and cook until lightly browned and fragrant. Add the milk gradually, stirring constantly, to form a thick sauce; turn off heat. Add the next six ingredients; mix well. Carefully fold mixture into egg whites. Coat a soufflé dish lightly with butter, then dust with remaining flour. Place soufflé mixture into dish and bake for 30 to 40 minutes, or until set.

Tofu Mincemeat

MAKES 5¼ CUPS

4 (tart) apples, peeled, cored, and diced
½ cup apple juice
1½ cups raisins
Grated rind of 1 orange
Juice of 1 orange
24 ounces tofu, pressed (p. 96) and mashed; or 10 ounces thick agé or ganmo, diced
½ to 1 cup nutmeats
½ teaspoon cinnamon
½ teaspoon cloves, allspice, or coriander (optional)
¼ cup Hatcho miso

Combine the first five ingredients in a heavy pot, bring to a boil, and simmer for 30 minutes. Add tofu, return to the boil, and simmer for 5 minutes more. Add the next three ingredients and miso creamed in a little of the cooking liquid; mix well and remove from heat. Allow to cool to room temperature, then cover and refrigerate for at least 8 hours. Use as a filling for mince pie or turnovers. Also delicious as a spread for buttered toast or served like chutney with curried dishes.

Tofu-Pineapple Sherbet

SERVES 3

¼ cup pineapple juice
1½ tablespoons lemon juice
1 tablespoon natural sugar or honey
1 egg, lightly beaten
½ cup crushed pineapple
1 cup finely-diced apple
¼ cup raisins
6 ounces tofu, rubbed through a sieve or puréed in a blender

Combine the first four ingredients in a saucepan. Simmer, stirring constantly, over very low heat for 4 to 5 minutes, or until thickened; allow to cool for 30 minutes. Stir in remaining ingredients, pour into a mold, and freeze for 1 hour, or until as firm as sherbet.

Tofu-Banana-Raisin Jelled Dessert

SERVES 3

½ stick of agar (4 gm), reconstituted and torn into small pieces (p. 37)
¾ cup milk
1 banana, sliced into thin rounds
1/3 cup raisins
6 ounces tofu, rubbed through a sieve or puréed in a blender
Dash of salt
¾ cup Honey-Lemon Whip (p. 148)

Combine the agar and milk in a saucepan and bring to a boil. Simmer, stirring constantly, for 3 to 4 minutes, or until agar dissolves. Mix in the next four ingredients and remove from heat. Pour into cups or a mold and allow to cool. Cover and refrigerate until firm. Serve chilled, topped with the whip.

Tofu-Peanut Butter Cookies
(High Protein)

MAKES 20

36 ounces tofu, crumbled (p. 98)
½ cup peanut butter
¼ cup brown sugar, sifted
¼ cup butter, beaten until soft
1 egg, lightly beaten
¼ teaspoon salt

Preheat oven to 350°. Combine all ingredients, mixing well to form a smooth dough. Roll dough into small balls, place balls on an oiled cookie tin, and press flat with a fork. Bake for about 15 minutes. Or press the dough into a loaf pan, bake, and serve cut into squares.

Tofu-Brown Rice Cookies

MAKES 15 TO 20

12 ounces tofu, squeezed (p. 97)
1 cup cooked Brown Rice (p. 50)
3 tablespoons natural sugar
1 tablespoon honey
¼ cup raisins
Cinnamon
¼ cup shredded coconut

Preheat oven to 350°. Combine the first five ingredients in a large bowl; mix well. Form mixture into small patties and arrange on a lightly-oiled cookie tin. Top with a sprinkling of cinnamon and the coconut. Bake for 15 to 20 minutes, or until nicely browned.

Marbled Tofu & Banana Delight

SERVES 2 OR 3

24 ounces tofu, crumbled (p. 98)
3 bananas, mashed
½ cup walnut meats (optional)
Dash of nutmeg
¼ teaspoon salt
1 tablespoon oil

Preheat oven to 350°. Combine the first five ingredients in a large bowl and mash together. Press the mixture into a small bread pan lightly coated with the oil, and bake for 20 to 30 minutes until lightly browned. Cool to room temperature before serving.

Tofu-Orange-Almond Dessert

SERVES 3

1 cup fresh orange juice
2 tablespoons honey or sugar
1½ teaspoons grated orange rind (optional)
1/8 teaspoon almond extract (optional)
12 ounces tofu, drained (p. 96) and cut into ½-inch cubes
1 cup tangerine sections, drained
3 tablespoons (toasted) sliced almonds

Combine orange juice and honey in a small saucepan and simmer uncovered until reduced to about ¾ cup. Stir in orange rind and almond extract, then combine with tofu and tangerine sections in a serving bowl. Cover and chill for at least 2 hours. Serve in dessert cups topped with sliced almonds.

Deep-fried Tofu Balls with Peanut Butter and Honey

SERVES 2 OR 3

6 ounces tofu, squeezed (p. 97)
¼ cup raisins
Dash of salt
Oil for deep-frying
1 tablespoon honey
2 tablespoons peanut butter
1 banana, sliced into thin rounds
2 tablespoons chopped peanuts

Combine tofu, raisins, and salt in a large bowl. Mix for several minutes to develop cohesiveness. Shape into 1-inch balls and allow to dry for 5 to 10 minutes.

Heat the oil to 350° in a wok, skillet, or deep-fryer. Drop in the balls and deep-fry until golden brown (p. 130); drain and allow to cool to room temperature. Arrange in a snug layer on a serving dish. Combine honey and peanut butter, mixing well, and pour mixture over deep-fried balls. Top with banana slices and peanuts. Chill in a freezer for 30 minutes, or until firm.

Tofu Custard Pudding

SERVES 3

12 ounces tofu
1 egg
2 to 2½ tablespoons honey
½ teaspoon salt
½ teaspoon vanilla extract
½ cup Tofu Whipped Cream (p. 148)

Combine first five ingredients in a blender and purée until smooth. Spoon the puréed mixture into 3 custard cups with tops. Cover cups, place in a heated steamer, and steam over low heat for 12 to 14 minutes, or until just firm. Or set the cups in a pan of hot water and bake at 325° for about 20 minutes. Serve hot or cold topped with the whipped cream.

Tofu also gives a delicious creamy texture to chocolate puddings.

Fig. 52. Gisei-dofu

Gisei-dofu
(Tofu Cheesecake-Like Dessert)

SERVES 8

Gisei means "fictitious or imitation." Traditionally, *Gisei-dofu* was any tofu preparation made to resemble a food prohibited by the precepts of Buddhism, like *ganmodoki* (p. 184) made to resemble the flavor of wild goose, and *yuba-no-kabayaki* (p. 245) designed to resemble the taste of broiled eels. In Zen Temple Cookery, regular Gisei-dofu was prepared in imitation of the flavor and texture of eggs, which the monks of most Japanese sects were forbidden to eat.

Gisei-dofu may also refer to any tofu preparation which contains—or rather conceals—a prohibited food. Whenever Buddhist monks drank sake, they referred to it as *hanya-to*, meaning "warm elixir of transcendental wisdom." When they dined on wild boar, they asked for some *yama kujira*, or "mountain whale." Likewise, they referred to eggs mixed with tofu as *Gisei-dofu*, or "mock tofu."

Gisei-dofu is one of the few representatives of tofu cuisine prepared in some traditional tofu shops. It usually contains no eggs and is broiled in sturdy copper pans over a charcoal brazier (fig. 86, p. 217).

24 ounces tofu, parboiled (p. 96) and squeezed (p. 97)
1 egg
¼ cup natural sugar

2 teaspoons shoyu
½ teaspoon (sesame) oil
3½ teaspoons *mirin*, sake, or white wine

Preheat oven to 350°. Combine the first four ingredients in a large bowl; mix well, stirring for about 5 minutes to develop cohesiveness. Press the mixture to a depth of 1 to 1½ inches into a small baking pan or pie tin coated with the oil. Place the bottom of a pan of equal size directly on top of the tofu mixture to serve as a pressing lid, then place an 8-ounce weight or 1 cup water in the upper pan. Bake for about 30 minutes, or until sides of tofu are a deep golden brown.

Remove from oven and immediately invert. Lift off upper pan so that tofu rests on top of the pressing pan. Brush and rub top and sides of tofu with *mirin*, then allow to cool. Cut into eighths to serve (fig. 52).

VARIATIONS

*Gisei-dofu Cookies: After mixing the first four ingredients in the basic recipe, shape mixture into cookies and bake on a lightly oiled tin for about 15 minutes. Brush with the *mirin* and allow to cool before serving.

*To the basic recipe add 2½ tablespoons ground roasted sesame seeds (p. 38), sesame butter, or *tahini*. Increase sweetening to 5 tablespoons honey or sugar, add ½ teaspoon salt, and omit *mirin*. Serve topped with a sprinkling of *sansho* pepper.

*Omit the egg and *mirin*. Increase sweetening to 5 tablespoons honey or sugar. This is the traditional recipe used in temple cookery.

*Sauté in (sesame) oil or simmer in Sweetened Shoyu Broth (p. 40) about ¼ cup slivered carrots, cloud-ear or *shiitake* mushrooms, green peas, or diced lotus root. Combine with 2 to 3 tablespoons diced walnut meats, ground roasted sesame seeds or roasted hemp seeds. Add to the tofu mixture before baking.

*Skewered Gisei-dofu: Cut the baked tofu into pieces 1½ by 1 by 1 inch. Pierce each piece from one end with a foodpick or a 2-pronged bamboo skewer 6 inches long. Sprinkle tofu with a dash of *sansho* pepper and garnish with 6 to 8 beefsteak seeds *(shiso-no-mi)*. Serve with shavings of *konnyaku* topped with Sweet Simmered Miso (p. 41). Or serve on a green beefsteak leaf garnished with pickled red gingerroot *(beni shoga)*.

Tofu-Egg Roll *(Datémaki)* SERVES 4

5 eggs, lightly beaten
12 ounces tofu, drained (p. 96)
¼ cup natural sugar
¼ teaspoon salt
1½ tablespoons oil

Preheat oven to 350°. Combine the first four ingredients in a blender and purée until smooth. Spread purée in a ¼-inch-thick layer over the bottom of a large baking pan (8 by 12 inches) lightly coated with oil. Bake for about 15 minutes until well set.

Using a large spatula, carefully remove freshly baked mixture from pan and transfer onto a dishtowel. Using the towel like a *sudare* (bamboo mat), roll the omelet from one end into a compact cylindrical spiral (fig. 57, p. 171). Fold both ends of towel over top of omelet to prevent spiral from unrolling, and allow to cool to room temperature. Cut roll into 1½-inch lengths and serve on small dishes with the cut spiral surface facing upward.

Additional Suggestions for Serving Tofu in Desserts

*Prepare cream puffs according to your favorite recipe. Fill with Tofu Whipped Cream (p. 148) topped with small strawberries.
*Use Sweetened Tofu Cottage Cheese (p. 109) in place of dairy cottage cheese or goat cheese in your favorite cheesecake recipe.
*Try tofu in applesauce cake or lemon pie.

9

Deep-fried Tofu

HREE TYPES of deep-fried tofu are prepared in most Japanese (and many American) tofu shops: *thick agé* (pronounced *ah-gay*), whole cakes of regular tofu which have been pressed and deep-fried; *ganmo*, deep-fried burger-shaped patties or small balls of firmly-pressed tofu containing minced vegetables and sesame seeds; and *agé*, small pouches or puffs of deep-fried tofu that can be filled with salads, grains, cooked vegetables, or other stuffings. We will begin by discussing the properties common to all three types and giving recipes in which they can be used interchangeably. In the sections that follow, we will speak more of their unique individual qualities.

Many Japanese chefs and tofu masters are of the opinion—with which we agree—that of the various types of tofu, deep-fried tofu may be most suited to Western tastes and cooking. All three varieties have a distinct, hearty flavor, golden-brown color, and firm, meaty texture that remind some of fried chicken. In fact the word *ganmo* actually means "mock goose," and this tasty tofu was originally developed by chefs who longed for the flavor of wild goose meat, a delicacy once forbidden to all but the Japanese nobility.

Deep-fried tofu can be used as a delicious and inexpensive substitute for meat in a remarkably wide variety of recipes. Grilled or broiled, it has a savory barbequed aroma; added to casseroles, sautéed vegetable dishes, or curry and spaghetti sauces, it adds body, texture, and plenty of protein; served in sandwiches, egg dishes, or atop pizzas, it may be used like cold cuts or bacon; and when frozen, its structure undergoes a total change, making it even more meatlike, tender, and absorbent.

Because the processes of pressing and deep-frying greatly reduce the water content in this tofu, it will stay fresh for long periods of time without refrigeration. Thus it is well suited for use in lunch boxes or on picnics and hikes, even during the warm summer months. Perhaps more important, it can serve as a basic daily food in tropical regions such as India or Africa where facilities for cold storage are not widely available. And, in fact, deep-fried tofu comprises a relatively large proportion of the tofu prepared in semi-tropical Taiwan and the warmer, southernmost provinces of China and Japan.

In addition to imparting a rich flavor and aroma to tofu, the process of deep-frying also adds highly digestible polyunsaturated fats, usually from either

Fig. 53. Serving freshly deep-fried agé

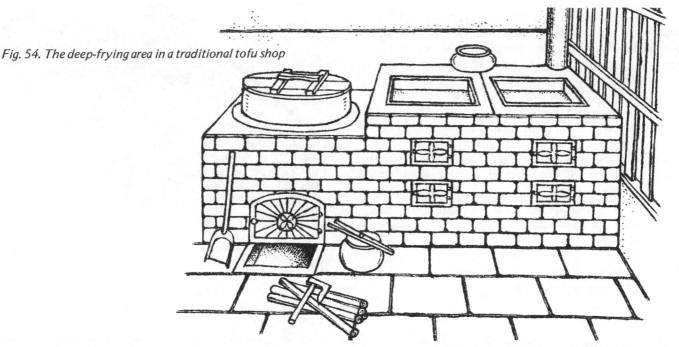

Fig. 54. The deep-frying area in a traditional tofu shop

rapeseed or soy oil. Thus when deep-fried tofu is used in place of meat, it serves as a source of the fatty acids necessary for a balanced diet and simultaneously helps to reduce the intake of saturated fats.

All varieties of deep-fried tofu are rich in protein: thick agé, ganmo, and agé contain respectively 10.1, 15.4, and 18.6 percent protein by weight. Thus both ganmo and agé have a higher percentage of protein than either eggs or hamburger (which have 13 percent each). A typical 5-ounce serving of thick agé, for example, provides about one-third of the daily adult requirement of usable protein.

Deep-fried tofu—like most deep-fried foods—is at its very best just after being prepared, while still crisp and sizzling (fig. 53). And each of the three basic types can easily be prepared at home from regular tofu using recipes given in the following three sections. Deep-fried tofu purchased commercially may be served as is, without reheating or further cooking, seasoned with any of the toppings or dipping sauces described on page 40. Or it may be lightly broiled to impart added flavor and aroma, then served in salads or other quick-and-easy preparations.

Deep-fried tofu is used in virtually every style of Japanese cuisine. Approximately one-third of all tofu served in Japan is deep-fried, and each day tofu makers prepare more than ten million pieces of agé alone!

In most Japanese tofu shops, the highly skilled work of preparing deep-fried tofu is entrusted entirely to the tofu maker's wife. She and her husband generally work side by side since, in most traditional

shops, the cauldron in which the soymilk is prepared is located next to the deep-frying area (fig. 54). Two containers of deep-frying oil are used in the preparation of ganmo and agé; one is kept at a moderate temperature and used for the initial, slow cooking; the other is kept at a high temperature, which causes the tofu to expand and imparts a handsome, golden-brown coating to each piece. Only the simplest tools are necessary to prepare fine deep-fried tofu: long chopsticks, two small skimmers, and a draining basket set over an earthenware container (fig. 55). The crisp, freshly-prepared tofu is transferred to attractive, handmade trays of woven bamboo (fig. 56) where it is allowed to cool.

Fig. 55. Deep-frying tools

In each of the following recipes, an equal weight of any of the three basic types of deep-fried tofu may be used interchangeably. However, since the texture and flavor of one type often seems to go best with each dish, that type will generally appear in the recipe title and be listed first in the ingredients, followed by the second and third choices. Because the size and weight of individual pieces of the basic types of deep-fried tofu differ widely from shop to shop and area to area, we have listed the total weight of tofu to be used in each recipe rather than the number of pieces. In our recipes we actually used pieces with the following weights and sizes:

Thick agé: 5¼ ounces (150 grams), 4 by 2¾ by 1¼ inches.

Ganmo patties: 3½ ounces (100 grams), 4¾ inches in diameter by 3/8 inch thick.

Agé pouches: 1 ounce (28 grams), 6 by 3¼ by ¼ inch.

PREPARATORY TECHNIQUES

Dousing

Dousing removes excess oil from the surface of deep-fried tofu, making the tofu lighter, easier to digest, and more absorptive of dressings and seasoned broths. In some dishes, dousing is also used to warm the tofu. Some cooks always douse deep-fried tofu, while others find the results are not worth the time and effort. Generally, we hold to the latter point of view. But if you are on a low-fat diet, douse!

Place uncut pieces of deep-fried tofu in a strainer or colander. Bring 2 or 3 cups of water to a boil in a saucepan. Douse first one, then the other side of the tofu. Allow to drain for about 1 minute before using.

Or, holding individual pieces of tofu with chopsticks.or tongs, dip tofu quickly into boiling water, then drain in a strainer.

Broiling

This technique, too, rids the tofu of some of its excess surface oil, while imparting a crispier texture and savory aroma to it. If you broil, do not douse beforehand. Some cooks like the broiled texture and aroma so much that they use this technique as a prelude to most deep-fried tofu preparations.

*If using a *stove-top burner* or bed of *live coals*, skewer tofu with a long-tined fork and hold just above the flames until lightly browned on both sides and fragrant.
*If using a regular *bread toaster*, simply drop in the deep-fried tofu and toast. Fast and easy. Serve immediately.
*If using an *oven broiler*, place tofu on a sheet of aluminum foil and broil under a high flame until lightly browned on both sides.

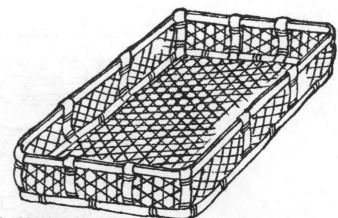

Fig. 56. A woven bamboo tray

*If using a grill over a *barbeque* or *brazier*, or a Japanese-style broiling screen over a stove-top burner (p. 36), broil tofu over high heat for 30 to 60 seconds on each side until speckled and fragrant. Turn with chopsticks or tongs. In our opinion, this method—used with a charcoal fire—gives the finest flavor and aroma.

*If using a *dry skillet*, preheat skillet over medium heat and drop in tofu. Pressing tofu down with chopsticks or fork, rub tofu over entire bottom of skillet until tofu is fragrant and lightly browned. Turn and brown second side.

DEEP-FRIED TOFU—QUICK AND EASY

The three basic types of deep-fried tofu are ready to serve in the form in which they are purchased or prepared at home. Thus, the following dishes require no cooking and can be prepared in less than 2 or 3 minutes.

Crisp Deep-fried Tofu   SERVES 1

This is our favorite recipe for serving deep-fried tofu, especially agé. If you live near or visit a tofu shop, the master may invite you to sample his sizzling, freshly deep-fried tofu served in this simple way.

4 to 5 ounces homemade agé, ganmo, or thick agé, freshly deep-fried; or storebought varieties lightly broiled (p. 156)
1 to 1½ teaspoons shoyu or Shoyu Dipping Sauces (p. 40)
½ teaspoon thinly sliced leeks or scallions, grated gingerroot, minced garlic, or any of the garnishes served with Chilled Tofu (p. 105)

Cut the hot tofu into bite-sized pieces and serve topped with the shoyu and garnish.

VARIATIONS
*Chilled Deep-fried Tofu: Serve as above using deep-fried tofu which has been well chilled. In Japan, this is a popular summertime lunch or dinner preparation. If the tofu is cut with chopsticks at the table, it will absorb the flavors of seasonings and garnishes more readily.
*Deep-fried Tofu with Miso Topping: Use either crispy hot

or well-chilled tofu. If using ganmo balls, break them open and fill with a little of the miso. Cut thick agé into thin slices. Spread one surface of the tofu with a thin topping of any of the following:

> Sweet white, red, barley, or Hatcho miso
> Yuzu Miso, Red Nerimiso, or any variety of Sweet Simmered Miso (p. 42)
> Kinzanji miso, moromi miso, or any variety of Finger Lickin' Miso (p. 31)
> Any variety of Miso Sauté (p. 43)
> Special Miso Toppings (p. 45)
> Vinegar Miso Dressings (p. 46)
> Nut & Seed Butter Toppings (p. 47)

*Deep-fried Tofu Topped with Sauces: Serve any of the following hot or cold over crisp or chilled deep-fried tofu:

> Ketchup-Worcestershire Sauce (p. 49), plain ketchup, or Worcestershire sauce
> All Basic Sauces (p. 48)
> Chinese Oyster Sauce
> Chili Sauce or Barbeque Sauces
> Mango or Apple Chutney

*Serve thick agé cubes (hot or cold) topped with maple syrup or honey. Chinese laborers enjoy this dish as a snack.

Grilled Thick Agé with Korean Barbeque Sauce   SERVES 2

5 ounces thick agé, ganmo, or agé
¼ cup Korean Barbeque Sauce (p. 49)

Broil the tofu over a barbeque fire, in a broiler, or in a hot unoiled skillet. Remove from heat and cut crosswise into sixths. Dip pieces briefly in the sauce and broil lightly once again. Serve topped with the remaining sauce.

Mock Peking Duck   SERVES 2

4 tortillas, cut into halves and warmed in a steamer
Butter
10 ounces thick agé or ganmo, cut into 4-inch-long-strips
2 or 3 tablespoons Peking Duck Dipping Sauce (p. 45)
1 leek or 3 green onions, cut into 4-inch slivers, soaked in water for 5 minutes and drained

Butter warmed tortillas lightly on one side. Divide tofu among tortillas, placing the strips in the center of each tortilla-half perpendicular to the tortilla's cut edge. Spread the dipping sauce on the tofu, then top with a sprinkling of the leek slivers. Roll up the tofu in the tortilla and, if desired, secure with a foodpick. Serve while still warm.

DEEP-FRIED TOFU HORS D'OEUVRE

Homemade deep-fried tofu served crisp and hot, or storebought tofu when lightly broiled, make hors d'oeuvre preparations with a wonderful flavor, aroma, and texture. During the summer the tofu can be served chilled.

Thick Agé with Curry Dip   SERVES 3

¼ cup cream cheese
2 teaspoons warm water
½ teaspoon shoyu
¼ teaspoon curry powder
10 ounces thick agé, ganmo, or agé, cut into thin strips

Combine the first four ingredients in a small bowl, mixing until smooth. Spread on tofu strips or use as a dip.

Thick Agé with Sesame-Cream Cheese Dip   SERVES 3

1 teaspoon sesame butter or tahini
5 tablespoons cream cheese
1 tablespoon warm water
1 teaspoon shoyu; or 1½ teaspoons red or barley miso
Dash of tabasco sauce or 7-spice red pepper
10 ounces thick agé, ganmo, or agé, cut into thin strips

Combine the first five ingredients, mixing until smooth. Spread on tofu slices or use as a dip.

Deep-fried Tofu Appetizers   MAKES 16

4 teaspoons Sweet Simmered Miso (p. 41), Miso Sauté (p. 43), or Finger Lickin' Miso (p. 31)
10 ounces thick agé, ganmo, or agé, cut into 16 bite-sized pieces
Toppings: Cut to fit on top of each piece of tofu
    Cheese
    Cucumbers
    Tomatoes
    Fresh mushrooms
    Bananas

Spread miso on one surface of each piece of tofu, cover with one or two slices of the toppings and, if desired, secure with a foodpick. Combinations with cheese are delicious if broiled until the cheese begins to melt.

Deep-fried Tofu Teriyaki Hors D'oeuvre   MAKES 12

10 to 14 ounces thick agé, ganmo, or agé, doused (p. 156) and cut into 1-inch-wide strips
2/3 cup Teriyaki Sauce (p. 48)
2 tablespoons (ground) roasted sesame seeds (p. 38)
Dash of (7-spice) red pepper (optional)

Cut shallow slits in the deep-fried surfaces to aid absorption of the sauce. Marinate, broil, and serve as for Tofu Teriyaki (p. 141), sprinkling each sizzling piece with the sesame seeds and, if desired, the red pepper.

For variety, add 2 teaspoons cornstarch to the sauce, bring to a boil, and simmer briefly until thick. Use hot as the marinade.

Spicy Broiled Ganmo Hors D'oeuvre

SERVES 2

7 ounces ganmo, thick agé, or agé
1 teaspoon shoyu
Dash of 7-spice red pepper

Broil ganmo lightly (p. 156), brush with the shoyu, and sprinkle with the red pepper. Cut into bite-sized pieces and serve hot or cold. If desired, pierce each piece with a foodpick.

Thick Agé Hors D'oeuvre with Cheese

SERVES 2

1 teaspoon oil
2 teaspoons butter
5 ounces thick agé, ganmo, or agé, cut crosswise into ½-inch strips
8 slices of cheese, each 1 by 3 by ¼ inch
¼ teaspoon salt

Heat a skillet and coat with the oil and butter. Add thick agé and fry on both cut faces until lightly browned. Lay a piece of cheese on top of each piece of tofu, cover skillet, and cook for 1 minute more. Salt lightly and serve hot.

For variety, top with a slice of green pepper or cucumber. Serve on small pieces of lettuce-covered bread, toast, or crackers.

VARIATION

*Cut and fry tofu as above. Omit cheese, and add 1 teaspoon shoyu and 1½ teaspoons sake or white wine to the skillet. Stir tofu into the seasoning liquid, then turn tofu over and simmer until liquid is absorbed. Top with a sprinkling of minced parsley and a mixture of 1 teaspoon each lemon juice and shoyu.

Marinated Thick Agé Hors D'oeuvre

SERVES 2

5 ounces thick agé, ganmo, or agé, doused (p. 156) and cut into six equal cubes
6 green *togarashi* peppers, or 1 green pepper cut lengthwise into sixths
2 tablespoons shoyu
½ clove garlic, crushed or minced
¼ teaspoon grated gingerroot
¾ teaspoon (sesame) oil
¾ teaspoon vinegar
2 teaspoons natural sugar

Combine all ingredients in a small bowl and marinate for 5 minutes. Heat an unoiled skillet, remove tofu and green peppers from marinade, and fry over medium heat until fragrant. Dip tofu and green peppers in marinade, then fry again for about 30 seconds. Place a piece of green pepper on top of each piece of tofu, secure with a foodpick, and serve piping hot.

This dish is also delicious if the ingredients are broiled over a charcoal brazier or barbeque fire, or in an oven broiler. For variety try the following marinade: 2 tablespoons shoyu,

1 tablespoon sugar, 1 teaspoon each sesame oil and *mirin*, ¼ teaspoon 7-spice red pepper.

Deep-fried Tofu Fondue

SERVES 2 TO 4

4 ounces Swiss or Gruyere cheese, grated or diced
2 teaspoons flour
1 teaspoon crushed garlic
5 to 7 tablespoon dry white wine or sake
2 teaspoons shoyu
1 teaspoon lemon juice
10 ounces thick agé or ganmo, cut into 1-inch cubes
Spices: your choice of grated gingerroot or powdered ginger, minced onion, pepper, paprika, nutmeg, or cloves

Mix cheese and flour in a small cup and set aside. Rub a small, heavy enamel pot (or a fondue pot) with the garlic, leaving garlic in pot. Add wine, shoyu, and lemon juice and bring almost to a boil over medium heat. Add floured cheese a little at a time, stirring constantly with a wooden spoon in a figure eight motion, until cheese melts and fondue is smooth. When fondue starts bubbling, stir in tofu and your choice of spices.

To serve: if you have a fondue table set with a warmer, place the pot on the warmer in the center of your serving table accompanied by long (fondue) forks. Invite each guest to spear the tofu while it's hot. Or serve the pot set in or over a container of hot water.

Tofu fondue may also be served cold or as a main dish.

DEEP-FRIED TOFU IN SALADS

Sliced, cubed, or diced, deep-fried tofu adds flavor, texture and protein to salads and harmonizes nicely with a wide range of popular dressings. The various Tofu Mayonnaise Dressings (p. 107) and Miso Salad Dressings (p. 46) also go nicely over salads containing deep-fried tofu. Thick agé may be substituted for regular tofu in all recipes where the tofu is served cubed or reshaped in salads. In most recipes, the flavor of the salad is greatly enhanced if the tofu is lightly broiled (p. 156). Roasted soybeans may be used with good results sprinkled lightly over the top of most deep-fried tofu salds. For a description of the differences between Western- and Japanese-style salads, see pages 111 and 114.

Western-style Salads

Ganmo-Tomato-Mayonnaise Salad

SERVES 2

3½ ounces ganmo, thick agé, or agé, lightly broiled (p. 156) and cut into ½-inch strips or squares
1 large tomato, diced fine
2 or 3 tablespoons (tofu) mayonnaise (p. 107)
¼ teaspoon salt or 1 tablespoon sweet white miso
Dash of white pepper
½ to 1 teaspoon lemon juice (optional)
¼ cup diced cheese or pieces of torn lettuce (optional)

Combine all ingredients in a large bowl; toss lightly.

Thick Agé Salad with Tangy Tofu Cottage Cheese

SERVES 4

10 ounces thick agé, ganmo, or agé
Shoyu
7-spice red pepper or paprika
Tangy Tofu Cottage Cheese (p. 109)
4 large lettuce leaves
1 tomato, cut into thin wedges
1 cucumber, sliced into thin diagonals
¼ to ½ cup raisins

Broil thick agé lightly (p. 156) and cut crosswise into thin strips. While still hot, dip into shoyu and sprinkle with the red pepper, then combine with the tofu cottage cheese, mixing well. Arrange lettuce leaves in individual salad bowls, mound with the tofu cottage cheese, and serve topped with tomato and cucumber slices and a sprinkling of raisins.

Fresh Sea-vegetable Salad with Thick Agé and Miso-Mayonnaise

SERVES 4

7½ ounces thick agé, ganmo, or agé, lightly broiled (p. 156) and cut crosswise into thin strips.
1 cucumber, thinly sliced
1 green pepper, thinly sliced
1 cup fresh or refreshed *wakame* (p. 37), cut into 2-inch lengths
½ cup raisins
Miso-Mayonnaise Dressing:
    5 teaspoons red, barley, or Hatcho miso
    3 tablespoons mayonnaise
    3 tablespoons lemon juice
    Dash of pepper (optional)
1 tomato, cut into thin wedges
4 lettuce leaves

Combine the first five ingredients and the dressing; mix lightly. Arrange tomato wedges on lettuce leaves in a large salad bowl. Top with the salad mixture and chill for several hours before serving.

    If *wakame* is unavailable, substitute 1 large diced apple or tomato.

Thick Agé & Brown Rice Salad with Mushrooms

SERVES 3 OR 4

1 teaspoon oil
1/3 cup minced onion
¾ cup minced mushrooms
1¼ cups cooked Brown Rice (p. 50)
1 tablespoon shoyu
Dressing:
    3 tablespoon mayonnaise
    2 tablespoons lemon juice
    ¼ teaspoon curry powder
5 ounces thick agé or ganmo, diced
3 or 4 lettuce leaves

Heat a skillet or wok and coat with the oil. Add onion and one-half the mushrooms and sauté for 3 to 4 minutes. Remove from heat and stir in rice and shoyu; allow to cool to room temperature. Now add the remaining mushrooms, dressing, and thick agé, mix lightly and, for best flavor, allow to stand for several hours. Serve mounded on lettuce leaves.

    Also delicious as a filling for Agé Pouches (p. 192).

Thick Agé-Kabocha Salad with Miso Mayonnaise Dressing

SERVES 4

10 ounces *kabocha*, pumpkin, or squash
½ teaspoon salt
10 ounces thick agé, ganmo, or agé, doused (p. 156) and cut into small bite-sized cubes
Miso Mayonnaise:
    4 tablespoons (tofu) mayonnaise (p. 107)
    2 tablespoons red, barley, or Hatcho miso
    1 tablespoon vinegar
    1½ tablespoons natural sugar
8 lettuce or Chinese cabbage leaves (optional)
4 teaspoons slivered Vinegared Gingerroot (p. 51) (optional)

Cut *kabocha* into large bite-sized cubes, sprinkle with the salt, and steam for about 20 minutes, or until soft (p. 38). Combine *kabocha*, tofu, and miso mayonnaise in a large bowl; mix lightly. Arrange lettuce leaves in salad bowls, mound with the *kabocha*-tofu mixture, and top with gingerroot slivers.

    This salad is also delicious dressed with Mustard-Vinegar Miso Dressing (p. 46).

Buckwheat Noodle Salad with Miso Mayonnaise

SERVES 4

3 ounces *(soba)* buckwheat noodles (or spaghetti), cooked (p. 50)
5 ounces thick agé, ganmo, or agé, diced
1 large tomato, diced
1½ cucumbers, cut into thin rounds
2/3 cup diced celery
½ cup grated cheese or walnut meats; or 2 diced hard-boiled eggs (optional)
Dressing:
    ¼ cup mayonnaise
    1½ tablespoons red, barley, or Hatcho miso
    1 teaspoon lemon juice
    Dash of pepper
4 lettuce leaves
¼ cup parsley

Combine the first five (or six) ingredients with the dressing; mix lightly. Arrange lettuce leaves in individual bowls, mound with the salad, and top with a sprinkling of parsley.

    Delicious served in Agé Pouches (p. 192).

Agé-Noodle Salad
SERVES 3 OR 4

4 ounces agé, ganmo, or thick agé, cut into thin strips
1½ cups cooked transparent noodles *(harusame)*, soba, or
   macaroni
2 small celery stalks, diced
2 teaspoons Sesame Salt (p. 51) or ¼ teaspoon salt
5 tablespoons (tofu) mayonnaise (p. 107)
Dash of pepper

Combine all ingredients in a large bowl; mix lightly. To serve,
divide among individual salad bowls.

Mock Tuna Salad with Deep-fried Tofu
SERVES 3 OR 4

1 tablespoon oil
1 small onion, thinly sliced
3 mushrooms, thinly sliced
2 green peppers or 12 green beans, slivered
3 eggs, lightly beaten
2 ounces of agé, ganmo, or thick agé, thinly sliced
¼ cup mayonnaise
2 teaspoons shoyu or 1 tablespoon red miso
Dash of pepper
1½ tablespoons minced parsley
2 or 3 lettuce leaves, torn into small pieces

Heat a skillet and coat with the oil. Add the next three ingredients and sauté for 4 to 5 minutes. Add eggs and agé, and
scramble until eggs are firm. Remove from heat and allow to
cool to room temperature. Combine mayonnaise, shoyu, and
pepper to make a dressing, then mix with the eggs. Just before serving, add parsley and lettuce; mix lightly.

Macaroni-Parsley Salad with Thick Agé
SERVES 4

4 lettuce leaves
¾ cup dry macaroni, cooked
2/3 cup chopped parsley
1 cup chopped celery
7½ ounces thick agé, ganmo, or agé, cut into small cubes
Dressing:
    2 tablespoons mayonnaise
    2 tablespoons vinegar
    1½ tablespoons lemon juice
    1½ tablespoons red miso or 1 tablespoon shoyu
    1 tablespoon oil
    1 tablespoon minced onion

Line 4 individual salad bowls with the lettuce. Combine the
next four ingredients and the dressing in a large bowl; mix
well. Spoon onto the lettuce leaves.

Thick Agé with Marinated Vegetables
SERVES 2

5 ounces thick agé, ganmo, or agé, diced
2 cucumbers, slivered
½ carrot, finely diced
1 tomato, finely diced
15 green beans, parboiled and diced
Dressing:
    3 tablespoons vinegar
    2 tablespoons sesame oil
    1 tablespoon salad oil
    3 tablespoons shoyu
    1 tablespoon sugar
    2 tablespoons ground roasted sesame seeds (p. 38),
        sesame butter, or *tahini* (optional)
    ¼ teaspoon salt
    Dash of 7-spice red pepper

Combine the first five ingredients and the dressing; marinate
overnight (or for at least 3 to 4 hours).

Garbanzo Bean Salad with Thick Agé
SERVES 6

2 cups garbanzo beans, rinsed, soaked overnight in 3 cups
    water, and drained
10 ounces thick agé, ganmo, or agé, cut into ½-inch cubes
2 stalks of celery, diced
½ onion, diced
¼ cup minced parsley or chives
½ cup diced green pepper, tomato, or carrot (optional)
Dressing:
    ¼ cup salad oil
    1½ teaspoons sesame oil
    2 tablespoons lemon juice or vinegar
    ½ cup Sesame Salt (p. 51) or 1 tablespoon salt
    1½ teaspoons shoyu
    ¼ teaspoon hot mustard
    1½ teaspoons powdered or 1 teaspoon grated gingerroot
    1 clove garlic, crushed
    Dash of pepper

Combine beans with 3 cups fresh water and bring to a boil.
Reduce heat to low, cover, and simmer for 2½ hours, or
until all liquid has been absorbed. Combine hot beans and
next five ingredients in a large flat-bottomed pan and add
dressing; mix well. Allow to stand for about 1 hour, or until
cool, before serving.

Japanese-style Salads
(Aemono)

Ganmo-Cucumber Salad with Miso Dressing
SERVES 2

3½ ounces ganmo, thick agé, or agé, cut into 1-inch squares
1 cucumber or *uri* melon, sliced into thin rounds
½ cup Mustard-Vinegar Miso Dressing (p. 46)

Combine all ingredients, mixing lightly. Serve chilled.

Vinegared Cucumber-Wakame Salad with Ganmo

SERVES 4

2 cucumbers, sliced into thin rounds
1½ cups fresh or refreshed *wakame* (p. 37) or slivered *kombu*
7 ounces ganmo or 4 ounces agé, cut into thin strips, each 1½ inches long
Dressing:
    2 tablespoons shoyu
    6 tablespoons vinegar
    2 tablespoons natural sugar
    3 tablespoons sesame butter

Combine the first four ingredients with the dressing, mix lightly, and serve.

Or try a *Sambaizu* dressing using 3 tablespoons each shoyu and vinegar, and 2 tablespoons sugar.

Pressed Salad with Agé and Sesame-Vinegar Dressing

SERVES 2 TO 3

2 ounces agé, ganmo, or thick agé, lightly broiled (p. 156) and cut crosswise into thin strips.
7 ounces *daikon*, cut into 2-inch matchsticks
¼ small carrot, cut into matchsticks
1 cucumber, cut diagonally into thin slices
2 teaspoons salt
2 tablespoons ground roasted sesame seeds (p. 38)
2 tablespoons (rice) vinegar
2 tablespoons natural sugar
1 teaspoon shoyu

Combine the first four ingredients in a small bowl; rub with 1½ teaspoons salt, rinse, and press (p. 37). Combine ½ teaspoon salt with remaining ingredients in a small bowl and mix well. Place pressed vegetables and tofu in a large bowl, sprinkle with the vinegar mixture, and mix lightly. Serve immediately.

Also delicious with *kombu*, fresh *(shiitake)* mushrooms, *konnyaku* noodles, or green beans.

DEEP-FRIED TOFU WITH SANDWICHES AND TOAST

These preparations are as delicious as they are easy to prepare. Lightly broiled, deep-fried tofu serves as a savory sandwich ingredient or may be used as a substitute for bacon or meat slices. The use of any variety of Finger Lickin' Miso (p. 31), Sweet Simmered Miso (p. 41), or regular miso in sandwiches with deep-fried tofu gives added flavor. Due to protein complementarity (p. 25), serving tofu and whole-wheat bread together can yield up to 32 percent additional protein.

Deep-fried Tofu Sandwiches

Use 2 ounces agé, ganmo, or thick agé, lightly broiled (p. 156), if desired, and cut lengthwise into 1-inch-wide strips. Place between 2 slices of buttered (whole-grain) bread or toast with any of the following combinations of ingredients:

    *Miso, Miso Toppings (p. 41), or salt; cheese, cucumber, lettuce, tomato, mayonnaise, mustard, ketchup.

    *1 egg fried in butter (see Fried Eggs with Deep-fried Tofu; p. 164) miso, ketchup, pepper, grated cheese, and parsley. Serve on toast.

    *Lettuce, mayonnaise, pepper
    *Cream cheese, tomato, lettuce
    *Nut Butter Spreads (p. 47), grated cheese, alfalfa sprouts
    *Cheese, *nori*, lettuce, miso
    *Grilled cheese, mayonnaise, tomato, lettuce, miso
    *Deep-fried Tofu Salads (p. 158), lettuce, tomato and mayonnaise; serve on toast.
    *Deep-fried tofu in onion sauce (p. 165) or with Fried Rice (p. 168); serve hot or cold on toast.
    *Deep-fried tofu simmered in seasoned broths (p. 174), cooled; serve on toast.

Pizza Toast with Deep-fried Tofu

MAKES 5

Use thin slices of deep-fried tofu in place of salami, sausage, or anchovies in your favorite pizza toppings. This variation on the traditional motif, now popular in many Japanese pizza parlors, can be prepared quickly and easily at home.

5 large, fairly thick slices of (whole-wheat or French) bread, buttered on one side
5 large, thin slices of (mozzerella) cheese
1¼ cups Tomato & Cheese Sauce (p. 49)
5 ounces thick agé or ganmo, thinly sliced

3 to 4 mushrooms, thinly sliced
1 to 2 green peppers, thinly sliced
½ tomato, thinly sliced
Olive oil
¼ cup minced parsley (optional)
Oregano and/or thyme
1 cup grated cheese (optional)
Parmesan cheese
Tabasco sauce

Preheat oven to 350°. Cover the buttered side of each piece of bread with a slice of cheese, and spread with the sauce. Arrange on top: slices of tofu, mushrooms, green peppers, and tomatoes, then sprinkle lightly with oil. If desired, top with grated parsley, herbs and cheese. Bake for 10 to 15 minutes, or until toast is nicely browned. Serve hot, topped with Parmesan cheese and tabasco sauce.

Tofu & Wakame Open-faced Toasted Sandwich

MAKES 6

7 ounces ganmo or thick agé, diced
2 cucumbers, thinly sliced
½ cup fresh or refreshed *wakame* (p. 37), thinly sliced
Dressing:
      3 tablespoons mayonnaise
      ½ cup walnut meats, mashed, ground, or minced
      2 tablespoons red, barley, or Hatcho miso
      1 tablespoon water
      Dash of pepper
6 pieces of buttered whole-grain toast

Combine the first three ingredients with the dressing; mix lightly. Spread in an even layer on the pieces of toast and serve immediately.

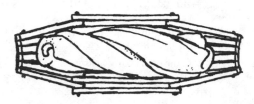

DEEP-FRIED TOFU IN SOUPS

Thin strips or bite-sized cubes of deep-fried tofu can add a tender, meaty texture and savory aroma to your favorite soups. Seasoning the soup with a small amount of miso or shoyu will often give it a delicious, distinguishing accent. Try broiling the tofu lightly before adding it to split pea, lentil, or tomato soups. Deep-fried tofu may also be substituted for regular tofu in most of the recipes beginning on page 117, or used in soymilk soups such as Creamy Corn (p. 207). Agé is also popular in Gôjiru (p. 74) and Kenchin-jiru (p. 120).

Onion Soup with Thick Agé

SERVES 4 OR 5

2 tablespoons oil
4 large or 6 medium onions, thinly sliced
10 ounces thick agé, ganmo, or agé, thinly sliced
1 tablespoon butter
¼ cup red miso (or 3 tablespoons shoyu) thinned in 1 to 2 cups warm water
2 ounces cheese, grated or diced

Heat a large casserole and coat with the oil. Add onions, cover, and simmer over lowest possible heat for 3½ hours, stirring the bottom once every 20 minutes. Add the thick agé, butter, and thinned miso; mix well. Allow to cool to room temperature, then refrigerate overnight. Add the cheese, bring just to a boil and, stirring constantly, simmer for 1 minute, or until cheese melts. Serve hot or, for a richer flavor, allow to cool to room temperature before serving. Or use as the basis for Baked Onion Soup (p. 165).

For variety, add 2 to 3 lightly beaten eggs and/or ½ cup thinly sliced lotus root 15 minutes before adding miso.

Thick Agé in Rich Kabocha Soup

SERVES 6

30 ounces *(kabocha)* pumpkin or winter squash, cut into 1-inch cubes
2½ cups water
10 ounces thick agé, ganmo, or agé, thinly sliced
¼ cup red or barley miso (or 3 tablespoons shoyu) thinned in 1 cup hot water
2 tablespoons butter

Bring the *kabocha* and 1 cup water to a boil in a large casserole or heavy pot. Reduce heat to low, cover, and simmer for 1 hour. Add tofu and 1½ cups water, and simmer for 1 hour more. Stir in thinned miso and butter and simmer for 10 minutes. Serve hot, or for a richer, sweeter flavor, allow to cool for 6 to 8 hours.

For an even meatier texture, use thick agé which has been frozen overnight and then thawed in warm water. Simmer ½ cup thinly sliced onions with the *kabocha*, and add 2 to 4 tablespoons sesame butter and a dash of pepper together with the butter.

Agé-Miso Soup with Wakame

SERVES 2 OR 3

This is one of Japan's favorite traditional ways of serving miso soup. The *wakame* supplies an abundance of calcium and other minerals, while the agé and miso supply protein and unsaturated oils. Requiring less than 3 minutes to prepare, this soup is particularly popular at breakfast, and is renowned for its fine aroma and flavor.

1¾ cups dashi (p. 39) or stock
¼ to 1/3 cup fresh or refreshed *wakame* (p. 37), cut into 1-inch lengths
1 to 2 ounces agé or ganmo, cut crosswise into thin strips
2 tablespoons red, barley, or Hatcho miso
1 tablespoon thinly sliced leeks or a dash of 7-spice red pepper

Bring dashi to a boil in a saucepan. Add *wakame* and agé and cook for 1 minute. Add miso creamed in a little of the hot broth and return just to the boil. Serve immediately, garnished with the leeks.

Thick Miso Soup with Onions and Agé

SERVES 2

1½ cups dashi (p. 39), stock, or water
1 onion, thinly sliced
2 ounces agé, ganmo, or thick agé, lightly broiled (p. 156) and cut into thin strips
2 tablespoons red, barley, or Hatcho miso
1 tablespoon minced parsley

Combine dashi and onion in a small saucepan and bring to a boil. Reduce heat to low, cover, and simmer for 10 minutes. Add agé, then the miso creamed with a little of the hot broth. Simmer for 1 minute more and serve garnished with parsley.

Although the Japanese almost always serve miso soup

piping hot, we find this dish to be just as tasy if served at room temperature or even chilled.

VARIATION

*Ozoni: This popular New Year's dish is prepared by adding *mochi* to any variety of miso soup. In the above recipe, use 2½ cups dashi and 3 tablespoons miso. Just before serving, add 3 cakes of *mochi* (each 2 by 2 by ½ inch) which have been broiled until they swell to twice their original size and are crisp and nicely browned. Serves 3.

Picnic Miso Soup with Agé   SERVES 3

3 tablespoons red, barley, or Hatcho miso
2 tablespoons bonita flakes or grated cheese
Dash of pepper (7-spice, red, or black)
1 to 2 ounces agé or ganmo, cut crosswise into thin strips
12 inches dry *wakame*, cut into 1-inch lengths; or 3 cakes of dried wheat gluten
2 to 3 tablespoons sliced leeks, minced chives, or minced parsley
2 cups hot or boiling water

Combine miso, bonita flakes, and pepper, mixing well, then shape into 3 balls. Skewer and broil each ball over a burner (as for Broiled Miso, p. 46) until it is well browned and fragrant. Place balls and the next three ingredients into a picnic container. Take the hot water in a thermos or heat water at the picnic site: To serve, divide all solid ingredients among 3 bowls, pour in the hot water, and mix until miso dissolves. Cover and allow to stand for several minutes before serving.

Other Ways of Serving Deep-fried Tofu in Miso Soups

In Japan, entire books and round-the-year calendars suggest hundreds of tasty ways to serve deep-fried tofu in miso soups. The following combinations containing deep-fried tofu appear on one such calendar. The first mentioned is the principal ingredient followed by its complements, the type of miso, and the garnish or seasoning. In the basic pattern for preparation, the fresh vegetables and deep-fried tofu are simmered together in dashi until the vegetables are just tender. The thinned miso is then added and the soup returned just to the boil before being served sprinkled with a garnish topping.

*Spring, Sunday morning: agé, chrysanthemum leaves, sweet white miso, slivered *yuzu* rind

*Spring, Tuesday evening: grilled tofu, agé, burdock root, red miso, grated gingerroot juice

*Spring, Thursday evening: *kampyo* (shaved dried gourd), agé, red miso, *fuki* buds *(fuki-no-to)*

*Spring, Friday morning: bracken or Osmund fern fronds, agé or ganmo, light-yellow miso, *sansho* pepper

*Summer, Sunday evening: tiny eggplants, agé, red miso, 7-spice red pepper

*Summer, Tuesday morning: snow peas, agé, sweet white miso and light-yellow miso, ground roasted sesame seeds

*Summer, Thursday evening: taro *(satoimo)*, agé, *shiitake* mushrooms, carrot, light-yellow miso, 7-spice red pepper

*Summer, Saturday morning: leeks, agé, red miso, *sansho* pepper

*Fall, Sunday morning: *hijiki*, thick agé, red miso, 7-spice red pepper

*Fall, Tuesday morning: cabbage, agé, light-yellow miso, pepper

*Fall, Wednesday morning: sweet potato, agé, light-yellow miso, pepper

*Fall, Friday morning: *kabocha*, fresh *shiitake* mushrooms, thick agé, red miso, beefsteak seeds *(shiso-no-mi)*

*Winter, Tuesday morning: small turnip, agé, red miso, hot mustard

*Winter, Wednesday morning: Chinese cabbage, agé, light-yellow miso, pepper

Noppei Soup *(Noppei-jiru)*   SERVES 3

This hearty vegetable soup is a traditional wintertime favorite in Japan's cold northwest provinces.

2 ounces agé, ganmo, or thick agé, cut into small rectangles
½ small carrot, cut into small rectangles
1 cup small rectangles of *daikon*
½ cake *konnyaku*, cut into small rectangles
3 *(shiitake)* mushrooms, thinly sliced
1½ cups half moons of sweet potatoes or taro
2 cups dashi (p. 39), stock, or water
5½ teaspoons shoyu
1 teaspoon salt
2 teaspoons sake
Dash of 7-spice red pepper (optional)
¼ cup slivered leeks

Combine all but the last two ingredients in a large pot or casserole and bring to a boil. Reduce heat to low, cover, and simmer for 30 minutes. Divide among 3 soup bowls and garnish with red pepper and leek.

For variety, simmer the agé in a mixture of dashi, shoyu, and sugar before combining it with the soup's other ingredients, or use grilled tofu in place of agé. This soup is also very tasty if it is allowed to cool for 4 to 6 hours before being served.

DEEP-FRIED TOFU IN BREAKFAST EGG DISHES

Use any variety of deep-fried tofu like bacon in your favorite egg dishes. Most Japanese tofu-and-egg preparations are lightly seasoned with a mixture of shoyu (or miso) and sugar. Or substitute diced deep-fried tofu for regular tofu in omelet recipes (p. 122).

Fried Eggs with Deep-fried Tofu   SERVES 2

2 tablespoons butter
2 eggs
5 ounces thick agé, ganmo, or agé, cut crosswise into very thin slices
¼ teaspoon salt or 1 teaspoon shoyu
Dash of pepper
1 tablespoon minced parsley (optional)

Melt the butter in a skillet. Break in the eggs and cover with tofu slices. Cover skillet, reduce heat to very low, and cook for 6 minutes. Season with salt and pepper, re-cover, and cook for 2 minutes more. Serve topped with a sprinkling of parsley.

For variety, butter-fry the tofu before breaking in the eggs.

Scrambled Eggs with Thick Agé and Onions   SERVES 3 OR 4

10 ounces thick agé or ganmo, cut into 1½-inch squares, each ½ inch thick
2 eggs, lighty beaten
½ onion, minced; or ½ cup chopped chives or wild onions
1 to 2 teaspoons shoyu
¼ teaspoon salt
1 tablespoon oil

Combine the first five ingredients, mixing lightly. Heat the oil in a large skillet. Pour in the egg-and-tofu mixture and scramble gently for 2 or 3 minutes, pressing tofu occasionally with back of spatula until each piece is golden brown and fragrant. Serve hot or cold.

Thick Agé & Scrambled Eggs with Mushrooms and Cheese   SERVES 2

5 ounces thick agé, ganmo, or agé, lightly broiled (p. 156) and cut into ½-inch cubes or thin slices
4 mushrooms, thinly sliced
1 tablespoon shoyu
1½ tablespoons natural sugar
1 tablespoon sake or mirin (optional)
2 eggs
3 tablespoons grated cheese or ¼ teaspoon sansho pepper

Combine the first five ingredients in a skillet and simmer, covered, for about 8 minutes. Break in the eggs and, stirring constantly, scramble until eggs are firm. Serve topped with the cheese or sansho.

If desired, sauté the mushrooms in butter before adding other ingredients. Or simmer the tofu and mushrooms in the sweetened shoyu broth used with Inari-zushi (p. 194), then add eggs after most of broth has been absorbed or evaporated.

Thick Agé Scrambled Eggs with Miso and Bonita Flakes   SERVES 3

2 eggs
2½ tablespoons red, barley, or Hatcho miso
1½ teaspoons bonita flakes
2 tablespoons minced onion
10 ounces thick agé or ganmo, cut into 1-inch squares, each ½ inch thick
4 teaspoons oil

Combine the first four ingredients, mixing until miso is well dissolved. Stir in the thick agé. Heat one-half the oil in a large skillet. Pour in one-half the egg-tofu mixture and scramble gently for 2 or 3 minutes, pressing tofu occasionally with back of spatula until each piece is golden brown and fragrant. Repeat with remaining oil and egg-tofu mixture. Serve hot or cold.

Swirled Eggs with Thick Agé and Onion   SERVES 3 OR 4

1½ cups dashi (p. 39) or stock
1 onion, thinly sliced
10 ounces thick agé or ganmo, cut into bite-sized pieces
3 tablespoons red, barley, or Hatcho miso; or 2 tablespoons shoyu
1½ tablespoons natural sugar
2 eggs, lightly beaten

Bring dashi to a boil in a small saucepan. Add onion, return to the boil, and simmer for 2 minutes. Add thick agé and return to the boil. Stir in miso (creamed in a little of the hot broth) and sugar, and return to the boil over high heat. Stir in eggs and remove immediately from heat. Serve hot or cold.

Poached Eggs with Deep-fried Tofu   SERVES 2

1 piece of thick agé, cut horizontally into 2 thin slices; 2 large ganmo patties; or 2 pieces of agé
1 teaspoon shoyu
2 eggs, poached
Dash of salt and pepper

Broil tofu lightly (p. 156), then sprinkle with shoyu. Serve topped with the poached eggs and seasoned with salt and pepper.

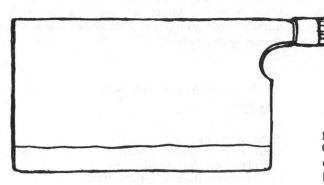

DEEP-FRIED TOFU BAKED

Diced or cut into thin strips, deep-fried tofu may be substituted for regular tofu in most baked preparations (p. 123). Ganmo and agé provide the chewiest, meatiest texture, while thick agé combines the soft tenderness of regular tofu with the savory deep-fried firmness of agé. To add extra flavor to your favorite baked dishes, simmer tofu cubes or slices in Sweetened Shoyu Broth (p. 40) for about 5 minutes before combining with your other ingredients.

Cheese-Onion Casserole with Thick Agé   SERVES 3 OR 4

3 tablespoons butter
3 tablespoons whole-wheat flour
1½ cups milk
1 to 1½ tablespoons red miso or 1 tablespoon shoyu
1 clove garlic, crushed
Dash of pepper
10 ounces thick agé or ganmo, cut into bite-sized pieces
½ cup grated cheese
1 onion, thinly sliced
1 carrot, grated
½ cup cracker or bread crumbs

Preheat oven to 350°. Melt butter in a skillet, stir in flour, and brown for about 1 minute. Stir in milk, reduce heat to low, and simmer for several minutes to form a thick sauce. Add miso, garlic, and pepper, mixing until miso is well dissolved. Add tofu, cheese, onions and carrot; turn off heat and mix thoroughly. Pour into a bread pan or casserole, sprinkle surface with cracker crumbs, and bake for about 25 minutes.

Baked Onion Soup with Thick Agé

Prepare Onion Soup with Thick Agé (p. 162). Place in a casserole and cover surface with large pieces of whole-wheat bread. Sprinkle liberally with grated cheese and bake in a moderate oven until cheese just begins to brown.

Or pour 2 or 3 lightly beaten eggs over the bread before adding cheese.

DEEP-FRIED TOFU SATUÉED, STIR-FRIED, OR TOPPED WITH SAUCES

Deep-fried tofu makes an excellent substitute for regular tofu in most tofu sauces (especially Sesame, Spaghetti, Onion-Curry, and Onion & Raisin White Sauce). It is also delicious topped with any of the Soymilk Sauces (p. 207) or Basic Sauces such as Onion, Gingerroot, Teriyaki, Sweet & Sour, or Tomato & Cheese (pp. 48-49).

Onion Sauce with Agé   SERVES 2 OR 3

1 1/3 cups Onion Sauce (p. 48)
3 ounces agé, ganmo, or thick agé, cut into small rectangles
1 tablespoon shoyu
¼ cup water
2½ ounces cheese, grated or finely diced
1 egg, lightly beaten

Combine Onion Sauce, agé, shoyu, and water in a casserole or heavy pot and, stirring constantly, bring just to a boil over medium heat. Now cover pot and simmer for 3 minutes. Add cheese and simmer, covered, for 10 minutes more. Mix in egg, increase heat to high and cook, stirring constantly, for 1 minute, or until egg becomes firm. Allow to cool for 5 to 6 hours, then serve as is or as a topping for brown rice or *(soba)* buckwheat noodles.

Or combine all ingredients in a casserole, sprinkle surface with cheese (and bread crumbs), and bake at 350° until nicely browned. Serve seasoned with *sansho* pepper.

Deep-fried Tofu with Barbeque Sauce   SERVES 4

10 ounces thick agé
7 ounces ganmo or agé, or substitute more thick agé
Sauce:
    2 tablespoons ketchup
    2 tablespoons shoyu
    1 tablespoon sake or white wine
    1 tablespoon melted butter
    ¼ small onion, diced
    1½ teaspoons sugar
    Dash of chili pepper or 7-spice red pepper
    ½ clove garlic, crushed

Heat an unoiled skillet and broil the thick agé and ganmo lightly on both sides until fragrant. Remove from pan and cut thick agé crosswise into 8 equal rectangles and ganmo into 12 equal wedges.

Combine all sauce ingredients in a small bowl; mix well. Mix sauce and tofu in the skillet and cook over medium heat for about 1 minute. Serve hot or cold.

Ganmo Sautéed with Green Pepper, Garlic, and Miso

SERVES 2

7 ounces ganmo, thick agé, or agé, cut into ½-inch strips
½ cup dashi (p. 39), stock, or water
3 tablespoons barley, red, or Hatcho miso
2 tablespoons natural sugar
2 teaspoons sake
2 tablespoons oil
1½ teaspoons crushed or minced garlic
5 green peppers, cut lengthwise into sixths
2/3 teaspoon shoyu

Combine ganmo, dashi, miso, sugar, and sake in a saucepan and bring to a boil. Cover and simmer for 5 minutes; set aside.

Heat a skillet or wok and coat with the oil. Add garlic and sauté for 1 minute. Increase heat to high, add green peppers and sauté for 1 minute more. Add ganmo, any remaining cooking liquid, and the shoyu. Stirring constantly, cook for 1 minute more. Serve hot or cold.

Apple & Onion Curry Sauce with Deep-fried Tofu

SERVES 3 OR 4

Any type of tofu may be used with excellent results in your favorite curry sauce. We like the tender yet meaty texture of deep-fried tofu in this richly-flavored preparation.

7½ ounces thick agé, ganmo, or agé, diced
1 apple, diced
2 potatoes, diced (1¾ cups)
1 cup water or stock
3 tablespoons butter
1 clove of garlic, crushed
1 teaspoon grated or 1½ teaspoons powdered gingerroot
1½ onions, minced
5 to 6 mushrooms, thinly sliced
1½ to 2 teaspoons curry powder
2 tablespoons whole-wheat flour
3 to 3½ tablespoons red miso or 2 tablespoons shoyu
1 tablespoon honey or natural sugar
2 tablespoons ketchup
Sambals: Sliced bananas, grated coconut, raisins, diced apples, peanuts or almonds, chopped hard-boiled eggs, and chutney

Combine the first four ingredients in a heavy pot or casserole and bring to a boil. Cover and simmer over low heat. Meanwhile melt the butter in a skillet. Add garlic and gingerroot, and sauté for 30 seconds. Add onions and mushrooms, and sauté for 5 to 6 minutes more. Mix in curry powder and flour, and cook, stirring constantly, for 1 minute. Cream miso with about 1/3 cup broth removed from the pot, then stir into the curried mixture together with the honey and ketchup to form a smooth, thick sauce. Now mix sauce into contents of pot, cover, and simmer for 20 to 30 minutes, stirring occasionally. Serve over brown rice or buckwheat noodles, topped with the *sambals*.

For a more elaborate sauce, add diced lotus root, cooked lentils, sweet potatoes, *kabocha*, or squash. To serve as an entrèe without grains, reduce the amounts of miso and curry powder by about one-fifth.

Thick Agé with Pineapple-Sweet & Sour Sauce

SERVES 4 TO 5

2 tablespoons oil
1 clove garlic, crushed or minced
1 small onion, thinly sliced
1 green pepper, cut into 1-inch squares
2 small tomatoes, diced; or 1 cup cherry tomatoes, cut into halves
Pineapple-Sweet & Sour Sauce:
    1¼ cups pineapple chunks, drained
    1½ tablespoons natural sugar
    3 tablespoons vinegar
    ½ cup water
    2 tablespoons shoyu or 3 tablespoons red miso
    2 tablespoons ketchup
    ½ teaspoon grated gingerroot or 1 teaspoon powdered ginger
    1 tablespoon cornstarch
7½ ounces thick agé, ganmo, or agé, cut into 1-inch cubes

Heat the oil in a large skillet or wok. Add garlic and onion and stir-fry over high heat, stirring constantly, for 2 minutes. Add green pepper, tomatoes and sauce ingredients, and cook, stirring contantly, for about 1 minute until thick. Mix in thick agé and remove from heat. Serve chilled. (To serve hot, increase amount of sugar and vinegar in sauce by 1 tablespoon each.)

Agé with Hijiki and Carrots

SERVES 5 TO 6

1 tablespoon oil
1/3 cup dried *hijiki*, reconstituted (p. 37)
2 ounces agé, ganmo, or thick agé, cut into thin strips
¼ small carrot, cut into matchsticks
4 teaspoons shoyu
4 teaspoons natural sugar or honey
¼ cup water
Dash of salt

Heat a skillet or wok and coat with the oil. Add all ingredients and sauté over low heat for about 15 minutes. Allow to cool or, for best flavor, chill for several hours before serving.

For a spicer taste, add 1 teaspoon grated gingerroot, ¼ to ½ cup diced lotus root, and 1 to 2 tablespoons ground roasted sesame seeds (p. 38) or sesame butter to the *hijiki*-agé mixture before sautéing. Or substitute ½ ounce dried-frozen tofu for 1 ounce agé.

Thick Agé with Zesty Steak Sauce   SERVES 2

1½ teaspoons butter
2 tablespoons finely chopped green onions
2 tablespoons ketchup
5 teaspoons Teriyaki Sauce (p. 48)
1 teaspoon mustard (optional)
Dash of black pepper
5 ounces thick agé, ganmo, or agé, cut into 1-inch cubes

Melt butter in a skillet. Add onions and sauté until tender. Stir in ketchup, Teriyaki Sauce, mustard, and pepper, and simmer for 1 minute. Arrange thick agé in bowls and top with the sauce. Serve hot or cold.

Sautéed Carrots with Agé, Wheat Germ, and Sunflower Seeds   SERVES 2

1 tablespoon oil
1 carrot, cut into matchsticks or thin rounds (1¾ cups)
3 ounces agé, ganmo, or thick agé
2 tablespoons water
3½ teaspoons shoyu or ½ teaspoon salt
2 or 3 tablespoons toasted wheat germ
2 or 3 tablespoons sunflower seeds or almonds

Heat a skillet and coat with the oil. Add carrots and sauté over high heat until just tender. Add next four ingredients, and reduce heat to low; cover and simmer for 4 to 5 more minutes. Remove from heat and mix in wheat germ and sunflower seeds. Serve hot or cold.

For variety, substitute 1¾ cups of 1-inch cubes of yam for the carrots. Serve with sunflower seeds or with wheat germ and walnuts.

Chinese-style Sweet & Sour Thick Agé   SERVES 4

2 tablespoons oil
½ carrot, cut into half moons
1 large onion, thinly sliced
½ small bamboo shoot (3 ounces), cut into half moons
5 mushrooms, cut into quarters
2 inches of lotus root, cut lengthwise into sixths
3 green peppers, cut lengthwise into sixths
15 ounces thick agé, ganmo, or agé, cut into ½-inch cubes
1½ tablespoons vinegar
3 tablespoons soy sauce
2 tablespoons sugar
1 tablespoon cornstarch dissolved in 3 tablespoons water

Heat a wok or skillet and coat with the oil. Add the vegetables consecutively, stir-frying each over high heat for about 1 minute. Mix in tofu, vinegar, soy sauce, and sugar, reduce heat to medium and cook, stirring constantly, for several minutes more. Stir in dissolved cornstarch and cook for 1 minute more. Serve hot or cold, as is, or as a topping for rice or (buckwheat) noodles.

Other Suggestions for Serving Deep-fried Tofu Sautéed

*Agé with Carrots and Burdock Root (Kinpira): Use 1½ cups each slivered carrots and burdock root, 1 tablespoon each sesame oil and salad oil, 2 ounces agé, ganmo, or thick agé cut into thin slices, 1 tablespoon shoyu and 2 tablespoons roasted sesame seeds. Sauté vegetables in oil over high heat for 5 minutes, or until almost tender. Add tofu and shoyu, reduce heat to medium, and sauté for 5 minutes more. Mix in sesame seeds and serve (hot or cold) seasoned with 7-spice red pepper.

*Tofu Sautéed with Vegetables: Sauté deep-fried tofu with any of the following: chard, spinach, Chinese cabbage or cabbage, wild greens or chrysanthemum leaves; green beans and almonds; winter squash or (kabocha) pumpkin. If desired, top with Ankake or Gingerroot Sauce (p. 49).

DEEP-FRIED TOFU DEEP-FRIED

Deep-frying chilled commercial thick agé, ganmo, or agé with any of the batters or coatings described on page 130 gives them a crisp texture similar to that of freshly deep-fried tofu. Try using deep-fried tofu in any of the recipes for deep-fried regular tofu.

Thick Agé Tempura with Miso Sauce   SERVES 2 OR 3

Orange-Sesame Miso Sauce:
    3 tablespoons barley, red, or Hatcho miso
    1 tablespoon sesame oil
    3 tablespoons boiling water
    ½ teaspoon grated orange rind
Oil for deep-frying
Tempura Batter (p. 134)
10 ounces thick agé or ganmo, cut into 1½-inch cubes

Combine all sauce ingredients in a small bowl; mix well. Heat oil to 350° in a wok, skillet, or deep-fryer. Dip tofu cubes in tempura batter and deep-fry until crisp and golden-brown (p. 130); drain briefly. Serve hot, topped with the sauce.

Breaded Thick Agé Cutlets   SERVES 2 OR 3

10 ounces thick agé, ganmo, or agé, frozen and thawed (p. 230) if desired
¼ cup flour
1 egg, lightly beaten
½ cup bread crumbs or bread crumb flakes
Oil for deep-frying
Worcestershire or Worcestershire-Ketchup Sauce (p. 49)

Dust uncut thick agé with flour, dip in eggs, and roll in bread crumbs. Place on a rack and allow to dry for 5 to 10 minutes.

Heat oil to 350° in a wok, skillet, or deep-fryer. Drop in tofu and deep-fry until golden brown (p. 130); drain briefly. Serve topped with the sauce.

Crispy Thick Agé in Miso Sauce
SERVES 3

6 tablespoons cornstarch or arrowroot
1 cup water
1 tablespoon oil
1 tablespoon red, barley, or Hatcho miso
1 tablespoon natural sugar
2 tablespoons sake or white wine
White of 1 egg
10 ounces thick agé or ganmo, cut into 1½-inch cubes
Oil for deep-frying
6 lettuce leaves

Mix the cornstarch and water in a bowl; allow to stand for 5 to 10 minutes until cornstarch settles and becomes firm. Meanwhile, heat the oil in a skillet. Add the miso and sugar, and sauté over medium heat for 2 or 3 minutes. Mix in the sake, cook for 1 minute more, and remove from heat.

Carefully pour off water from cornstarch. Mix egg white with cornstarch in bowl, then add thick agé cubes, mixing until each cube is covered with batter. Heat the oil to 350° in a wok, skillet, or deep-fryer. Slide in the tofu cubes and deep-fry until crisp and golden brown (p. 130); drain.

Reheat miso sauce, stir in the deep-fried tofu and cook for 1 minute. Serve in individual bowls, mounded on the lettuce leaves.

DEEP-FRIED TOFU WITH GRAINS

Combining soy and grain proteins gives a substantial increase in the total protein content of each of these preparations, as explained on page 25. Deep-fried tofu mixed with sauces (Sweet & Sour, Curry, Spaghetti, etc.) makes delicious toppings for brown rice, noodles, or other cooked grain dishes. Try also using deep-fried tofu in Chop Suey or Chow Mein (p. 67), or in grain salads (pp. 111 and 158).

Fried Buckwheat Noodles with Deep-fried Tofu (Yaki-soba)
SERVES 3 OR 4

2 tablespoons oil (used tempura oil is excellent)
1 clove garlic, crushed or minced (optional)
½ cup slivered carrot
1 small onion, thinly sliced
1 green pepper, diced
2 thinly sliced mushrooms or ½ cup thin rounds of lotus root
¼ cup raisins
3½ ounces ganmo, agé, or thick agé, thinly sliced
4½ to 5 ounces (soba) buckwheat noodles, cooked (p. 50)
1 tablespoon shoyu or ½ teaspoon salt
3 tablespoons ketchup (optional)
½ teaspoon salt
4 Paper-thin Omelets (p. 51), cut into thin strips; or substitute ¼ cup diced cheese
Crumbled toasted nori

Heat a wok or skillet and coat with the oil. Add the next six ingredients and sauté for about 4 minutes. Add ganmo and sauté for 1 minute more. Add the next four ingredients and cook, stirring constantly, for 1 minute more. Divide among deep bowls and top with the omelet strips and nori. Serve hot or, for a richer flavor, allow to stand for 4 to 6 hours before serving.

For variety, add 2 lightly beaten eggs together with the shoyu. Add ¼ to ½ cup thinly sliced lotus root, snow peas or Chinese cabbage together with the mushrooms. Season with curry powder or black pepper. Serve topped with ¼ cup roasted soybeans or peanuts or Sweet Simmered Miso (p. 41). Serve in Agé Pouches (p. 192) or Inari-zushi Pouches (p. 194).

Sizzling Rice with Deep-fried Tofu (Chahan or Yaki-meshi)
SERVES 3 OR 4

This recipe may also serve as a simple and delicious way of using leftover vegetables.

2 tablespoons oil
1 or 2 cloves of garlic, crushed or minced
1 small onion, diced; or ¼ cup minced chives or nira
5 to 10 ounces thick agé, ganmo, or agé, cut into bite-sized pieces
2 to 4 eggs, lightly beaten
2 cups cooked Brown Rice (p. 50)
2 to 3 tablespoons ketchup (optional)
2½ teaspoons shoyu
½ teaspoon salt
Dash of pepper
2 Paper-thin Omelets (p. 51), cut into thin strips (optional)
¼ cup crumbled toasted nori

Heat the oil over high heat in a wok or skillet. Add garlic and stir-fry for 1 minute. Reduce heat to medium-high, add onion, and stir-fry for 3 minutes. Add thick agé and stir-fry for 2 minutes more. Add egg and cook, stirring occasionally, for about 1 minute until egg becomes firm and bubbly. Mix in rice and stir-fry for 1½ to 2 minutes more, using spatula to cut egg into small pieces. (If using a wok, hold the wok handles and flip the cooking foods into the air 3 or 4 times to create a drier texture.) Mix in the ketchup, shoyu, salt, and pepper and sauté for 2 to 3 minutes more. Transfer to serving bowls, top with a sprinkling of the omelet strips and nori, and serve hot or cold.

VARIATIONS

*Add ¼ to ½ cup of any of the following chopped vegetables together with the onion: green peppers, green or snow peas, fresh corn, celery, bamboo shoots, Chinese cabbage, or takuan pickles. Add 3 (shiitake) mushrooms together with the thick agé.
*Serve topped with a dab of Sweet Simmered Miso (p. 41) or miso pickles.
*Serve on buttered toast or in Agé Pouches (p. 192).

Curried Buckwheat Noodles with Thick Agé

SERVES 4 TO 6

2 tablespoons oil (used tempura oil is excellent)
1 carrot, sliced into thin rounds
1 onion, thinly sliced
1/3 cup raisins
½ apple, diced
¼ cup water
1½ teaspoons curry powder
1 teaspoon salt
2 teaspoons shoyu or 1 tablespoon red or barley miso
10 ounces thick agé or ganmo, cut into thin 1-inch squares
4½ to 5 ounces buckwheat noodles, cooked (p. 50)
Dash of pepper
¼ cup roasted soybeans or peanuts (optional)
¼ cup diced or grated cheese (optional)
¼ cup chutney (optional)

Heat the oil over high heat in a skillet or wok. Add carrots and stir-fry for 2 minutes. Add onions and stir-fry for 2 minutes more. Add raisins and apple and stir-fry for 3 minutes. Stir in water, curry powder, salt, shoyu, and thick agé; reduce heat to medium and cook for 3 minutes. Stir in noodles, season with pepper, and remove from heat. Serve hot or cold. If desired, top with roasted soybeans, peanuts, cheese, and/or chutney.

Crumbly Agé Soboro with Brown Rice

SERVES 4

Soboro refers to dishes which have the texture of sautéed hamburger.

5 ounces agé, ganmo, or thick agé, doused (p. 156) and diced
    fine (and, if desired, ground in a meat grinder or *suribachi*)
1 cup dashi (p. 39), stock, or water
2 tablespoons shoyu
1½ tablespoons natural sugar
2 tablespoons sake
2 teaspoons minced gingerroot
1½ cups brown rice, cooked (p. 50)
1 tablespoon roasted sesame seeds (p. 38)
1 tablespoon minced parsley
1½ tablespoons diced red pickled gingerroot (beni shoga)
    (optional)

Combine the first six ingredients in a small saucepan and bring to a boil. Reduce heat to low and simmer for 5 to 6 minutes. Stirring constantly with 4 or 5 chopsticks held in the fist of one hand, simmer until all liquid has been absorbed or evaporated.

Divide hot brown rice among large individual bowls, top with the *soboro,* and serve garnished with sesame, parsley, and gingerroot.

Soboro may also be served as an entrée.

Five-color Sushi Rice with Agé
(Maze-gohan or Gomoku-zushi)

SERVES 3

This dish is served each year during Japan's week-long spring and autumn equinox celebrations. Known also as *Kayaku Gohan,* it is a close relative of *Chirashi-zushi* which is served at *sushi* shops and generally contains fish. Since the weeks of the equinox are considered sacred seasons, fish is traditionally omitted.

½ cup water
1½ tablespoons shoyu
2 tablespoons natural sugar
4 (shiitake) mushrooms, thinly sliced
½ carrot, cut into matchsticks
2 ounces agé, ganmo, or thick agé, thinly sliced
1 green pepper, thinly sliced
2 tablespoons ground roasted sesame seeds (p. 38) (optional)
1½ cups Sushi Rice (p. 50; made from 2/3 cup raw brown rice)
2 Paper-thin Omelets (p. 51), cut into thin strips
¼ cup crumbled toasted *nori*
12 to 15 snow peas, parboiled (p. 37)
2 to 4 tablespoons diced trefoil (optional)

Combine water, shoyu, and sugar in a small saucepan and bring to a boil. Add mushrooms, carrots, and agé, cover pan, and simmer for about 5 minutes. Increase heat to medium and simmer, stirring constantly, for 3 to 5 minutes more, or until all liquid has been absorbed or evaporated. Set aside and allow to cool.

Combine cooked vegetables, green pepper, sesame, and rice in a large wooden salad bowl or sushi tray; mix well. Sprinkle with the omelet strips, *nori,* snow peas, and trefoil; place at the center of the dining table.

Substitute or add any of the following to the cooked vegetables: green beans or peas, lotus root, bamboo shoots, or *kampyo.* Four ounces of lotus root may also be simmered separately in a mixture of 1½ tablespoons vinegar, 1 tablespoon sugar, and ½ teaspoon salt. Or add sliced cucumber or *udo* which has been marinated in equal parts vinegar and sugar. Other toppings include slivered red pickled gingerroot or parsley. Serve in Agé Pouches (p. 192) or Inari-zushi Pouches (p. 194).

Chinese-style Thick Agé and Bean Sprouts

SERVES 2

2 tablespoons oil
1½ teaspoons crushed or minced garlic
2 cups bean sprouts
¼ cup thinly sliced chives, *nira*, or green onions
5 ounces thick agé, ganmo, or agé, cut into 1-inch cubes
1 teaspoon grated gingerroot
1 teaspoon sake or white wine
¾ teaspoon salt
3 tablespoons soy sauce
½ teaspoon cornstarch or arrowroot, dissolved in 2 tablespoons water

Heat a skillet and coat with the oil. Add garlic and sprouts and stir-fry over high heat for about 1 minute. Mix in chives and agé and stir-fry for 1 minute more. Reduce heat to medium, stir in gingerroot, sake, salt, and soy sauce and sauté briefly. Mix in dissolved cornstarch and cook for 1 minute more. Serve hot.

VARIATIONS

*Omit the garlic and chives. Sauté the sprouts in 1 tablespoon sesame oil. Add the tofu together with ¼ cup water, 1 teaspoon vinegar, 4 teaspoons each soy sauce and sugar, and ¾ teaspoon grated gingerroot. Simmer for 5 minutes, then stir in 1 teaspoon cornstarch dissolved in 1 tablespoon water.

Crisp Tortillas with Taco Sauce and Deep-fried Tofu

SERVES 5

Taco Sauce:
    2/3 cup ketchup
    1¼ cups grated cheese
    2 tablespoons red miso
    2 tablespoons minced onion or leek
    1 teaspoon grated gingerroot
    1 teaspoon sake or white wine
    Dash of tabasco sauce or pepper
    1 tablespoon water
2½ cups shredded lettuce or cabbage
15 ounces thick agé, ganmo, or agé, thinly sliced
10 seven-inch *tortillas*
Butter

Place taco sauce, lettuce, and tofu in separate serving bowls. Heat *tortillas* in a medium oven for 5 to 7 minutes until lightly browned and crisp, then butter immediately and arrange on a large serving platter. Invite each guest to spread *tortillas* with sauce, sprinkle with lettuce, and top with sliced tofu.

    Or, use Mushroom Sauce (p. 48) in place of the taco sauce.

Deep-fried Tofu Gruel with Leftovers

Combine plenty of deep-fried tofu with leftover cooked grains and vegetables. Add enough leftover soup, stock, or water to give the consistency of a thick stew; bring to a boil and simmer for 5 to 10 minutes. Add shoyu or creamed miso and, if desired, curry powder or ketchup to unify the flavors. To thicken, stir in lightly roasted whole-wheat or barley flour and cook for several minutes more. Serve hot or cold. To use leftover gruel as the basis for full-bodied breads, knead in flour to earlobe consistency, allow to rise overnight, and bake in a slow oven for several hours.

Thick Agé with Gingerroot Miso

SERVES 2 OR 3

1½ tablespoons oil
10 ounces thick agé, ganmo, or agé, cut into ½-inch-thick, bite-sized rectangles
2 tablespoons red, barley, or Hatcho miso
2 to 2½ tablespoons natural sugar
1 teaspoon grated gingerroot
Minced parsley or lettuce leaves

Heat a skillet or wok and coat with the oil. Add thick agé and sauté over high heat for 3 to 4 minutes until slightly crisp and well browned. Add miso, sugar, and gingerroot, and cook, stirring constantly, for about 2 minutes more, or until all ingredients are well mixed. Serve hot or cold, garnished with parsley or placed on individual lettuce leaves.

Nori-wrapped Sushi with Agé (Norimaki-zushi)

SERVES 3 OR 4

3½ tablespoons vinegar
2 tablespoons natural sugar
3 ounces agé, ganmo, or thick agé, doused (p. 156)
3 sheets of *nori*
3½ cups Sushi Rice (p. 50)
½ cucumber, cut into long, 1/8-inch-square strips
3 tablespoons shoyu

Combine vinegar and sugar in a small saucepan and bring to a boil. Add agé, cover pan, and reduce heat to low; simmer for 3 to 4 minutes. Uncover pan and simmer over medium heat, stirring constantly, until all liquid evaporates. Set aside to cool, then cut agé lengthwise into very thin strips.

Place 1 sheet of *nori* on a *sudare* or small dry dishcloth. Spread one-third of the rice evenly over the *nori*, leaving a 1-inch-wide strip uncovered along the far edge (fig. 57). Place one-third of the agé and cucumber strips in a row about 2 inches from the near edge of the *nori*. Now roll up *nori* and moisten edge of *nori* with water to seal. With a sharp knife, cut the roll crosswise into 10 small discs. (Wipe knife with a moist cloth to prevent sticking.) Repeat with remaining ingredients until all are used. Serve the shoyu in small dishes for dipping.

For variety, add or substitute for the cucumber: thin strips of Paper-thin Omelets (p. 51), Walnut Miso (p. 42), or slivered walnuts simmered in a mixture of honey, shoyu, and sugar; *kampyo* or *hijiki* simmered in Sweetened Shoyu Broth (p. 40).

Fig. 57. Making Nori-wrapped Sushi with Agé

Fox Domburi *(Kitsune Domburi)*   SERVES 4

This and the following dish are named after foxes which, in Japan, are said to be very fond of agé. A *domburi* is a deep serving bowl, usually heaped high with rice. Fox Domburi is one of the most popular dishes served in the many thousands of *soba* shops throughout Japan.

1 cup water, stock, or dashi (p. 39)
3 tablespoons shoyu
3 tablespoons natural sugar
1 tablespoon *mirin* (optional)
4 ounces agé, ganmo, or thick agé, cut into ½-inch-wide
     strips
1 onion, thinly sliced
1 cup brown rice, cooked (p. 50)
Dash of *sansho* pepper (optional)

Combine the first four ingredients in a saucepan and bring to a boil. Add agé and onion, then simmer for 7 minutes. Divide cooked rice among bowls and pour on hot broth, onions, and agé. Serve seasoned with the pepper.

If desired, top with crumbled toasted *nori* or slivers of Sweet Vinegared Gingerroot (p. 51).

Fox Noodles *(Kitsune Soba or Udon)*   SERVES 3

3 pieces of agé or ganmo, doused (p. 156) and each cut into 4
     equal triangles or diagonal ½-inch-wide strips
1 cup dashi (p. 39), stock, or water
1½ to 2 tablespoons natural sugar
1 tablespoon shoyu
2 teaspoons *mirin* (optional)
Dash of salt
2¼ cups Noodle Broth (p. 40)
1 onion, cut into very thin wedges
4½ ounces *soba* or *udon* noodles, cooked (p. 50) and drained
7-spice red pepper

Combine the first six ingredients in a small saucepan and bring to a boil. Reduce heat to low and simmer uncovered, stirring occasionally, until all liquid has been absorbed or evaporated.

Meanwhile, combine Noodle Broth and onion in a large pot and bring to a boil. Add cooked noodles and agé and return to the boil. Serve in deep bowls, inviting each person to season his portion to taste with red pepper.

Buckwheat Noodles with Grated   SERVES 3
Glutinous Yam and Agé *(Yamakake Soba)*

4½ ounces *(soba)* buckwheat noodles, cooked (p. 50)
2¼ cups Noodle Broth (p. 40)
Grated Glutinous Yam with Agé (p. 174)

Divide the cooked noodles among 6 deep bowls. Pour in the hot broth and top with the yam-and-agé. Serve hot or cold.

Noodles & Deep-fried Tofu in   SERVES 4 TO 6
Chilled Broth *(Hiyashi-soba)*

A popular summertime recipe in both China and Japan, *Hiyahsi-soba* is often prepared with slivers of ham rather than ganmo.

6 to 7 ounces *(soba)* buckwheat noodles, cooked (p. 50) and
     doused with cold water
7 ounces ganmo, thick agé, or agé, slivered
½ cucumber, slivered
½ tomato, cut into thin wedges
4 Paper-thin Omelets (p. 51), slivered
Broth:
     2/3 cup dashi (p. 39) or stock
     2½ tablespoons shoyu
     3 tablespoons vinegar
     ½ teaspoon sesame oil
     Dash of 7-spice red pepper
     ¼ cup slivered leeks, rinsed and pressed (p. 37)
Crumbled toasted *nori* (p. 38) (optional)

Place the first five ingredients in separate bowls, cover, and chill. Bring the dashi to a boil in a saucepan. Add shoyu and return just to the boil. Remove from heat and allow to cool. Stir in remaining broth ingredients, cover, and chill.

To serve, mound noodles on individual plates or in bowls. Arrange tofu, cucumber, tomato, and omelet slivers in equal portions atop each serving. Pour on the chilled broth and, if desired, top with a sprinkling of *nori*.

Eating noodles in old Japan (from Hokusai's sketchbooks)

Ganmo Simmered with Homemade Noodles and Miso (Nikomi Udon)

SERVES 6

This dish is a favorite in the village of Uehara, which is renowned for its many vigorous centenarians. They claim the key to their long life is eating unrefined barley and vegetables, little or no animal foods, and plenty of miso. In this nutritious dish, the water in which the noodles are cooked is not discarded but is used as the basis for a thick miso sauce that closely resembles a Western white sauce. For best flavor, allow this dish to stand overnight so that the noodles further contribute to the thickening of the sauce. Then serve either cold or reheated.

2 cups flour, half of which is whole-wheat
8½ cups warm water
¼ teaspoon salt
6 tablespoons sweet white miso
5 tablespoons red or barley miso
10½ ounces ganmo, thick agé, or agé, cut into bite-sized pieces
3 large leeks, cut diagonally into 2-inch lengths
1½ small leeks or green onions, cut into thin rounds
7-spice red pepper
Crumbled toasted *nori* (optional)

Put the 2 cups flour into a large bowl and, adding ½ cup water a little at a time, mix and knead to form a heavy dough. Roll out dough on a floured board to 1/8-inch thickness, sprinkle surface lightly with flour, and fold lengthwise accordion fashion into quarters (fig. 58). Now cut crosswise into 1/8-inch-wide strands to make noodles. Spread noodle strips on the floured board to dry briefly.

Bring remaining 8 cups water to a boil in a large pot. Drop in noodles and salt, and simmer until noodles float to surface. Cream the miso with a little of the hot cooking water and add to the pot. Add ganmo and large leeks and simmer for 10 minutes. Serve garnished with thin rounds of leeks, red pepper, and *nori*.

Use about 10 ounces dried noodles in place of the homemade variety.

Deep-fried Tofu with Tabbouli (Lebanese Grain Salad)

SERVES 4

¾ cup raw bulgur wheat
2 2/3 cup boiling water
10 ounces thick agé, agé, or ganmo, diced; or 24 ounces regular tofu, crumbled (p. 98)
½ cup minced mint
1 cup minced parsley
½ cup minced scallions
2 tomatoes, diced
3 tablespoons olive oil
6 tablespoons lemon juice
1 teaspoon salt
1 clove of garlic, crushed
Dash of pepper
4 large lettuce or (Chinese) cabbage leaves

Combine bulgur and boiling water in a saucepan, cover, and allow to stand for 2 hours. Drain bulgur, press between the palms to expel excess water, then mix with all remaining ingredients except the lettuce. Chill for 1 hour. Serve mounded on the lettuce leaves.

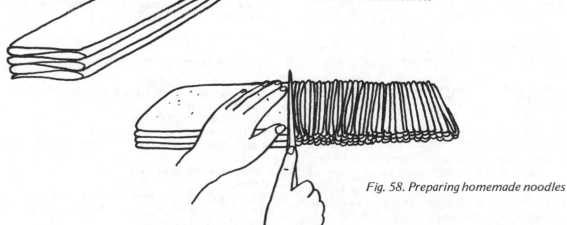

Fig. 58. Preparing homemade noodles

DEEP-FRIED TOFU BROILED

Try using your favorite barbeque sauces with deep-fried tofu. When cooked over a bed of live coals, the tofu develops a delicately crisp texture and savory barbequed aroma.

Grilled Thick Agé with Korean Barbeque Sauce
SERVES 2

5 ounces thick agé, ganmo, or agé
¼ cup Korean Barbeque Sauce (p. 49)

Broil the tofu over a barbeque fire, in an oven broiler, or in a hot unoiled skillet (p. 156). Remove from heat and cut crosswise into 6 equal pieces. Dip briefly in the sauce and broil lightly once again. Serve in bowls, topped with the remaining sauce.

Savory Thick Agé with Broiled Miso
SERVES 1 OR 2

5 ounces thick agé, ganmo, or agé
1½ to 3 teaspoons red, barley, or Sweet Simmered Miso (p. 41)

Pierce thick agé from one end with a large fork or 2 chopsticks. Holding tofu just above a strong flame (or use an oven broiler), broil quickly on both sides until lightly browned. Spread both sides of the tofu with a thin layer of miso and re-broil for about 15 seconds per side, or until miso is fragrant and speckled. Cut tofu into bite-sized pieces and serve immediately.

Or cut thick agé or ganmo crosswise into fourths, skewer, and prepare as for Tofu Dengaku (p. 139); use Egg Yolk Miso (p. 43) or any variety of Sweet Simmered Miso for the topping. If using agé, spread one surface of each piece with miso, then roll from one end to form a tight cylinder. Insert skewers from the side, fastening the roll; broil (fig. 100, p. 245).

Agé Mock Broiled Eels
(Kabayaki or Yaki-Shinoda)
SERVES 4

2 tablespoons shoyu
2 tablespoons natural sugar
2 green peppers, cut lengthwise into quarters
1 tablespoon oil
8 ounces agé, ganmo, or thick agé, cut into bite-sized triangles
Dash of *sansho* pepper

Combine shoyu and sugar in a small bowl for use as a dipping sauce. Brush peppers lightly with the oil. Place peppers and tofu over a charcoal brazier or barbeque, or in an oven broiler, and grill on both sides until lightly browned and fragrant. Set peppers aside. Dip tofu into sauce, then broil again lightly and sprinkle with the pepper. Serve tofu and peppers on small plates accompanied by the remaining dipping sauce.

Thick Agé Shish Kebab
SERVES 4

Ingredients for skewering: (Use four or more)
    5 ounces thick agé or ganmo, cut into bite-sized cubes
    4 green peppers, cut into 2-inch triangles
    8 mushrooms
    1 apple, cut into bite-sized chunks or rounds
    8 chunks of firm pineapple
    4 firm small tomatoes
    4 small blanched onions
    1 celery stalk or cucumber, cut into bite-sized sections
2/3 cup Teriyaki Sauce (p. 48)

Place basic ingredients in a shallow pan and pour on sauce. Marinate for 1 hour, turning ingredients serveral times. Skewer pieces on 4 to 8 skewers and broil for 2 to 3 minutes, basting occasionally, until nicely speckled and fragrant.

VARIATIONS

*Broil tofu without basting. Substitute ½ teaspoon grated gingerroot and/or 2 teaspoons grated *daikon* for the sugar in the dipping sauce. Serve broiled tofu accompanied by sauce garnished with thinly sliced leeks (or scallions) and 7-spice red pepper.
*While broiling, baste tofu with a mixture of 2 tablespoons shoyu and 1½ teaspoons *mirin*. Serve garnished with a mixture of ¼ cup grated *daikon* and ½ teaspoon grated gingerroot.

DEEP-FRIED TOFU SIMMERED IN SEASONED BROTHS

Deep-fried tofu absorbs simmering liquids or broths best if first doused (p. 156). Avoid simmering for too long, lest a chewy, web-like structure and many small bubbles form in the tofu. Most of these dishes attain their peak of flavor if served 4, or as much as 48, hours after they have been prepared. During this time they should be allowed to stand in the remaining broth, covered and refrigerated. If thick agé is frozen overnight, then thawed in warm water, it develops a very absorbent texture somewhat like tender meat (p. 230) and makes an excellent replacement for regular thick agé in most of the following recipes, or for regular tofu in Sukiyaki (p. 224) and other *nabe* preparations.

Grated Glutinous Yam with Agé
SERVES 3

1 2/3 cups dashi (p. 39), stock, or water
4 tablespoons shoyu
2 tablespoons natural sugar
1 tablespoon *mirin*
4 ounces agé, ganmo, or thick agé, doused (p. 156) and cut into thin strips
1 cup grated glutinous yam
3 eggs
¼ cup thinly sliced rounds of leek or scallion
Dash of 7-spice red pepper or *sansho* pepper
Crumbled toasted *nori*

In a saucepan combine the dashi, 2 tablespoons shoyu, sugar and *mirin*, and bring to a boil. Add agé and reduce heat to low. Cover pan and simmer for 10 minutes, then transfer agé from pan and allow agé to cool separately.

Stir 1½ tablespoons shoyu into cooled broth. Divide the grated yam among 3 deep bowls and break an egg into each. Top with the agé and seasoned broth, and garnish with leeks, pepper, and *nori*. Invite each guest to beat the ingredients together with chopsticks or fork before eating.

This dish also makes a delicious topping for buckwheat noodles or brown rice. Or use in Yamakake Soba (p. 172).

Deep-fried Potatoes & Thick Agé in Seasoned Broth

SERVES 6

Oil for deep-frying
7 small potatoes, quartered
2 cups water or dashi (p. 39)
5 tablespoons shoyu
5½ tablespoons natural sugar
10 ounces thick agé, ganmo, or agé, cut into 1-inch cubes

Heat the oil to 350° in a wok, skillet, or deep-fryer. Drop in the potatoes and deep-fry until golden brown (p. 130); drain well.

Combine water, shoyu, and sugar in a saucepan and bring to a boil. Add potatoes, cover pan, and simmer for 30 minutes. Add thick agé, return to the boil, and remove from heat. Cover pan and allow to stand for 6 to 8 hours. Serve cold.

Deep-fried Tofu Simmered in Seasoned Broth

SERVES 2

5 ounces thick agé, ganmo, or agé, cut into bite-sized pieces
Basic Seasoned Broth:
   ½ cup water, stock, or dashi (p. 39)
   1½ tablespoons shoyu or 2 tablespoons red miso
   1 to 1½ tablespoons natural sugar
   1½ teaspoons sake or white wine (optional)

Combine all ingredients in a small saucepan and bring to a boil. Reduce heat to low and simmer for about 10 minutes, then set aside to cool. Divide thick agé and broth among serving bowls. Garnish with a sprig of *kinome*, a dab of grated gingerroot or mustard, or a dash of *sansho* pepper.

VARIATIONS
*Agé Simmered with Vegetables: In the basic broth simmer 2 ounces agé, ganmo, or thick agé cut into small rectangles and 2 cups of any of the following vegetables cubed or diced: *kabocha*, sweet potatoes, small yams or taro, celery, butterbur, bracken ferns, or green beans. Prepare as above and serve cold, sprinkled with ground roasted sesame seeds or sesame salt.
*Ganmo Treasure Balls with Snow Peas: In the basic seasoned broth above simmer 2 Homemade Ganmo Treasure Balls (p.

188) or 3 ounces agé and 4 to 5 ounces (1½ cups) snow peas. Serve chilled. Use deep lacquerware bowls for greater aesthetic effect.
*Thick Agé Sandwiches: Cut a 5-ounce cake of thick agé horizontally into halves and simmer in the seasoned broth as above. Place each half on a plate, cover with a slice of cheese and mound with sautéed onions, carrots, green beans, and burdock root. Serve like open-faced sandwiches.
*Mother's Favorite (*Ofukuro no aji*): In the basic seasoned broth, simmer bite-sized pieces of thick agé, ganmo, lotus root, *daikon*, carrot, and *konnyaku*. Meanwhile prepare finely diced green beans, burdock root, and carrots; mix with thick tempura batter and deep-fry as for Kaki-age (p. 136). Arrange deep-fried patties in deep bowls with the simmered tofu and vegetables. Serve topped with a little of the seasoned broth.

Agé Simmered with Shredded Dried Daikon

SERVES 4 TO 6

1½ cups (2½ ounces) shredded dried *daikon (kiriboshi)*
2 ounces agé, ganmo, or thick agé, cut lengthwise into halves, then crosswise into ½-inch-wide strips
3 tablespoons natural sugar or honey
2 tablespoons shoyu
1 tablespoon sake or white wine

Pour 1½ cups water into a large bowl. Rinse *daikon* quickly in the water, then press *daikon* lightly between the palms of both hands so that water is returned to the bowl. Rinse and press 3 more times. Combine *daikon* and 1 cup of the pressing water in a small saucepan. Cover and simmer over low heat for about 40 minutes, or until *daikon* is quite soft. Mix in the agé, sugar, shoyu, and sake; cover and simmer for about 30 minutes more, stirring well every 10 minutes. Set aside uncovered and allow to cool to room temperature before serving.

Deep-fried Tofu in Western-style Stews

All three varieties of deep-fried tofu make excellent additions to your favorite stews, as well as tasty meat substitutes. Try using deep-fried tofu in place of regular tofu in Tofu-Miso Stew (p. 145). To give the stew a meatier flavor, season with miso or shoyu. Use lightly roasted whole wheat or barley flower as a thickener. Add curry powder or ketchup, if desired, to help marry the various flavors.

Oden (*Japanese Stew*)

SERVES 4 TO 8

When October nights grow chilly, Oden carts become a familiar and welcome sight along Tokyo's streets. Each old-fashioned wooden stall, mounted on two bicycle wheels, is equipped with a gaslight lantern illuminating a compact, self-contained kitchen. Two pans of foods simmering in a fragrant, dark broth are heated by a small charcoal brazier. Large bottles of shoyu, sake, and water stand ready to replenish the steaming bubbling liquid, and a knife and pair of long chopsticks are kept busy serving the many customers who gather around this little oasis of warmth for a quick night meal or snack. Here you can find tofu and deep-fried tofu of all types simmering together with as many as twenty other different foods. In nearby suburban neighborhoods, the "Oden man" roams the night streets at dinnertime, pulling his cart behind him and ringing his familiar bell. Stopping at homes when someone hails him from the doorway, he provides one of Japan's oldest ready-made meals and leaves a wake of savory aromas floating in the cold air behind him as he goes on his way (fig. 59).

Fig. 59. The "Oden man"

Throughout Japan, huge red papper lanterns hung outside the doorway of working class taverns and bars bear the name Oden in bold jet-black brushstroke letters. Each evening throughout the year—but especially during the cold months—steaming hot Oden is served inside as the favorite accompaniment to hot sake. And in fine Kyoto Oden shops such as *Takocho* (p. 308) or Kyoto-style shops in Tokyo such as *Otako* (p. 312), Oden is served in an atmosphere of quiet refinement. Seated at high, square stools along a simple but elegant counter made of thick, unfinished wood, each customer orders his favorite items from the wide selection of ingredients cooking in a brightly polished one-by-three-foot copper tray located just behind the counter. As the guest refreshingly wipes hands and face with a hot, damp towel, the cheery, white-clad shopkeepers whisk his order onto a small plate, cut the tofu, *daikon,* or potatoes into smaller pieces with quick strokes of a razor-sharp knife, pour a little of the hot broth over the food, add a dab of mustard, and place the dish before the guest with no time lost. As the evening progresses, the shopkeeper keeps a running tally of what was ordered on an inconspicuous card behind the counter. Each item has its own, very reasonable price.

In Japanese farmhouses, Oden is one of the most ancient and most popular forms of *nabe* cookery. Prepared in a heavy iron pot hung over the coals of the living-room open-hearth fireplace (fig. 69, p. 186), the Oden is simmered slowly and leisurely, which allows fullest development of its fine flavors.

The name Oden is an abbreviation of *Nikomi Dengaku* or "Dengaku simmered in seasoned broth." Tofu Dengaku (p. 139) was originally made of grilled tofu topped with a layer of miso. After about 1750, *konnyaku* began to be prepared in somewhat the same way. At a later stage, instead of being broiled, the *konnyaku* was cut into large triangles and simmered in a broth seasoned with miso. Gradually other ingredients such as potatoes, *daikon* and various types of fish sausage were added to the stew, and the miso was replaced by a topping of tangy hot mustard.

The name Oden seems to have first been used in a well-known play called *Keian Taiheki,* written about 1850. In it, one character says, "It looks like they're enjoying Nikomi Oden with their sake." Oden itself originated in the Tokyo area where it was generally served together with hot sake in working class and lower class bars. The broth was quite dark and richly seasoned with shoyu and *mirin* or sugar; the ingredients were simmered for many hours until they turned a deep amber. As Oden spread to then more aristocratic Kyoto area, it underwent some basic transformations. Served as a high-class food in fine shops, it contained a much wider variety of ingredients. The relatively light-colored broth was conservatively seasoned with pale *(usukuchi)* shoyu, salt, and sake. After the great earthquake of 1923, the new Kyoto style was brought back to Tokyo where it now co-exists with its lower-class, but none the less delicious, progenitor as well as an increasingly popular blend of the two styles.

Oden's ingredients, broth, and manner of preparation are closely related to Nishime (p. 178), except than Oden is a cold weather dish usually served hot with plenty of broth and various toppings and seasonings. Using a pressure cooker, both dishes can be prepared in about 20 minutes. Like Nishime, Oden is very delicious if allowed to stand overnight and then served cold or reheated the next day. In the following recipe, the basic ingredients are listed in order of popularity in Japan.

Broth:
- 5 cups dashi (p. 39), stock, or water
- 7 to 8 tablespoons shoyu
- 2 to 3 tablespoons natural sugar
- 1½ tablespoons sake or white wine (optional)

Basic Ingredients: choose about 8
- 10 inches of *kombu*, wiped clean with a damp cloth and cut crosswise into 2-inch-wide strips
- 1 cake of *konnyaku*, cut into 4 triangles
- 3 to 4 small potatoes, cut into quarters or halves
- 5 to 10 ounces regular or frozen thick agé, cubed; or thick agé cubes
- 4 to 8 small taro, cut into halves
- 5 to 6 ounces lotus root, cut into half moons
- 12 ounces *daikon*, peeled and cut into ½-inch-thick half moons
- 2 large ganmo patties, quartered; 4 ganmo treasure balls (p. 188) or 8 small ganmo balls
- 4 hard-boiled eggs, peeled
- 4 Kinchaku Agé Pouches (p. 196)
- 12 ounces tofu, grilled tofu, or kinugoshi, quartered
- 4 cabbage rolls (see below)
- 4 *kombu* rolls (see below)
- 4 agé rolls (see Shinoda Maki, p. 197)
- 4 *konnyaku* noodle bundles (see below)
- 4 prepared skewers (see below)
- 1 carrot, cut into large irregular chunks
- 4 rolls of *Oharagi* yuba (p. 241)
- 10 ounces bamboo shoots, cut into large irregular pieces
- 2 sweet potatoes, quartered
- 2 turnips, quartered

Seasonings:
- 2 teaspoons hot mustard
- 4 tablespoons thinly sliced leek or scallion
- Dash of 7-spice red pepper

Pour dashi into a large pot or casserole. Tie 4 of the *kombu* strips into simple overhand knots, and arrange remaining *kombu* pieces over bottom of pot. Chose about 7 more basic ingredients from the list. Arrange those which require the longest cooking (*daikon, konnyaku*) atop *kombu* and bring dashi to a boil over high heat. Reduce heat to low and simmer for 10 minutes. Add remaining uncooked vegetables (potatoes, taro, lotus root) and simmer for 10 minutes more. Stir in shoyu, sugar, and sake, then add tofu ingredients. Return broth to the boil, then reduce heat to very low and cover pot. Simmer for at least 40 to 60 minutes, lifting pot and shaking it gently every 20 minutes to mix broth. Do not change the order of layering. For best flavor, allow Oden to stand for at least 6 to 8 hours, then serve reheated or as is. Divide the ingredients and broth among individual serving bowls and invite each guest to top his portion to taste with mustard and, if desired, other seasonings.

TO MAKE:

*Cabbage Rolls: Dip a large cabbage leaf into boiling water until pliable. On the concave surface place 2 to 4 tablespoons of any of the following: diced or slivered onions, carrots, lotus root, *shiitake* or cloud-ear mushrooms (fresh or sautéed); cooked transparent or rice flour noodles, or yuba.

Roll the cabbage leaf from one end, tucking in the sides, then tie with a piece of *kampyo* which has been soaked for a few minutes in water until pliable.

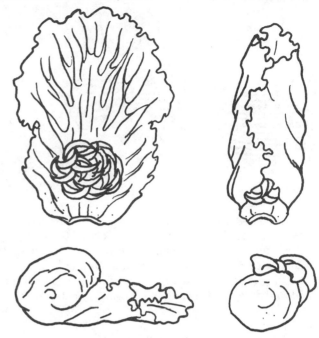

*Kombu Rolls: Refresh a large piece of *kombu* until pliable by soaking in water, then cut into a piece about 6 inches square. Cut eight 6-inch-long strips of carrot, burdock, lotus root, or butterbur and arrange in a bundle at the center of *kombu*. Roll up cut vegetables in the *kombu*, tie in 4 places with refreshed *kampyo*, and cut crosswise to form 4 rolls about 1½ inches long.

*Konnyaku Noodle Bundles: Wrap about 10 *konnyaku* noodles around the tips of 2 fingers, then tie in the center with a single *konnyaku* noodle.

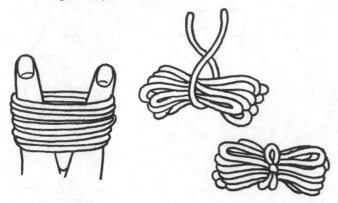

*Prepared Skewers: Skewer 4 ginkgo nuts or green beans on a foodpick or small bamboo skewer. Or make tiny balls or dumplings of glutinous rice flour or wheat flour kneaded with a little water, and skewer. Or mix grated lotus root and grated carrot with a little whole-wheat flour and salt; deep-fry, and skewer alternately with brussel sprouts.

*Other Ingredients: Additional ingredients may include dried wheat gluten cakes, tempura, eggplants, deep-fried fresh wheat gluten or any of the following commonly used sea foods: fish sausage *(tsumire, hanpen, satsuma agé, chikuwa, kamaboko)*, octopus or squid, *sakura* shrimp, or shark marrow *(suji)*. Alternative seasonings include: grated gingerroot, grated orange peel, or a few drops of *yuzu* juice.

Fig. 60. Making konnyaku "twists"

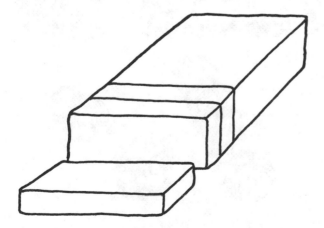

Nishime

A popular dish at equinox rituals or ceremonial occasions and national holidays, *Nishime* is also frequently included in picnic box lunches as a special treat. At New Year's, grilled tofu is generally used in place of or together with the usual deep-fried tofu. Enough *Osechi* (New Year's) *Nishime* is made on the last day of the "old year" to last throughout the following week of festivities, and the flavor is said to improve with each passing day.

Many recipes include only 3 or 4 of the vegetables listed below, so omit or substitute according to what is available. Adjust the amount of cooking liquid accordingly. Some cooks prefer to cook each of the ingredients separately for a different length of time in a broth seasoned to match the food's unique character. Each cooked ingredient is allowed to marinate overnight in its own broth, but is served without broth in a bowl together with all the other ingredients.

If Nishime is simmered in a relatively small amount of broth until all is absorbed and a soft luster forms on each ingredient, the dish is called *Uma-ni*. If the vegetables are first cooked in unseasoned dashi, to be seasoned toward the end of the cooking and served with a large amount of broth, the dish is called *Fukume-ni*. All three of these types of popular *Ni-mono*, or "foods simmered in seasoned broths," include tofu.

3 cups dashi (p. 39), stock, or water
7 tablespoons shoyu
7 to 9 tablespoons natural sugar or *mirin*
3 tablespoons sake or white wine
½ teaspoon salt
1 cake of *konnyaku*, cut crosswise into ¼-inch-thick pieces
1 carrot, cut into large random chunks
½ burdock root, cut lengthwise into halves, then into 1½-inch lengths and parboiled for 10 minutes
1 large taro or potato, cut into eighths
2 inches *daikon*, cut into half moons
½ lotus root, cut into half moons
8 inches *kombu*, wiped clean with a moist cloth and cut crosswise into 1-inch-wide strips
1 small bamboo shoot, cut into large random chunks
3 *(shiitake)* mushrooms, cut into quarters
10½ ounces ganmo (patties or small balls), thick agé, or agé, doused (p. 156) and cut into bite-sized pieces
10 ounces grilled tofu, cut into large triangles (optional)
8 sprigs of *kinome*

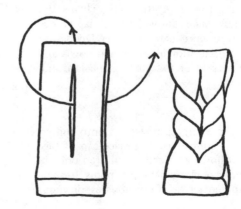

Combine the first five ingredients in a large pot or casserole and bring to a boil. Meanwhile, cut a slit lengthwise down the center of each small piece of *konnyaku* and thread one end up through the slit and back again (fig. 60). Add *konnyaku* and next 8 ingredients to the broth, and return to the boil. Reduce heat to low, cover pot, and simmer for about 40 minutes. Add tofu, stir vegetables so that uppermost ones are transferred to bottom of pot, re-cover, and continue simmering until all but about ¾ cup of broth has been absorbed or evaporated. Remove from heat and allow to cool for at least 5, preferably 24 hours. Divide ingredients among individual serving bowls, pour on remaining liquid, and garnish with a sprig of *kinome*.

For variety, add or substitute a small amount of frozen-, or dried-frozen tofu, or frozen thick agé.

DEEP-FRIED TOFU DESSERTS

In these tasty treats, the combination of apples and agé makes healthful and satisfying desserts. Other treats using agé pouches are found beginning on page 196.

Cooked Apples with Agé and Tofu Whipped Cream

SERVES 4

3 apples, cut into thin wedges
¼ cup raisins
1 cup water
1½ tablespoons natural sugar
2 ounces agé, ganmo, or thick agé, cut into small triangles
¼ teaspoon cinnamon
12 ounces tofu made into Tofu Whipped Cream (p. 148)

Combine 2 apples, raisins, water, and sugar in a pressure cooker. Bring to full pressure, reduce heat to low, and cook for 15 minutes. Remove from heat and let stand under pressure for 10 minutes. Add tofu and remaining apple, and simmer uncovered over low heat for 15 minutes more. Sprinkle with cinnamon and allow to cool. Serve topped with Tofu Whipped Cream.

Cooked Apples with Agé and Creamy Topping

SERVES 3 TO 4

2 apples, thinly sliced
1½ tablespoons natural sugar
2 ounces agé, cut crosswise into fourths
¼ cup water
¼ teaspoon cinnamon
Soymilk Thick Sweet Cream (p. 206)

Combine the first four ingredients in a small saucepan and simmer until apples are just tender and most of the liquid has evaporated. Allow to cool, then sprinkle with cinnamon and serve topped with soymilk cream.

For variety, add 1 to 2 teaspoons lemon juice before cooking.

Thick Agé
(Deep-fried Tofu Cutlets)

IN JAPAN thick agé, whole deep-fried cakes of tofu, are referred to both as *nama-agé*, meaning "fresh or raw deep-fried tofu," and as *atsu-agé*, meaning "thick deep-fried tofu." Both names are used interchangeably, and the former is used frequently in the United States. The word "thick" is used to contrast thick agé with agé and ganmo, which are usually made in fairly thin sheets or patties, while the words "fresh" or "raw" refer to the fact that only the surface of the tofu cake is affected by the quick deep-frying in very hot oil; the center remains almost as tender and soft as firmly-pressed regular tofu.

Of the many and varied types of Japanese and Chinese tofu, we feel that thick agé is perhaps the best suited to Western tastes and cuisine. We use more thick agé in our daily cookery than any other type of tofu. It is unique in combining the softness and substantial quality of regular tofu with the crisp firmness and deep-bodied flavor and aroma acquired from deep-frying. Costing no more on a protein basis than regular tofu, it keeps its form better during cooking and tossing in salads, and works better in casseroles and most other baked dishes due to its lower water content and tender, meaty texture. It is also easier to transport, maintains freshness longer and, due to its lower water content, absorbs seasoned broths and other flavors more readily than regular tofu. When frozen, it becomes more porous and tender than ganmo or agé and is therefore particularly delicious in sauces, stews, and sautéed vegetable preparations.

In most parts of Japan, thick agé is prepared from whole, 12-ounce cakes of regular tofu. (In some cases, day-old tofu is used.) The cakes are arranged on bamboo mats placed on top of large boards. Several layers of boards, mats, and tofu are combined to form a sort of "sandwich" that is placed (with one end raised) on a barrel and topped with two buckets filled with water (fig. 61). The tofu is pressed for 20 to 40 minutes in order to reduce its water content and make it suitable for deep-frying. The firm, individual cakes are then dropped into high-temperature oil and deep-fried (without batter) for several minutes until crisp and golden brown (fig. 62). The resulting thick agé contains all of the protein from the original 12 ounces of tofu, but now weighs only 5¼ ounces (44% of its original weight) and is slightly reduced in size.

All of the thick agé in Japan, like its Chinese predecessor, was originally made in triangular form. It is said that Tokyo craftsmen first changed to rectangular pieces because they were easier to prepare and to cut into cubes. However, in the Kyoto area, most thick agé is still sold in the original design and is called "three-cornered agé" (*sankaku-agé*). These triangles, as thick as the rectangular variety, have sides which range from 2 to 3½ inches in length. In most semi-traditional or modern tofu shops, 20 to 30 triangles are arranged on each of several large screen trays during deep-frying (fig. 63).

In both Tokyo and Kyoto, many shops also cut pressed cakes of regular tofu into fourths—each piece being about 2 by 1½ by 1½ inches—then deep-fry these to make "agé cubes" (*kaku-agé*). Sometimes these cubes are only 1 inch on a side and, when that small, are excellent for use in soups or as hors d'oeuvre.

Fig. 61. Pressing tofu for thick agé

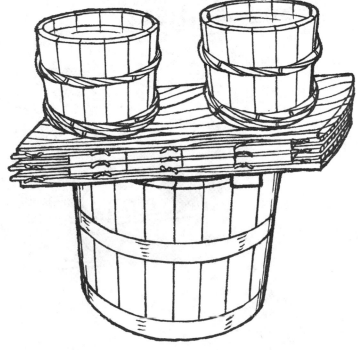

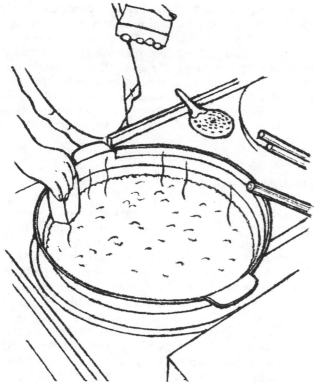

Fig. 62. Deep-frying tofu for thick agé

A fourth and rarer type of thick agé, called "five-color agé" (*gomoku-agé*), contains ingredients such as green peas, sesame seeds, minced carrots, burdock root, mushrooms, *kombu*, or *hijiki*. These are stirred gently into the soymilk curds just before the curds are ladled into the settling boxes. After this tofu is pressed and deep-fried, it has a unique flavor and texture somewhat resembling that of ganmo.

In Taiwan and China, where ganmo and agé are rarely if ever seen, most of the deep-fried tofu is made from very firm Chinese-style Pressed Tofu (p. 251) and sold as triangles each 2 inches on a side and 3/8 inch thick (see Chapter 15). In some areas small cubes of thick agé are eaten as a snack served with maple syrup or honey.

In Western-style cookery, thick agé is particularly delicious cooked whole, grilled, broiled, or barbequed like a steak. If you have a small charcoal brazier, try preparing the tofu indoors. Connoisseurs say it tastes best if the surface is lightly scored during cooking, then sprinkled with shoyu and served sizzling hot as an hors d'oeuvre.

In traditional Japanese cuisine, thick agé is most commonly used in *nabe* dishes, where it is simmered with a variety of vegetables in a seasoned broth. Thick agé triangles are always found in Oden, Japan's favorite wintertime potpourri, and are the most commonly used variety of tofu in the popular Nishime (p. 178). Thick agé holds its shape well even after many hours of simmering, adds its own fine flavor to the cooking broth, and absorbs and retains the flavors of each of the many other ingredients with which it is cooked. It will absorb flavors even better if first doused with boiling water to remove excess surface oil.

In the United States at present, thick agé is available at many stores that sell regular tofu. The Japanese-style cakes are golden-brown and about 3 by 2 by 1 inch in size. From 3 to 8 cakes are generally sold in a small polyethylene tub covered with an airtight seal of transparent film. Chinese-style thick agé cubes are sold by the dozen in sealed plastic bags.

Most of the recipes in this book using thick agé are included in the previous section. The few recipes that follow are those in which thick agé is used in unique ways and cannot be replaced by ganmo or agé.

Fig. 63. Deep-fried thick agé triangles on screen trays

Homemade Thick Agé

SERVES 2 TO 4

Use fresh or day-old regular tofu. Tofu that is just beginning to spoil is rendered fresh and tasty by deep-frying. When short on time, pat the tofu with a dry dishtowel instead of pressing it to remove excess surface moisture. A 12-ounce cake of tofu usually weighs about 5¼ ounces after pressing and deep-frying. Consequently, the protein content by weight increases from 7.8 to about 15 percent.

2 cakes of tofu (12 ounces each), pressed (p. 96)
Oil for deep-frying

Heat the oil to 375° in a wok, skillet, or deep-fryer (p. 130). Carefully slide in both cakes of tofu. Deep-fry for about 2½ to 3 minutes, or until tofu is floating on surface of oil. Stir occasionally to prevent tofu from sticking to pan. Turn tofu over and deep-fry for 30 seconds more, or until crisp and golden brown. Drain on a wire rack for several minutes, then pat dry with absorbent paper. For best flavor, serve immediately, topped with a few drops of shoyu and garnished with grated gingerroot (or *daikon*) and thinly sliced leek or scallion rounds. Or serve as for Crisp Deep-fried Tofu (p. 156).

To store, allow to cool, then refrigerate in an airtight cellophane bag.

VARIATIONS

*Thick-Agé Triangles or Cubes: After pressing, cut each cake of tofu diagonally into halves or into 4 equal cubes before deep-frying. Serve hot with shoyu, honey, or maple syrup. Or simmer with vegetables in *nabe* cookery or Sweetened Shoyu Broth (p. 40).
*Five-Colored Deep-fried Tofu: Prepare any of the various types of Five-Colored Tofu (p. 105). Cut into 12-ounce cakes, press, and deep-fry. Serve immediately with shoyu and desired garnish, or simmer with vegetables in Sweetened Shoyu Broth (p. 40).

*Chinese-style Thick-Agé Net: Press a 12-ounce cake of tofu until very firm. Score the tofu diagonally to half its depth about 6 to 8 times (fig. 109, p. 254). Turn cake over and score other side in exactly the same way. Holding the tofu with one hand at each end, gently pull and twist the two ends to open the cuts slightly into a coarse net. Now deep-fry the tofu as above. After deep-frying, recut each of the original cuts with a knife. Simmer the entire cake of deep-fried tofu with vegetables in Sweetened Shoyu Broth (p. 40) or use in place of thick agé in any of the recipes on pages 156 to 179.

Thick Agé Pouches

These pouches are an excellent substitute for regular agé pouches which are difficult to prepare at home and are not yet widely available in the West. They can be filled with cooked grains, vegetables, eggs, or noodles and served like luncheon sandwiches. Or they may be coated with batter and deep-fried, or simmered in Sweetened Shoyu Broth (p. 40). Start with either homemade or storebought thick agé.

To make *two pouches*, cut a (4- by 3- by 1-inch) piece of thick agé crosswise into halves. Carefully spoon out most of the soft white tofu inside each half and reserve for use in other cooking. Use the hollow pouches in recipes calling for Agé Pouches (p. 192).

To make *one large pouch*, cut a 1/8-inch-thick slice from one end of a piece of thick agé, then spoon out the tofu.

Stuffed Thick Agé Triangles

SERVES 2 TO 4

This preparation is similar to Stuffed Agé Pouches (p. 192), except that the soft tofu scooped from within the thick agé is mixed with other ingredients and used as a filling. Any of the fillings used with agé pouches may also be used with thick agé cut and hollowed out this way.

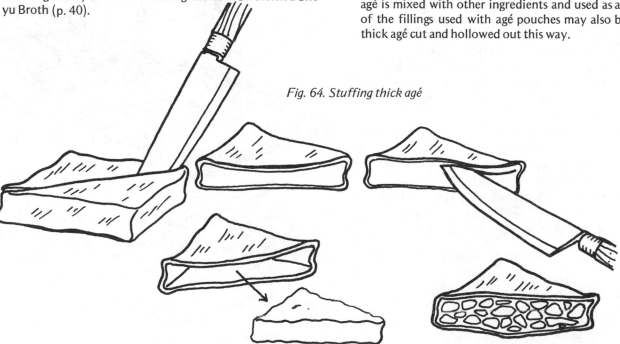

Fig. 64. Stuffing thick agé

2 cakes of thick agé (5 ounces each), lightly broiled (p. 156)
    and cut diagonally into halves
2 hard-boiled eggs, minced
¼ cup mayonnaise
2 tablespoons minced onion
1 tablespoon red, barley, or Hatcho miso
Dash of pepper

Cut the thick agé halves as shown in fig. 64; using a knife or two fingers, cut or scoop out the soft white tofu from the deep-fried covering. Combine this soft tofu with remaining ingredients and mash well, then use mashed mixture to stuff the 4 triangular pouches.

Homemade Frozen Thick Agé

When we freeze thick agé, we transform its internal structure. Like frozen tofu, it becomes highly absorbent and acquires a firm texture similar to that of tender meat or gluten meat. Reconstituted, frozen thick agé may be cut into cubes or thin slices and then deep-fried like Frozen Tofu Cutlets (p. 232). Or it may be substituted for regular thick agé in dishes simmered in seasoned broths (pp. 174 to 179).

Frozen Thick Agé Cutlets   SERVES 4 TO 6

18 ounces thick agé, frozen (p. 230), reconstituted (p. 229),
    and cut crosswise into ½-inch-thick strips
6 tablespoons flour
2 eggs, lightly beaten
½ cup bread crumbs or bread crumb flakes
Oil for deep-frying
Salt
Lemon wedges or Tofu Tartare Sauce (p. 109)

Dust tofu strips with flour, dip into beaten egg, and roll in bread crumbs; place on a rack and allow to stand for 10 minutes. Heat oil to 350° in a wok, skillet, or deep-fryer. Slide tofu into oil and deep-fry until crisp and golden brown (p. 130). Serve sprinkled with salt and garnished with lemon wedges.

VARIATIONS

*Omit salt and serve with shoyu, topped with a small mound of grated gingerroot or a few drops of lime or lemon juice
*Substitute 9 ounces thick agé or frozen thick agé for the tofu in Frozen Tofu Cutlets (p. 232).

Crisp and Crunchy Thick Agé Cubes   SERVES 2 TO 4

Cut 9 ounces thick agé into 1½-inch cubes. Roll each cube in *kuzu* (or, for a less crisp texture, substitute arrowroot powder); deep-fry and serve as for Frozen Thick-Agé Cutlets (see above).

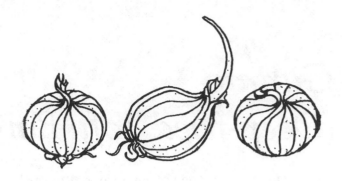

Thick Agé Stuffed with Onions   SERVES 2 TO 4
(Horoku-yaki)

2 cakes of thick agé (5 ounces each), cut diagonally into
    halves
¼ onion, thinly sliced
1 teaspoon oil
3/8 cup White Nerimiso, Rich Red Nerimiso or Yuzu Miso (p. 42)
Dash of *sansho* pepper

Cut a deep slit from end to end of the cut surface of each piece of thick agé (fig. 65). Open this slit to form a pouch and stuff with the sliced onion. Heat a skillet and coat with the oil. Sauté the thick agé on both sides for 3 minutes, or until fragrant. Serve topped with the miso and seasoned with the *sansho* pepper. Or top with shoyu and grated *daikon* or gingerroot.

Fig. 65. Thick Agé Stuffed with Onions

Ganmo
(Deep-fried Tofu Burgers)

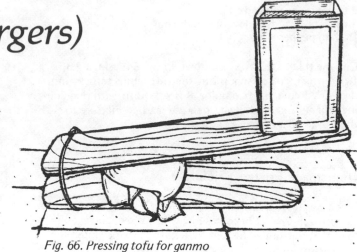

Fig. 66. Pressing tofu for ganmo

A T DAITOKU-JI, one of the great, centuries-old temples in Kyoto, an entire ceiling is covered with the monochromatic, writhing coils of a Chinese dragon. Portrayed with spiky whiskers and sharp horns, it races through a dark sky among swirling clouds. Two thick, whip-like whiskers stream back from flaring nostrils along its long snout. In one scaly claw, this fierce creature clutches the precious wish-fulfilling gem of Complete Perfect Enlightenment. Zen masters say that the awakening to one's true nature is like the shock of seeing the True Dragon.

The Zen dragon of enlightenment also appears in the world of tofu. Each morning in shops throughout Japan, the tofu maker's wife places all tofu remaining from the previous day into a coarse-weave sack, twists the sack's mouth closed, and presses the tofu between two boards arranged like a kind of nutcracker (fig. 66). After several hours, during which time all excess moisture has been expelled, she mixes sesame seeds and finely-slivered vegetables into the tofu (fig. 67), then kneads the mixture in a large basin or bowl as if she were kneading bread. Finally she kneads in a little grated glutinous yam and, sometimes, salt. After shaping the mixture into burger-sized patties or 2-inch balls, she deep-fries them, first in moderate and then in hot oil, until they

puff up and turn golden brown (fig. 68). For some reason, deep-frying causes the slivered vegetables to stick out helter-skelter from the surface of the tofu. Seeing this, the Japanese are reminded of the terrifying Chinese sky dragons with their bristling whiskers and spiky horns. Thus, in the Kyoto area, the unassuming little balls or patties are commonly given the awesome name "Flying Dragon's Heads" (*Hiryozu*).

Fig. 68. Deep-frying ganmo

Fig. 67. Adding seeds and vegetables

The method for preparing deep-fried tofu is thought to have originated in Buddhist temples and monasteries about 500 years ago. At that time, the rarest, most expensive, and most sought-after food of the nobility was wild goose (*gan*). The story is told that when these freshly deep-fried tofu creations were first served to the monks, they praised their flavor as surely being equal to that of the finest wild goose. As a result, in all parts of Japan (except Kyoto) these patties are still most frequently known as *gan-modoki*, or simply *ganmo*, which means "mock goose."

Although most scholars believe that ganmo were first developed by the Japanese, there are several other interesting theories concerning their origin. The first suggests that they were an adaptation of the Portuguese skewered meatballs (called *hirosu*) which became popular in Japan during the 15th century. Since the Japanese word *gan* can mean "ball" as well as "goose," and since the names *hirosu* and *hiryozu* are very similar and are still used interchangeably to refer to Kyoto's round ganmo, this theory seems quite plausible. The second theory suggests that ganmo were first developed by the Chinese, who still prepare a similar type of homemade deep-fried tofu containing ground meat instead of minced vegetables. This tofu, however, is not available in most Chinese or Taiwanese tofu shops.

In the Tokyo area, and throughout most of Japan (except Kyoto), ganmo are prepared in the shape of patties ranging from 3½ to 5 inches in diameter. A typical patty weighs 3½ ounces, about the same as a good-sized hamburger. The flavor and chewy texture of ganmo are also quite similar to those of hamburger. Only the price is different: in 1975 one thick patty cost only 19 cents. Indeed, ganmo makes an excellent replacement for meat in hefty, Western-style cheeseburgers and hamburgers; who, we wonder, will be the first to start a chain of ganmo-burger restaurants?

Probably the most famous ganmo in Japan are the Ganmo Treasure Balls prepared at the Morika tofu shop and others in the Kyoto area. Each 2-inch-diameter ball contains seven different vegetable ingredients including ginkgo nuts and lilly bulb sections. These delicacies are a popular ingredient in the *nabe* dishes served at many of Kyoto's finest restaurants.

Most tofu shops presently use only two or three vegetable ingredients in ganmo, the favorites being grated carrots, slivered *kombu*, and burdock root. Many shops, in addition to patties or balls, also prepare Small Ganmo Balls which swell up to no larger than 1½ inches in diameter and are often served stuffed with minced vegetables and nuts. Some shops prepare firm ganmo ovals containing a large proportion of varied ingredients; these are sometimes said to be Japan's earliest form of ganmo. To please children and for use in one-pot cookery and Dengaku, the tofu craftsman will occasionally use a cookie cutter to make ganmo in the shape of tiny gourds, flowers, or maple leaves.

Each year as the weather turns cold, ganmo makes its appearance in various *nabe* dishes. Since earliest times, the Japanese have believed in heating the body, not the house. The methods they use for doing so, developed out of necessity in a country where fuel and other energy resources have always been scarce, could serve as practical models for ecological living in generations to come. Able to absorb and retain heat unusually well, tofu, and especially deep-fried tofu, is served in the winter as much for its ability to warm the body as to please the palate.

Beginning in about November, Japanese homemakers bring out their earthenware, casserole-shaped *nabe* (pronounced nah-bay; p. 176). A good *nabe* may be many generations old, and is usually rustically beautiful, simple, and rugged. Its heavy lid fits snugly down inside the pot's lips to prevent boiling over—a necessary precaution when cooking over wood fires. The earliest Japanese *nabe*—still found in many farmhouses—was a heavy iron pot that hung suspended from a large overhead hook above an open-hearth fireplace located at the center of the main room of the house (fig. 69). During the long winter months, when the thick straw roofs of the farmhouses were heaped with snow, the small fire or bed of live coals and the bubbling *nabe* became a center of warmth and brightness. Since the rest of the house was dark and cold, the family gathered around the *nabe* while its steam danced and delicious aromas curled into the cold night air. Here one could feel that ancient and primitive magic of conviviality. We moderns, children of the electric lightbulb and central heating, easily forget that for most of man's several million years on this planet, he has cooked over wood fires and had no other source of light and heat at his table. This was not fire from slender white candles or a flame neatly contained in the glass chimney of a kerosene lamp. Rather, it crackled, spit sparks, and sent smoke up into the dark, arching roofbeams. The *nabe* and the many fine deep-fried tofu dishes associated with it were developed during this earlier age.

Today, the context has changed. The *nabe* has acquired a sense of elegance that makes it the featured dish in many of Japan's finest restaurants. Set over a portable burner at the family dining table, it is associated with celebration: holding a large family reunion, welcoming an old friend or an honored guest, or even bringing home the monthly paycheck. Yet the *nabe* and tofu—and especially ganmo—have maintained their centuries-old association. Because they serve as the focus of an atmosphere filled with good cheer, they are always warmly welcomed. Best known and most widely used in Oden (p.175), ganmo is indeed one of Japan's favorite wintertime foods.

Ganmo also makes an excellent addition to many Western-style dishes. It combines the substantial quality of thick agé with the firm and meaty texture of agé pouches. Lower in water content than thick agé, it stays fresh longer and therefore is ideal for use on picnics and short hiking trips. Ganmo patties, cut into small cubes and seasoned with a miso topping, make very tasty hors d'oeuvre, while small ganmo balls make a creative addition to vegetarian shish kebab. If you have tried making soyburgers and were disappointed to find that they were heavy and hard to keep from falling apart, try preparing homemade ganmo patties instead.

Ganmo is made by relatively few tofu shops in America today. However, since it can be prepared easily at home from regular tofu and your choice of nuts, seeds, and minced vegetables, anyone can enjoy this special treat served fresh and crisp, at its peak of flavor.

Fig. 69. A farmhouse open-hearth fireplace with nabe kettle

186 THE BOOK OF TOFU

Homemade Ganmo   MAKES 8 PATTIES OR 12 BALLS

Ganmo can be prepared quite easily at home. Experiment with different combinations of ingredients to suit your taste. The various vegetables, nuts, and seeds used should comprise about 15 to 20 percent of the total volume of the ganmo mixture. In tofu shops, ganmo is usually deep-fried, first in low or moderate oil and then in hot oil, and contains grated glutinous yam as a binding agent. Ganmo balls seem to hold together better than large patties and, having a smaller surface area, they absorb less oil during deep-frying. Patties are better for use in Ganmo Burgers (p. 188).

30 ounces tofu, squeezed (p. 97)
2 tablespoons grated carrots
2 tablespoons diced onions, scallions, leeks, or gingerroot
2 tablespoons slivered or diced mushrooms
2 tablespoons green peas (use only with ganmo balls)
2 tablespoons sunflower seeds, peanuts or chopped nut meats
2 tablespoons roasted sesame or poppy seeds, whole or ground
2 tablespoons raisins
¾ teaspoon salt
Oil for deep-frying

Combine the first eight ingredients in a large shallow bowl; mix well. Knead the mixture for about 3 minutes, as if kneading bread. Add the salt and knead for 3 minutes more until "dough" is smooth and holds together.

Fill a wok, skillet, or deep-fryer with 2 to 2½ inches of oil and heat to 300° (p. 130). Moisten your palms with a little oil or warm water and shape the dough into 8 patties 3 to 3½ inches in diameter or 12 balls about 1½ inches in diameter. Deep-fry patties or balls for 4 to 6 minutes, or until they float high in the oil. Turn patties over and deep-fry for several minutes more until crisp and golden brown; drain ganmo on a wire rack or absorbent paper. Serve sprinkled with a little shoyu as Crisp Deep-Fried Tofu (p. 156), or in any of the ganmo recipes in Chapter 9.

Fig. 70. Preparing homemade ganmo

Refrigerated in an airtight container, ganmo will keep for up to 1 week; frozen, it will last indefinitely.

VARIATIONS

*When preparing large patties, add 1½ tablespoons grated glutinous yam or lightly beaten egg to the ganmo mixture to serve as a binding agent.
*Sauté vegetables lightly in oil before combining with the tofu. For a richer flavor, simmer the sautéed vegetables in Sweetened Shoyu Broth (p. 40) until all the liquid is absorbed or evaporated.
*For lighter, airier ganmo, heat two woks filled with oil, one to 340° and the other to 385°. Deep-fry patties or balls in the moderate oil for 2 to 4 minutes until they float to the surface. Now transfer them to the hot oil and deep-fry both sides for 30 seconds each.

* Small Ganmo Balls: Form the dough into balls about 1 inch in diameter and deep-fry as in the basic recipe. Serve as Stuffed Ganmo Balls (below) or Crisp Deep-fried Tofu (p. 156). Or use in Oden (p. 175), Udon-tsuki (p. 144), or Nishime (p. 178).

*Japanese-Style Ganmo: Combine 2 cups squeezed tofu, 1½ tablespoons grated carrots, 3 tablespoons refreshed shredded *kombu*, 1½ teaspoons whole roasted sesame seeds, ¾ teaspoon salt, and 1 tablespoon grated glutinous yam. Prepare as for the basic recipe.

* Simple Hokkaido-style Ganmo: Make ganmo patties using only squeezed tofu, salt and, if desired, grated glutinous yam. Pat a sprinkling of sesame seeds into both surfaces of each patty and deep-fry. Quick, easy, and delicious.

*Make ganmo balls using only squeezed tofu. Before deep-frying, fill the center of each ball with 1 teaspoon Yuzu Miso (p.42), Sweet Simmered Miso (p. 41), or sweet white miso.

*Form the ganmo dough into cylinders 10 inches long and 1½ inches in diameter. Wrap each cylinder in 2 pieces of agé opened into flat sheets (p. 191). Deep-fry in 340° oil for 8 to 10 minutes. Cut cylinders crosswise into 1-inch lengths and simmer for 5 minutes in Sweetened Soy Broth (p. 40). Cool and serve topped with a sprig of *kinome*.

Ganmo Treasure Balls *(Hiryozu)*   MAKES 6

This popular traditional recipe comes from the Morika tofu shop located in the countryside town of Arashiyama west of Kyoto.

36 ounces tofu, squeezed (p. 97)
1 tablespoon matchsticks of carrot
1½ teaspoons whole roasted sesame seeds (p. 38)
1 refreshed cloud-ear mushroom, cut into ¼-inch-wide strips
1½ teaspoons paper-thin half moons of burdock root
1½ teaspoons flax or hemp seeds
2 tablespoons grated glutinous yam
6 shelled ginkgo nuts, boiled for 30 minutes
30 thin sections of lilly bulbs
Oil for deep-frying

Combine the first six ingredients in a large bowl; mix well, then knead for 3 minutes. Add yam and knead for 2 minutes more. With moistened hands, shape dough into 6 balls. Press a ginkgo nut and 5 lilly bulb sections into the center of each ball; seal hole. Deep-fry at 240° for 10 minutes, or until balls float high in the oil, then increase heat to 350° and deep-fry for 1 or 2 minutes more, or until balls are crisp and golden brown. Drain on a wire rack or absorbent paper. Serve as Crisp Deep-Fried Tofu (p. 156).

Stuffed Ganmo Ball Hors D'oeuvre

Cut a small slit in one side of regular or small ganmo balls and fill with any of the following: Applesauce or diced apples (fresh or cooked), cinnamon and raisins; sliced bananas, nutmeg, and raisins; Tofu Whipped Cream (p. 148) and fresh strawberries; a dab of Yuzu Miso (p. 42), Sweet Simmered Miso (p. 41), or sweet white miso; peanut butter or peanuts, raisins, and honey; regular or Tofu Cream Cheese (p. 109), chopped dates and grated lemon rind; diced cheese and cucumbers with Tofu Mayonnaise (p. 107).

Ganmo Cheeseburger   MAKES 1

1 toasted hamburger bun or 2 slices of whole-wheat bread
1 tablespoon (tofu) mayonnaise (p. 107)
2 teaspoons butter
1 tablespoon ketchup
1 teaspoon mustard
1½ teaspoons miso or ½ teaspoon shoyu
1 ganmo patty—4 to 4½ inches in diameter—lightly broiled (p. 156)
1 large, thin slice of onion
1 large slice of tomato
1 large slice of cheese
1 lettuce leaf

Cut the bun horizontally into halves and spread with mayonnaise, butter, mustard, and ketchup. Spread the miso on one side of the ganmo pattie, then place pattie on the lower half of the bun. Stack onion, tomato, cheese, and lettuce on top of ganmo. Top with upper half of bun.

For variety, douse ganmo in boiling water (p. 156), then simmer for 5 minutes in Sweetened Shoyu Broth (p. 40). Drain briefly before assembling burger. Substitute cucumber pickles or relish for the miso.

Ganmo in a draining tray

Agé
(Deep-fried Tofu Pouches)

THE MORIKA tofu shop, located in the country-side west of Kyoto, is spacious and quiet, with the well-ordered look that comes from a long tradition of careful craftsmanship. Early one morning, we visited the shop to watch agé being prepared. Sunlight streamed in through the shop's tall windows falling on the large sinks filled with cold, clear well water and on the glistening hand-cut granite blocks making up the shop's floor. By 4 o'clock in the morning, the first batch of tofu was ready and cooling in the sinks. Now the master's wife would use this specially-prepared tofu to make agé.

She carefully lifted one large block of tofu out of the water on a thick cutting board. Using a long, wide-bladed knife which she wielded with stacatto swiftness, she sliced off thin pieces of the tofu, trimmed their tops to precisely the same thickness, then scooped them up with the knife and placed them carefully on a bamboo pressing mat (fig. 71). The tofu seemed to come alive, each small piece dancing with the knife, leaping onto the shining blade.

After the sandwiched layers of thinly-sliced tofu—called *kiji*—had been pressed under heavy weights for several hours (as in the preparation of thick agé; p.180), they were taken to the deep-frying area. A grandmother, wearing a blue kerchief and traditional Japanese apron, worked with a pair of long chopsticks in front of two deep-fryers filled with bubbling, golden-brown oil. She carefully explained to us each step in the process of making agé, her gold teeth sparkling whenever she laughed.

Into the first container of moderate oil, she lowered a flat screen tray neatly spread with 16 thin tofu kiji, each about 5½ by 2½ by ½ inch thick. The oil hissed and steamed as the kiji sank out of sight. After several minutes, they began to reappear, slowly floating upward until their soft white edges were just above the surface of the oil. The woman carefully turned over each piece, and soon they were floating high and light. Lifting up the screen tray, she transferred it and all of the kiji into the second container of hot oil. The oil came alive, crackling and filling the air with steam. In an instant, as if by magic, each kiji had puffed up and swelled to almost twice its original size. Light, airy, and golden-brown, the little "fleet" bobbed in the sunlight on the surface of the deep-brown oil (fig. 72). The whole room filled with agé's deep aroma, and all the cats in the neighborhood awoke, stretched, and sniffed the suddenly-fragrant morning air.

After turning the agé twice more, lifting it out of the oil on the screen, and allowing it to drain briefly, our new friend said that we must try a piece right away while it was crisp, light, and steaming hot. That morning, sizzling-crisp agé, served topped with a few drops of shoyu, became one of our favorite ways of enjoying tofu.

Tofu makers say that it is only when a young

Fig. 71. Cutting tofu to make agé kiji

Fig. 72. Deep-frying agé

189

apprentice is able to prepare fine agé that he may call himself a full-fledged craftsman and receive permission to leave his master in order to start his own shop. Making agé takes more time and skill than making any other type of tofu. The tofu from which agé is prepared is treated somewhat differently from regular tofu: the soymilk is cooked for only a short time and then cooled quickly by adding a large amount of cold water to it; the curds, solidified with nigari, are broken up very fine and a relatively large amount of whey is removed; the curds are then pressed with heavy weights for a long time in the settling boxes. This complex procedure is designed to make the tofu swell during deep-frying so that, when cooled, the agé can be cut crosswise into halves and the centers opened to form small pouches.

A typical tofu shop prepares about 300 pieces of agé each morning. These come in three different sizes; in general, most pieces are about 6 by 3¼ by 3/8 inch thick; some shops make 2½-inch-square pieces which are specially used as Inari-zushi; and Kyoto shops make pieces up to 9 inches long and 3½ inches wide.

All agé has a tender, slightly chewy texture and much less body than either of the other types of deep-fried tofu. Since it has a high oil content (31%) and is the most expensive type of deep-fried tofu on a weight basis, it is generally used in fairly small quantities. Yet its remarkable versatility makes it popular in almost the entire panorama of Japanese cuisine, where it is used in three basic forms: as pouches, flat sheets, and thinly-sliced strips.

Agé pouches may be filled with almost any fresh or cooked ingredients and served as light hors d'oeuvre or hearty main dishes. Leftovers placed in agé pouches are transformed instantly into new and tasty dishes which may be used in lunch boxes in much the same way as a sandwich. In Japan, pouches are often filled with grains, noodles, or vegetables and simmered in stews or *nabe* dishes. Stuffed pouches are also very delicious when deep-fried with batter. The most popular way of using agé pouches in Japanese cookery is with Inari-zushi; the pouches are simmered in a sweetened shoyu broth, filled with vinegared rice, and served as a favorite lunch-box ingredient at picnics and special occasions.

If a piece of agé is used as is, or is cut along three sides and opened to form a flat sheet, foods such as cucumbers and strips of cheese seasoned lightly with miso or shoyu may be rolled up inside. The roll can be pierced with food picks, cut crosswise, and served as an hors d'oeuvre.

Sliced into thin strips, agé may be used interchangeably with thick agé and ganmo. It is partic-

ularly popular in miso soups, especially in combination with *wakame*, and may also be used like bacon or ham in breakfast egg dishes, or sautéed like thinly-sliced beef with a wide variety of vegetables.

It seems likely that the Japanese invented agé, since it is not presently found in Taiwan or China. While most of the agé in Japan is still made in neighborhood tofu shops, an increasingly large proportion is prepared in huge, mechanized factories (the largest of which produces 200,000 pieces daily!) and sold at supermarkets for about two-thirds the price of traditional agé.

Traditional masters say that there are four requirements for making the most delicious agé: the tofu must be solidified with nigari from soymilk cooked in a cauldron; the agé must be made to expand without the addition of chemical agents; each slab of tofu used must be sufficiently thick so that the agé has body and can be opened easily to form pouches; and the agé must be deep-fried (by hand) in rapeseed oil. Unfortunately, the tofu used to prepare agé in most factories is solidified with calcium sulfate from soymilk cooked in a pressure cooker, and the agé is made to expand with a chemical agent consisting primarily of calcium carbonate (a white powder found in limestone, chalk, and bones) and phosphate salts. The tofu is cut into very thin slabs (which sometimes tear upon opening) and is deep-fried in inexpensive soy oil using an automatic conveyorized machine. The difference in quality is readily apparent.

Japan's most unique variety of agé is Crisp Agé (*Kanso Aburagé*), which comes in light crisp sheets that are mild in flavor, golden-brown in color, and about 6 by 8 by ¼ inch in size. Rich in protein (24%) and natural oils (64%), it has a very low water content (4½%) which allows it to be stored for more than 3 months at room temperature without spoiling. Like its two long-lasting relatives (dried-frozen tofu and dried yuba), Crisp Agé is very well suited for areas such as Africa and India where spoilage is a major problem. A traditional, natural food, it has been prepared for several hundred years in the city of Matsuyama on the large island of Shikoku, as well as on Okinawa. (It is often sold as Milk Agé, since 1 part of dairy milk curds [resembling cottage cheese] is mixed with 5 parts of soymilk curds to give the tofu additional calcium and amino acids). The curds are ladled into shallow, cloth-lined trays which are then stacked and pressed under a hydraulic press until the tofu is very thin. These tofu sheets are then deep-fried in 5 temperatures of oil ranging from 250 to 392°F until the agé is almost as crisp as a light biscuit. Crisp Agé is generally served in miso soups or sautéed and simmered with vegetables. In Western-style preparations it may be topped with various spreads and crisp vegetables like canapés, used like croutons in salads and soups, or mounded with lettuce and cheese like *tacos* or *tortillas*.

At present, two unique varieties of agé are made and sold in the United States. The first—which we call Agé Puffs—is prepared at most Japanese tofu shops. Made from pressed tofu shaped like a small square rod, this variety puffs up during deep-frying until it looks like a golden-brown sausage 4½ inches long and 2 inches in diameter. Unlike Japanese agé, it stays puffed up even after it cools. Some varieties also puff up to form triangular shapes. Three Agé Puffs (weighing a total of 1½ ounces) are often sold in plastic bags under such names as Fried Soybean Cakes, Fried Tofu, or simply Agé. Each puff is meant to be slit open at one end. Unlike Japanese agé, these puffs are not easily opened into flat sheets.

The second variety—which we call Hollow Agé Cubes—is made in many Chinese tofu shops. Like agé puffs, these 1-inch cubes stay puffed up after deep-frying and can therefore be stuffed with other foods and cooked or served as hors d'oeuvre. One or two dozen cubes are generally sold at Chinese markets in plastic bags under such names as Nama-agé or Raw-fried Bean Curd.

Imported, canned Japanese agé is now sold in Japanese markets as Shinoda-maki and Inari-zushi no Moto, or Prepared Fried Bean Curd. Filled with vinegared rice, the latter may be served without further preparation as Inari-zushi.

Opening Agé into Pouches, Puffs, and Large Sheets

In the recipes that follow, the word *agé* refers to pieces 6 by 3¼ by 3/8 inches. One piece of agé makes 2 pouches. Agé Puffs sold in the U.S. may be slightly smaller, so when using them, decrease the filling proportionally.

Agé pouches: Cut agé crosswise into halves. To open the center, carefully work your thumbs between the two deep-fried surfaces (fig. 73).

Large agé pouches: Cut a thin slice from one end of

each piece of agé, then open the center by working your thumbs between the deep-fried surfaces.

Agé puffs: One piece of hollow (Western-style) agé makes one sausage-shaped puff about 4½ inches long and 2 inches in diameter. With the point of a sharp knife, cut a slit across one end of each agé puff. If desired, pull or scoop out any tofu which may remain inside.

Large sheets: Using a knife or pair of scissors, open agé into a sheet 6 inches square by cutting into 1 long and 2 short sides.

Homemade Agé Pouches   MAKES 4 TO 6
(from Storebought or Homemade Tofu)

This is the quick and easy way to prepare homemade agé pouches although they will not expand quite as much as when you use the lengthier process starting with whole soybeans described below. Twelve ounces of unpressed tofu will yield 5 ounces of agé pouches.

---

12 to 20 ounces tofu
Oil for deep-frying.

Cut tofu horizontally into ½-inch-thick slices, 4 to 6 inches long and 3 to 3½ inches wide. Press slices using the sliced tofu method (p. 97), except place a cutting board and a 5- to 10-pound weight on the tofu and press for about 40 minutes.

Fill a wok, skillet, or deep-fryer with 2 inches of oil and heat to 240°. Slide in the pressed tofu and deep-fry over high heat until temperature of oil reaches 310°. Reduce heat to medium-high and continue to deep-fry until agé pieces float on the surface of oil. Return heat to high, turn agé with chopsticks, and deep-fry until oil reaches 385°. Reduce heat to medium and deep-fry until agé are crisp and golden brown. Remove agé from oil, drain briefly on a wire rack or absorbent paper, and allow to cool for about 10 minutes.

Cut a thin slice from the end of each piece of agé. Carefully insert the point of a knife between the deep-fried surfaces from the cut end and separate the surfaces to form a pouch. Using a small spoon, scoop out any tofu remaining inside the pouch. (To make 2 small pouches, cut each piece of agé crosswise into halves, then proceed to open as above.)

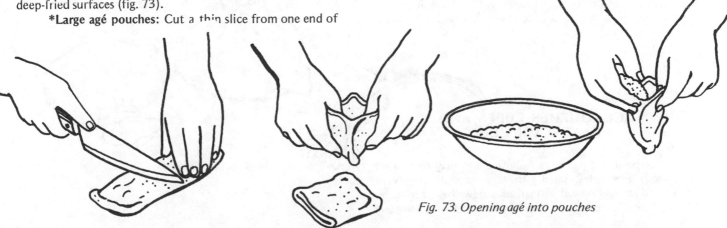

Fig. 73. Opening agé into pouches

Homemade Agé Pouches
(from Storebought or Homemade Thick Agé)

If thick agé is available at your local market, it can easily be transformed into agé pouches by following the method for Homemade Thick Agé Pouches (p. 182).

Homemade Agé Pouches *(from Whole Soybeans)*

This recipe should be attempted only after you have mastered the process for Homemade Tofu (p. 99). Although quite time consuming, it yields excellent agé which expands nicely and is light and crisp.

1½ cups whole dry soybeans
18 cups water
¾ teaspoon baking powder or calcium carbonate
Solidifier as for Homemade Tofu
Oil for deep-frying

Prepare the tofu for homemade agé as for Homemade Tofu but with the following modifications: 1) Begin by heating 5¼ cups water in cooking pot. 2) Rinse pressed okara with 1½ cups warm water. 3) Bring soymilk to a boil and simmer only 3 minutes; turn off heat and immediately stir 6 cups (unheated) water into soymilk. 4) Add baking powder to solidifier solution before stirring solution into soymilk. 5) After removing whey, stir curds slowly, then set colander or strainer back on curds, place ½-pound weight into colander, and ladle off any remaining curds which settle in colander. 6) Ladle curds quickly and rather roughly into settling container. 7) Press curds in the container with a 3- to 4-pound weight for about 30 minutes.

Remove tofu from container and proceed to cut and deep-fry it as for Homemade Agé Pouches (from storebought or homemade tofu; p. 191).

Homemade Agé Slices
(from Storebought or Homemade Tofu)

Many of the recipes in Chapter 9, Deep-fried Tofu, call for regular pieces of agé which do not need to be opened into pouches or large sheets. This type of agé can be quickly and easily prepared at home as described in the recipe for Crisp Agé Slices (p. 131).

AGÉ POUCHES, PUFFS, AND HOLLOW AGÉ CUBES

Agé pouches, puffs, or hollow cubes may be stuffed with fresh vegetables, salads, fruits, or a wide variety of cooked foods and served instead of sandwiches or as finger foods. The pouches may first be simmered in a sweeten-

ed shoyu broth, then filled with sushi rice or other cooked grains. Once filled, pouches can be simmered (in seasoned broths), deep-fried, baked, steamed, or even smoked to create a rich variety of flavors and textures. To create a dappled, felt-like exterior, turn pouches inside-out before filling. Leftovers can be rejuvenated and transformed when used as fillings.

In most of the following recipes 4 to 6 hollow agé cubes may be substituted for 1 pouch or puff.

Fresh Vegetable Salads in Agé Pouches   SERVES 2

½ tomato, diced
¼ cucumber, diced
¼ onion, diced
¼ cup diced cheese
3½ ounces ganmo or thick agé, diced (optional)
1½ tablespoons (tofu) mayonnaise (p. 107)
1½ tablespoons ketchup
Dash of pepper
4 agé pouches or puffs (p. 191), broiled (p. 156) if desired

Combine the first eight ingredients in a small bowl; toss lightly. Spoon the mixture into agé pouches until each is one-half to two-thirds full. Fold over mouth of each pouch and fasten with a foodpick (fig. 74).

Or substitute 2 teaspoons red miso for the ketchup and add 2 thinly sliced lettuce, cabbage or Chinese cabbage leaves, and ½ teaspoon hot mustard to the ingredients listed above. Serve on a piece of hot buttered toast.

VARIATIONS: Use any of the following as filling for the agé pouches:
*1 cup fresh mung, soy, or alfalfa sprouts, 1 tablespoon red miso, ½ diced tomato and ¼ diced cucumber.
*Waldorf Salad, Potato Salad, Tossed Green Salad, Tomato-Mayonnaise Salad, or any of the various tofu (p. 111) or deep-fried tofu salads (p. 158).
*Grain or noodle salads made with deep-fried (p. 159) or regular tofu (p. 111).

Agé Treasure Pouches

Fruits in Agé Pouches SERVES 2

2 bananas, cut into thin rounds
½ teaspoon nutmeg
½ cup yogurt or cottage cheese
½ cup raisins
¼ cup walnut meats
4 agé pouches or puffs (p. 191), broiled (p. 156) if desired

Mix the first five ingredients and spoon into agé pouches. Fold over mouth of each pouch and fasten with a foodpick (fig. 74).

VARIATIONS

*Cut 2 bananas into thin slices and fry in plenty of butter until slightly soft. Season with nutmeg and serve hot as a filling.
*Use only sliced fresh bananas mixed with 1 tablespoon sweet white miso.
*Substitute apple wedges for the bananas, and cinnamon for the nutmeg. If desired, add sesame or peanut butter and 2 teaspoons lemon juice.

Cooked Grains and Noodles in Agé Pouches SERVES 3

In the following recipe for Sizzling Rice, the use of green peppers, carrots, mushrooms, bean sprouts, or lotus root sautéed with the onions will give a variety of flavors. Or mix into the cooked rice: ground roasted sesame seeds, sunflower seeds, nutmeats, or diced cheese.

2 tablespoons oil
1 small onion, diced
2 eggs, lightly beaten
2 cups cooked Brown Rice (p. 50)
3 tablespoons ketchup
½ teaspoon salt
Dash of pepper
9 agé pouches or puffs (p. 191), lightly broiled (p. 156) if
    desired

Heat a wok or skillet and coat with the oil. Add the onion and sauté over high heat for 2 minutes, or until lightly browned. Add beaten eggs and stir briefly until light and dry, then immediately add rice. Reduce heat to medium high and fry rice for 3 to 4 minutes, stirring constantly. Add ketchup, salt, and pepper and fry for 2 minutes more; turn off heat. Spoon 3 to 4 tablespoons of the rice mixture into each pouch. Fold over mouth of pouch to form a flap and fasten with a foodpick (fig. 74). Serve hot or cold.

VARIATIONS

*Fried Buckwheat Noodles with Vegetables: In 1 tablespoon oil sauté ½ onion cut into thin wedges and 1 small carrot grated or cut into matchsticks. When carrot is tender, add 2 cups cooked buckwheat noodles (soba), 2 tablespoons each roasted sesame seeds and shoyu, ¼ cup diced cheese, and a dash of salt. Sauté for several minutes more, then cool briefly.

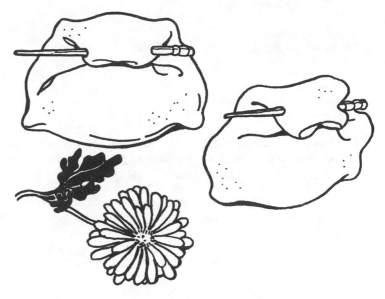

Fig. 74. Agé pouches sealed with foodpicks

If desired, mix with a little crumbled toasted nori. Use to fill pouches; broil pouches (p. 156) before serving.
*Grain Fillings with Sauces: Prepare Curry Sauce (p. 121), Onion Sauce (p. 48), Mushroom Sauce (p. 48), Spaghetti Sauce (p. 121), or your favorite and combine with brown rice or noodles. If using curry sauce, just before filling the pouches, add peanuts, raisins, coconut, diced hard-boiled eggs, sliced bananas or diced apples. With the other sauces, you may wish to add diced or Parmesan cheese. Serve cold.
*Adzuki Rice (Sekihan): Soak 1 cup brown rice and 2 tablespoons adzuki beans over night in 1¾ cups water. Pressure cook for 40 minutes, then season with Sesame Salt (p. 51). Use as filling.

Tofu Dishes in Agé Pouches

Use any of the following as filling for agé pouches: Shira-ae (p. 114), Iri-dofu (p. 128), all sautéed okara dishes (p. 80), Okara Salad with Rice-flour Noodles (p. 79), Tofu with Onion Sauce (p. 116), Tofu with Mushroom Sauce (p. 127), Vinegared Okara (p. 83).

Eggs in Agé Pouches SERVES 3

4 hard-boiled eggs, diced
4 tablespoons (tofu) mayonnaise (p. 107)
2 teaspoons red miso or ½ teaspoon salt
¼ cup minced parsley
6 agé pouches or puffs (p. 191)

Mix the first four ingredients, then spoon into pouches. Fold over the mouth of each pouch to form a flap. Scrambled eggs work well too.

Agé Treasure Pouch with Egg and Onion

SERVES 2 OR 3

3 eggs, lightly beaten
1 small onion, diced
¼ teaspoon salt
1½ cups water
2 tablespoons shoyu
2 tablespoons natural sugar
6 agé pouches or puffs (p. 191)

Combine eggs, onion, and salt; mix well. Combine water, shoyu, and sugar in a small saucepan and bring to a boil. Meanwhile spoon the egg and onion mixture into each of the agé pouches, fold over the mouth of each pouch, and seal with a foodpick (fig. 74, p. 193). Place pouches into shoyu broth, return to the boil and cook over medium heat for 5 10 minutes. Pierce each pouch in several places with a fork or chopsticks and simmer for 30 to 40 minutes more, or until most of the liquid is absorbed or evaporated. Serve hot or cold.

For variety, add diced carrots, mushrooms, snow peas, green peppers, and/or cubes of deep-fried tofu to the filling.

Treasure-Pouch Poached Egg

SERVES 1

1 egg
1 agé pouch or puff (p. 191)
Shoyu, or salt and pepper

Fill a small saucepan with several inches of water and bring to a boil. Break egg into pouch without breaking yolk. Seal mouth of pouch with a foodpick (fig. 74 p. 193) and place pouch in water. Return to the boil and simmer for 2 or 3 minutes, or until egg is just firm. Using a mesh skimmer, remove pouch and any egg white in the water. Serve hot, seasoned with a sprinkling of shoyu.

Cooked Vegetables in Agé Pouches

SERVES 3

2 cups small cubes of steamed *kabocha*, winter squash, or pumpkin
2 tablespoons minced onion
3 tablespoons (tofu) mayonnaise (p. 107)
2 teaspoons red, barley, or Hatcho miso
2 tablespoons ground roasted sesame seeds (p. 38)
6 agé pouches or puffs (p. 191), broiled (p. 156) if desired

Mix the first five ingredients, then spoon into the pouches. Fold over the mouth of each pouch to form a flap and fasten with a foodpick (fig. 74, p. 193). For variety omit the onion, mayonnaise, and miso; and 1½ tablespoons butter and ¼ teaspoon salt.

VARIATIONS: Use any of the following combinations as a filling for agé pouches; serve topped with a sprinkling of shoyu:

*½ cup diced steamed sweet potato or yam, ¾ cup cubes of steamed cauliflower, 3 tablespoons mayonnaise, ¼ teaspoon salt and a dash of pepper.

*Steamed, baked, or boiled sweet potatoes or yams and any of the following: yogurt, sunflower seeds, sautéed onion, and shoyu; butter, salt, pepper, cinnamon, orange juice, and grated orange rind; raisins, butter, and salt or miso.

*Baked or boiled potatoes, sour cream, salt, pepper, butter, crushed garlic, and grated cheese.

*Hashed brown potatoes seasoned with a little shoyu or salt.

Agé Pouches Served in Thickened Sauces

Fill agé pouches with cooked (or stir-fried) brown rice, noodles, buckwheat groats, or millet. Seal each pouch with a foodpick. Prepare Sweet & Sour, Ankake, or Gingerroot Sauce (p. 49). Arrange 2 or 3 pouches in individual serving bowls and serve with a topping of the hot sauce.

Inari-zushi *(Vinegared Sushi Rice in Sweetened Agé Pouches)*

SERVES 5

In Japan, the most popular way of serving agé is in the form of *Inari-zushi*. Packed into lightweight wooden boxes and topped with thin slices of vinegared gingerroot, Inari-zushi are often found at picnics and outings of all kinds where they play much the same role as do sandwiches in the West. Served at most sushi shops, they are very inexpensive and are prepared in a different way by each chef.

Inari-zushi is said to have originated in Tokyo about 1848, the creation of one Jiro Kichi, chef at the *Jukkenten* restaurant. Kichi peddled his new culinary treats at night through the streets of Tokyo carrying a four-sided paper lantern called an *andon*. On this he painted a red Shinto *torii* gateway, the hallmark of the Inari shrine where the Goddess of rice is said to abide. Since foxes are said to be very fond of agé, and since the fox is the patron animal of Inari shrines, this pictorial symbolism and its curious logic seemed natural and appropriate; Inari-zushi soon spread throughout Japan.

20 agé pouches or puffs, doused with boiling water (p. 156)
1 2/3 cups water
7½ tablespoons sugar
5 tablespoons shoyu
2 teaspoons *mirin* (optional)
3¾ cups Sushi Rice (p. 50)
20 slices Sweet Vinegared Gingerroot (p. 51)

Combine the first five ingredients in a large saucepan, cover, and bring to a boil. Reduce heat to low and simmer for 20 minutes. Set aside and allow to cool overnight. (Meanwhile begin soaking the rice for Sushi Rice.)

The next morning while cooking the rice, simmer the agé until just heated through. Drain pouches thoroughly in a strainer set over a bowl and allow to cool to room temperature. Reserve the remaining broth for use as a cooking liquid for potatoes or other vegetables.

Using your fingertips, gently form 2½ to 3 tablespoons of the rice into egg-shaped ovals. Place one oval into each agé pouch so that the pouch is 1/3 to ½ full. Fold over the mouth of each pouch, and arrange pouches on a serving tray or place in Japanese-style wooden lunch boxes. Top each sushi pouch with a slice of the gingerroot.

VARIATIONS

*Add 4 to 8 tablespoons ground or whole roasted sesame seeds (black or white), flax seeds, or hemp seeds to the hot rice just before cooling. Or mix ¼ cup toasted okara with the rice.

*Add any or all of the following diced vegetables: mushrooms, carrots, burdock root, *kampyo*, green beans, or green peas. Simmer vegetables in Sweetened Shoyu Broth (p. 40), drain and add to the rice before cooling. Or use Five-Colored Sushi (p. 169) as the filling for the pouches.

*Turn each pouch inside out before simmering. Tie each filled pouch with a strip of *kampyo* that has been soaked for 20 minutes in the broth used to simmer the pouches.

*Cut each piece of agé diagonally into halves to form 2 triangular pouches. Starting from the short side, roll up the filled pouch along the diagonal.

*Prepare Inari-zushi pouches, but instead of filling them with sushi rice, use plain cooked buckwheat noodles, brown rice (plain, seasoned with sesame salt, or sautéed with vegetables), or Sushi Okara (p. 83).

*Lima Ohsawa's Inari-zushi: This recipe uses no sugar or vinegar. Simmer 8 agé pouches in a mixture of ½ cup water and 1 tablespoon each shoyu and *mirin* until all of the liquid has evaporated or been absorbed. Simmer ½ cup diced lotus root and 2 minced *umeboshi* in ¼ cup water for about 5 minutes or until liquid has been absorbed. Sauté ¼ cup slivered or grated carrot and 3 tablespoons reconstituted *hijiki* seaweed in 2 teaspoons oil, then season with a dash of salt and a little shoyu. Mix all of the vegetables and the juice of ½ lemon with 1 cup of hot cooked brown rice; allow to cool to room temperature. Divide this mixture among the agé pouches and proceed as above.

Agé Treasure Pouches with Crunchy Vegetables (Fuku-bukuro)

SERVES 4

Small agé pouches loaded with vegetables and tied with *kampyo* are known as "bags of wealth and good fortune" *(fuku-bukuro)* or "treasure sacks" *(takara-zutsumi).*

½ cake of *konnyaku*, cut into small rectangles
1 small carrot, cut into matchsticks
4 inches of lotus root, cut into thin quarter moons
4 *(shiitake)* mushrooms, cut into thin strips
¼ cup reconstituted, diced cloud-ear mushroom (optional)
2 tablespoons green peas
8 agé pouches or puffs (p. 191), turned inside-out
8 strips of *kampyo*, each 13 inches long, reconstituted (p. 37)
3 cups dashi (p. 39), stock, or water
4 tablespoons shoyu
2 tablespoons natural sugar
2 tablespoons sake

Heat an unoiled skillet. Put in *konnyaku* and cook over medium heat for several minutes, or until surface of *konnyaku* is dry. Transfer to a large bowl and combine with the next five ingredients. Spoon *konnyaku*-and-vegetable mixture into each of the agé pouches. Fold over the mouth of each pouch, then tie with *kampyo* (fig. 75).

Combine the last four ingredients in a small saucepan and bring to a boil. Add agé pouches, cover, and simmer for 20 to 25 minutes; allow to cool. Now divide pouches among individual serving bowls, top with any remaining broth, and serve hot or cold.

For variety, add to each pouch: 1 ginkgo nut, 3 thin sections of lilly root, or 1 small roll of yuba.

VARIATIONS

*Sacks of Gold *(Takara-zutsumi):* Combine cooked buckwheat groats, millet, or transparent noodles with sautéed onions, carrot, lotus root, mushrooms, and burdock root (all diced). Spoon the mixture into long agé pouches (p. 191) and tie the mouth of each pouch with *kampyo*, or seal with a foodpick. Simmer in a sweetened shoyu broth, as above.

*Matchstick Vegetables Wrapped in Agé Pouches *(Shinoda-maki):* Cut burdock root, *daikon*, carrot, or butterbur into matchsticks 3 inches long. Use the vegetables individually or in combination to completely fill agé pouches. Tie each pouch with *kampyo*. Simmer in sweetened shoyu broth as above until vegetables are tender. Or cook in Oden or *nabe* dishes.

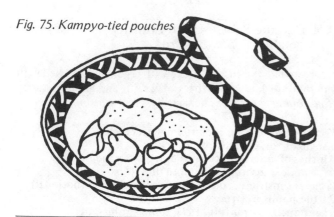

Fig. 75. Kampyo-tied pouches

Drawstring Purses and Treasure Bags (Kinchaku and Takara-bukuro)

SERVES 4

Also known simply as "bags" (fukuro) or "bags of wealth and good fortune" (fuku-bukuro), these handsome preparations are most widely used in Kyoto-style Oden (p. 175) and occasionally in Nishime (p. 178). Prefilled, uncooked kinchaku are often sold in Kyoto's bustling outdoor markets.

4 agé pouches or puffs (p. 191)
Fillings: konnyaku noodles or threads, carrots, cabbage, cubes of fresh or dried wheat gluten, small balls of mochi, transparent noodles, bean sprouts, cubes of thick agé or ganmo, shiitake mushrooms, burdock root, Osmund fern, lotus root, quail egg, daikon, diced konnyaku, snow peas, bamboo shoots (all diced or slivered)
4 pieces of kampyo, each 13 inches long, reconstituted (p. 37)

Turn the agé pouches inside-out, then fill each pouch with your choice of 6 to 8 of the different filling ingredients. Tie each pouch closed with kampyo (fig. 75), then use the pouches as one of the ingredients in Oden or Nishime.

Deep-fried Agé Apple Turnover

SERVES 2

1½ small apples, cut into thin wedges
¼ cup raisins
1 tablespoon natural sugar
3 tablespoons water
¼ teaspoon cinnamon
4 agé pouches or puffs (p. 191)
1 tablespoon whole-wheat flour
Oil for deep-frying

In a small saucepan simmer apples, raisins, sugar, and water for 6 to 8 minutes until apples just begin to soften. Sprinkle with cinnamon, then spoon mixture into agé pouches. Fold over the mouth of each pouch and fasten with a foodpick. Combine flour with just enough water to make a thick paste and use to seal the mouth of each pouch.
Heat the oil to 350° in a wok, skillet, or deep-fryer. Slide in the pouches and deep-fry until crisp and golden brown (p. 130). Remove foodpick, drain, and serve piping hot.

Or dip each pouch into tempura batter (p. 134) and roll in bread crumbs (or dust with flour, dip in lightly beaten eggs, and roll in bread crumbs) before deep-frying.

Mashed Potatoes Deep-fried in Agé Pouches (Hasami-agé)

SERVES 3 OR 4

1½ tablespoons oil
¼ onion, diced
1 green pepper, diced
1¼ potatoes, boiled and mashed
1 tablespoon butter
¼ teaspoon salt
8 agé pouches or puffs (p. 191)
2 tablespoons whole-wheat flour, combined with enough water to form a thick paste
Oil for deep-frying
Dipping Sauce:
    2 tablespoons ketchup
    1 tablespoon Worcestershire sauce
    ½ teaspoon salt

Heat a wok or skillet and coat with the oil. Add onions and green pepper and sauté until onions are transparent. Transfer onions and pepper to a large bowl and combine with potatoes, butter, and salt. Spoon mixture into agé pouches. Fold over the mouth of each pouch and seal with the flour paste.
Heat the oil to 350° in a wok, skillet, or deep-fryer. Slide in the pouches and deep-fry until crisp and golden brown (p. 130); drain. Serve hot, accompanied by a small dish of dipping sauce.

Baked or Steamed Agé Pouches

SERVES 2

1 large mushroom, diced
½ onion, diced
2 tablespoons diced cheese
2 eggs, lightly beaten
1 tablespoon shoyu
4 agé pouches or puffs (p. 191)

Preheat oven to 350°. Combine the first five ingredients in a bowl; mix well. Place agé pouches on a well-oiled baking tin and fill with equal portions of the egg-and-vegetable mixture. Fold over the mouth of each pouch and fasten with a foodpick. Bake for 15 to 20 minutes, or until egg is just firm.

VARIATIONS
*Add first these ingredients, then carefully break 1 egg into each pouch (do not break yolk). Proceed as above, and serve topped with a sprinkling of shoyu. This method helps prevent the egg from leaking from the pouch.
*Use as fillings any of your favorite casserole mixtures or the ingredients used for stuffing baked green peppers or other vegetables.
*Steam the prefilled pouches for about 15 minutes. Or begin by frying the filled pouches in a well-oiled skillet, then add a little water, cover, and steam for about 10 minutes.

Smoked Tofu

SERVES 4

Smoked tofu is now sold commercially as a canned food in Japan.

24 ounces tofu, well pressed (p. 96)
¾ cup chopped mushrooms, chestnuts, or walnut meats
½ teaspoon salt
4 large agé pouches (p. 191)
Oil for marinating

Combine the tofu, mushrooms, and salt in a large bowl; mix until cohesive. Spoon the mixture into the agé pouches, then seal the mouth of each pouch with 2 foodpicks. Place the pouches on a *(sudare)* bamboo mat, screen, or grill. Place a cutting board on top of the pouches, and a 5- to 10-pound weight on top of the board; press for 30 minutes. Remove weight and board, and transfer mat and pouches to a smoke-house or place above a barbeque, wood-burning stove, or fireplace; smoke for 2 or 3 hours.

Cut smoked tofu crosswise into slices 3/8 inch thick and marinate for several hours in salad oil. Serve as hors d'oeuvre on crackers or toast, or in tossed green salads.

FOODS ROLLED IN AGÉ AND LARGE AGÉ SHEETS

Fresh crisp vegetables or cheeses may be rolled up in a single piece of agé and served as hors d'oeuvre. Or the agé may be opened into large sheets and used to wrap various ingredients into a compact roll which may then be simmered in seasoned liquids, steamed, or deep-fried.

Shinoda-maki *(Agé-Cabbage Rolls)*

SERVES 4

The name *Shinoda* is given to numerous dishes in which a large sheet of agé is used as a wrapper for a cylindrical core of other ingredients. This name—like the name *Inari*—is connected with foxes, an animal whose favorite food is said to be agé. In a well-known *kabuki* play, a fox turns into a lovely woman—as foxes often do in Japan to deceive gullible men—marries, and has a child. Eventually the time comes when she must turn back into a fox. At the difficult moment of parting from her child she says: "If you miss me and long to be together, come to the forest of Shinoda in Izumi." Thus Shinoda became known as a favorite hangout for foxes, and the name soon came to be used with agé rolls. Shinoda-maki are often used as an ingredient in Oden (p. 175) or other *nabe* dishes. Fasten the rolls with foodpicks if *kampyo* is not available.

4 large leaves of Chinese or regular cabbage
4 pieces of agé, opened into large sheets (p. 191)
6 carrot strips, 3/8 inch square and 6 inches long
8 strips of *kampyo*, each 12 inches long, refreshed (p. 37)
1½ cups water
2 tablespoons shoyu
1½ tablespoons natural sugar
½ teaspoon salt
4 slivers of *yuzu* or lemon rind

Trim the stems of cabbage leaves smooth, then dip leaves in boiling water until pliable. Place 1 sheet of agé with its deep-fried surface facing downward on a cutting board or *sudare*. Cover agé sheet with 2 cabbage leaves. Lay 3 carrot strips crosswise near one end of the leaves, and top with a second sheet of agé with its deep-fried surface facing downward. With the carrot strips as the core, roll up the layered preparation and tie with *kampyo* in 4 places (see p. 177). Repeat with remaining ingredients to form a second roll.

Combine the water, 1 tablespoon shoyu, and ¾ tablespoon sugar in a 2-quart saucepan and bring to a boil. Add the rolls (*kampyo* bow facing down) and simmer for 15 minutes. Add remaining shoyu and sugar, and the salt, and simmer for 10 minutes more; allow to cool. Cut each roll crosswise into fourths and divide among 4 deep bowls. Serve topped with the remaining broth, garnished with a sliver of *yuzu*.

VARIATIONS

*Single Sheet Rolls: Wrap 8 to 10 long strips of any of the following vegetables in one sheet of agé: carrot, burdock root, bracken fern, *daikon*, butterbur, or celery. Tie as above and cook in the seasoned broth until tender.

*Fragrant Agé-Cabbage Roll: Roll up 1 large cabbage leaf in 1 large sheet of agé and fasten with foodpicks. Make 2.

In a skillet, combine 2 tablespoons shoyu, ½ clove of crushed garlic, 2 teaspoons natural sugar, and ¼ teaspoon each grated gingerroot, vinegar, and sesame oil. Bring just to a boil, then add the cabbage rolls and 6 green *togarashi* peppers (or 1 green pepper cut lengthwise into strips). Sauté over low heat until cabbage is tender. Serve hot or cold as hors d'oeuvre.

Rolled Agé Hors D'oeuvre

SERVES 2

2 pieces of agé, lightly broiled (p. 156) if desired
Vinegar-Miso Spread:
    2 teaspoons vinegar
    1 teaspoon red, barley, or Hatcho miso
    1 tablespoon natural sugar
    Dash of *sansho* green pepper (optional)
½ cucumber, cut into 3-inch-long matchsticks

Coat the surface of each piece of agé with the spread. Lay cucumber matchsticks at one end of the coated surface, then roll up agé (fig. 76). Secure each roll with 3 foodpicks. Cut rolls crosswise into thirds to serve.

Or use 4 strips of cheese, 6 parboiled green beans, and 6 strips of cucumber for the core of each roll. Substitute red, barley, or Sweet Simmered Miso (p. 41) for the miso spread used above. Sauté the rolls briefly in butter before cutting them into thirds.

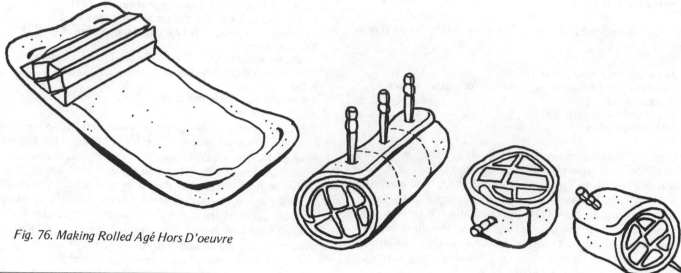

Fig. 76. Making Rolled Agé Hors D'oeuvre

Steamed Agé Roll with Tofu and Vegetables (Shinoda-mushi)

SERVES 3 OR 4

2 small mushrooms, diced
¼ cup diced carrots
¼ cup water
2 tablespoons natural sugar
2½ teaspoons shoyu
12 ounces tofu, well pressed (p. 96) and mashed
3 2/3 tablespoons cornstarch
1 teaspoon salt, approximately
1 egg, separated into white and yolk
1 teaspoon oil
3 pieces of agé, doused in boiling water (p. 156) and opened
    into large sheets (p. 191)
2 tablespoons green peas, parboiled in lightly salted water (p.
    37)
12 seven-inch strips of kampyo, reconstituted (p. 37)
¾ cup dashi (p. 39), stock, or water
1 tablespoon sake

In a small saucepan combine carrots, mushrooms, ¼ cup water, 2 teaspoons sugar, and 1 teaspoon shoyu. Cover and bring to a boil, then reduce heat to low and simmer for 3 minutes. Uncover, simmer until all liquid is absorbed, then set aside to cool briefly.

In a large bowl combine tofu, 2 tablespoons cornstarch, 1 tablespoon sugar, ½ teaspoon salt, and the egg white. Mix well, then stir in the carrots and mushrooms.

Heat a skillet and coat with the oil. Scramble the egg yolk with a dash of salt; set aside to cool.

Spread the 3 agé sheets on a cutting board with the deep-fried surface facing downward and 1 piece resting on a *sudare* bamboo mat (if available). Sprinkle 1 teaspoon cornstarch evenly over each of the 3 sheets. Spread the tofu mixture in an even layer over the 3 sheets. Arrange the green peas and scrambled eggs in a line about 1 inch from one edge of each of the layers of tofu. With the aid of the bamboo mat, roll up each of the sheets firmly from this edge so that the peas and eggs form the core of the roll. Tie each roll in 4 places with *kampyo* strips (see p. 177), place in a preheated steamer, and steam over high heat for 10 minutes.

In a small saucepan combine ¾ cup dashi, 1½ teaspoons shoyu, 1/3 teaspoon salt, 1 tablespoon sake, 1 teaspoon sugar, and 2 teaspoons cornstarch. Stirring constantly, heat until thick. Cut the steamed rolls crosswise into 4 sections, divide among the bowls and serve hot or cold, topped with the thick sauce.

For variety, add a little grated *yuzu* or lemon rind to the sauce, and garnish with a sprig of *kinome* and several parboiled green beans. And/or substitute diced burdock root for the mushrooms and use a core of fresh wheat gluten *(fu)* in place of the scrambled eggs.

10
Soymilk

ON A CLEAR cold morning in late October, Akiko and I paid out first exploratory visit to a Japanese tofu shop. Above the shop's steam-matted windows was written its name, San-gen-ya, in bold, black characters. The shop's master, Mr. Toshio Arai, greeted us cheerfully, accepted our gift of crisp autumn apples, then quickly returned to the bubbling cauldron behind him. Into it he ladled some 25 gallons of freshly-ground gô (fig. 77) and on top of it he placed a 3-foot cedar lid, all the time explaining that he was preparing soymilk later to be made into kinugoshi tofu. After about 10 minutes, steam billowed up from beneath the lid, filling the shop with a delightful aroma. The master uncovered the cauldron and with a specially-made split bamboo rod, stirred down its swelling contents just before they were about to overflow (fig. 78). Lowering the

flame, he continued to simmer the bubbling gô for about 10 minutes more, stirring it down from time to time. As he worked, he explained that there were four basic requirements for preparing the very finest soymilk: first, the soybeans used had to be bestgrade whole beans, and the water well water; second, a relatively small amount of water had to be used to give the resulting soymilk a thick, rich consistency; third, the gô had to be cooked in a cauldron and, ideally, over a wood fire to evoke its full flavor; and finally, the gô had to be simmered long enough to ensure lasting freshness and make best use of its potential nutrients (see p. 70).

When the gô had finished cooking, he ladled it into a large, coarsely woven sack set into a cedar barrel next to the cauldron. He raised the sack with a hand-turned hoist and allowed the soymilk to drain

Fig. 77. Ladling gô into the cauldron

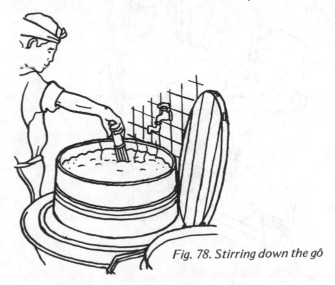

Fig. 78. Stirring down the gô

into the barrel through a layer of finely-woven silk cloth. Lowering the sack onto a sturdy rack placed across the mouth of the barrel, he then pressed it thoroughly (below) until the okara had yielded its last drop of precious soymilk.

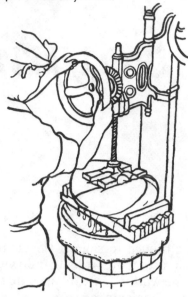

Pressing soymilk from okara

Now, from the deep wooden barrel, he scooped out a large ladleful of this steaming soymilk and used it to fill seven earthenware mugs (fig. 79): one for each of his three children, his wife, his visitors and, of course, for himself. Into each mug he spooned a little wildflower honey—chunks of the honeycomb still suspended in it. A tiny pinch of salt and *kampai*—"bottoms up."

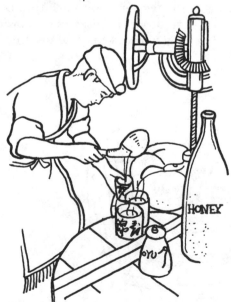

Fig. 79. Serving fresh soymilk

Within the space of less than 40 minutes, we had witnessed a truly remarkable process: the transformation of soybeans into milk. Its consistency and appearance resembling that of creamy, fresh dairy milk, this delicious drink had a natural full-bodied flavor, a mellow aroma, and a subtle, mild sweetness. Highly nutritious and low in cost, it soon became a regular part of our daily meals; we picked up a bottle each morning together with our day's supply of tofu.

Nutritionally, soymilk compares very favorably with dairy milk, as will be seen by comparing the following figures showing the composition of a 100 gram portion of soy, dairy, and mother's milk:

	SOYMILK	DAIRY MILK	MOTHER'S MILK
Water (grams)	88.6	88.6	88.6
Protein	4.4	2.9	1.4
Calories	52	59	62
Fat	2.5	3.3	3.1
Carbohydrates	3.8	4.5	7.2
Ash	0.62	0.7	0.20
Calcium (mg.)	18.5	100	35
Sodium	2.5	36	15
Phosphorous	60.3	90	25
Iron	1.5	0.1	0.2
Thiamine (B_1)	0.04	0.04	0.02
Riboflavin (B_2)	0.02	0.15	0.03
Niacin	0.62	0.20	0.2

(SOURCE: *Standard Tables of Food Composition* [Japan])

When prepared with the same precentage of water as that found in dairy milk (it is usually made with less), soymilk contains 51 percent more protein, 16 percent less carbohydrate, 12 percent fewer calories (18 percent fewer calories per gram of protein), and 24 percent less fat (48 percent less saturated fat). At the same time, it contains 15 times as much iron, many of the essential B vitamins, and no cholesterol. Finally it contains one-tenth the amount of dangerous agricultural chemicals (DDT among them).

(Unlike some varieties of commercial soymilk or that described above for the sake of comparison, the rich kinugoshi soymilk sold in most tofu shops and described in the recipe for Homemade Soymilk [p. 204] contains an average of 5.5 percent protein and, in some cases, as much as 6.3 percent; its complement of minerals and vitamins is also, of course, about 25 percent higher.)

Because it contains only 52 percent as much calcium as mother's milk (18 percent as much as found in dairy milk), soymilk is often enriched with calcium or calcium lactate when used in baby formulae. But whereas 7 to 10 percent of all American babies—as well as many adults—are allergic or otherwise sensitive to dairy milk (an even larger percentage find that it creates digestive difficulties), there is no evidence of similar reactions to regular or enriched soymilk.

Although various types of "vegetable milks" can be prepared from nuts (almonds, peanuts, walnuts, coconut) and seeds (sunflower and sesame), the soybean is, perhaps, the only plant known to man capable of yielding milk in large quantities at reasonable cost. And it strikes us as a deeply mysterious coincidence that the substance of a simple seed, ground and cooked with water, should be so similar to the life-giving milk produced in the bodies of mammals and used to suckle their young.

Soymilk has been used for centuries throughout East Asia in much the same way that dairy milk is now used in the West. Today many people who could not possibly afford cow's milk find that soymilk's greatest appeal lies in its remarkably low cost. Whether prepared at home or in tofu shops, specialty shops, or factories, it can be produced for about one-half to one-third the cost of cow's milk. Thus, in many parts of the world where dairy milk is not generally consumed and does not give promise of ever being able to meet the needs of growing populations, soymilk could serve as a practical source of high-quality, essential nutrients both for infants and growing children in their crucial formative years, and for adults of all ages. Moreover, it is already finding popular appeal in the affluent West, especially among the many people interested in natural, health, and diet foods, and in a growing number of communities that find they can produce their own soymilk fresh each morning for a fraction of the price they would have to pay for dairy milk. *The Farm* (see p. 316), a community of seven hundred, for example, has recently started its own soy dairy capable of producing 80 gallons of rich soymilk every day at a cost of only 7½ cents per quart. *Farm* spokesmen report that the community's "babies love soymilk" and that most of its 250 children have been weaned onto it directly. And many tofu shops in America now sell bottled soymilk (available plain, or sweetened with honey or honey-carob) to a growing number of patrons.

As we studied the tofu-making process in Taiwan, we noticed a continuous stream of people, each bringing a teapot or kettle to the local tofu shop to purchase several quarts of fresh soymilk. We learned that this is commonly served as part of the family breakfast and is considered an essential source of protein for babies and young children. Here, as well as on the mainland, soymilk is also bottled on a large scale by shops and factories and is delivered each morning to regular customers: workmen are said to consider it an excellent source of energy and stamina. We found that most tofu makers took special pride in the flavor of their own preparation; in every shop we visited, we were unfailingly offered a large cup of hot soymilk, generally sweetened with a little brown sugar. And almost every block in the city of Taipei seemed to have at least one shop or cafe specializing in spicy hot soymilk soups and sweetened soymilk drinks available from early morning until well after midnight.

In the 1950s, soymilk appeared in a new form, as a bottled, non-carbonated soft drink produced on a large scale by industrial methods. Aimed at replacing the empty calories of conventional soft drinks with protein and other essential nutrients, this product has been given an up-dated image by means of modern advertising techniques and slogans emphasizing health and nutrition. *Vitasoy*, the first beverage of its kind, was developed by Mr. S.K. Lo, an idealistic Hong Kong businessman, whose primary motivation was to provide nourishment for the masses at a price they could afford. Each 6½-ounce bottle contains 3 percent protein (6.8 grams) and retails for less than 3½ U.S. cents, or about two-thirds the cost of the same sized bottle of Coca Cola. Sold from sampans, sidewalk stands, and grocery stores, it is enjoyed ice cold in summer and piping hot in winter. By 1974, *Vitasoy's* sales had skyrocketed to more than 150 million bottles per year, making it Hong Kong's best selling soft drink.

Soon after *Vitasoy* caught on in Hong Kong, *Vitabean*, a similar beverage marketed by the Yeo Hiap Seng Company, came on the scene in Singapore and Kuala Lumpur (Malaysia). Pasteurized and packaged in decorative, aseptic tetrapak cartons containing 10 fluid ounces (284 cc), *Vitabean* can stay fresh for weeks without refrigeration. By the late 1960s, America's Monsanto Corporation had formed a joint venture with the Vitabean Company to market a variety of soymilk beverages (among them, *Puma*) in South America. Not long thereafter, the Coca Cola Corporation, apparently deciding to join rather than fight, opened its own soymilk soft drink plant in Rio de Janeiro, where it is producing *Saci*. And in India, Africa, and a growing number of other areas, protein-rich soymilk drinks flavored to suit local tastes (malt, orange, coffee, cinnamon, and vanilla) are now being sold for about one-fourth the price of cow's milk.

Recognizing the nutritive value of these soymilk beverages, prestigious international organizations such as UNICEF and the Food and Agricultural Organization (FAO) have recently given them their endorsement. The World Health Organization (WHO) has gone so far as to build a one-million-dollar soymilk factory in Indonesia and smaller plants in the Philippines (Manila) and other areas where soymilk has long been a traditional breakfast drink. Perhaps the world's most modern soymilk plant, privately owned by a Mr. Cheng, is located in Bangkok, Thailand; it is fully automated from the time the beans are dehulled until the finished product is bottled and packed for distribution. A product comprised of a mixture of soymilk and ordinary skim milk is also being marketed here.

In the West, the growing recognition of the value of soymilk has been greatly stimulated by the work of Dr. Harry W. Miller, now a resident of Southern California. Strong, alert, and very active at age 95, he is a living testimony to the health-giving virtues of soymilk. In 1936, while working as a medical missionary in Shanghai, Dr. Miller started the first soy dairy where soymilk was prepared on a large scale, sterlized in bottles, and distributed daily. Largely through Dr. Miller's efforts, soymilk fortified with vitamins and minerals has finally come to be used in the United States, too, primarily for feeding infants. His life's dream has been to see soymilk made available to people throughout the world, especially to the increasing number of children suffering from malnutrition.

The research work of Dr. Miller and other nutritionists around the world, based on experiments with large numbers of infants and young children, shows clearly and conclusively that soymilk can be used as a complete and effective substitute for dairy or human milk. When fortified with sulphur-containing amino acids, calcium, and vitamins A,B,C, and D, the nutritional balance of the product approaches its ideal as a baby food. In 1937, when Dr. Miller patented the first such formulated drink, he was advised that if he called it by its common and obvious name, soymilk, he would be fought by the dairy industry; so he latinized the name to *Soyalac*. The actual cost of preparing this milk in the United States is about one-half the cost of obtaining dairy milk (before bottling and distribution). Reports in various publications suggest that, for this reason, the American dairy industry may be growing increasingly concerned about the use of soymilk and other soy products to extend, or even replace, dairy products.

In Japan, soymilk is prepared by a number of large companies and sold in tetrapak cartons or, in condensed form, in cans. Now available in a variety of flavors (plain, honey, barley-malt, strawberry, or chocolate) at virtually all natural and health food stores and at most supermarkets, some types are even dispensed from vending machines or delivered door to door. (Many Japanese tofu makers used to deliver a bottle of soymilk each morning to a large number of their regular customers, but the tradition has gradually declined with the increasing availability of commercial soymilk and the post-war trend toward drinking dairy milk.) A formulated, canned soymilk for infants (and those allergic or sensitive to dairy milk) and at least four varieties of powdered, spray-dried soymilk packaged in cartons are available at most pharmacies or natural food stores. Plain powdered soymilk contains 44 to 52 percent protein, 28 percent fat (mostly polyunsaturated), and 12 percent carbohydrates; stored at room temperature, it will keep its flavor indefinitely and is an excellent lightweight ingredient for use on camping trips or picnics. One type of powdered soymilk, called *Bonlact*, is especially formulated for infants and growing children. Another, used primarily as a health food by adults on low-fat or reducing diets, is fortified with lecithin and linoleic acid, methionine, fruit sugar, plus vitamins and minerals. The most popular spray-dried soymilk is packaged together with a small envelope of lactone solidifier and sold at most food markets as instant homemade tofu.

Soymilk is well thought of by medical practitioners as well as laymen. Many Japanese doctors view it as an effective natural medicine and prescribe it as a regular part of the diet for diabetes (because it is low in starch); heart disease, high blood pressure, and hardening of the arteries (because it is free of cholesterol, low in saturated fats, and rich in lecithin and linoleic acid); and anemia (because it is rich in iron and is thought to stimulate the production of hemoglobin). It is also used to strengthen the digestive system (since health-giving lactic acid bacteria thrive and multiply in its presence) and alkalize—hence fortify—the bloodstream (since it is among the most alkaline sources of protein).

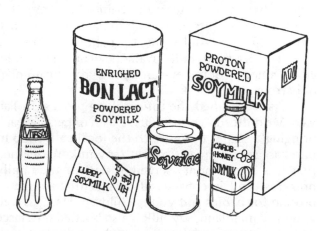

Commercial Japanese soymilk products

In his full-length book, *The Wonders of Soymilk*, Mr. Teisuke Yabuki carefully documents case after case where doctors or patients attribute the cure of various diseases to soymilk. Some prescribe it as an effective remedy for chronic nosebleed or bruises that won't heal; others find that it alleviates arthritis, softens corns, or restores healthy black hair. Some doctors assert that since soymilk contains an abundance of water-soluble vitamins (some of which dissolve in the whey during the tofu-making process), they actually prefer soymilk to tofu for use in diets related to vitamin-deficiency diseases.

Tofu makers have frequently told us that a number of their customers order soymilk daily for use as a medicine as well as a tasty beverage. Many Japanese claim that soymilk helps bring out the natural luster of the skin, and, in fact, people who work in tofu and yuba shops are well known for their fine complexions. Many a tofu maker has told us how, when his nursing wife's milk supply decreased or failed, she fed the baby soymilk, often using it as a basic food until weaning time. And even today, many pregnant and nursing women drink soymilk to increase the quality and flow of their milk. Soymilk is also thought to be effective in curing constipation and intestinal disturbances in children.

In Japanese tofu shops, soymilk is the source of each of the six types of tofu. The rich soymilk served as a drink is generally used to make kinugoshi tofu, while regular tofu is made from soymilk with a much thinner consistency. The secret of delicious soymilk lies above all in its thickness, which varies widely from shop to shop.

The point can well be made that soymilk is a better and more convenient way of using soybeans as a food than tofu: it is considerably easier to make, takes less than one-half the time, requires less fuel and equipment, and therefore costs less; it contains 83 percent of the protein originally present in the soybeans (tofu contains only 73½ percent due to losses in the whey and soaking water); it is a simpler food since no solidifier need be added in its manufacture; it contains the full, subtle sweetness of the soybeans, which gradually diminishes in proportion to the length of time the resultant kinugoshi or regular tofu is soaked in water; and it can be fed even to babies who are too young to eat tofu.

In recent years, a number of large commercial manufacturers of soymilk have developed methods for producing soymilk with a flavor quite similar to that of dairy milk. The characteristic soy flavor, which is found in water-soluble soybean enzymes rather than in the protein or oil, is removed by dehulling the beans, washing and draining them thoroughly several times before and after soaking, and cooking the gô for a fairly long time at a high temperature (about 8 minutes at 238°). Some makers then pasteurize the soymilk at 293° for a few seconds and package it in foil-lined tetrapak cartons in which it will keep for up to 1 month without refrigeration. Although this mild-flavored, modern product is said to have a wider appeal than its traditional counterpart, we—like almost all people in China and most Japanese tofu makers—definitely prefer the flavor of the natural product.

Used for centuries to make doufu-ru, a soft Chinese cheese-like product fermented in brining liquor (p. 262), soymilk can also be used to make Western-style cheeses (p. 88). Furthermore, it can be fermented with the same starters as dairy milk to make delicious and inexpensive homemade yogurt (p. 205). In Western-style cookery, soymilk may be used in any recipe calling for dairy milk.

The soymilk used in the recipes that follow may be the type freshly prepared at home (you can prepare excellent soymilk in a blender in less than 20 minutes) or any one of the varieties of fresh, powdered, or canned soymilk now available throughout the United States at most natural- and health food stores, many Japanese and Chinese markets, and a growing number of supermarkets.

"Kids love soymilk" (The Farm)

Homemade Soymilk

The recipe given below is the traditional one used in Japanese tofu shops. This rich, thick soymilk contains 5.5 percent protein (vs. 3% for dairy milk). Using storebought soybeans, it can be prepared at home for less than one-half the cost of dairy milk and should be ready to serve 20 minutes after you start. If you are not preparing homemade kinugoshi or yuba and desire a slightly larger yield of soymilk, heat 1 (instead of ½) cup water in the cooking pot initially. The utensils you will need are included among those required for preparing Homemade Tofu (p. 99).

1 cup soybeans, washed and drained 3 times, soaked in 2 quarts water for about 10 hours (see graph; p. 289), then rinsed and drained twice
4 cups water, approximately

Prepare pressing pot and sack in advance as for Homemade Tofu.

1) Heat ½ cup water over very low heat in covered cooking pot. While water is heating, combine beans and 2 2/3 cups water in a blender and purée at high speed for about 3 minutes, or until very smooth. (If using a grain mill, food mill, or meat grinder, grind beans without adding water and add 2 2/3 cups more water to cooking pot.)

2) Add soybean purée to water heating (or boiling) in cooking pot, rinsing out blender with ¼ cup water to retrieve any purée that may cling to blender's walls. Increase heat to medium-high and continue cooking, stirring bottom of pot constantly with a wooden spatula or spoon to prevent sticking (fig. 34b, p. 101). When foam suddenly rises in pot, quickly turn off heat and pour contents of pot into pressing sack (fig. c). Using a rubber spatula, retrieve any soybean purée that may still cling to sides of cooking pot and transfer to pressing sack. Quickly fill cooking pot with water and set aside to soak.

3) Twist hot sack closed. Using a glass jar or potato masher, press sack against colander, expressing as much soymilk as possible (fig. d). Open sack, shake okara into one corner, close and press again. Now open sack wide in colander and stir okara while blowing on it to hasten cooling, then allow okara to stand for 3 to 5 minutes while you wash cooking pot. Sprinkle ½ cup water over surface of okara. Close sack and press well as before, then squeeze sack by hand to express last of soymilk (fig. e). Empty okara into any large container and set aside.

4) Pour soymilk into cooking pot and bring to a boil over medium-high heat, stirring bottom constantly to prevent sticking. Reduce heat to medium and cook for 5 to 7 minutes, then turn off heat.

Serve soymilk hot or cold as Rich Soymilk (p. 205). To serve chilled, stir desired sweeteners and seasonings into hot soymilk, cover pot, and set into cold water for 10 minutes. Pour into a bottle, cover, and refrigerate.

Substitute soymilk for dairy milk in all cooking, or use to prepare Homemade Kinugoshi (p. 215) or Yuba (p. 242).

The leftover okara is especially rich in nutrients; be sure to use it (Chapter 6).

VARIATIONS
*For soymilk with a refreshing but subtle citrus fragrance and a slightly richer creaminess, add a very thin wedge of lemon, lime, or *yuzu* to soymilk at the beginning of step 4, and remove wedge just before serving.
*For soymilk with a milder flavor (more like that of dairy milk), remove hulls from soaked beans by rubbing under water, then skimming off with a mesh skimmer.

Homemade Chinese-style Soymilk
(Doufu-chiang)

Chinese-style soymilk is usually thinner than the Japanese variety and, in our opinion, considerably more difficult to prepare. Moreover, since unheated purée does not pass as easily through the pressing sack, this method gives a 10 percent lower yield of nutrients. If the okara is to be used in other recipes, be sure to cook it thoroughly since it is not cooked with the soymilk.

1 cup soybeans, washed and drained 3 times, soaked in 2 quarts water for 10 hours, then rinsed and drained twice
5½ to 6 cups water

Combine beans with 3½ cups (warm) water in a blender and purée at high speed for 3 minutes. Empty purée into a moistened cloth pressing sack lining a colander set over a large pot. Twist sack closed and squeeze sack gently but thoroughly to expel as much soymilk as possible. Remove okara and return to blender with 2 to 2½ cups more (warm) water; purée for about 1 minute. Return okara to pressing sack and squeeze again.

Bring soymilk to a boil over high heat, stirring constantly. Reduce heat to low and simmer for 5 to 7 minutes. (If foam begins to rise, remove with a skimmer.) Serve hot or cold with sweetening, as for Rich Soymilk (p. 205).

Homemade Soymilk
(from Powdered Soymilk)

Although soymilk prepared from powder is somewhat more expensive than (and not quite as delicious as) that made from whole soybeans, the process is naturally much faster since it is unnecessary to grind the beans or press the milk from okara. The soymilk will be ready less than 10 minutes after you start. This recipe is good for use on camping trips or when the soymilk is blended with other ingredients. Powdered soymilk is now available at many natural food stores and Japanese markets and when prepared according to the following recipe can be used to prepare Homemade Kinugoshi (p. 215).

1 cup powdered soymilk
3 cups water

Combine powder and water in a 3 to 4 quart saucepan and whisk well until dissolved. Bring to a boil over high heat, stirring constantly. Reduce heat to low and simmer for 3 minutes. Serve hot or cold.

Homemade Soymilk
(from Soy Flour)
MAKES 4¼ CUPS

Here is a recipe you can use if you are unable to obtain whole soybeans or powdered soymilk, or if you do not have a blender or grinder.

1 cup soy flour
3½ cups water

Combine soy flour and 3 cups water in a small saucepan and bring to a boil over medium heat, stirring constantly. Proceed as for Homemade Soymilk (p. 204), pressing soymilk through a cloth sack; rinse okara with ½ cup water and re-press. Now bring soymilk to a boil and simmer for 5 minutes before serving.

For variety, the soymilk may be cooked in a double boiler for about 50 minutes; omit the second cooking.

Soymilk Yogurt
MAKES 3¼ CUPS

Since soymilk ferments faster than dairy milk, soymilk yogurt takes less time and less starter, and involves much less trouble than dairy yogurt. Soymilk yogurt requires no special incubating and heating equipment and can be prepared at room temperature. When prepared from homemade soymilk, the cost is about one-sixth that of commercial dairy yogurt, while the protein content is often twice as high. The bacteria in the starter—fresh plain yogurt—produce lactic acid which acts as a protein solidifier in much the same way as nigari.

3¼ cups Homemade Soymilk (p. 204)
1 teaspoon yogurt

Allow freshly made soymilk to cool to slightly warmer than body temperature (105° to 110°). Remove thin yuba film from surface of soymilk and reserve. Stir yogurt into soymilk, then pour innoculated milk into a clean jar. Cover and allow to stand at room temperature (70°F or above) for 14 to 18 hours. When ready, set aside several tablespoons of the new yogurt to use as a starter for the next batch. Serve yogurt as is, sweetened with a little honey, or mixed with sliced bananas, raisins, toasted wheat germ, grated coconut, apple wedges, chopped nuts, sunflower seeds, or granola. Serve yuba sprinkled with a few drops of shoyu.

If cultured for too short a time, the tang and subtle sourness of fine yogurt will not develop; if cultured for too long, the yogurt will sour and separate into curds and whey.

Storebought soymilk can be made into yogurt by simply mixing in starter at room temperature and proceeding as above. To decrease fermentation time, add 1 teaspoon honey before innoculation, or use a little more starter or an incubator set at 100° to 110°.

SOYMILK QUICK AND EASY

Chilled soymilk can be served just as is, like dairy milk, on your favorite dishes such as hot or cold applesauce, crunchy granola, or fresh strawberries.

Rich Soymilk
SERVES 1

This is the most popular way of serving soymilk throughout East Asia. Generally soymilk is served steaming hot out of the tofu shop cauldron; but during the summer it is also served chilled. The latter has a richer, creamier consistency, a deeper natural sweetness, and a flavor more like that of dairy milk. In China and Taiwan, a well-known breakfast drink called *tento-chiang* or *tien-chiang* (sweet soymilk) consists of soymilk sweetened with sugar or molasses. It is usually served with deep-fried bread sticks wrapped in a *chapati*.

Serve Homemade Soymilk plain, or stir into 1 cup, hot or cold:

*1 to 2 teaspoons honey, natural sugar, molasses, *mizuame*, or barley sugar; and a dash of salt or several drops of shoyu. (The latter may also be used without the sweetening.)

*1 egg yolk. This greatly improves the drink's nutritional value.

*2½ teaspoons carob powder, 1 tablespoon honey or sugar, and a dash of salt. If desired, add several teaspoons malt and a few drops of vanilla to make malted milk or malted carob cocoa.

*2 teaspoons honey or sugar, ¼ teaspoon grated gingerroot (or 1/8 teaspoon powdered ginger), and 1/8 teaspoon each nutmeg and salt.

*1 tablespoon honey or *mizuame*, 2 tablespoons ground roasted sesame seeds and, if desired, 1 tablespoon grated glutinous yam.

*Cream ¼ cup nut butter (cashew, almond, peanut), 1½ teaspoons honey or natural sugar, and a dash of salt with a small amount of the warm milk, then stir in remainder of milk.

Sesame Soymilk for Children
MAKES 1 CUP

Soymilk is richer than dairy milk in almost every nutrient except calcium, a mineral which is essential for babies and growing children. The world's richest source of calcium is the sesame seed which contains over six times as much calcium by weight as dairy milk. Since soy and sesame proteins are complementary, their combination yields an abundance of high quality protein.

1 cup (warm) soymilk
1½ to 2 tablespoons *tahini* or sesame butter
1 to 1½ teaspoons honey or natural sugar
Dash of salt
1 egg yolk (optional)

Combine all ingredients, mixing well.

PURÉED SOYMILK BEVERAGES, FRUIT-WHIPS, AND DRESSINGS

Frothy Soymilk with Honey   MAKES 2 CUPS

2 cups chilled soymilk
1½ tablespoons honey or natural sugar

Combine ingredients in a blender and purée for 1 minute at high speed until light and frothy. Serve immediately in chilled mugs, over ice if desired.

Whipped Creamy Soymilk   SERVES 3

The lemon juice partially solidifies the soy protein which, when puréed, gives this beverage a thick, rich texture; the lemon adds a tasty tang. If a blender is not available, use an egg beater or whisk.

3¼ cups fairly hot soymilk, preferably homemade (p. 204)
1½ tablespoons honey
1½ teaspoons lemon juice and/or 2 tablespoons oil

Combine soymilk and honey in a blender and purée for 15 seconds. Slowly add lemon juice while continuing to purée for 30 seconds more. Allow mixture to stand for at least 1 minute, then purée again briefly just before serving.

Banana-Raisin Whip   MAKES 2 CUPS

½ cup chilled soymilk
2 chilled or frozen bananas
1/3 cup raisins
1 teaspoon lemon juice

Combine all ingredients in a blender and purée until smooth.

Healthy Banana Milkshake   MAKES 2 CUPS

1 cup chilled soymilk
¼ cup toasted wheat germ or Okara Granola (p. 84)
1 raw egg
1 or 2 chilled or frozen bananas
1 to 2 teaspoons honey or natural sugar
Dash of nutmeg

Combine all ingredients in a blender and purée until smooth. For variety, add a few dried fruits or nuts.

Nutty Soymilk   MAKES 2½ CUPS

2 cups soymilk
½ cup nutmeats, sunflower seeds, or roasted sesame seeds
1½ teaspoons honey or natural sugar
Dash of salt (if nuts are unsalted)

Combine all ingredients in a blender and purée until smooth. For extra sweetness, add a few dates, bananas, or raisins before puréing. Substitute nut butters, *tahini*, or sesame butter for the whole nuts. Serve chilled as a drink or topping for crunchy granola, or serve warm as a topping for cooked vegetables.

Fresh Fruit Whip   MAKES 2½ CUPS

2 cups chilled soymilk
½ to 1 cup fresh or frozen fruits or berries

Combine all ingredients in a blender and purée until smooth.

Thick Sweet Cream   MAKES 2½ CUPS

1 cup soymilk
12 ounces tofu
2 tablespoons honey or natural sugar

Combine all ingredients in a blender and purée until smooth. Serve over desserts, salads, cooked vegetables, or Cooked Apples with Agé (p. 179).

Soymilk Mayonnaise Dressing   MAKES 1 CUP

½ cup soymilk
½ cup oil
Juice of 1 lemon or 2½ tablespoons vinegar
½ teaspoon salt

Combine soymilk and ¼ cup oil in a blender and purée for 1 minute. Slowly add remaining oil in a thin stream. When mixture is fairly thick, add lemon juice and salt, and purée for 30 seconds more. For variety add minced onions, garlic, grated gingerroot, paprika, or your choice of herbs or seasonings. Or add any of the combinations of ingredients used in the variations to Tofu Mayonnaise (p. 107).

SOYMILK IN SOUPS OR SAUCES, WITH EGGS, AND IN OVEN COOKERY

Use soymilk as you would dairy milk in cream soups or scrambled eggs. It lends a creamy rich quality to casseroles, quiches, soufflés, and other baked dishes. In white, cheese, and cream sauces, soymilk may be used as either milk or cream depending on the soymilk's thickness.

Creamy Soymilk-Corn Soup with Thick Agé

SERVES 4 OR 5

Kernels from 1 ear of fresh corn
1 potato, diced
½ small carrot, diced
1½ small onions, minced
1¾ cups water
¾ teaspoon salt or 2 tablespoons red miso
¾ cup soymilk
1 tablespoon butter
Dash of pepper
10 ounces thick agé, ganmo, or agé, cubed (optional)
¼ cup minced parsley

Combine the first six ingredients and bring to a boil over medium heat. Reduce heat to low, cover pot, and simmer for 30 minutes. Allow to cool for a few minutes, then combine with soymilk in a blender and purée until smooth. Return mixture to pot and bring to a boil over medium heat. Add butter, pepper, and thick agé, and return to the boil. Serve hot or chilled, garnished with parsley.

Chinese Breakfast Soymilk Soup
(Siento-chiang)

SERVES 5

This soup is served morning and night in small shops throughout the cities and towns of Taiwan and China. It is given a special name if the raw egg is mixed with the soymilk before the various garnishes are added.

5 cups soymilk
Seasonings and Garnishes:
 Diced *cha-t'sai* or *takuan* salt pickles
 "Bits" of *yu-chiao* deep-fried bread sticks
 Grated *yuson* dried shrimp
 Bonita flakes or fish meal
 Diced leeks
 Sesame oil
 Salt
 Soy sauce
 Minced or 7-spice red pepper
 Raw egg (optional)

Heat the soymilk but do not bring to a boil; serve in individual bowls. Arrange small dishes filled with garnishes and allow each guest to select garnishes to taste.

Rich and Creamy Potatoes

SERVES 4

3 tablespoons butter
4 potatoes, cut into ½-inch cubes
2 small onions, cut into thin wedges
2½ cups soymilk
½ teaspoon salt
Dash of pepper
2 tablespoons natural sugar
¼ cup diced parsley

Melt the butter in a skillet. Add potatoes and onions, and sauté until onions are transparent. Add soymilk, salt, and pepper and simmer until potatoes are thoroughly cooked. Mix in sugar and simmer for several minutes more, then remove from heat and allow to cool. Serve topped with parsley.

Lemon-Miso White Sauce

SERVES 2

2 tablespoons butter or oil
2 tablespoons (whole-wheat) flour
1 cup soymilk
4 teaspoons red or barley miso; 2½ teaspoons shoyu; or 2/3 teaspoon salt
2 teaspoons lemon juice
¼ teaspoon grated lemon rind (optional)
12 ounces tofu or 7½ ounces thick agé, cut into bite-sized cubes
Dash of pepper, paprika, or cayenne
1 tablespoon minced parsley (optional)

Use the first four ingredients to prepare a White Sauce (p. 48). When sauce is partially thickened, add lemon juice (and rind) together with tofu. Continue to cook, stirring gently, for about 2 minutes more, or until sauce is well thickened. Stir in pepper and, if used, the parsley, and remove from heat.

VARIATIONS

*Soymilk-Mushroom Sauce: After adding milk, add ¼ diced onion and 6 thinly-sliced mushrooms. Simmer over low heat, stirring constantly, for 4 to 5 minutes, then add 1 teaspoon lemon juice, a dash of pepper, and 1 tablespoon white wine or sake. Add tofu or substitute 5 ounces thick agé, ganmo, or agé. Finish cooking as above.
*Soymilk-Cheese Sauce: Sauté 1 clove crushed garlic in the butter for 15 seconds, then add flour, soymilk, and miso as above. Omit lemon juice. Stir in pepper and ½ teaspoon powdered hot mustard. Simmer, stirring constantly, for 2 minutes, or until sauce has thickened. Stir in ½ to 1 cup (1½ to 3 ounces) grated cheese and 5 ounces deep-fried tofu (or 12 ounces regular tofu) cut into cubes. Serve hot or cold.
*Herb Sauce: Use 2 teaspoons each minced chives and parsley, and 1/8 teaspoon marjoram. Sauté chives and parsley for 3 minutes, then add marjoram with flour and proceed as for basic recipe.

SOYMILK WITH GRAINS

Use soymilk as you would dairy milk in pancakes or waffles, breads, French toast, or muffins, and as a topping for hot breakfast cereals such as rolled oats or oatmeal.

Buckwheat Noodles Cooked in Soymilk   SERVES 2

1½ cups soymilk
1 small onion, diced
2 tablespoons shoyu or 2½ tablespoons red miso
2 tablespoons butter
½ cup grated cheese or 2½ tablespoons sesame butter
3½ ounces *(soba)* buckwheat noodles, cooked (p. 50) and well drained
Dash of pepper
2 tablespoons minced parsley or ground roasted sesame seeds (p. 38)
Crumbled toasted *nori* (optional)

Combine soymilk and onion in a large saucepan and bring to a boil over medium heat, stirring constantly. Mix in the next three ingredients, add noodles, and return to the boil. Season with pepper and remove from heat. Allow to stand until soymilk clabbers. Serve garnished with parsley and, if desired, the *nori*.

SOYMILK IN COOKED DESSERTS AND STEAMED DISHES

Use soymilk in puddings, cakes, ice cream, and other treats, or as a base for delicately-flavored Japanese-style steamed custards.

Soymilk Custard Pudding   SERVES 4

2 tablespoons melted butter
1½ to 2 cups soymilk
3 tablespoons honey or natural sugar
Dash of salt
½ teaspoon vanilla (optional)
4 eggs, well beaten
1 cup Tofu Whipped Cream (p. 148)

Preheat steamer (p. 38) or oven to 300°, and use the butter to coat 4 custard cups. Combine soymilk, honey, and salt in a small saucepan and heat to body temperature. Add vanilla and stir well.

Place eggs in a large bowl and stir vigorously with a whisk. Add the warm soymilk while stirring, then pour mix-

ture through a strainer into the 4 custard cups. Cover cups with paper and lid (p. 38) and steam over low heat for 13 to 15 minutes. (Or, if using an oven, place cups in a pan of hot water and bake for 20 to 30 minutes.) Chill thoroughly and serve topped with Tofu Whipped Cream.

For variety, add a little grated lemon rind or 2 teaspoons minced raisins to the custard just before steaming. Or omit eggs and substitute 6 tablespoons cornstarch, arrowroot, or *kuzu*.

Brown Rice Pudding   SERVES 4 TO 6

1¼ cups cooked Brown Rice (p. 50)
2 cups soymilk
2½ tablespoons honey
2 tablespoons butter
½ cup raisins
½ teaspoon salt
½ teaspoon cinnamon

Combine rice and soymilk in a small pan and bring to a boil over low heat. Add remaining ingredients and simmer, stirring constantly, for 10 minutes or until soymilk is completely absorbed. Serve chilled.

For variety, add 2 thinly sliced bananas and substitute ½ teaspoon nutmeg for the cinnamon. Or add ¼ cup *tahini*, 2 eggs, and 1 teaspoon vanilla. Any of these dishes may be baked at 350° for 20 minutes.

Oatmeal Pudding   SERVES 3 TO 4

2½ cups soymilk
½ cup oatmeal
½ cup raisins
1½ cups chopped apple
2 or 3 tablespoons brown sugar
¼ to ½ teaspoon cinnamon
½ teaspoon salt

Bring soymilk to a boil over medium heat in a small pan. Slowly stir in the oatmeal, then the remaining ingredients. Reduce heat to low and simmer, stirring constantly, for about 10 minutes, or until thick. Serve chilled.

Apple Soymilk Dessert

SERVES 2

In this Chinese dish, the natural acid from the apple clabbers the soymilk to yield a pudding consistency.

1 cup soymilk
½ cup water
1 to 2 tablespoons natural sugar or honey
Dash of salt
1 teaspoon cornstarch or arrowroot dissolved in 1 tablespoon water
1 small apple, peeled and grated

Combine the first four ingredients in a saucepan and bring to a boil over medium heat. Stir in dissolved cornstarch and grated apple, and return just to the boil. Serve chilled.

For variety, add 1 tablespoon butter, 3 tablespoons raisins, and a dash of cinnamon.

Soymilk Egg Tofu

SERVES 2

Soymilk gives this richly-textured tofu a creamier, more custard-like quality than its close relative, Egg Tofu (p. 267).

¾ cup (homemade) soymilk, cooled to room temperature
1 egg, lightly beaten
¼ teaspoon shoyu

Combine all ingredients in a small bowl; mix well. Divide the mixture among 2 custard cups, cover, and place in an unheated steamer (p. 38). Bring steamer to a boil, reduce heat to low and steam for 13 to 15 minutes. (Oversteaming will create tiny bubbles in the tofu and spoil its delicate texture.) Serve as is or topped with a few drops of shoyu.

For a richer flavor, include an additional egg, 1 tablespoon butter, and 1 teaspoon *mirin*. Or add 2 tablespoons peanut butter. This dish may also be steamed in a rectangular pan (as for Egg Tofu, p. 267) or baked in a 300° oven for 20 minutes (as for custard).

Soymilk Chawan-mushi

SERVES 4

2 cups soymilk
1 egg, lightly beaten
2½ tablespoons shoyu
2 mushrooms, thinly sliced
1/8 onion, thinly sliced
¼ cup green peas or fresh corn, parboiled
½ ounce agé, thinly sliced; or 4 small ganmo balls (p. 188) (optional)
2 tablespoons diced sweet potatoes (optional)

Combine the first three ingredients in a small bowl; mix well. Divide the remaining ingredients among 4 Chawan-mushi or custard cups, then pour in the soymilk mixture. Steam for 15 minutes as for Chawan-mushi (p. 147).

For variety, add small amounts of fresh or deep-fried yuba, chestnuts, cubes of fresh wheat gluten, or sections of lilly bulbs and ginkgo nuts.

JELLED AND MOLDED SOYMILK DISHES
(Yose-dofu)

A number of dessert or semi-dessert dishes can be prepared from soymilk jelled with agar, *kuzu*, or arrowroot starch.

Soymilk Kuzu Mochi

SERVES 4

3¼ cups soymilk
½ cup powdered *kuzu*
¼ cup brown sugar
¼ cup kinako

Combine soymilk and *kuzu* in a small saucepan and cook over medium heat, stirring constantly, until the mixture begins to thicken. Reduce heat to low and stir vigorously for 2 or 3 minutes or until mixture thickens and becomes transparent. Smooth surface of mixture with a wooden spatula, then remove from stove and allow to cool thoroughly. Cut jelled mixture into small triangles or break into bite-size pieces and arrange on 4 plates. Mix the sugar with enough water to form a thick syrup, and pour over each serving. Serve topped with a sprinkling of kinako.

For variety, add the sugar (or 2 teaspoons powdered green *matcha* tea) to the soymilk with the *kuzu*. Serve topped with Sweet Peanut Sauce (p. 91).

Banana Blancmange

SERVES 4 TO 6

1¼ cups soymilk
¼ cup powdered *kuzu*
1 banana
2 tablespoons honey
1 tablespoon lemon juice
Tofu Whipped Cream (p. 148)

Combine the first four ingredients in a blender and purée until smooth. Transfer to a small saucepan and cook, stirring constantly, over medium heat until mixture begins to thicken. Reduce heat to low and stir for 2 or 3 minutes more, until mixture becomes partially transparent. Stir in lemon juice and spoon the mixture into a mold partially immersed in cold water; allow to cool to room temperature, then refrigerate until well chilled. Serve topped with Tofu Whipped Cream.

VARIATIONS

Egg Blancmange: Substitute 1 egg for the banana.
Egg-Lemon Blancmange: Combine in a blender: ¾ cup soymilk, 2 tablespoons *kuzu*, 1 egg, 2 teaspoons lemon juice, and 1 tablespoon honey; prepare as above but serve without the whipped cream.

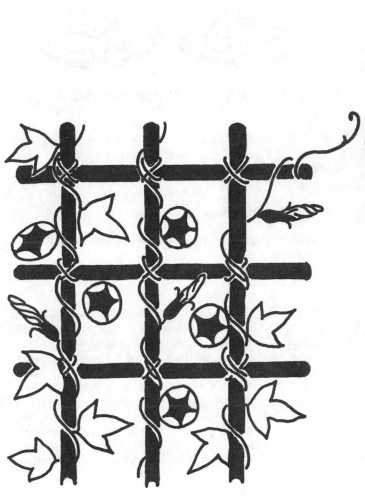

Jelled Soymilk Dessert with Bananas and Raisins

SERVES 4

1 banana, sliced into thin rounds
1/3 cup raisins
¼ cup chopped walnut or almond meats
2 tablespoons honey
1½ cups soymilk
1 stick of agar (8 gm), reconstituted and torn into small pieces (p. 37)
Nutmeg

Divide the banana slices, raisins, and nutmeats among 4 (custard) cups. Combine honey, soymilk, and agar in a saucepan and bring to a boil. Simmer, stirring constantly, for 3 minutes, or until agar dissolves. Pour soymilk-agar mixture through a (warmed) strainer into the cups. Top each serving with a pinch of nutmeg and allow to cool. Chill thoroughly before serving.

Or substitute 1½ cups fresh strawberries for the first three ingredients and omit nutmeg.

Fig. 80. Takigawa-dofu

Takigawa-dofu (Swirling Jelled Soymilk)   SERVES 4

The two Chinese characters in the name *Takigawa* mean "waterfalls and rivers." The jelled soymilk in this popular dish is cut lengthwise into noodle-like strips and arranged in the serving container to resemble the swirls and eddies of a meandering river (fig. 80). Some varieties are also prepared with jelled puréed tofu (p. 114).

1 stick of agar (8 gm), reconstituted and torn into small pieces (p. 37)
2¾ cups (homemade) soymilk (p. 204)
4 (marischino) cherries (optional)
Sauce:
       ¾ cup dashi (p. 39) or stock
       1 tablespoon shoyu
       ½ teaspoon salt
       1½ tablespoons *mirin*
2 tablespoons grated gingerroot or *wasabi*
4 green beefsteak leaves, minced

Combine agar and soymilk in a large saucepan. Stirring constantly, bring soymilk to a boil over medium heat, then simmer for 3 minutes, or until agar dissolves. Pour through a strainer into a shallow rectangular pan so that soymilk fills the pan to a depth of about 1½ inches. Allow to cool to room temperature, then cut into 4 equal rectangular pieces. Cut each piece lengthwise and horizontally to form thin noodle-like strips (or press each piece through a *tentsuki* or *konnyaku* noodle slicer available at Japanese markets or hardware stores). Place 1 cherry at the center of each of four serving dishes (or in large hollow sections of fresh bamboo), then arrange strips around cherries so that they seem to swirl around them. Chill.

Combine dashi, shoyu, salt, and *mirin* in a saucepan and bring just to a boil. Allow to cool to room temperature, then refrigerate. Pour over each serving of tofu, then top with dabs of gingerroot and beefsteak leaves.

VARIATIONS
*Substitute ¼ cup Yuzu Miso (p. 42) for the sauce.
*Gohoji-dofu: Cook ¼ cup parboiled green soybeans together with the soymilk and agar; serve without cutting into strips. Top with shoyu and grated gingerroot.

11

Kinugoshi or Silken Tofu

KINU MEANS "silk"; *kosu* means "to strain": well-named, *kinugoshi* tofu has a texture so smooth that it seems to have been strained through silk. Soft and white, it melts in the mouth like custard or firm yogurt. Made from thick soymilk, kinugoshi has a subtle bouquet (especially when prepared with nigari) and natural sweetness resembling that of rich, fresh cream.

The Japanese language contains an abundance of words used to describe nuances of feeling, texture, and taste. *Shita-zawari*, for example, refers to the particular feeling that a food makes as it touches the tongue, and *nodo-goshi* to the gentleness with which it goes down the throat: kinugoshi is the epitome of exquisite *shita-zawari* and *nodo-goshi*. Free of even the fine-grained structure and internal cohesiveness of regular tofu, kinugoshi is so delicate that a chopstick slices—almost glides—evenly and effortlessly through it, leaving behind a nearly smooth surface.

At the tofu shop or market, a cake of kinugoshi is almost indistinguishable from one of regular tofu. Their shape and proportions appear the same, but the kinugoshi is usually slightly smaller, its color is a bit whiter, and its surface is smoother and less porous. The two types are made from the same basic ingredients and sell for about the same price.

Nevertheless, kinugoshi is prepared by a fundamentally different process, one characterized above all by its use of relatively thick soymilk. The boxes used to give form to the kinugoshi have neither draining holes nor lining cloths. While still hot, kinugoshi soymilk is simply poured in (fig. 81) and, in most neighborhood shops, solidified with calcium sulfate placed at the bottom of the boxes just before the soymilk is added. (Traditionally, kinugoshi was prepared by carefully stirring a solution of nigari and water into the soymilk just after it had been poured into the box [fig. 82]). The kinugoshi is allowed to stand in the boxes for 20 to 30 minutes until it becomes firm. *The curds and whey never separate and the tofu is never pressed.* Finally, the tofu is trimmed away from the sides of each box with a long knife (fig. 83), the box and tofu are immersed in cold water, and the tofu is carefully removed and cut into 12-ounce cakes.

When making regular tofu, some of the protein, vitamin B, natural oils, and sugars dissolve in the whey and are removed with it. Since whey is never removed from kinugoshi, the latter contains more of the nutrients originally in the soybeans. At the same time, it has a slightly higher water content, hence a somewhat lower percentage of protein than that contained in regular tofu (5.5% vs. 7.8%). It is this higher water content that gives kinugoshi its softer consistency. Its homogenous, fine-grained structure prevents the loss of natural sugars (as well as solidifier) when the tofu is soaked in water, so that kinugoshi generally retains more of the soymilk's sweetness. However, because of its delicate, fine grain, kinugoshi cannot be pressed and firmed, and when simmered with sauces or in seasoned broths, it does not readily absorb other flavors. Although its versatility in cooking is, therefore, limited, its sensuous texture and creamy sweetness make it a much favored delicacy.

In Japan, kinugoshi, like cool silk, is associated with summer. When served chilled, it can be as lus-

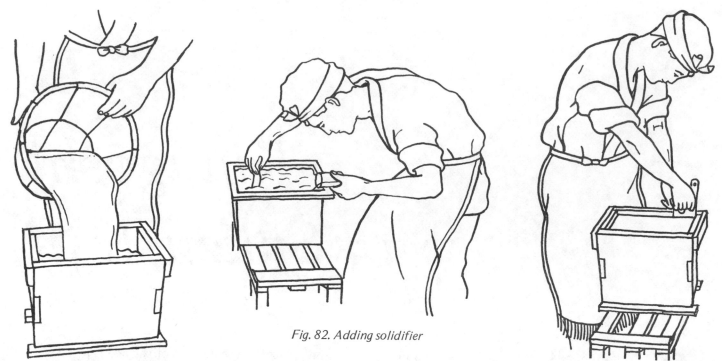

Fig. 81. Pouring the soymilk

Fig. 82. Adding solidifier

Fig. 83. Trimming kinugoshi from sides of box

cious as a succulent melon. Refreshingly light, it quenches thirst and cools both body and spirit while providing the energy to carry one through a hot day's work. During the hottest months, most kinugoshi in Japan is served as Iceberg Chilled Tofu, a simple refreshing dish designed to bring to life and celebrate the tofu's flavor.

With the first autumn colors on the maple leaves, kinugoshi begins to appear in the second of its most popular roles, Simmering Tofu, the cold-weather equivalent of Chilled Tofu and one of Japan's most popular *nabe,* or one-pot cookery, dishes. At many fine restaurants, the *nabe* is heated over a charcoal brazier and served outdoors, with no sources of light or heat other than the glowing coals, perhaps a paper lantern, and the piping-hot tofu.

Other main uses of kinugoshi are in miso soups, clear soups, and dishes served with various shoyu dipping sauces or miso toppings. Regular tofu can always be substituted for kinugoshi, but keep in mind that the texture of the dish may not be quite as soft and smooth. Kinugoshi, however, *cannot* always be substituted for regular tofu, particularly if the recipe calls for the tofu to be pressed, skewered, broiled, or sautéed in cube form. Kinugoshi is also not generally used in dishes such as scrambled eggs, omelets, or casseroles since it may contribute more water than is desirable. Kinugoshi yields good results when steamed or puréed to make cream sauces, spreads, dips, dressings, or foods for babies or elderly adults.

In many Japanese tofu shops, kinugoshi is prepared only during the warm months from about May until October and, during this time, the demand is often greater than that for regular tofu. In some shops, a little freshly-grated *yuzu* (or lime) rind or gingerroot is mixed into the soymilk before adding the solidifier to impart a light fragrance.

At present, there are five different types of kinugoshi sold in Japan. The primary factors determining the quality of each are the thickness of the soymilk and the type of solidifier used. The most traditional varieties, those solidified with nigari, were probably first developed in Japan. However, since the preparation of this tofu required a great deal of skill, and since nigari kinugoshi was too fragile to be easily transported, it was made at only a small number of Japan's finest tofu shops. Hence it was considered a rare delicacy—which most Japanese never had an opportunity to taste.

The earliest form of nigari kinugoshi, *shikishi-dofu,* was prepared in about 30 to 50 tiny wooden kegs, each about 4 inches deep, 4 inches in diameter, and coated inside with lacquer. Hot soymilk was poured into each container, nigari stirred in, and the kinugoshi allowed to form. The individual kegs were then immersed in water and the tofu removed, to be sold in its cylindrical form.

Beginning in the year 1703, a second form of nigari kinugoshi came to be prepared in Japan at Tokyo's Sasa-no-yuki tofu shop and restaurant. Today, as far as we now, no other shop in Japan makes nigari kinugoshi, primarily for lack of a sufficiently talented master. (The present master asserts that it took him six years to learn the process.) Sasa-no-yuki's delicious kinugoshi, with its unmatched nigari-evoked sweetness, is the delight of tofu connoisseurs throughout Japan. The words *sasa-no-yuki* mean "the snow on small bamboo leaves," a precise description of the delicate softness of this tofu from which the shop took its name. For three centuries, the terms "nigari kinugoshi" and "Sasa-no-yuki" have been almost synonymous, and today, too, the restaurant offers 12 separate dishes, each featuring its kinugoshi. (Many of these recipes and the method for preparing homemade nigari kinugoshi are included in this chapter.)

The transformation of kinugoshi from a rare and somewhat aristocratic food into one that was truly democratic came about through a quirk of history. At the beginning of World War II, the Japanese government siezed all of the nigari from the country's salt fields to use as a source of magnesium to build lightweight aircarft. Tofu makers were suddenly forced to switch to calcium sulfate solidifier. Although considered at the time to make less delicious tofu, it required less skill and less time to use and produced firmer tofu that was easier to transport. This made it possible for virtually every craftsman in the country to begin making kinugoshi. Thus most Japanese first tasted kinugoshi in the 1950s. And although it is now as common as regular tofu, and takes less time and effort to make, even calcium sulfate kinugoshi retains a sense of its aristocratic origins, being sold in equally priced but slightly smaller cakes than regular tofu. This second type of kinugoshi, which is still the most popular variety in Japan, has been prepared in China using gypsum (natural calcium sulfate) since ancient times.

The third type of kinugoshi is made with lactone (glucono-delta lactone or GDL), an organic acid that solidifies soymilk in much the same way that lactic acid or a yogurt starter is used to curdle dairy milk. A newly discovered solidifier made from natural gluconic acid, lactone makes it possible for the first time to solidify very thin soymilk, and even cold soymilk, by simply heating it to somewhat below the boiling point. When used in neighborhood tofu shops, lactone is generally combined with calcium sulfate. It is also included with the powdered soymilk in the packages of instant homemade tofu now sold in most Japanese supermarkets.

The fourth type of kinugoshi available in Japan, Packaged Lactone Kinugoshi, is also solidified with lactone, but the chilled soymilk is mixed with the solidifier right in the plastic container in which the tofu is eventually sold. The top of the container is covered with a sheet of plastic film, sealed thermally, and immersed in hot water at the factory for about 50 minutes during which time the tofu solidifies. (In some cases the tofu is solidified in sausage-shaped plastic bags [fig. 84].) This method allows the tofu to be mass-produced in highly automated factories, the largest of which have a daily output of 60,000 cakes (fig. 85). Japan's least expensive tofu, the 10½-ounce packaged cakes are distributed over an area of several hundred miles and sold at supermarkets at about 68 percent the cost (on a usable protein basis) of regular tofu and 60 percent the cost (on an equal weight basis) of the kinugoshi sold in neighborhood tofu shops. Furthermore, since the tofu is sterilized and sealed in the container, it stays fresh for up to 1 week if refrigerated. In many cases, however, the low price of the tofu only too faithfully reflects the thinness of the soymilk from which it is made. Although its flavor is often rather weak and the use of lactone gives it a texture somewhat like that of jello, however, it presently retails for as low as 15 cents per pound and consequently has found a very large market. Recently a number of higher quality (and slightly higher priced) varieties of Packaged Lactone Kinugoshi have become available. Made with richer soymilk (containing 5.5 rather than the typical 4.4 percent protein), they are solidified with a combination of lactone and calcium sulfate.

The fifth type of kinugoshi, and the most recently developed, is called Sealed Lactone Kinugoshi. The soymilk-lactone mixture is funneled into thick-walled polyethylene containers through a very small opening. The opening is then pinched closed and thermally sealed so that (unlike the previous type of kinugoshi) absolutely no air can enter. After being heated and solidified as above, this tofu (which contains no preservatives) stays fresh for 2 to 3 months. Moreover, the sturdy container makes it

Fig. 84. Modern lactone kinugoshi

possible to carry the tofu (in box lunches, for example) without fear of leakage or crushing the delicate curd structure. Although the cost of the container makes the retail price of this tofu about 85 to 90 percent higher than the previous variety, it is still relatively inexpensive and its convenience is winning it wide acceptance. Sealed Lactone Kinugoshi is now sold in three different flavors: regular, peanut, and egg. In the peanut type, nuts are ground together with the soybeans and made into soymilk; in the egg type, eggs are stirred into the chilled soymilk and the mixture reheated slightly before it is funneled into the containers. These two varieties contain up to 26 percent more protein than regular kinugoshi and are popular items at many natural- and health food stores.

Another type of modern tofu, closely resembling but nevertheless different from kinugoshi, is called "soft tofu." Like kinugoshi, it is solidified using calcium sulfate without the separation of curds and whey. But it is solidified in the curding barrel rather than in the kinugoshi box, and the solidified curds, ladled into the settling boxes used for regular tofu, are pressed with heavy weights until the tofu is firm. Soft tofu has almost the same smooth, homogeneous texture as kinugoshi, plus some of the internal strength and cohesiveness of regular tofu. Very fine-grained and difficult to press, it is generally used in recipes calling for kinugoshi.

It has been estimated that during the summertime in Japan, the total consumption of regular tofu is only about one-fourth that of the five types of kinugoshi plus "soft tofu."

Kinugoshi is now prepared by many Japanese and Chinese tofu shops in the United States. Sold in 12-ounce cakes in the same type of containers as regular tofu, it is commonly called Kinugoshi Soft Tofu or, in some Chinese shops, *Sui-dofu*. It is usually solidified with either lactone (GDL) or calcium sulfate. Some Japanese markets and co-op stores now

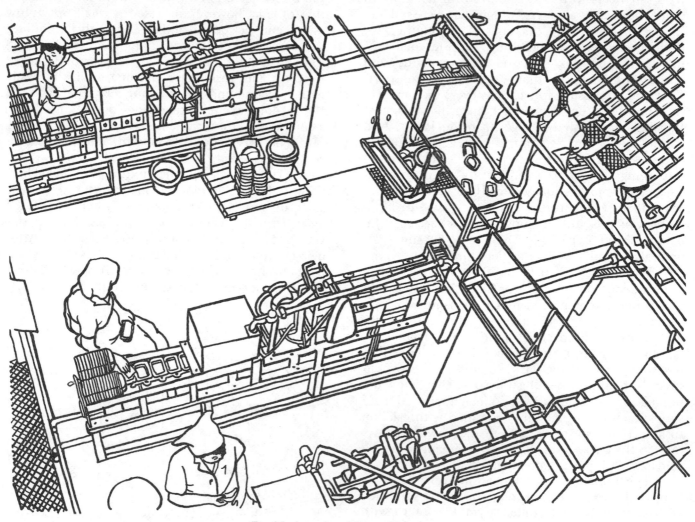

Fig. 85. A modern kinugoshi factory

also sell an instant homemade kinugoshi consisting of powdered soymilk and a small envelope of lactone solidifier. One package makes about 21 ounces and takes 15 to 20 minutes to prepare; directions are given on the package. A high-priced, canned kinugoshi is available in some Japanese markets but, in our opinion, its flavor does not meet up to expectation. Fortunately, fresh kinugoshi is very easy to prepare at home, even using nigari-type solidifier.

HOMEMADE KINUGOSHI

Homemade Kinugoshi *(from Whole Soybeans)*	MAKES 27 OUNCES

Kinugoshi is easier and faster to prepare than regular tofu and requires no special settling container. The yield is also considerably greater—1 pound of beans makes about 4½ pounds of tofu—and only half as much solidifier is required. We feel that kinugoshi made with natural nigari or magnesium chloride nigari is the most delicate and delicious. However, kinugoshi made with calcium sulfate is the firmest and easiest to prepare. Kinugoshi is usually ready to serve about 50 minutes after you start to prepare soymilk. In the following method, the kinugoshi is served like a custard or molded salad. In the last variation, the kinugoshi is first removed from the settling container so that it can be cut into cakes, as is usually done in Japan. This latter procedure is a bit difficult to master. For information about solidifiers, see pp. 282-285.

3¼ cups Homemade Soymilk (p. 204)
Solidifier:
    1) **For delicate, subtly-sweet nigari kinugoshi:** ½ teaspoon magnesium chloride or calcium chloride; 3/8 teaspoon granular or powdered natural nigari; 1/3 to 1 teaspoon liquid natural nigari from (home-processed) sea salt; or ½ to 1½ teaspoons liquid natural nigari from a salt refinery
    2) **For firm, mild kinugoshi:** ½ teaspoon Epsom salts (magnesium sulfate) or calcium sulfate; or 1 teaspoon lactone (GDL)
    3) **For firm, subtly tart kinugoshi:** 4 teaspoons lemon or lime juice, or 1 tablespoon (apple cider) vinegar
2 tablespoons water

Prepare Homemade Soymilk (p. 204). Place a 1½- to 3-quart serving bowl or a casserole on a firm surface (where it will not be jiggled or disturbed for 20 minutes) and pour in the freshly-made hot soymilk; cover. In a small cup quickly mix the solidifier with 2 tablespoons water and stir until dissolved. Stir soymilk back and forth briskly for 3 to 5 seconds, then quickly pour in all of the solidifier solution. Continue stirring soymilk for 3 to 5 seconds more, making sure to stir to bottom of container. Now stop spoon upright in center of soy-

milk and wait until turbulence ceases; lift out spoon. Let soymilk stand uncovered and undisturbed for 20 to 30 minutes while it cools and solidifies. Now cover with plastic wrap and refrigerate, or float bowl in cold water until chilled. To serve, bring the bowl to the table or ladle the kinugoshi into individual serving dishes. Serve as for Chilled Tofu (p. 105).

VARIATIONS

*Fragrant Kinugoshi:** Just before adding the solidifier, stir any of the following into the hot soymilk: ¼ teaspoon grated rind of *yuzu*, lemon, or lime; ¼ to ½ teaspoon grated ginger-root; 10 to 15 minced mint leaves; 10 green beefsteak leaves which have been soaked in water for 10 minutes, drained, squeezed gently in a dry towel, and minced. Serve the latter garnished with 2 teaspoons *benitade*.
*Peanut Kinugoshi:** Cream 2 or 3 tablespoons smooth peanut butter with a little of the hot soymilk, then stir into the soymilk just before adding solidifier. Or purée 3 to 4 tablespoons whole peanuts with the soybeans when preparing soymilk, and increase the amount of solidifier used by about 25 percent.
*Kinugoshi with Eggs:** Whisk 2 lightly beaten eggs into the hot soymilk just before stirring in solidifier.
*Jade-Green Kinugoshi:** Just before adding solidifier, stir 1 tablespoon powdered green tea *(matcha)* and 3 tablespoons honey into the soymilk. Serve chilled without topping or garnish.
*Sweet Kinugoshi:** Stir 1 tablespoon honey or natural sugar into the hot soymilk just before adding the solidifier.
*Subtly-Sweet & Firm Kinugoshi:** Solidify the soymilk with a combination of ¼ teaspoon Epsom salts (or calcium sulfate) and ¼ teaspoon magnesium chloride (or calcium chloride) nigari.
*Gelatinous Kinugoshi:** Solidify 3¼ cups soymilk with a combination of ½ teaspoon lactone (GDL) and ¼ teaspoon calcium sulfate (or Epsom salts).
*Reheated Lactone Kinugoshi:** Mix 3¼ cups soymilk at room temperature (below 86°) with 1 teaspoon lactone. Pour into one or more heat-resistant containers (plastic tubs serve well) and seal or cover. Float or partially immerse containers in water at about 185° for 50 minutes until solidified. Cool in water below 68° for 50 minutes more. This method is used commercially to prepare Packaged Lactone Kinugoshi.
*Tofu Shop-style Kinugoshi:** In place of a large bowl or casserole, use a 5- to 7-inch diameter, 1½-quart saucepan or box (wooden or metal) as a settling container. After 15 to 20 minutes, when kinugoshi is quite firm, float the pan in a large basin or sink filled with cold water for several minutes more. Carefully separate kinugoshi from walls of container using a narrow spatula or knife, then cut kinugoshi into quarters. Slowly press one edge of container under water so that it gradually fills with water. Wait several minutes as tofu cools further and firms. If kinugoshi quarters do not float, use spatula to carefully separate each quarter from bottom of container. Wait 5 to 10 minutes until center of tofu is firm. Now slip a small plate under each piece, lift out, drain, and serve. Or store in a cool place.

Kinugoshi Custard (Shikishi-dofu)   SERVES 3 OR 4

The earliest kinugoshi made in Japan was prepared in this simple but attractive way. If possible, use calcium sulfate solidifier: it curdles the soymilk slowly, and the curds and whey do not separate while the soymilk-solidifier mixture is being poured into the serving cups.

Prepare Homemade Soymilk (p. 204). Place 3 or 4 custard or coffee cups where they will be undisturbed. Mix the solidifier with 2 tablespoons water as for Homemade Kinugoshi (p. 215), then stir quickly into hot soymilk in the cooking pot. Immediately pour this soymilk-solidifier mixture into the cups. Cool and chill as for Homemade Kinugoshi. Serve in the cups seasoned with shoyu, or top with Ankake Sauce (p. 49), or any of the dipping sauces or toppings used with Chilled Tofu (p. 105).

VARIATIONS

*Kinugoshi Custard with Crisp Vegetables: This dish bears a close resemblance to *Chawan Mushi*. Dice or sliver any or all of the following: lotus root, carrot, mushroom, ginkgo nuts, green peas, trefoil, burdock root. Simmer in Sweetened Shoyu Broth (p. 40) until just tender. Place 3 tablespoons of the vegetables in the bottom of each custard cup before pouring in the soymilk-solidifier mixture; wait several minutes. Poke a few vegetable pieces into the surface of the solidifying curds and sprinkle a few pieces on top.

*Sweetened Kinugoshi with Fruits: Fill each of 5 custard cups about two-thirds full with fresh strawberries, thinly-sliced peaches, bananas, or apples. Prepare one-half of the regular recipe for Homemade Soymilk (p. 204). Stir quickly into the hot soymilk: 1 to 2 tablespoons honey, ¼ teaspoon vanilla extract, and 3/8 teaspoon calcium sulfate solidifier. Pour the mixture immediately into the cups to cover the fruits. Allow to cool, then cover with plastic wrap and chill before serving.

*Rich Kinugoshi Custard Dessert: Add ½ cup powdered milk (soy or dairy) to 3¼ cups hot soymilk just before stirring in ¾ teaspoon calcium sulfate solidifier. Pour mixture immediately into cups. Serve chilled as is, or top with a small amount of honey, dark brown sugar, maple syrup, or crunchy granola. Or serve accompanied by any of the shoyu dipping sauces and garnishes used with Chilled Tofu (p. 105).

Homemade Soft Tofu   MAKES 23 TO 25 OUNCES

"Soft Tofu" is made by pressing kinugoshi in a cloth-lined settling container. The result is firmer, more cohesive, and less delicate than kinugoshi, but softer, smoother, and higher-yielding than regular tofu. Always use calcium sulfate solidifier.

Prepare Homemade Soymilk (p. 204), but heat 2½ (rather than ¼) cups water in the cooking pot and rinse the okara with ½ (rather than ¼) cup water. Solidify as for Homemade

Kinugoshi (p. 215), using ½ teaspoon calcium sulfate. After stirring in solidifier, allow tofu to stand for about 8 minutes, then carefully ladle the soft curds in large, unbroken scoops into the cloth-lined settling container (as for regular Homemade Tofu, p. 99.) Avoid leaving gaps between adjacent scoops of curds. Put on the lid and press with a ½-pound weight for about 5 minutes, then add 1½ pounds more and press for an additional 20 minutes, or until whey no longer drips from the settling container. Cool under water for 10 to 15 minutes before removing cloths from tofu. Serve as for Chilled Tofu (p. 105).

Homemade Kinugoshi   MAKES 25 OUNCES
(from Powdered Soymilk)

This is a good way to make tofu on a camping trip since the ingredients are lightweight and the only utensils required are a 2-quart pot and a measuring cup. The tofu takes only 8 to 10 minutes to prepare and 20 minutes more to cool and firm. We find the flavor of the tofu is greatly improved by the addition of any of the ingredients mentioned in the variations for Kinugoshi Custard (p. 216), or the first 5 variations to Homemade Kinugoshi (p. 215).

Using 1 cup powdered soymilk, prepare Homemade Soymilk (p. 204). Using any of the solidifiers in the same amounts listed in the recipe for Homemade Kinugoshi (p. 215), quickly combine the solidifier with 2 tablespoons water in a small cup, stirring until dissolved. Now stir the solidifier solution into the hot soymilk. If calcium sulfate solidifier is used, the soymilk-solidifier mixture may be poured into cups to make Kinugoshi Custard (p. 216).

Rich Kinugoshi with Milk   MAKES 24 OUNCES
(Mineoka-dofu)

Using 1 cup powdered soymilk, 1½ cups dairy milk, and 1½ cups water, prepare Homemade Soymilk (from powdered soymilk, see above). Solidify with ¾ teaspoon calcium sulfate and allow to cool and firm either in a pot or in individual cups (as for Kinugoshi Custard). Serve chilled as is, or top with a little honey, maple syrup, or dark brown sugar.

Modified Kinugoshi

True kinugoshi is solidified with a salt (such as nigari or calcium sulfate) or an acid (such as lactone or lactic acid) each of which coagulates soybean protein. But soymilk can also be solidified with other jelling agents to create tofu with a soft, homogeneous texture similar to kinugoshi. To solidify 3¼ cups (homemade) soymilk use any of the following: 2 sticks (16 gm) of agar, as for Takigawa-dofu (p. 210); ½ cup *kuzu*, arrowroot, or cornstarch, as for Kuzu Mochi (p. 209); a mixture of ½ teaspoon each calcium sulfate and cornstarch; 3 or 4 well beaten eggs, as for Egg Tofu (p. 267).

KINUGOSHI DISHES FROM SASA-NO-YUKI

The following ten recipes come from Tokyo's famous *Sasa-no-Yuki* restaurant (p. 307) where the kinugoshi is made "on the spot."

Chilled Kinugoshi *(Hiya-yakko)*   SERVES 1

Most of the kinugoshi served in Japan is prepared in this simple way, which makes possible the full enjoyment of the kinugoshi's subtly sweet flavor and delicate texture. The kinugoshi at Sasa-no-Yuki is so soft that you can just barely pick it up with chopsticks. This and the recipe that follows are the owner's favorites.

6 to 8 ounces fresh kinugoshi
1 to 2 tablespoons shoyu
1 tablespoon thinly sliced rounds of leeks, soaked in cold
    water for 1 minute and drained
½ teaspoon grated gingerroot

Cut kinugoshi into 1-inch cubes and float with ice cubes in a shallow bowl of iced water. Serve accompanied by 2 tiny dishes (2½ inches in diameter and ¾ inch deep), one containing shoyu and one containing the leeks and gingerroot. Add condiments to shoyu to taste, then transfer several kinugoshi cubes into shoyu using a slotted spoon. For best flavor, cut and eat tofu with chopsticks.

Kinugoshi with Yuzu-Miso   SERVES 2
    (Yuzumiso-dofu)

6 ounces kinugoshi
2 teaspoons Yuzu Miso (p. 42)

Parboil tofu (p. 37), then cut into four ½-inch-thick pieces. Divide tofu pieces between 2 small, shallow bowls. Top each piece with a dab of the miso. Serve immediately, while still warm.

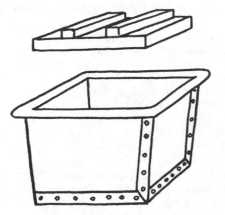

Fig. 86. Sasa-no-Yuki's Gisei-dofu container

Kinugoshi Gisei-dofu   MAKES 25 SERVINGS

At Sasa-no-Yuki—as at many traditional tofu shops—this tasty dish is cooked in a specially designed copper container into which fits a 1-inch-thick wooden pressing lid (fig. 86). The Sasa-no-Yuki container is 6 inches deep, 7½ inches square at the bottom, and 8½ inches square at the top. This recipe may also be prepared in an 8-inch skillet or baking tin: when doing so, omit paper and reduce oil by one-half.

5 tablespoons oil
3 pounds kinugoshi, ground (p. 98) (about 4½ cups)
1 3/8 cup sugar
4 2/3 tablespoons shoyu
8 2/3 tablespoons *mirin*
3 eggs

Heat copper container or skillet over a burner for 30 seconds, then coat bottom and lower walls of container with 2 tablespoons oil. Line bottom with a sheet of white *(washi)* stationery paper cut to just cover the entire surface. Brush paper with 1½ teaspoons oil.

In a large pot, combine tofu, sugar, shoyu, and 6 2/3 tablespoons *mirin*. Mix for 2 minutes with a large wooden paddle or spoon to develop cohesiveness. Cook over medium heat, stirring constantly, for about 5 minutes. Remove from heat, break in eggs, and stir for 2 minutes more.

Spoon tofu-egg mixture into the paper-lined container, press firmly into the corners with backs of fingers, and smooth surface with fingertips. Cover with a wooden pressing lid and a 6- to 8-pound weight. Cook over low heat for 15 minutes, turning container ¼ turn every 5 minutes to ensure even heating. Now and then, run a metal spatula down the walls of the container to help release steam and prevent cracks from forming in center of tofu.

Remove from heat. Pressing lid against tofu with one hand and holding container in the other, invert container and lift off, leaving tofu inverted on lid. Now place a second pressing lid on top of tofu and invert again so that tofu is upright on the second lid. Remove used paper, re-oil bottom of container with 2 tablespoons oil, and re-line bottom with a fresh piece of paper. Brush paper with remaining 1½ teaspoons oil. Holding cooking container with one hand and pressing lid topped with tofu in the other, invert container over lid. Pressing tofu against bottom of container, quickly return container to upright position leaving tofu with uncooked surface facing downward. Re-weight and cook for 10 minutes over medium heat. Invert tofu on pressing lid once again and remove from container. Brush top and sides of golden brown tofu with 2 tablespoons *mirin* and allow to cool. Cut tofu into 25 equal squares, cut each square into halves, and serve 2 halves on a small plate to each person (fig. 52, p. 152).

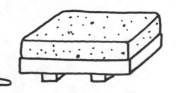

Fig. 87. Kinugoshi with Ankake Sauce

Place tofu in a small—4½-inch-diameter, 2½-inch-deep—heat resistant bowl. Break in the egg and place the fish on the tofu. Place bowl in a heated steamer (p. 38) or over a pan of hot water in an oven. Steam for 10 minutes or until egg is just firm. Pour on shoyu and top with lemon. Serve hot.

Warm Kinugoshi with Ankake Sauce (Ankake-dofu)

SERVES 2

From the year 1704, when Sasa-no-Yuki first began to make and serve tofu, until 1926, this was the only dish offered at the restaurant. The story is still told that many generations ago a famous samurai, having enjoyed one dish of Ankake-dofu, asked if he might be permitted to order another. In memory of that occasion, two small dishes of this speciality have been offered to each guest ever since (fig. 87).

12 ounces kinugoshi
1¼ cups Mild Ankake Sauce (p. 49), well warmed
½ teaspoon hot mustard

Parboil tofu (p. 96). Cut tofu horizontally, then crosswise into halves. Divide among 4 small bowls and top with warm sauce and a dab of mustard. Offer each guest 2 servings.

Warm Kinugoshi with Shoyu, Mustard, and Leeks (Kijoyu)

SERVES 1

4 ounces kinugoshi
1 tablespoon shoyu, warmed
1/8 teaspoon hot mustard
1½ teaspoons thinly-sliced rounds of leek, soaked in cold water for 1 minute and drained

Parboil tofu (p. 96), then cut tofu into halves and place in a small bowl. Mix shoyu with mustard and pour over tofu. Serve topped with leeks.

Chiri-mushi
(Kinugoshi Steamed with Egg in Lemon-Shoyu)

SERVES 1

3 ounces kinugoshi
1 egg
1 thin slice of white fish meat (2 by 3 inches), or substitute 1 large mushroom
1 tablespoon shoyu
A thin half-moon of lemon

Kinugoshi-Egg Custard with Ankake (Kuya-dofu or Kuya-mushi)

SERVES 4

8 ounces kinugoshi
1 egg
2 teaspoons shoyu
1½ teaspoons sugar
1 cup dashi (p. 39), stock, or water
¼ cup Mild Ankake Sauce (p. 49)
2 tablespoons cooked hamburger (optional)
Dash of pepper
15 to 20 strips of toasted *nori*, each 1½ by 1/8 inch

Cut tofu into fourths and divide among 4 custard or *Chawan-mushi* cups. Combine egg, shoyu, sugar, and dashi in a bowl, mixing well, then divide among the 4 cups filling each ½ to 2/3 full. Place cups in a heated steamer (p. 38), and steam for about 10 minutes or until custard is firm. Pour in warm Ankake Sauce to a depth of about 3/8 inch. Divide hamburger among the 4 cups and top with a sprinkling of pepper and the "pine needles" of *nori*. Cover with a small lid and serve while still hot.

Scrambled Kinugoshi (Iridofu)

SERVES 4 TO 6

½ cup thinly sliced *shiitake* mushrooms
1 tablespoon bamboo shoots, cut into thin ginkgo leaves (p. 37)
1 tablespoon diced chicken (optional)
2 tablespoons sugar
½ teaspoon salt
2 teaspoons shoyu
2 tablespoons water, stock, or dashi (p. 39)
2 cups ground kinugoshi (p. 98) (use about 2 pounds fresh kinukoshi)
2 eggs, lightly beaten
2 tablespoons green peas, parboiled (p. 37)

Combine the first seven ingredients in a skillet; simmer, stirring occasionally, for about 5 minutes. Meanwhile combine ground tofu and eggs in bowl, mixing well. Stir tofu-and-egg mixture into cooking vegetables and simmer, stirring constantly, for about 10 minutes, or until mixture is light, dry, and crumbly. Allow to cool. Divide among small bowls and serve topped with green peas.

Kinugoshi Miso Soup

SERVES 6

The following is a description of how miso soup is prepared each morning at Sasa-no-Yuki; the amounts have been reduced to about one-eighth their actual figures.

1½ cups (5 ounces) dried *shiitake* mushrooms, soaked overnight in 2 cups water
½ cup (¾ ounce) round-herring flakes *(urume iwashi)*
½ cup (medium salty) light-yellow miso
1/3 cup Hatcho miso
5½ cups water
60 (canned) *nameko* mushrooms
12 ounces kinugoshi, cut into 3/8-inch cubes
18 trefoil leaves (including stems)

Pour mushrooms into a colander set over a pot. Press mushrooms gently but firmly against bottom of colander to expel remaining liquid, then reserve mushrooms for use in other cooking. Bring mushroom soaking water to a boil over high heat. Skim off any foam that may develop, then add herring flakes and return to the boil. Reduce heat to low, simmer for 5 minutes, and turn off heat.

Meanwhile, combine light-yellow and Hatcho miso with ¾ cup warm water in a mixing bowl. Mix well until miso is dissolved. Pour herring dashi through a fine-mesh strainer set over the mixing bowl and press the herring flakes (in the strainer) to expel all remaining liquid.

Combine herring flakes with 2 cups water in a saucepan to make a Number 2 Dashi (p. 39). Bring dashi to a boil, reduce heat to low, cover pan, and simmer for 5 minutes.

While Number 2 dashi is simmering, pour miso-dashi mixture through a fine-mesh strainer set over the pot. Remove particles of miso grain left in strainer, and mix with 2 cups warm water. Pour mixture back through strainer into pot, reserving miso grain particles for use in other cooking.

Pour Number 2 dashi through strainer into pot; discard herring flakes remaining in strainer. Bring the dashi in pot just to a boil, then add *nameko* mushrooms and tofu. Serve piping hot, garnished with trefoil leaves.

OTHER WAYS OF SERVING KINUGOSHI

Kinugoshi can be used in place of regular tofu in many preparations. It is particularly delicious in Fruit Cocktail Chilled Tofu (p. 148), on toast and sandwiches, with fried eggs, in soups, and topped with sauces. In Japan, during the wintertime, it is very popular in Simmering Tofu (p. 142) and many of the various tofu *nabe* dishes (p. 143).

Deep-fried Kinugoshi

SERVES 2 OR 3

Although kinugoshi's delicate texture and high water content make it somewhat difficult to deep-fry, it can be done, and the results are well worth the effort. Its crisp breaded crust enfolds a soft, creamy texture.

12 ounces kinugoshi, cut into 1½-inch-squares about ½ inch thick
2 tablespoons sweet white miso
1½ teaspoons natural sugar
Dash of *sansho* pepper (optional)
¼ cup flour
1 egg, lightly beaten
Oil for deep-frying
Shoyu

Arrange tofu squares on a large plate. Combine miso, sugar, and pepper, mixing well, then use the mixture to coat the upper surface of each tofu square. Matching their coated surfaces, gently press the pieces together, two at a time, to form "sandwiches." Carefully dust each sandwich with flour, dip in beaten egg, and deep-fry until golden brown (p. 130). Serve topped with a few drops of shoyu.

12
Grilled Tofu

S MORNING and evening cool and late summer turns into early fall, many tofu shops gradually stop making kinugoshi and shift their attention to grilled tofu (*yaki-dofu*). Easily recognized by its speckled brown surface and distinctive barbecue-broiled flavor and aroma, a cake of grilled tofu is a little longer and thinner than one of regular tofu. And unlike regular tofu, which is so soft and yielding, grilled tofu is firm and compact, its texture resembling that of Chinese-style doufu. Simmered in Sukiyaki and other types of *nabe* cookery, or skewered and broiled to make Dengaku, it always keeps its shape. And because it contains relatively little water, it readily absorbs the flavors of seasoned broths, soups, or casseroles.

Grilled tofu is prepared from the same curds used to make regular tofu. However, to create a strong, cohesive structure, the tofu maker stirs these curds in the curding barrel until they break into fine particles. Then, after ladling off more whey than usual, he places the curds quickly (and rather roughly) into the settling box and presses them with a heavy weight (10 to 12 pounds) for a relatively long time (40 to 50 minutes). Finally, he cuts the finished tofu into cakes about 5 inches long, 3 inches wide, and 2 inches thick, and these he presses for about one hour between alternate layers of bamboo mats sandwiched between large wooden boards (as when pressing tofu to make thick agé; fig. 61, p. 180). At each step in the process, the tofu becomes firmer and more compact so that it will hold together when skewered and grilled over a charcoal fire.

A traditional master grills tofu with the effortless precision of a circus juggler and the speed of a chuckwagon flapjack cook. Sitting squarely in front of a small, round charcoal brazier, he places two iron bars on opposite sides of its glowing mouth. Using a sturdy, metal skewer about 12 inches long, he then pierces a cake of well-pressed tofu to the hilt and sets it over the hot coals (fig. 88). Quickly skewering a second cake, he flips over the first and slides it to the opposite side of the brazier, while setting the second in its place and skewering a third. At just the right instant—a second too long and the tofu will burn, too short and it will lack the proper color and aroma—the master snatches the first cake from the fire, checks to see that its surfaces are nicely browned, and plunges it into a tub of cold water, withdrawing the skewer. He then flips over the second cake, sets a third in its place, and skewers the next piece. With a small paper fan, he sends several quick strokes of air down into the live embers. The charcoal-broiled fragrance of the sizzling tofu fills the shop and a thin curl of white smoke rises through a shaft of morning sunlight.

(In the spirit of traditional craftsmanship, nothing is wasted. When the work is done, the coals—which were originally scooped from the dying fire under the cauldron—will be placed in a charcoal brazier and used to warm the living room and boil the morning tea.)

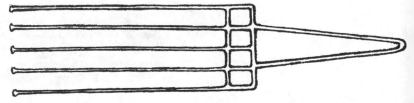

Fig. 88. Traditional master making grilled tofu

Grilled tofu may have been one of the earliest ways of preparing tofu in Japan. Since it is not found at all in present-day Taiwan or mentioned in writings on Chinese tofu, this variety may be another Japanese invention. In many Japanese farmhouses, regular tofu was generally broiled around a bed of coals in the open-hearth fireplace. Country-style tofu, made very firm (see p. 271), lent itself well to skewering without the need for additional pressing. And broiling the tofu—especially during long winter evening—gave the family a chance to come together near the warmth and light of the fire. Skewered on specially-cut pieces of bamboo (below), the freshly-

grilled tofu was either served sizzling hot, seasoned with a little miso or shoyu, or used as a basic ingredient in miso soups, Nishime, Oden, or Simmering Tofu.

Even today, many of Japan's rural festivals are not considered complete unless they end with a fireside feast featuring grilled tofu. We've witnessed one such feast in a small village in Japan's snowy northeast provinces. At its conclusion, a large bonfire was built and all the members of the village gathered round. After each person had prepared a 2-foot-long bamboo skewer, the village tofu makers passed around cakes of freshly prepared tofu. With flames

leaping and everyone singing and clapping in time to the rhythmic beating of huge drums, the skewered tofu was stuck upright in the ground as near to the fire as possible, then snatched back when done. The grilled tofu, together with hot sake, was served late into the night.

Grilled tofu's ancient ancestor may have been prepared without skewers on a lightly oiled, hot iron griddle—a method still used in a few rural tofu shops and farmhouses. Apparently, the predecessor of the present round charcoal brazier used in tofu shops was an oblong brazier about 2 feet long. We have watched one highly-skilled tofu maker prepare five cakes of grilled tofu at once on such a brazier using an elaborate version of the method described earlier (fig. 89). On the whole, the use of live coals and the traditional skewers is rapidly disappearing. Most Japanese shops now arrange cakes of well-pressed tofu on metal trays or thick wooden boards and broil them under the flame of a hand-held, propane blow torch. In more modern shops, the tofu-containing metal tray is placed on rollers and passed slowly under several rows of propane burners. This modern variety of grilled tofu—recognizable by the absence of skewer holes—is similar in appearance to traditional grilled tofu, but lacks the latter's charcoal aroma and some of its ability to absorb flavors during cooking.

Open-hearth grilling

Fig. 89. An early method of elaborate grilling

Grilled tofu is one of the featured ingredients in Japan's New Year's cuisine. In accordance with an ancient custom, no fresh food is cooked during the first three—and sometimes the first seven—days of the new year. Thus, during the last two days in December, most housewives are busy from morning until night preparing the New Year's food and setting it aside in special layered, lacquerware boxes reserved for the occasion. Since the basic New Year's dishes were standardized in the centuries before refrigeration, the only foods used traditionally were those which could be kept fresh for a fairly long time. Since grilled tofu stayed fresh longer than regular tofu (due in part to its low water content and in part to the effects of broiling) it was chosen as the ideal variety for use in the holiday menu. Moreover, since it was very firm, grilled tofu could be simmered in sweetened shoyu broths—which acted as a natural preservative—without losing its form so that it looked attractive when served. Today used most widely

in a dish called New Year's Nishime (p. 178), grilled tofu is said to reach its peak of goodness several days after it has been cooked, when the flavors of the broth and fresh vegetables have mellowed and permeated it.

The tofu maker spends the last few days of the old year working from morning until night trying to fill all his orders for grilled tofu. At the end of the year's work, as the great temple bells throughout Japan sound the midnight hour, the master may use his freshly-made grilled tofu to prepare a special type of Dengaku. He spreads one entire surface of the cake with a thin layer of miso, then broils the miso quickly until it is fragrant and flecked with brown. This steaming hot Dengaku, a small feast in itself, is meant to welcome in the new year.

Many of our fellow Westerners have been surprised to learn that tofu is one of the indispensable ingredients in Japan's most famous overseas dish: Sukiyaki. If you have ever tasted real Sukiyaki, you have also tasted grilled tofu. Indeed, in Japan, more grilled tofu is used in Sukiyaki than in any other type of cuisine.

In Western cookery, grilled tofu is particularly suited to the barbeque and broiler. You can prepare your own over the live coals of an outdoor barbeque, a small indoor Japanese-style brazier, or in an oven broiler. Or try cooking pre-grilled tofu in these various ways, treating it almost as if it were a large steak and basting it with a favorite sauce. Grilled tofu can also be substituted in most recipes calling for regular tofu and is especially delicious in Western-style egg dishes.

Grilled tofu is usually about 10 percent more expensive than regular tofu since each cake is larger, contains less water, and requires additional time, effort, and fuel to prepare. In Japan, its season usually comes to an end in March or April, when the tofu maker packs away his charcoal brazier and begins to prepare kinugoshi.

At present in the United States, fresh grilled tofu is available in only a few areas. An imported, canned variety called *yaki-dofu* or Baked Bean Curd is sold at some Japanese markets, but the tofu loses much of its flavor and fine texture in canning and after lengthy storage. For best results, make your own.

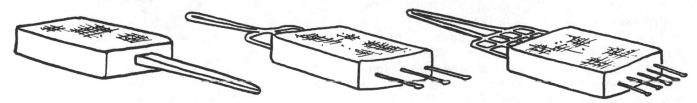

Homemade Grilled Tofu

Grilled tofu can be prepared quickly and easily at home.

Preparing the Tofu: Firm Chinese-style doufu may be grilled without additional preparation. Regular commercial tofu should be thoroughly pressed between layers of toweling or bamboo mats (p. 97) before skewering, but may be broiled in an oven broiler without pressing if you are in a hurry or want a softer texture. When preparing Homemade Tofu (p. 99) to be made into grilled tofu, use a nigari-type solidifier if possible, ladle the curds into the settling container rather quickly and roughly, and press the curds with a fairly heavy weight for a longer time than usual. Cut the finished tofu into 2-inch-thick pieces and press again in toweling or between bamboo mats.

Grilling or Broiling: The appropriateness of the cooking method depends first on whether or not the tofu is to be skewered, and second on the nature of your heat source. A charcoal or wood fire gives the best flavor.

Skewered Tofu

1. *Charcoal Brazier:* Skewer 12-ounce cakes of pressed tofu from one end using a pronged metal skewer, two metal shish kebab-type skewers, two sturdy bamboo skewers which have been soaked in (salted) water, or a large fork with tynes longer than the tofu. Place 2 parallel bars across the brazier to support both ends of the skewers. Grill each piece of tofu for about 15 to 30 seconds on each side, or until nicely browned.

2. *Open-Hearth Fireplace or Campfire* (planted skewer style): Prepare skewers 12 to 18 inches long by sharpening both ends of a flat, 1-inch-wide piece of bamboo or wood; skewer tofu from one end. Plant the base of the skewer upright in the ashes or ground near the bed of coals so that the tofu leans slightly over the coals and each side of the tofu browns in 1 to 2 minutes.

3. *Open Fire or Stove-Top Burner* (marshmallow style): Skewer the tofu with a long metal fork or forked stick. Hold just above the flames or coals and brown on both sides.

Unskewered Tofu

1. *Oven Broiler:* Place 12-ounce cakes of tofu (pressed or unpressed) on a lightly-oiled baking sheet or sheet of aluminum foil and broil for 3 to 5 minutes on both sides until nicely browned.

2. *Barbeque or Brazier:* Place well-pressed tofu on the grill or grating like a steak. When one side is nicely browned, turn over with a large spatula or fork.

3. *Griddle:* Heat a heavy griddle and coat lightly with oil. Fry each cake of tofu on both sides until golden brown. Turn with a wide-blade knife or spatula. Country-style grilled tofu is still prepared in this way.

Serving or Storing Grilled Tofu: Grilled tofu is most delicious when served still hot and fragrant, as in the following recipe. However if you wish to save some homemade grilled tofu for later use, plunge the hot tofu into a large container of (circulating) cold water as soon as the tofu is removed from the fire. Allow tofu to cool thoroughly, then place in a covered container and refrigerate. If tofu is to be stored for more than 24 hours, refrigerate in cold water to cover.

Sizzling Grilled Tofu *(Quick and Easy)*

These simple serving suggestions are for connoisseurs who prepare their own grilled tofu at home and want to enjoy it "fresh from the fire" when its flavor and aroma are at their peak.

Grilled Tofu with Miso: Cut the cake of freshly grilled tofu horizontally into halves. Place each half on a plate with the grilled side up. Coat with your favorite variety of Sweet Simmered Miso (p. 41) or Finger Lickin' Miso (p. 31). Serve immediately.

Country-style Tofu Dengaku: Prepare grilled tofu skewered and grilled over a bed of coals. When tofu is golden brown, spread both large surfaces with a thin coating of red, barley, or Hatcho miso; broil for about 1 minute more on each side until miso is fragrant. Invite each guest to hold the tofu "popsicle-style" while eating.

Grilled Tofu Steak: Marinate tofu for 30 to 60 minutes before grilling, using Teriyaki (p. 48) or your favorite steak sauce. Grill slowly, basting lightly with the marinade. Serve topped with marinade or Ketchup-Worcestershire Sauce (p. 49).

*Serve the hot tofu with any of the dipping sauces and garnishes used with Chilled Tofu (p. 105). Cut tofu as for Grilled Tofu with Miso, above.

*Serve cubes of freshly grilled tofu topped with Ankake Sauce (p. 49) and a little slivered gingerroot; or with grated *daikon* and a little shoyu.

Sukiyaki

A Japanese cookbook written over 350 years ago contains the following recipe for *Sukiyaki:* "Obtain either wild goose, wild duck, or antelope, and soak the meat in *tamari shoyu*. Heat a well-used Chinese plow *(kara-suki)* over an open fire. Place the meat on the plow, garnish with thin rounds of *yuzu*, and broil on both sides until the color changes. Serve and be happy."

The word *sukiyaki*—pronounced skee-ya-kee—means "broiled on the blade of a plow." Although the modern preparation generally features beef as the basic ingredient, sukiyaki was traditionally prepared with wild game, fowl, fish, or shellfish. Wild boar was also a favored ingredient, and seafoods such as tuna, yellowtail, whale, wreath shells, and scallops were and, in areas such as Kyoto, still are widely used in the dish.

Before reaching its present form, sukiyaki passed through a number of unusual historical transformations. The earliest preparation was undoubtedly developed by farmers, hunters, and fishermen who broiled their catch over an open fire using a plow or whatever other utensil was available. Since the earliest plow, the predecessor of the present *nabe*, was nothing but a flat iron plate, it was unable to hold cooking liquids. It was probably for this reason that the meat came to be marinated or basted with tamari shoyu, a technique that is still practiced in some Japanese restaurants. Gradually, sake or *mirin* came to be used in the marinade, various vegetables and grilled tofu were broiled with the meat, and the traditional flat plow or griddle became inadequate to hold the juices of this cornucopia of new ingredients. A new container was needed, and at this point, the ancient tradition of broiling wild meat on a plow merged with the newly-imported tradition of *shippoku*, a type of beef-*nabe* cookery which originated about 300 years ago, just after the first contact with Western traders and missionaries.

Developed in the international port town of Nagasaki, *shippoku* was said to have its historical culinary roots in Holland, Portugal, China, and Korea. As a result of the merger, the original sukiyaki ingredients eventually came to be cooked in heavy iron or Korean-style stone pots, and the dish was served as a one-pot meal prepared at the table. Consequently "sukiyaki" became a misnomer, for the new dish was neither broiled nor prepared on a griddle-like plow. But neither was the new sukiyaki a true *nabe* dish, since its ingredients were not simmered in a seasoned broth. Rather, this unique Japanese creation straddled three categories: it was a broiled dish insofar as the meat was first cooked in a sizzling-hot pan; it was a *nabe* dish since it was a one-pot dish prepared at the dining table; and it was a *nimono*, or simmered dish, insofar as the meat and vegetables were simmered together in a rich mixture of shoyu, sake, and dashi.

Up until this time, the Japanese had never apparently considered using beef or other livestock in sukiyaki. According to a popular legend, *kamado-gami*, the god of the kitchen hearth, is said to have instructed the Japanese people in ancient times to refrain from eating the meat of all four-legged animals, especially of livestock. This admonition was reinforced by the nation's emperors and the vegetarian teachings

of Buddhism, so that for about 1200 years—from the 8th until the 19th century—most Japanese did not eat meat. However with the arrival of Christianity in the 16th century, and the public knowledge that missionaries considered meat important in the diet, some Japanese—and particularly Christian converts—came to know its taste. But with the expulsion of Christianity from Japan in the late 16th century, the eating of beef was also forbidden, and sukiyaki was once again prepared exclusively with seafood, wild game, or poultry. Those who developed a longing for broiled meat, but who were not allowed to prepare it in the family's common pot or in the presence of those who kept the faith, were compelled as a last resort to prepare their sukiyaki in the traditional way, substituting a plow or mattock for the kettle and enjoying the forbidden delicacy alone and in secret in the barn, field, or forest. This tradition of "underground sukiyaki" is said to have continued until about 1900.

With the opening of Japan to the West in the mid 19th century and the relaxation of traditional prohibitions, meat eating gradually became fashionable in the cities. Yet most Japanese tasted their first beef with considerable trepidation, having been warned by priests and traditionalists that their action was an affront to their ancestors and that dire consequences would befall them. Little by little, however, beef sukiyaki came to be accepted.

The first Japanese who worked up the courage to actually eat beef did not prepare it Western-style as steak or roast beef. Rather, they cut the meat into paper-thin slices, employing the same method they had used for centuries to prepare *sashimi*, or raw fish. And they seasoned this meat with shoyu in much the same way they would season simmered vegetable or tofu dishes. Many Japanese probably ate their first beef in the form of sukiyaki, and different parts of the country soon developed unique styles of serving it. To this day in the Kyoto area, restaurants place dispensers of shoyu, *mirin*, and sugar on the table and allow each guest to season his food to taste, whereas restaurants in Tokyo have developed their own unique mixtures of these ingredients to form standard cooking liquids.

Throughout the world people now associate sukiyaki with fine Japanese cookery. In a sense, this is ironic because Japanese cuisine still makes relatively little use of meat, and much of sukiyaki's historical influence came from abroad. The ancient delicacy of Japanese hunters and the imported *nabe* preparation have now been totally transformed to become Japan's most famous international dish. And although tofu plays a relatively inconspicuous role in creating the flavor of this dish, sukiyaki has nevertheless been the vehicle whereby thousands of Westerners have had their first taste of "soybean curd."

Although most present-day sukiyaki uses beef as the featured ingredient, our recipe uses ganmodoki—mock goose—in deference to the earliest traditions of using wild fowl. Homemade frozen tofu and frozen thick-agé, the textures of which resemble that of tender beef, make excellent substitutes. Although regular tofu is occasionally used in sukiyaki, grilled tofu is generally preferred for its ability to absorb the flavors in the rich broth; its substantial, almost meaty texture; its ability to keep its form during the frequent stirring; and its barbeque flavor. In Japan, more grilled tofu is used in sukiyaki than in any other type of cuisine.

3 tablespoons oil
12 ounces ganmo; or 4 pieces of frozen or dried-frozen tofu (p. 229); or 12 ounces (frozen) thick-agé or gluten cutlets, cut crosswise into ¾-inch-thick strips
12 ounces grilled tofu, cut into ¾-inch cubes
4 leeks, including green portions, cut diagonally into 2-inch lengths; or 10 green (or 4 regular) onions, thinly sliced
4 ounces trefoil or spinach leaves
8 ounces *konnyaku* noodles, parboiled and cut into thirds
8 small cakes of dried wheat gluten, reconstituted (p. 37) (optional)
8 *(shiitake)* mushrooms, thinly sliced
4 ounces chrysanthemum leaves, watercress, or Chinese cabbage, cut into 2-inch-wide strips
2 small bamboo shoots, thinly sliced and parboiled (p. 37)
Sukiyaki-Shoyu Mixture:
  ¼ cup dashi (p. 39), stock, or water
  ½ cup shoyu
  ¼ cup sake
  ¼ cup *mirin* or 3 tablespoons natural sugar
4 eggs

Arrange tofu and vegetables on a large platter. Preheat a 10- to 12-inch skillet set on a tabletop burner, or set an electric skillet to 350°. Coat skillet with the oil, add about one-third of each of the tofu and vegetable ingredients, and sprinkle with one-third of the shoyu mixture. Cook over medium heat for 5 to 6 minutes, turning ingredients gently from time to time. Using chopsticks or long-handled forks, serve from the skillet an ingredients become done. Replenish the sauce and each ingredient, and continue cooking while the guests eat.

To serve, each person breaks a raw egg into his serving bowl and beats it lightly with chopsticks. The tofu and vegetables are dipped into the egg, then eaten. The usual accompaniment for sukiyaki is plain rice. Reserve any leftover sauce to use when sautéing other vegetable dishes, or as a broth for noodles.

Alternate ingredients and seasonings include celery stalks, bean sprouts, green peppers, thinly sliced carrots or *daikon*, and slender white *enokidake* mushrooms. Season with pepper and hot mustard, and garnish with a little parsley.

Other ways of Serving Grilled Tofu

Grilled tofu may be used in place of regular tofu with excellent results on sandwiches and toast, in egg dishes and soups, and in sautéed vegetable and grain dishes. In Japan it is particularly popular in Tofu Dengaku (p. 139), Simmering Tofu (p. 142) and most other *nabe* cookery, Oden or Nikomi Oden (p. 175), New Year's *Osechi* Nishime (p. 178), Noppei Soup (p. 163), and Miso Soup (p. 118).

In country farmhouses grilled tofu is used in a Nishime stew in which it is combined in a large iron pot with *daikon*, potatoes, *konnyaku*, seasonal vegetables, and an unsweetened miso broth which may include dried fish. The stew is simmered for at least 30 minutes and served steaming hot on winter evenings.

Farmhouse Sukiyaki with grilled tofu

13

Frozen
and Dried-frozen Tofu

THE METHOD for preparing frozen tofu was first discovered in the cold mountainous regions of northern China about 1,000 to 1,500 years ago. It was found that if regular tofu was cut into ½-inch-thick slabs, arranged on boards or bamboo mats, and then set out in the snow overnight until frozen solid, the structure and basic character of the tofu underwent a radical transformation. All the water in the tofu—about 86 percent of the tofu's total weight—turned to ice, and the protein and other solids congealed into a lacy but firm network. When the frozen tofu was later placed in warm water, the ice thawed, leaving only the network of protein and solids; this network looked like a beige, fine-grained natural sponge or a zwieback biscuit. With the loss of water, the tofu became a highly concentrated source of protein and energy. Like a delicate sponge, it was resilient, highly absorbent, and cohesive enough to hold together when pressed or cooked. Its soft texture was appealing and, in some types of cooking, seemed remarkably similar to that of very tender meat. This tofu had its own special flavor, which was enhanced by the flavors it so readily absorbed when simmered or sautéed.

As well as showing a way to transform regular tofu into a completely new food with unique uses in cooking, the discovery of frozen tofu also made it possible to preserve tofu—otherwise highly perishable—for long periods of time. After the arrival of frozen tofu in Japan over 1,000 years ago, it became possible for families in country farmhouses or monks in snowbound temples to make a large quantity of tofu, freeze what wasn't eaten, and then enjoy tofu daily for as long as the supply lasted, or until

the snows melted. In rural areas, where there were no tofu shops, this saved the time and fuel required to make a small batch of fresh tofu every few days. Since it was almost impossible to obtain fish or other seafoods during the winter in the snowy mountain provinces, frozen tofu became a popular element in the daily diet and was soon known throughout much of Japan as "one-night frozen tofu."

Made almost exclusively in rural farmhouses and temples, frozen tofu has never been sold at neighborhood tofu shops. At present, many people make it at home by placing fresh tofu into the freezing compartment of their refrigerator. And it is sold on a limited scale in the frozen foods section of some department stores as six ½-inch-thick slices sealed in a cellophane bag. However, it is no longer a common commercial food in Japan, because modern, lightweight, dried-frozen tofu is now available at low prices in the dry goods section of most markets.

For us in the West, though, the process of freezing tofu can be an easy way to ensure a ready supply, either after making a large batch of homemade tofu or after purchasing a large quantity from a store. Homemade frozen tofu will generally have a better flavor than, but will not be quite as light, fine-grained and expansive as, the commercial dried-frozen variety. Since storebought dried-frozen tofu is generally permeated with ammonia gas, baking soda, or other chemical agents which cause the tofu to expand during cooking, homemade frozen tofu will be more natural. The less water the tofu contains and the faster it freezes, the finer will be the grain structure and the more delicate the texture of the finished product. Good quality frozen tofu can be prepared with less than 12 hours of freezing, and may be used immediately or stored under refrigeration indefinitely. It makes an excellent, low-cost replacement for gluten meat or cutlets in vegetarian menus. Thick agé and kinugoshi can also be used to make frozen tofu: the first develops a firm, meaty texture; the second, a fine, delicate consistency.

Dried-frozen Tofu

But preserving tofu by freezing it outdoors had two basic limitations: first, the tofu could only be stored in its frozen form for as long as the air temperature remained below freezing; and, second, the tofu was very heavy and susceptible to thawing when transported from place to place. The Japanese, therefore, began to experiment with drying frozen tofu to create a lightweight, staple food that could be preserved well into springtime. Since this idea seems never to have occurred to the Chinese, dried-frozen tofu is thought to have originated in Japan. Two different traditional methods of freezing and drying arose independently in the snowy, mountainous regions of the nation.

The home of the first experiment, Mount Koya, stands high and solitary in a vast forest of cedars south of Kyoto, Japan's ancient capital. Kobo Daishi, one of Japan's great Buddhist saints, founded a monastery there in 816, and it continues to serve as the headquarters of the Shingon sect of esoteric Buddhism. Tradition has it that the method for making dried-frozen tofu was first discovered there some 750 years ago by a Shingon priest.

The priests and monks living in Mount Koya's snowbound temples chose a day for making tofu when the night temperatures were expected to be bitterly cold and there were winds to help hasten the freezing process in order to give the tofu the desired fine-grained texture. Beginning work in the late afternoon, they prepared a large quantity of firm tofu, cut the cakes into ½-inch-thick slabs, and pressed these in layers between bamboo mats or boards to expel excess water. Waking at about 3 a.m., the coldest hour, they set the tofu out in the snow on the mats or boards in a place that received no direct sunlight during the day.

The next morning, after the tofu slabs had been out in the cold for about 8 hours and were frozen solid, the monks took them into a specially built shed, arranged them on shelves, and allowed them to stand undisturbed (out of direct sunlight) at temperatures below freezing for about one to three weeks. During this second freezing, the tofu slabs developed an even finer grain and firmer structure and became more resilient. They were then thawed in warm water and pressed lightly to expel the melted ice. The entire shed was then heated in much the same way as a sauna (using large charcoal braziers) and each slab was dried until it turned light beige and was as hard and crisp as a zwieback biscuit. It was found that if this dried tofu was stored in a cool, dry place, it could be preserved for about 4 months after the last snows had melted.

Farm villages in the area learned the technique from the monks, and many large freezing and drying sheds were built in the mountain valleys. "Koya-dofu" soon came to be made on a fairly large scale as a communal wintertime occupation and source of income during the lean months. In some areas, an entire village would turn out on cold days and work together, freezing and drying the tofu. By the Edo period (1600-1868) Koya-dofu was known throughout Japan. In 1911, it started to be made on an even larger scale throughout the year using artificial refrigeration.

The second traditional experiment with dried-frozen tofu began about 400 years ago in the cold mountains of Nagano north of Tokyo. A famous samurai warrior, Takeda Shingen, thought of drying frozen tofu to make a lightweight, nutritious food that his soldiers could carry in their backpacks. The soldiers apparently learned how to prepare the tofu, then taught the method to local farmers. After the pieces of well-pressed tofu had been placed overnight in the snow and frozen solid, they were wrapped in straw mats, placed in the shade in a barn or tool shed, and left at below-freezing temperatures for about one week. Then five pieces of tofu at a time were tied together with several pieces of rice straw (fig. 90), and these strands were hung from poles under the eaves of farmhouses (where they received no direct sunlight). After several weeks of thawing during the day and freezing again at night, the tofu became completely dry and crisp.

This technique, which obviated the special drying shed and equipment used on Mount Koya, was simple and inexpensive, so that most tofu of this type came to be made on a small scale by individual farmers. Carrying the light tofu in backpacks, these farmers often walked from village to village selling it as a source of wintertime income. To this day, strands of drying tofu can be seen hanging under the verandas of farmhouses and the eaves of temples throughout the Nagano area (fig. 91).

Today, dried-frozen tofu is produced year round in huge automated factories (most of which are still located in the Nagano area.) Since the tofu is neither perishable nor fragile, it is well suited to centralized, large-scale production and nationwide (or worldwide) distribution. If kept sealed in the airtight cellophane bag in which it is sold, and if stored at room temperature, it has a shelf life of 6 to 8 months during the colder seasons and 4 to 6 months during the warmer ones. Each package is stamped with the date of manufacture to encourage quick use. If stored for too long, dried-frozen tofu loses its softness, freshness, and ability to expand and absorb cooking liquids.

In 1928, it was found that if thawed tofu was steeped in a solution of baking soda before being dried, it swelled during cooking and become softer and more absorbent than the traditional dried-frozen variety. In 1929 it was discovered that thoroughly dried tofu, when permeated with ammonia gas, became even softer and swelled even more than the tofu containing baking powder. Moreover, if the tofu was reconstituted in hot water before use in cooking, the odor and flavor of the ammonia completely disappeared. (The ammonia was not intended as a preservative and, in fact, if the tofu was not treated with ammonia, it stayed fresh longer.)

At present the largest dried-frozen tofu factory employs about 250 workers and over 23 tons of soybeans daily. The only ingredients used are whole soybeans, well water, and calcium chloride nigari solidifier—plus ammonia gas added at the end of the process. The tofu is made in a continuous production line that takes about 25 days from start to finish. The basic techniques are essentially the same as those developed for making Koya-dofu 750 years ago. The first freezing is carried out in a very cold refrigerated room with strong winds provided by huge electric fans. The frozen tofu is then stored in a refrigerated warehouse for 20 days. Finally it is placed on a wide conveyor belt, thawed under a spray of warm water, pressed between heavy rollers, and dried in a 100-yard-long tunnel dryer. Permeated with ammonia in large vacuum chambers, it is

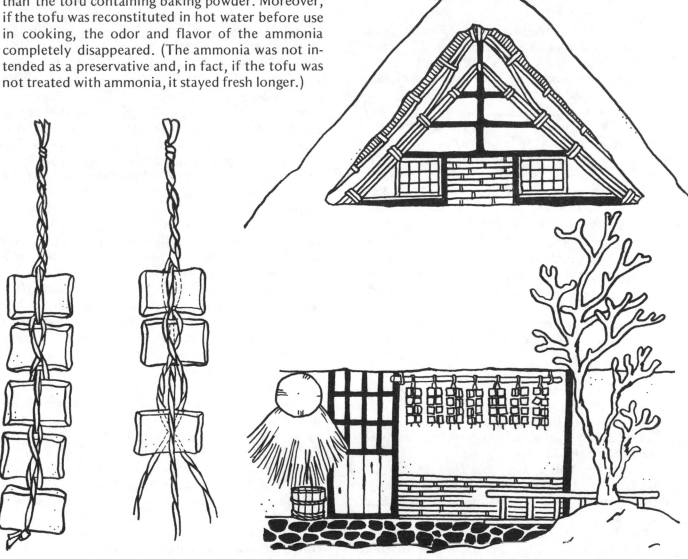

Fig. 90. Tying frozen tofu with rice straw   Fig. 91. Drying farmhouse frozen tofu

sealed 5 to 10 pieces at a time in airtight cellophane bags, packaged in small paper boxes, stamped with the date, and shipped throughout Japan. A small portion of the tofu is also cut into ½-inch cubes for use as soup croutons or ground into meal for use in baked or sautéed dishes. Some of the large factories still make strands of dried tofu tied with rice straw, which are sold mostly as a tourist item.

Present-day dried-frozen tofu differs from both its traditional counterpart and from homemade frozen tofu in that it has a very fine, firm grain structure, and is much softer and more absorbent. When reconstituted, it swells by about 26 percent, as compared with 7 percent in the case of tofu containing no ammonia. Dried-frozen tofu has relatively little flavor of its own: it is used mostly for its texture and ability to acquire flavor from seasoned broths and sauces.

Dried-frozen tofu is also highly valued as a concentrated source of nutrients. It contains 53.4 percent protein and 26.4 percent natural oils, and is only 7 percent carbohydrate and 10 percent water. An excellent energy source, it provides 436 calories per 100 grams, and contains more than 7 times the amount of protein and energy as an equal weight of regular tofu. In Japan, it is advertized as providing both the highest percentage of protein and the least expensive energy of any known food. The economies of large-scale production make it possible to produce dried-frozen tofu at about 96 percent the cost (on a usable protein basis) of regular tofu made in small shops. Its relatively low cost has been a major factor in its growing popularity and, combined with its durability even when not refrigerated, would make it an excellent food for use in developing areas such as India, Africa, and South America.

In Japan, a carton containing ten pieces of dried-frozen tofu (each 2½ by 2 by 5/8 inches thick) weighs only 5.8 ounces (165 grams). The same amount of protein in the form of fresh tofu would weight about 6 times as much. Thus, its light weight and ease of preservation obviously make dried-frozen tofu an ideal back-packing food, now available in the West at prices far below those of most freeze-dried camping foods.

Highly versatile and requiring only a few minutes of cooking, dried-frozen tofu is well suited to a wide variety of Western-style dishes. We have found it preferable to regular tofu in a number of sautéed vegetable preparations, egg dishes, and casseroles. Preliminary experiments in Japan indicate that it can be flavored to resemble meat and can therefore be used in many of the same ways as textured soybean protein.

In Japanese cookery, it is commonly used in *nabe* cookery, Sukiyaki, simmered and sautéed dishes, and sushi rice preparations. Properly seasoned, dipped in tempura batter or eggs, then rolled in bread crumbs and deep-fried, it makes an excellent cutlet. While still dry, it can be grated, and the gratings added to almost any dish. It is also, of course, a popular ingredient in Zen Temple Cookery.

At present in the United States, dried-frozen tofu is available at most Japanese markets and some co-op stores at very reasonable prices. It can also be prepared quite easily at home.

Reconstituting Frozen and Dried-frozen Tofu

IMPORTANT: In the following recipes, "1 piece of frozen tofu" refers either to 5 or 6 ounces of tofu made into Homemade Frozen Tofu (p. 230), or an equivalent weight of regular tofu which has been frozen and sold commercially. The phrase "1 piece of dried-frozen tofu" refers to a standard ½ ounce (16.5 gram) piece of the commercial variety, measuring about 2½ by 2 by ½ inches. In many recipes the two types can be used interchangeably.

Frozen Tofu (or natural dried-frozen tofu). Remove tofu from freezer and place in a large pan or bowl. Add several quarts boiling water, cover, and allow to stand for 5 to 10 minutes until completely thawed. (If a large cake of tofu was frozen initially, cut crosswise into ½-inch-thick slices after cake is partially thawed to hasten the process.) Pour off hot water and add lukewarm or cold water. Gently but firmly press tofu several times between the palms of both hands to expel all hot water. Lift tofu out of water and press firmly before using (fig. 92). This last pressing makes the tofu light and dry so that it will readily absorb liquids during cooking.

Dried-frozen Tofu (containing ammonia or baking soda): The stronger the smell of ammonia when the tofu package is opened, the fresher the tofu. When reconstituted, the volatile ammonia gas disappears and the tofu becomes soft and absorbent as it expands.

Remove dried tofu from airtight package, place in a pan

Fig. 92. Pressing frozen tofu

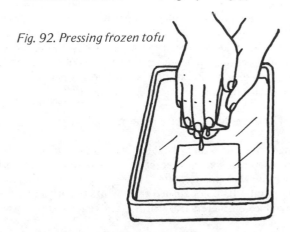

or bowl, and add just enough hot water (175°) to cover. (Do not pour water directly onto tofu.) Cover pan and allow to stand for 3 to 5 minutes while tofu swells. Do not allow to stand for too long, lest the tofu fall apart. Pour off hot water and cover with lukewarm or cold water. Press tofu several times under water gently but firmly between the palms of both hands to expel hot water and milky ammonia residue. Discard soaking water and add fresh water. Repeat pressing and discarding of water twice more, or until water pressed from tofu is no longer whitish. Lift tofu out of water and press very firmly once more before using.

Some Japanese chefs insist that dried-frozen tofu should be reconstituted by placing it in cold (rather than hot) water for 5 to 10 minutes and then pressing it repeatedly in clear cold water until the milky liquid no longer emerges. This technique is said to produce a softer texture and prevent the tofu from falling apart during lengthy simmering.

Grated Dried-frozen Tofu: Grate dried-frozen tofu on a metal grater to give a fine, granular texture. Place gratings in a bowl, cover with hot water (175°), and soak for 2 minutes. Pour into a dishcloth set over a strainer, allow to drain, then squeeze or press to expel excess water. Rinse twice with cold water, squeezing after each rinsing. Squeeze very firmly the last time to expel as much water as possible.

Storing and Cooking Dried-frozen Tofu

During summer, use commercial dried-frozen tofu within 4 months of the production date printed on the package; during winter, use within 6 months. After opening the airtight cellophane package, try to use all of the tofu as soon as possible, preferably within several days, to prevent it from losing its ability to expand and soften. Any tofu not used immediately should be placed in a small polyethylene bag sealed with a rubber band.

If fresh tofu is simmered for too long or over very high heat, it will begin to fall apart. If too much shoyu is used in the cooking broth, the tofu may shrink somewhat and become firmer than desirable.

Homemade Frozen Tofu   MAKES 2 "PIECES"

Although regular tofu is generally used as the basis for frozen tofu, both kinugoshi and whole cakes of thick agé may also be used. Due to freezing, the latter develops a texture remarkably similar to tender meat. If using homemade tofu (p. 99), make it as firm as possible by pressing with a heavy weight for a long time in the settling container.

10 to 12 ounces tofu, cut crosswise into halves

Arrange tofu pieces on a plate, leaving at least ½ inch between pieces, then place in the freezer with the temperature turned down as cold as possible. (Or place outdoors on a very cold winter night.) Its color turned from white to dark amber, the tofu will be completely transformed and ready to use after 48

hours; the most porous and resilient texture, however, is attained after 1 week of freezing. If you do not wish to use the tofu immediately, seal it in a polyethylene bag and store in the freezer. Lengthy storage actually improves the texture.

VARIATIONS

*For tofu with a very soft texture but little resiliency, freeze for only 24 hours. Use in soups and simmered dishes.
*For tofu with a very fine-grained structure similar to that of commercial dried-frozen tofu: Press tofu (p. 96), then cut crosswise into ½-inch-thick pieces. (For an even finer grain, press again briefly using the sliced tofu method, p. 97). Place pieces on a porous surface—such as a bamboo mat *(sudare)* or colander *(zaru)*—or on a large plate or tray, leaving at least ½ inch between pieces. Freeze as in the basic recipe.

Homemade Dried-frozen Tofu   MAKES 10 TO 20 PIECES

For a description of the traditional methods of preparing *Kori-dofu* and *Koya-dofu* see page 227. During winter, we have had good results using the former method, which requires no special equipment. Our 20-ounce batch of tofu was ready and well-dried after about 1 week.

To prepare homemade dried-frozen tofu in any season for use in camping or traveling, try the following:

10 to 20 pieces of (homemade) frozen tofu, reconstituted (p. 229) and cut crosswise into ¼-inch-thick slices

Preheat oven to 170°. Arrange the thin, slightly moist tofu slices on large baking sheets, leaving at least ½ inch between slices. Place in oven for about 2 hours, or until tofu color has turned from amber to light beige and slices are crisp and dry. Remove and allow to cool. Seal in polyethylene bags and store in a cool dry place. Use within 2 to 3 months.

Scrambled Eggs with Frozen Tofu   SERVES 2

Because of its excellent ability to absorb flavors and its tender, almost meaty texture, frozen tofu makes an excellent addition to many egg dishes. Frozen kinugoshi may be used to lend a soft, delicate texture to the dish, while frozen thick agé adds a substantial, hearty quality similar to that provided by ham or bacon.

1 piece of frozen or dried-frozen tofu, reconstituted (p. 229) and torn into small pieces
2 eggs
2 teaspoons shoyu
1 tablespoon natural sugar
1/3 cup dashi (p. 39), stock, or water

Combine all ingredients in a small bowl; beat lightly. Pour into a skillet and scramble without oil over medium heat until just firm. Serve hot or cold, seasoned lightly with Sesame Salt (p. 51) or ketchup, if desired.

Frozen Tofu in Scrambled Egg Salad with Tofu Dressing

SERVES 4

1 piece of frozen or dried-frozen tofu, reconstituted (p. 229) and torn or diced into very small pieces
4 eggs
¼ teaspoon salt
½ teaspoon butter or oil (optional)
2 cucumbers, cut into thin strips
2 tomatoes, cut into thin wedges
½ cup Tofu Mayonnaise Dressing (with onion) (p. 107)

Combine tofu, eggs, and salt in a small bowl; mix well. Heat a skillet and, if desired, coat with the butter or oil. Add tofu-egg mixture and scramble until dry and crumbly. Arrange cucumber and tomato pieces in serving bowls, sprinkle on the eggs-and-tofu, and top with the mayonnaise.

Frozen Tofu & Scrambled Eggs with Ankake

SERVES 2

2 teaspoons oil
1 piece of frozen or dried-frozen tofu, reconstituted (p. 229) and torn into small pieces
1 onion or leek, diced
1 clove of garlic, crushed
1 tablespoon grated gingerroot
2 eggs
2 teaspoons shoyu
Dash of salt and pepper
Ankake Sauce (p. 49)

Heat a skillet and coat with the oil. Add tofu, onion, garlic, and gingerroot, and sauté until onion is lightly browned. Add eggs, shoyu, salt, and pepper and scramble until egg is just firm. Serve topped with the sauce.

Or omit the sauce and use as a filling for Gyoza (p. 232).

Frozen Tofu & Egg Casserole with Cheese and Raisins

SERVES 4

Frozen tofu makes an excellent substitute for regular tofu in many baked dishes, but because the tofu is so absorbent, it may be necessary to increase the amount of liquid in the recipe slightly. Use the tofu cubed, grated, or cut into thin strips to create a variety of textures. Especially delicious in *gratin* preparations (p. 124).

2 pieces of frozen or dried-frozen tofu, reconstituted (p. 229) and torn into small pieces
2 ounces cheese, chopped fine or grated
¼ cup raisins
¼ cup milk (soy or dairy)
½ to ¾ teaspoon salt
Dash of pepper
2 tablespoons butter

Preheat oven to 350°. Combine the first six ingredients in a large bowl; beat lightly. Pour into a lightly oiled casserole and dot with butter. Bake for 25 minutes or until firm.

Frozen Tofu with Eggs and Onions (Tamago-toji)

SERVES 2 OR 3

1 piece of frozen or dried-frozen tofu, reconstituted (p. 229) and cut into ½-inch cubes; or 7 ounces (frozen or regular) deep-fried tofu, cut into strips
½ cup dashi (p. 39), stock, or water
2 tablespoons natural sugar
1½ tablespoons shoyu
1 tablespoon oil
1 onion or leek, thinly sliced
1 egg, lightly beaten

Combine tofu, dashi, sugar, and shoyu in a bowl; beat lightly. Heat a skillet and coat with the oil. Sauté onion for about 1 minute, then add tofu-dashi mixture and simmer, stirring occasionally, for 7 to 10 minutes. Turn heat to high, mix in egg, and cook, stirring constantly, for about 1 minute more, or until egg is just firm.

Frozen Tofu & Onion Sauce with Eggs and Cheese

SERVES 4

Frozen tofu makes a good addition to most sautéed or stir-fried dishes, especially when seasoned with shoyu or miso. Try substituting it for regular tofu in the recipes beginning on page 126. It is also delicious used in (or topped with) sauces such as Mushroom (p. 48), Spaghetti (p. 121), Onion-White (p. 207), or Curry (p. 166). Or try the following:

2 tablespoons oil
6 onions, thinly sliced
3 pieces of frozen or dried-frozen tofu, reconstituted (p. 229) and torn into ½-inch pieces
3 tablespoons red or barley miso; or 2 tablespoons shoyu
2 or 3 eggs
2 ounces cheese, cut into small cubes
2/3 cup water

Using the oil and onions, prepare an Onion Sauce (p. 48); simmer for 1½ hours. Stir in tofu and remaining ingredients and simmer for about 15 minutes more, or until sauce is well thickened. For best flavor, allow to cool to room temperature. Serve either cold or reheated.

For variety, omit eggs and cheese. Add ½ cup lotus root (cut into gingko leaves, p. 37) to the sauce together with the tofu.

Frozen Tofu in Soups

The addition of cubes, thin strips, or gratings of frozen tofu to any soup means added protein and body. Add reconstituted tofu about 10 minutes before the soup is done to allow it time to absorb the soup's unique flavors. In Japan, frozen tofu is popular in wintertime miso soups, especially in combination with white miso, hot mustard, and various greens.

Gyoza

MAKES 6; ONE SERVING

We use frozen tofu rather than hamburger in this famous Chinese dish.

2½ tablespoons oil
1 piece of frozen or dried-frozen tofu, grated and reconstituted (p. 229)
1 onion or large leek, minced
1 clove garlic, crushed
1 tablespoon grated gingerroot
1 teaspoon shoyu
¼ teaspoon salt
Dash of pepper
1 teaspoon cornstarch, arrowroot, or *kuzu,* dissolved in 2 tablespoons water
¼ cup dashi (p. 39), stock, or water
½ cup flour
Dipping Sauce:
    1½ tablespoons shoyu
    1 teaspoon (rice) vinegar
    ½ teaspoon sesame oil
    ¼ teaspoon hot mustard

Heat a skillet and coat with 1 tablespoon oil. Add the next seven ingredients and sauté over low heat for 10 minutes. Stir in dissolved cornstarch and dashi, simmer for 30 seconds more, and set aside to cool.

Add enough water to the flour to prepare a stiff dough. Divide dough into sixths and roll out on a floured breadboard into thin rounds about 3½ inches in diameter. Divide the tofu filling into sixths and place a dollop of the filling at the center of each round. Fold rounds in half and seal with the tynes of a fork, like a turnover. Heat a large skillet and coat with remaining 1½ tablespoons oil. Add the *gyoza* and fry over high heat for about 1 minute on each side. Add 2½ tablespoons water, reduce heat to low, cover pan, and steam for 5 minutes more. Serve hot with the dipping sauce.

Or use Frozen Tofu & Scrambled Eggs (p. 231) as the gyoza filling, or substitute Crumbled Tofu (p. 98) for frozen tofu. Gyoza may also be deep-fried (with or without batter).

Frozen Tofu Cutlets

SERVES 2

One of our favorite tofu recipes, these cutlets often bear a remarkable resemblance to fish or veal cutlets, depending on the type of sauce with which they are served.

2 tablespoons grated gingerroot
4 tablespoons shoyu
1½ cups water
4 pieces of frozen or dried-frozen tofu, reconstituted (p. 229) and cut into large 3/8-inch-thick slices
½ cup flour
1 egg, lightly beaten
½ cup bread crumbs or bread crumb flakes
Oil for deep-frying
1 lemon, cut into 4 wedges

Combine gingerroot, shoyu, and water in a large saucepan and bring to a boil. Reduce heat to low, add tofu, and simmer for 15 to 20 minutes. Lift out tofu, allow to cool slightly, then press each piece lightly with your fingertips to expel about one-fourth of the liquid. Dust well with flour, dip in egg, and roll in bread crumbs. Heat the oil to 375° in a wok, skillet, or deep-fryer. Drop in tofu and deep-fry until golden brown (p. 130). Serve hot or cold with lemon wedges.

To lend more of a seafood flavor, serve with Tofu Tartare Sauce (p. 109) or Tangy Ketchup & Lemon Sauce (p. 109). To give the feeling of breaded veal, serve with Worcestershire or Ketchup- Worcestershire Sauce (p. 49).

VARIATION
*Frozen Tofu Tempura: Simmer the tofu as above, then dip in Tempura Butter (p. 137) and deep-fry. Serve as above or with a Tempura Dipping Sauce (p. 137).

Frozen Tofu in Breads

Adding reconstituted frozen or dried-frozen tofu to breads is an easy way to add plenty of inexpensive protein. Use 2 to 3 pieces of grated (or diced), reconstituted tofu for each loaf of bread.

Dried-frozen Tofu French Fries

SERVES 2

1 piece of dried-frozen tofu, reconstituted (p. 229) and cut into pieces the size of French-fried potatoes
¼ cup *kuzu,* arrowroot, or cornstarch
Oil for deep-frying
¼ teaspoon salt
2 lemon wedges

Dust tofu pieces liberally with *kuzu* or arrowroot and set aside on a rack to dry briefly. Heat the oil to 375° in a wok, skillet, or deep-fryer. Drop in the tofu and deep-fry until crisp and golden brown (p. 130). Drain briefly, sprinkle with salt, and serve garnished with lemon.

Or omit the salt and lemon and sprinkle with a little shoyu or Lemon-Shoyu (p. 40).

Deep-fried Frozen Tofu with Chinese Sauce

SERVES 2

1½ pieces of frozen or dried-frozen tofu, reconstituted (p. 229) and torn into 12 pieces
6 tablespoons *kuzu,* arrowroot, or cornstarch
Oil for deep-frying
Chinese Sauce:
    1 teaspoon grated gingerroot
    2 tablespoons water or stock
    3 tablespoons natural sugar
    2 tablespoons soy sauce or shoyu
    1 tablespoon ground roasted sesame seeds (p. 38)
    1 tablespoon vinegar
15 snow peas, parboiled (p. 37) and cut crosswise into halves

Roll tofu in 4 tablespoons *kuzu* or arrowroot, then set aside briefly to dry. Heat oil to 350° in a wok, skillet, or deep-fryer. Drop in tofu and deep-fry until golden brown (p. 130); drain briefly.

Combine all sauce ingredients and bring just to a boil. Stir in 2 tablespoons *kuzu* or arrowroot dissolved in 3 tablespoons water. Add snow peas, then simmer for 30 seconds more. Divide tofu pieces among two serving bowls and serve topped with the hot sauce.

You can also serve this dish as a topping for deep-fried noodles or fried rice.

Deep-fried Frozen Tofu & Chinese Sauce with Fried Noodles
SERVES 4

1½ pieces of frozen or dried-frozen tofu, reconstituted (p. 229) and cut into 20 thin rectangles or triangles
6 tablespoons cornstarch
Oil for deep-frying
1 onion, diced
½ carrot, cut into matchsticks
3 mushrooms, sliced
1 green pepper, thinly sliced
10 to 15 snow peas or green beans
Tangy Chinese Sauce:
    3 tablespoons soy sauce or shoyu
    2 tablespoons vinegar
    1 clove crushed garlic
    1 teaspoon grated gingerroot
    2 tablespoons water or stock
    3 tablespoons natural sugar
2 cups cooked noodles (p. 50), well drained

Dust tofu with cornstarch and deep-fry as in the previous recipe. Heat 2 tablespoons oil in a skillet, add all the vegetables and sauté for 4 to 5 minutes until carrots are just tender. Combine all the sauce ingredients in a small saucepan and bring just to a boil. Stir in 2 tablespoons cornstarch dissolved in 3 tablespoons water. Add tofu and vegetables and simmer for 30 seconds more. Deep-fry the noodles (without batter) until crisp in oil heated to 350°, then drain well. Serve hot or cold, topped with the vegetables-and-sauce.

Deep-fried Frozen Tofu with Sweet Miso
SERVES 4

1 piece of frozen or dried-frozen tofu, reconstituted (p. 229) and cut into 4 equal cubes
2 tablespoons Yuzu Miso (p. 42) or Sweet Simmered Miso (p. 41)
2 tablespoons cornstarch, arrowroot, or *kuzu*
Oil for deep-frying
4 tablespoons kinako
2 tablespoons natural sugar
Dash of salt

Cut a ¾-inch-deep, 1-inch-square piece out of one surface on each piece of tofu (see fig. 51, p. 147). Fill this "well" with 1½ teaspoons of the miso. Trim bottom of square and replace

on top of miso. Roll filled tofu pieces in cornstarch. Heat oil to 350° in a wok, skillet, or deep-fryer. Drop in tofu and deep-fry until golden brown (p. 130); drain briefly.

Combine kinako, sugar, and salt in a small bowl; mix well. In a saucepan, bring 2 cups water to a boil. Dip tofu into boiling water, drain briefly, then roll in the sweetened kinako. Serve with the meal, or as an hors d'oeuvre or dessert.

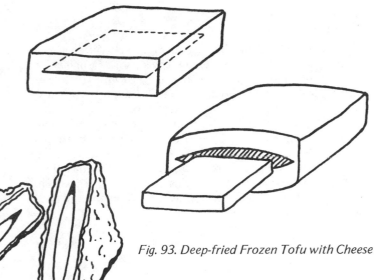

Fig. 93. Deep-fried Frozen Tofu with Cheese

Deep-fried Frozen Tofu Stuffed with Cheese
SERVES 2

2 pieces of frozen or dried-frozen tofu, reconstituted (p. 229)
1 tablespoon shoyu
½ cup water
2 slices of cheese, each 3 by 2 by ¼ inch
2 tablespoons flour
1 egg, lightly beaten
¼ cup bread crumbs or bread crumb flakes
Oil for deep-frying
Tofu Tartare Sauce (p. 109), Ketchup-Worcestershire (p. 49), or ketchup

Combine tofu, shoyu, and water in a small saucepan and bring to a boil. Reduce heat and simmer for 5 minutes, pressing tofu occasionally to aid absorption of the liquid. Remove tofu and allow to cool briefly.

Make a horizontal slit from one end of each piece of tofu to the other, leaving about ¼ inch of uncut tofu along each side so that tofu can be opened like a tube (fig. 93). Slide the cheese into the slit tofu.

Combine flour and egg in a small bowl and mix lightly to form a thick batter. Dip stuffed tofu into batter, then roll in bread crumbs. Heat oil to 350° in a wok, skillet, or deep-fryer. Drop in tofu and deep-fry until golden brown (p. 130). Drain briefly, then cut each piece diagonally into halves. Serve hot or cold topped with the sauce.

Deep-fried Frozen Tofu in Lemon Sauce (Oranda-ni)

SERVES 3

3 pieces of frozen or dried-frozen tofu, reconstituted (p. 229)
1 cup water, stock, or dashi (p. 39)
3 tablespoons natural sugar
2 tablespoons shoyu
½ cup cornstarch, arrowroot, or kuzu
Oil for deep-frying
3 lemon slices
3 sprigs of parsley

Combine the first four ingredients in a small saucepan and bring to a boil. Reduce heat to low, cover pan, and simmer for 10 minutes, pressing the tofu once or twice with a spatula to aid absorption of the cooking liquid. Remove tofu and allow to cool, then dust liberally with cornstarch.

Heat oil to 350° in a wok, skillet, or deep-fryer. Drop in tofu and deep-fry until golden brown (p. 130). Return initial cooking liquid to a boil, drop in the hot deep-fried tofu, and simmer for 1 minute more. Cut tofu pieces diagonally into halves, then divide among 3 serving bowls. Top with remaining cooking liquid and serve garnished with lemon and parsley.

Onion-Sauce Flavored Frozen Tofu Cutlets

MAKES 18

We like to prepare a large batch of these cutlets and freeze the leftovers for use on hiking trips.

2 tablespoons oil
7 onions, thinly sliced
¼ cup red, barley, or Hatcho miso
2 tablespoons shoyu
2½ cups water
Dash of pepper
9 pieces of Homemade Frozen Tofu (p. 230), reconstituted (p. 229) and cut into ½-inch-thick slices
½ cup flour
2 eggs, lightly beaten
½ cup bread crumbs or bread crumb flakes
Oil for deep-frying
Ketchup-Worcestershire Sauce (p. 49) or lemon wedges

Heat the oil in a casserole or heavy pot. Add onions, cover, and simmer over very low heat for 2 hours, stirring occasionally, to form an Onion Sauce (p. 48). Mix in miso, shoyu, water, and pepper, and return to the boil. Add tofu, cover, and simmer for 40 to 60 minutes more. Now remove tofu and allow to cool briefly. Press tofu lightly between your fingers to expel about one-fourth of the liquid it contains.

Dust cutlets with flour, dip in egg, and roll in bread crumbs; set aside briefly to dry. Heat oil to 350° in a wok, skillet, or deep-fryer. Drop in tofu and deep-fry until golden brown (p. 130). Serve topped with Ketchup-Worcestershire Sauce or garnished with lemon wedges; or top with remaining Onion Sauce.

VARIATIONS

*Shish Kebab Cutlets: Cut frozen tofu into bite-sized cubes before simmering in the onion sauce. On 6-inch bamboo or metal skewers place 1 tofu cube, a piece of vegetable (onion, carrot, green pepper) and finally another tofu cube. Dust all ingredients with flour, dip in beaten egg, and roll in bread crumbs. Deep-fry and serve as above, placed on a bed of slivered cabbage.
*Serve cutlets on buttered whole-wheat bread or toast with mustard, shredded cabbage, and Ketchup-Worcestershire Sauce. Add thin slices of tomato, cheese, or onion, if desired.

Deep-fried Frozen Tofu Dengaku

SERVES 2

2 pieces frozen or dried-frozen tofu, reconstituted (p. 229)
1 cup dashi (p. 39), stock, or water
2 tablespoons natural sugar
¼ cup cornstarch, arrowroot, or kuzu
Oil for deep-frying
Sweet Simmered Miso (p. 41)

Combine tofu, dashi, and sugar in a small saucepan; bring to a boil and simmer for 5 minutes. Remove tofu and allow to cool briefly, then cut into 6 rectangular pieces. Roll pieces in cornstarch.

Heat oil to 350° in a wok, skillet, or deep-fryer. Drop in tofu and deep-fry until golden brown (p. 130). Pierce each piece of tofu from one end with 1 or 2 small bamboo skewers (fig. 46, p. 141). Spread the upper surface of each piece with the miso and serve.

Soboro (Grated Frozen Tofu Rice Topping)

SERVES 2 OR 3

2 teaspoons oil
1 onion, minced
3 pieces of frozen or dried-frozen tofu, grated and reconstituted (p. 230)
1 tablespoon shoyu
¾ teaspoon salt
1 carrot, grated
15 to 20 green beans, parboiled (p. 37)
2 to 3 cups cooked Brown Rice or Sushi Rice (p. 50)

Heat a skillet and coat with the oil. Add onion and sauté until transparent. Add tofu and sauté for 2 minutes more. Season with shoyu and ¼ teaspoon salt, and simmer for 30 seconds more; set aside.

Reheat skillet and add grated carrot. Stirring constantly, parch for about 1 minute. Season with ¼ teaspoon salt and cook for 1 minute more, or until just tender; set aside.

Cut beans diagonally into thin strips and sprinkle with remaining ¼ teaspoon salt. Divide cooked rice among 3 individual serving bowls or lunch-box compartments. Cover one-third of surface of rice in each bowl with each of the three cooked vegetables to form an attractive pattern.

Deep-fried Frozen Tofu Sandwich
(Hakata-agé)

SERVES 2

An *hakata obi* is a brightly colored woman's belt or sash with a horizontal stripe design from which this dish takes its name.

2 pieces of dried-frozen tofu, reconstituted (p. 229)
½ cup water
1 tablespoon shoyu
1 tablespoon natural sugar
2 teaspoons red, barley, or Hatcho miso (optional)
3 ounces cheese
1 sheet of *nori*, cut crosswise into fourths
¼ cup (whole-wheat) flour
Oil for deep-frying

Before pressing water from reconstituted tofu, cut each piece crosswise into halves, then horizontally into thirds. Now, using your fingertips, firmly press out any remaining water.

Combine tofu, water, shoyu, and sugar in a small saucepan, and bring to a boil. Reduce heat to low, cover, and simmer for 5 minutes. Uncover pan, increase heat to medium and cook for 2 or 3 minutes more, or until all liquid has been absorbed or evaporated. Set aside to cool.

Cut cheese into eight 1/3-inch-thick slices the size of each piece of tofu, and coat one side of each slice with miso. Combine 2 pieces of cheese and 3 pieces of tofu to form a double-layer sandwich (fig. 94). Wrap each sandwich with a strip of *nori*, leaving the sandwich ends exposed and sealing the ends of the *nori* with water.

Mix the flour with just enough water (about ¼ cup) to form a thick batter. Heat the oil to 350° in a wok, skillet, or deep-fryer. Dip each sandwich in batter, drop it into the oil, and deep-fry until golden brown (p. 130). Drain and allow to cool briefly. Cut each sandwich crosswise into thirds and serve with the cut surface facing up.

Or substitute for the cheese thinly-sliced carrots which have been simmered in the shoyu broth. Cut each sandwich diagonally into halves and serve standing on end. Garnish with parsley.

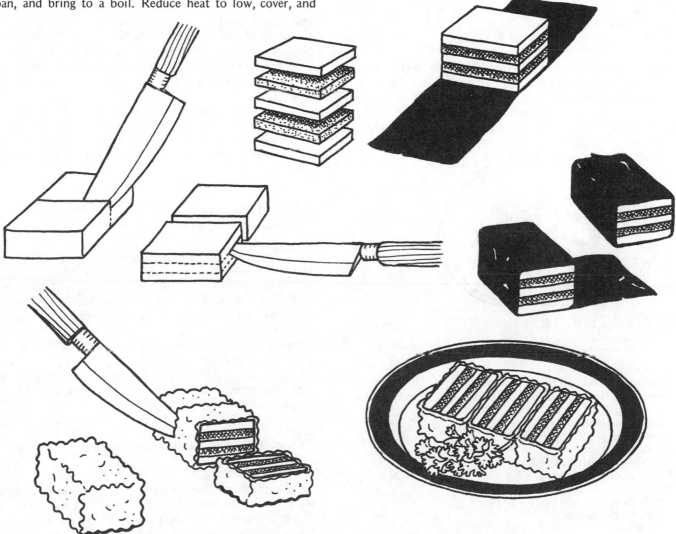

Fig. 94. Making deep-fried frozen tofu sandwiches

Fig. 95. Frozen Tofu Wrapped in Kombu

Frozen Tofu Wrapped in Kombu
(Koya-dofu no Kombu-maki)

SERVES 3

3 pieces frozen or dried-frozen tofu, reconstituted (p. 229) and cut lengthwise into halves
6 pieces of *kombu,* each 2½ by 8 inches, wiped with a moist cloth
6 strips of *kampyo,* each 12 inches long, reconstituted (p. 37)
1 cup dashi (p. 39), stock, or water
1½ tablespoons shoyu
2 tablespoons natural sugar
3 tablespoons *mirin* or sugar (p. 322)

Wrap each piece of tofu with a piece of *kombu* and tie around the middle with a piece of *kampyo* as shown in figure 95. Combine in a pressure cooker with the dashi, shoyu, sugar, and *mirin* and bring to full pressure (15 pounds). Simmer for 10 minutes, then remove from heat and allow pressure to come down naturally. Chill rolls and broth before serving.

Three-color Brown Rice
(Sanshoku Gohan)

SERVES 3

2 teaspoons vegetable oil
1 teaspoon sesame oil
2 pieces of frozen or dried-frozen tofu, grated and reconstituted (p. 229)
2 mushrooms, diced
½ cup dashi (p. 39), stock, or water
3 tablespoons shoyu
3 tablespoons natural sugar
1 tablespoon sake or white wine
1 tablespoon grated gingerroot
3 tablespoons Sesame Salt (p. 51)
2 eggs, lightly beaten
Dash of salt
8 green beans, parboiled (p. 37)
3 cups cooked Brown Rice or Sushi Rice (p. 50)

Heat a skillet and coat with the vegetable and sesame oil. Add the next eight ingredients and sauté for 3 to 5 minutes, or until dashi has been absorbed or evaporated. Set aside.

Using eggs and salt, prepare 1 Paper-thin Omelet (p. 51). Allow omelet to cool, then cut into 2-inch-long, thin strips.

Cut beans diagonally into thin strips and season lightly with salt. Place the rice into 3 individual bowls or lunch-box compartments. Cover one-third of the surface of the rice in each container with a sprinkling of each of the toppings: tofu, omelet, and beans.

Frozen Tofu Simmered in One-Pot Cookery and Seasoned Broths

Frozen and dried-frozen tofu are used widely in Yose-nabe and Mizutaki (p. 144), and Sukiyaki (p. 224), as well as in most other types of one-pot cookery. The tofu may be either simmered in Sweetened Shoyu Broth (p. 40) for 10 to 15 minutes and added to the *nabe* at the last minute, or simmered in the *nabe* together with the other ingredients. If homemade frozen tofu is used in Sukiyaki, it adds a texture and flavor resembling tender meat to the dish.

Frozen tofu is often added to Chinese-style Happosai (p. 249), simmered with vegetables in Nishime (p. 178), or topped with Ankake Sauce (p. 49).

Frozen Tofu Simmered in Sweetened Broth (Fukuyose-ni)

SERVES 2

Probably the most popular way Japanese restaurants serve frozen tofu, the following recipe is that provided us by Tokyo's Sasa-no-Yuki. There the tofu is served with young butterbur, tiny "maiden" bamboo shoots, and a roll of deep-fried, fresh yuba which has been simmered in a lightly seasoned broth.

2 pieces of frozen or dried-frozen tofu, reconstituted (p. 229)
1 cup water
3 tablespoons sugar
1 tablespoon shoyu
Vegetables: butterbur *(fuki)*, carrot slivers, tiny bamboo shoots, *(shiitake)* mushrooms, green beans, snow peas, *konnyaku* rectangles, wheat gluten cakes, or deep-fried fresh yuba rolls

Combine tofu, water, sugar, and shoyu in a saucepan and bring to a boil. Reduce heat to low, cover pan, and simmer for 15 to 20 minutes. Remove tofu and allow to cool, then cut into bite-sized cubes.

Add your choice of vegetables to the remaining cooking liquid and simmer until tender. Arrange tofu and vegetables in individual bowls, pour any remaining cooking liquid over the top of each portion, and serve cold or chilled.

For variety, garnish each serving with a sprig of *kinome*.

VARIATIONS

*Try the following cooking liquid: 1 cup dashi (p. 39), 1½ teaspoons shoyu, 2 tablespoons sugar, 1½ teaspoons each sake and *mirin*, and a dash of salt. For added richness, mix in 2 to 3 tablespoons sesame butter.
*Simmered Frozen Tofu Wrapped in Agé and Kampyo *(Shinoda-maki):* Cut each piece of reconstituted tofu lengthwise into thirds. Using 6 pieces of agé, cut each piece along 3 sides, then open to form flat sheets. Roll up one piece of tofu in each of the sheets and tie in two places with pieces of refreshed *kampyo*. Simmer rolls for 15 minutes in the dashi described in the recipe above. Cut rolls crosswise into halves and serve with the simmered vegetables.
*Add 1 piece of reconstituted frozen or dried-frozen tofu cut into thin rectangles to Agé with Hijiki and Carrots (p. 166), and simmer together with the other ingredients.

Deep-fried Frozen Tofu Dessert with Apples

SERVES 2

Two of our favorite recipes for frozen tofu are dessert preparations. Reconstituted frozen tofu can also be substituted for regular tofu in Tofu-Rice Pudding (p. 150). Or it can be grated and added in small amounts to cookies, cakes, or muffins.

1 apple, cut into thin wedges
3 tablespoons raisins
1 teaspoon natural sugar
½ cup water
1 piece frozen or dried-frozen tofu, reconstituted (p. 229)
¼ cup flour mixed with 3 tablespoons water
½ cup bread crumbs or bread crumb flakes
Oil for deep-frying
¼ teaspoon cinnamon
½ to 1 cup milk (soy or dairy)

Combine the first four ingredients in a small saucepan and simmer for about 5 minutes. Cut tofu into 6 or 8 equal pieces, add to the cooking apples, and continue to simmer until apples are tender and most of the liquid is absorbed or evaporated. Set aside and allow to cool briefly.

Mix the flour and water to form a thick batter. Remove tofu pieces from the cooked apples, dip into the batter, and roll in bread crumbs. Heat the oil to 350° in a wok, skillet, or deep-fryer. Drop in the tofu and deep-fry until golden brown (p. 130). Divide drained tofu between 2 serving bowls and top with the apples, a sprinkling of cinnamon, and the milk.

VARIATIONS

*Use 2 pieces of dried-frozen tofu. After reconstituting, cut each piece horizontally into 4 thin sheets. Cook with the apples as above; allow to cool. Spread the cooked apple mixture on 4 of the tofu sheets, then top with remaining sheets to make 4 "sandwiches." Cover each sandwich with a thick batter prepared by mixing flour with lightly beaten eggs. Sprinkle with bread crumbs, then carefully deep-fry until golden brown. Serve as is, or top with applesauce or cooked apples, a dash of cinnamon, and 1 cup milk.
*Combine the first four ingredients in the above recipe and 1 tablespoon butter in a pressure cooker. Bring to full pressure (10 pounds) and cook for 10 to 15 minutes. Cool under running cold water to release pressure. Cut tofu into 12 equal rectangles, mix into the cooked apples, and return to full pressure. Cook for 5 minutes more, then release pressure. Chill the tofu-apple mixture and serve topped with (soy or dairy) milk and a pinch of cinnamon.

Abekawa-dofu
(Frozen Tofu Rolled in Sweetened Kinako)

SERVES 2

This dish takes its name from *Abekawa Mochi,* a popular New Year's confection made by rolling moist, freshly-made *mochi* (pounded rice cakes) in a mixture of roasted soy flour and sugar.

1 piece frozen or dried-frozen tofu, reconstituted (p. 229)
¼ cup dashi (p. 39), stock, or water
3 tablespoons natural sugar
¼ cup *kuzu,* arrowroot, or cornstarch
Oil for deep-frying
3 tablespoons kinako
Dash of salt

Cut tofu crosswise into sixths. Combine with dashi and 1 tablespoon sugar in a small saucepan and bring to a boil. Reduce heat to low, cover pan, and simmer for about 10 minutes. Remove tofu and allow to cool, then roll in the *kuzu* or arrowroot.

Heat oil to 350° in a wok, skillet, or deep-fryer. Drop in tofu and deep-fry until golden brown (p. 130). Drain and allow to cool briefly. While tofu is cooling, combine kinako, 2 tablespoons sugar, and the salt in a bowl, mixing well. Bring 2 cups water to a boil in a saucepan. Dip cooled tofu into the boiling water, drain, then roll in the sweetened kinako. Serve immediately.

Or cut the tofu horizontally into 2 thin sheets, then cut each sheet crosswise into thirds. Proceed as above, but roll in a mixture of 3 tablespoons ground roasted sesame seeds, 2 to 3 tablespoons sugar, and a dash of salt.

14
Yuba

*I*F YOU HAVE ever simmered a pot of milk over very low heat or set a bowl of hot milk aside to cool, you have no doubt noticed the thin, delicate film that soon forms on the milk's surface. The longer it is allowed to set, the firmer and thicker it becomes. And if you have ever tried lifting this film off and tasting it, you may well have found it to be soft, warm, and delicious. In the same way, if fairly thick soymilk is gently heated, a thin film soon covers its surface. In Japan this film is called *yuba*, and since ancient times it has been considered a true delicacy. It is easily prepared at home, and since it is best when fresh and warm, yuba made in your own kitchen and served as an hors d'oeuvre or as part of a meal will have a tenderness and fragrant richness that can far surpass that of the yuba ordered from even the finest traditional shops.

Yuba in its commonly-sold dried form is a nutritional treasure-trove containing a remarkable 52.3 percent high-quality protein. This makes it one of the richest natural sources of protein known to man. Easy to digest, yuba also contains 24.1 percent natural oils (mostly polyunsaturated), 11.9 percent natural sugars and, in its dried form, 8.7 percent water. Thus it is extremely lightweight and easy to carry. Furthermore, a 100-gram portion contains some 432 calories, making it a highly concentrated energy source that is ideal for camping. Finally, yuba is rich in minerals, as shown in figure 5 on page 24. Because of its nutritional excellence, yuba is a popular item at Japanese natural food and health food stroes. Recommended to mothers before and after childbirth, it has been said for centuries to stimulate the flow of milk. Widely used in Japanese hospitals as a concentrated source of protein, doctors also recommend it to patients suffering from high blood pressure (it is believed to aid in the removal of cholesterol) and diabetes.

In spite of its nutritional excellence, yuba is appreciated primarily for its unique flavor and texture. The Japanese say that the natural sweetness and the subtle richness of yuba remind them of the flavor of fresh cream. Like cream, yuba rises to the surface of the soymilk from which it is made and embodies the condensed essence or elixir of the soymilk's flavor and nutrients. The most popular way of enjoying yuba's fine flavor is also the simplest: a delicate half-done sheet is lifted with the fingertips from the surface of steaming soymilk and placed in a small bowl; sprinkled with a few drops of shoyu, it is served immediately. Soft and warm, it melts on the tongue—and is gone.

Fresh yuba looks like a diaphanous veil of creamy silk and is usually sold in single sheets about 15 by 17 inches. When dried, it turns beige and has a crisp, brittle texture. yet it softens as soon as it is refreshed or added to soups, stocks, egg dishes, or the like. In Japan, the dried form is also popular as a deep-fried hors d'oeuvre; it turns as crisp and crunchy as a potato chip.

The art of making yuba was transmitted from China to Japan about 1,000 years ago. During the following centuries, yuba developed a well-established role as one of the indispensable delicacies in both Zen Temple and Tea Ceremony Cookery. Today, in restaurants serving these two varieties of haute cuisine, yuba will often appear in more than half the dishes in a typical six-course meal. The beautiful *Sorin-an* restaurant (p. 311), which specializes in yuba cuisine, features homemade fresh yuba in a selection of more than 15 delectable dishes. Likewise, many Chinese restaurants—including those in the United States—generally have a special section on the menu devoted solely to yuba or "bean curd skin" preparations.

In Japan, yuba is (and has traditionally been) served largely as a gourmet food. A special product of the ancient capital, Kyoto, where most of the country's yuba shops are still located, it gradually acquired an aura of aristocracy, refinement, and elegance through its close association with the Imperial Court. And because it is made by slow traditional methods on a small scale, most of Japan's yuba is quite expensive. In Taiwan, China, and Hong Kong, on the other hand, yuba is a very popular food sold at prices anyone can afford. Although much of the yuba there, too, is still made in tiny cottage shops, modern methods have also been developed for preparing good-quality yuba on a large scale. This yuba, in its dried form, is now sold throughout the world.

Although, strictly speaking, yuba is not a type of tofu and is not made or sold at neighborhood tofu shops, it is nevertheless grouped together with tofu in most books on Japanese foods and cooking. This is partially because yuba, like all tofu, is made from soymilk; partially because its history parallels that of tofu; and partially because the two foods have closely related flavors and are therefore used in many of the same types of cookery.

Yuba and tofu shops have a great deal in common. And although yuba is made commercially only in special shops, a small amount is produced inadvertently each day at neighborhood tofu shops when soymilk cools in the curding barrel just before it is solidified into curds. This yuba is picked off to prevent it from entering the tofu, where it could form an interface and cause a large block of tofu to split apart. It is either eaten fresh at the tofu shop by the tofu maker and his family, served to guests or visitors as a special treat, or set aside and dried to be used later in cooking.

Like tofu shops, virtually all of Japan's yuba shops are run by a single family whose home adjoins the shop. Many of Kyoto's 23 shops have been in the family for centuries. Yuba Han, for example, is a beautiful example of classical Kyoto architecture; the building itself is 120 years old with massive rafters arching below a 20-foot-high ceiling. Here one can find a unique collection of all the ancient tofu-making tools still in daily use: large granite grinding stones, an iron cauldron heated by a wood fire, and a lever press weighted by heavy granite pendants. This historic shop and its tools were used as the basis for the drawing on the cover of this book. The Yuba-cho shop is run by a master (now assisted by his two sons) who has been making yuba in the same shop for fifty years. This cheerful old man, now a Living National Treasure, prepares his yuba for the Imperial Household.

In most shops, yuba is prepared in large copper or stainless steel steaming trays supported by a sturdy brick dais. One steaming table may be 8 to 10 feet long and 3 feet wide (fig. 96); most shops will have at least two such tables. Thick soymilk, prepared with the same tools and in the same way as in tofu shops, is poured into the trays to a depth of about 1½ inches. Each tray is divided into rectangular compartments by removable wooden frames. The soymilk is heated from below by steam or low flames until it is steaming but not bubbling (about 175°F). After 5 to 7 minutes, when a firm film has formed in each compartment, the master makes his or her rounds, lifting off each sheet with a 2-foot-long bamboo skewer, then hanging the yuba-draped skewer in a rack over the steaming table. Here the yuba drains and begins to dry.

Fig. 96. Steaming table in a yuba shop

To visit Kyoto's yuba shops early in the morning and watch the craftsmen at work is an unforgettable experience. Sunlight shines from the high windows down through the steam rising from heating soymilk and makes pinpoint rainbows in the air. Falling on the sheets of translucent yuba, the light renders them shimmering white. The delicious fragrances of fresh soymilk and wood-smoke are everywhere. At times, the entire shop can suddenly take on a surrealistic, almost unreal appearance as through this hushed world, half-visible figures move slowly along the steaming white pools. Hundreds of sheets of pale yuba teem and hover in the thick mist like the frail ghosts of a vision and flutter in the magical netherworld light like silken banners on the lances of dream knights. As the day warms or the sun's position shifts, the visual reverie can vanish as quickly as it came, leaving us in a world only slightly less enchanted.

Types of Yuba

Yuba is commonly sold in three different states: fresh, half-dried, and dried. The first pieces of yuba to be lifted off the steaming soymilk are considered to be the best grade: their color is creamy white, their flavor mild and light with relatively little sweetness, and their texture firm. This yuba stays relatively soft and flexible even when dried. After about half of the yuba sheets have been removed from the soymilk, the remaining sheets begin to have a faintly reddish tinge and a sweeter flavor. Having less internal cohesiveness, they tear more easily and become somewhat brittle when dried. This yuba is regarded as second grade.

Fresh yuba (*Nama-yuba*), served as soon as possible after it has been made, is usually thought to be the most delicious. Highly perishable, it keeps, for only 2 to 4 days in summer and 3 to 5 days in winter, even when refrigerated. To prevent molding, it must be kept dry and well sealed. In yuba shops, it is allowed to drain and begin to dry in the moisture-laden air over the steaming tables before it is wrapped, five pieces at a time, in paper-thin, shaved wood, placed in airtight plastic bags, and whisked away on dry ice to the finest restaurants and Japanese inns.

Half-dried yuba (*Nama-gawaki* or *Han-gawaki*) keeps longer than its fresh counterpart but not nearly as long as dried yuba. It is usually prepared by inserting a bamboo skewer under the center of a sheet of yuba in the steaming tray and lifting it up so that the two halves of the sheet hang down on each side of the skewer and stick together. The resulting half-sized piece, having a double thickness and firm exterior, is then cut from the skewer when it has dried enough so that it is no longer moist but is not yet brittle. Packed in an airtight plastic bag and stored on regular or dry ice, it is used mostly in restaurants.

Dried Yuba (*Kanso-* or *Hoshi-yuba*) is the most common of the three forms sold in Japan; its five most popular varieties (flat sheets, long rolls, small rolls, large spirals, and *Oharagi*), are illustrated below. Thoroughly dried yuba will last for 4 to 6 months if stored in a cool dry place and sealed tightly to prevent the entry of moisture. Since the flavor diminishes with time, dried yuba should be used as soon as possible. The various rolled or folded forms of yuba are usually prepared when the yuba is half-dried and still pliable; they are then dried thoroughly. All types of commercial yuba are understood to be dried unless the name specially states that they are fresh or half-dried.

At present in the United States, Chinese-style dried yuba is available at most Chinese dried-goods markets in two forms: dried yuba sheets (called Dried Bean Curd, Bean Curd Sheets, or Bean Curd Skin) and u-shaped rolls (called Bamboo Yuba or Bean Curd Sticks). Five varieties of Japanese dried yuba (flat sheets, long rolls, small rolls, large spirals, and *Oharagi*) are available at some Japanese markets and natural food stores. We know of no yuba shops in the United States nor of any commercial sources of fresh yuba. The latter, however, is easy to make at home. And its fine flavor can always be enjoyed when preparing homemade soymilk, for then yuba inevitably appears of its own accord.

The Varieties of Yuba

Fresh Yuba Sheets (*Nama-yuba*): A typical yuba sheet is 12 to 15 inches wide and 14 to 17 inches long. In recipes calling for "large sheets of fresh yuba," use sheets with the larger dimensions, if possible. Each sheet weighs about 0.8 ounces or 23 grams. When fresh sheets are gathered like a cloth, draped over individual skewers to drain, and then packaged, the yuba is called "fresh gathered sheets" (*hikiage*).

Flat Yuba Sheets (*Hira-* or *Taira-yuba*): These are prepared from fresh yuba sheets, usually folded into thirds before being dried. In some cases, yellow food coloring is added to the soymilk to make "yellow yuba sheets" (*kiyubu*), often used as a colorful topping in sushi shops.

Fresh Yuba Rolls (*Maki-yuba*): A "long roll of fresh yuba" is about 16 inches long and 1 inch in diameter. It is made by folding a piece of fresh or sweet yuba lengthwise into halves, laying it lengthwise on a second sheet together with fresh yuba trimmings, and rolling the second sheet up lengthwise. "Small rolls of fresh yuba" are prepared by cutting this long roll into 1½-inch lengths.

Long Yuba Roll (*Komaki*): About 1 inch in diameter and 15 inches long, *komaki* are prepared by rolling fresh yuba trimmings in several fresh yuba sheets. After partial drying, the roll is wrapped in still another sheet of fresh yuba, dried again, and then trimmed at both ends.

Small Yuba Rolls (*Kiri-komaki*): Prepared by cutting a long yuba roll into 1½- to 2-inch lengths, these delicate rolls are used in thin soups, one-pot cookery, or with sautéed vegetables.

Tied Yuba (*Musubi-yuba*): Prepared from a piece of regular or yellow fresh yuba about ½ inch wide and 5 inches long, *musubi-yuba* is tied into a simple loop and used in thin soups.

Large Yuba Spirals (*Omaki-, Futomaki-,* or *Uzumaki-yuba*): To make yuba spirals, about 40 sheets of half-dried yuba are rolled up to form a long cylinder 1½ to 2 inches in diameter and 1½ feet long. This is wrapped in a single sheet of fresh yuba, dried until crisp, then cut crosswise into discs about ½-to 1-inch thick. They are used widely in thin soups, one-pot cookery, and seasoned broths.

Ginkgo-leaf Yuba: Prepared by cutting fresh yellow or regular fresh yuba sheets with a cookie cutter, these dried pieces resemble 3-inch-diameter ginkgo leaves and are used as a garnish in thin soups and on top of sushi.

Oharagi Yuba: This slightly-flattened yuba roll, tied with a thin piece of *kombu*, is about 2½ inches long, 2 inches wide, and ¾ inch thick. It is prepared by loosely rolling one sheet of half-dried yuba inside a sheet of fresh yuba, tying the oval-shaped roll with 5 strips of *kombu*, then cutting the roll crosswise into fifths. (This variety derives its name from the large bundles of firewood tied around the center with a length of rope which the women of Ohara village near Kyoto are famous for carrying on their heads.)

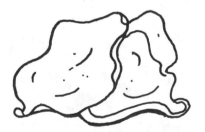

Sweet Yuba (*Amayuba*): This is the last sheet of yuba lifted (and often partially scraped) from the bottom of the steaming tray. It has a sweet rich flavor and slightly reddish color. Thicker and less delicate than most yuba, its edges are often ragged and uneven. Eaten fresh and warm at the yuba shop, it is ambrosial. It is usually dried and sold in large pieces of various sizes in sealed cellophane bags. The least expensive of all types of yuba, sweet yuba is, in our opinion, the most delicious, especially when deep-fried, lightly salted, and served like potato chips. Dried pieces may be added to soups, egg dishes, or sautéed vegetable preparations.

Fresh Yuba Trimmings (*Kirehashi*): These small pieces and scraps, left over after trimming the ends of yuba rolls or sheets, serve as an excellent ingredient in fillings for other rolls or pouches. When dried, they are called yuba flakes.

Yuba Flakes (*Kuzu-yuba* and *Mimi*): These dried yuba trimmings, sold in sealed bags at a very low price, are used in many of the same ways as sweet yuba. They are also served in many hospitals as an inexpensive source of high-quality protein.

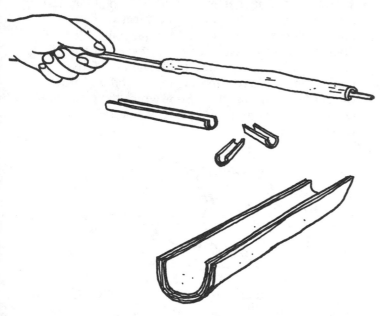

Trough-shaped Yuba (*Toyuba*): When dried sheets of yuba are cut off their bamboo skewers, the part of the yuba that was in contact with the top and sides of the skewer remains attached in the form of a long, inverted trough. After 8 to 10 sheets of yuba have been cut away, the "trough" is about 1/8 inch thick and composed of 8 to 10 layers of dried yuba. Pried off the skewer with a knife, it is cut into 2-inch lengths. Often served deep-fried, it is also used in Sukiyaki, one-pot cookery, and all types of Zen Temple Cookery.

Reconstituting Dried Yuba

Since dried yuba is very brittle, before being used in cooking it is briefly reconstituted in water or dashi until it becomes soft and pliable. It should be added to most dishes just before they are served, and should never be simmered for much more than a minute lest it begin to fall apart and lose its delicate flavor. When unrefreshed dried yuba is added to a dish, it tends to absorb a large amount of liquid; be sure to use enough stock or water to cover this loss. Reconstituted dried yuba may be substituted for fresh yuba in any of the following recipes.

Dried Yuba Rolls: Dip rolls into a bowl of water, or place on a plate or bamboo colander and sprinkle lightly with water. Moisten a dish towel, arrange the yuba atop one half of it, and fold the other half over to rest atop the yuba. Allow to stand for 5 to 10 minutes.

Dried Yuba Sheets: Dip sheets into a bowl of water. Place on a cutting board or other flat surface, roll up, and cut into 1½-inch lengths. Soak in the water for 5 to 10 minutes.

Homemade Fresh Yuba   MAKES 12 TO 14 SHEETS

This dish takes about an hour to make, but it's worth it. Prepare yuba while you have other work to do in the kitchen. For the steaming container, use either a shallow enamel pan (about 9 by 12 inches) or a heavy iron skillet about 12 inches in diameter. Be sure that the steaming container is at least 1½ but no more than 3 inches deep. Two different steaming arrangements may be used: 1) Place the steaming container on a broiling screen, perforated metal plate, or asbestos pad set directly over a low flame. 2) Use a double boiler arrangement with a large pot on the bottom at least one-half full of rapidly boiling water, and a shallow pan on top that fits into the lower pot. Since each piece of yuba takes about 7 minutes to form, you can save time by using more than one steaming container at the same time.

Prepare Homemade Soymilk (p. 204) and pour into steaming containers to a depth of 1 to 1½ inches. Skim off foam with a spatula. Heat soymilk to about 175° (until steaming but not quite boiling). Wait about 7 minutes until a firm yuba film has formed over entire surface of soymilk. Trim film away from walls of steaming container with the tip of a knife. Using your fingertips, lift up one edge of yuba film, and insert a long moistened chopstick, skewer, or knitting needle under center of yuba sheet (fig. 97). Carefully lift yuba away from soymilk, drain for a few seconds over steaming container, then set chopstick across the mouth of a deep pot allowing yuba to drain and cool for 4 to 5 minutes. Slide yuba off chopstick and arrange on a small plate. Serve immediately as hors d'oeuvre seasoned with a dash of shoyu, or reserve and serve with other yuba during the meal.

Continue lifting off yuba sheets at 7-minute intervals until all soymilk has evaporated from steaming containers and only a thick reddish film remains on bottom of pan. This is "sweet yuba" *(amayuba)*, a true delicacy. Carefully scrape

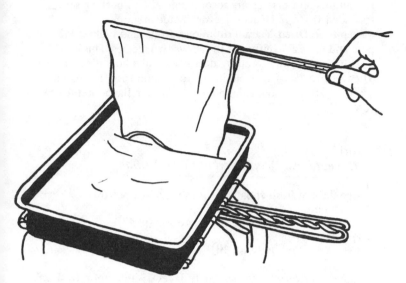
Fig. 97. Lifting yuba away from soymilk

it off with a spatula and arrange with the other yuba. Place any crisp scraps or soft scrapings into a small bowl and serve together with the yuba as Warm Fresh Yuba (p. 243).

VARIATIONS

Half-formed Yuba (Tsumami-ugé): Using your fingertips, lift the delicate yuba sheets off the surface of the steaming soymilk at about 4 to 5 minute intervals, just before the yuba has had a chance to become attached to the sides of the container. Place yuba directly into a small cup and serve immediately.

Large Sheets of Fresh Yuba: Prepare homemade fresh yuba, however when lifting yuba off surface of soymilk, insert moistened chopstick or skewer along one edge of sheet (rather than under the center) so that sheet hangs like a flag from chopstick. Allow yuba to drain as above for 15 to 20 minutes until it is no longer moist; carefully remove chopstick and lay flat sheet on a dry cutting board. Use as called for in the following recipes. For larger sheets use a 12- by 15-inch pan.

Fresh Yuba Rolls (Maki-yuba): After yuba has dried on the chopstick for 4 to 5 minutes, place the flat yuba sheet on a cutting board or other flat surface and roll into a cylinder; then cut into 1-inch lengths. Use in recipes calling for small yuba rolls.

Dried Yuba: Prepare yuba sheets or rolls. Leave sheets drying on chopsticks and put rolls into a screen basket. Place in a warm dry place—such as over a hot water heater or in a very low temperature oven—for 10 to 20 hours, or until dry and crisp. Store in an airtight bag in a cool dry place until ready to use.

YUBA HORS D'OEUVRE

In Japan, yuba is prized for its use in delicate and ambrosial hors d'oeuvre. The variety of shapes, textures, and flavors which you can offer your guests is almost unlimited.

Warm Fresh Yuba — SERVES 3

If you prepare your own yuba at home, this is the only recipe you need to know. Here is how most yuba masters offer fine yuba to their guests. The simpler, fresher, and warmer the yuba, the more completely your guests will enjoy it.

12 sheets of homemade fresh yuba, half-formed yuba, or fresh yuba rolls
3 tablespoons shoyu, Wasabi-Shoyu, or Yuzu-Shoyu (p. 40)

Serve the yuba warm and fresh in small bowls or arranged on a serving platter accompanied by tiny dishes containing the dipping sauce. Or serve with any of the following mixtures:

*Honey- Vinegar Dipping Sauce
    3 teaspoons honey or sugar
    2 teaspoons (rice) vinegar
    1 teaspoon *mirin*, sake, or white wine

*Honey-Lemon Dipping Sauce
    3 teaspoons honey
    4 teaspoons lemon or lime juice

*White Miso Dipping Sauce
    1½ teaspoons sweet white miso
    1 teaspoon sugar or honey
    1 teaspoon vinegar

Yuba-Cucumber Rolls — MAKES 8 TO 10

1 small cucumber, cut lengthwise into quarters and crosswise into 4-inch lengths
2 or 3 sheets of fresh yuba
Wasabi-Shoyu, Yuzu-Shoyu (p. 40), or shoyu

Arrange cucumber pieces in groups of 3 and wrap with a sheet of fresh yuba. Cut crosswise into 1-inch rounds (above) and serve with the dipping sauce.

Yuba-Nori Rolls — MAKES 8 TO 10

4 sheets of *nori*
4 sheets of fresh yuba
Shoyu

Arrange equal-sized sheets of *nori* and fresh yuba on top of each other in alternate layers. Roll up lengthwise, secure with foodpicks, and cut into 1-inch lengths. Serve topped with a sprinkling of shoyu.

Yuba Canapés

12 Fresh Yuba Rolls (p. 243)
12 bite-sized pieces of (lightly buttered) toast or crackers
Shoyu
Sweet White miso, Yuzu Miso, or Red Nermiso (p. 42)

Arrange yuba rolls on toast and crackers. Sprinkle one-half the rolls with a few drops of shoyu and top the remainder with a dab of the miso.

Fresh Yuba Sashimi

SERVES 1

2 sheets of (homemade) fresh yuba (p. 242)
¼ cup slivered *daikon* or fresh *daikon* threads
2 green beefsteak leaves
Wasabi-Shoyu (p. 40), Vinegar-Shoyu, Gingerroot-Shoyu, or shoyu garnished with crumbled *nori;* or plain shoyu

Fold the yuba from one end to form a many-layered, 4-inch-wide sheet; cut diagonally into ¾-inch-wide strips (fig. 98). Arrange strips on a mound of the *daikon* slivers or threads, garnish with the beefsteak leaves, and serve accompanied by the dipping sauce.

Served this way, fresh yuba bears a close resemblance to *sashimi,* or Japanese-style raw fish.

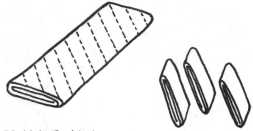

Fig. 98. Yuba Sashimi

Crunchy Sweet-Yuba Chips

This is one of our very favorite yuba preparations. The crisp texture resembles that of potato chips, but the flavor and aroma are truly unique.

Oil for deep-frying
10 to 15 sheets of dried sweet yuba (p. 241)
Salt

Heat the oil to only 275° in a wok or skillet. Drop in yuba and Deep-fry for about 3 to 5 seconds, until yuba turns reddish golden brown and is covered with tiny bubbles. Drain thoroughly, salt lightly and serve immediately. Also delicious served with a dip of Tofu Mayonnaise (p. 107) seasoned with a little extra lemon juice and sweetened with sugar.

VARIATIONS
*Deep-fried Trough-shaped Yuba *(Toyu Yuba):* Deep-fry yuba pieces without batter for about 1 minute, salt lightly and serve like yuba chips. This crisp hors d'oeuvre is especial-

ly prized in Zen temple cookery where it is sometimes referred to as "Flowers of Kyoto." It is also served in high-grade restaurants and bars as an accompaniment to beer or sake, sprinkled as a topping over rice, or floated in soups.
Deep-fried Dried Yuba Trimmings, Rolls, and Flakes: Prepare and serve as in either of the above two recipes. This is the least expensive way to enjoy deep-fried yuba hors d'oeuvre. They also make a nice addition to scrambled eggs, tossed green salads, and soups, lending a bacon-like flavor and texture.

Kaori Yuba

MAKES 6

(Sweet Miso Deep-fried in Fresh Yuba)

1 large sheet of fresh yuba, cut into six 4½-inch squares
9 tablespoons fresh yuba trimmings
3 tablespoons Yuzu Miso or Red Nerimiso (p. 42)
Oil for deep-frying
Shoyu or Wasabi-Shoyu (p. 40)

In the center of each yuba square layer 1 tablespoon fresh yuba trimmings, 1½ teaspoons Yuzu Miso, and ½ teaspoon yuba trimmings, in that order. Fold over the four corners of the yuba to form an envelope (fig. 99). Deep-fry at 350° for about 40 seconds, turning from time to time with chopsticks. Drain briefly, place on absorbent paper, and serve with dipping sauce.

VARIATIONS
*Omit yuba trimmings and use 1 tablespoon Mushroom Miso Sauté (p. 43) as the filling for each yuba "packet."
*On a large sheet of fresh yuba, spread a thin layer of Yuzu Miso, sweet white miso, or Sweetened Tekka Miso (p. 44). Roll up the sheet to form a cylinder, cut crosswise into 1-inch lengths, and deep-fry. Serve with shoyu and a mixture of equal parts grated *daikon* and grated gingerroot.

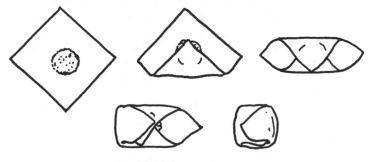

Fig. 99. Yuba envelopes

Deep-fried Yuba Dengaku

MAKES 6

1 large sheet of fresh yuba, cut crosswise into thirds
Oil for deep-frying
Sweet white miso or Red Nerimiso (p. 42)
Roasted sesame seeds

Fold each yuba piece into thirds, then roll up from the folded end to form a cylinder (fig. 100). Wrap each cylinder with a second yuba piece moistened along one edge to seal. Pierce

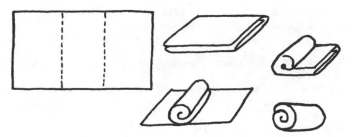

yuba cylinder from one end with a (green) bamboo dengaku skewer (or two foodpicks) and deep-fry for about 1 minute until golden brown. Spread tops of rolls with the miso and top with a sprinkling of sesame seeds. Serve while crisp and hot.

The freshly deep-fried rolls —called *Agé-maki* Yuba— may also be served as is, sprinkled with a little shoyu. Simmered in Sweetened Shoyu Broth (p. 40), they make a tasty addition to soups and *nabe* dishes.

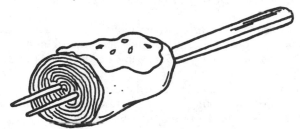

Fig. 100. Deep-fried Yuba Dengaku

Yawata-maki *(Yuba-Burdock Root Roll)*   MAKES 6

8 to 10 strips of burdock root (or carrot), each 12 inches long and 1/8-inch square
Sweetened Shoyu Broth (p. 40)
2 large sheets of fresh yuba, each 12 by 14 inches
5 to 6 fresh yuba trimmings, each 12 inches long
Oil for deep-frying

Soak burdock root strips in cold water for 15 minutes; drain. Combine with the broth in a saucepan and simmer, covered, for 1 to 2 hours. Place 1 yuba sheet congruently atop the other. Arrange burdock and yuba strips in a bundle crosswise at one end of the sheets. Roll to form a cylinder 1½ inches in diameter and 12 inches long. Deep-fry in 350° oil until crisp and golden brown; drain well. Cut roll crosswise into thirds, then cut each third diagonally into halves. Serve upright (below).

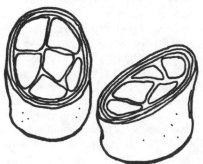

Toji Yuba *(Deep-fried Yuba* *with Ginkgo Nuts and Lilly Bulbs)*   MAKES 6

1 large sheet of fresh yuba, cut into six 6-inch squares
3 teaspoons refreshed cloud-ear mushroom
10 tablespoons fresh yuba trimmings
6 ginkgo nuts
18 small sections of lilly bulbs
Oil for deep-frying
Wasabi-Shoyu (p. 40) or shoyu

Arrange the yuba squares on a cutting board or other flat surface. Divide the next four ingredients evenly among the squares, placing them in a small mound at the center of each square. Fold over the two opposing corners (below), then roll up lengthwise from one end. Secure with a foodpick and deep-fry in 350° oil until golden brown. Serve with the dipping sauce or use as an ingredient in one-pot cookery.

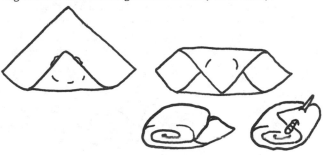

Deep-fried Yuba-Nori Rolls   MAKES 10

10 pieces of fresh yuba, each 2½ inches square
10 pieces of *nori*, each 2½ inches square
10 tablespoons grated glutinous yam or 10 teaspoons Red Nerimiso (p. 42)
Oil for deep-frying
Shoyu (optional)
Parsley sprigs

Place each of the *nori* pieces congruently on top of a piece of yuba. Spread the surface of each piece of *nori* with either 1 tablespoon yam or 1 teaspoon miso. Roll each square into a tight cylinder, and deep-fry until golden brown. Serve with shoyu and garnish with parsley.

Yuba-Mock Broiled Eels *(Yuba no Kabayaki)*   MAKES 12

1 small roll of fresh yuba, cut crosswise into 1-inch lengths
Oil for deep-frying
Sweetened Shoyu Broth (p. 40)
Sansho pepper

Deep-fry yuba rolls until crisp and golden brown, drain briefly, then simmer in the broth for 10 minutes. Drain well and gently press out excess broth. Now broil rolls over a low flame (on a screen) until lightly browned and fragrant. Serve topped with the pepper.

Or simply baste fresh or trough-shaped yuba with shoyu while broiling over charcoals.

Buddha's Chicken

SERVES 4

1½ tablespoons soy sauce
¼ teaspoon salt
2 teaspoons sugar
1½ teaspoons sesame oil
½ cup stock or water
6 large sheets of fresh yuba
Oil for deep-frying
Parsley and radish roses

Combine the first five ingredients in a small saucepan, bring just to a boil, and remove from heat; allow to cool briefly. Place 1 yuba sheet in a baking pan and coat with a little of the warm sauce. Continue to add sheets in layers, coating each, until all ingredients are used. Roll up sheets from one end to form a compact sylinder. Wrap in cheesecloth, place into a preheated stemer (p. 38), and steam for 10 minutes; remove cheesecloth. (Or bake over a pan of water in a 350° oven.)

Heat oil to 350° in a wok, skillet, or deep-fryer. Drop in yuba roll and deep-fry until golden brown (p. 130). Cut diagonally into ½-inch-thick rounds and serve garnished with parsley and radish roses.

Homemade Buddha's Ham
(Suhuo-t'ui)

SERVES 3 OR 4

3 tablespoons oil
2 cups dried yuba flakes and trimmings, well-packed
¼ cup grated carrot
1 tablespoon grated gingerroot
2½ tablespoons soy sauce

Heat a skillet and coat with the oil. Add the remaining ingredients and sauté over low heat for about 5 minutes. Remove from heat and allow to cool for several minutes, then press ingredients into a 3- by 8- inch mold, or tupperware container of comparable size. Cover with a pressing lid, and press with a 6- to 8-pound weight for 1 hour. Cut into this slices and serve like ham as an hors d'oeuvre.

In China, another variety of Buddha's Ham is prepared as follows: Spread one surface of a large sheet of fresh (or refreshed) yuba with sesame oil. Roll the sheet into a tight cylinder and tie with string in 3 or 4 places (p. 177); steam for 30 to 40 minutes. When cut crosswise into slices, this preparation looks remarkably like rolled meat. It is often used as a key ingredient in an elaborate vegetarian dish known as the Arhat's Feast or Monk's Dish (p. 261).

Chinese Smoked Yuba Sausage
(Su-tsang or Su-shiang tsa)

MAKES 6

The aroma and the deep red filling of this savory hors d'oeuvre make it resemble a high-grade sausage. Used widely in Chinese vegetarian restaurants, these mock sausages are also sold in most traditional marketplaces.

1 cup red fermented rice (ang-tsao)
¼ cup sake lees (chu-tsao)
¼ cup each sliced mushrooms and wheat gluten, simmered until tender in a mixture of wine, brown sugar, salt, and dashi
6 large sheets of fresh yuba

Combine the red rice, sake lees, mushrooms, and wheat gluten; mix well. Spread in a thin layer over the yuba sheets. Roll up each sheet to form a tight cylinder 9 inches long and ½ inch in diameter. Deep-fry until golden brown, then wrap from end to end with a single strand of rice straw. Now smoke over a wood fire for about 3 hours.

Chinese-style Deep-fried Yuba Hors D'oeuvre

Each of these tasty preparations are sold ready-made in many traditional marketplaces and some modern food stores in Taiwan and China (p. 257). Many are illustrated in figure 111.

*Yuba Chicken (Ssu-chi): Mix diced fresh yuba trimmings with a little soy sauce, salt, sugar, sesame oil, and minced mushrooms. Spread the mixture on a large sheet of fresh yuba, roll into a tight cylinder and cut into 4-inch lengths. Wrap each roll tightly in a 6-inch square of cotton cloth, tying both ends and the middle with string to form a sausage-like shape. Simmer rolls for 15 to 30 minutes in Sweetened Shoyu Broth (p. 40), or steam for the same time in a preheated steamer. Remove cloth, wrap each roll with a sheet of *nori*, and deep-fry until golden brown.

*Deep-fried Buddha's Yuba: Cut Buddha's Ham, Fish, or Chicken (above) diagonally into 3/8-inch-thick strips and deep-fry without batter until crisp. Serve with sautéed mushrooms and topped with a sprinkling of soy sauce.

*Yuba-Nori Roll: Simmer diced carrots, cabbage, and bamboo shoots in Sweetened Shoyu Broth, then roll in sheets of fresh yuba to form cylinders 9 inches long and ¾ inch in diameter. Wrap cylinders in *nori* and deep-fry. Cut into 1-inch lengths and serve with soy sauce.

*Yuba Drumstick (Sso-tsai): On a sheet of fresh yuba place a mixture of diced yuba trimmings, minced carrots, cabbage, *konnyaku*, mushrooms, bamboo shoots and hot spices. Roll the yuba to form a cone about 6 inches long and 2 inches in diameter at the mouth. Tuck in the edge of the yuba at the mouth of the cone to hold in the filling. Simmer cone in sweetened shoyu broth for 15 minutes, then drain well. Deep-fry without batter and serve with a sprinkling of soy sauce. The yuba may also be folded as a pouch rather than a cone.

*Glutinous Rice Roll: On a large sheet of fresh yuba, spread a mixture of cooked glutinous rice combined with diced carrots which have been simmered in sweetened shoyu broth. Roll up tightly to form a cylinder 9 inches long and ¾ inch in diameter. Deep-fry and cut into 1-inch lengths. Serve with soy sauce.

YUBA IN SALADS, SOUPS, AND SAUCES

Add yuba trimmings or sweet yuba to tossed green salads just before adding the dressing. Or deep-fry the yuba and allow to cool before adding. Use yuba in Shira-ae (p. 114) or other *Aemono* (Japanese-type salads) in the recipes described in the chapters on tofu and deep-fried tofu cookery. Or serve yuba with thinly-sliced fresh cucumbers, carrots, and mushrooms marinated with Vinegar-Miso (p. 46) or Sambai-zu (p. 41).

Flakes or trimmings of dried or sweet yuba make a delicious addition to most thick soups. For thinner soups, add small yuba rolls, large yuba spirals, or *Oharagi*-yuba.

Yuba trimmings and flakes go well in all types of sauces. In China and Taiwan, yuba is often served in gravy or thick brown sauces generally seasoned with plenty of red pepper and other fiery spices. Favorite combinations of ingredients in the sauces include: yuba and mushrooms; yuba, bamboo shoots, and mushrooms; yuba, green soybeans, leeks, and cabbage. The yuba is added shortly before the sauce is ready to be served.

Yuba in Miso Soups

Yuba is most commonly used in thick miso soups made with sweet white miso. Add 1 or 2 small yuba rolls per serving to the broth when you add the miso. In Zen Temple Cookery, trough-shaped yuba is floated on miso soups as a savory garnish or is crumbled and used as a replacement for bonita flakes. Ingredients which combine well with yuba in sweet white miso soups are *mochi*, wheat gluten, trefoil, and slivered *yuzu* or lemon rind. Try adding yuba to any of the miso soups beginning on page 118.

Yuba in Clear Soups

Place several pieces of yuba —fresh or dried, flat or rolled— into a soup bowl, then carefully pour in Clear Broth (p. 40). Allow to stand for about 5 minutes before serving. The following combinations make nice garnishes: *(shiitake)* mushrooms, (Japanese) spinach, and slivered *yuzu* rind; green beans, mushrooms simmered in Sweetened Shoyu Broth (p. 40), and several drops of *yuzu* or lemon juice; trefoil, crumbled *nori*, and *junsai* (water shield).

YUBA IN SANDWICHES, EGG DISHES, AND OVEN COOKERY

Sheets of fresh yuba lightly seasoned with shoyu are delicious served on lightly-buttered pieces of hot toast or with fresh vegetable slices on open-face sandwiches.

Add yuba trimmings and flakes, or sweet yuba to your favorite casseroles, quiches, gratin dishes, or vegetable pies, using about ¼ cup yuba to each cup of casserole ingredients.

Mixed with a little milk, yuba makes a good addition to scrambled eggs and omelets. Deep-fried dried or sweet yuba may be used with excellent results to lend a bacon-like flavor and texture to all egg dishes. Yuba Ham and Smoked Yuba Sausage (p. 246), too, are delicious with most breakfast egg preparations.

Tamago-toji Yuba   SERVES 1
(Raw Eggs Cooked Over Hot Yuba)

---

3 to 4 small yuba rolls or 2 large yuba spirals
¼ to ½ cup Sweetened Shoyu Broth (p. 40)
1 egg, lightly beaten

Combine yuba rolls and broth in a small saucepan and simmer for 3 to 4 minutes. Place rolls steaming hot into a small bowl. Quickly mix egg with 1 tablespoon hot broth, then pour over yuba. Serve as is, or use as a topping for hot brown rice or noodles.

YUBA SAUTÉED AND DEEP-FRIED

Add yuba trimmings and flakes, or sweet yuba, to vegetable dishes near the end of sautéeing, or use in Okara with Vegetables (p. 80).

Yuba is always deep-fried without batter in moderate oil for a very short time. For deep-fried yuba hors d'oeuvre see pp. 244-246.

Simmered Roll of Deep-fried Fresh Yuba   SERVES 1

---

1 large yuba spiral, 1½ inches in diameter and 1 inch thick, containing about 30 layers of rolled yuba
Oil for deep-frying
½ cup water
1½ tablespoons sugar
1 teaspoon shoyu
1 tiny "princess" bamboo shoot (2 inches long and 3/8 inch in diameter)
2 cubes of dried-frozen tofu, each 1 inch on a side
3 sections of butterbur stem, each 2 inches long

Deep-fry the yuba roll until very lightly browned; drain. Now drop into boiling water and simmer for 5 minutes to remove excess oil. Rinse twice in cold water, then soak for 5 minutes in circulating cold water.

Combine the water, sugar, and shoyu in a small saucepan and bring to a boil. Add the yuba, vegetables and frozen tofu, return to the boil, and simmer for about 7 minutes. Allow yuba and vegetables to cool, then arrange in a bowl (fig. 87, p. 218). Serve topped with a little of the cooking liquid.

This preparation is a specialty at Tokyo's *Sasa-no-Yuki* restaurant (p. 307).

Deep-fried Yuba in Ankake Sauce
(Tamago Yuba)
SERVES 4

4 large sheets of fresh yuba
Oil for deep-frying
1½ cups Ankake Sauce (p. 49)
2 teaspoons grated gingerroot or 1 teaspoon hot mustard

Fold each yuba sheet lengthwise into thirds, then fold in 2-inch lengths from one end to form compact bundles (fig. 101). Secure each bundle with a foodpick and deep-fry in 350° oil until golden brown. Divide yuba bundles among 4 deep bowls and top with the sauce and a dab of grated gingerroot or mustard.

Kenchin-maki
(Large Yuba Rolls with Tofu and Vegetables)
MAKES 2

¼ cup green peas
¼ cup diced or grated carrots
¼ cup sliced mushrooms
¼ cup diced burdock root, soaked for 15 minutes in water and drained
2 cups Sweetened Shoyu Broth (p. 40)
24 ounces tofu, pressed (p. 96)
2 large sheets of fresh yuba
Oil for deep-frying

Combine the first five ingredients in a saucepan and bring to a boil; simmer, covered, for 20 minutes. Drain vegetables, reserving broth, and combine vegetables with tofu; mash together thoroughly. Lay yuba sheets on *sudare* bamboo mats. Cover each sheet with a ½-inch-thick layer of the tofu-vegetable mixture, then roll up yuba as for Nori-wrapped Sushi (p. 170) to form a 1½-inch-diameter, 10-inch-long cylinder. Deep-fry yuba rolls until golden brown (p. 130); drain well. Return rolls to the Sweetened Shoyu Broth and simmer for 5 minutes. Cut rolls crosswise into 1-inch lengths to serve.

VARIATIONS
*Shinoda-maki: Across one end of a large sheet of fresh yuba, lay a long bundle of Osmond fern fronds and butterbur stems. Roll up yuba, secure in several places with foodpicks, and deep-fry. Now simmer in the shoyu broth. Serve as above.
*Chinese-style Yuba Spring Rolls *(Yuba Harumaki):* In a large bowl combine thinly sliced leeks, bamboo shoots, mushrooms, and minced gingerroot. Season with salt, sugar, sake, pepper, and sesame oil. Mix in 1 egg and cornstarch. Place ¼ cup of the mixture in the center of each of a number of fresh yuba rectangles, then fold over edges to form envelopes (fig. 99). Seal edges with a thick paste of flour and water. Deep-fry in moderate oil, first with the seam-side down. Cut crosswise into 1-inch-wide strips and serve with the cut surface facing upwards accompanied by Mustard-Shoyu Dipping Sauce (p. 40).

For variety, add or substitute diced onion, sweet potatoes, carrots, slivered burdock root or green peas. After deep-frying, dip in hot water to remove surface oil, then simmer in Sweetened Shoyu Broth (p. 40). Serve as is or top with Gingerroot Sauce (p. 49).

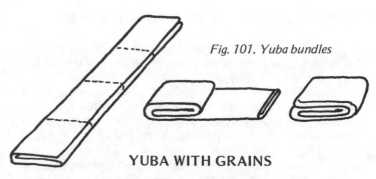

Fig. 101. Yuba bundles

YUBA WITH GRAINS

When used as a topping for grain dishes, yuba adds rich flavor, delicate sweetness, and plenty of protein. In China, Bamboo Yuba (p. 259) is often added to or sprinkled on top of breakfast rice gruel.

Yuba with Noodles

*Lay several pieces of *Oharagi* yuba or small yuba rolls atop buckwheat or whole-wheat noodles in a deep bowl. Pour on Noodle Broth (p. 40) and serve hot.
*Sauté onions and cabbage until just tender. Add thinly-sliced Buddha's Ham (p. 246) and sauté for 1 minute more. Stir in several cups of cooked noodles and season to taste with shoyu and Sesame Salt. Serve topped with a sprinkling of crumbled toasted *nori*.
*Serve cooked buckwheat noodles topped with a mixture of thinly-sliced, parboiled green beans, carrot matchsticks sautéed in lightly salted oil, slivers of uncooked leeks, and fresh yuba rolls which have been simmered for several minutes in Sweetened Shoyu Broth (p. 40). Top with hot Noodle Broth (p. 40) and season with 7-spice red pepper.

Yuba with Rice and Sushi

*Deep-fry dried yuba flakes, trough-shaped yuba, or dried sweet yuba. Sprinkle with salt, break into small pieces, and serve as a topping over hot rice.
*Sliver fresh yuba and use as one of the toppings for Five-color Sushi (p. 169). Prepared in this way, the yuba is called "threads of gold."
*Simmer yuba in Sweetened Shoyu Broth (p. 40) then use with or in place of agé as the core of Nori-wrapped Sushi (p. 170). Yellow yuba is often used in this preparation.

YUBA IN ONE-POT COOKERY AND SEASONED BROTHS

In Japan, all varieties of yuba are used widely in the various *nabe* dishes described on pages 143 to 144, and in Sukiyaki (p. 224). Add the yuba toward the end of cooking. Yuba is also preserved as *tsukudani* by simmering it for a long time in a mixture of shoyu and a little sugar, grated gingerroot, and water.

Fresh or refreshed yuba is delicious simmered for 10

minutes in a broth of 1 cup water, 2 tablespoons sake or white wine. In Chinese cookery a more potent broth is used: ½ cup water, 4½ tablespoons soy sauce, 1½ tablespoons sugar, and 1 tablespoon sake. Simmer vegetables in the broth with the yuba. Garnish with slivers of *yuzu* or lemon peel and/or minced trefoil leaves. Yuba-rolled vegetables are also delicious when simmered in seasoned broths.

In Chinese-style *Happosai*, yuba is simmered for 10 minutes in a lightly seasoned broth thickened with cornstarch and containing lotus root, burdock root, carrots, bamboo shoots, *(shiitake)* mushrooms, green peas, and cloud-ear mushrooms.

YUBA STEAMED

Yuba is a favorite addition to Chawan-mushi (p. 147). Use small yuba rolls, fresh yuba trimmings, or a small square of fresh yuba folded around a dab of slivered vegetables and secured with a foodpick. If desired, simmer any of these forms of yuba in Sweetened Shoyu Broth (p. 40) before adding to the Chawan-mushi.

Yuba Kenchin-maki (p. 248) is often prepared by steaming rather than deep-frying yuba rolls before simmering them in Sweetened Shoyu Broth.

Yuba Shinjo *(Yuba Steamed with Eggs)* SERVES 2

1 cup fresh yuba trimmings, ground in a meat grinder or
 suribachi
2 eggs, lightly beaten
2 tablespoons shoyu
4 teaspoons natural sugar

Combine all ingredients and divide among 2 custard or Chawan-mushi cups. Cover and steam as for Chawan-mushi (p. 147). Serve hot or cold.

Chinese-style Steamed Yuba

*Yuba-filled Steamed Buns: Combine equal volumes of diced yuba trimmings, mushrooms, and carrots, and simmer until tender in Sweetened Shoyu Broth (p. 40). Place 1 heaping tablespoon of the drained vegetables at the center of 2-inch diameter patties of leavened dough. Fold dough around filling and seal to form a bun, then steam in a pre-heated steamer for 30 minutes. Serve hot, topped with a sprinkling of soy sauce.

*Pressed Yuba with Peanut Sauce: Dice fresh yuba trimmings and press into a mold the shape of a bun. Steam until firm, then serve topped with a sauce made from a mixture of peanut butter, miso, sugar, and vinegar.

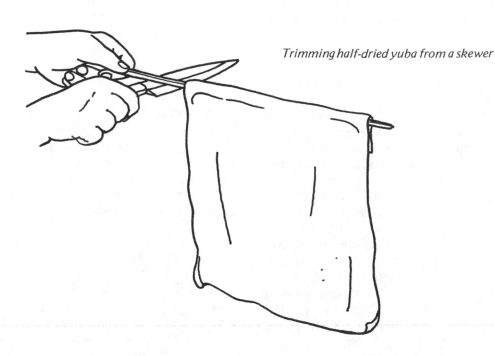

Trimming half-dried yuba from a skewer

15
Tofu and Yuba in China, Taiwan, and Korea

TOFU ORIGINATED in China over two thousand years ago and today serves as one of the most popular basic foods of that nation's more than 800 million people. Costing only about 8 cents per pound—roughly one-third the price of regular Japanese tofu (which has a lower protein content)—firm Chinese-style tofu plays a crucial nutritional role in the life of most Chinese. The average Taiwanese, for example, is said to eat as much as 64 pounds of tofu every year.

The subject of Chinese tofu is so vast, and the varieties of tofu and tofu cuisine so numerous and unusual, that this short chapter actually merits an entire volume. For every Chinese province makes its own varieties of tofu and has its own names (and pronunciations) for the many varieties found throughout the other provinces. This proliferation of titles, combined with the presence in China of numerous dialects and the difficulties of phonetic translation from Chinese into English, has resulted in the fact that these various types of tofu often appear in cookbooks and other contemporary literature under differing and sometimes contradictory names. Fortunately, even though each of the basic varieties is referred to in speech differently by the Mandarin-speaking people of Peking, the Cantonese-speaking residents of the south, and the citizens of Taiwan, each is nevertheless written with the same ideographic characters by all. Thus we have learned (the hard way) that the easiest way to make ourselves understood by Chinese chefs or tofu masters—whether in Japan, Taiwan, or America—is to carry a list of the names of all the different types of tofu written in Chinese!

In what follows, we have consistently used the standard Mandarin, which is slowly becoming China's national language. The word "tofu" will be used as a general term to refer to all varieties of tofu, Japanese or Chinese. In Mandarin, the word for tofu is *doufu*, with the first syllable pronounced like a combination of the two English words "doe" and "toe." It is called *dowfu* (also spelled *dow-foo*) in Cantonese, with the first syllable being pronounced like the "Dow" of Dow Jones.

At present, many excellent Chinese tofu shops are in operation throughout the United States (see Appendix B). Most produce several varieties of Japanese-style tofu as well as uniquely Chinese tofu products such as doufu, pressed tofu, savory tofu, white *doufu-ru*, and hollow agé cubes. In addition, Chinese grocery stores carry red *doufu-ru*, Chinese dried yuba, and bamboo yuba. A list of the size, shape, and Chinese name(s) of each of these products together with the types of stores at which they are sold can be found on page 22.

Although many more varieties of tofu are found in China and Taiwan than in Japan, a number of common Japanese varieties (such as grilled and dried-frozen tofu, agé, ganmo, and kinugoshi cakes) are rarely if ever seen there. China's southern provinces have produced the greatest number of tofu products, possibly because of the necessity to find ways to keep the tofu from spoiling in their semi-tropical climate.

Three Varieties of Tofu

Regular Chinese tofu can be divided into three basic types according to moisture content and texture: *doufu*, which is about as firm as Japanese-style grilled tofu; *pressed tofu*, which is even firmer; and *Chinese kinugoshi*, which is often so much softer than Japanese kinugoshi that it cannot be cut into cakes.

Doufu: Known in the West as Chinese-style firm tofu, *doufu* is the most common variety of tofu found in China. It is closely related to regular Japanese tofu, although it has a firmer texture and contains less water (about as much as does Japanese tofu after being pressed). By using doufu in all recipes calling for pressed Japanese tofu, or in stir-fried or sautéed dishes, you can be assured of excellent results while saving the time otherwise needed for pressing. (Substitute 9 ounces of doufu for 12 ounces of regular Japanese tofu.) Having a firm, cohesive texture, doufu keeps its form well—when transported over China's back roads as well as during the vigorous process of stir-frying. In semitropical areas such as Canton and Taiwan, its low water content helps it to stay fresh for up to several days without refrigeration or the addition of preservatives; thus doufu is especially well suited for tropical or semitropical areas such as India, Africa, and South America. Its protein content averages about 10 percent (versus Japanese tofu at 7.8 percent and ground beef at about 13 percent).

As it spread throughout East Asia, doufu was transmitted first to Japan where it became known as tofu. Its close relative can still be found in Japanese farmhouse tofu which, like its Chinese progenitor, is so firm it can be tied with rope and carried hanging from one hand (fig. 112, p. 271). In the Philippines, this variety of Chinese tofu was to become known as *tojo* or *tokua;* in Indonesia as *tahu.*

Since doufu is often solidified with a mixture of nigari and calcium sulfate, and since (like farmhouse tofu) it is not generally soaked in water after being removed from the settling box, it has a rich, subtly sweet flavor. Whereas Japanese tofu is prepared in large, deep settling boxes, then cut into 12-ounce cakes sold individually by the tofu maker at his shop and in the neighborhood, doufu is prepared in the form of 5½ pound "flats" about 10 to 12 inches square and 1½ inches thick. Each flat is cut to yield 16 squares, each square weighing about 4½ ounces and measuring 2½ to 3 inches on a side and 1½ inches thick. Venders buy entire flats from the maker, place them on wooden pallets for easy transport, then sell the doufu in marketplaces or by the roadsides. The flat is usually cut into individual squares for each customer (fig. 102).

Although most doufu is quite firm, a less com-

Fig. 102. Cutting doufu
at the marketplace

mon variety with about the same water content as regular Japanese tofu can also be found in parts of China and Taiwan. In the West, fresh doufu is now widely available at Chinese food markets, natural food stores, and some supermarkets, where it is sold immersed in water in sealed plastic tubs.

Pressed Tofu: The firmest variety of Chinese tofu, pressed tofu or *doufu-kan*, contains about 22 percent protein and only 62 percent water. It can be prepared at home from Japanese tofu by means of the reshaping process described on page 98. The character *kan* means "dry" or "containing little water." In the actual process of making pressed tofu, cloth-lined trays or small cloth-wrapped bundles of firm curds are pressed in multiple layers under a large hand-turned screw press until as much whey and water as possible have been expelled (fig. 103). The finished tofu has a chewy, meaty texture like that of smoked ham, sausage, or firm cheese. The use of nigari, or a mixture of nigari and calcium sulfate solidifiers, adds to the tofu's solidity.

Regular pressed tofu is sold in individual squares about 3 inches on a side and ¾ inch thick. Although many squares are sold as is, with their natural white color and subtly-sweet flavor, others are simmered in solutions of water and either burnt millet sugar, molasses, turmeric, or tea to create a variety of colors and flavors and to further help preserve them. Thus, some squares are dark chocolate brown and others are brilliant saffron yellow. The latter, stamped with a vermilion red Chinese character, are used as offerings at household altars.

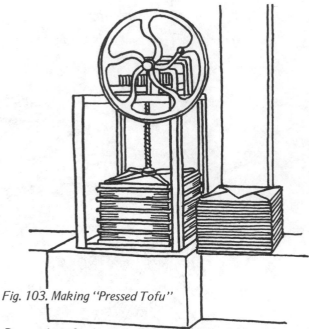

Fig. 103. Making "Pressed Tofu"

Pressed tofu is usually cut into thin strips, shredded, or diced. It is stir-fried with vegetables, used in thickened Chinese sauces, added to soups, marinated with fresh (or cooked) vegetables and nuts in salads, or served in thin slices like cuts of cold meat. Its firm texture and high protein content make it an excellent meat replacement in many Western-style preparations including casseroles and breakfast egg dishes.

Savory Pressed Tofu (Wu-hsiang kan): This variety of pressed tofu is prepared by simmering pressed tofu squares in a mixture of soy sauce, oil, and seasonings. The latter, which vary widely from maker to maker and from province to province, include anise, garlic, minced scallion, cinnamon, cloves, peppermint, and bay leaves as well as a number of spices which have no English equivalent. The name *wu-hsiang kan* means literally "five fragrances dry" indicating that a combination of five or more spices and seasonings is generally used. This tofu ranges in color from light to dark brown and has a texture and flavor resembling smoked ham. In the San Francisco area it is freshly prepared daily and sold as Flavored Bean Cake. Savory Pressed Tofu is served as an hors d'oeuvre, thinly sliced like cold cuts, and is often accompanied by drinks. Or it is sometimes used as a side dish or topping for rice gruel, or in salads with peanuts and a sesame oil dressing.

Soy-sauce Pressed Tofu (Chiang-yu doufu-kan): Sold in most market places and tofu shops in China and Taiwan (but not yet available in the West), these 1½-inch squares, pressed to a thickness of only 3/8 inch, are simmered in a mixture of soy sauce and water until they turn dark brown. Some varieties, prepared at delicatessens, are simmered (whole or diced) in a chicken or pork broth seasoned with soy sauce and red peppers. Others are smoked after being simmered and served as an hors d'oeuvre, like smoked ham, or used as a seasoning for rice dishes.

Pressed Tofu Sheets (Pai-yeh): Perhaps the most unusual variety of pressed tofu, *pai-yeh* is written with the characters meaning either "one hundred pages" or "one hundred leaves." Sometimes called bean curd "sheets" or "wrappers" in Chinese cookbooks, each sheet looks like a 6- to 12-inch square of canvas with a clothlike pattern imprinted on both sides, and each has a soft flexible texture. They are prepared by ladling a thin layer of firm curds onto each of about 100 pieces of cloth stacked consecutively in a tall wooden frame. The alternate layers of cloth and curds are then pressed for several hours beneath a very heavy weight. Most of the finished sheets are sold in outdoor marketplaces and are generally used in cooking as wrappers for various steamed or deep-fried foods, just like *wonton,* spring-roll (*harumaki*), or egg-roll skins. Since the sheets resemble and are used in many of the same ways as Chinese yuba (*tou-p'i*), they are sometimes called by the same name. Sheets which have been cut (by hand or with a noodle-cutting machine) into very thin strips are known as "pressed tofu noodles" or "beancurd shreds" (*doufu-ssu* or *kan-ssu*), and sheets which have been cut into ½-inch-wide strips that are tied into simple overhand knots are known as "pressed tofu loops" or *pai-yeh chieh* (fig 104). These preparations are very popular in soups, *nabe* dishes or firepots, and in simmered or sautéed vegetable dishes.

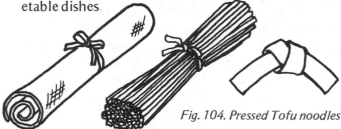

Fig. 104. Pressed Tofu noodles

Pressed tofu sheets are also rolled up tightly to form a cylinder, wrapped and bound in a piece of cloth, and simmered in water until they are tender yet maintain their form when unwrapped. Sold in Chinese markets as varieties of Buddha's Chicken (*su-chi*) or Buddha's Ham (*suhuo-t'ui*), this firm tofu is generally used like rolled meat. It is usually either simmered in sweetened soy broth or stir-fried with vegetables, or it is sometimes allowed to mold for several days, and is then deep-fried in sesame oil

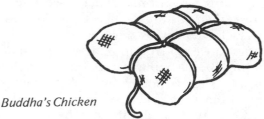

Buddha's Chicken

to give it a flavor resembling that of fried chicken. Another preparation, also called Buddha's Chicken, is made by first softening pressed tofu sheets in a solution of natural soda and water, then coating each sheet with sesame oil and pressing a number of sheets into individual molds. After being steamed, the "chicken" is cut into ½-inch-thick slices and deep-fried until crisp and golden brown. (A third variety of Buddha's Chicken is prepared in a similar way from pressed fresh yuba.)

Salted-Dried Tofu (*Doufu-kan*): This variety is prepared from squares of regular pressed tofu which are rubbed with salt, tied together with rice straw like the dried-frozen tofu made in Japanese farmhouses (p. 228), and hung in sunlight until thoroughly dried. Very similar to Japanese *rokujo-dofu* (p. 94), salted-dried tofu is dark brown and has a consistency resembling that of a very firm dry cheese. It is generally shaved or sliced into paper-thin strips and used in vegetable soups, in dashi as a substitute for bonita flakes, or as an hors d'oeuvre with drinks. Although the Chinese name is pronounced exactly like the *doufu-kan* meaning "pressed tofu," it is written with a different character for *kan*, one meaning "to dry thoroughly."

Chinese Soft Kinugoshi (*Shui-* or *Sui-dofu*):Not nearly as common in China or Taiwan as is kinugoshi in Japan, this product has a very soft texture due largely to the thinness of the soymilk from which it is made and to the practice of storing it under water to prevent spoilage. Two varieties are available in the Far East, both solidified with calcium sulfate. The first is prepared like Japanese kinugoshi and is sold in cakes which are only slightly softer than the average Japanese-style product. The second, which is more common, is curded in a large kettle and is too soft to be cut and sold as individual cakes. Rather, it is scooped like pudding into large bowls brought by each customer to the tofu shop and is generally eaten with a spoon, topped with a little soy sauce or sugar, or served in soups and delicate sautéed dishes. Both varieties are also knows an "young" or "soft" tofu (*nen-* or *nan-doufu*) in contrast to firm doufu and pressed tofu, both of which are known as "old" tofu (*lao-doufu*); the word "old" being used here in the figurative sense to indicate that lack of softness and flexibility often connected with old age. Chinese kinugoshi is often referred to as "calcium sulfate tofu" (*shin-kao doufu* or *sekko-dofu*) to contrast it with most traditional firm tofu which was solidified with nigari.

Warm Soymilk Curds

A popular delicacy throughout China and Taiwan, curds play a much more important role in the nutritional life and cookery of these countries than they do in Japan.

Chinese Smooth Curds (*Doufu-nao* or *Dounao*): A close relative of the softer variety of kinugoshi, this product's Chinese name means "tofu brains": when ladled into a bowl, the warm curds apparently remind the Chinese of their namesake. Most widely served in southern China, Taiwan, and Nanking, smooth curds are now available in the West as Tofu Pudding or Fresh Soybean Pudding. In China, they are made in special shops and hawked along city streets early each morning by men who either carry the curds in wooden buckets dangling from shoulder poles or who sell the curds out of small pushcarts (fig. 105). In some areas the venders chant the name of their product as they roam the awakening streets. Customers seat themselves at stools around the cart and get ready for a hearty breakfast (costing less than 5 cents). The vender ladles out scoops of custard-like curds into deep bowls, tops them with a warm syrupy sauce (*hung t'ang*) containing peanuts and brown sugar, and places them (together with porcelain spoons) on the edge of the cart, which serves as a table. In some areas the curds

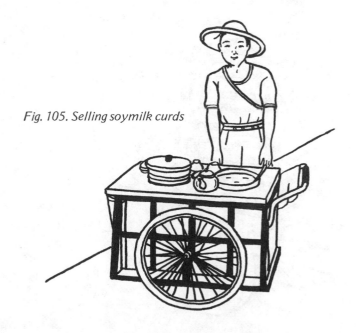

Fig. 105. Selling soymilk curds

are mixed with *cha-t'sai* pickles, tiny dried shrimp, soy sauce, and a dash of sesame oil, then served as a thick soup. In others, they are mixed with sweet oil, vinegar, finely chopped meat, or spices.

Most smooth curds are prepared at special soy-milk shops rather than at tofu shops. Soymilk is cooked in a large kettle over a very hot fire and is solidified in the kettle; the hot fire imparts a fragrant, slightly nutty flavor to the curds. When solidified with nigari, the curds have an extremely soft texture, more delicate than that of yogurt; when calcium sulfate or natural gypsum is used, they have much the same texture as soft Japanese kinugoshi.

Curds-in-Whey (*Doufu-hua*): The Chinese name for this variety of curds means "tofu flowers," since the curds have somewhat the same appearance as eggs swirled in hot broth to make egg-flower soup. Although most varieties are identical to Japanese *oboro* (p. 86), in some areas they are prepared by simmering smooth curds over a low fire to give them a firmer texture.

Deep-fried Tofu

Deep-fried tofu is not as readily available in China and Taiwan as it is in Japan, and the art of deep-frying has not reached the level of sophistication in Chinese tofu shops that it has in their Japanese counterparts. This may be partly because many Chinese chefs and housewives prefer to deep-fry their tofu at home so as to serve it hot and crisp. All Chinese deep-fried tofu is called *yu-dofu* ("oil tofu") or *cha-dofu* ("frying-tofu"). Chinese thick-agé triangles, the most common variety, are prepared by

pressing curds very firmly under a weighted lever (fig. 106), then cutting the sheets of finished tofu into triangles 1½ inches thick and 1½ inches on a side. These are deep-fried in a single large pot of very hot oil (fig. 107). Another popular variety now available in the West is hollow agé cubes (*doufu-kuo*) prepared from 1-inch cubes of doufu which swell up during deep-frying and can later be stuffed with meats or vegetables; they are often added to thickened sauces or soups. Thick agé cubes (*cha-dofu*) or agé balls are sometimes sold strung on a loop of bamboo fiber (fig. 108) and are eaten with syrup like fritters by Chinese laborers as a popular lunchtime snack. In some tofu shops, entire cakes of medium-firm doufu may be cut on both sides in a criss-cross pattern, opened up by pulling gently on both ends to create a netlike structure, and deep-fried (fig. 109). When simmered in seasoned broths or sauces, this structure helps the netlike thick agé to absorb flavors and is quite attractive when served. Neither agé nor ganmo are generally prepared in Chinese tofu shops; the technique of deep-frying in moderate and then hot oil to make the tofu expand has apparently not yet been developed. Sautéed Tofu (*kuo-lao doufu*), a cross between Japanese thick agé and grilled tofu, is thinly sliced doufu fried in oil until it turns a rich brownish yellow.

Fig. 109. Net-like thick agé

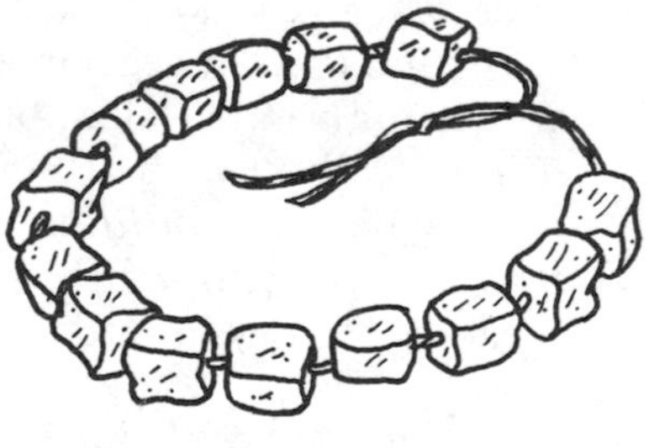

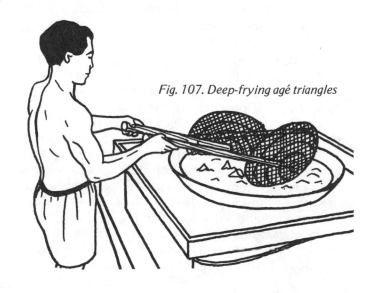

Fig. 108. Threaded thick-agé cubes

Fig. 106. Pressing curds

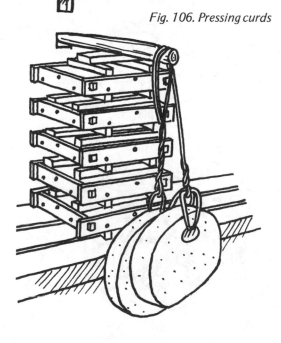

Fig. 107. Deep-frying agé triangles

Frozen Tofu

Frozen tofu, called *tung-doufu* or *ping-doufu*, has been prepared in China since ancient times by setting firm tofu out in the snow overnight. It is the exact counterpart of the "one-night frozen tofu" traditionally prepared in the Japanese countryside. However, dried-frozen tofu, a Japanese invention, has come into production only very recently in China and does not yet play an important role in Chinese cookery. It is sold in small paper boxes as Dried Bean Curd.

Doufu-ru

Surely the most distinctive genre of tofu prepared in China is *doufu-ru*, or fermented tofu. Doufu-ru, in its many forms, is completely unlike anything prepared in Japan or, for that matter, any food familiar to most Westerners. Known in English as Chinese cheese, tofu-, bean curd-, or soybean cheese, or preserved- or pickled bean curd, it is called *doufu-ru*, *furu*, *rufu*, or *dou-ru* in Mandarin, *fuyu* or *funan* in Cantonese (and in most Western tofu shops run by Cantonese masters), and *sufu* or *dou-sufu* in Shanghai and in most scientific literature. The latter terms, which mean "molded milk," are not at all familiar to most Chinese.

Doufu-ru has a soft—almost creamy—consistency and strong flavor and aroma reminiscent of Camembert cheese. Most varieties, seasoned with minced red peppers, are quite sharp and hot on the tongue, so that a little bit goes a long way. Widely enjoyed as a relish and seasoning, doufu-ru is prepared and sold in special Chinese pickle-and-miso shops rather than in neighborhood tofu shops. Traditionally, it was also prepared in many homes and farmhouses. The process of fermentation and preservation in a brining liquor enables this variety of tofu to last for as long as one to two years, even in semitropical climates, and its low cost makes doufu-ru especially popular among the poorer classes. Like cheese, wines, miso, shoyu, and many other fermented foods, doufu-ru gradually improves in flavor, aroma, and texture as it ages. As mold enzymes break down and digest the protein in the tofu, the latter's sharp flavors mellow and its consistency softens: well-aged doufu-ru virtually melts on the tongue. After the tofu has ripened for 6 to 8 months, its color turns from yellowish white to a soft light-brown, and the wine-and-salt brining liquor, too, grows richer and mellower.

Fermented tofu is the only traditional soybean product made in the manner of Western cheeses, that is, by ripening tofu with a mold. Although one would think that soymilk could easily be made into cheeses similar to those prepared from dairy milk, repeated attempts to produce such cheeses—even in modern Western laboratories—have until very recently met with failure. But unlike Western cheeses, doufu-ru is immersed in an alcoholic brine during ripening and is generally sold still immersed in the brining liquor in pint bottles or small cans. To prepare doufu-ru, ¾- to 1¼-inch cubes of doufu or firm tofu are innoculated with spores of a mucor-type mold, then incubated in a warm place for about 3 to 7 days until each cube is covered with a dense mat of fragrant white mycelium. The molded cubes are immersed in the brine, which generally contains Chinese rice wine and red peppers (or other spices and seasonings). After ripening for one to two months in the brining liquor, the bottled tofu is shipped to Chinese markets where it is often allowed to age for another two to four months before being placed on sale. It is said that if the doufu-ru remains motionless when the jar is spun quickly on its axis, it has been properly aged and is ready to use.

In China, the most popular ways of serving doufu-ru are as a seasoning for *congee* (hot breakfast rice porridge) or rice, as an appetizer or hors d'oeuvre with drinks, or as an ingredient in stir-fried dishes or simmered sauces, used to add zest and flavor. The brining liquor is also used in many of these preparations. In Western cookery, doufu-ru is delicious used like Camembert or Roquefort cheese in dips, spreads, dressings, and casseroles. Recipes for each of these preparations are given at the end of this chapter.

The ideographic character for *fu* in doufu-ru (also used in the word doufu) means "spoiled." The character for *ru* means "milk." These characters have an unusual and very ancient etymology. Although the Chinese had a highly developed civilization long before the beginning of the Christian era, they never developed the art of dairy farming or, consequently, of making cheese. But their northerly neighbors, the Mongols, whom the Chinese regarded as uncivilized barbarians, were quite skilled in the preparation of fine goat's cheese. The Chinese called this cheese *furu*, or "spoiled milk." Centuries later, the Chinese learned how to prepare their own variety of fermented cheese, but from soy rather than dairy milk, probably with some help (or at least inspiration) from the Mongols. And the name which they had used derogatorily for the Mongolian cheese gradually came to be used for their own tofu cheese: their insult boomeranged and remains with them to this day. Consequently some modern Chinese and

Japanese—especially those operating expensive restaurants—write the character *fu* in the words tofu, doufu, and doufu-ru with a different character which, although pronounced "fu," means "affluent, ample, or abundant."

Records show that doufu-ru was being produced in China by the fifteenth century and that it may have originated much earlier. The technique for making fermented tofu spread from China to Vietnam (where similar a food called *chao* is now prepared) and to the East Indies (where *tao tuan* is made.) A type of fermented tofu called *tahuri* is also produced in the Philippines by packing large (4- by 4- by 2½-inch) cakes of firm molded tofu into cans with a large quantity of salt. Neither sake nor brine is used in the process. After ripening for several months, the tofu is yellowish brown and has a distinctive salty flavor.

The four basic types of Chinese fermented tofu are white doufu-ru, red doufu-ru, *tsao*-doufu ("tofu fermented in sake less"), and *chiang*-doufu ("tofu fermented in miso or soy sauce"). The brining liquor used for each is also a popular ingredient in many Chinese recipes, especially in dipping sauces. Called doufu-ru *chih*, it often contains various spices or minced red peppers which make it a zesty seasoning.

White Doufu-ru (*Pai doufu-ru*): In most of China and in the West, this is the most popular type of fermented tofu. Unless it is specifically being contrasted with the red variety, it is generally called simply doufu-ru. The tofu's flavor, color, and aroma can be modified either by changing the salt or alcohol composition of the brining liquor or by adding different combinations of spices and seasonings. The most common brine contains about 10 percent alcohol and 12 percent salt; some contain little or no alcohol, while others may contain more than twice as much alcohol as salt. One brine of the latter type yields "drunken cheese" (*tsui-fang*) and another yields "small cheese cubes" (*chih-fang*).

At least five different varieties of white doufu-ru are sold in markets and marketplaces throughout Taiwan and China. The most popular is red pepper doufu-ru (*la doufu-ru, la-chiao furu*, or *la furu*). Available in the West as Fermented Bean Curd, it contains a hearty portion of minced red peppers which make the flavor hot and spicy while also serving as a natural preservative. When sesame oil is added to this type of fermented tofu it is known as sesame-red pepper doufu-ru (*mayu-la* foufu-ru). Some milder and particularly delicious types of doufu-ru are made in liquors containing only rice wine, salt, and water plus an occasional small amount of sesame oil. Other seasonings include anise, cinnamon, lemon juice, slivered lemon peel, tiny dried shrimp, and diced ham. Spiced, fermented tofu with five seasonings is called *wu-hsiang furu*, and a variety of fermented tofu called *hsia-tsu* doufu-ru is dried after brining, then sold in paper cartons.

Red Doufu-ru (*Hung doufu-ru, Nanru,* or *Nanyu*): This product is prepared in basically the same way as its white counterpart except that Chinese red fermented rice (*ang-tsao*) is added to the brining liquor (to give it a deep-red color, thick consistency, and distinctive flavor and aroma) and soy sauce is generally used in place of rice wine. The liquor may or may not contain minced peppers. Red doufu-ru is now available in the West packed in a hot red sauce in small (4- to 6-ounce) cans labeled Red Bean Curd. One popular variety is "rose-essence doufu-ru" (*mei-kui doufu-ru, mei-kui hung nanru*, or *nanyu*), made in a brining liquor similar in appearance to ketchup and seasoned with small amounts of rose essence, caramel, and natural sugar. The seasonings lend a distinctive fragrance to any dish in which it is served. Red doufu-ru is especially popular in spicy hot sauces served with *nabe* dishes, meats, and fresh or even live "dancing" shrimp.

Tsao-doufu: Prepared by aging either fresh or molded tofu in rice wine and its lees (*chu-tsao*), this product has a heady alcoholic flavor and aroma. Green tsao-doufu (*ch'ou doufu*), a popular Taiwanese food, is prepared in homes and marketplace stalls by placing pressed tofu squares into a crock containing sake less, crushed leaves, and a green mucor mold. After the tofu has fermented for 12 hours or more, venders peddle it in the streets. *Ch'ou doufu* means "foul-smelling tofu." While many Chinese themselves dislike its strong aroma and flavor, slippery texture, unusual color, and aftermath of bad breath, its devotees claim that once a taste is acquired for this unique food, it is for evermore regarded as a great delicacy.

Chiang-doufu: Prepared by pickling firm cubes of tofu for several days in either Chinese-style miso (*chiang*) or soy sauce (*chiang-yu*), this product has a reddish-brown color and a salty flavor. In some cases it is dried briefly or fermented with mold before being pickled; sake lees are occasionally mixed with the *chiang*. This tofu often has much the same rich sweetness as Japanese Finger Lickin' Miso (p. 31). Chiang-doufu sauce (*chiang-doufu chih*) is prepared by mixing the pickled tofu with its pickling brine, then grinding the mixture until it is smooth; it is used as a condiment for Chinese lamb or beef dishes.

Soymilk

Chinese-style soymilk (*doufu chiang, dou-chiang, dou-nai*, or *dou-ru*) has been an essential source of protein for Chinese infants, children, and adults since long before the Christian era and continues to play a much more important role in the nutritional life of the people than does soymilk in Japan. It is widely enjoyed as a spicy hot breakfast soup or warm, sweetened beverage (pp. 204 and 207). Every morning many Chinese bring large containers to the local tofu shop to purchase their family's daily supply of soymilk. Whereas the Japanese drink only the rich, thick soymilk used to make kinugoshi tofu, the Chinese drink the thinner soymilk used to make regular tofu, since neither thick soymilk nor Japanese-style kinugoshi are prepared in Chinese tofu shops. Many small shops and some large factories are engaged solely in the production of soymilk and most of the shops serve their specialty from early morning until late at night in adjoining streetside cafes or restaurants. Accompanied by 18-inch-long deep-fried bread sticks and Chinese wheat *tortillas*, the soymilk serves as the basis of a snack or light meal. In some cities, it is bottled and sold by street venders (fig. 110).

Fig. 110. A soymilk vender

Yuba

Yuba is much more popular and much less expensive in China and Taiwan than it is in Japan. There are hundreds of yuba shops throughout Taiwan and probably thousands in China, and yuba plays an important role in the nutritional life of the people in home and restaurant cookery. Called bean curd "skin" or "sheets" in most Chinese cookbooks, yuba is known in Mandarin as *doufu-p'i*, "tofu skin," or *doufu-i*, "tofu robes." In any public market, especially in the old quarter of many cities, there will be a number of special shops or stalls selling only yuba in a variety of forms. In two of Taiwan's largest cities, Taipei and Taichung, for example, we saw more than 35 different types of fresh, dried, or pre-cooked yuba for sale.

One of the most obvious differences between the uses to which yuba is put in China as compared to Japan is the remarkable ingenuity and inventiveness employed by the Chinese in giving yuba the semblance of meat. Imagine walking by the display case of an attractive restaurant or marketplace yuba shop and seeing perfect replicas of plucked hens, roosters and ducks, light-brown fish (complete with fins, gills, eyes, and mouth) juicy hams, tripe, liver and rolled meats—all made from yuba (fig. 111)! Rich red sausage links hang in rows and deep-fried drumsticks are handsomely arranged on a large platter—together with a lifesized pig's head. Most of these imitation meat dishes are prepared by pressing fresh yuba into a hinged (wooden or aluminum) mold, then placing the well-packed mold in a steamer until the yuba's shape is fixed. In some cases the finished products are deep-fried or simmered in a sweetened or seasoned soy broth (in the same way the Chinese "whole-cook" many fish and other animals). Served at *su-tsai* restaurants which specialize in Buddhist vegetarian cookery, each has its own well-known name: Buddha's Chicken (*suchi*), Buddha's Fish (*suyu* or *sushi*), Buddha's Duck (*suya*), Vegetarian Tripe (*taoto*) or Liver (*sukan*); Molded Pig's Head (*tutao*), and Molded Ham (*suhuo*). The Sausage Links (*enchan*) are made of a mixture of fresh yuba, agar, and Chinese red fermented rice (*ang-tsao*) packed into real sausage skins. Buddha's Drumsticks (*sutsai tsui*) are prepared by rolling fresh yuba into a conical shape which is filled with minced mushrooms and then deep-fried. Deep-fried Duck (*suya*) is made by pressing together sheets of soft fresh yuba, then tearing these into irregular pieces about 6 to 8 inches across; finally the pieces are deep-fried. Each of these dishes is served at fine restaurants or family banquets as part of eleborate cold plates. Occasionally they are served whole in soups and *nabe* dishes, or sliced and deep-fried. Recipes for a number of these basic preparations are given in Chapter 14.

Fig. 111. Yuba mock meats

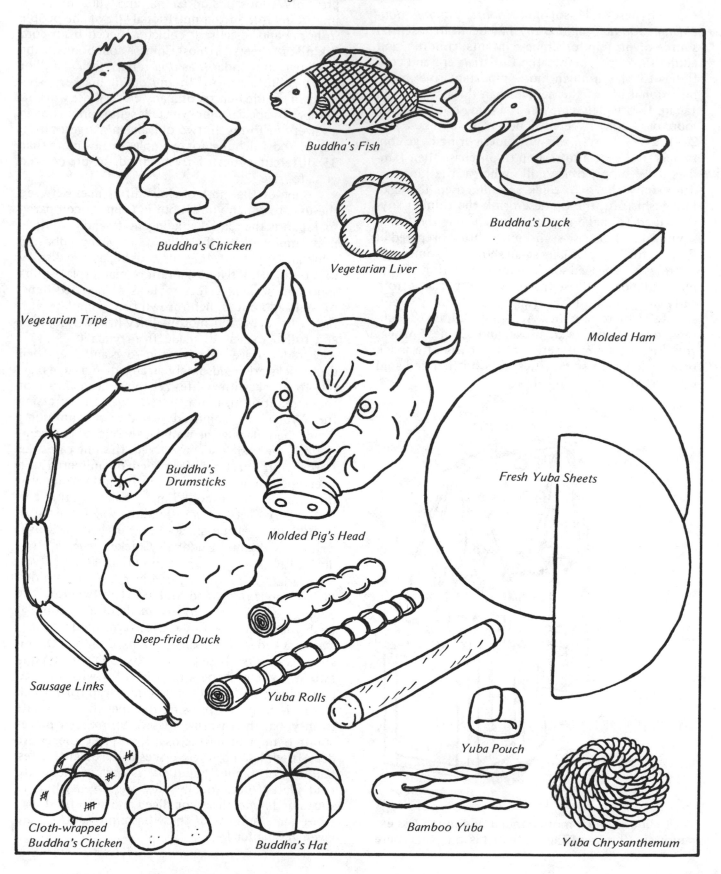

Buddha's Fish

Buddha's Duck

Buddha's Chicken

Vegetarian Liver

Vegetarian Tripe

Molded Ham

Buddha's Drumsticks

Molded Pig's Head

Fresh Yuba Sheets

Sausage Links

Deep-fried Duck

Yuba Rolls

Yuba Pouch

Cloth-wrapped
Buddha's Chicken

Buddha's Hat

Bamboo Yuba

Yuba Chrysanthemum

Yuba in China and Taiwan is remarkably inexpensive. Most fresh yuba sells for as little as 27 cents per pound; higher quality varieties cost about 40 cents. Dried yuba, containing 53 percent protein, sells for about the same prices. In Japan, comparable yuba is roughly 15 *times* as expensive! Consequently, in China, yuba is available to everyone, whereas in Japan, since ancient times, it has been enjoyed mostly by the affluent. Chinese yuba is sold in particularly large amounts to temples, Buddhist laymen, vegetarians, and the nutrition-conscious.

Fresh Yuba: About 90 percent of all yuba made in Taiwan and China is sold fresh, while in Japan, the majority is sold dried. The most common form of fresh yuba is sheets, some of which are round or semi-circular since the yuba is often prepared in large (16-inch-diameter) steaming pots (fig. 112). Some sheets are so thin they are almost trans-

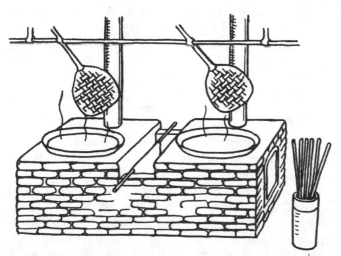

Fig. 112. Yuba steaming pots

parent, and others, sold by weight, are as thick as cotton cloth. Whole or cut sheets are folded into many forms and sizes to make rolls and pouches later simmered in sweetened soy broths, deep-fried, steamed, or smoked. Long rolls are often bound with a strand of rice straw to hold them together during deep-frying. One particularly delicious variety of roll is filled with Chinese red fermented rice, sake lees or glutinuous rice, and minced pickles; it is wrapped with a sheet of *nori* before being deep-fried or smoked. Pouches are generally filled with diced bamboo shoots, mushrooms, or other vegetables. Fresh yuba sheets, often in combination with pressed tofu sheets, are shaped into different forms by wrapping them in cloth, tying the bundle with twine, and steaming or boiling until set. Cloth-wrapped Bud-

dha's Chicken (*suchi*) is prepared this way and may bo sold either wrapped in the cloth or a sheet of *nori*, or simmered in a sweetened or seasoned broth. Buddha's Hat (*taobo*) is prepared by mixing diced mushrooms with the yuba before cloth-wrapping and steaming.

Dried Yuba (*Kan doufu-p'i*): Much of the dried yuba sold in Taiwan and Hong Kong is prepared in the world's most modern yuba factories using completely natural methods to make a high-quality, low-priced product that can be stored for up to 6 months. The great majority of dried yuba is sold in plain sheets—either round or rectangular—in 1¼-pound bundles. Sweet yuba (*amayuba*) and deep-fried yuba sheets and rolls are also available. Most Chinese rolled dried yuba is sold as Bamboo Yuba (*fuchu*), so called because the color and form of the u-shaped rolls resemble a pair of young bamboo shoots. This variety is now available in many Chinese food markets in the West. Yuba Chrysanthemums are one of the most elaborate and decorative of the many yuba forms; to make them, fresh yuba is folded and twisted into a three-dimensional spiral about 4 inches in diameter and 4 inches high. Many thin slits are then cut along the yuba's perimeter to resemble chrysanthemum petals. After the flowers have dried, they are painted with natural red, yellow, and green food dyes, then deep-fried to be used as ingredients in soups and *nabe* dishes. One of the most famous dried yuba preparations is a variety of Buddha's Ham (*suhuo-t'ui*) made by sautéing crumbled dried yuba with grated gingerroot, soy sauce, and (diced or grated) carrots, pressing the warm mixture into a rectangular mold, and allowing it to cool. Served in thin slices as an hors d'oeuvre, it is as juicy and delicious as its meat counterpart.

Tofu and Yuba in Chinese Cookery

Gourmets have long recognized Chinese cuisine to be one of the finest in the world, and in it, tofu and yuba arc highly esteemed foods which form an integral part of each of the main schools of Chinese cookery. In Canton, China's culinary capital, tofu is used to create the light and subtle flavors and textures which characterize Cantonese cookery. In Shanghai, tofu is used in dishes prepared by the technique known as "red cooking," wherein foods are simmered in a rich mixture of soy sauce, stock, anise, and other seasonings to yield hearty, robust flavors. In the Imperial cuisine of Peking, firm tofu is a favorite ingredient in stir-fried dishes and in the many powerfully-flavored sauces with contrasting seasonings: sweet-and-sour or hot-and-sour. In Szechwan and Taiwan, the mild flavor of fine tofu makes an excellent base for the fiery and exciting flavors created by *fagara* red peppers and spicy sauces. In the boldly-seasoned, hot cookery of Hunan, the famous firepots of Mongolia, and the distinctive red broths of Fukien, too, tofu is a popular ingredient. And tofu is widely used in *Mandarin* cooking as well, *"Mandarin"* referring not to a regional cooking style but to a level of quality suitable for the emperor and the members of the court. Thus, a fine tofu dish prepared in any of the regional styles may bear the proud Mandarin title; it need not be prepared in the Peking or northern style.

Tofu is also popular in the thousands of Chinese restaurants in Japan where dishes such as Mabo-doufu (p. 128), and Oyster Sauce Tofu (p. 129) are particularly popular. In America's many Chinese restaurants—a majority of which are Cantonese—tofu can be enjoyed in traditional Chinese preparations as well as dishes modified to Western tastes and expectations. On the menu of virtually every Chinese restaurant in the world is a section entitled "bean curd," which generally contains at least five, and often as many as ten or fifteen dishes. Tofu also appears in soups, firepots and sandpots, vegetable, meat or seafood dishes, and even hors d'oeuvre and desserts. And in many Chinese delicatessens, ready-made preparations such as Oyster Sauce Tofu and Marinated Pressed Tofu are available.

In Japan, the great majority of tofu dishes contain no meat at all and tofu is honored in and of itself; in China, however, and particularly in restaurants, tofu is often cooked together with or used in conscious imitation of seafoods and meats. Since most varieties of Chinese tofu have the firm texture of ham or smoked sausage, they lend themselves well to their role as meat substitutes in a way the softer, more delicate Japanese varieties cannot match. In many Chinese cookbooks and restaurants, more than three-fourths of all tofu dishes contain shrimp, fish, pork, chicken, or beef. Studying restaurant menus and cookbooks, one could easily get the impression that the Chinese eat meat as a regular part of their diet. In fact, however, most Chinese—including the pre-revolution affluent—have traditionally eaten only small quantities of meat (see fig. 2, p. 18). The Chinese nutritional equilibrium has become a source of great interest to nutritionists and doctors, and should serve as a source of data and inspiration for the growing number of Westerners who are now moving away from a meat-centered diet.

For most Chinese farmers, laborers, and office workers, meals of rice and tofu, cabbage, a hearty soup and, perhaps, soymilk epitomize daily home cooking. In many homes in China, as in Japan, tofu is served at all three meals. At breakfast it accompanies the course of *congee* (rice porridge), and at lunch and dinner it appears most commonly in stir-fried dishes, sauces, soups, and/or steamed preparations. In this diet, in which 95 percent of all protein comes from vegetable sources, tofu plays a role worthy of the name "meat of the fields." And since most Chinese do not drink cow's milk or use other dairy products, tofu (solidified with calcium sulfate) and soymilk also serve as essential sources of calcium.

Whereas the Japanese delight in the simple light flavors of the tofu itself, and generally give tofu the leading role in any particular dish, the Chinese often serve their tofu as an extender in dark-brown, corn-starch-thickened sauces generally made from a meat, chicken, or oyster-sauce base and seasoned with plenty of sesame oil. Many of these "red broiled" sauces (*hong-sao*)—especially those in the cookery of Szechwan and Taiwan—are fiery hot, peppery, and spicy, and in restaurants will often contain small pieces of meat, chicken, or seafood. A crisp texture may be supplied by such exotic delicacies as water chestnuts, bamboo shoots, tiger lillies, bean sprouts, "wood-ear" mushrooms, Chinese cabbage, or hair-like black seaweeds. In some cases these rich tofu sauces are served over noodles or fried rice, a practice almost never met with in Japan.

Over a period of several thousand years, Chinese tofu has been adapted to the unique tools and cooking techniques used in a typical Chinese kitchen: especially stir-frying. In preparation for the actual cooking, the Chinese chef or housewife first uses a razor-sharp cleaver to mince tofu and vegetables on massive chopping blocks set near a great black stove—which is actually more like a forge or blast furnace—holding three or four different-sized woks. Neatly arranged on a long table near the stove are at least 16 open-top bowls or crocks, each containing a commonly-used oil, sauce, or seasoning. After the ingredients are assembled and the wok to be used is surrounded by a cushion of dancing flames, oil is scooped in to sizzle and crackle for an instant as the brisk fire leaps higher. Tofu and vegetables are then added, stirred, and flipped with such dexterity and split-second timing that not a single piece is broken. Scooped from their respective crocks with a large metal ladle and measured by eye, red-pepper oil, miso sauce, salt, and/or minced gingerroot are then added to season the tofu dish to perfection. A half-ladleful of water, and the wok's contents are tossed lightly into the air three, four, five times. At just the right instant—and fast as magic—the wok is snatched from its nest of fire and the stir-fried tofu-and-vegetables transferred to elegant serving platters. The tofu's firm texture enables it to retain its form during this vigorous process.

At certain times each month and year, the average family's meals contain no meat or fish at all. Since ancient times, many Chinese—especially orthodox Buddhists—have refrained from eating such foods on the first and fifteenth days of each lunar month. And during the entire sultry sixth month, the hottest period of summer, many people also take no wine, eggs, or cooked foods, a practice which gives a rest to both the cook and the digestive system (and one related perhaps to the ancient Christian tradition of fasting or eating more simply during Lent). At these times, a great deal of imagination is expended in using tofu and yuba in daily family meals or banquets at which many of the dishes bear all of the appearance of delicately layered or rolled meats, fresh fowl, or fish. One popular main dish served on meatless days is called The Arhat's (Buddhist Saint's) Fast or the Vegetarian's Ten Varieties. Containing hollow agé cubes, pressed tofu sheets, plus eight varieties of land and sea vegetables, it is a large stew or soup said to improve in flavor for up to one week. Tofu also plays an important part in the large repasts served in connection with funerals and memorial services, meals in which meat and eggs are generally not allowed.

The many Su-tsai or Shojin Ryori restaurants throughout China and Taiwan which specialize in Buddhist or Taoist vegetarian cookery are filled to capacity on Sundays and during those periods when people eat no meat. Laymen and house-holders—as well as the usual monks and nuns with their shaved heads, rosary beads, and long gray robes—enjoy sumptuous meals featuring dishes such as "baked ham," roast duck," or "sliced chicken breast." Tofu, yuba, and wheat gluten (mien tien) are indispensable foods which appear in more than half the dishes on the menu. In each of the su-tsai restaurants we visited in Taiwan, the large rooms were bustling with activity. Bare neon lights, large linoleum tables, canned foods, and white plaster walls created an atmosphere in sharp contrast to that of the lovely Japanese Zen temple restaurants where the guests are served in a garden setting of rocks, sand, water, bamboo, and trees, and each dish is served with a sense of refined simplicity and artfulness. Tofu is also served to the guests and visitors in China's temples, but many temples are so improverished that the monks only rarely enjoy the tofu themselves.

In most places in China and on most occasions when tofu is served, yuba is also to be found. Most Chinese restaurants, including those in the West, will generally offer 10 to 15 dishes featuring yuba. Any of the different types of yuba may be sautéed or stewed with vegetables, topped with thickened sauces, deep-fried, or added to soups or nabe dishes. Recipes for many of these preparations are given in Chapter 14.

Since most of the basic varieties of Chinese tofu, soymilk, and yuba available in the West are closely related to their Japanese counterparts, we have included Chinese-style recipes in many of the preceeding chapters. However, since fermented tofu is not found in Japan, we have presented recipes for its use in the pages that follow.

The Chinese Tofu Shop

In most Chinese tofu shops, the gö is cooked in a cut-off drum can (fig. 113) using steam from a coal-heated boiler. It is then run into a cloth-lined cone set over a curding barrel into which the soymilk filters before being solidified, usually with a mixture of calcium sulfate and nigari. Using this simple, inexpensive equipment, large batches of tofu can be prepared in rapid succession (at intervals of about 17 minutes) and the finished product sold at a very low price (about one-third that of Japanese tofu). Although the tofu lacks some of the subtle flavor of traditional Japanese tofu and the work is often done rather hastily, the basic process (described in detail in the companion volume to this work) could provide an excellent model for use in developing countries.

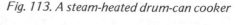
Fig. 113. A steam-heated drum-can cooker

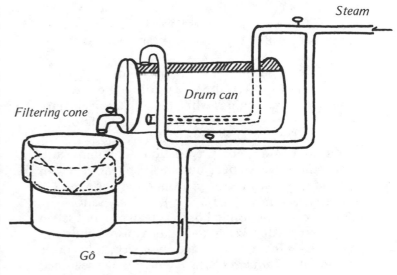

Tofu in Korea

Although tofu is an important staple in Korean cookery, it does not play quite the essential role that it does in China, Taiwan, and Japan. Koreans eat about one-third as much tofu as do the Japanese. This tofu is made at the more than one thousand small tofu shops (*tubu kong jang*) scattered throughout the country, 150 of which are located in the capital city of Seoul. Most shops use a fire-heated cauldron and calcium sulfate solidifier. A great deal of tofu is still prepared at home in farmhouses, especially on festive occasions.

Regular Korean tofu, called *tubú*, is slightly firmer than its Japanese counterpart but not as firm as Chinese tofu (*doufu*). This tofu is widely sold in outdoor marketplaces. Shopkeepers and venders buy flats of tofu from tofu shops in returnable wooden boxes, each 10 by 13 by 2 inches deep. The tofu is placed on wooden pallets, then cut into cakes weighing 12 to 16 ounces. Tubu is the only traditional variety of Korean tofu.

During the Japanese occupation, the Koreans developed a number of varieties of deep-fried tofu (*tofu kuii* or *twigin tubu*). Agé strips (*yubu*) are pieces of deep-fried tofu about 7 by 1 by ¾ inches. Ten strips are sold together in a sealed plastic bag. This food is unlike any deep-fried tofu in Japan or China. Agé pouches (*fukuro*) are similar to Japanese agé but are sold in different sizes; the smallest is 2½ inches square, the medium size is 4½ by 2½ inches, and the largest size is 8½ by 3 inches. Each variety can be opened and filled with various stuffings, and many are used to make Inari-zushi (p. 194) or Oden Kinchaku (p. 196).

Okara (*piji*), soymilk curds (*sun tubu*), and whole soybeans (*kung kong*) are used widely in Korean cookery. Fermented tofu (*tubu kuppa*), available mostly in Chinese food markets, is not. Kinugoshi, grilled tofu, soymilk, and yuba are rarely if ever seen.

Korean cuisine is extremely hot and spicy. Tofu serves to soften the flavors of red peppers and other strong seasonings while lending body and protein to soups, stews, and sautéed vegetable dishes. The most famous Korean tofu dish is *Tubu Chige* or "tofu soup," a fiery preparation containing tofu cubes, thin slices of beef, and shellfish seasoned with red and green hot peppers, ground red peppers, Korean soybean miso (*kotsu jang*), and soy sauce. The soup is served bubbling hot in a small iron pot set on a wooden platter. When it contains miso as the dominant seasoning and is served with rice, it becomes the popular *Tenjang Chige Pekpen*. When seasoned with *kimchi* pickles, it is known as *Kimchi Chige*, and when it contains more broth and is prepared with less salt, it is known as *Tubu Kuk*. Tofu is also sautéed in oil until golden brown, then cooked with vegetables for 5 to 10 more minutes to create the favorite household preparation *Tubu Puchim*. Sautéed with bean sprouts, tofu becomes the dish known as *Konamul Kuge Tubu*.

DOUFU-RU DRESSINGS, SPREADS, DIPS, AND HORS D'OEUVRE

Tangy and flavorful, rich and zesty, these are some of our favorite recipes. If you like Roquefort or Camembert, Cream Cheese or Sour Cream, try some of the following.

Doufu-ru Salad Dressing

3 small cubes of white or 2 large cubes of red doufu-ru
1 teaspoon doufu-ru brining liquor
6 ounces tofu
3 tablespoons lemon juice
¼ cup oil
¼ teaspoon salt

Combine all ingredients in a blender and purée until smooth. Serve over a salad of fresh vegetables. Or simply blend or mash the dofu-ru and brining liquor with ¾ cup mayonnaise.

Tangy Doufu-ru & Cream Cheese Spread

MAKES ¾ CUP

6 cubes of doufu-ru, well drained (about 4 ounces)
4 ounces cream cheese
2 teaspoons sake or white wine
½ small onion, grated or minced
1 tablespoon softened butter
1½ teaspoon Worcestershire sauce

Combine all ingredients and mash together until smooth. For best flavor, refrigerate in a covered container for at least 2, preferably 7 days. Serve on crackers, potato chips, toast rounds, cucumber slices, or celery stalks.

Cream Cheese & Doufu-ru Dip

MAKES 1 CUP

3 cubes of white doufu-ru
6 ounces cream cheese
2 tablespoons mayonnaise
2 teaspoons shoyu; or 1 teaspoon Worcestershire sauce and ¼
    teaspoon salt
1½ teaspoons minced onion

Combine all ingredients and mash together until smooth. Serve as a dip for crackers, potato chips, toast rounds, or crisp vegetables; or as a sandwich spread. Also good as a stuffing for celery stalks.

Sour Cream & Doufu-ru Dip

MAKES 1¼ CUPS

1 cup sour cream (dairy or tofu, p. 109)
2 or 3 cubes of white doufu-ru
1 tablespoon minced chives
1 tablespoon minced parsley
¼ teaspoon salt
Dash of curry powder
Dash of paprika or 7-spice red pepper

Combine all ingredients and mash together until smooth. Serve chilled as a dip or sandwich spread.

Oriental Doufu-ru & Sour Cream Dip

MAKES ¾ CUP

2 cubes of white doufu-ru
½ cup sour cream (dairy or tofu, p. 109)
1 tablespoon grated gingerroot
1½ teaspoons shoyu
¼ cup minced leeks, onions, or scallions
2 tablespoons minced parsley
¼ teaspoon fresh coriander (optional)

Combine all ingredients and mash together until smooth. Serve chilled as a dip for crackers.

Doufu-ru & Egg Spread

MAKES ½ CUP

1 or 2 cubes of doufu-ru
2 hardboiled eggs, minced
1 teaspoon Worcestershire sauce
1 tablespoon cream cheese (dairy or tofu, p. 109)
1 tablespoon cucumber pickles (optional)

Combine all ingredients and mash together until smooth.

Doufu-ru Hors D'oeuvre

Place a single cube of white or red doufu-ru on a tiny dish and serve with other hors d'oeuvre, appetizers, or drinks, or as a side dish or relish with the main meal. Each guest uses the tips of his chopsticks to take a tiny piece of the doufu-ru from time to time between sips of the drinks, bites of grain or vegetables, or courses of the meal.

In some Chinese restaurants in Japan, the doufu-ru cube is served topped with 1 tablespoon sesame oil and ½ teaspoon sugar.

Doufu-ru Spread

Use doufu-ru like Camembert or Roquefort cheese as a spread for crackers, canapés, or small pieces of toast. If desired, garnish with a small slice of cheese, hard-boiled egg, tomato, cucumber, or a sprig of parsley.

DOUFU-RU IN SAUCES, EGG DISHES, AND WITH GRAINS

Creamy and mellow Western sauces; fiery Chinese dipping sauces. In scrambled eggs and with steaming hot rice, doufu-ru can bring any dish to life.

Spicy Red Doufu-ru Dipping Sauce

SERVES 2 TO 4

1 cube of red doufu-ru
½ teaspoon doufu-ru brining liquor
2 tablespoons sake or white wine
½ teaspoon soy sauce
1 teaspoon grated gingerroot
Dash of salt
¼ teaspoon minced fresh coriander (optional)

Combine all ingredients and mix together until smooth. Serve as a dipping sauce with lightly roasted strips or cubes of deep-fried tofu, tempura, or, as in China, with live "dancing shrimp" or shrimp cocktail.

In Szechwan, a simplified version of this sauce is prepared using only 1 tablespoon each doufu-ru brining liquor and soy sauce, 1 teaspoon sake, and ¼ teaspoon sesame oil.

Simmering Tofu Dipping Sauce a là Chinois

Doufu-ru
Chinese rice wine or cooking wine
Chinese vinegar
Minced chives
Sesame oil
Sesame butter (or sesame jam)
Pickled garlic
Fresh coriander, minced
Hot pepper oil
Shrimp Sauce

Arrange all of the ingredients on separate plates or in bottles at the dining table. Invite each guest to combine the ingredients to taste in the small saucer provided at his place setting.

A somewhat simpler version of the above sauce is used as a dipping sauce for lamb.

Doufu-ru White Sauce

SERVES 2

2 cubes of white doufu-ru
¼ teaspoon doufu-ru brining liquor
Dash of salt
Dash of Pepper
1 cup milk (soy or dairy)
2 tablespoons butter
2 tablespoons (whole-wheat) flour

Combine the first four ingredients and mash together. Slowly stir in the milk, mixing until smooth. Melt the butter in a skillet. Add the flour and proceed as for White Sauce (p. 48). Serve as a topping for deep-fried tofu or cooked vegetables.

Stir-fried Thick agé and Greens with Doufu-ru Sauce

SERVES 2 OR 3

2 tablespoons oil
7 ounces spinach, Chinese cabbage, or *komatsuna*, cut into 2-inch lengths
Dash of salt
½ cup stock or water
1 tablespoon soy sauce
3 tablespoons natural sugar
2 teaspoons sake or white wine
1¼ teaspoons sesame oil
10 ounces thick agé, cut crosswise into ½-inch-wide strips
1 large or 3 small cubes of doufu-ru, preferably red
1 tablespoon doufu-ru brining liquor
1 teaspoon cornstarch or arrowroot, dissolved in 2 tablespoons water

Heat a wok and coat with the oil. Add the greens and stir-fry for 1 or 2 minutes until just tender. Add salt and stock and cook for 2 minutes more. Remove wok from heat and transfer only the greens to a large bowl. Add the next five ingredients to the liquid remaining in the wok, return to the boil, and simmer over low heat for 5 minutes. Meanwhile combine doufu-ru and brining liquor in a cup and mash together until

smooth. Remove only the thick agé from the wok and transfer to the bowl with the greens. To the broth in the wok, add the mashed doufu-ru thinned in a few tablespoons of the hot broth. Mix well, then stir in the dissolved cornstarch and cook for about 30 seconds, or until thickened. Return the greens and thick agé to the thickened broth in the wok. Mixing gently, cook for 1 minute. Serve hot in large bowls.

Brining Liquor Dipping Sauce

MAKES 3/8 CUP

The brining liquor remaining in the bottle or can after the doufu-ru has been served can be used in sauces, dips, or dipping sauces.

2½ tablespoons doufu-ru brining liquor
2½ tablespoons shoyu
2 teaspoons sake or white wine
¼ teaspoon sesame oil
1 to 2 tablespoons thinly sliced leeks (optional)

Combine all ingredients, mixing well. Serve as a dipping sauce for deep-fried tofu or barbequed foods.

Tangy Ketchup & Lemon Sauce with Doufu-ru

SERVES 2 TO 4

1/3 cup ketchup
5 tablespoons lemon juice
2 cubes of doufu-ru, preferably red
½ teaspoon shoyu
1 teaspoon minced onion

Combine all ingredients and mash or blend until smooth. Serve with deep-fried tofu, tempura, or shrimp cocktail.

Doufu-ru with Hot Rice

SERVES 2

This is the most popular way of serving doufu-ru in China. The dish is generally served for breakfast. Some people prefer to use the tips of their chopsticks to take a tiny piece of doufu-ru with each bite, whereas others like to mix the doufu-ru with the hot rice or rice porridge *(congee)* before starting the meal.

2½ cups freshly cooked Brown Rice or Rice Porridge (p. 50)
2 to 4 cubes of doufu-ru (white or red)
2 tablespoons thinly sliced scallions or leeks (optional)

Place the hot rice in large individual serving bowls and top with doufu-ru cubes and, if used, sliced scallions.

A street-side doufu vender

16

Special Tofu

ESAME-, peanut-, walnut-, and egg tofu are subtly flavored tofu-like preparations served with traditional Japanese cuisine. Since these dishes have somewhat the same appearance and custard-like texture as real tofu, each bears the tofu name. However they are all fundamentally different from tofu: they are not made from soybeans or solidified by curding; they are never stored under water; and they are not made or sold in tofu shops. Sesame-, peanut-, and walnut tofu are prepared by blending or mixing the respective ground nuts or seeds with water, simmering the mixture with *kuzu* (Japanese arrowroot) or other starches until thick and transparent, and then cooling it in a mold until firm. These dishes are usually served with various shoyu dipping sauces or miso toppings. Egg tofu looks like and is made in somewhat the same way as rich egg custard.

Sesame tofu, the most popular variety of special tofu, is served at the beginning of the meal in most restaurants featuring Zen Temple Cookery or Tea Ceremony Cuisine. Each chef has his own unique (and highly secret) way of preparing both it and the sauce that accompanies it. All four types of special tofu are available at large food markets and some natural food stores in Japan. They are usually sealed in plastic containers accompanied by a separate container of dipping sauce.

In China and Taiwan another type of special tofu, Annin-dofu, is a popular dessert. Made with milk, sugar, and a little almond extract, and jelled with agar (*kanten*), it is cut into small cubes and served with sections of mandarin oranges and other sweet fruits.

Recipes for Western-style sesame tofu have re-cently appeared in a number of natural food cookbooks in America. Often made with sesame butter (or *tahini*), honey, and *kuzu*, and generally containing nuts, dried fruits, and coconut, it is a delicious innovation on the more subtly flavored, unsweetened Japanese sesame tofu.

Most of the following recipes may be served as side dishes, desserts, or hors d'oeuvre.

TOPPINGS AND SAUCES

The various types of special tofu are often served with the following toppings and sauces.

Shoyu-Wasabi Topping   FOR 1 SERVING

Place each serving of special tofu in a deep bowl, sprinkle with about 1 teaspoon of shoyu, then top with a small dab (about ¼ teaspoon) of *wasabi*. Freshly grated *wasabi* —which is mixed with water just before use— is more readily available and less expensive.

Rich Shoyu Sauce   FOR 6 TO 8 SERVINGS

5 tablespoons dashi (p. 39), stock, or water
2 tablespoons shoyu
2 teaspoons natural sugar or honey
1 teaspoon sake or white wine
2 teaspoons *wasabi* (grated or powdered)

Combine the first four ingredients in a saucepan and bring to a boil. Reduce heat to low and simmer for 1 minute. Cover and set aside to cool, or refrigerate. Pour over individual serving of special tofu and top with a small dab of *wasabi*.

Thickened Shoyu Sauce

FOR 4 SERVINGS

1 cup dashi (p. 39), stock, or water
¼ cup shoyu
3 tablespoons natural sugar or honey
5 teaspoons *kuzu*, cornstarch, or arrowroot
1 teaspoon *wasabi*

Combine the first four ingredients in a small saucepan and, stirring constantly, bring to a boil. Reduce heat and simmer until transparent and quite thick. Cover pan and set aside to cool, or refrigerate. Pour over individual servings of special tofu and top with *wasabi*.

Sweet Miso Topping

FOR 8 SERVINGS

5 tablespoons red, barley, or Hatcho miso
1½ teaspoons *mirin*
2 tablespoons natural sugar or honey
1½ teaspoons sake or white wine
¼ cup dashi (p. 39), stock, or water

Combine all ingredients in a small saucepan and simmer, stirring constantly, until mixture becomes almost as thick as the original miso. Set aside to cool. Serve in large dabs atop individual portions of special tofu. Refrigerated, unused portions will last indefinitely.

Shoyu-Mirin Sauce

FOR 4 SERVINGS

2½ tablespoons shoyu
4 teaspoons *mirin*
2 teaspoons sake
½ cup dashi (p. 39), stock, or water

Combine all ingredients in a small saucepan, cover, and bring just to a boil. Allow to cool before serving over Egg Tofu (p. 267).

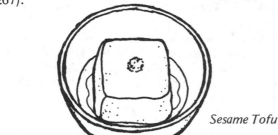

Sesame Tofu

Sesame Tofu (*Goma-dofu*)

SERVES 6 TO 8

In the following basic recipe, the tofu is prepared in a blender using whole roasted sesame seeds. Roasting gives the tofu a rich brown color and delicious, nutlike fragrance, while the blender makes the process quick and easy. Some Japanese chefs prefer to use either unroasted or only lightly roasted sesame to obtain a subtler, more delicate flavor. The seeds are generally ground by hand in a *suribachi* (p. 34) until they turn into a smooth, slightly oily paste. In shops making com-

mercial sesame tofu, the seeds are ground by machines for about 5 hours to obtain the ideal consistency. The finest sesame tofu is solidified with genuine *kuzu*, now available in the West in many natural food stores. Powder from the root of the bracken fern *(warabiko)* may also be used. Arrowroot or cornstarch are fair substitutes; add about 25 percent more than if using *kuzu*. The longer the tofu is stirred while thickening, the finer the texture: shops and restaurants often mix large quantities vigorously for up to 30 minutes.

6 tablespoons (white) sesame seeds
2½ cups water
5½ tablespoons *kuzu*, or 7 tablespoons arrowroot or cornstarch
½ teaspoon salt
Shoyu-Wasabi Topping (p. 265)

Roast sesame seeds over medium heat in a heavy skillet, stirring constantly, until they are well browned and begin to pop. Place in a blender with ¼ cup water and purée for 20 to 30 seconds, gradually increasing blender's speed. Turn off blender, rinse down walls with ½ cup water, and purée again. Rinse off walls and lid of blender with 1½ cups water, add *kuzu* and salt, and purée for about 3 minutes more. Immediately pour contents of blender into a fine-mesh strainer set over a small saucepan. Using your fingertips, rub as much of the solids as possible through the strainer, then douse the sesame seeds hulls in the strainer with the remaining ¼ cup water. Again rub sesame residue against strainer, then discard any remaining seed hulls.

Heat contents of saucepan over medium heat, stirring constantly with a wooden spoon, until mixture begins to thicken. Reduce heat to low and stir for about 12 minutes more. Pour sesame mixture into a metal or glass mold —preferably one with square corners and a flat bottom— and smooth surface of mixture with moistened fingertips. Partially immerse mold in cold water and allow to cool, then cover with a sheet of plastic wrap and refrigerate until thoroughly chilled and firm. Cut into individual portions with a moistened knife, apportion among deep (lacquerware) bowls or individual serving dishes, and top with shoyu and *wasabi*.

If a mold is not available, the sesame mixture may be cooled in the saucepan.

VARIATIONS

*Any of the following topping may also be used:
    Rich Shoyu Sauce (p. 265)
    Thickened Shoyu Sauce (p. 266)
    Sweet Miso Topping (p. 266)
    Red Nerimiso (p. 42) garnished with a sprig of *kinome*
    Gingerroot Sauce (p. 49)
    Ankake Sauce (p. 49) topped with a dab of grated gingerroot or hot mustard
    Mustard-Shoyu Dipping Sauce (p. 40)
    Yuzu Miso (p. 42)
    Any variety of Finger Lickin' Miso (p. 31)
    A mixture of 1 cup dashi, ¼ cup shoyu, several drops of grated gingerroot juice, and a pinch of grated *yuzu* rind

*Tahini Tofu: Substitute 4 tablespoons *tahini* for the whole sesame seeds in the basic recipe. Mix all ingredients thoroughly using a spoon, egg beater or blender, before cooking. Or, for a richer version, use 2½ cups water or dashi, ½ cup *tahini*, 6 tablespoons *kuzu*, 2 tablespoons sake, and ½ teaspoons each salt and sugar.

*Sesame Butter Tofu: Substitute 3 tablespoons sesame butter for the sesame seeds in the basic recipe. Prepare as for Tahini Tofu.

*Use almonds, cashews, filberts, Brazil nuts, sunflower or poppy seeds, substituting 6 to 8 tablespoons of any one of these for the sesame seeds in the basic recipe.

Sweet & Crunchy Sesame Tofu SERVES 3 OR 4

This Western dessert-style adaptation of the traditional Japanese favorite has a rich and hearty flavor.

3 tablespoons sesame butter or ¼ cup *tahini*
2½ cups water
5½ tablespoons *kuzu*, or 7 tablespoons arrowroot or cornstarch
¼ cup natural sugar
½ cup raisins
2/3 cup shredded coconut
½ cup walnut meats

Combine sesame butter, water, *kuzu*, and sugar in a large bowl or blender and mix or purée until smooth. Pour into a saucepan, add raisins, and cook as for Sesame Tofu. Sprinkle one-half the coconut over the bottom of a mold or shallow pan, and spoon in the sesame-*kuzu* mixture. Smooth surface of mixture, press in the walnut meats, and sprinkle on the remaining coconut. Serve chilled.

If using honey instead of sugar, increase the amount of *kuzu* by ½ tablespoon.

Peanut Tofu SERVES 4 TO 6

½ cup peanuts or ¼ cup peanut butter
2½ cups water
5½ tablespoons *kuzu*; or 7 tablespoons arrowroot or cornstarch
¼ to ½ teaspoon salt; or 2 to 4 tablespoons honey or natural sugar

Combine peanuts and 1 cup water in a blender and purée at high speed for about 2 minutes, or until smooth. Without turning off blender, rinse off inside walls with remaining water, add *kuzu*, and purée for 30 seconds more. Pour mixture quickly into a small saucepan and proceed as for Sesame Tofu. Serve chilled, topped with Shoyu-Wasabi (p. 265) or, if preparing the sweetened version, top with a sprinkling of shredded coconut and chopped nutmeats.

If using peanut butter, the ingredients may be mixed with a spoon rather than a blender.

VARIATION

*For **Walnut Tofu** *(Kurumi-dofu)*, substitute ½ cup chopped walnut meats for the peanuts in the above recipe. Do not use sweetening. Serve topped with *Wasabi*-Shoyu. This delicious preparation is a specialty at many fine Japanese temple restaurants.

Egg Tofu *(Tamago-dofu)* SERVES 4

Resembling a mild and delicate custard, Egg tofu is a Japanese summertime favorite, whether sold packaged in food stores or prepared at the finest restaurants. The only type of special tofu not solidified with *kuzu*, this dish made with dashi should not be confused with Soymilk Egg Tofu (p. 209) which is prepared with soymilk and sold commercially in Japan. It is very important to steam Egg Tofu for just the right length of time; oversteaming causes it to develop internal bubbles and a porous structure, spoiling its delicate texture.

4 large eggs
¾ to 1 cup dashi (p. 30), stock, or water
½ teaspoon shoyu
1 teaspoon *mirin* or honey
1½ teaspoons sake or white wine
Shoyu-Mirin Sauce (p. 266)
1½ teaspoons *wasabi* or grated gingerroot
4 sprigs of *kinome* (optional)

Break eggs into a measuring cup and add an equal volume of dashi. Pour egg-and-dashi mixture into a large bowl and combine with shoyu, *mirin*, and sake. Mix well with chopsticks, trying to make as few bubbles as possible. Strain through a fine-mesh strainer or piece of cheesecloth into a small pan (one 5 inches in diameter is ideal) so that egg mixture fills pan to a depth of 1½ to 2 inches. Skim off any bubbles, then cover pan with a cloth or piece of paper and place in a preheated steamer (p. 38). Steam over high heat with lid slightly ajar for about 5 minutes until tofu surface is just firm. Reduce heat and steam for 5 to 10 minutes more, checking frequently to see that bubbles have not formed within the tofu. When a chopstick or foodpick inserted into tofu comes out dry, remove pan from steamer and allow to cool. Cut tofu into fourths and serve in deep (lacquerware) bowls, topped with the sauce, a dab of *wasabi*, and a sprig of *kinome*.

Other garnishes include slivers of *yuzu* or lemon peel, a mixture of grated *wasabi* and gingerroot, or a combination of grated *yuzu* rind and thin rounds of cucumber.

VARIATIONS

*Add ½ cup refreshed *wakame* cut into 3-inch lengths. Mix into the strained egg mixture just before steaming.

*Cut Egg Tofu into 1½- by 2-inch pieces and serve in Clear Soup (p. 119) in place of regular tofu.

*Serve topped with hot or chilled Ankake Sauce (p. 49).

Emerald Tofu (Uguisu-dofu)

SERVES 3 TO 4

Made from fresh green soybeans, this tofu is a brilliant emerald green, as green as the *uguisu*, the Japanese nightingale.

10¼ cups water
1¼ teaspoons salt
2½ to 3 cups green soybeans in their pods
5½ tablespoons *kuzu;* or 7 tablespoons arrowroot or cornstarch

Bring 8 cups water to a boil in a large pot and add 1 teaspoon salt. Drop in the soybeans, return to the boil, and simmer for 4 minutes. Rinse beans in a colander under cold running water; drain. Remove pods and measure out ½ cup green soybeans, reserving any remaining beans. Combine the ½ cup beans, 2½ cups water, *kuzu*, and remaining ¼ teaspoon salt in a blender, and purée for 3 minutes, or until smooth. Pour into a saucepan and proceed as for Sesame Tofu. Serve chilled, topped with Thickened Shoyu Sauce (p. 266).

Kinako Tofu

SERVES 4 TO 6

This recipe is the result of our experiments using Kinako Butter (p. 65) to develop an easy-to-make special tofu similar in flavor to Sesame Tofu but richer in protein and less expensive.

10½ tablespoons kinako (roasted soy flour)
3 tablespoons oil
2½ cups water
5½ tablespoons *kuzu;* or 7 tablespoons arrowroot or cornstarch
¾ teaspoon salt
Sweet Miso Topping (p. 266) or Shoyu-Wasabi Topping (p. 265)

Combine kinako and oil in a small bowl, mixing well, then stir in water, *kuzu*, and salt. Pour through a fine-mesh strainer into a saucepan. Bring just to a boil over high heat, reduce heat to medium, and cook, stirring constantly, for 3 to 4 minutes after mixture thickens. Proceed as for Sesame Tofu (p. 266). Serve chilled with the miso topping.

VARIATION
*Prepare like Sweet & Crunchy Sesame Tofu (p. 267) but substitute the kinako-and-oil mixture in the above recipe for sesame butter.

Annin-dofu
(Milk & Almond Tofu with Fruit Cocktail)

SERVES 4 OR 5

This famous Chinese-style dessert preparation is often called Almond Bean Curd in Western-style Chinese cookbooks. In Japan, where it is sold in cans or prepared fresh in Chinese-style restaurants, it is known variously as *Kyonin-, Chinden-* or *Shinrin-dofu.*

1 stick of agar (8 gm), reconstituted and torn into small pieces (p. 37)
2/3 cup milk
2/3 cup water
1 tablespoon honey
½ teaspoon almond extract
3 cups fruit cocktail

Combine agar, milk, and water in a small saucepan. Stirring constantly, bring to a boil over medium heat, then simmer for 3 minutes or until agar is completely dissolved; stir in honey and almond extract. Pour through a strainer or fine cheesecloth into a flat-bottomed container (one about 9 inches in diameter is ideal) and allow to cool. Cover container and chill. Cut tofu into 1½-inch-long diamond-shaped pieces and mix with the fruit cocktail. For best flavor, chill for about 6 hours before serving.

Milk Tofu

MAKES 8 OUNCES

Dairy milk can be solidified with an acid, as when preparing cottage cheese, then shaped and pressed in a mold like homemade tofu. Although the flavor and texture are good, the yield is only about one-third that obtained from an equal volume of powdered soymilk.

1 cup powdered (non-fat) dairy milk
6 cups water
Solidifier:
        1 tablespoon vinegar
        1¼ tablespoons fresh lemon juice

Prepare as for Homemade Tofu (from powdered soymilk) (p. 99), except 1) stir bottom of pot constantly while heating milk and 2) omit 3 minute simmering and stir in solidifier as soon as milk comes to a boil. Serve cubed in tofu salads with or in place of regular tofu, or serve as for Chilled Tofu (p. 105) topped with any variety of Sweet Simmered Miso (p. 41) or Finger Lickin' Miso (p. 31).

PART III

Japanese Farmhouse Tofu:

Making Tofu for More and More People

Why have we failed to realize our Buddha Nature? It is only because our practice has not been based on the true method. We know, for example, that doufu can be made from soybeans. Yet knowing this and actually making the doufu are two completely different things. First we must grind the beans and add the purée to boiling water. Removing the lees from the soymilk, we must then stir in the correct amount of gypsum. In this way we will certainly get doufu.
—From a sesshin lecture
by the Chinese Zen Master Shu Yun;
Ku Shan Monastery, 1930

17

The Quest

OUNTRY-STYLE tofu has become something of a legend in Japan, a legend that has arisen not just from the deep reverence the Japanese feel for their rich cultural heritage, nor simply from the feeling of separation from a life which was rooted for millenia in the earth and surrounded by the mystical dance of the four seasons. Perhaps the memory is being romanticized as the reality becomes more and more remote, yet many modern Japanese speak with a sense of profound nostalgia of a way of life characterized by the fragrance of woodsmoke and freshly harvested sheaves of rice, a way of life which helped men to grow strong on grandma's cooking and strenuous work under a vast sky, and which made people want to sing and dance together in celebration of the birth of new life into the world, of sons and daughters being given in marriage, of house-building, rice-planting, and village festivals: a way of life both simple and sacred, partially lost forever, partially vanishing, and partially dissolving into yet another dream.

For fine tofu craftsmen who sustain and nourish the legend, country-style tofu-making represents both a pure and early stage of their art and a standard of excellence for which they continually strive. "Once you have enjoyed the satisfying flavor of homemade country tofu," they say, "you will never forget it." They tell how, in the old days, farmhouse tofu was made so firm it could be tied into a package with rice-straw rope and carried over long distances without breaking apart (fig. 114). One piece was two to four times the size of the present 12-ounce cake and was always solidified with nigari, which the farmers extracted from natural salt. Fine craftsmen praise the farmhouse tofu-making art for its simplic-

ity (its use of only basic natural ingredients and hand-crafted tools) and elegance—its mastery of the art of simplicity itself. The closer one comes to the perfection of this art, it is said, the more one has the heart and mind of a true beginner.

But when we asked the tofu craftsmen with whom we studied where we might go to observe this tofu being made, no one seemed to know. Some surmised that we might find it in remote villages where the traditional culture was still alive. Although we inquired about country-style tofu during our travels in the towns and villages of rural Japan, however, we met again and again with disappointment.

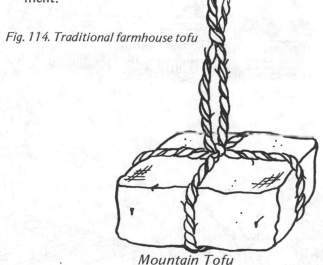

Fig. 114. Traditional farmhouse tofu

Mountain Tofu

Finally, on the suggestion of friends, we set out one spring for the picturesque mountain village of Shirakawa-go. It is believed that the survivors of the defeated Heike clan, immortalized in the epic

Tale of Genji, took refuge in this village at the end of the twelfth century when chased from Kyoto, Japan's early capital, by the victorious Genji family. After the Heike fled, they were never seen or heard of again. The village's unique, aristocratic architecture, its well-preserved ancient traditions, and its history of genetic inbreeding all serve as evidence in support of it's unusual origin. If the traditional way of making tofu had been preserved in this isolated village, we realized we might catch a glimpse of the way tofu was first prepared when it came to Japan's capital from China more than 1,000 years ago.

Carrying backpacks and feeling an inevitable kinship with the many wanderers who have fallen victim to the power of Japan's spring, we began our journey, walking and hitch-hiking. As we followed the Nagara River higher and higher into the mountains, it seemed as if its bright cold headwaters and a strong current of life from traditional Japanese culture flowed down from a single distant source. As we left the murky cities behind, we felt that we were moving back through time. The roofs on the houses turned from tile to thatch, the windows from glass to paper, the people's clothes from Western-style suits to well-worn farming attire. The air grew radiant, creeks cascaded down the steep mountainsides, flowers and birds were more abundant, and people's faces seemed more and more expressive of the shaping forces of wind, snow, and sun.

When we finally arrived at the village, its surrounding ridges were still crowned with snow and the mountain cherry trees were in brilliant full bloom. We spent the night at a traditional farmhouse inn (fig. 115) and immediately inquired of the old woman who ran it whether or not she knew of any-

Fig. 115. Shirakawa-go farmhouses with water-powered rice-husker in foreground

one in Shirakawa-go who still made old-fashioned tofu. She replied that while she and many other women her age had made tofu when they were younger, everyone had stopped during the last decade, either because they were no longer able to turn the heavy grinding stones or because they could no longer obtain unrefined salt from which to make nigari. She also pointed out that it had become possible to buy ready-made tofu from a shop that had opened in a neighboring village. The next day, though, she introduced us to Kidoguchi-san, an energetic old woman with laughing eyes, and together these two women led us to the village temple's attic museum. Showing us the tools they had once used, they described in detail how traditional country-style tofu was made. To our disappointment, however, no one in the village under 70 knew how to make tofu, and no one over 70 was making it any more. What's more, no one knew where we might continue our search.

We left Shirakawa-go somewhat downhearted, but our spirits were immediately lifted by the first man who offered us a ride. He informed us that one old woman who lived in his village still made the kind of tofu we were looking for. Excited, we asked that he drop us off at her home. We waited there until evening, when Ozawa-san returned from the rice fields. Kindly but firmly, she explained that we had come at a bad time—she was too busy with her rice planting to make tofu for us—but she spent several hours showing us the traditional tools she used and the small shed behind her house specially built for preparing tofu. After describing her method in detail, she invited us to return after the harvest in late fall when, she said, she would be happy to prepare farmhouse tofu for us. Unfortunately, she, too, knew of no one else in the area who could help.

We took to the road again next morning and, after walking quite a ways, met a solitary woman working in the fields. She told us of Kaminonomata, a small village nearby, where she thought a number of villagers still made tofu on special occasions. Kaminonomata was so small it wasn't even listed on our map! Undaunted, we headed out in the direction the woman had indicated and, after tramping for several hours, arrived and were directed to the home of one Watanabe-san, a 72-year-old grandmother. To our surprise, we found that we had arrived at just the right moment. Watanabe-san ushered us into her home just as she and a friend were about to make tofu in commemoration of the seventh anniversary of the passing of a former member of the village. We felt blessed.

Watanabe-san and her friend seemed as pleased as they were surprised at our sudden, yet timely, arrival. Soon the four of us were laughing and joking together as the transmission of the ancient art of farmhouse tofu-making began to take place. We watched the beans ground into gô between hand-turned stones, then cooked in a wide-mouthed iron pot set over a wood fire. We noticed how rice bran was sprinkled into the pot and how the head of foam that formed on the cooking gô was stirred down with a bamboo rod. Once transferred to a pressing sack set on a rack made of tree limbs and placed across the mouth of an old wooden barrel, the cooked gô was pressed with one of the heavy grinding stones. The soymilk in the barrel was solidified with (store-bought) nigari and the curds were then pressed in a homemade settling box under a lid weighted by a large rock. Without soaking the tofu in water, Watanabe-san cut it into small pieces for us all to sample.

The flavor of this tofu was graced with the faintest aftertaste of woodsmoke. Country-style pressing had given it a firmness and slight coarseness of texture quite unlike the soft, smooth tofu common to the cities. By not placing the tofu in water after it was pressed, a shade of beige and a fine edge of bouquet had been preserved; these we had never seen or experienced before. Beneath the subtle sweetness and fragrance of home-grown soybeans was a faint and even subtler bitterness left by the nigari. Somehow this tofu seemed to embody and share completely in the total configuration out of which it had been born. The wine-sweet morning air, the water drawn from the deep farmhouse well, the pleasure of communal down-home craftsmanship all participated in its essence. Wholesome, rustic, and deeply satisfying, this tofu seemed imbued with a genuine warmth that was the heart's warmth; and this was the loveliest flavor of all.

Seawater Tofu

Having recorded three detailed accounts of how nigari tofu was traditionally made in the mountain villages of central Japan, we decided to travel to Kyushu, Japan's southernmost main island, to see if the same method was employed there. In Kyushu, too, we found that only elderly women seemed to know about farmhouse tofu-making and that the traditional method in the south was basically the same as that used farther north. But several of the women mentioned to us in passing that they had heard of a rather simple way of preparing tofu which made use of seawater as the solidifier rather than nigari, the seawater's concentrated essence. We were advised that if this method were still being practiced any-where, it would probably be on some of the tiny, sparsely-populated islands that extend in a chain from the southern tip of Kyushu as far south as Okinawa. We had already planned a visit to the Banyan Ashram located on Suwanose island, one of the smallest islands in the chain. The ashram (which has been described by the poet Gary Snyder in *Regarding Wave* and *Earth Household*) is a commune founded by the Japanese wanderer-poet Nanao Sasa-ki together with numerous other young people. Devoted to a simple life-style based on farming and meditation, Suwanose is 17 hours by boat from the mainland.

Upon our arrival at Suwanose, we asked the native farmers and fishermen if they had ever heard of solidifying tofu with seawater. We were surprised to find that not only was the tofu made in the small village always solidified with it, but that the ashram's members had already learned the process, built or acquired the necessary tools, and were now making their own tofu once or twice a week! Within a few days we were—with a little help from our friends—making seawater tofu for the whole ashram. Fortunately, the island, surrounded by a spectacular coral reef and presided over by its own active volcanoe, is set like a tiny jewel in a vast expanse of remarkably clear water. At night, after starting the soybeans to soak, we walked several miles to the ocean along dirt paths, making our way by moonlight. At the shore, we filled large sake bottles with foaming brine dipped from the dark waves. Next morning we ground the beans between hand-turned stones, cooked the gô outdoors over a wood fire (fig. 116), and served the tofu for lunch at long, rustic tables under the nodding bamboos. Its fine flavor, firm texture, and down-home feeling closely resembled the nigari tofu we had enjoyed so much in the mountains.

"Long-Life" Tofu

Just one and a half years after visiting Suwano-se, we traveled to the northernmost tip of Japan's main island to study Ugemura, one of the nation's many "long life" villages, where people regularly live past the age of 90. We had recently heard that these snowy northeast provinces were one of the few places in Japan where the traditional culture was still very much alive and where farmhouse tofu was still prepared in many homes. When we arrived at this small village situated high in the mountains of Iwate prefecture, the family to whom we had been introduced by letter had just finished preparing their day's supply of firm nigari tofu. The woman of the house had skewered a number of cakes and was preparing farmhouse-style grilled tofu (see p. 221)

Fig. 116. Making seawater tofu at Suwanose

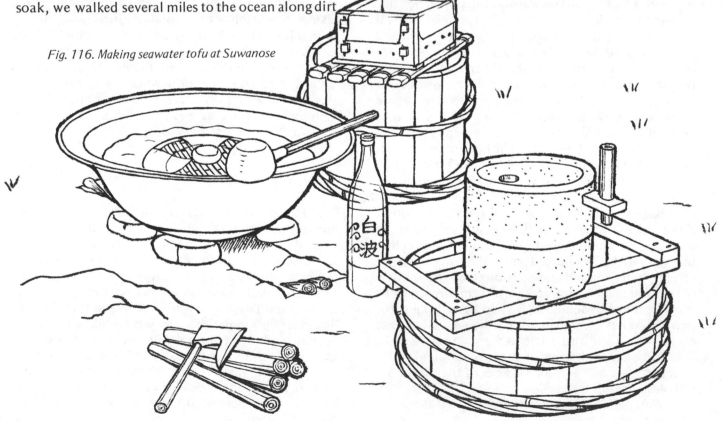

which she served to her family and to us in the form of Dengaku as a mid-morning treat. We soon learned that every home in the village was equipped with a small-scale tofu shop and that each family prepared country-style tofu on a regular basis. Furthermore, each batch of tofu was about 5 times as large as that prepared at Suwanose or most of the other villages we had visited, so that tofu could be served three meals a day to a large family for several days. An illustrated description of this tofu-making process is given on page 288. Here, we felt, was an historic link between the earliest farmhouse tofu and the traditional tofu shop.

Village Tofu

In villages throughout Japan, tofu and tofu makers have traditionally had their own special place in a tightly interwoven pattern of social relationships and the yearly cycle of festivals. In most villages, tofu has been regarded as a delicacy served on no less than ten to fifteen special occasions each year, and it was largely because a single batch (made from 8 cups of dry soybeans) could serve 15 to 20 people that tofu became a communal as well as a family treat. In most villages, the soybeans were never purchased and the tofu was never sold. Rather, the beans were gathered from the local fields and given to the tofu makers who, in turn, offered the fruits of their craft gratis to the community. The resulting tofu was usually served at the feast accompanying most of the year's major events, including the week of New Year's celebrations, the week of *Obon* (the Buddhist All-Souls' Festival), weddings, funerals and memorial services, *Sekku* Holidays (such as the third day of the third month or the fifth of the fifth), the various agricultural and religious festivals, and other special times of shared communal life. In the ancient chronicles of the village of Shirakawa-go, it is recorded that gifts of tofu were often brought to the ceremony that followed the completion of a new house or thatch roof. Served at most religious events held in the village temple or shrine, a portion of tofu was usually placed on the temple altar by a priest before the rest was enjoyed by the villagers. In remote villages, these customs still perservere.

During the winter months, tofu was prepared by individual families and served around an open-hearth fireplace. From about the beginning of May until the end of October, most villagers were busy from sunrise until sunset working in the fields; except on holidays, therefore, there was little time to make tofu. But after the crops had been harvested and the world had filled with snow, there was more free time. The new crop of soybeans was as its peak of flavor, and the clear water's low temperature would help to keep the tofu fresh. Now, even if there were no festival or special occasion to use as an excuse, a farmer's wife might take the time to prepare a batch of tofu for family and friends.

Farmhouse tofu was—and in villages where it is still made continues to be—served in relatively simple preparations: country people seem to find the greatest pleasure in the unmasked flavor and bouquet of the tofu itself. During the cold months, tofu will often be served sizzling hot as grilled tofu or Dengaku, prepared on skewers around a huge communal bonfire or over the dying embers of the family's open-hearth fireplace. Or the tofu may be served in Oden, Nishime, Miso Soup, or Simmering Tofu, prepared in a heavy iron *nabe*, or kettle, suspended over the living-room fire. Wrapped in fresh rice straw, the tofu may be simmered to make Komo-dofu. And during the summer months, it is most widely served as Chilled Tofu.

The history of the art of preparing farmhouse tofu has several interesting parallels with that of homemade bread-baking in America. In both cultures, the art was first practiced primarily by women. In Japanese communities, there were as many as 10 to 15 women, all in different households, who had their own grinding stones and a complete set of tofu-making tools. Sometimes working in pairs, these women often began the slow, difficult work of grinding the beans in the wee hours in order to have the tofu fresh and ready to serve by mid-morning. And just as home-baked bread started to disappear from American culture as soon as commercial bakeries were established and mass-produced bread became available at local stores, so did the practice of making tofu at home tend to die out in Japan shortly after tofu shops spread into rural areas. Since there are now about 38,000 commercial shops throughout the country, farmhouse tofu has survived only in the most remote villages. And finally, just as there has been a revival in America of the traditional art of baking bread among people who have re-discovered the beauty of the work and the superior flavor and nutritional quality of the end product, so in Japan, too, among people seeking to re-establish a simpler, more natural way of life and to revive ancient Japanese crafts, there is now a growing interest in making country-style tofu.

In many villages, especially after motor-driven grinding wheels came into use, either a widow or a poor farmer's wife would open a small shop as a means of augmenting the family income. These shops not only supplied tofu on a regular basis but were also known as favorite places to sit and gossip. In some rural areas, several families lived in farmhouses which were too far apart to be called a village and were also a long distance from the nearest tofu shop. These families often made tofu on a rotating basis, each family delivering it to the other families in turn. Gradually in these and other ways, farmhouse tofu makers began to practice their art as a profession. Tofu which was once shared was now sold. Yet, no doubt, the villagers were happy to have a readily available source of fresh, inexpensive tofu, and the craftsman was glad to have a source of income.

Traditionally, the tofu shops that grew up in both the cities and villages of Japan used the same ingredients and methods. The differences between country-style and city-style tofu first began to appear in the postwar period. Needless to say, in villages where farmhouse tofu is still prepared, it is considered incomparably superior to its modern, commercial counterpart, and we would have to agree. Thus we have asked every village tofu maker we have met what she or he considers the most important elements in preparing fine tofu. The following, listed in order of priority, are believed to be the essentials of the farmhouse process:

1. Use nigari or seawater as solidifier.
2. Press the tofu in the settling boxes with a heavy weight for a long time to create a firm texture and rich, dense flavor.
3. Do not soak the finished tofu in water; serve it as soon as possible.
4. Use a wood fire.
5. Use high-quality, organically-grown whole soybeans, preferably a Japanese variety.
6. Use a moderately coarse pressing sack so that a small amount of very fine-grained okara enters the tofu to give it a more substantial texture and slightly increase the yield.
7. Use pure water, from a deep well or clear stream if possible.
8. Prepare the tofu in a heavy iron pot or cauldron (rather than in a pressure cooker or aluminum container).
9. Learn to work with single mindedness and care, giving life to each ingredient and each action, wasting nothing, preparing tofu as a festive offering for the delight of both gods and men.
10. Use simple tools, make them yourself, treat them with respect.
11. Grind the soybeans with slowly-turning granite stones which yield a fine-textured, smooth purée.
12. Serve the tofu in the simplest possible way to allow full appreciation of its flavor.

Mortar and pestle for pounding mochi

18
Making
Community Tofu

Learning to make country-style tofu and bringing this fine tradition to the West can be as easy—and joyous—as learning to bake bread. Only about 1½ hours of work are required from the time the beans are ground until the curds are ladled into the settling container. An additional hour or more is then necessary for the curds to settle and the tofu to cool. If the soybeans are purchased inexpensively in bulk, the following recipe can be prepared for about one-sixth the cost of the same amount of commercial tofu. Since tofu will stay fresh if kept under cold water, a single batch of farmhouse tofu will feed a family of four for 3 or 4 days. For best results, be sure you have mastered the method for preparing Homemade Tofu (p. 99) before starting to make the farmhouse variety.

The finest flavor will be obtained by following the traditional farmhouse method as closely as possible. (Be assured, however, that a blender or handmill can be used in place of the grinding stones with no loss in quality.) The basic recipe that follows is a description of the easy-to-use "island method" practiced at Suwanose. The "mainland method" used in most mountain villages and tofu shops is explained as a variation.

Frequent variations and adaptations to both the traditional tools and method have been suggested so that the recipe can be followed easily in any Western kitchen. Although it is always easier to make country-style tofu if two or more people work together, one person working alone can do the job.

This method, which uses simple, traditional tools and natural ingredients, is also well suited to people living in even primitive conditions, such as in the villages of Africa, India, or South America, or in Western communities or communes practicing voluntary (or involuntary) poverty. In either situation, the method might be used as the basis for a new vocation, craft, or small family-based enterprise which can be started easily in one's home or community with little or no initial investment. If a person begins work at 6 o'clock in the morning, he or she should be able to make 4 batches (about seventy 12-ounce cakes) of this tofu by noon.

The following recipe (and the scale of the tools) is designed for making each batch of tofu from 8 cups of dry soybeans. While this size batch is the most common in Japan, some farmhouse craftsmen use 16 (or in large families as much as 40) cups of soybeans at a time. If you have a large enough cooking pot and can assemble the other utensils you will need, it is much faster to prepare one large batch than two or three small ones. In either case, however, the method is the same.

Use the same basic ingredients as for homemade tofu, giving special attention to the quality of the soybeans and water. Contact your nearest tofu shop (p. 313) to learn more about the best available soybean varieties, and ask the craftsman or a local natural foods dealer about prices for bulk (100 pound) purchases. Using the latter (at about 17 cents per pound), you can produce tofu costing about 6 to 7 cents per pound.

Tools and Utensils

The basic tools needed to prepare country-style tofu resemble those used for homemade tofu; most are simply larger. Those which cannot be made at home are easily obtainable and relatively inexpensive.

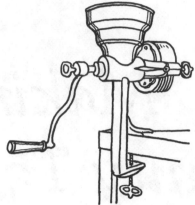

Blender, Foodmill, Grinder, or Grinding Stones: If electricity is available, use a fairly large electric blender, mill, or grinder. The former is now used in many Japanese farmhouses for recipes of this size. A small electric grinder with 6-inch-diameter, vertically mounted stone wheels is used in farmhouses where slightly larger batches of tofu are made on a regular basis. A good grinder is the key to the tofu-making process since the most difficult and time consuming step is the grinding of the beans. If electricity is not available, use a handmill (such as the inexpensive Corona Hand Mill or a Quaker City

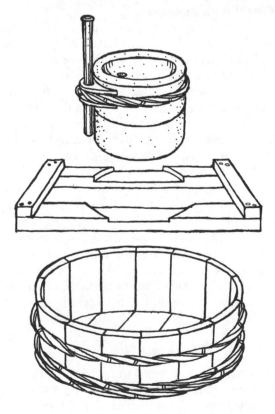

Hand Grain Grinder) or a meat grinder with a hopper on top and a fine blade attachment.

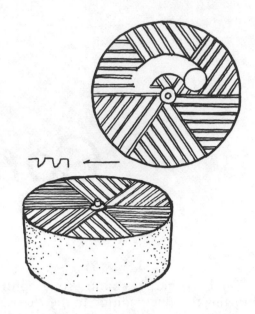

Traditionally, farmhouse tofu makers grind their soybeans with hand-turned granite grinding stones. Each of the two granite stones, weighing about 40 to 50 pounds, is about 13 inches in diameter and 4 to 5 inches thick. In the concave upper surface is a 2-inch-diameter hole into which the soaked beans are ladled. A metal rod in the center of the upper face of the bottom stone fits into a metal sleeve in the center of the lower face of the top stone to hold the stones in place while they are turning. Both grinding faces are cut with 1/8-inch-deep grooves beveled as illustrated. For the preparation of smooth, fine-grained gô, it is essential that the two stones be well balanced and aligned and that the grooves be well cut and sharpened once every 3 to 6 months.

During grinding, the lower stone remains stationary while the upper stone is turned by means of its vertical wooden handle. Larger stones, used for making larger batches of tofu, can be turned more easily by the push-pull action of a 3½-to 4-foot-long handle supported at one end by a rope from the ceiling (fig. 16, p. 70). The craftsman stands in one place while turning the stones. A grinding platform, which supports the stones, usually rests directly on top of a sturdy wooden catch-barrel about 22 inches in diameter and 10 to 12 inches deep. If the catch-barrel is not sturdy enough to support the weight of the stones, or if you wish to remove the barrel without moving the platform, set the stones on a platform supported by four sturdy legs, as in the design shown on the cover of this book.

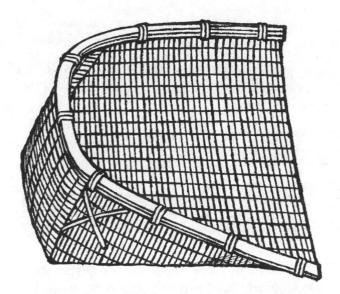

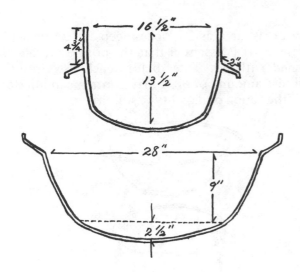

Colander: Any metal or plastic colander, sieve, or large strainer will work well. It should be at least 10 inches in diameter but smaller than the diameter of the cooking pot. Farmhouse tofu makers generally use a shallow, round colander made of tightly woven bamboo. In some farmhouses the soaked beans are rinsed in the colander; in others, they are rinsed in a large scoop-shaped basket made of woven, split bamboo and used for winnowing grains.

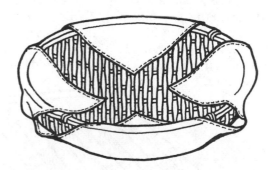

Colander Cloth: A piece of cotton cloth 18 to 24 inches square is used to cover the underside of the colander to prevent tiny particles of curd from entering and being ladled off with the whey.

Colander Weight: Use a clean stone or half brick weighing about 1 pound.

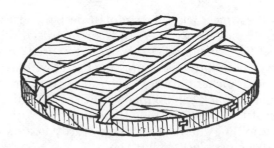

Cooking Pot and Lid: Use a heavy metal (or earthenware) pot with a capacity of at least 6, and preferably 8 to 10, gallons to minimize spilling. If the pot is to be used over an open wood fire, the lid should be thick enough so that its edges will not burn.

Farmhouse tofu makers prefer a pot with a rounded bottom made of fairly thick iron or steel. Two designs commonly used are shown above. The upper design, with its flaring mouth and lower center of gravity, is excellent for use over an open wood fire or drum-can cooker. The lower design, similar to the cauldron used in most tofu shops, is meant to be placed over a large wood-burning stove or firebox. In some farmhouses where large batches of tofu are made regularly, the pot is built into a brick dais and

may be as large as 20 inches deep and 36 inches in diameter. It is essential that the pot be thoroughly washed with hot water before each use since the slightest amount of oil it may contain can interfere with the action of nigari-type solidifiers.

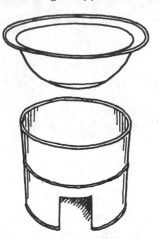

Heat Source: All farmhouse craftsmen agree that the most delicious tofu is that prepared over a wood fire. However, 1 or 2 large (gas or electric) stovetop burners also give good results. In farmhouses, four different systems are used to support the cooking pot over the fire: 1) It is placed on top of 4 solid rocks set 2 on each side of a shallow trench located outdoors (fig. 116, p. 274) or in a small shed; 2) It is set into the mouth of a 2-foot-high cut-off drum can which has a 10-inch-square opening cut out at the bottom of one side for feeding in firewood and letting out woodsmoke (see above); 3) It is placed over the typical earthen stove located in most farmhouse kitchens; 4) It is built into a permanent brick dais (similar to that in many tofu shops) that has a chimney in the rear and firebox door at the lower front (see p. 279).

Hot Water Pot: Use a large tea kettle or covered pot with a capacity of at least 5 quarts.

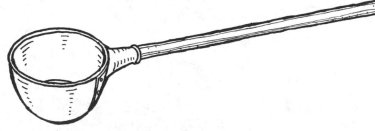

Ladle: Any small saucepan works well. Farmhouse craftsmen prefer a ladle similar to that shown here. The 12- to 24-inch handle makes it easy to reach over the fire into the large pot, and the rounded bottom and 5- to 6-inch-diameter mouth aid in handling the curds gently. The ladle used with a Chinese wok (p. 35) is also satisfactory.

Measuring Utensils: Use one container having each of the following capacities: 1 gallon, 1 quart, 1 cup, 1 tablespoon. When measuring whole dry soybeans, most farmhouse craftsmen use a standard 1 *sho* wooden box (fig. 10, p. 56) which holds 1800 cc, or about 8 cups.

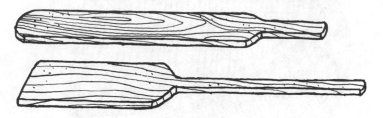

Paddle: Any large wooden spoon or spatula, or a thin wooden board may be used. Or make a paddle from a piece of wood about ¾ inch thick, 4 to 6 inches wide, and 2½ to 3 feet long.

Purée Container (Gô Catch Barrel): Use any container with a capacity of at least 3 gallons to hold the freshly-puréed gô or to catch the gô beneath the grinding stones.

Pressing Pot or Barrel: Use any sturdy pot, barrel, or tub made of wood or metal and having a capacity of 6 to 8 gallons. If using the mainland method (p. 287), try to use a wooden container in order to help keep the soymilk hot. Typical farmhouse pressing barrels, 18 to 22 inches in diameter and 16 to 18 inches deep, are made of sturdy cedar staves bound together with 2 or 3 hoops of plaited bamboo or twisted wire.

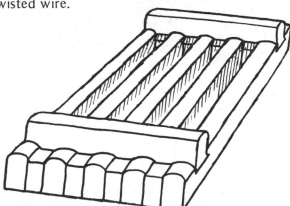

Pressing Rack: The simplest design consists of about 5 strong wooden rods or boards (broom-, shovel-, or axe-handles can also be used) placed across the mouth of the pressing barrel with a space of several inches between each rod. A sturdier, more permanent rack can be made either by notching the ends of the rods and tying them together with rope or by joining the rods or other sturdy boards with wooden cross pieces at both ends.

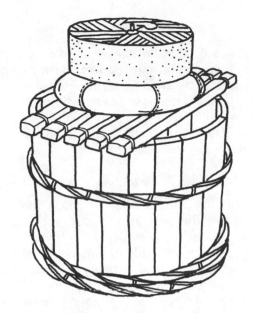

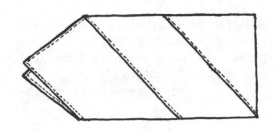

Pressing Sack: Use a rectangular sack (such as a small flour sack) about 24 inches long and 13 to 15 inches wide made of rather coarsely-woven, undyed cotton, hemp, nylon, or other strong fabric. If the weave of the cloth is too fine, the okara will be difficult to press and a large quantity of it will be left in the sack, causing a decline in the tofu yield and a lack of that certain substantial quality in the tofu cherished by farmhouse tofu makers. Furthermore, the mesh opening in such a sack will also gradually become clogged after 8 to 10 batches of tofu. However, if the weave of the sack is too coarse, too much okara will pass through the sack into the tofu. The strongest homemade pressing sacks are prepared with the seams running diagonally.

Pressing Weight and Lever: For a weight, use any clean object or objects weighing at least 50, and preferably 80 to 100 pounds. A large rock with at least one flat surface is ideal. In Japan, a grinding stone is often employed for this purpose (see above). A slightly more complicated but more effective design for pressing the okara is the simple lever press. The pressing lever is a 2-by-4 board about 3½ feet long. Some farmhouse craftsmen simply place the paddle they are using across the top of the closed pressing sack and press with the weight of their body (p. 288).

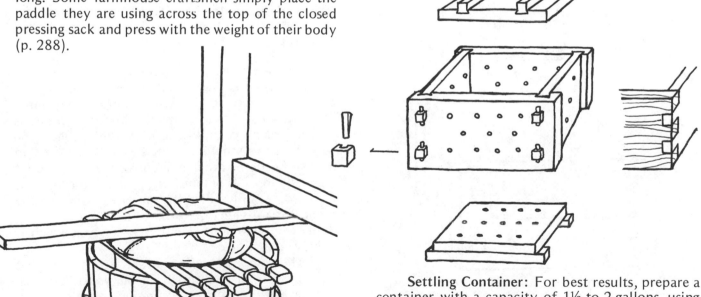

Settling Container: For best results, prepare a container with a capacity of 1½ to 2 gallons, using the design shown here, or any of the 3 designs in figure 33 on page 100. Use ¾-inch-thick (cedar or oak) boards, and make the box about 4 to 5 inches deep and 10 to 12 inches square (inside dimensions). Drill about eleven 3/8-inch-diameter holes in each of the four sides and about 13 holes in the bottom. The lid may be made with or without holes and the sides joined with or without nails, using either of the two designs shown in the inset. A box of this size will hold the curds made from 8 cups of dry soybeans. A large flat or round-bottomed colander may also be used as the settling container.

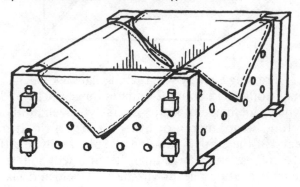

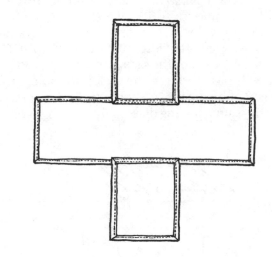

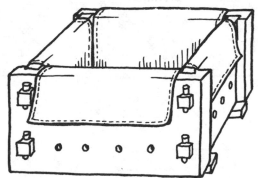

Settling Container Cloths: The simplest design is a piece of cheesecloth or a light cotton dishtowel about 20 to 24 inches square which can be arranged diagonally into a square (or round) settling container. A design that allows for slightly better drainage and gives the tofu a smoother surface is made by sewing the cloths to form a square and arranging them in the settling box as illustrated. Sew the cloth to fit your box and seam the edges to prevent fraying.

The Care of Your Tools

Wooden boxes and barrels should be dried in the sun after use and stored in a clean dry place. Cloths and sacks should be thoroughly scrubbed in hot whey or hot water as soon as possible after use to prevent soymilk from gradually clogging the mesh; rinse well, dry in the shade, and store in a dry, well-ventilated place to prevent molding.

Solidifiers

Farmhouse tofu makers in Japan have traditionally used either seawater or natural nigari to solidify their tofu. At present, the refined forms of nigari (magnesium chloride or calcium chloride) are also widely used and give virtually the same fine flavor. Although we, like most traditional craftsmen, prefer to use and recommend simple, natural ingredients, the level of contamination of seawater in most parts of the world makes it necessary for us to advise caution in the use of natural seawater or nigari and suggest the use of their refined forms. Nevertheless, for people who still have access to clean seawater, and in the hope that man's large-scale pollution of the environment will soon stop, we would like to give detailed information concerning the composition, preparation, and use of the traditional farmhouse solidifiers. In the process, we will try to explain why the refined forms of nigari make good substitutes.

Seawater: Clean seawater is highly recommended as a solidifier because it is easy to use, makes delicious tofu, requires no further processing or preparation and, if taken directly from the ocean, is available at no cost. Whenever possible, collect the seawater shortly before it is to be used and store it in a clean bottle or other non-corrosible container; it gradually loses its potency as a solidifier the longer it is stored. Do not collect the seawater from near the mouth of a stream or river since it will be relatively dilute and impotent. Do not use water which is cloudy or unclear.

The composition of seawater varies somewhat from place to place throughout the world. A typical sample has the following composition by weight. The remainder is water (H_2O):

	Percent
Sodium chloride (common salt)	2.72
Magnesium chloride	0.38
Magnesium sulfate	0.17
Calcium sulfate	0.13
Potassium chloride	0.09
Magnesium bromide	0.01

Seawater also contains over 60 trace elements, all of which are of nutritional value. In approximate order of abundance are strontium, boron, silicon, nitrogen, aluminum, rubidium, lithium, phosphorous, barium, and iodine, among others.

It is interesting to note that magnesium chloride, magnesium sulfate (Epsom salts), and calcium sulfate are each effective tofu solidifiers used (separately) in modern tofu shops. By using seawater to solidify tofu, their combined action seems to bring out a wide range of complementary flavors and ensure more complete solidification of the different types of soy protein.

Since all seawater contains approximately the same concentration of nigari, it is easy to specify exactly how much seawater will be necessary to solidify tofu made from a given quantity of soybeans. By remarkable coincidence, the required volume of seawater is just equal to the volume of dry soybeans used. Since the concentration of liquid nigari, on the other hand, varies widely and is difficult to measure, it is not easy to specify exactly how much to use in a given recipe.

Tofu prepared with seawater does not taste "salty" because all the salt dissolves in the whey as the latter separates from the curds. However, since a very small amount of whey is inevitably contained in the tofu, even after thorough pressing, the salt contained therein serves as a seasoning, further enhancing the tofu's flavor. Thus, if you have a supply of clean seawater, by all means use it to solidify your tofu. Only if you wished to make your own natural salt would it make sense to first extract salt from seawater, then extract nigari from the salt.

Natural Nigari: Called "bittern" or "bitterns" in the West, *nigari* is the mineral-rich mother liquor that remains after salt is extracted from seawater. All natural sea salt contains some nigari, which gives the salt its hygroscopic propensity to absorb and retain water from the air and imparts to it a subtle bitterness, a slightly gray color, and a concentrated flavor that makes natural salt taste "saltier" and more potent than refined salt. In fact, the refining process is basically the removal of nigari from natural salt to create a pure-white product that is about 99 percent sodium chloride. Generally containing magnesium carbonate additive, refined salt bears about as much resemblance to natural salt as do white bread, white rice, or white sugar to their whole, natural counterparts. The Japanese call natural salt *nami-no-hana*, "the flowers of the waves." It has been regarded as a symbol of purity and is used in a wide array of sacred ceremonies and rituals.

Anyone can make natural salt: to do so, take a large, wide-mouth pot to a clean stretch of ocean, use seawater to fill the pot two-thirds full; then simmer its contents over a driftwood fire until all of the water has evaporated and only moist solids remain. Transfer the solids to a glass jar and cover. (This is a beautiful and fruitful way to spend a day at the ocean!) One gallon of seawater (weighing 8¼ pounds) yields about ¼ pound natural sea salt, almost one-fourth of which consists of minerals other than sodium chloride. Containing all of the trace elements found in seawater, its composition on a moisture-free basis is:

	Percent
Sodium chloride	77.8
Magnesium chloride	9.5
Magnesium sulfate	6.6
Calcium sulfate	3.4
Potassium chloride	2.1
Magnesium bromide	0.2

Using your moist salt (or natural sea salt available at most natural foods stores) you can now prepare your own nigari. For small-scale production, place the salt into a fine-mesh bamboo (or plastic) colander set over the mouth of a non-corrosible (earthenware, glass, wood, or plastic) container (fig. 117). If the salt is dry, sprinkle it lightly with water,

Fig. 117. Making nigari with bamboo colander

then place the salt and container in a cool, damp place. (Or, for faster results, place a large bowl filled with water next to the container and cover the salt, bowl, and container with a large plastic bag or box to form a simple humidifier.) As the salt absorbs moisture from the air, the nigari, a slightly reddish, concentrated liquid, will begin to drip into the empty container. After several days, depending on the amount of salt and the humidity, there should be enough nigari to solidify the tofu made from 8 cups of soybeans.

For larger-scale production, obtain at least 10 pounds (or as much as 50 to 100 pounds) of sea salt. Place the salt in a moistened sack (such as a flour or gunney sack) or on a piece of cotton or linen cloth which is then gathered at the corners to form a sack. Suspend the sack above a large container or, if the container is sturdy and has a wide mouth, place the sack on top of several boards resting across the container's mouth. Set in a cool damp place and allow the nigari to factor out.

In traditional Japanese farmhouses, about 100 pounds of unrefined sea salt were placed in a sack 3 feet long and 2½ feet wide made of woven rice straw. This was either set directly on top of a specially-made wooden container called a "salt boat" (fig. 118) or suspended from the farmhouse rafters over an empty wooden barrel. These sacks could be seen

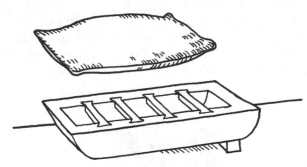

Fig. 118. A "salt boat"

working throughout the year as farmers "refined" their own salt while simultaneously collecting the valuable nigari: thus, full use was made of the natural salt purchased from oceanside salt fields, nothing was wasted, and no energy was consumed in the refining process. The nigari was used for solidifying homemade tofu. The well-drained topmost portions of the salt were used in the preparation of farmhouse miso and shoyu, and for seasoning foods at the dinner table. The lowermost portions, which still contained a small amount of nigari, were used for pickling, since farmers found that the nigari gave vegetables (such as *daikon*) and fruits (such as the *ume*) a crisper texture, firmer skin, and better flavor. Over a period of several weeks during the warm, humid months when nigari could be collected most rapidly, 100 pounds of unrefined (grade 5) natural salt yielded about 10 to 20 quarts of the liquid usually with the following composition (not including its water content):

	Percent
Magnesium chloride	31
Magnesium sulfate	2
Potassium chloride	2
Sodium chloride	1

It will be seen why refined magnesium chloride and natural nigari produce almost identical flavors in tofu.

Natural nigari is also available from salt refiners (such as Leslie Salt in the U.S.) using natural salt fields. Enormous quantities of bittern are produced as a byproduct of the salt refining process. Although this bittern has not been approved for use in foods by the Food and Drug Administration, it is purified by natural processes; algae eat any organic matter in the salt fields, brine shrimp are introduced to eat the algae, and the shrimp are carefully removed before the brine is made into salt. Most of this nigari is sold for commercial use in tank-truck quantities to produce magnesium chloride, magnesium metal, Epsom salts, potash, or bromine, or to remove the ice from frozen road surfaces. Weighing 10.7 pounds per gallon (specific gravity 1.28 at 60°F), a typical sample of the solids in this nigari shows the following composition by weight:

	Percent
Magnesium chloride	11.8
Sodium chloride (common salt)	6.9
Magnesium sulfate	6.7
Potassium chloride	1.8
Potassium bromide	0.2

For over 1,000 years, up until the beginning of World War II, almost all the tofu made in Japanese farmhouses and tofu shops, and much of the tofu made near the seacoast in China, was solidified with natural nigari. The word "nigari" is composed of the two characters meaning "bitter" and "liquid." Unlike the word "bittern" in the West, "nigari" is well known and widely used in Japan due to its long-standing association with natural sea salt and salt-pickled vegetables as well as with tofu. Magnesium chloride, the main active ingredient in nigari, coagulates the soy protein in soymilk to form curds; in chemical terms, the double-bonded, positive magnesium ion (Mg^{++}) combines with a double-bonded negative ion in the protein to form a fruitful and happy marriage.

Until the postwar period, most of Japan's nigari and natural salt were produced by the solar evaporation of seawater in small salt farms located on the seashore in areas with low rainfall, plenty of sunshine, and a high average temperature. Using the ancient "raised beach" method, the salt maker carried sea water from the ocean in large wooden buckets suspended from the ends of a shoulder pole. On hot, sunny days, he scattered this water over the surface of a small, level field consisting of clean sand spread several inches thick over a base of hard clay. (In the early part of the twentieth century, the salt fields came to be built at sea level, and the water was run in by a type of irrigation system.) The salt water in the wet sand rose to the surface of the field by capillary action. Here it evaporated and salt crystals formed. These were raked up and placed in a double-level draining vat. The latter consisted of a shallow wooden tub on top of which was mounted a slightly deeper wooden vat with a slatted bamboo bottom covered with a matting of woven rice straw. The sand (in which was deposited the crystallized salt) was placed in the upper vat. Sea water was then poured over it so that the salt dissolved and drained into the lower tub as a concentrated brine. The well-drained sand was scattered back over the field and raked smooth. The brine was then transferred to a large cauldron in which it was further evaporated (simmered) over a wood fire. As the concentration of the brine increased, sodium chloride (common salt) reached its saturation point and crystallized on the bottom of the pot. The crystals were scooped up with a shallow strainer and placed in a tightly-woven bamboo basket. The basket was set on a draining board attached to the edge of the cauldron so that the liquid (nigari) in the salt drained back into the cauldron. The well-drained salt was then put into a 6-foot-deep double-level draining vat—similar in design to but larger than the one used to wash the sand—and was allowed to drain for one week. The liquid remaining in the cauldron, "fresh nigari," was set aside and conserved. The well-drained salt was then sorted into 5 grades. That at the top of the vat, which drained best and contained the least nigari, was considered top-grade and sold at the highest price. That at the bottom of the barrel, grade 5, was relatively moist and bitter; it was sold at the lowest price and was widely used in farmhouses where it was further refined, as described above.

The nigari that remained in the cauldron after all the salt had been removed was cooled, placed into well-seasoned cedar shoyu vats (fig. 9, p. 32), and shipped to tofu shops throughout the country. In some cases it was condensed (by simmering) to twice its concentration or even until it became a solid. Because of its light weight, concentrated (or solid) nigari was easier to transport and was therefore often sold to tofu makers at a lower price.

As the simple salt farms throughout the country were gradually replaced by large scale, industrial salt factories, the lower grades of salt gradually disappeared. By 1931, grades 4 and 5 were no longer available, and by the end of World War II all salt made in Japan was either grade 1 or 2. This meant that farmers could no longer produce their own nigari. Although some farmhouse tofu makers began to order nigari from commercial sources, country tofu gradually started to disappear from the culture.

Food-grade natural nigari is now available at low prices from natural food distributors in both the United States and Japan (see p. 315). It is usually sold in its solid form, which has a coarse, granular texture resembling sea salt, is tan to reddish gray in color, and will dissolve in cold water in less than 1 minute. The solid form is preferable to liquid nigari primarily because the amount necessary to solidify a given quantity of tofu can be specified exactly, whereas with liquid nigari the amount required depends on the concentration. One pound of solid nigari will solidify about the same amount of tofu as 6½ cups of typical liquid nigari or 114 pounds (14 gallons) of seawater. It is obvious from these figures why nigari rather than seawater has been used in most farmhouses and tofu shops in Japan.

Refined Nigari: Because of the present level of contamination in the oceans and the difficulty of obtaining food-grade natural nigari, most Japanese farmhouse craftsmen and many tofu shops throughout East Asia and the United States now use refined nigari—either magnesium chloride or calcium chloride. Although both evoke much the same delicate natural sweetness and bouquet as natural nigari, magnesium chloride gives tofu that is slightly closer in flavor to the traditional, natural product, while calcium chloride is valued for yielding tofu that is rich in calcium. On a farmhouse scale, both solidify the tofu more quickly and are easier to use than the two solidifiers listed below. Both are sold in the form of a granular or crystalline white solid.

Calcium Sulfate and Magnesium Sulfate: When used with soymilk cooked in a metal pot over a wood fire, both of these solidifiers yield delicious, though rather mild-flavored, soft tofu. Natural calcium sulfate (gypsum) has been used to solidify farmhouse and commercial tofu in China for about 2,000 years. Although it has never been used by Japanese farmhouse craftsmen, it is now the most widely used solidifier in tofu shops throughout the world. Its recent popularity is due primarily to its ability to give a slightly larger bulk yield (by incorporating more water into the tofu) and to the ease and speed with which it can be used on a commercial scale. (Keep in mind, however, that nigari gives tofu with the same yield of solids and nutrients as calcium or magnesium sulfate.) Although present-day natural gypsum is about 97 percent pure, the remaining portions may contain lead or other impurities. To be safe, therefore, use only natural gypsum certified as a food ingredient.

Regardless of the variety of solidifier, use the *minimum amount necessary* to curdle the soymilk. If too much is added, the bulk yield (but not the yield of solids or nutrients) will drop, and the end product will be relatively hard, coarse, and crumbly. Its surface will be less smooth and glossy and contain tiny holes or air pockets. It may also have a slightly bitter taste (which can be alleviated by soaking in cold water as soon as the tofu is removed from the settling container). If the curds forming in the cooking pot separate from the pot's walls and the space in between fills with yellow whey, you have probably added too much solidifier.

Country Farmhouse Tofu   MAKES 15 TO 20 SERVINGS

8 cups soybeans
5 gallons water, approximately
Solidifier:

   For subtly sweet nigari tofu use: 3 tablespoons solid granular magnesium chloride or calcium chloride; or 2½ to 4 tablespoons granular or powdered natural nigari; or 2½ to 5 tablespoons homemade liquid nigari, or 3 to 8 tablespoons commercially prepared liquid nigari; or 8 cups clean seawater (freshly collected)

   For mild soft tofu use: 3 tablespoons Epsom salts (magnesium sulfate) or calcium sulfate

   For subtly tart or slightly sour tofu use: 1¼ cups lemon or lime juice (freshly squeezed), or 1 cup (apple cider) vinegar

Prepare in advance:

   On the evening of the previous day: Place beans in pressing pot and rinse with water, stirring vigorously with paddle or hands. Drain in colander, rinse again, and re-drain. Combine beans and 1½ gallons water in pressing pot and soak for 8 to 10 hours (or in very cold weather for as long as 15 to 20 hours).[1]

   If using a wood fire, gather firewood, preferably oak or other fragrant hardwood. Prepare cooking site and lay (but do not light) a small fire.

   Rinse out pressing pot, sack, and rack. Place sack and rack in pressing pot and set pot 6 to 8 feet away from fire.

Moisten settling-box cloths and use to line bottom and sides of settling container. See that cloths fit closely against all inside edges and corners of container and are free of large wrinkles. Set container aside for later use.

   Pour soaked beans into colander, rinse well under running water, and allow to drain.

After making the above preparations, proceed as follows:

   1) Light fire and begin to heat 4¾ gallons water in covered cooking pot. While water is heating, combine about 2½ cups soaked beans with 2 2/3 cups water in blender and purée at high speed for 2 to 3 minutes or until smooth. Transfer purée (gô) to purée container and repeat until all beans are used. (If using a foodmill or meat grinder, grind beans without adding water, and add 5½ quarts more water to cooking pot. If using grinding stones, see Note 2.)

   2) When water in cooking pot comes to a boil, transfer 1 gallon to hot water pot. Add soybean purée to water in cooking pot, rinsing out purée container and blender with a little water from hot water pot to retreive any remaining purée. Taking care that pot does not boil over, heat over high heat, stirring bottom of pot frequently with wooden paddle to prevent sticking. When foam suddenly rises in pot, quickly lift pot off fire (or use tongs or a shovel to remove fire from under pot) or turn off heat.

   3) Place pressing pot next to cooking pot. While a second person holds sack down inside pressing pot with mouth of sack open, ladle and then pour hot purée into sack. Rinse out cooking pot with a little water and pour into sack. Lift sack out of barrel, quickly place pressing rack across barrel's mouth, and set sack on top of rack. Twist hot sack closed and fold neck across top of sack. Balance a heavy pressing weight directly on top of neck in center of sack and press for 2 to 3 minutes. (Or press sack with lever press.) Adding your full body weight, press for about 1 minute more to expel as much soymilk as possible.

   4) Remove weight and bounce sack on rack to loosen pressed okara. Open sack on rack and pour in 1 gallon hot water from hot water pot, dampening entire surface of okara. Stir okara briefly with paddle or ladle, then twist sack closed and re-press for 2 to 3 minutes. Open sack, shake okara into one corner of sack, twist closed again, and press for 1 to 2 minutes more. Adding your full body weight, press for several minutes more, or until soymilk no longer drips into pressing pot. Bounce sack on rack to loosen okara, then empty okara into purée container and set aside. Dry hot water container thoroughly, measure in solidifier, and set aside.

   5) Scrub out and rinse cooking pot, return it to the fire and pour in soymilk. Stoke fire, increasing heat to medium-high. Bring soymilk to a boil, stirring bottom of pot frequently to prevent sticking. Reduce heat to medium and cook for 5 minutes, then turn off heat. (Or place lid on pot, then rake or shovel all burning wood and coals out from under pot.)

   6) Add 1½ quarts water to solidifier in hot water container. (Do not add additional water to seawater.) Using paddle or ladle, stir soymilk clockwise to form a swift whirlpool, stop paddle abruptly near side of cooking pot with blade

broadside to swirling soymilk, and pour 2 cups solidifier solution down upstream side of paddle.[3] (Pour from a height of 1 foot above surface of soymilk so that solidifier penetrates to bottom of pot.) Stir soymilk 1 turn counter clockwise, bring paddle to a halt upright in soymilk and wait until all turbulence ceases; lift out paddle. Sprinkle 2 cups more solidifier solution over surface of soymilk, cover pot, and wait for 4 minutes while curds form. Stir remaining 2 to 3 cups solidifier solution, uncover pot, and sprinkle solution over surface of soymilk.[4]

7) Very slowly stir the upper 1-inch-thick layer of the curdling liquid for 30 to 40 seconds, then cover pot and wait for 5 to 6 minutes. (Wait 8 to 10 minutes if using Epsom salts or calcium sulfate.) Uncover and stir surface layer again for 30 to 40 seconds, or until all milky liquid curdles.

(White "clouds" of delicate curd should now be floating in the whey, a clear, pale yellow liquid. If any milky, uncurdled liquid remains, wait for 3 minutes, then gently stir until it has curdled. If milky liquid persists, dissolve a small amount of additional solidifier [about ¼ of the original amount] in 2 cups water and pour directly into the uncurdled portions; stir gently until curdled.)

8) Set pressing pot next to cooking pot. Place pressing rack across mouth of pressing pot and set cloth-lined settling container in center of rack. Cover outside surface of colander with colander cloth, and set colander on surface of liquid in cooking pot, allowing colander to sink until it is half-filled with whey. Ladle all of this whey into the settling container to remoisten the lining cloths. Place the 1-pound colander weight at center of colander. After about 1 minute, when colander is almost filled with whey, remove weight and ladle whey into pressing pot. Move colander to a place in cooking pot where whey still remains, replace weight, and repeat ladling off whey. When most of whey has been removed from surface of curds, remove colander and set aside.

9) Smooth out any wrinkles in cloths. Now, working rather quickly, ladle curds —and any remaining whey— into settling container one layer at a time. Rinse out pot with a little water to retrieve any remaining curds, and pour into settling container. Fold edges of cloths neatly over curds, place settling container lid on top of cloths, and set a 4- to 6-pound weight on top of lid for about 5 minutes. Increase weight to about 10 pounds and press for 30 to 40 minutes more, or until whey no longer drips from settling container.

10) Remove weight and lid from atop tofu. If using settling box with removable bottom, lift off sides, leaving cloth-wrapped tofu resting on bottom of box. (If bottom is not removable, leave lid resting atop tofu and invert box, leaving cloth-wrapped tofu resting on lid as in figure 35, p. 104.) Allow tofu to cool for 10 to 15 minutes more, then carefully unwrap cloths. Tofu may be served immediately, allowed to cool to room temperature, or chilled before serving. Serve (or reserve) tofu and use okara and whey as described at Homemade Tofu (p. 99).

VARIATIONS

*The Mainland Method: This method, used in most Japanese farmhouses (and virtually all tofu shops), may be thought of as the major tradition of country-style tofu making; the is-

land method comprises a minor —even esoteric— tradition in the sense that even most professional tofu makers in Japan are not aware of its existence.

The main differences between the two methods can be summarized as follows:

Island Method	Mainland Method
1. Cook gô partially in pot	1. Cook gô throughly in pot
2. Omit use of bubble extinguisher (see below)	2. Stir in bubble extinguisher 3 times
3. Extract soymilk, return soymilk to pot, and cook throughly	3. Extract soymilk and leave in pressing barrel
4. Solidify soymilk in pot while soymilk is very hot	4. Solidify soymilk in pressing barrel while soymilk is only fairly hot

For people who are just learning to make tofu and who wish to prepare only one cauldronful at a time, there are three basic advantages to using the island method: 1) It obviates the need for bubble extinguisher; 2) A smaller-sized cooking pot may be used; 3) The soymilk can be solidified more quickly and easily with the use of a smaller quantity of solidifier. The main advantage of the mainland method is that it permits the preparation of additional batches of tofu while the soymilk from the first batch is being solidified in the pressing barrel. (In the island method too, however, the soymilk can be returned to the pressing barrel before it is solidified.) Seawater or nigari can be used as the solidifier with either method, although the former is of course generally used with the island method and the latter with the mainland method.

Any of three types of bubble extinguisher may be used to prevent foam from rising and overflowing as the gô cooks: most farmhouse craftsmen use either rice bran (nuka), which is rich in natural oils, or cold water. Professional craftsmen use 1 part cooking oil—preferably thick oil which has been used several times for deep-frying tofu—and 1 part finely-ground natural limestone or its refined counterpart, calcium carbonate.

When preparing tofu with the mainland method, use the same tools as for the island method except make sure to use a pot with a thick bottom and a capacity of at least 8 gallons, and use a wooden (or split-bamboo) rod about 1 inch in diameter and 18 inches long for stirring in bubble extinguisher (see page 301). If possible, use a wooden pressing barrel. Use the same ingredients and methodology but:

1. Do not remove 1 gallon hot water from cooking pot before adding gô; cook gô in 4 ¾ gallons boiling water.

2. After gô first comes to a boil in cooking pot, reduce heat immediately to low. When foam rises, sprinkle 1 to 2 cups water or 1 to 2 tablespoons rice bran over surface of foam while stirring slowly with paddle or large spoon. (Or dip the wooden stirring rod into a mixture of limestone and oil until 1 inch of the tip is coated, then stir down.) Return to a boil twice more, stirring down foam each time, then simmer over very low heat for about 5 minutes.

3. Ladle cooked gô into pressing sack and press okara thoroughly. Omit rinsing and re-pressing of okara.

4. Increase amount of solidifier used by about 15 percent to compensate for soymilk's lower temperature. Dissolve solidifier in 2 quarts warm or hot water, then add immediately to soymilk as in basic method.

5. After all solidifier has been added, let curds stand in covered barrel for 10 to 20 minutes before ladling off whey.

*Large-scale Farmhouse Tofu Making: In some farmhouses (as in the village of Ugemura described earlier), a typical batch of tofu is made from 40 cups of dry soybeans, or 5 times the amount used in our basic recipe. A cooking pot about 3 feet in diameter at the mouth and 20 inches deep is used. Either traditional push-pull grinding stones (fig. 119a) or small electric grinders are employed to grind the soaked soybeans into gô. Using the mainland method, the cooked gô is ladled into the pressing sack (fig. b). A wicker or bamboo support is used to hold open the sack's mouth obviating the need for a co-worker. The okara is pressed in the sack using the bubble-extinguisher rod (fig. c). Nigari, (diluted only slightly) is stirred into the soymilk in the pressing barrel (fig. d). After the whey has been removed, the curds are ladled into the settling box set on the pressing rack over the cauldron (fig. e) and are then pressed with a 6- to 8-pound weight for about 1 hour (fig. f).

Fig. 119. Making farmhouse tofu

e)

f)

NOTES

1. *Soaking Time for Soybeans:* The correct soaking time varies with the air temperature, as shown in figure 120. If tiny bubbles have begun to form on the surface of the soaking water, the beans have been soaked too long. Examine

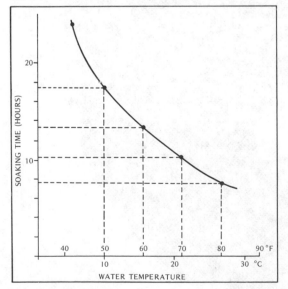

Fig. 120. Soaking Time for Soybeans

the inside of a bean by breaking it lengthwise into its two halves with your fingertips. If the faces of the two halves are flat and the same color in the center as at the edges, and if each half can be easily broken crosswise into halves, the soaking time has been correct. However, if the faces of the two halves are slightly concave and a little more yellow at the center than at the edges, and if the halves are flexible and rubbery, the beans have not been soaked long enough.

2. *Using Hand-turned Grinding Stones:* If one person turns the stone and another person ladles in the beans and water, the work of grinding goes more quickly and easily. Proceed as follows: place well-washed grinding stones on grinding platform over gô catch-barrel. Place colander containing soaked, rinsed soybeans together with a pot of water next to catch-barrel. Using a small cup or ladle, pour about ½ to ¾ cup soybeans into hole in top stone so that entire hole and part of concave upper surface of stone are filled with beans. Pour about 1/8 to ¼ cup water from pot over beans and begin to turn top stone counter clockwise at about 1 revolution every 1 to 2 seconds. After 8 to 10 revolutions (or when almost all soybeans in the hole have been ground), add another dose of beans and water.

Watch for the following: If too much water is added, the gô will be thin and will contain chunks of unground beans. If too little water is added, the gô will be thick and pasty, making it difficult to turn the stones. If the hole in the upper wheel is too small or if too little water is used, the beans may get clogged in the hole; poke them down by hand. The smoother and finer the gô's texture, the higher the yield of tofu. If the gô contains chunks of soybeans, it may be worth the time and effort to regrind (without adding more water). Grinding 8 cups soybeans generally takes about 45 minutes. Light the fire under the pot 5 to 10 minutes before you have finished.

3. *Adding Solidifier to Soymilk:* Each farmhouse (and commercial) tofu maker has his own unique way of adding solidifier. Some stir in a circle and some stir back and forth across the pot; some stir rapidly, some slowly; some add all of the solidifier at once, some in two or three installments; some pour in the solidifier from 6 to 12 inches above the soymilk surface, some sprinkle it gently over the soymilk surface, and some do both; many add liquid nigari in concentrated form without first diluting it in water. Some craftsmen using the mainland method return the soymilk to the cauldron, bringing it to a boil, before adding the solidifier. Craftsmen using the island method, but wishing to prepare a number of tofu batches in quick succession, transfer the heated soymilk to the pressing barrel just before stirring in the solidifier.

4. *Making Softer Tofu with a Higher Yield:* The use of magnesium sulfate or calcium sulfate will generally give yields 10 to 20 percent larger than other solidifiers: remove less whey from the curds; ladle the curds slowly and carefully into the settling container; after all curds are in the box, wait for about 5 minutes before pressing; press with a 1- to 2-pound weight during the first 5 minutes, then double the weight and press for 15 to 20 minutes more. Remove tofu from box underwater (see Homemade Tofu), cut into cakes, and allow to cool underwater for 15 to 20 minutes before serving.

PART IV

The Practice of Making Tofu:

The Traditional Tofu Shop

"Tofu-making possesses that stillness so cherished by one who wishes to practice. Daily work is a moment by moment apprenticeship in stillness."
— A Tofu Master

19

The Traditional Craftsman

IN TRADITIONAL Japan, the daily work of the craftsman was regarded as a spiritual path or *sadhana* that had as its goal self-realization, liberation, and the expression of inner awakening in artistic perfection. The *sumi-e* painter realized this state of Being when, in complete selflessness, he became one with the bamboo and the bamboo effortlessly painted itself. The archer approached mastery of his practice when he in no way interfered with the arrow releasing itself from the bow and flying to its true destination at the center of the target. It was the same with the swordsmith, the potter, the calligrapher, the martial artist, and others—including the tofu master.

In Japanese, each of the traditional disciplines—which Westerners usually refer to as "arts"—is called a "Way": *Sado,* the Way of Tea; *Kado,* the Way of Flowers; *Butsudo,* the Way of the Buddha, or of meditation. More broadly, however, the Chinese character that means "Way" also refers to the *Tao,* the fundamental ordering principle of the universe, the ineffable Logos. Thus, although each Way has its own unique outward form, all are united by a single underlying principle and animated by a common spirit: the spirit of *practice.*

Practice is a way of working that transforms work into art. Paradoxically, he who is engaged in practice is not primarily concerned with an explicit result—striking the bull's eye, painting the bamboo—but rather with the moment to moment realization of selflessness; through selflessness, supreme beauty is enabled to express itself.

For the true tofu master, practice is a living reality, giving energy and an ungraspable, deep meaning to daily work. To watch such a master at work is a rare and beautiful experience. His every gesture seems to emerge from a deep, still center. Grace and economy of movement give a feeling of dance to even the most mudane of his actions. A sense of rhythm, alertness, and precision shows the result of years of patient training and untiring striving for excellence. A panoramic awareness allows the master to be wholly concentrated on the one activity before him while being simultaneously attentive to the full field of activity around him.

Work done in the spirit of practice is its own fulfillment and reward. Moment to moment, the true craftsman touches reality and gives it life. In each moment, through practice, he dies and is reborn, continually reborn in the giving of selfless service. When a craftsman learns to work with his whole body and mind, time becomes for him an unbroken Being-in-Nowness. Repetition is no longer repetition, but perpetual new creation. Everything extra falls away in the direct contact with the wellspring of living reality.

Entering into his work wholeheartedly, the craftsman loses himself. He discovers a silence that cannot be broken by sounds and finds a new home at the very center of his work. The work flows freely through him into the world, finding its own way. In the midst of the world of time, he becomes free of time, and so he neither hurries nor wastes his precious moments. Through constant and patient practice, the mysteries and inner harmonies of his calling are revealed to him. Like a fish in the great ocean or a bird in the air, he reaches a clear and boundless space. Here he discovers humility. Then others may see that a fine tofu master has appeared in the world.

Master, Disciple, and Lineage

In traditional Japan, a young man's decision to enter a craft meant, initially, becoming the disciple of a master and undertaking practice as an apprentice. If the young man came from a family of tofu makers, which was often the case, the master would be his father, and he would eventually inherit his father's work. If he were bold and determined enough to start out on his own, he would probably have to obtain an excellent recommendation to a tofu master from an influential person. In either case, his relationship with his master was bound to be a trying experience. Japanese masters, whether in the arts, the crafts, or the spiritual disciplines, were known to express their kindness and compassion in what appeared at first sight to be a harsh, sudden, and unexpected manner. The story is told, for example, of a boy who, having apprenticed himself to a master swordsman, was told to chop wood, carry water, and pound rice all day. At every opportunity, the old master would sneak up behind him and whack him with a broom, a pot lid, or a stick of firewood. At first the boy was continually caught off guard, and retired each night dejected and covered with bruises. But he quickly developed a hair-trigger alertness and catlike agility which began to permeate all his work. This new sixth sense gradually deepened until his master could no longer touch him. When, after five years of housework apprenticeship, the boy was finally given a sword for the first time and showed how to hold it, he was actually well on his way to absorbing the spirit of his mentor.

In being required to become as dust before the master, the disciple learned humility. The master, by demanding complete and unquestioning obedience, self-effacement, and self-surrender, compelled the disciple to "let go" of everything he identified with himself—all old habits of thought and behavior—and thus realize selflessness. By requiring the disciple to give of himself again and again with no expectation of reward, the teacher helped him realize that only the perfect servant could eventually become the perfect master. This was the essential background or underlying spirit of all the arts, crafts, and practices. The teaching of particular forms, techniques, or methodology—the foreground—was either left until the very end of the apprenticeship or, as was generally the case in tofu shops, allowed to take place as an inevitable result of prolonged contact with the master.

As an apprentice's skill and understanding developed, he advanced through stages corresponding roughly to those designated in the West as journeyman, craftsman, and, finally, master. But the process went slowly—the average apprenticeship lasted about 8 years—since no true master wished to place his seal of approval on an apprentice with whom he was not well pleased. Of course, the master benefitted from the presence of a strong, semi-skilled helper receiving only subsistence wages. In addition, he was generally hesitant to part with the hard-earned secrets of his profession. Young apprentices, meanwhile, were expected to keep busy washing pots and tidying the shop. They peddled most of the shop's tofu and were generally allowed to keep about 10 percent of their receipts. Many apprentices were allowed to use leftover okara to prepare special treats sold to earn them a little pocket money.

Although they were never taken by the hand and instructed—especially in the master's secrets, which often had to be learned almost surreptitiously—apprentices were gradually taught fundamentals: placement of the feet, distribution of the weight when ladling or lifting to conserve energy, use of the body's inherent momentum and natural rhythms to give ease to each movement. They learned shop ecology: regard for each drop of precious hand-pumped well water, each bit of hand-cut firewood, each soybean. Principles of recycling were stressed: the mixing of used deep-frying oil and sifted ashes to make bubble-extinguisher, the use of live coals at the end of each morning for preparing grilled tofu and then for heating the home.

When each disciple was finally approved by the master as a full-fledged craftsman, he was often expected to work for one more year in the shop as a token of gratitude for having received his training. If he planned to starts his own shop—rather than take over his master's—he would receive the treasured gift of his master's lineage name, which he would inscribe in bold letters above his shop door, on his lapel and apron, and on certain tools. The Sangen-ya lineage, my master's, for example, was started more than 200 years ago and now includes about 30 shops, all in Tokyo. Most of these shops take pride in continuing to use traditional methods; their masters meet monthly for business and fraternizing. At the Sasa-no-yuki shop, the lineage has remained in the one shop for 270 years; each master transmitted his knowledge to only one disciple who then succeeded him.

Quality

The traditional craftsman placed great importance on the quality of his work and the quality of his tofu. He was first and foremost a craftsman, not a businessman or merchant. As the tofu sold, it provided sufficient income but, like all true craftsmen, he wasn't in it primarily for the money. He worked in a shop that was simple, well-ordered and immaculate; a perfect union of the aesthetic and the practical. His tools had their own character and charm. He honored them, cared for them, made them his friends, and they helped him. Work was the movement of the body in space, the feeling of water on the hands and arms, the fragrance of woodsmoke, the exertion of lifting, grinding, and pressing. Work had an intrinsic richness that was life itself. Through work, the spirit of the craftsman found concrete expression in the world of forms—as tofu. And the quality of a master's tofu bore living witness to the depth of his understanding and practice.

Each year, throughout Japan, tofu-making contests were held among master craftsmen. First on the city, then on the provincial, and finally on the national level, master craftsmen met for a period of several days and were judged by retired masters on the speed and accuracy of their cutting, their ability to grind smooth thick gô or make agé that expanded well, and, above all, on their ability to make tofu with fine flavor, texture, bouquet, and appearance.

Balance and the Middle Way

The tofu craftsman is involved in a dynamic process whose central principal is balance. Throughout the day, he must constantly seek the optimum middle way between the two extremes: he must soak the beans for neither too long nor too short; grind the gô neither too thick nor too thin; have the fire neither too high nor too low; cook the gô for neither too long nor too short a time; add neither too much nigari nor too little. To continually find the precise point of balance or perfection requires sustained attention, careful observation, and considerable experience. Furthermore, this point of balance is constantly changing with the weather and air temperature, the type and freshness of the beans, the concentration of the nigari, and the flavor and texture of the tofu desired at a particular season or on a particular day. Fine traditional craftsmen with over twenty years of experience have said that of the 25 or 30 batches of tofu they make each week, there are usually no more than one or two with which they feel completely satisfied. Such a statement points not only to the high personal standards of these men but also to the depth and subtlety of the process itself.

The Cycles and Rhythms of the Day and Year

In Japan's neighborhood tofu shops, it is the tradition for the tofu maker and his wife to rise together early in the morning. At that hour, except for the light in the tofu shop, the streets are usually dark. Although most craftsmen begin work at about 5 or 6 o'clock, those who make a large quantity of tofu—and especially those using a cauldron and the slower, traditional methods—may rise as early as 2 or 3 o'clock. In Taiwan and China, most shops start work at about 10 o'clock at night and work straight through until morning.

Upon awaking, the tofu maker begins to heat the water in the cauldron for the first batch of tofu. He then fills the sinks with cold water, rinses off his tools, and begins to prepare at least three consecutive batches of tofu: one of regular tofu that can also be made into thick agé, grilled tofu, or ganmo; one of kinugoshi made from relatively thick soymilk; and one of agé, made from very thin soymilk. As soon as the first batch has been completed and is cooling in the water-filled sinks, the tofu maker is joined by his wife who has finished her morning housework. She cuts and begins pressing the fresh tofu to prepare it for deep-frying, then gathers up any tofu leftover from the previous day and begins pressing it to make ganmo. Working together in the confined space of the small shop, the skilled tofu maker and his wife develop a dance-like sense of harmonious movement and a close feeling of cooperation and sensitivity to each other's work.

By about 7 or 8 o'clock, housewives from the neighborhood begin stopping by to purchase fresh tofu for their breakfast miso soup (fig. 121). Since the neighborhood markets are not open at this early hour, many tofu shops also sell miso, eggs, sea vegetables, dried mushrooms, and other breakfast food staples as a service to their customers as well as a means of supplementing their income. At about this same time, the tofu maker may cut the freshly-made tofu into 12-ounce cakes and make quick early morning deliveries to local markets, restaurants, hospitals, or school cafeterias. At times, he also fills special orders for meetings or other large gatherings. Returning to the shop, he will continue work if there is more tofu to be made for that day.

Since the craftsman's wife usually has complete responsibility for all deep-frying, her work continues after her husband has finished washing the tofu-making tools and cleaning up the shop. She waits on customers who come to the shop's window and, at the end of the morning's work, enjoys a leisurely breakfast with her husband.

Fig. 121.
Morning shopping

At about 3 o'clock in the afternoon, the tofu maker resumes his deliveries. He carefully immerses the tofu in cold water in a special wooden delivery box placed on the back of a bicycle or motor bike, then drives through the streets of those neighborhoods which are a long walk from his shop. When housewives hear the sound of his small, trumpet-like horn, they come quickly into the street, usually carrying their own containers, and buy their choice of the five or six types of tofu being offered.

During the afternoon or evening, depending on the season and the air temperature, the tofu maker washes and begins soaking the beans for the following day's tofu; a typical shop uses 70 pounds of soybeans daily. In deciding how much tofu he will prepare, the craftsman must first try to predict the coming day's weather: if it rains, many housewives will not leave their homes to go shopping and sales will drop; if it is a hot summer's day, people will probably eat a lot of Chilled Tofu; if it is a cold winter's day, people will want to gather around a tabletop brazier to enjoy Simmering Tofu or other types of one-pot cookery. The tofu maker must also consider the day of the week (tofu is often served at large elaborate meals on the weekend), the time of the month (tofu sales rise shortly after payday), and the season (peak sales are in June, the hottest month).

Since the busiest time of the day for selling tofu at the shop window is in the evening, most shops stay open for several hours after dinner, or until all of the day's tofu has been sold. The craftsman and his wife take turns waiting on customers. The family ordinarily goes to bed quite early.

Most tofu makers take a one-day vacation in the middle of each week. On either the previous or following day, the shop will be cleaned and scrubbed with even more care than usual; all wooden boxes and barrels are dried in the sun, and brass barrel hoops and the cauldron's rim are polished until they shine. The wooden barrels and boxes are then stacked as usual on top of the cauldron where they continue to dry during the night. Japanese tofu shops have a long history of the highest standards of cleanliness which, in recent times, the government health department has helped to maintain by strict, periodic inspections.

For the tofu maker, the year, too, like the day, has its inborn rhythms. January and February are ideal months for making tofu. Ice cold water helps keep the tofu fresh for long periods, and the air in the shop is brisk but not too chilly, being warmed slightly by the fires under the cauldron and deep-fryer. The windows steam up and the shop becomes a small, cozy world unto itself. With the advent of

spring, many shops begin to prepare silken-smooth kinugoshi. By mid-March, at the time of school graduations, the tofu maker works from morning until night to fill orders for agé which are made into Inari-zushi, the little rice-filled pouches so popular at graduation-day picnic lunches. As summer approaches, masters begin work even earlier than usual while the pre-dawn air is still cool. As the demand for tofu increases, so do working hours. During the warm months, additional care is required to keep the tofu fresh and the shop up to hygenic standards. By September, the blessed cool of fall ushers in Japan's most welcomed season. Kinugoshi is replaced by grilled tofu as the nights become chilly and families start to prepare *nabe* dishes. Restaurants, bars, and small pushcart venders order different types of tofu for use in steaming-hot Oden, and families use grilled tofu in Sukiyaki and other dishes which are warming and satisfying. In some parts of Japan, tofu makers hold a public festival each September in honor of the God or Spirit of water, *Suijin-sama*, who provides an abundant supply of pure cold water to each shop's well. Their parade begins at the local shrine, winds through the town, and concludes at a warm tavern for an evening of fraternizing. (It is said that from the earliest of these gatherings grew Japan's first tofu unions.)

In late fall, the new crop of soybeans arrives, and the tofu suddenly has a sweetness, softness, and bouquet that sends customers hurrying to their neighborhood shops. Shops also begin to sell more okara, which keeps well when the air is cold. With the coming of the New Year's season, the demand for grilled tofu reaches its peak. During the two or three days preceding the last day of the year, the tofu maker is busy from early morning until late at night grilling tofu that will be used in the traditional New Year's cuisine. (Up until the postwar era, tofu makers also prepared a variety of special tofu treats for New Year's Day and other ceremonial occasions.) On New Year's Eve, all of Japan's tofu shops close and, like most Japanese, the tofu maker and his family spend at least three, and as many as seven, days resting and celebrating the most important holiday of the year. Masters from the same shop lineage often gather at large parties. Few true masters are unhappy, however, when the vacation ends and they can get back to their work and practice—and once again have fresh tofu at family meals.

Basic Characteristics of the Traditional Shop

The traditional shop is characterized by the use of an iron or steel cauldron, a wood fire, nigari solidifier, whole (Japanese-grown) soybeans, and a simple lever press or hand-turned screw press for pressing the okara. Most of these shops use well water; their settling boxes and curding barrels are made of wood. Some have also preserved the use of granite grinding stones driven by a small motor, and homemade bubble-extinguisher prepared from finely-ground natural limestone or wood ash mixed with thick oil used previously for deep-frying. Of course, no preservatives or other chemical additives are used. The tools in the shop are generally simple, inexpensive, and beautiful. The atmosphere is quiet, and work is done slowly and carefully with little waste and a feeling of genuine craftsmanship.

The traditional shop is a small-scale family enterprise or "cottage industry." The master and his wife often receive help from one of their elder sons, or from their parents who share the home. Workers hired from outside the family are almost never found in traditional shops. Most of the tofu is sold either from the shop window or in the nearby neighborhood rather than through a middleman or other retail outlets. This system helps keep the price of the tofu low and encourages decentralization, since each neighborhood has its own tofu shop. At present over 95 percent of Japan's 38,000 tofu shops are small neighborhood outlets, although very few of these have all the characteristics of a traditional shop.

The traditional workshop itself is generally quite small—often no larger than 12 by 15 feet—and almost always adjoins the tofu maker's home. The front of the shop usually faces the street so that tofu can be sold from the store-front window and customers may look into the shop to see what varieties of fresh tofu are in the sink or cold storage unit ready for sale. In many shops there is a view from the family kitchen or living room to the shop front so that the master and his wife can see when customers arrive. A small shop is advantageous in that is saves unnecessary movement during work, allows the shop to fit easily into the architecture of the home, and keeps building and remodeling costs to a minimum. The floor plan of a typical traditional shop is shown in figure 122. The spatial relationships between each of the main pieces of equipment have been determined during centuries of experimentation with different layouts and designs. Like the cabin of a small boat (or a Japanese garden), the traditional tofu shop is a model of compactness and utility.

The traditional shop has a low rate of energy consumption and causes almost no pollution. For these reasons, Japanese neighborhood tofu shops are given the same zoning status as family dwellings. Although the traditional process is not as fast as its modern counterparts—which utilize a pressure cooker, a boiler heated by fuel oil, and an hydraulic

press—only about 90 minutes are required between successive batches of tofu, each consisting of 120 twelve-ounce cakes.

The traditional shop is particularly well suited for two types of social and economic environments. First, those in which people have a genuine interest in high-quality, natural foods and desire the very finest tofu, and where the tofu maker places importance on the feeling and quality of the work. Second, areas where there is a critical need for inexpensive sources of protein, a lack of capital for investment in expensive equipment, and a shortage of energy and high level technology. Thus the traditional tofu shop can serve both the post-industrial nations where many people are seeking meaningful work and a return to simpler, more independent and decentralized life-styles, and the great majority of mankind who have always lived simply and are now in need of both protein and employment.

A typical shop can be built and equipped at a relatively low cost. The only two pieces of equipment that cannot be easily built or inexpensively purchased are the cauldron and the grinding stones (or grinder). The total cost of setting up a small traditional shop can be less than $1,500 if you improvise and do the construction work yourself. In Japan, a complete neighborhood shop with all new tools installed cost about $2,900 in 1975. Yet as described in Part III, a farmhouse-style tofu shop using large pots, a sturdy blender, and other tools found in most homes can be started at virtually no expense and slowly expanded into a small-scale traditional shop.

Fig. 122. A tofu-shop floor plan

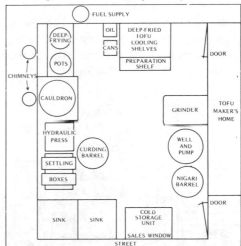

The Traditional Shop in the Modern World

The basic tools, ingredients, methodology, and spirit which characterize the traditional shop remained almost unchanged from the time that tofu was first introduced into Japan over 1,000 years ago up until the outbreak of World War II. Unlike much of the rest of Japanese society, the traditional arts and crafts—and especially that of tofu-making—were surprisingly unaffected by the period of Westernization and modernization that began in 1868. Only after World War II did traditional shops feel the full impact of the industrial revolution, which led to their gradual modernization—and decline.

With this late coming of the industrial revolution, a new consciousness began to replace the traditional one. Work came to be seen primarily as an economic enterprise and, for many, producing tofu became just another job or business. The spirit of craftsmanship was gradually diluted or largely forgotten as emphasis shifted to productivity, efficiency, cost reduction, and growth. Profits took on a new importance as commercialism became the order of the day. The master-disciple relationship was eventually reduced to a 3-month training period or eliminated altogether, and tofu-making contests were gradually discontinued. With the decline in the perceived value of the work itself and the importance of daily practice came an inevitable decline in the quality of the tofu.

During the 1960s Tokyo's prestigious Food Research Institute did the first scientific study of the tofu making process with the intent of increasing yields, reducing production times, and replacing traditional methods based on personal intuition and experience with modern methods arrived at rationally and objectively. Hoping to standardize tofu making throughout the country, the institute urged makers to use calcium sulfate (to yield tofu with high water content) and pressure cookers (to reduce cooking time). The question of the tofu's flavor was never raised. Replete with graphs and scientific data, the institute's final report played a major role in the modernization of traditional shops.

As simple tools and natural ingredients were replaced by machines and a number of new synthetic ingredients, the traditional tofu shop evolved into its modern form. Cauldrons were replaced by boilers and high-speed pressure cookers (fig. 123), wood fires by fuel-oil burners, simple lever presses or hand-turned screw presses by centrifuges and hydraulic presses (fig. 124), natural nigari by refined calcium sulfate, and whole soybeans in part by defatted soybean meal. In many shops, well water, contaminated by industrial pollution, was replaced by municipal water, wooden boxes and barrels by their aluminum counterparts, stone grinding wheels by higher-speed grinders, and charcoal braziers by propane burners. During the decade of the 1960s the traditional tofu shop reached its lowest ebb and its very existence was threatened by the new shops and factories, with their faster production time and higher output. By 1970, the wood fire, granite grinding stones, lever press, and charcoal brazier were still being used in only a very few shops throughout the country. It was estimated that a mere 1 percent of all tofu makers used only nigari solidifier (although some 14 percent used a mixture of nigari and calcium sulfate). About 60 percent continued to use cauldrons (heated by fuel-oil burners) and 55 to 60 percent used hand-turned screw presses.

Fortunately, however, the crisis seems to be passing. In Japan, as in many other industrialized nations, an appreciation of high-quality natural foods and traditional craftsmanship is re-emerging. Nigari is coming into wider use, as are many of the other traditional ingredients and tools. The small number of masters who have weathered the storm now hold the key to a rejuvenation, the promise of a potential renaissance.

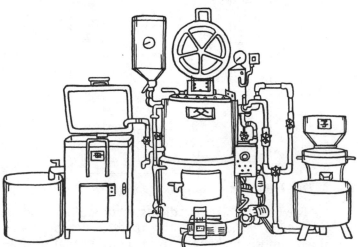

Fig. 123. A modern pressure cooker with hydraulic press

Fig. 124. A modern centrifuge with 3 soymilk barrels

20

Making Tofu
in the Traditional Way

"How would you prepare tofu to serve the Emperor?" is a question we asked of every master we met, and each responded only after careful deliberation. Our question allowed each craftsman to go directly to the heart and essence of his art, leaving aside all consideration of cost, time, and economic profitability. And almost all tofu makers, both young and old, both modern and old-fashioned, answered our question quite simply: "To make the very finest tofu, we would use the traditional method."

This chapter briefly describes that method in words and pictures. An in-depth discussion of the basic principles and practical techniques for starting your own tofu plant and making all the different types of tofu and soymilk on any of six different scales (from community and traditional shops up to a modern factory) is given in our book *Tofu & Soymilk Production: The Book of Tofu, Volume II* (see inside back cover). To the best of our knowledge, the process has never before been committed to writing since, traditionally, it was seen as a living transmission, handed down from master to disciple in relative secrecy.

Making Tofu for the Emperor

The basic ingredients required to make one batch (or cauldronful) of tofu yielding 120 twelve-ounce cakes are:

13¼ quarts (7 *sho*) whole Japanese soybeans (22.5 pounds)
30½ gallons well water, approximately (191 pounds)
4½ cups natural liquid nigari solution (relative density 1.14)
Natural bubble extinguisher
Hardwood firewood (preferably oak)

In the afternoon or evening, the tofu maker uses a handsome 1-*sho* box to measure dry soybeans into a large cedar barrel. Adding fresh water, he churns the beans vigorously with a wooden paddle to rinse them thoroughly, then pours off the water. After repeating this process several times, he adds 10 to 12 gallons of fresh water and allows the beans to soak overnight. Before retiring, the craftsman ladles about 22½ gallons of water into the cauldron; this will save him time next morning—and serve as an emergency reservoir in case of fire in the neighborhood.

Early the next day, the tofu maker dresses in the traditional garb of his craft. His raised wooden *geta* keep his feet high and dry above the shop's wet stone floor; his cloth apron bears the name of his shop and lineage; in Japan, his headband, which keeps his brow free of perspiration during the hot summer, has long been a symbol of exertion.

After lighting a large wood fire under the covered cauldron, the tofu maker washes his hands thoroughly, then scrubs out and fills the sinks with cold water. He transfers the soaked beans into a bucket with a perforated bottom. After draining the beans briefly, he then pours them into the hopper above the grinding stones (or grinder) and runs in a steady trickle of water. The beans are transformed into gô which runs into the cedar catch-barrel.

When the water in the cauldron has come to a boil, the tofu maker ladles about 1½ gallons into a separate container for later use. The gô catch-barrel is moved next to the cauldron, into which the craftsman now ladles most of the gô.

Lifting the catch-barrel onto the lip of the cauldron, all remaining gô is poured and scooped in.

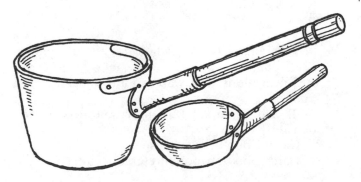

The gô is brought to a boil a total of three times and is stirred down each time with a little bubble extinguisher; it is then simmered for about 5 minutes. While the gô simmers, the tofu maker rinses out the cedar curding barrel, the straining bag, and the pressing sack. The straining bag is used to line the barrel; the sack is hung down inside the bag. When the gô has finished cooking, the craftsman removes the cauldron's wooden rim, fits a special wooden trough just inside the mouth of the pressing sack,

Held over the cauldron, the ladle is then rinsed with some of the hot water set aside previously. A small dipper is used for this purpose.

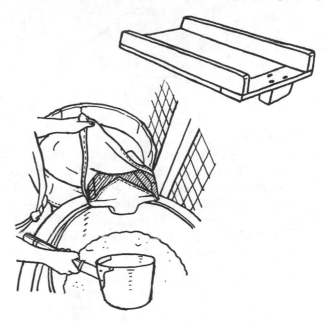

and hangs the sack and trough on the cauldron's lip. Now, holding the sack open with one hand, he ladles in the cooked gô.

The tofu maker now cooks the gô over high heat, placing a wooden rim on the lip of the cauldron to prevent the gô from overflowing. (The cauldron lid is set aside during cooking so that the fragrance of the woodsmoke can permeate the gô.) When a head of white foam rises in the cauldron, the craftsman dips the tip of a split bamboo rod into a container of bubble extinguisher, then uses the coated rod to briskly stir down the rising foam.

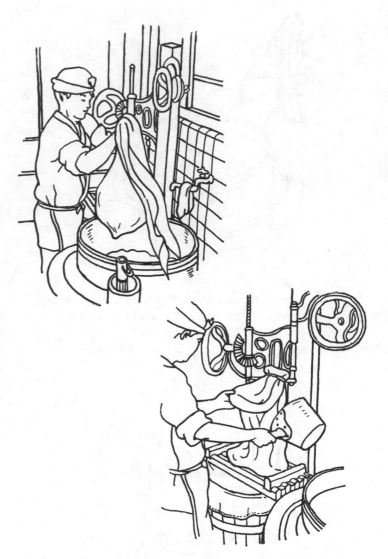

After rinsing out the cauldron with a few dippersful of hot water and transferring all gô into the sack, the tofu maker refills the cauldron with about 9½ gallons of fresh well water and stokes the fire. Using the cable from a hand-turned cogwheel winch located just above the curding barrel, he hoists the heavy sack into the air: soymilk drains into the curding barrel; okara remains in the sack.

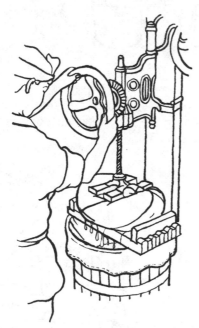

After several minutes, the craftsman places a wooden pressing rack across the mouth of the barrel directly below the sack, then lowers the sack onto the rack. After twisting closed the sack's neck and folding it across the top of the sack, he presses the sack for about 4 to 5 minutes using either a simple lever press or a hand-turned screw press.

The master now opens the pressing sack and empties the okara into the water heating in the cauldron. A small amount of fine-grained okara has found its way into the straining bag; this okara, too, is drained briefly, then emptied into the cauldron. The heavy wooden lid is now placed on the cauldron to hasten the reheating process. The tofu maker meanwhile stretches a rinsed, fine-weave straining cloth over the mouth of the curding barrel and sets the pressing rack on top of it. He places the sack on top of the rack, drapes one edge of the sack's mouth over the hanging-bar, and secures it with a piece of rope. When the okara comes to a boil in the cauldron, it is stirred briefly with the bamboo rod, then ladled into the sack. The cauldron is rinsed out with a little hot water, the rinsings are ladled into the sack, and the cauldron is then refilled with water for the next batch of tofu. The okara is re-pressed, then emptied into a special container and put outside the shop to be picked up later by a local dairyman.

The master covers the curding barrel with the cauldron lid to keep the soymilk from cooling, then ladles 4½ cups of nigari solution from the sturdy cedar nigari barrel into a wooden bucket, where it is diluted with about 3 gallons of warm water.

Another one-third of the nigari is sprinkled over the surface of the soymilk, poured first onto the paddle to give a finer spray. The curding barrel is re-covered and the curding soymilk allowed to stand for 10 minutes. The master then sprinkles the remaining one-third of the nigari over the surface of the curding soymilk and slowly stirs the upper 2 inches of the surface of the curds for about 20 seconds; the barrel is re-covered and allowed to stand for 10 minutes more.

Using the paddle, the tofu maker stirs the soymilk into a swift clockwise whirlpool. Stopping the paddle suddenly and holding it against the side of the barrel with its face broadside to the soymilk's flow, he uses the dipper to pour about one-third of the nigari solution down the upstream side of the paddle.

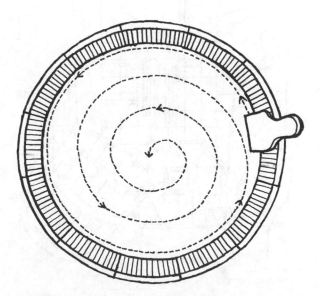

Removing the barrel's lid, the tofu maker now uses the paddle to cut a slow, deep spiral through the curds, thereby helping any unsolidified soymilk at the bottom of the barrel to rise to the surface, where it will curdle.

The master moistens the settling-box cloths and uses them to line the settling boxes. He then covers a large bamboo colander with a cloth, and places the cloth-lined colander into the liquid in the curding barrel. The colander fills with whey which is ladled off into the whey catch-box located beneath the settling boxes. Weighting the colander with a brick or stone, he allows it to fill with whey several more times.

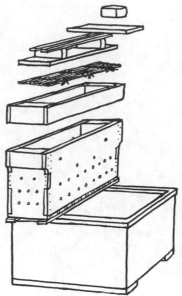

If the settling boxes are too small to hold all the curds initially, the tofu maker places a special frame atop each box to increase its depth. When all of the curds are in the boxes, the settling-box cloths are folded over the top of the curds, and a bamboo pressing mat and wooden pressing lid are set atop the cloths. Across the tops of the lids is laid a small board; atop this board is placed an 8- to 10-pound weight.

Removing the colander, the tofu maker carefully ladles the soymilk curds into the cloth-lined settling boxes. He tilts the barrel to one side to reach the curds at the very bottom.

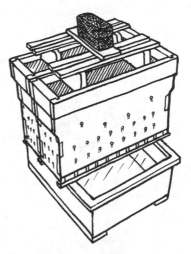

After 4 or 5 minutes the curds will have settled several inches in the boxes. The pressing apparatus and frames are removed, the cloths on all four sides of each box are gently pulled up to smooth out any wrinkles that may have formed, and the pressing apparatus is replaced, this time topped with a 20- to 25-pound weight; the curds are pressed for 10 to 15 minutes more, or until whey no longer drips from the boxes. The pressing apparatus is once again removed, the cloths are unfolded, and the boxes carried to the water-filled sinks.

Immersed in the water, each settling box is inverted, then lifted out, leaving the cloth-wrapped tofu resting on the bottom of the sink.

About one-half of the tofu remains in the sinks until it is sold to customers at the shop window; the rest is sold in the neighborhood. In many shops, up until the end of World War II, the tofu was placed in special water-filled wooden containers and carried throughout the neighborhood by means of a shoulder pole.

The tofu maker unwraps the cloths, slips a wooden cutting board under the tofu, and cuts the tofu (under water) crosswise into fifths. Each fifth is then cut lengthwise into halves, and each half crosswise into sixths. The resulting 12-ounce cakes (120 in all) are allowed to cool under water.

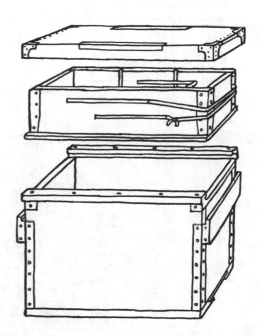

At present the tofu is placed in a large double-layer wooden box. The bottom compartment (which is lined with rustproof metal) is partially filled with water, into which is placed regular tofu, kinugoshi, and grilled tofu; the top compartment holds deep-fried tofu.

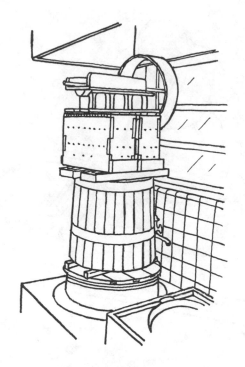

The entire box is strapped onto the back of a bicycle or motorbike which the tofu maker rides through the neighborhood as he sells the fruits of his labor.

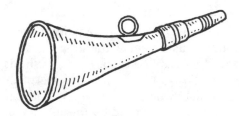

Whenever he makes his rounds, the craftsman carries a small horn tied around his neck; he blows it to announce his arrival.

At the end of work each day, the tofu maker washes all his tools with hot whey, rinses them with well water, then stacks them neatly above the cauldron to dry.

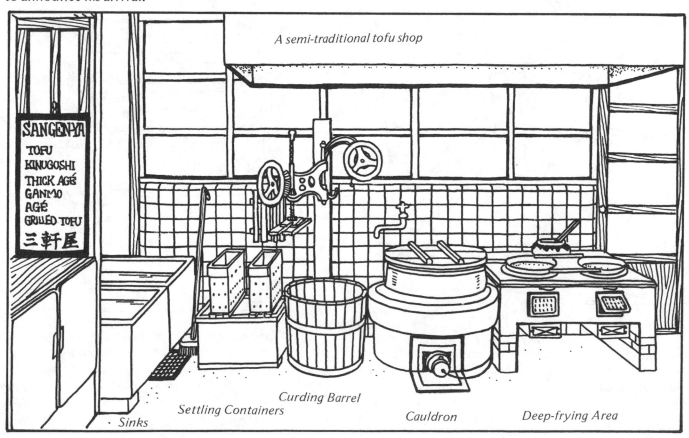

A semi-traditional tofu shop

SANGENYA
TOFU
KINUGOSHI
THICK AGÉ
GANMO
AGÉ
GRILLED TOFU
三軒屋

Sinks *Settling Containers* *Curding Barrel* *Cauldron* *Deep-frying Area*

Appendix A
Tofu Restaurants in Japan

THIS SECTION has been included first, to give Western readers a sense of the key role tofu plays and the excellent reputation it enjoys in the most distinguished traditions of East Asian cuisine; second, to provide creative suggestions for Westerners who might like to start tofu restaurants or include tofu on the menu of restaurants now in operation; and finally, to serve as a guide for those living or traveling in Japan who wish to enjoy tofu restaurant cookery. A listing of each of the restaurants mentioned in the following pages is given at the end.

Some of Japan's oldest and finest restaurants have built their reputation around tofu cuisine. If you ask a Japanese to recommend one restaurant where you can enjoy tofu cookery at its best, though, he will probably suggest Sasa-no-yuki. Founded in 1703, Sasa-no-yuki has been managed by one family for twelve generations and has long been known throughout Japan for its unequalled nigari kinugoshi, its delicious variety of tofu dishes at democratic prices, and its warm and friendly atmosphere. The name of the restaurant is proudly displayed in flowing characters written on two cloth *noren* that hang in front of the doorway. As you duck under these into the traditional Japanese entrance room, two doormen greet you with a hearty welcome. They check your shoes as you step onto long, thick beams of smoothly polished wood. Their loosely fitting blue coats—resembling *Happi* coats—give an added taste of old Japan. Perhaps the true genius of Sasa-no-yuki is that everyone feels welcome and at home here: aristocrat or working man, country grandmother or schoolboy. As in the Japanese tea house, where all are asked to come together as equals and friends, the charm here is found in refined simplicity. This book began, quite unexpectedly, with the first evening we enjoyed tofu at Sasa-no-yuki. We ended up trying one dish of every type on the menu!

The Nakamura-ro restaurant, too, has a long and distinguished history. Said to be the oldest of all existing Japanese restaurants, it began about 400 years ago as a simple tea shop serving travelers, pilgrims, and townspeople who came to pay homage at the revered Yasaka Shrine in Kyoto's Gion Quarter. Over the centuries, the shop grew into a restaurant and became famous for its "Gion-dofu." In front of the shop, kneeling behind small wooden tables and wearing distinctive kimonos and elaborate hairdos (fig.125), women cut cakes of tofu into thin slices with a speed and synchopated rhythm that have become legendary. Visitors were entertained by a *shamisen* player who took her rhythms from the beat of

Fig. 125. Cutting tofu for Dengaku (from the "Tofu Hyaku Chin")

the knives. Each small piece of tofu was pierced with bamboo skewers, spread with miso, broiled over a charcoal fire, and served piping hot as Dengaku (fig. 126).Gradually the shop's spirited atmosphere and its savory tofu became the subject of poem and song, and its spacious interior gradens attracted writers, poets, and other distinguished figures throughout the four seasons. The present master and head chef, Mr. Shigemitsu Tsuji, is famous throughout Japan as

307

Fig. 126. Busy Making Dengaku (from the "Tofu Hyaku Chin")

a cook, lecturer, and author. He has recently published an entire volume devoted solely to tofu cuisine, his specialty. In the seven rooms adjoining the famous old gardens, he and his staff offer both a moderately-priced luncheon of tofu dishes and an expensive but exquisite meal of Tea Ceremony Cuisine, served in the banquet style and featuring tofu in many of the dishes. The original tea shop at Nakamura-ro retains the charm and familial warmth of old Japan. In one corner of the room is the original stone grill where Dengaku used to be broiled (fig.

Fig. 127. Nakamura-ro

127).Two gracefully-curved tea kettles with elegant wooden lids fit down into the raised stone hearth at the center of the room; here hot *amazake* (thick sweet sake) is kept simmering. In one corner of the room, an old, hand-carved bucket and pulley hang from the ceiling above an indoor well. This is a delightful setting for enjoying Dengaku considered by many to be the best in Japan.

Another of Japan's oldest and most well-known tofu restaurants is Okutan, founded over 300 years ago and now in its twelfth generation. Started originally as a tea house inside the spacious grounds of Nanzenji temple in Kyoto, Okutan soon began serving Zen Temple Cookery and Simmering Tofu to the many pilgrims, worshippers, and visitors who came to the famous temple from throughout Japan. The restaurant continues to preserve an atmosphere of quiet serenity which reflects the spirit of Zen. While strolling along Kyoto's historic tree-lined "Philosopher's Path," hungry students, statesmen, poets, and gourmets have for centuries entered Okutan's rustic front gate and stopped to enjoy a light meal. Today, for many Japanese, the name Nanzenji is associated just as much with Simmering Tofu as it is with Zen. At Okutan, lunch and early dinner are served both indoors in teahouse-style rooms or outdoors on raised *tatami* mats set among the trees and greenery around a large, meandering pond. In summer the shaded garden is cool and filled with the rock-splitting sound of a thousand cicadas. In winter the trees are bare and the only sound to be heard is the bubbling of Simmering Tofu in the earthenware *nabe* set over a tabletop charcoal brazier (fig.128).

Like Sasa-no-yuki with its kinugoshi tofu, Nakamura-ro with its Dengaku, and Okutan with its Simmering Tofu, many of Japan's oldest and finest tofu restaurants have a single specialty, the preparation of which is a carefully guarded secret. Takocho, perhaps the most famous place in Kyoto to enjoy Oden, is no exception to this rule. Founded in 1888, Takocho is known for the savory broth that makes this Oden a true delicacy. A generations-old secret of the shop, it has a fragrance that fills the shop's single cozy room and makes passers-by want to step inside and see "what's cooking." More than 15 separate Oden ingredients (including five types of tofu) simmer in a shiny brass pot behind the thick, natural-wood counter. The elegant, dark beams and white plaster walls create something of the same convivial atmosphere found in the inns of Old England.

Tofu is one of the key ingredients used in both of Japan's main schools of haute cuisine: Tea Ceremony Cuisine (*Kaiseki Ryori*) and Zen Temple

Fig. 128. The garden at Okutan

Cookery (*Shojin Ryori*). Often called Buddhist Vegetarian Cookery, the *Shojin* school began to flourish in Japan in the thirteenth century and served as one of the first vehicles for introducing laymen to the many tofu dishes prepared by monks in monasteries and temples. Restaurants soon opened in the major temples of Japan's larger cities and led the way in developing much of the tofu cookery now famous throughout the country. Today, many of Japan's best known centers of tofu cuisine are located in or near major temples. At one of Kyoto's largest temples, Daitokuji, the *Shojin* restaurant Izusen is known for its attractive garden atmosphere, its selection of more than eight different tofu dishes, and its reasonable prices. Tenryuji, an active Zen temple in Arashiyama near Kyto, is surrounded by about eight restaurants specializing in tofu cookery, and Nanzenji temple in eastern Kyoto by at least this many tofu restaurants. *Shojin* Cookery is said to be the art of simplicity raised to perfection. From it have originated almost all of the basic principles which characterize the best in Japanese cuisine. Rich in protein, inexpensive, and highly-versatile, tofu serves as the backbone of the *Shojin* meatless diet.

Tea Ceremony Cuisine, an offshoot of Zen Temple Cookery, was taken to the level of a fine art during the sixteenth century by the great tea master Sen-no-Rikyu. Though originally the school of gourmets who cherished the life of tasteful frugality, *Kaiseki* is now among the most elegant and expensive types of cookery served in Japan. And tofu will often appear in over half the dishes on the menu. The Nishiki restaurant in Kyoto offers a type of modified *Kaiseki* cuisine at prices available to everyone. Yet a full *Kaiseki* banquet can serve as an unforgettable introduction to the finest in Japanese

culture and tofu cookery, an aesthetic experience that will refresh the senses, delight the intellect, and nourish the soul.

Closely related to *Kaiseki* and *Shojin* cookery are *Fucha Ryori*, the tea ceremony cookery developed in Chinese temples, and *Sansai Ryori*, the tradition which features edible wild plants gathered fresh from the mountains throughout the four seasons. When the great Chinese priest Ingen came to Japan in 1661 to found Manpukuji temple and transmit the Zen teachings of the master Huang Po, he also introduced the Japanese to *Fucha* cuisine and to Chinese-style Pressed Tofu (*doufu-kan*). The headquarters of this school is at the attractive Hakuun-an restaurant located next to Ingen's temple; and here they still serve Pressed Tofu and a wide variety of other tofu dishes. *Sansai* restaurants, usually located in rural areas, offer more than 30 different varieties of tasty mountain vegetables and numerous tofu preparations. Many of these restaurants are located in temples and reflect the finest of the spirit of Zen Temple Cookery.

In many Japanese tofu restaurants, the beauty of the setting is considered as important as the food itself. In most cases, the setting is one of natural beauty permeated by a sense of the season, which is also reflected in the ingredients appearing on the menu. The Rengetsu tofu restaurant, set snugly at the foot of Kyoto's eastern mountains, is composed of a number of private dining rooms opening onto a lovely courtyard beneath the spreading branches of an 800-year-old tree. Rengetsu means "lotus moon," and these two Chinese characters are written in weather-worn brush strokes on a plank of wood that hangs before the restaurant's welcoming gate. In the evening, each room seems filled with the same warm and golden light that glows in the paper-covered windows of the large stone lantern near the entranceway, while on balmy summer nights, Rengetsu becomes a harbor of coolness. A cedar dipper, set across the mouth of a stone basin overflowing with water, invites guests to drink and rinse their hands. The young bamboos in the garden and the flat, natural stones underfoot are kept moist and glistening with an occasional sprinkling of water. Along one side of the courtyard, a tiny stream emerges from a grotto of rushes and ferns, and flows around both sides of a large granite grinding stone (once used in a tofu shop) which now serves as a stepping stone. Crossing the brook, guests step onto a large, flat rock at the entranceway to their room, where they remove their shoes before entering.

In restaurants such as the Dengaku in Kamakura, the atmosphere is contained entirely within the walls of a single room no larger than 12 feet square. In the center of a floor made of jet-black river pebbles is a large open-hearth fireplace similar to that found in country farmhouses but raised several feet above floor level. Four massive timbers form the edges of the hearth and serve simultaneously as the dining table for guests seated around the perimeter on low stools with seats of woven rice straw. In the rectangular hearth, partially filled with black sand, glows a small charcoal fire. Several wooden platters are piled with neatly-arranged pieces of grilled tofu, three varieties of deep-fried tofu, and numerous fresh vegetables. Antique pottery bowls are filled with three varieties of Sweet Simmered Miso. The hostess pierces each guest's choice of foods with a foot-long bamboo skewer, daubs on his or her choice of miso with a wooden spatula, and sticks the base of the skewer firmly into the sand at a slant so that the tofu or vegetables are close to the live coals. Now and then she pours out water for tea from an iron pot suspended near the fire on a rustic hook hanging from the ceiling. The sizzling hot Dengaku is as delicious as the mood is warm.

In temple restaurants the atmosphere is one of utter simplicity: the uncluttered *tatami* room with its single scroll and flower; the garden of raked sand broken by a single outcropping of rocks; the fragrance of incense and perhaps the sound of a bamboo flute that helps us, in its pauses, to hear the silence. The simplicity of tofu seems to harmonize perfectly with this atmosphere.

In most tofu restaurants, the menu changes continually with the seasons, creating both a challenge for the chef and a delightful sense of variety for the regular customer. During the peak of winter, a piece of dried-frozen tofu in white miso soup may bring to mind the image of a snowbound temple. In the spring, Chilled Tofu may be garnished with a sprig of *kinome* from the tree in the garden. It has been rightly said that, in the finest Japanese cuisine, the right food is honored at the right season in the right setting. In fact, many Japanese tofu cookbooks arrange their recipes according to the four seasons rather than by types of food. It is precisely tofu's adaptability and versatility that allows it to be used throughout the year as host to an unending parade of seasonal delicacies.

In most of the restaurants mentioned above, great attention is given to the way in which the food is served and the care with which each guest is treated. The Japanese believe that a dish must please the eye as well as the palate. Thus chefs have made an art

of cutting and slicing so that each ingredient is given added character. Generally, a meal is composed of a large number of small courses, each served in a distinctive container, each a work of art in itself, carefully arranged and meticulously prepared. The colors, shapes, and textures are as carefully balanced as the flavors. Each ingredient is honored in and of itself; the chef works to enhance and bring to life its innate natural flavors. Thus Japanese cookery is an excercise in nuance and subtlety, the use of restraint and reserve in the highest sense to do full honor to every food.

At the Sagano restaurant in western Kyoto, for example, guests are ushered into private rooms facing a large and carefully manicured garden of emerald moss, inlaid with several clusters of large rocks and set against a background of towering bamboos. The rooms are decorated with original woodblock prints, earthenware sake jugs, and antique Japanese lutes. The waitress serving each room is dressed in a kimono of hand-dyed indigo *kasuri* cloth. A *tasuki*, or band of bright red cloth, passes over both shoulders and crosses in front to tie up the kimono's sleeves as she works. An *obi*, or wide brocade sash, is wrapped firmly around her waist, and white *tabi*, or Japanese socks, make her feet look light and cool. First she brings in a large cup of tea, then chopsticks which she rests upon a small coral support, then a moist towel for refreshing each guest's hands and face. In summer, Chilled Tofu is served floating with chunks of ice in a handsome wooden container, and a variety of fresh and colorful garnishes are served in tiny dishes. The tofu dessert, Gisei-dofu, is presented on handmade square ceramic plates and decorated with a sprig of maple.

At the tofu restaurant Goemon, located in the center of a busy section of Tokyo, the guests enter down a long path lined on both sides with stone lanterns lit with candles. An unexpected oasis of beauty and quiet amid the cacophony of modern Tokyo, the restaurant garden surrounds a small stream. A large cauldron—the type used in tofu shops—is filled with water from a bamboo pipe and overflows to form the stream's headwaters. The sound of a windbell fills the spacious rooms. In the winter, guests are seated at low tables, each containing a charcoal brazier filled with live coals. The hostess places an earthenware *nabe* over the brazier and invites guests to add their choice of several types of tofu and other carefully cut ingredients arranged on a large platter. Tofu and yuba are served in various forms in many of the delicate portions accompanying the main dish. In summer, Chilled Tofu is served in handsome lacquerware boxes accompanied by a thin crescent of watermelon and surrounded by chunks of ice. In a half section of fresh bamboo, a single red cherry is surrounded by strips of Takigawa-dofu arranged to swirl like a meandering river.

Most tofu restaurants bear living witness to tofu's remarkable versatility. At Hisago in Tokyo, over 200 tofu dishes are served throughout the four seasons and more than 85 are available at any one time. The inspirational source of many of these recipes is a two-volume book of tofu cusine written about 200 years ago. The *Tofu Hyaku Chin*, which combines the virtues of a travel and restaurant guidebook and a cookbook, was written to introduce the Japanese people to about 230 different varieties of tofu cuisine served in the different provinces. The famous novelist Tanizaki Junichiro is said to have personally prepared each of the 100 tofu recipes described in the first volume. Ms. Fukuzawa, the founder of Hisago, worked with these traditional vegetarian recipes to develop much of her present repertoire.

At Sorin-an, located in a temple surrounded by rice fields in the countryside west of Kyoto, homemade yuba is the featured ingredient in each of the restaurant's 15 dishes. Likewise, at Sasa-no-yuki, each of the twelve dishes on the menu, several of which are also available on a "take out" basis, has kinugoshi tofu as its main ingredient. In many Zen temple restaurants, tofu will be used in more than half of all dishes made throughout the four seasons. And in Japan's most famous book on *Shojin* Cookery, more than one-quarter of the recipes use tofu and many more use yuba.

One might well expect that at most of the restaurants described here, the cost of a meal would be relatively high. Yet because tofu itself is so inexpensive, most restaurants featuring tofu can offer very reasonable prices—especially considering the beautiful setting, gracious hospitality, and elegant service that invariably accompany the fine food. At Sasa-no-yuki, for example, the average price in 1975 for any of the 12 dishes on the menu was only 41 cents. In many Zen temple restaurants, a full 7-course meal costs between $2.50 and $3.50.

Most of these restaurants purchase their tofu wholesale from a nearby tofu shop, often going out of their way to obtain tofu made with nigari and prepared in the traditional way. The many excellent tofu restaurants of Arashiyama, west of Kyoto, have grown up around the famous Morika tofu shop and built their reputations on Morika tofu's fine flavor. Sasa-no-yuki is the only tofu restaurant we know of that prepares its own tofu. The restaurant's owner, Mr. Takichi Okumura, is himself a master of the tofu-making process; he learned it when he was a boy from the former master, his father. A distinguished restauranteur and tofu connoisseur, he feels strongly that the flavor of the tofu itself is the indispensable foundation for fine tofu cuisine: "Unless the tofu exhibits its own natural sweetness and bouquet, it can never become a dish worthy of the Japanese cuilinary tradition, not even in the hands of the most talented chef." Thus he insists on serving tofu made with nigari and the best-grade Japanese soybeans, prepared fresh each day in the shop located in the basement of the restaurant.

In addition to restaurants specializing in tofu cookery, there are many more which serve tofu regularly in dishes such as Sukiyaki, Miso Soup, Nishime, Chilled Tofu, or Simmering Tofu. Each of Japan's Chinese restaurants has a special section devoted to tofu cookery, and most of the thousands of *soba* shops use deep-fried tofu in a variety of noodle dishes. In the large number of restaurants specializing in Inari-zushi and in most sushi shops, agé is one of the main ingredients. And in the shops, bars, and wintertime street stalls featuring Oden, tofu is found in its many forms.

Japan's most bizarre—indeed barbaric—restaurant tofu dish is called Yanagawa-dofu. Several small, live loaches (fresh-water eels) are placed in a large tureen containing cold water and a cake of tofu. The pot is placed over a tabletop burner in front of the diners and the water is slowly brought to a boil. The loaches frantically burrow into the soft, cool tofu, trying to escape the heat. Once inside, they are cooked.

Tofu is also one of the main items on the menu at the many natural food restaurants which have opened throughout Japan in recent years. Most of these restaurants make a special point of advertizing the tofu as nigari-based and using it in both traditional Japanese and Western-style preparations. Surely, tofu salads, soups, egg dishes, sauces, sandwiches, and burgers would make excellent additions to the menus of many natural food and other restaurants in the West, as well.

TOKYO AND ENVIRONS

SASA-NO-YUKI: *Tofu Cuisine*
67 Kaminegishi Machi
Daito-ku, Tokyo
Uguisudani Station
Tel: 03-873-1145

GOEMON: *Tofu Cuisine*
Hongomagome 1-1-26
Bunkyo-ku, Tokyo
Sugamo Station
Tel: 03-811-2015

SANKO-IN: *Zen Temple Cookery*
Honcho 3-1-36
Koganei-shi, West Tokyo
Musashi Koganei Station
Tel: 0423-81-1116

SHINODA-ZUSHI: *Inari-zushi*
25 restaurants in Tokyo
For information call:
03-666-4561

TOFUYA: *Tofu Cookery*
Akasaka 3-5-8
Minato-ku, Tokyo
Akasaka Mitsuke Station
Tel: 03-582-1028

TENMI: *Natural Foods Restaurant*
Sakuragaoka 4-3
Shibuya-ku, Tokyo
Shibuya Station
Tel: 03-461-7988

MISUZU: *Tofu Cuisine*
Kogawa-cho 3-3, Kawasaki-ku
Kawasaki City (south of Tokyo)
Tel: 044-244-6845

DENGAKU: *Dengaku Cuisine*
Komachi 1-6-5
Kamakura (South of Tokyo)
Kamakura Station
Tel: 0467-23-2121

KYOTO AND ENVIRONS

OKUTAN: *Simmering Tofu*
Nanzenji Keidai, Fuji-cho
Sakyo-ku, Kyoto
Tel: 075-771-8709

JUNSEI: *Tofu Cuisine*
Nanzenji Keidai, Fuji-cho
Sakyo-ku, Kyoto
Tel: 075-761-2311

NAKAMURA-RO: *Dengaku and Kaiseki Cuisine*
Yasaka Jinja-nai
Higashiyama-ku, Kyoto
Tel: 075-561-0016

RENGETSU: *Tofu Cuisine*
Chion-in, Kitaohairu
Higashiyama-ku, Kyoto
Tel: 075-561-4589

IZUSEN: *Zen Temple Cookery*
Daitokuji-nai
Kita-ku, Kyoto
Tel: 075-4891-3806

TAKOCHO: *Oden*
Miyazawa-suji 1-237
Higashiyama-ku, Kyoto
Tel: 075-525-0170

SORIN-AN: *Yuba Cuisine*
Higashi-no-kuchi-cho 45
Kami-katsura, Ukyo-ku, Kyoto
Hankyu Line, Katsura Station
Tel: 075-381-7384

NISHIYAMA SODO: *Simmering Tofu*
Tenryuji-nai
Ukyo-ku, Kyoto
Arashiyama Station
Tel: 075-861-1609

SAGANO: *Tofu Cuisine*
Susuki-no-baba 45
Saga, Tenryuji
Ukyo-ku, Kyoto
Arashiyama Station
Tel: 075-861-0277

NISHIKI: *Kaiseki Cuisine*
Nakanoshima Koen
Ukyo-ku, Kyoto
Arashiyama Station
Tel: 075-871-8888

OHARA: *Simmering Tofu and Kaiseki*
Torii-moto, Saga
Ukyo-ku, Kyoto
Arashiyama Station
Tel: 075-871-1788

TAKEMURA: *Simmering Tofu*
Tenryu-ji, Hokuzoji-cho 48
Ukyo-ku, Kyoto
Arashiyama Station
Tel: 075-861-1483

HAKUUN-AN: *Fucha Cuisine*
Obaku, Manpuku-ji
Uji-shi (South of Kyoto)
Obaku Station
Tel: 0774-31-8017

UNITED STATES

ALASKA
Anchorage 99502—Northland Soy Products, 5650 Old Seward Hwy Unit J. Ph. 907-349-4235. Bernie Soupanauong.

ARKANSAS
Fayetteville 72701—Summercorn Tofu Shop, 401 Watson St. Ph. 501-521-9338. Steve Kectner & David Druding.

ARIZONA
Tucson 85705—Unicorn Village Soyfoods, 332 7th St. Ph. 602-622-4963. Les Snyder.

CALIFORNIA
Alhambra 91803—American Food Co, 800 S Palm Ave. Ph. 213-570-1620. Jackson Wu.
Arcata 95521—The Tofu Shop, 768 18th St. Ph. 707-822-7409. Matthew Schmit.
Carmel Valley 93924—Jack and the Beanstalk, 65 W Carmel Vlly Pob 525. Ph. 408-659-4366. Paula & Nobukatsu Terui.
Chico 95926—California Kitchen, 903 Cherry St. Ph. 916-893-0986. Al Parrott.
Duarte 91010—Soyfoods of America, 1091 E Hamilton Rd. Ph. 213-358-4526. Ken Lee.
Escondido 92025—Palomar Mountain Soyfood, 31405 N Highway 395. Ph. 714-749-2476. Alex Press.
Fairfax 94930—Wildwood Natural Foods, 135 Bolinas Rd. Ph. 415-459-3919. Paul Orbuch & Bill Bramblett.
Fresno 93706—Goto Tofu Co/Star Tofu, 943 E Street. Ph. 209-268-1717.
Gardena 90247—Meiji-Ya, 1569-F Redondo Beach Blvd. Ph. 213-770-4677. Charles Iwana.
Los Angeles 90066—Aloha Grocery Store, 4515 Centinela Ave. Ph. 213-822-2288. Mr Uehara.
Los Angeles 90021—C.R. Food, 1701 E 7th St. Ph. 213-622-0556. Munung Peter Kang.
Los Angeles 90013—Hinode Tofu Co, 526 S Stanford Ave. Ph. 213-624-3615. Shoan Yamauchi, Largest Plant In Western World Mdrn Fac.
Los Angeles 90023—Mighty Soy, 2805 E Washington Blvd. Ph. 213-266-6969. Mr Maung Ming.
Los Angeles 90037—Sam Woong Foods Corp, 4607 S Main St. Ph. 213-232-5197. Mr Aoki.

Los Angeles 90031—Wy Ky, 237 San Fernando Rd. Ph. 213-222-0779. William Lee.
Mt Shasta 96067—Many Happiness Tofu, 305 Smith St. Ph. 916-926-3939. Susan Ergas.
Nevada City 95959—Ananda Tofu Shop, 14618 Tyler Foote Rd. Ph. 916-292-3505. Michael Moody.
Ojai 93023—Ojai Tofu Co, 602 E Ojai Ave. Ph. 805-646-3285. Carl G Tolbert.
Petaluma 94953—Sonoma Natural Foods, 100A Poultry PO Box 603. Ph. 707-778-8638. Dik & Sharon Rose.
S San Francisco 94080—Quong Hop & Co, 161 Beacon St. Ph. 415-873-4444. Stanley Lee & Jim Miller.
Sacramento 95814—Sacramento Tofu Mfg Co, 1915 6th St. Ph. 916-447-2682. Mr Kunishi.
San Diego 92103—San Diego Soy Dairy, 2965 Fifth Ave. Ph. 714-296-8029. Gary Stein.
San Francisco 94124—Azumaya Inc, 1575 Burke Ave. Ph. 415-285-8500. Jack & Bill Mizono, #2 Largest Us Tofu Plant.
San Francisco 94133—Silver Sprout Co, 124 Russ St. Ph. 415-431-5031. Paul Louie.
San Francisco 94107—Wo Chong Co, 1001 16th St. Ph. 415-431-5666. Walter W Louie.
San Francisco 94108—Wo Hop Co, 759 Clay St. Ph. 415-982-7176.
San Jose 95112—Fuji Tofu Co, 248 Jackson St. Ph. 408-297-1666. Reiso And Steve Kake.
San Jose 95112—San Jose Tofu Co, 175 E Jackson St. Ph. 408-292-7026. Kenny Takeshi Nozaki.
Santa Cruz 95061—Clearway Soyfoods, 1037 17th Ave. Ph. 408-476-6390. Buddy Hamel.
Watsonville 95076—Murata's Market, 226 Riverside Dr. Ph. 408-724-5118. Mr Murata.
Whitethorn 95489—Yerba Santa Tofu Shop, Whitethorn Star Route. Ph. 707NL.

COLORADO
Boulder 80301—White Wave, 1990 N 57th Ct. Ph. 303-443-3470. Steve Demos.
Denver 80221—Denver Tofu Co, 6150 N Federal Blvd. Ph. 303-426-0122. Mr Haruhisa Yamamoto.
Ft Collins 80526—Nupro Foods, 1819 W Prospect Rd. Ph. 303-493-0138. Carol & John Hargadine.

CONNECTICUT
Middletown 06457—The Bridge, 598 Washington St. Ph. 203-346-3663. Roberto Marrocchesi & Bill Spear, Trad Fds For Modern Times.

DISTRICT OF COLUMBIA
Washington 20002—Sam Sung Food Inc, 409 Morse St. Ph. 202-544-6660. Henry & Kim Salazar.

FLORIDA
Coral Gables 33146—Sunshine Soy Co, 4015 Laguna. Ph. 305-447-1277. Danny Paolucci.
Lake City 32055—Lecanto Tofu, Rte 3 Box 150. Ph. 904-746-5374. Jean Huffman.
Longwood 32750—Aqua Agra, 100 Highline Dr. Ph. 305-339-8157. Don Wilson.
Miami 33127—Bob & Toni's Tofu Works, 764 NW 29th St. Ph. 305-635-6052. Bob & Toni Heartsong.
Miami 33127—Swan Gardens, 1111 NW 22nd. Ph. 305-324-8910. Dick Mcintyre.
Miami 33142—Tropi-Pak, 3664 NW 48th St. Ph. 305-635-1968. Dennis Murasaki.
Plant City 33566—Marjon Foods, 3508 Sydney Rd. Ph. 813-752-3482. John Miller.
Pompano Beach 33060—Aberdeen Foods Inc, 631 S Dixie Hwy E. Ph. 305-782-2685. Tony.

GEORGIA
Atlanta 30317—The Soy Shop, 1863 Memorial Dr SE. Ph. 404-377-8433. Sara & Steve Yurman.

HAWAII
Hilo/Hawaii 96720—Kreston's Enterprise, 265-D Kekuanaoa St. Ph. 808-935-6973.
Hilo/Hawaii 96720—Natural Pacific Tofu, 153 Makaala St PO Box 4352. Ph. 808-935-3220. David Gantz.
Hilo/Hawaii 96720—Puueo Poi Factory, 265-D Kekuanaoa St. Ph. 808-935-8435. Leslie Ahana Chang.
Honolulu/Oahu 96817—Aala Tofu Co, 513 Kaaahi St. Ph. 808-845-0221. Mr Shojin Yamauchi.
Honolulu/Oahu 96817—Aloha Tofu Factory, 961 Akepo Ln. Ph. 808-845-2669. Jack & Kazu Uehara, Largest Plant In Hawai.
Honolulu/Oahu 96819—Better Food Tofu Factory, 727 Bannister St. Ph. 808-841-8616. Richard Higa.

Honolulu/Oahu 96814—Green Mill Food Mftrs, 914 Coolidge St. Ph. 808-949-2370. Tom Uehara.
Honolulu/Oahu 96814—Kanai Tofu Factory, 515 Ward Ave. Ph. 808-538-1305. Richard & Mark Kaneda, 2Nd Largest Plant In Hawaii.
Honolulu/Oahu 96822—Manoa Soy Works, 2561 Manoa Rd. Ph. 808-949-1815. Bev Lum.
Honolulu/Oahu 96816—Mrs Cheng's China Bean, 1829 E Palolo Ave. Ph. 808-737-2571.
Kapaa/Kauai 96746—Kapaa Poi Factory, RR 1 Box 366. Ph. 808-822-5426. Kenneth Lai.
Lihue/Kauai 96766—Matsumoto Tofu Shop, 3469 Maono St. Ph. 808-245-6141. Mr Matsumoto.
Wahiawa/Oahu 96786—Hawaii Tofu, PO Box 26. Ph. 808-621-6941. Mrs Nemoro.
Wahiawa/Oahu 96786—Rural Food Products, 117 Mango St. Ph. 808-621-5603. Mr Haruo Honda.
Wailuku/Maui 96793—Tamashiro Tofu Shop, 326 Alahee Dr. Ph. 808-244-5215. Mr Tokusaburo Tamashiro.
Wailuku/Maui 96793—Teruya Tofu Factory, 1830 Mill St. Ph. 808-244-5313. Mr Takeshi Teruya.

IOWA
Fairfield 52556—American Pride, 208 N 2nd St. Ph. 515-472-9244. Earl Kaplan.

IDAHO
Boise 83702—Boise Co-Op, 1515 N 13th St. Ph. 208-342-6652.

ILLINOIS
Champaign 61820—Midwest Soy Products Inc, 608 S Belmont Ave. Ph. 217-398-5756. Anthony & Patricia Kao.
Chicago 60657—Chicago Tofu Co, 3255 N Holstead. Ph. 312-525-3823. Mr Minoru Kanki.
Chicago 60613—Korea Farm, 3456 N Clark. Ph. 312-348-1625. Mr Young Sun Yo.
Chicago 60614—Nomura Tofu Co, 2119 N Clark St. Ph. 312-935-9766. Mr Willer Woo.
Chicago 60640—Phoenix Bean Products, 5438 N Broadway. Ph. 312-784-2503.
Chicago 60660—Sam Hwa Beansprout Co, 5642 N Broadway. Ph. 312-271-0330. Sam Hwa.
Morton Grove 60053—Tofu Inc, 6216 Madison Ct. Ph. 312-967-0090. Eileen Friedman.

INDIANA

Bloomington 47401—Love Life Foods, 901 S Rogers St. Ph. 812-332-9662. Jay Mckinney.

Ft Wayne 46804—Zakhi Soyfoods, 124 S Hadley Rd. Ph. 219-432-1291. Victor Zakhi.

Greenwood 46142—Tris Inc, 340 Greenhills Ct. Ph. 317-881-1299. David Yang.

Indianapolis 46239—Jomar Inc, 8404 E Brookville Rd. Ph. 317-353-1008. Fred Mark.

Mishawaka 46544—Michiana Soyfoods, 2027 N Merrifield Ave. Ph. 219-259-1729. Kris Klawitter.

KANSAS

Lawrence 66044—Central Soyfoods, 832 Louisiana. Ph. 913-843-0653. Jim Cooley.

Wichita 67202—Rose Kitchen Tofu, 515 E Central. Ph. 316-267-8024. John Guffey.

MASSACHUSETTS

Boston 02111—Cheng Yah Wong, 83 Tyler St. Ph. 617-426-7588. Mr Wong.

Boston 02111—Tung Hing Lung Co, 9 Hudson St. Ph. 617-426-4827.

Greenfield 01301—New England Soy Dairy, 305 Wells St. Ph. 413-772-0746. Tom Timmins, Largest New-Age And Caucasian Tofu Plant.

Leominster 01453—Nasoya Foods, Mechanic St Exit Box 841. Ph. 617-537-0713. John Paino & Bob Bergwall.

Webster 01570—Soy Magic Coop Inc, 39 Tower St. Ph. 617-943-3049. Lucy Morrison.

MARYLAND

Baltimore 21218—American Soyfood Indus, 2222 Aisquith St. Ph. 301-235-5554. Larry Betzler.

Baltimore 21230—Bud Inc Soyfoods. Raleigh Industrial Ct, 1100 Wicomico St. Ph. 301-837-4034. Aaron Liu & Wang Chen.

Chevy Chase 20015—Swan Tofu, 4812 Leland St. Ph. 301NL. Terrence Billotte.

Laurel 20810—Eastern Food Products Co, 9157-3 Whiskey Bottom Rd. Ph. 301-792-0440. Mr Kim.

MAINE

Anson 04911—Mainley Tofu, PO Box 209. Ph. 207-696-5845. Peter Beane.

Bar Harbor 04609—Island Tofu Works, %Golbitz-Kingma 318 Main. Ph. 207-288-4969. Peter Golbitz.

Waterville 04901—Soy Beings, 13-C Railroad Sq. Ph. 207-872-8790. Richard Tory.

MICHIGAN

Ann Arbor 48104—Soy Plant, 771 Airport Blvd #1. Ph. 313-663-8638. A Collective.

Detroit 48208—Abbey Hearth Inc, 6327 14th St. Ph. 313-895-9366. Brother David.

Detroit 48205—Wah Hing Co, 12347 Gratoit. Ph. 313-527-2210.

Traverse City 49684—Oryana Food Cooperative, 601 Randolph. Ph. 616-947-0191.

MINNESOTA

Duluth 55804—Greatwater Soyfoods, 1039 E Pioneer Rd. Ph. 218-525-3913. Doug Hamdorf And Demetria Nanos.

Minneapolis 55414—Continental Soyfoods, 510 Kasota Ave. Ph. 612-378-0464. Pat Aylward.

Minneapolis 55413—Eastern Foods Corp, 3225 E Hennepin Ave. Ph. 612-331-3353. Mr Lee R Lee & Calvin Lutzke.

MISSOURI

Drury 65638—Brush Creek Tofu, PO Box 129. Ph. 417-261-2553. Marie Steinwachs.

Jamestown 65046—Imagine Foods Inc, RR 1 Box 11. Ph. 816-849-2583. David Carlson.

Kansas City 64141—Chunco Foods Inc, PO Box 883. Ph. 913-362-8097. Peter Chun.

Springfield 65802—Muckfoot Farms, 300 N Waverly. Ph. 417-866-1337. Paul Day.

Springfield 65802—Springfield Comm Tofu, 300 N Waverly. Ph. 417-866-1337.

St Louis 63133—Light Foods, 6144 Bartmer. Ph. 314-721-3960. Bob Davis.

MONTANA

Helena 59601—South Fork Tofu Cafe, 322 Fuller Ave. Ph. 406-443-5586.

St Ignatius 59865—The Tofu Factory, Rte 1 Box 216. Ph. 406-745-4538. Gerald Minsk & Brenda Adley.

NORTH CAROLINA

Asheville 28801—White Clouds of Tofu, 300 Hillside St. Ph. 704-252-0854. Joelen Bell.

Boone 28607—Bean Mountain Soy Dairy, 121 W Howard St. Ph. 704-264-0890. Jerry Mckinnon.

Fletcher 28732—Blue Ridge Soyfoods, PO Box 5321. Ph. 704-684-8501. Bob Hunt.

Hillsborough 27578—Fertile Hills, Rte 1 Box 171-E. Ph. 919-732-6626. Ken Dawson.

Hillsborough 27278—Libby Outlaw Tofu Shop, Box 34. Ph. 919-732-3359.

NEBRASKA

Lincoln 68504—Prairie Soyl, 4029 Progressive Ave #4. Ph. 402-466-8638. Julie Diegel & Marla Lowell.

Omaha 68124—Midwest Oriental Foods, 8243 Hascall. Ph. 402-391-7730. Mr Kim.

Omaha 68103—Omaha Oriental Foods, 2763 Farnam St. Ph. 402-345-1736. Mr Iksu Shin.

NEW HAMPSHIRE

Ashland 03217—Sugar Ridge Soyfoods, Box 726. Ph. 603NL. Mary Bates.

Bethlehem 03574—North Country Soyfoods, Box 572 Jefferson St. Ph. 603-869-2677. Jay & Pat Gibbons.

Gilsum 03448—Willowbrook Soyfoods, Vessel Rock Rd. Ph. 603-357-3762. Viney Loveland Robert Clark.

NEW JERSEY

Paterson 07505—Cnk Corp, 165 Main St. Ph. 201-742-3830. L H Cho.

NEW MEXICO

Dixon 87527—Tofu Shop, Box 94. Ph. 505NL. Mr Toufic Haddad.

Espanola 87532—Golden Temple Foods, PO Box 747. Ph. 505-753-3270. Hargobind S Khalsa.

Jemez Springs 87025—Bodhi Mandala Tofu Shop, Box 8. Ph. 505-829-3854. Bob Mammoser & Michael Arnold.

Santa Fe 87501—Southwest Soyfoods, 2889 Trades West. Ph. 505-471-8979. Richard Jennings.

NEW YORK

Albion 14411—Sopro Products Inc, 111 West Ave. Ph. 716-589-7074. Stephen Hwa.

Brooklyn 11237—Tokyo Food Processing, %Japan Food 40 Varick Ave. Ph. 212-456-8805. Mr Shirata & Mr Terry Terahira.

Buffalo 14223—Sung's Oriental Grocery, 471 Englewood Ave. Ph. 716-836-3611.

Haverstraw 10927—Local Tofu, 26 Main St. Ph. 914-429-2292. Sam Weinreb.

Ithaca 14850—Ithaca Soy, 403 N Plain St. Ph. 607-272-4903. David Scovronick + Robt Shapiro.

Long Island City 11101—Hashizume Food Products, 2-01 50th St. Ph. 212-392-2860. Kiyuu Yokoyama.

New York 10014—Caldron Tofu Shop, 308 E 6th St. Ph. 212-473-9543. Gloria Bremmer.

New York 10013—Chia Sheung, 376 Broome St. Ph. 212-226-3838. Mr Wu.

New York 10013—Fong-Inn, 46 Mott St. Ph. 212-962-5196. Kevin Chan, Started In 1935.

New York 10023—K Tanaka & Co, 326 Amsterdam Ave. Ph. 212-874-6600. Mr Eisuke Murakami.

New York 10013—Mandalay Food Products, 450 Broome St. Ph. 212-966-0338. Mr U Han Kyu & John Tun.

New York 10013—Sun Hop Hing, 4 Bowery St. Ph. 212-227-4812.

Ogdensburg 13669—Soyanara, 711 Montgomery St. Ph. 315-393-3836. Pat Duprey.

Rochester 14607—Northern Soy, 30 Somerton St. Ph. 716-442-1213. Andy Schecter & Norman Holland.

Woodhaven 11421—Panda Food Products, 79-20 Jamaica Ave. Ph. 212-271-4669. Hal Siegel.

OHIO

Cincinnati 45214—Soya Food Products Co, 2356 Wyoming Ave. Ph. 513-661-2250. Ben & Nina Yamaguchi Edw Willwerth.

Cleveland Hts 44118—Cleveland Tofu Co, PO Box 18153. Ph. 216-791-5100. Bob Carr & Brooks Jones.

Columbus 43227—Rising Sun Soy Farms, 2810 Banwick Rd. Ph. 614-231-4073. Tim Nusser & C H Burnett.

OREGON

Ashland 97520—Ashland Soy Works, 280 Helman. Ph. 503-482-1865. James Muhs.

Corvallis 97330—Sunbow Farm Products, Rte 2 Box 46. Ph. 503-929-5782. Mia Posner & Harry Mccormack.

Durham 97223—Dae Han and Company, 18300 SW Boones Ferry Rd. Ph. 503-620-8983. Yeun Mo Koo.

Eugene 97405—Devis Country Soy Sausg, 2240 Lorane Hwy. Ph. 503-344-7454. Virginia Ruffulo.

Eugene 97402—Surata Soyfoods, 302 Blair Blvd. Ph. 503-485-6990. Cal Miller & Lisa Rein.

Jacksonville 97530—Ruch Co-Op Soy Dairy, 6091 Hwy 238. Ph. 503NL.

Ontario 97914—Kanetomis Soybean Prods, 336 SW 5th St PO Box 568. Ph. 503-889-6584. Jim Kanetomi.

Portland 97214—Ota Tofu Factory, 812 SE Stark. Ph. 503-232-8947. Mr Ota.

PENNSYLVANIA

Allentown 18103—Real Foods, 1501 Lehigh St. Ph. 215-791-4100. Jim Saunders.

Avondale 19311—Green Valley Farms Tofu, PO Box 506. Ph. 215-268-2456. Warren Reynolds.

Honesdale 18431—Liberty Soyfoods, 111 W 11th St. Ph. 717-253-0245. Jamie & Nancy Stunkard.

Mertztown 19539—Cricklewood Soyfoods, Rd #1 Box 161. Ph. 215-682-4109. Karl & Renate Krummenoehl.

Philadelphia 19120—Formosa Foods, 5146 N Fifth. Ph. 215-457-6724. Steve Sieh.

Summit Station 17979—Kirpalu Yoga Retreat, Box 120. Ph. 717-754-3051. Chris Yorsten.

TENNESSEE

Greenbriar 37073—Millers Soy Inc, Rt 2 Box 2088. Ph. 615-643-7506. Harry Miller Jr & Mike Bishop.

Memphis 38117—Mid South Soyfoods, PO Box 17254. Ph. 901-365-7003. G Barzizza.

Summertown 38483—The Farm Soy Dairy, 156 Drakes Ln. Ph. 615-964-3584.

TEXAS

Austin 78721—Purist Foods, 4100-A Ed Bluestein St 105. Ph. 512-928-0191. Reed Murray.

Dallas 73204—Jung's Oriental Foods, 2519 N Fitzhugh. Ph. 214-827-7653.

Dallas 75204—Yong Ho Pak Food Inc, 3201 Ross Ave. Ph. 214-821-0542. Yong Ho Pak.

Elgin 78621—Yaupon Soyfoods, 404 S Main. Ph. 512-285-3810. Chico Wagner & Doug Cox.

Houston 77081—Banyan Enterprise Usa, 7332 Rampart St #113. Ph. 713-995-6885. David Chiu.

UTAH

Hurricane 84737—Knitty Gritty City Inc, PO Box 736. Ph. 801-635-4369. Joanne Michaels.

VIRGINIA

Crozet 22932—Virginia Soyworks, Rte 2 Box 505. Ph. 804-823-2364. Shag Kiefer.

Floyd 24091—Annelies Breads & Tofu, Rte 2 Box 72. Ph. 703-789-7080. Annelies Brady.

Norfolk 23508—Lucky Bean Cake, 3925 Hampton Blvd. Ph. 804-489-1493. Dan Nguyen.

Stanley 22851—New Ark Foods, Rte 1 Box 252B. Ph. 703-778-3890. Melinda Siska.

VIRGIN ISLANDS

St Croix 00840—Tofu in-Sted, Box 805 Frederickstead. Ph. 809NL. Monty Thomson.

St Thomas 00801—Veggie Table, PO Box 8029 31 Altona. Ph 809-774-1810. P A Callwood.

WASHINGTON

Seattle 98104—Hoven Foods Co, 502 6th Ave S. Ph. 206-623-6764. Yung-Ching Lui.

Seattle 98112—M.K. Tofu Co, 1800 Yessler Way. Ph. 206-622-1365.

Seattle 98104—Star Tofu Mfg Co, 608 S Weller St. Ph. 206-622-6217.

Seattle 98104—Uwajimaya Inc, 519 Sixth Ave S. Ph. 206-624-6248. Tommie Oiye.

Twisp 98856—Methow Valley Foods, General Delivery. Ph. 509-996-2372. Bernie Bigelow & Joyce Campbell.

Vashon 98070—Island Spring, PO Box 747. Ph. 206-622-6448. Luke Lukoskie.

WISCONSIN

Chilton 53014—Beantime Soyfoods, N4469 Highway 55. Ph. 414-439-1746. Glenny Whitcomb.

Madison 53703—Bountiful Bean Plant, 903 Williamson St. Ph. 608-251-0595. Chris Burant.

Milwaukee 53212—Magic Bean, 2310 N Richards St. Ph. 414-263-1297.

River Falls 54022—Creative Soyfoods Inc, 526 N Clark St. Ph. 715-425-0467. David Nackerud.

WEST VIRGINIA

Charleston 25414—Happy Dragon Tofu, Box 112. Ph. 304-725-4437. Elizabeth Martin.

Spencer 25276—Spring Creek Soy Dairy, 136 Main St. Ph. 304-927-1815. Stan Kenner.

TOFU: FOREIGN

AUSTRALIA. Colac 3250—Kims Bean Curd, 1/53 Calvert St. Kim West.

AUSTRALIA. Gembrook 3783—Blue Lotus Foods, Po Box 44. Ph. NL. Eng Eu.

AUSTRALIA. Leichhardt 2040—Soyfoods Australia, 355 Parramatta Rd. Ph. 025600792. Marcea Newman & John Fenwick.

AUSTRALIA. Marrakville NSW—Sin Ma Trading Co, 9 Meeks Rd.

AUSTRALIA. Melbourne—Tofu Shop, 78 Bridge Rd Richmond. Ph. 034296204. Malcolm Green.

AUSTRALIA. Melbourne VIC—Chung Hing Bean Curd Mfg, 268 Victoria St. Ph. 033284596.

AUSTRALIA. Melbourne VIC—Hong Oriental Food, 189 Lt Bourke St. Ph. 036632811.

AUSTRALIA. Melbourne VIC—Jon Weekes Tofu, 6/405 Alma Rd Caulfield.

AUSTRALIA. Mt Waverly 3149—Earth Angel Soyfoods, 53 Stanley Ave. Ph. 035448020. Debbie Schmetzer.

AUSTRALIA. Mullumbimby 2482—Chinese Farmhouse Tofu, Motts Rd Main Arm. Ph. NL. Ian Mott & Yuen Har Louie.

AUSTRALIA. N Adelaide 5006—Protein City, 28 Lombard St. Ph. 082673635. Terrell & Laryssa Neuage.

AUSTRALIA. NSW 2492—Homeland Tofu Shop. Homeland Foundation, Upper Thora Bellingen. Ph. 066558514. David Wilson.

AUSTRALIA. Randwick NSW—Castle Trading Pty Ltd, 93 Belmore Rd.

AUSTRIA. Merzg 34—Weg Der Natur, A2380 Perchtoldsdorf. Lawrence Dreyer.

BELGIUM. B-2070 Ekeren—Jonathan Pvba, Kapelsesteenweg 693. Ph. 031644173. Jos Van De Ponseele, Near Antwerp.

BELGIUM. Hallaar—Alternatur, Korte Spekstraat. Makes Soymilk And Yogurt.

BELGIUM. 9830. St Martens-Latem—Lima Foods, Edgar Gevaertdreef 10. Ph. 09824176.

BELGIUM. 1000 Brussels—Establissents Takanami, Rue Antoine Dansaert 107. Ph. 02--511-6635. Mr Takanami, Also Makes Miso.

BELGIUM. 1070 Bruxelles—Establissements Takanami, Rue Des Trefles 128. Ph. 025228192. Mr Takanami.

BELGIUM. 2000 Antwerp—De Brandnetel, Consciencestreat 48. Ph. 0313961. Jan Lansloot.

BELGIUM. 3000 Leuven—Seven Arrows Tofu, Hoogaardenstr 83.

BRAZIL. Sao Paulo—Agro Nippo Productos. Vila Clarice 210-350 Pir, Ave 15 De Novembro. Ph. 2612348. A Large Tofu And Soymilk Factory.

BRAZIL. Sao Paulo—Agro-Nippo Produtos Alim. Piribuba, Av Jose Alves De Mira 185.

BRAZIL. Sao Paulo—Proteija Ind & Comercio, Estrada D No 1300 Itaquera.

CANADA M1V1N9. Agincourt ONT—Nutri Soy Foods, 20 Big Red Ln. Ph. 416-291-6823. Harry Kwok.

CANADA G0C1E0. Bonaventure PQ—La Maison Du Tofu Carmel, Cp 567. Ph. 418-752-5869. Dennis Connolly.

CANADA. Calgary ALTA—Norman Leong Tofu, 2031 53rd Ave Sw. Ph. 403-243-6531. Norman Leong.

CANADA G1H2M7. Charlesbourg/PQ—Tofu Quebec Inc, 451 47th St E. Ph. 418-622-0471. Pierre Laflanne.

CANADA B0E1J0. Cleveland NS—Rubenstein Tofu Shop, Rr 1. Mark Rubenstein.

CANADA V0R1T0. Denman Island BC—Metta Tofu Products, Wren Road. Ph. 604-335-0108, Ray Lipovsky.

CANADA V9L4T6. Duncan BC—Thistledown Soyfoods, Rr 5 Church Rd (5855). Ph. 604-748-9514. Jean & Jan Norris.

CANADA V0G1J0. Edgewood BC—Winnie Imrie Tofu, Rte 1 Comp 9 Site 1. Ph. 604-269-7275. Winnie Imrie.

CANADA J8X1H5. Hull PQ—La Soyarie, 25 Rue St Etienne. Ph. 613-235-5356. Koichi & Francine Watanabe.

CANADA. Montreal PQ—Soy-Can Dairy Ltd, 59 St James St W #601. Ph. 514NL.

CANADA H2W1V3. Montreal QUE—Nanda-Line Soy Products, 4058 Rue St Urbain. Ph. 514NL. Nantha Kumar.

CANADA H1Z2J9. Montreal/QUE—Tofuco Foods Inc, 3637 Cremazie E #1215. Ph. 514-376-5010.

CANADA J0R1T0. Prevost QUE—Unisoya Inc, Cp Box 278. Ph. 514-224-2628. Norbert Argiles.

CANADA G1K6S2. Quebec QUE—Tofu Quebec, 344 Rue St Roch. Ph. 418-525-7207. Guy De Valter & Pierre La Flamme.

CANADA E0A2L0. Rexton NB—Robert Richard Tofu, Box 225.

CANADA V6X1T3. Richmond BC—Mandarin Enterprises, 11031 Bridgeport Rd #1107. Ph. 604-270-1815. Mr Eng Lim.

CANADA S7H4K1. Saskatoon SASK—Flying Dragon Foods, 3311 8th St E. Ph. 306-373-9040. Tak K Sue.

CANADA S7M1N4. Saskatoon SK—Oriental Trading Co, 340 Ave C South. Ph. 306-652-3697. Art Mark.

CANADA M1L2C9. Scarborough ONT—Victor Food Products, 102 Hymus Rd. Ph. 416-752-0161. Stephen Yu.

CANADA V0S1N0. Sooke BC—Sooke Soyfoods, 2625 Otter Pt Rd Rr 2. Ph. 604-642-3263. Wayne Jolley.

CANADA J0N1L0. St Janvier PQ—Soybios, Cp 929. Ph. 514-430-0305. Norbert Argiles & Ron Bazar.

CANADA P7E2P6. Thunder Bay ONT—Cantai Tofu Corp, 700 S Leland Ave. Ph. 807NL.

CANADA M6R1X1. Toronto ONT—Pyung Hwa Food Co, 2139 Dundas St W. Ph. 416-534-0237. Mr Jhasun Koo.

CANADA M4L1Z9. Toronto ONT—Shaw Grocery, 1447 Gerard St E. Ph. 416-466-8058. Mr Yen Yung Shaw.

CANADA M6P1Y6. Toronto ONT—Soy City Foods, 2847 Dundas St W. Ph. 416-762-1257. Pat Guardino & Paul Whitehead.

CANADA M5T2R4. Toronto ONT—Wah Chong Co, 80 Ossington Ave. Ph. 416-532-0841. Anthony Kim.

CANADA. Toronto ONT—Yet Sing Co, 11 Baldwin St. Ph. 416-977-3981.

CANADA V6A1C5. Vancouver BC—Shinbo Tofu Co, 450 Alexander St. Ph. 604-255-8141. Philip Saburo.

CANADA V6A1G4. Vancouver BC—Sunrise Co, 300 Powell St. Ph. 604-685-8019. Mr Leslie Joe.

CANADA V6A1G4. Vancouver BC—Yet Chong Co, 348 Powell St. Ph. 604-681-2712. Mr Chong Kok.

CANADA V9B4Z3. Victoria BC—Dayspring Soyacraft Corp, Po Box 7285 Station D. Ph. 604-382-2144. Michael & Paul Hsieh.

CANADA. Winnepeg MAN—Yees Grocery, 209 Pacific Ave. Ph. 204-942-7668. Philip Yee.

DENMARK. 2500 Valby—Tofu Denmark, Valbylanjady 231. Per Freurgaard.

ECUADOR. Quito—Fundacion Tofu, Casilla 252-a. Ph. 540288. Richard Jennings.

ENGLAND. Bristol 16—Cauldron Foods. Sunny Bank Chapel Lane, Fishponds. Ph. 658881. Philip Marshall & Peter Fagan.

ENGLAND. E Sussex BN71XH—Full of Beans Wholefoods, 97 High St Lewes. Ph. 079162627. John & Sara Gosling.

ENGLAND. Leicester LE21BU—the Regular Tofu Company, 75 Chandos St. Ph. 053-354-9839. John Holt.

ENGLAND. London—Hong Kong Supermarket, Shaftsbury Ave.

ENGLAND. London N1—Dragon & Phoenix Co. Kings Cross, 172 Pentonville Rd. Ph. 018370146.

ENGLAND. London N64NA—Paul's Tofu, 155 Archway Rd Highgate. Ph. 013481192. Paul Jones.

ENGLAND. Newport/Pemb—Bean Machine, 45 Maes Ingli. Ph. 820896. Zorah Groom.

ENGLAND. Surrey KT66QN—Yu's Tofu Shop, 21 Langley Ave Surbiton. Joseph Yu.

FRANCE. Castelnau Montmr—Presb St Paul De Marmiac, Penne Du Tarn. Olivier Hattier.

FRANCE. Paris—Sojatour Tofu Shop,

FRANCE. 13007 Marseille—Ets Co-Lu, 38 Rue Chateaubriand. Ph. 91314414. Andrew Mooney.

FRANCE. 74330 Poisy—Les Sept Marches. Les Cruesettes, Chemin Des Mouille.

FRANCE. 75011 Paris—Institut Tenryu, 2 Rue Rochebrune. Ph. 8059135. Tsuyoshi Ito.

FRANCE. 75013 Paris—Le Bol En Bois, 35 Rue Pascal. Ph. 7072724. Noboru Sakaguchi, Combination Nat Foods Restaurant/Tofu.

FRANCE. 81140 Penne Tarn—Olivier Attie Tofu. Par Castelnau, Presb De St Paul D'mammiac.

FRANCE. 81140 Penne Tarn—Olivier Attie Tofu. Par Castelnau, Presb De St Paul D'mammiac.

FRANCE. 91590 Cerny—Soy Sarl, Plateau De L'ardenay. Ph. 64575201. Bernard Storup & Jean De Preneuf.

GUATEMALA. Solala—Solala Soy Dairy, %C Figallo Molina Belen. Run Jointly With Members Of The Farm Tennessee.

GUYANA. Ecd—Sarvodaya Dev Educ Org, 423 Golden Grove. Peter Kempadoo.

INDIA. Dalhousie Hp—Himalayan Tofu, Jeet Villa. Ph. 15. Susan Jootla.

INDIA 605104. Kottakuppam—Pour Tous Food Process, Aspiration Auroville. Alain Bernard.

INDIA. Tamil Nadu—Hannes Bakery. Kottakarai, 605101 Auroville.

INDONESIA. Jakarta—Duta Proteina Indonesia, Po Box 3137. Lusiani T Saputro.

ISRAEL. Doar Na Hamercaz—Pillar of Dawn Tofu, Moshav Me'or Modi'im. Ben Zion Solomon.

ISRAEL. Jerusalem 91061—Golden Jerusalem Tofu, Zichron Tuvia 19 Pob 6212. Ph. 02249569. Zvi Weisberg.

ISRAEL. Ramat Gan—Little Prince, Rehov Mac-Donald 16. Joseph Fresco.

ITALY. Rome—Ohnichi Intl Foods Co. Lottizzazione Indus, V Salaria Km 25.

ITALY. Rome—Small Tofu Shop,

ITALY. Torino—Aldo Fortis Tofu, Ph. 017263503.

ITALY. 46100 Mantova—Circolo L'aratro, V Cavour 35. Ph. 037-636-8760. Sergio Mambrini.

ITALY. 47037 Rimini—Centro Macrobiotico Tofu, Via Cuoco 9. Gilberto Bianchini.

ITALY. 50123 Firenze—Fondazione Est-Ouest, Via De Serragli #4. Ferro Ledvinka.

JAPAN 039-01. Aomori-Ken—Taishi Shokuhin Kogyo. Oaza-Gawa Mito-Cho, Okinaka 68 Morita-Aza. Ph. 017-923-5111. Large Tofu Factory.

JAPAN. Fujisawa-Shi 251—Maruka Shokuhin. Kanagawa-Ken, Fujigaoka 2-10-2. Ph. 046-626-3261. Large Factory.

JAPAN 822-01. Fukuoka-Ken—Taiyo Shokuhin. Wakamiya-Cho, Shimofujiwara 400-1 Oaza. Ph. 094-952-3141. Large Factory.

JAPAN. Fukuoka-Ken 838—Okay Shokuhin, Miwa-Cho. Ph. 094-622-7131. Large Factory.

JAPAN. Ina-Shi 396—Tokiwa Reito Shokuhin, Nagano-Ken Ina 5057. Ph. 026-572-7277. Tsuru Habutae Frozen Tofu.

JAPAN. Isezaki-Shi 372—Nihon Beans. Gunma-Ken, Kita Senmoku-Cho 1435. Ph. 027-024-8111. Large Factory.

JAPAN. Ishikawa-Shi 272—Takatsuka Marugo, Chiba-Ken Soya-Cho 7-30-12. Ph. 047-372-2581. Japan'S Largest Mfgr Of Reg Tofu.

JAPAN. Kamakura-Shi—Masuda Tofu-Ten, Ogigandani 119. Ph. 046-722-3503. Hiroshi Matsuda, Traditional.

JAPAN. Kanagawa-Ken 252—Home Shokuhin, Ayase-Cho 1090 Takaza-Gun. Ph. 046778617. Nigari Tofu Factory.

JAPAN. Kanazawa-Shi 921—Habutae-Dofu. Ishikawa-Ken, Nishi Kanazawa 2-162. Ph. 076-249-1171. Frozen Tofu.

JAPAN. Kobe Hyogo-Ken—Nada Kobe Seikyo. Higashi 5-1-9, Higashinada-Ku Sumiyoshi. Ph. 078-811-0001. Large Factory.

JAPAN 616. Kyoto Arashiyama—Morika Tofu-Ten. Saga Ukyoku, Fujinoki-Cho 42 Shakado. Ph. 075-872-3955. Shinji Morii, Traditional.

JAPAN 399-25. Nagano-Ken—Asahi-Matsu Kori-Dofu, Dashina 1008 Iida-Shi. Ph. 026-526-9031. Largest Mfgr Of Dried-Frozen Tofu.

JAPAN 399-46. Nagano-Ken—Daiya-Dofu. Kamiina-Gun, Minowa-Machi 9945-2. Ph. 026-579-2572. Dried-Frozen Tofu, Asahimatsu Subsidiary.

JAPAN. Nagano-Shi 380—Misuzu-Dofu. Nagano-Ken, Wakazato-Cho 1606. Ph. 026-226-1671. Dried-Frozen Tofu.

JAPAN 663. Nishinomiya-Shi—Nagai Sogo Shokuhin. Hyogo-Ken, Takamatsu-Cho 15-26. Ph. 079-866-2001. Large Tofu Factory.

JAPAN. Saitama-Ken 361—Asahi Shokuhin. Ooza-Mochida Gyoda-Shi, Aza-Nagamachi 1991. Ph. 048-555-2351. Silken Tofu.

JAPAN 062. Sapporo-Shi—Nichiryo Daily Shokuhin. Hokkaido, Higashi X 148 Toyohira-Ku. Ph. 011-851-1364.

JAPAN 166. Tokyo—Yamato Tofu. Suginami-Ku, Horinouchi 3-16-45. Ph. 033121101. Large Factory.

JAPAN. Tokyo 100-91—Mitoku Co Ltd, Cpo Box 780. Ph. 032016706. Akiyoshi Kazama.

JAPAN. Tokyo 130—Tengu Tofu. Kotobashi 4-29-16, Sumida-Ku. Ph. 036534411. Large Factory.

JAPAN 440. Toyohashi-Shi—Yamaguchi-Ya. Shimoji, Aichi-Ken Higashiguchi. Ph. 053-254-4105. Large Tofu Factory.

MEXICO. Col De Valle—Sr Natural, Vasconcelos 143 Ote Nl. Mr Hugo Victoria.

MEXICO. Guadalajara/Jal—Jamie Valencia Tofu, Ave Ninos Heroes 1633-307. Jaime Valencia.

MEXICO. Mexico 13 DF—Eng D Figueiroa Tagle, Proquide Sa 5 Febrero 743.

MEXICO. Mexico 22 DF—Americo Larralde, Timantitla 15 Tlalpan.

NEPAL. Kathmandu—Kathmandu Tofu Shop,

NETHERLANDS. Amsterdam 1054—Michel Horemaus, Le Helmerstraat 67-I.

NETHERLANDS. Arnheim—Hwergelmir Foundation. For A Natural Life, Eiland 2.

NETHERLANDS. Heerewaarden—Jakso, Voorne 13 6624 Kl. Ph. 088772189. Tomas Nelissen & Peter Dekker.

NETHERLANDS. 1017 Amsterdam—Stichting Oost W Centrum, Achtergracht 17-19. Ph. 020240203. Adelbert Nelissen.

NETHERLANDS. 1021JK Amsterdam—Manna, Meeuwenlaan 70. Ph. 020323977. Sjon Welters & Robt Hendriks.

NETHERLANDS. 2518 Ck Den Haag—Witte Wonder Prod, Piet Heinstraat 80. Ph. 070-464-5225. Cees Van Rest & Niko Van Hagen.

NETHERLANDS. 3615 Westbroek—Soy-Lin, Burgemeester Huydecoper 18. Mr F M Lin.

NETHERLANDS. 9243WC Bakkeveen—De Morgenstond, Kreilen 3. Ph. 05169651. Wout Gerritsma.

NEW ZEALAND. Auckland I—Harvest Wholefoods, 403 Richmond Rd Grey Linn. Greg - Ricky - Eliz Chalmers.

NEW ZEALAND. Christchurch 1—Soysource Tofu, Flat 3 39 Fendalton Rd. Ph. 558691. Jon Judson.

NEW ZEALAND. Wanganui—John Francis, Brunswick Rd 1.

PHILIPPINES. Manila—Feliciano Laiz Tofu, 1518 Sande St Tondo. Ph. 269761.

PHILIPPINES. Metro Manila—Chinese Tofu, 25 Mauban St Caloocan.

PHILLIPPINES. Quezon City—Cherry Food Industry, 74 Speaker Perez. Ph. 613424.

PORTUGAL. Setubal—Jose Parracho Tofu. Quinta Da Portugesa, Fieguesia Da Annuciada. Jose Parracho.

PORTUGAL. 1200 Lisboa—Unimave Tofu, R Mouzinho Da Silveira 25.

PORTUGAL. 1300 Lisboa—Shogun Produtos Alimen. 44-Rc-Dto, R Gen Joao De Almeida. Ph. 644868. Joaquim Reis & Francisco Varatojo.

S AFRICA. 7925 Capetown—Cedric Lindholm Tofu, 203 Lwr Main R Observatory. Cedric Lindholm.

SRI LANKA. Colombo—Boncheese, 128 Kitulwatte Rd. Ph. 596992. Mr U N Gunasekera.

SWEDEN. 19063 Orsundsbro—Aros Sojaprodukter, Bergsvagen 1. Ph. 017160456. Ted Nordquist.

SWITZERLAND. Bern—Restaurant Sesam, Byouxstr. Ph. 032257077.

SWITZERLAND. CH-8002 Zurich—Soyana, Friedensgasse 3. Ph. 012028997. Walter Daenzer.

SWITZERLAND. CH-8810 Horgen—Gauthier Loeffler Tofu, Zugerstr 1401. Ph. NL. Gauthier Loeffler.

SWITZERLAND. CH8913 Ottenbach—Sojalade, Dorfplatz. Ph. 017690349. Verena Krieger.

SWITZERLAND. Geneva CH-1201—Le Grain D'or, Rue Voltair 29.

SWITZERLAND. 1227 Geneva—Natural Products Promo. Carouge, 11 Ch Faubourg-Cruseilles. Ph. 022432416. Eric W Dougoud.

SWITZERLAND. 1260 Nyon—Soy Joy, Ch De La Prelaz 1. Martin Halsey.

SWITZERLAND. 1345 Vaud—Joya, Le Lieu. Joanna White.

SWITZERLAND. 6330 Cham—Opplinger Tofu, Weinbergsstrasse 13. Hans R Opplinger.

W GERMANY. D-5000 Koln 1—Bittersuss, Handelstr 35. Thomas Kasas.

W GERMANY. Prien-Chiemsee—Auenland Tofu/Sojaprod, Hub 4. Peter Wiegand.

W GERMANY. 8000 Munchen 19—Alexanders Tofu Shop, Leonrodstr 19. Ph. 089160474. Alexander Nabben.

W GERMANY. 8492 Furth Wald—Svadesha Pflan-Feinkost, Aussere Kotzingerstr 52a. Ph. 099-73--1066. Ruediger Urban.

Appendix C
People and Institutions Connected with Tofu

PEOPLE AND INSTITUTIONS IN EAST ASIA

Abe, Koryu, Sarugaku-cho 1-4-2, Chiyoda-ku, Tokyo. Tel: 03-291-6324. Japan's foremost tofu historian and author of several books on tofu.

American Soybean Association, Akasaka Tokyo Bldg., 11th Floor, 2-14-3 Nagata-cho, Chiyoda-ku, Tokyo 100, Japan. Tel: 03-593-2501. Ms. Yoshiko Kojima. Good source of information about tofu, soyfoods, and soybeans in Japan.

Japan Packaged Tofu Assoc., Fujikanda Bldg #6F, 2-21 Kanda, Tsukasa-cho, Chiyoda-ku, Tokyo, Japan. Tel: 03-233-1226. Represents makers of lactone silken tofu.

Japan Soymilk Assoc., c/o Asahi Food Co. Ltd., Sunshine 60 Bldg., Higashi Ikebukuro 3-1-1, Toshima-ku, Tokyo 170, Japan. Tel. 03-987-2175.

Japan Frozen Tofu Assoc., Muromachi 3-1, Nihonbashi, Chuo-ku, Tokyo 103, Japan. Tel: 03-241-7331.

Japan Tofu Association, 1-16-12 Ueno, Taito-ku, Tokyo 110, Japan. Tel: 03-833-9351. The coordinating organization for all smaller tofu shops in Japan.

Korean Tofu Union, Seoul, Korea, Tel: 28-8461. The main coordinating organization.

Machida, Yoshiro, 4-17-20 Nishihara-cho, Fuchu-shi, Tokyo 183. Tel: 0425-72-8576. Founding director of Japan's first tofu research institute. A prolific writer on the manufacture of tofu and a wide variety of creative and unusual foods which can be prepared from tofu. Presently a retired consulting engineer for many tofu and soymilk factories.

Nishiki-aji, Kita Otsuka 2-30, Toshima-ku, Tokyo. Tel: 03-918-7244. Japan's largest maker of tofu delicatessen foods.

Taiwan-American Soybean Association, 386-12 Tun Hua South Rd., Room 603 Kwang-Wu Bldg., Taipei, Taiwan. Tel: 781-2110. Dr. Steve Chen. Complete information about soyfoods and soybeans in Taiwan.

Taiwan Tofu Association, No. 9, Lane 133, Tai-yuan Rd., Taipei. Tel: 551-9633 or 541-4494. Mr. Rien Tsan Tin, president and owner of a large tofu factory.

Tsuji, Shigemitsu, contact at Nakamura-ro (see Appendix A). A great chef and author of books on tofu.

Watanabe, Tokuji, Kassei Gakubu, Kyoritsu Joshi Daigaku, Hitotsubashi 2-2-1, Chiyoda-ku, Tokyo 101, Japan. Tel: 03-237-2482. Dr. Watanabe is one of Japan's leading authorities on Tofu.

Yanaihara, Toshio, Yanaihara Ryori Kyoshitsu, Akasaka 2-23, Tokyo. Tel: 03-582-5927. Teacher of Japanese cuisine and author of numerous articles on tofu.

TOFU PLANTS IN JAPAN

A complete listing of Japan's finest traditional and modern tofu companies is given in our book *Tofu & Soymilk Production.* The following four traditional shops are of particular interest:

Morika, Fujinoki-cho 42, Shaka-do, Saga, Ukyo-ku, Kyoto 616. Tel: 075-872-3955. Mr. Shinji Morii, master.

Masuda, Ogidadani 119, Kamakura-shi. Tel: 0467-22-3503. Mr. Hiroyoshi Masuda, master.

Sangen-ya, Shakujiidai 6-19-30, Nerima-ku, Tokyo. Tel: 03-922-2354. Mr. Toshio Arai, master.

Yuba Han, Fuyacho Oike Agaru, Kyoto. Tel: 075-221 5622. Ms. Kisa Asano.

Of the many large tofu and dried-frozen tofu factories which have appeared in Japan in recent years, several are of particular interest.

Toko Daily Shokuhin, Kobayashi, Uchihara-cho, Higashi, Ibaragi-gun, Ibaragi prefecture. Tel: 0292-59-4121. Japan's most modern producer of Packaged Lactone Kinugoshi, Toko makes over 50,000 cakes daily. Contact Mr. Takato.

Asahimatsu Shokuhin, 1008 Dashina, Iida-shi, Nagano-ken 399-25, Japan. Tel: 0265-26-9031. Dr. Shiro Kudo. Japan's largest maker of dried-frozen tofu.

Misuzu-dofu, Wakazato-cho 1606, Nagano-shi 380, Nagano-ken, Japan. Tel: 026-226-1671. Large maker of dried frozen tofu.

Takatsuka Marugo, Soya-cho 7-30-12. Ishikawa-shi 272, Chiba-ken, Japan. Tel: 047-372-2581. Japan's largest maker of regualr tofu.

FOR INSTITUTIONAL USERS

Tofu is used as an inexpensive and healthful source of protein in school-, hospital-, cafeteria-, and other institutional feeding programs throughout Japan. Perhaps one of the most nutritious and creative cuisines of this type is that prepared in the modern kitchens of Tokyo's prestigious Seventh-day Adventist Hospital. Here a staff of three nutritionists and 11 cooks has developed a unique repertoire of about 50 tofu dishes, some half of which are especially suited to the tastes of Western patients. A number of our favorites—such as Tofu Italian Meatballs (p. 123)—have been included in this book. Since no meat is served at the hospital, each day's menu usually offers at least one protein-rich Western- or Japanese-style tofu preparation. Enjoyed daily by 120 Western and Japanese patients and 180 staff members, the menu changes throughout the four seasons.

Seventh-day Adventist Hospital, 17-3 Amanuma 3-chome, Suginami-ku, Tokyo 167 (Ogikubo Station). Tel: 03-392-6151.

PEOPLE AND INSTITUTIONS IN AMERICA

The Soyfoods Center, P.O. Box 234, Lafayette, CA 94549. Tel: 415-283-2991. William Shurtleff and Akiko Aoyagi. The leading source of basic information on tofu, plus books including *Tofu & Soymilk Production* and *Soyfoods Industry and Market: Directory and Databook;* also has a soyfoods business consulting service.

Soyfoods Magazine, 100 Heath Rd., Colrain, MA 01340. Tel: 413-624-5591. Richard Leviton, editor. The world's best publication for current, quality information on tofu and other soyfoods.

Bean Machines, Inc., P.O. Box 1145, Sebastapol, CA 95472. Tel: 707-829-2952. Larry Needleman. America's best source of tofu making equipment; all sizes and types.

Soycrafters' Apprenticeship Program, c/o Island Spring, P.O. Box 747-SC, Vashon, WA 98070. Tel: 206-622-6448. Luke Lukoskie. A basic course in how to start a tofu company and make tofu in a commercial plant.

Soyfoods Association, 526 East 20th St., New York, NY 10009. Tel: 212-254-6698. Michael Austin. The trade association for all makers of tofu and other soyfoods.

PEOPLE AND INSTITUTIONS IN EUROPE

For an up-to-date list of leaders of the tofu and soyfoods movement in each country in Europe, send a self-addressed envelope to The Soyfoods Center, at the address given below.

Appendix D
Table of Equivalents

TEMPERATURE

C = 5/9 (F-32)
F = 9/5C + 32
350°F = 177°C
375°F = 191°C

VOLUME

1 tablespoon = 3 teaspoons = 14.75 cc.
1 cup = 236 cc = 16 tablespoons
1 quart = 4 cups = 0.946 liters
1 U.S. gallon = 4 quarts = 3.785 liters = 231 in³ =
    5/6 Imperial gallon.
1 bushel = 8 gallons = 4 pecks
1 *sho* = 10 *go* = 1800 cc = 7.63 cups

WEIGHT

1 ounce = 28.38 grams
1 pound = 16 ounces = 454 grams
1 ton (U.S.) = 2,000 pounds = 0.907 metric tons

NATURAL EQUIVALENTS

1 gallon of water weighs 8.33 pounds
1 quart of soybeans weighs 1.69 pounds
1 bushel of 1st grade soybeans weighs 56 pounds

PUBLICATIONS ON TOFU

Additional publications relating to the manufacture of tofu and soymilk will be found in *Tofu and Soymilk Production* by Shurtleff and Aoyagi.

Abe, K. 1964. Outlook for fewer tofu producers, more production. *Soybean Digest*. May. p. 48.

Abe, Koryu. 1972. *Tofu Hyakuchin to Zokuhen*. Tokyo: Shinshu Shorin. (Original edition, 1782).

Abe, Koryu and Tsuji, Shigemitsu. 1974. *Tofu no Hon*. Tokyo, Japan: Shibata Shoten. 328 p.

Adolph, W.H. and Kiang, P.C. 1919. The nutritive value of soy bean products. *National Medical J. of China* 5:40-49.

Adolph, W.H. 1922. How China uses the soy bean as food. *J. of Home Economics* 14:63-69.

Agricultural Research. 1968. Better sufu. Nov. p. 6.

Aihara, Cornellia. 1972. *The Chico-san Cookbook*. Chico, CA: Chico-san Inc. Reissued as *Macrobiotic Kitchen* by Japan Publications in 1982. 140 p.

Aihara, H. 1974. *Soybean Diet*. Oroville, CA: George Ohsawa Macrobiotic Foundation, 164 p.

Andersen, J. 1980. *The Tofu Primer*. Berkeley, CA: Creative Arts Communications. 41 p.

Andersen, J. 1981. *Juel Andersen's Tofu Kitchen*. New York: Bantam Books. 211 p.

Andersen, Juel. 1982. *Tofu Fantasies: A Cookbook of Incomparable Desserts*. Berkeley, CA: Creative Arts. 88 p.

Anson, M.L. 1958. Potential uses of isolated oilseed proteins in foodstuffs. In *Processed Plant Protein Foodstuffs*, A.M. Altschul, ed. New York: Academic Press. p. 279.

Asahimatsu Shokuhin. 1981. *Asahimatsu Sanju-nen no Ayumi*. Iida-shi, Nagano-ken, Japan: Asahimatsu. 290 p.

Bannar, R. 1980. Let's talk tofu. *Food Engineering*. May. p. 126-28.

Barrett, C. 1982. The Hilton Hotel's gourmet tofu dishes. *Vegetarian Times*. Oct. p. 32-36.

Bauer, C. and Andersen, J. 1979. *The Tofu Cookbook*. Emmaus, PA: Rodale Press. 188 p.

Belenki, D.E. and Papowa, N.N. 1933. Soy cheese. Russian Patent 32,907 and 32,908. Oct. 31. C.A. 28:3808 (1934).

Beltzer, F.J.G. 1911. Extended utilization of soya bean products: Milk, cheese, and a variety of other products from a vegetable seed. *Scientific American Supplement*. 72(1859): 115. Aug. 19.

Beltzer, Francis J.G. 1911. Le lait vegetal, la caseine vegetale. *Revue de Chimie Industrielle et le Moniteur Scientifique Quesneville* 22(259):209-215, 22(260):241-51.

Blasedale, W.C. 1899. Some Chinese vegetable food materials. USDA OES Bull 68:32-36.

Bloch, A. 1906. Quelques mots sur la fabrication et la composition du Teou-Fou. *Bulletin des Sciences Pharmacologiques, Paris*. 13:138-143. Also in the 1906 *Archives d'Hygiene et de Medicine Coloniales*. p. 298.

Bloch, A. 1907. Le Soja. Sa culture, sa composition, son emploi en medecine et dans l'alimentation. *Bulletin des Sciences Pharmacologiques, Paris* 14:536-51, 593-606. Sept.-Oct.

Boyd, B.R. 1980. Tofu in public schools. *East West Journal*. June. p. 46-50.

Bretschneider, Emilii Vasilevich. 1881-95. *Botanicon Sinicum*. Notes on Chinese Botany from Native and Western Sources. London: Trübner & Co. 3 Vols. Issued originally in the Journal of the Royal Asiatic Society, North China Branch. Series 2, Vols. 16, 25, 29.

Bui, Quang Chieu. 1905. Les cultures vivrieres au Tonkin. *Bulletin Economique de l'Indo-Chine*. New Series 2. No. 48. p. 1152-53, 1157-68.

Bulkeley, W.M. 1979. Good old bean curd; It's suddenly popular but you call it tofu. *Wall Street Journal*. April 12. p. 1-2.

Bulkeley, W.M. 1979. The Americanization of bean curd. *Washington Post*. May 24. p. E1, E11, E26.

Burkill, I.H. 1935. *A Dictionary of the Economic Products of the Malay Peninsula*. London: Crown Agents. p. 1080-86. (The work is 2 volumes, 2400 p.)

Champion, P. 1866. Sur la fabrication du fromage de pois en Chine et au Japon. *Bull. de la Societe d'Acclimatization*. p. 562-65.

Champion, Paul. 1869. *Industries Anciennes et Modernes de l'Empire Chinois*. (Translated by Stanislas Julien.) Paris: Eugene Lacroix. p. 185-89.

Champion, P. and Lhôte, M. 1869. *Fabrication du fromage de pois*. In Julien and Champion. p. 185-89.

Chang, I.C.L. and Murray, H.C. 1949. Biological value of the protein and the mineral, vitamin, and amino acid contents of soy milk and curd. *Cereal Chemistry* 26:297-305.

Chang, K.C. ed. 1977. *Food in Chinese Culture*. New Haven, CT: Yale University Press. 429 p.

Chen, P.S. 1956. Soybeans for Health, Longevity, and Economy. Revised ed. 1973. *Soybeans for Health and a Longer Life*. New Canaan, CT: Keats Publ. Co. 178 p.

Cherniske, S.S. 1980. *Tofu: Everybody's Guide*. East Woodstock, CT: Mother's Inn Center for Creative Living. 90 p.

Chiang, Cecelia S. 1974. *The Mandarin Way*. Boston: Little, Brown and Co.

Chiu, W.C.L. 1960. Soy curd can add variety to diet. *Soybean Digest*. June. p. 8.

Chiu, W.C.L. and Van Duyne, F. 1961. Soybean curd. *Illinois Research* (Univ. of Ill. Ag. Expt. Station). Fall. p. 6-7.

Chiu, W.C.L. 1961. *The Calcium Content and Palatability of Soybean Curd from Field and Vegetable Varieties*. MSc thesis, University of Illinois, Dept. of Home Ec.

Church, M.B. 1920. Laboratory Experiments on the Manufacture of Chinese Ang-Khak in the United States. *J. of Industrial and Engineering Chemistry* 12:45-46.

Church, M.B. 1923. Soy and related fermentations. USDA Department Bulletin No. 1152, May 12. 26 p.

Clarke, Christina. 1981. *Cook with Tofu*. New York: Avon Books. 223 p.

Cohen, Richard L. 1981. Local tofu makers and sellers trying to stir up interest within food market. *San Francisco Business Journal*. Oct. 20. p. 18-19.

Colchie, E.S. 1981. Light, low calorie, and versatile tofu. *Bon Appetit*. Aug. p. 52-55.

Concepcion, I. 1943. Significance of soybean in the dietary of Filipinos. *Proceedings of the Sixth Pacific Science Congress of the Pacific Science Assoc*. July 24-Aug. 12, 1939. Vol VI. p. 437-47. Berkeley, CA: Univ of Calif. Press.

Coville, F.W. 1929. Soybean cheese. *Science* 70(1812):282-83. Sept. 20.

Cummins, J.S. 1962. *Travels and Controversies of Friar Domingo Navarrete 1618-1686*. Hakluyt Soc. Ser. 2. No. 118, Cambridge.

Dänzer, A.W. 1982. *Tofu, die Einladung ins Schlaraffenland*. Zurich: Verlag Bewusstes Dasein. 97 p.

Dänzer, A.W. 1982. *Tofu, l'invitation au pays de cocagne*. Zurich: Editions Bewusstes Dasein. 107 p.

Dänzer, A.W. 1982. Tofu—Ein neues altes produkt aus Asien. *Reform + Diät*. June. p. 2.

Deroin, N. 1980. Tofu. *Cuisine* (Cover story). June. p. 32-38, 40, 73-75.

Dittes, F. 1929. The calcium content of soybean cheese. *J. of Home Economics*. October:779.

Dittes, Frances Linda. 1935. *Food For Life*. Madison, Tennessee: Associated Lecturers, Inc. 332 p.

Dominguez, Blanca. 1978. *Alimentacion Integral Para Una Vida Plena: Los Mil Usas de la Soya*. San Angel, Mexico: Editorial Posada. 232 p.

Drown, M.J. 1943. *Soybeans and Soybean Products as Food*. USDA Misc. Publ. No. 534. 14 p.

Dukess, K. 1981. Tofu, tofu everywhere. *New York Times*. Aug. 2.

DuSablon, Mary Anna. 1981. *Cooking with Tofu*. Charlotte, VT: Garden Way Publishing. 32 p.

Dyson, G.M. 1928. Mould food of the Far East. *The Pharmaceutical Journal and Pharmacist* 121:375-77. (Oct. 20, London).

Ebine, Hideo et al. 1965. *Daizu cheezu no seizoho* (Preparation of a soy cheese.) Japanese Patent 16,737. July 30.

Escuenta, E.E. 1979. *Effect of Boiling Treatment and Gata (Coconut Cream) Addition to Soymilk on the Chemical, Rheological, and Sensory Properties of Tofu*. Cornell University. PhD thesis. 155 p.

Family Circle. 1979. Tofu—The Oriental way to high-protein, low-calorie meals. July. p. 140, 157, 164.

Farm, The. 1974. *Hey Beatnick*. Summertown, TN: The Book Publishing Co. 100 p.

Farm, The. 1974. *Yay Soybeans*. Summertown, TN: The Book Publising Co. 14 p.

Farm, The. 1975. *The Farm Vegetarian Cookbook*. Summertown, TN: The Book Publishing Co. 128 pp. Revised edition by L. Hagler. 1978. 223 p.

Farm, The. 1977. *Vegetarian Prenatal Nutrition and High Protein Recipes*. Summertown, TN: The Book Publishing Co. 14 p.

Farm, The. 1979. Soybean project in Guatemala Highlands. *Plenty News* 1(2):1-3.

Farm, The. 1981. Soy Demonstration Program: *Introducting Soyfoods to the Third World*. Summertown, TN. 16 p.

Fesca, M. 1898. Die Sojabohne. *Tropenpflanzer* 2(8):233-46.

Fillip, J. 1981: The amazing tofumobile. *East West Journal*. May. p. 38-40.

FIND/SVP. 1981. *The Tofu Market: Overview of a High-Potential Industry*. New York: FIND/SVP. The Information Clearing-house, 500 Fifth Ave., 10110. 140p.

Forbes, R.M. et al. 1983. Bioavailability of zinc in coagulated soy protein (tofu) to rats and effects of dietary calcium at a constant phytate:zinc ratio. *J. of Nutrition* 130(1):205-10.

Ford, R. 1981. *Soy Foodery Cookbook*. Santa Barbara, CA: Self published. 78 p.

Fox, Chloe and Abraham. 1983. *The Au Naturel Tofu Manual: Modern Jewish Tofu Cooking*. Montreal QUE, Canada: Au Naturel, 6110 Monkland Ave., H4A 1H4. 47 p.

Fox, M. 1980. Tofu and special diets. *Soyfoods*. Summer. p. 9.

Fox, M., O'Connor, K. and Timmins, J. 1981. *Delights of Tofu*. Greenfield, MA: Soy to the World Publishing Co. 42 p.

Fuerstenberg, Maurice. 1917. *Die Soja*. Berlin: Paul Parey. 43 p.

Gibbs, H.D. and Agcaoili, F. 1912. Soy-bean curd, an important Oriental food product. *Phillipine J. of Sci.* (A) 7:47-51.

Giraud-Gillet, J. 1942. *Le Soja: Aliment d'Avenir*. Saigon: SIDI Anct. C. Ardin. 282 p.

Goldman, S. 1977: Charles Atlas versus the Bodhisattva: An Interview with Bill Shurtleff and Akiko Aoyagi. *East West Journal*. Jan. p. 32-35.

Gurafusha. 1973. *Tofu no Ryori* (Tofu Cookery). Tokyo: Gurafusha, My Life Series, No. 15.

Haberlandt, Friedrich. 1878. *Die Sojabohne: Ergebnisse der Studien und Versuche über die Anbauwürdigkeit dieser neu einzufuhren-den Culturpflanze*. Vienna: Carl Gerold's Sohn. 119 pp.

Hagler, Lousie, ed. 1978. *The Farm Vegetarian Cookbook*, revised ed. Summertown, TN: The Book Publishing Co., 156 Drakes Ln., 38483. 223 p.

Hagler, L. 1982. *Tofu Cookery*. Summertown, TN: The Book Publishing Co., 156 Drakes Ln., 38483. 160 p.

Hall, Janice. 1981. *A Taste for Tofu*. Avalon, CA: A Marjanal Publication (P.O. Box 1363; 90704) 50 p.

Harris, R.F. et al. 1949. The composition of Chinese foods. *J. of the American Dietetic Association* 25:28-38.

Hayashi, S. 1957. Tofu takes large volume of soybeans. *Soybean Digest*. Aug. p. 26-27.

Hayashi, S. 1960. A visit to a leading tofu factory. *Soybean Digest*. May. p. 26.

Heartsong, Toni & Bob. 1977. *The Heartsong Tofu Cookbook*. Miami, FL: Banyan Books. 80 p. Revised 1978.

Hepburn, J.S. and Sohn, K.S. 1930. Do fu: An Oriental food. *American J. of Pharmacy* 102(10): 570. Oct.

Hesseltine, C.W. and Wang, H.L. 1972. Fermented soybean food products. In A.K. Smith and S.J. Circle. 1972. *Soybeans: Chemistry and Technology*. Westport, CT: AVI Publ. Co. p. 389-419.

Hoffman, J. and Keough, C. 1981. *Home Soyfood Equipment*. Emmaus, PA: Rodale Press. 80 p.

Holthaus, Fusako. 1982. *Tofu Cookery*. Tokyo: Kodansha International. 159 p.

Hommel, Rudolph P. 1937. *China at Work*. New York: John Day. p. 105-09.

Honcamp, F. 1910. Die sojabohne und ihre verwertung. *Tropenpflanzer* 14(12):613-634.

Horvath, A.A. 1927. The soybean as human food. Peking: Chinese Government Bureau of Economic Information. *Bulletin Series No. 3*. 86 pp. Also published as a series in *Chinese Economic Journal*. Sept. 1926 to April 1927.

Hosie, A. 1901: *Manchuria: Its People, Resources, and Recent History*. London: Methuen & Co. (or 1910, Boston: J.B. Millet Co.)

Hymowitz, T. and Newell, C.A. 1981. Taxonomy of the genus Glycine, domestication and uses of soybeans. *Economic Botany* 35(3):272-88.

Immegart, M. and Dansby, P.J. 1981. *The Incredible Tofu Cookbook: California Style*. P.O. Box 1146, Yorba Linda, CA 92686. 128 p.

Inouye, M. 1895. The preparation and chemical composition of tofu. *Bulletin of the College of Agriculture, Tokyo* 2(4):209-15.

Jackobs, S.L. 1983. Company finds a niche selling frozen foods made with tofu. *Wall Street Journal*. Jan. 24. p. 23.

Japanese National Tofu Assoc. 1972. *Tofu Shusetsu*. Tokyo. 20 p. Tools and techniques for making tofu in the traditional way.

JDAC: Japan Dietetic Assoc. Corp. 1964. *Standard Composition of Japanese Foods*. Tokyo: Daiichi Shuppan K.K. Bilingual: Japanese/English.

Jones, D.V.G. 1963. *The Soybean Cookbook*. New York, NY: Arco Publ. Co. 240 p.

Jordan, S. 1918. Soy beans from soup to nuts. *Country Gentleman* 83(39):7, 34, Sept 28.

Julien, S. and Champion, P. 1869. *Industries Anciennes et Modernes de L'Empire Chinois, d'Apres des Notices Traduites du Chinois*. Paris: Eugene Lacroix. p. 185-89.

Kano, S. and Iishima, S. 1899. Digestion experiments with single food materials. *Gun-i Gakko Gyofu (Bul. Army Medical College)*, Tokyo. No. 3, p. 101.

Katayama, T. 1906. On the preparation of a vegetable cheese from the protein of the soy bean. *Bulletin of the College of Agric. Tokyo Imp. Univ.* 7(1):117-119.

Kato, Yogoro. 1909. Physico-chemical studies on tofu. Chem. La. Higher Tech. School, Tokyo. *Mem. Coll. Sci. Eng.*, Kyoto. 1:325-31.

Kellner, O. and Mori. Y. 1887. Beiträge zur Kenntniss de Ernährung der Japaner. *Mitteilungen der Deutschen Gesellschaft für Natur and Völkerkunde Ostasiens, Tokyo*. 4(37):305-21.

Kellner, O. and Mori, Y. 1889. Untersuchungen über die Ernährung der Japaner. *Zeitschrift für Biologie* 25:102-22.

Kellner, O.J. 1889. Tofu Cakes. *Bulletin of the College of Agriculture. Tokyo Imperial University* 1(4):24-25.

Kellner, O., Nagaoka, M. and Kurashima, Y. 1889. Researches on the manufacture and composition of "miso." *Bulletin of the College of Agriculture, Tokyo Imperial University* 1(6):1-24.

Kempski, Karl E. 1923. *Die Sojabohne: Geschichte, Kultur und Verwendung unter besonderer Berucksichtigung der Verhältnisse in Niederländisch-Indien*. Berlin: Paul Parey. 88 p.

Kikuchi, Grace. 1974. *Tofu Recipes*. Ann Arbor, MI: Mrs. Chihiro Kikuchi, 260 Sumac Ln., 48105. 47 p.

Kinch, E. 1879. (About tofu and kori-dofu). In *A Classified and Descriptive Catalog of a Collection of Agricultural Products*, Tokyo.

Kinderlehrer, J. 1979. Tofu, Food of 10,000 flavors. *Prevention*. Jan. p. 111-23.

Krieger, V. 1981. Gestern steak, morgen tofu. *Tages Anzeiger Magazin*. Aug. 22. p. 6-12.

Krieger, V. 1982. Die tausend talente von tofu. *Naturlich* 2(5):69-73.

Kudo, S. 1976. Kori-dofu. *Shoku no Kagaku*. No. 29. p. 122-27.

Lager, Mildred. 1942. *Soy Bean Recipes: 150 Ways to Use Soy Beans as Meat, Milk, Cheese & Bread*. Los Angeles: House of Better Living. 44 p.

Lager, M. 1945. *The Useful Soybean: A Plus Factor in Modern Living*. New York, NY: McGraw-Hill. 295 p.

Lager, M. 1946. The meat without a bone. *Soybean Digest*. April. p. 22.

Lager, Mildred. 1955. *How to Use the Soybean: A Plus Factor in Modern Nutrition*. Burbank, California. Self published. 115 p.

Lager, M. and Jones, D.V.G. 1963. *The Soybean Cookbook*. New York, NY: The Devin-Adair Co. 240 p.

Landgrebe, G. 1978. *Tofu Goes West*. Palo Alto, CA: Fresh Press. 114 p.

Landgrebe, G. 1981. *Tofu at Center Stage*. Palo Alto, CA: Fresh Press. 114 p.

Langgaard, A. 1878. Bemerkungen ueber den naehrwerth des tofu nach analysen von J. Schimoyama. *Mitteilungen der Deutschen Gesellschaft fur Natur- und Volkerkunde Ostasiens* 2:268-69, 271.

Langworthy. C.F. 1897. Soybeans as food for man. *USDA Farmers Bulletin* No. 58. p. 20-23. Revised 1899.

Lappe, F.M. 1971. *Diet for a Small Planet*. New York: Ballantine Books. 410 p. Revised 1975 and 1982.

L'aurore. 1979. *La Cuisine au Tofu: Un Art Japonais*. Montreal, QUE, Canada. 191 p. Based on *The Book of Tofu* by Shurtleff & Aoyagi.

Leviton, R. 1979. The soy delicatessen. *Soyfoods*. Summer. p. 12-18.

Leviton, R. 1980. Soyfoods and the media. *Soyfoods*. Winters: 56-59.

Leviton, R. 1981. Putting tofu in the lunch boxes of America. *Soyfoods*. Winter. p. 54-61.

Leviton, R. 1981. The world's best tofu cheesecake. *Vegetarian Times* No. 52. Nov. p. 74-77.

Leviton, R. 1982. *Tofu, Tempeh, Miso and Other Soyfoods*. New Canaan, CT: Keats Publishing Inc. 26 p.

Leviton, R. 1982. Tofu for institutions. Recipes for 225. *Soyfoods*. Winter. p. 66-67.

Leviton, R. 1983. Jack's Beanstalk: The American tofu dream on trial in Salt Lake City. *Soyfoods*. Winter. p. 18-27.

Leviton, R. 1983. Profile: Hinode Tofu Company. *Soyfoods*. Winter. p. 33-36.

Li, Ch'iao-p'ing. 1948. The Chemical Arts of Old China. Easton, PA: *Journal of Chemical Education*.

Li, Shih-chen. 1597. *Pen ts'ao kang mu*. 1965 ed. Hong Kong: Commercial Press (in Chinese). p. 360-371.

Li, Yu-ying. 1910. Vegetable milk (from soya beans) and its derivatives. English Patent 30,275. Dec. 30.

Li, Yu-ying. 1910. *Ta Tou: Le Soja*. Paris: Societe biologique de l'Extreme Orient. 65 p.

Li Yu-ying and Grandvoinnet, L. 1912. *Le Soja. Sa Culture. Ses Usages Alimentaires, Therapeutiques, Agricoles et Industriels*. Paris, France: A. Challamel. 141 p.

Li Yu-ying and Grandvoinnet, L. 1911-12. Le soja. *L'Agriculture Pratique des Pays Chauds* 11:177-96, 270-94, 360-75, 459-74. 12:28-38, 120-32, 213-23, 302-08.

Lin, H.Y. Shia, C.L. and Shia, C.M. 1975. *Chinese soybean curds*. Chun Wen Hsueh Publisher. Taipei, Taiwan.

Lin, Hai-ying et al. 1975. *Chung-kuo toufu (Chinese Tofu)*. Taipei, Taiwan: Wen-hsueh ch'u-pan-she. 249 p.

Linder, U.V. 1912. Soybean cheese. *J. of Industrial and Engineering Chemistry* 4(12):897-98.

Liu, P.W. 1932. Hakko-dofu no koso ni tsuite (About the enzymes of fermented tofu). *Nippon Nogei Kagaku Kaishi* (J. of the Agricultural Chemical Socy. of Japan) 8(3):273-79.

Lockwood, L.B. and Smith, A.K. 1952. Fermented Soy Foods and Sauce. *Yearbook of Agri*. 1950-51. p. 357-361.

Loetterle, F. 1977. Tonyu to tofu. *California Living*. April 17. p. 40, 42, 44.

Loew, O. 1904. Ueber die anwendung des frostes bei herstellung einiger japanischer nahrungsmittel. *Mitteilungen de Deutschen Gesellschaft fur Natur- und Volkerkunde Ostasiens* 10(1):75-76.

Loew, O. 1906. Ueber einige sonderbare Japanische nahrungsmittel. *Mitteilungen der Deutschen Gesellschaft fur Natur- und Volkerkunde Ostasiens* 11(1):109-11.

Loomis, H.M. 1914. Food products from the soy bean. *American Food Journal*. 9(8):472-74.

Loureiro, Juan de. 1793. *Flora Cochinensis*. Vol. 2. p. 537-38.

MacCormack, H. 1982. The place of small tofu shops in the industry. *Soyfoods*. Summer. p. 28-29.

MacCormack, H. 1982. *The Soy Dairy: A Way to Save the Small Farm*. P.O. Box 229, Philomath, OR: Sunbow Publishing. 26 p.

Madison Food Co. ca. 1933. *Madison Soy Cheese*. Madison, TN. 6 p.

Madison Health Messenger. 1939-44. Early articles on tofu at Madison College. 1939, Vol. 2(3): 1944. Vol 6(1) and 7(1).

Madison Survey. 1929-32. Early articles on tofu at Madison College. 1929: May 15, June 19, Oct. 23; 1932: Dec. 7. Madison, TN: Madison College Press.

Madison Health Foods. ca. 1934. *Vegetable Milk and Cheese*. Madison, TN. 21 p.

Makino, Magotaro. 1918. *Soy-bean Food*. U.S. Patent 1,258,427. Mar. 5.

Maruhi. 1972. *Tofu Ryori, Hyaku-sen* (Tofu Cookery, One Hundred Favorites). Tokyo: Sankosha Katei Buhen, Maruhi.

McGruter, P.G. 1979. *The Great American Tofu Cookbook*. Brookline, MA: Autumn Press. 124 p.

Melhuish, W. J. 1913. *Artificial milk from soy beans*. British Patent No. 24,572. Oct. 29.

Miller, C.D. 1933. Japanese foods commonly used in Hawaii. *Hawaii Agric. Exp. Station. Bulletin* No. 68. p. 1-10, 28-43.

Miyashita, A. 1962. *Kori-dofu no Rekishi (History of Dried-frozen Tofu)*. Tokyo: Japanese National Frozen Tofu Association. 571 p.

Moore, Karen. 1979. Tofu, a Far East import offers potential as meat, fish, cheese substitute. *Food Product Development* 13(5): 24. May.

Moriyama, Yukiko. 1982. *Quick & Easy Tofu Cookbook*. Tokyo: Joie. c/o J.P. Trading Inc., 300 Industrial Way, Brisbane, CA 94005. 104 p.

Morse, W.J. 1918. The soybean industry in the United States. *USDA Yearbook* (1917):101-111. (Separate No. 740).

Morse, W.J. 1929-31. *Log of the Dorsett-Morse Expedition to East Asia*. Typewritten manuscript in 17 volumes and handwritten notebooks. Only copy located at offices of American Soybean Assoc., St. Louis, Missouri. 6,000 p.

Motoyama, T. 1958. *Inshoku Jiten* (Encyclopedia of Food and Drink). Tokyo: Heibonsha. 604 p.

Murakami, Kamekichi. 1916. *Bean curd and process of making same*. U.S. Patent 1,195,843. Aug. 22.

Nakano, M., Ebine, H. and Ota, T. 1967. *Hakko Shokuhin* (Fermented Foods). Tokyo: Korin Shoin.

Nakayama, Tokiko. 1973. *Chugoku Meisaifu* (Chinese Cuisine: Famous Recipes). Tokyo: Shibata Shoten. 4 Vols.

Nasoya Foods. 1981 *Nasoya Tofu Cookbook*. P.O. Box 841, Leominster, MA. 28 p.

Natural Foods Merchandiser. 1981. Soyfoods report. Sept. 16 p.

Nelson, J.H. and Richardson, G.H. 1967. Molds in flavor production. In *Microbial Technology* (H.J. Peppler, ed.). New York: Reinhold.

New York Times Magazine. 1917. Woman off to China as government agent to study soy bean. June 10, Section VI, p. 9.

New Yorker. 1982. Tofu 'n Tab (cartoon). May 3, p. 44.

Newman, Marcea. 1975. *Sweet Life*. Boston: Houghton Mifflin.

Ng Sock Nye, 1979. *Soya Bean—Nutritious Food for the People*. Malaysia: Institut Masyarakat Berhad, 9 Lorong Kucing, Pulau Tikus, Penang. 19 p.

NHK. 1979. *Tofu Ryori* (Tofu Cookery). Tokyo: Nihon Hoso Kyokai. 128 p.

Nordquist, Ted, and Öhlund, Tim. 1981. *Tofu-Boken*. Orsundsbro, Sweden: Aros Sojaprodukter. 52 p.

Norinsho. 1964. *Nihon Shokuhin Hyojun Seibunhyo*. (Standard Composition of Japanese Foods). Tokyo: Norinsho (Japanese Ministry of Agriculture and Forestry).

Norton, R. and Wagner, M. 1980. *The Soy of Cooking: A Tofu and Tempeh Recipe Book*. Eugene, OR: White Crane, P.O. Box 3081, 97403. 24 p. 1983 revised ed. 58 p.

Ochomogo, M.G. 1974. *An unfermented cheese from soy-cow's milk mixture.* Thesis. Louisiana State University.

Ochse, J.J. 1931. *Vegetables of the Dutch East Indies.* Buitenzorg (Bogor), Java: Archipel Drukkerij. p. 366, 372, 389-93, 398, 407-08, 732, 943-71.

Ohsawa, Lima. 1971. *Makurobiotiku Ryori* (Macrobiotic Cookery). Tokyo: Nihon CI Kyokai. 199 p.

Ohsawa, Lima. 1974. *The Art of Just Cooking.* Brookline, MA: Autumn Press. 216 p.

Okada, K. et al. 1976. *Method of Manufacturing an aseptic soya bean curd.* Morinaga Milk Industry Co. Ltd. U.S. Patent 4,000,326.

Olszewski, N. 1978. *Tofu Madness.* Vashon, WA: Island Spring. 64 p.

Omura, Y. 1981. *The Tofu-Miso High Efficiency Diet.* New York: Arco Publishing Inc. 221 p.

Orosa, Maria Y. 1932. Soybeans as a component of a balanced diet and how to prepare them. *Popular Bulletin 13*, Science Bureau, Manila. 53 p.

Osawa, K. and Ueda. 1887. Digestion experiment with tofu. *Chugai Iji Shimpo* (Medical News, Foreign and Domestic), Tokyo. No. 177. p. 16.

Osawa, K. 1889. Shoka shiken tsuika ("additional investigations on digestion"). *Chugai Iji Shimpo* 211:6-8.

Osbeck, Peter. 1771. *A Voyage to China and the East Indies.* (Trans. by J.R. Forseter; original edition publ. 1757 in Swedish). London: Benjamin White. pp. 218, 253, 305 (Vol. 1).

Oshima, Kintaro. 1905. A digest of Japanese investigations on the nutrition of man. *USDA OES Bulletin* 159. p. 23-33, 145-53, 168-73.

Paillieux, A. 1880. Le soya, sa composition, chimique, ses varietes, sa culture et ses usages. *Bulletin de la Societe d'Acclimatization* 27 (or 3rd Series vol. 7):414-71, 538-96.

Piper, C.V. and Morse, W.J. 1923. *The Soybean.* New York: Mc Graw-Hill. 329 p.

Poirier, Marie. 1982. *Le Plaisir de la Cuisine au Tofu.* Prevost, Quebec, Canada: Unisoya Inc. 52 p.

Pontecorvo, Aldo J. and Bourne, M.C. 1978. Simple methods for extending the shelf life of soy curd (tofu) in tropical areas. *J. of Food Science* 43:969-72.

Prinsen-Geerligs, H.C. 1895. Eenige Chineesche voedingsmiddeln uit Soja boonen bereid. *Pharmaceutisch Weekblad Voor Nederland* 32(33):1-2. Dec. 14.

Prinsen-Geerligs, H.C. 1896. Einige chinesische Sojabohnenpraparate. *Chemiker-Zeitung* 20(9):67-69 (Jan. 29).

Rein, J.J. 1899. *The Industries of Japan.* London: Hodder and Stoughton. pp 105-07. A translation of volume II of his *Japan nach reisen und studien.* publ. 1886.

Richard, C. 1959. Le chao. Fromage de soja fermente, sale, et alcoolise. *Societe des Etudes Indochinoises, Bulletin* (Saigon) 34:317-24.

Ritter, D. 1874. Tofu, yuba, ame. *Mitteilungen der Deutschen Gesellschaft fur Natur- und Volkerkunde Ostasiens* 1(5):3-4.

Rose, M.S. and MacLeod, G. 1925. Maintenance values for the proteins of milk, meat, bread and milk, and soy bean curd. *J. of Biological Chemistry* 66:847-67.

Rouest, L. 1921. *Le Soja et son Lait Vegetal: Applications Agricoles et Industrielles.* Carcassonne (Aude), France: Lucie-Grazaille. 157 p.

Rovira, E. ed. 1979. *The What to Do with Tofu Cookbooklet.* Philadelphia, PA: The Grow-cery, 6526 Landsowne Ave, 19151. 28 p.

Rudzinsky, Russ. 1969. *Japanese Country Cookbook.* San Francisco: Nitty Gritty Productions. 192 p.

Ruhräh, John. 1909. The soy bean in infant feeding. Preliminary report. *Archives of Pediatrics* 26:496-501. (July).

Saio, K., Sato, I. and Watanabe, T. 1974. Food use of soybean 7S and 11S proteins. High temperature expansion characteristics of gels. *J. of Food Science* 39:777-82.

Saio, K., Terashima, M. and Watanabe, T. 1975. Food use of soybean 7S and 11S proteins. Heat denaturation of soybean proteins at high temperature. *J. of Food Science* 40:537-40.

Sass, L.J. 1980. A couple on a tofu mission in the West. *New York Times.* Sept 24.

Sass, L.J. 1981. Soyfoods: Versatile, cheap and on the rise. *New York Times.* Aug. 12. p. C1, C6. Widely syndicated.

Satow, E.M. 1900. The Voyage of Captain John Saris to Japan, 1613. *Hakluyt Society,* London. Vol. 5, Series 2. p. 124.

Schmit, Matthew. 1978. *Peaking Out on Tofu.* Telluride, CO: Self published. 16 p.

Schroder, D.J. and Jackson, H. 1972. Preparation and evaluation of soybean curd with reduced beany flavor. *J. of Food Science* 37:450-51.

Science News Letter. 1943. Soybean curd makes good cottage cheese substitute. Dec. 4:360.

Senft, E. 1872. Untersuchung von chinesischen Oelbohnen. *Chemische Ackersmann.* p. 122-25.

Senft, E. 1907. Ueber einige in Japan verwendete vegetabilische nahrungsmittel mit besonderer beruecksichtigung der japanischen militaerkonserven. *Pharmazeutische Praxis* 6(3):81-89; 6(4):122-24, 131-32.

Shaw, Norman. 1911. *The Soya Bean of Manchuria.* Shanghai: Statistical Dept. of the Inspectorate General of Customs. II. Special Series No. 31. 32 p.

Sheppard, Sally. 1981. *Tofu Cookbook.* Salt Lake City, UT: Jack's Beanstalk. 99 p.

Shih, Chi-yien. 1918. *Beans and Bean Products.* Shanghai: Soochow Univ. Biology Dept. 13 p.

Shinoda, Osamu. 1971. Tofu-ko ("Thoughts on Tofu"). *Sekai.* p. 30-37.

Shinoda, Osamu. 1974. *Chugoku Shokumotsu-shi ("History of Chinese Foods").* Tokyo: Shibata Shoten. 389 p.

Shufu-no-tomo. 1972. *Ryori Hakka* (Encyclopedia of Japanese Cookery). Tokyo: Shufu-no-tomo.

Shurtleff, W. and Aoyagi, A. 1975. *The Book of Tofu.* Brookline, MA: Autumn Press. 336 p.

Shurtleff, W. and Aoyagi, A. 1977. *The Book of Kudzu.* Lafayette, CA: The Soyfoods Center. 104 p.

Shurtleff, W. and Aoyagi, A. 1979. *The Book of Tempeh: Super Soyfood from Indonesia.* New York: Harper & Row. Paperback 160 p. Professional hardcover 248 p.

Shurtleff, W. and Aoyagi, A. 1979. *Tofu & Soymilk Production.* Lafayette, CA: The Soyfoods Center. 336 p.

Shurtleff, W. and Aoyagi, A. 1979. *The Book of Tofu.* New York: Ballantine Books. 434 p. Extensively revised.

Shurtleff, W. and Aoyagi, A. 1981. *Das Tofu Buch.* Soyen, W. Germany: Ahorn Verlag. 286 p.

Shurtleff, W. and Aoyagi, A. 1981. La Soya y Sus Derivados: Tofu, Miso, Tempeh. *Quadernos de Natura.* No. 20. 87 p.

Shurtleff, W. and Aoyagi, A. 1982. *Using Tofu, Tempeh & Other Soyfoods in Restaurants, Delis & Cafeterias.* Lafayette, CA: The Soyfoods Center. 116 p.

Shurtleff, W. and Aoyagi, A. 1983. *The Book of Miso.* Berkeley, CA: Ten Speed Press. 256 p.

Shurtleff, W. and Aoyagi, A. 1983. *Soyfoods Industry and Market: Directory and Databook.* Lafayette, CA: The Soyfoods Center. 116 p.

Simonds, N. 1979. Chinese cuisine: Bean curd. *Gourmet.* Sept., p. 28-29, 84-91.

Sinclair, P. et al. 1974. Soybean in family meals. *USDA Home and Garden Bulletin* No. 208. 26 p.

Smith, A.K. and Beckel, A.C. 1946. Soybean or vegetable milk. *Soybean Digest* 6(7):18-23 or *Chemical and Engineering News.* 24:54-56.

Smith, A.K. 1949. Oriental use of soybeans as food. *Soybean Digest.* Feb:15-17, March:26-34, April:23-31, May:24-30, June:15-22.

Smith, A.K. 1949. *Oriental methods of using soybeans as food with special attention to fermented products.* USDA, AIC-234. June. 40 p. Reissued as ARS-71-17, July 1961. 65 p.

Smith, A.K. 1958. Use of U.S. soybeans in Japan. *USDA Bulletin* ARS-71-12. 36 p.

Smith, A.K., Watanabe, T. and Nash, A. 1960. Tofu from Japanese and United States Soybeans. *Food Technology.* July:332-36.

Smith, A.K. 1961. *Oriental Methods of Using Soybeans as Food. With Special Attention to Fermented Products and Notes on Oriental Farming Practices.* USDA/ARS-71-17. 65 p.

Smith, A.K. 1962. Problems involved in increasing world-wide use of soybean products as foods—technical assistance in developing soybean markets. In *Proceedings of Conference on Soybean Products for Protein in Human Foods.* USDA-NRRC, Peoria, IL, Sept 13-15, 1961. p. 214-16.

Smith, A.K. 1963. Foreign uses of soybean protein foods. *Cereal Science Today* 8(6):196, 198, 200, 210.

Smith, A.K. and Circle, S.J. eds. 1972. *Soybeans: Chemistry and Technology.* Vol 1, Proteins. Westport, CT: AVI Publishing Co. 470 p. Slightly revised, 1978.

Soyanews. 1978-83. Articles about tofu in Sri Lanka. Colombo, Sri Lanka. P.O. Box 1024. Feb. 1978; Aug., Sept. 1980; Feb., June 1981; April, May, Oct. 1982.

Soybean Digest. 1950. Soy foods from a unique college (Madison). Nov. p. 14-15.

Soybean Digest. 1960. USDA research may put more U.S. soybeans in Japanese foods. Feb. p. 20-21.

Soybean Digest. 1965. Research leads to a new food market for soybeans. June. p. 16.

Soyfoods magazine. 1979 to date. Every issue has articles about tofu. 100 Heath Rd., Colrain, MA 01340.

Stahel, G. 1946. Foods from fermented soybeans as prepared in the Netherlands Indies. I. Taohoo, a cheese-like substance, and some other products. *J. of the New York Botanical Garden* 47:261 67.

Standal, B.R. 1963 Nutritional value of proteins of Oriental soybean foods. *J. of Nutrition* 81:279-85.

Steiman, H. 1980. Tofu: Trader Vic Americanizes an Asian staple. *San Francisco Examiner.* Sept 3. p. B7-8.

Stein, E. 1978. Making money making tofu. *Whole Foods.* Jan. p. 32-37.

Steinberg, Raphael, 1969. *The Cookery of Japan.* New York: Time-Life Books.

Stern, Arthur M. 1952. *Studies on the Physiology of Mucor mucedo and its Role in the fermentation of Soybean Curds.* Univ. of Illinois Thesis. (from University Microfilms, 3150).

Strayer, G.M. 1956. Japanese tofu makers don't like green beans or foreign material. *Soybean Digest.* March. p. 20, 22.

Stuart, G.A. 1911. *Chinese Materia Medica:* Vegetable Kingdom. Shanghai: American Presbyterian Mission Press. p. 189-96.

Suchi, T. 1888. Digestion experiments with rice and tofu. *Tokyo Igakkai Zasshi* (J. of the Tokyo Medical Socy.) 2:457, 511.

T'ao Ku. 10th century A.D. *Ch'ing I Lu.* Earliest known Chinese reference to tofu.

Time magazine. 1980. Climbing curd. Feb. 25. p. 62.

Timmins, T. 1978. New England's tofu shop. *Soycraft Newsletter* 1(2):1-3. Winter.

Tremblay, Yvon and Boyte, Frances. 1982. *La Magie du Tofu.* Montreal and Paris: Stanké Ltee. 101 p.

Trimble. H. 1896. Recent literature on the soja bean. *American J. of Pharmacy* 68:309-13.

Tseng, R.Y.L., et al. 1977. Calcium and phosphorous contents and ratios in tofu as affected by the coagulants used. *Home Economics Research Journal* 6(2):171-75.

Tsuda, Tadao et al. 1974. *Shojin Ryori* (Zen Temple Cookery). Tokyo: Fujokai Shuppansha. 242 p.

Tsuji, Kaichi. 1962. *Tofu Ryori* (Tofu Cookery). Tokyo: Fujin Gaho.

Tsuji, Kaichi. 1971. *Zen Tastes in Japanese Cooking.* Tokyo: Kodansha. 207 p.

USDA Weekly News Letter. 1918. Cooking soy beans. 5(21):6. Soy beans as food. 5(34):6. Soy beans, used like navy kind, make valuable food. 5(42).

U.S. Dept. of Health, Education, and Welfare. 1972. *Food Composition Table for Use in East Asia.* Nutrition Program, Center for Disease Control, HEW, Atlanta, GA 30333. 334 p.

Van Gundy, Dorothea. 1936. *La Sierra Recipes.* Ontario, CA: Self published. 47 p.

Vitale, E. and Brock T. 1977. Plowboy interview with Shurtleff and Aoyagi. *Mother Earth News.* No. 44. March-April. p. 8-18.

Waggoner, D. 1980. With his *Book of Tofu* William Shurtleff hopes to bring soy to the world. *People* magazine. Oct. p. 57-58.

Wai, Nganshou. 1929. A new species of mono-mucor, *Mucor sufu,* on Chinese soybean cheese. *Science* 70:307-08.

Wai, Nganshou. 1964. Soybean cheese. *Bulletin of the Institute of Chemistry* (Taiwan). Academia Sinica 9. July. p. 75-94.

Wai, Nganshou. 1968. *Investigation of the various processes used in preparing Chinese cheese by the fermentation of soybean curd with mucor and other fungi.* Final Technical Report. Institute of Chemistry, Academia Sinica, Taiwan.

Wai, N. 1968. *Final Technical Report: Chinese Cheese.* USDA Grant No. FG-Ta-100, Project No. UR-A6-(40)-1. 90 p.

Wang, H.L. 1967. Products from soybeans. *Food Technology* 21: 115-16.

Wang, H.L. 1967. Release of protease from mycelium of *Mucor hiemalis. J. of Bacteriology* 93:1794-99.

Wang, H.L. and Hesseltine, C.W. 1970. Sufu and lao-chao. *J. of Agricultural and Food Chemistry* 18(4):572-75.

Wang, H.L., Ellis, J.J. and Hesseltine, C.W. 1972. Antibacterial activity produced by molds commonly used in Oriental food preparations. *Mycologia* 64(1):218-21.

Wang, H.L. et al. 1977. *An Inventory of Information on the Utilization of Unprocessed and Simply Processed Soybeans as Human Food.* Peoria, IL: USDA Northern Regional Research Center. AID AG/TAB-225-12-76. 197 p.

Wang, H.L. and Hesseltine, C.W. 1979. Mold-modified foods. In *Microbial Technology,* 2nd ed. Vol. II, H.J. Peppler ed. New York: Academic Press. p. 95-129.

Watanabe, T. et al. 1960. Tofu seizo kotei no hyojunka ni taisuru kenkyu. (Research into the standardization of the tofu making process.) *Report of the Food Research Institute No. 14B.* Tokyo. Part 1, regular tofu; part 2, silken tofu; part 3, bagged lactone silken tofu. p. 6-30.

Watanabe, T. 1969. Industrial Production of Soybean Foods in Japan. Presented at *Expert Group Meeting on Soya Bean Processing and Use,* Peoria, IL 17-21 No. 1969. United Nations Industrial Dev. Org. 38 p.

Watanabe Tokuji, Ebine Hideo, and Ota Teruo. 1971. *Daizu Shokuhin* (Soyfoods). Tokyo: Korin Shoin. 270 p.

Watanabe, T., Ebine, H. and Okada, M. 1974. New protein food technologies in Japan. In *New Protein Foods. Vol. 1A. Technology.* (A.M. Altschul, ed.). New York: Academic Press. p. 414-53.

Watt, B.K. and Merrill, A.L. 1963. *Composition of Foods.* USDA, Food Economics Research Div., Agriculture Handbook No. 8. 190 p.

Wells, P. 1978. What is this thing called tofu? *New York Times,* May 3, p. 19-20.

Whiteman, Elizabeth F., and Keyt, Ellen K. 1938. *Soybeans for the Table.* USDA Leaflet No. 166. 6 p.

Whole Foods. 1979. The soyfoods revolution (Cover story). Jan. 44 p.

Winarno, F.G. et al. 1976. *The Present Status of Soybean in Indonesia.* Bogor, Indonesia: FATEMETA, Bogor Agricultural University. 128 p.

Women's College of Nutrition. 1969. *Tofu, Mame, Miso Ryori: Ju-ni Kagetsu* (Tofu, Soybean, and Miso Cookery Throughout the Twelve Months). Tokyo: Joshi Eiyo Daigaku.

Wood, B.J.B. and Hounan, L.L. 1981. 'Dairy' products from soya beans. *Proceedings of Dairy Symposium at the Food Industries Exhibition, London.* 19 p.

Wu, Ch'i-chun. 1848. Ta Tou (the soy bean). In *Chih wu ming shih t'u k'ao.* T'ai-yuan-fu, Shansi, China. 98 p. Translated into English and indexed by W.J. Hagerty, USDA, Washington, D.C. 1917. With photocopies of plates.

Yamaguchi, H.S.K. 1934-50. *We Japanese.* Yokohama, Japan: Yamagata Press. 590 p.

Yao, M.Y. and Peng, A.C. 1979. New chemical coagulant for making soybean curd. *Ohio Report* 64(1):11.

Yeo, V. and Wellington, G.H. 1974. Effects of soy curd on the acceptability and characteristics of beef patties. *J. of Food Science* 39:288-92.

ABOUT WORLD HUNGER

The three most important works are starred.

Berg, Alan. 1973. *The Nutrition Factor.* The Brookings Institute, 1775 Massachusetts Ave., N.W., Washington, D.C. 20036. A nutrition expert on the staff of the World Bank, Berg discusses the way hunger in the Third World is linked to underdevelopment and malnutrition.

Borgstrom, Georg. 1974. *The Food/People Dilemma.* New York: Duxbury Press.

_____. 1973. *World Food Resources.* New York: Intext.

_____. 1972. *The Hungry Planet.* New York: Collier-Macmillan. A professor at Michigan State Univ., Borgstrom examines the food/population problem from an environmentalist's point of view, focusing on the effects of uneven food distribution between the rich and poor nations.

Brown, Lester R. 1974. *By Bread Alone.* New York: Praeger. One of the best books on the world food crisis. Head of the newly formed Worldwatch Institute in Washington, D.C., Brown is a highly articulate agricultural economist with a clear vision of the present problem and its solutions. His other recent writings include *In the Human Interest* (1973), *World Without Borders* (1972), and *Seeds of Change* (1970).

*Brown, Lester R. 1978. *The Twenty-Ninth Day: Accommodating Human Needs and Numbers to the Earth's Resources.* New York: W.W. Norton, 363 p. Outstanding!

Brown, Lester R. 1981. *Building a Sustainable Society.* New York: W.W. Norton & Co. 433 p. A great work.

George, Susan. 1977. *How the Other Half Dies: The Real Reasons for World Hunger.* Montclair, NJ: Allanheld, Osmun & Co. 308 p.

Lappé, Frances M. 1982. *Diet for a Small Planet* (Revised Edition). San Francisco: Ballantine/Friends of the Earth. 498 p. A two million-copy bestseller and one of the most influential books ever written concerning the world food crisis and basic nutrition. Emphasis on protein complementarity, meatless meals, and the wisdom of eating low on the food chain.

*Lappé, F.M., and Collins, J. 1978. *Food First:: Beyond the Myth of Scarcity.* New York: Ballantine Paperback. Revised edition. 19 p. The finest and most up-to-date book on the world food crisis. A must! Available at reduced rates from the Institute for Food and Development Policy, 2588 Mission Street, San Francisco, Calif. 94110.

Lerza, Catherine, and Jacobson, Michael, ed. 1975. *Food for People Not for Profit.* New York: Ballantine. This official handbook for Food Day 1975 contains a wealth of information concerning every aspect of the food crisis; each chapter written by an authority in the field.

Manocha, Sohan L. 1975. *Nutrition and Our Overpopulated Planet.* Springfield, Ill: Charles C. Thomas. An extensive and up-to-date treatment of the population/food crisis and means for its solution.

*Mesarovic, M., and Pestel, E. 1974. *Mankind at the Turning Point: The Second Report to the Club of Rome.* New York: Signet. The successor to *The Limits of Growth,* this highly readable and condensed book, based on sophisticated computer models, spells out clearly what we can and must do to avoid worldwide famine and catastrophe in the near future.

Miller, G. Tyler. 1975. *Living in the Environment.* Belmont, CA: Wadsworth. An excellent ecology textbook with extensive material concerning the population/food crisis and the means of its solution.

Japanese sea-vegetables

Glossary

The following Japanese-style ingredients, referred to in the recipe sections of this book, are generally available in the West at Japanese food markets and at a growing number of natural and health food stores. For local addresses look in the Yellow Pages under Japanese (or Chinese) Food Products or Oriental Goods.

AGAR *(kanten):* A sea vegetable gelatin made from the genera *Gelidium* and *Gracilaria.* Sold in the form of flakes, bars, powder, and strands.

AMAZAKÉ: Literally "sweet sake." A creamy thick drink with a rich, sweet flavor and virtually no alcohol content. Made from rice *koji* or steamed rice overgrown with a fragrant white mycelium of *Aspergillus oryzae* mold.

AZUKI BEANS: These small red beans *(Vigna angularis)* are cooked with glutinous rice or used to make a sweet filling for confections.

BEEFSTEAK PLANT *(shiso):* This fragrant herb *(Perilla nankinensis)* is prized for its versatility: beefsteak buds and blossoms *(mejiso and hojiso)* are garnishes, beefsteak seeds *(shisonomi)* are a condiment, green beefsteak leaves *(aojiso)* can be used like mint, and red beefsteak leaves *(shisonoha)* are used in making salt plums, pickles, and confections.

BENI-TADÉ: Also called *akamé* or "red bud," these tiny purple leaflike sprouts are used as a garnish for chilled tofu.

BONITO FLAKES *(Hana katsuo):* A popular garnish and basis for soup stocks made by shaving hard-as-wood, dried fermented bonito *(katsuobushi).*

BRACKEN FERN *(warabi):* The olive green young fiddlenecks of *Pteridium aquilinum.* Parboiled and served as a delicacy.

BREAD CRUMB FLAKES *(panko):* Similar to bread crumbs except that each particle has been rolled under pressure to form a tiny, thin flake. Used in deep-fried breadings.

BURDOCK ROOT *(gobo):* *Arctium lappa* has a long, dark-brown tapering root ½ to 1 inch in diameter and 18 to 24 inches long.

BUTTERBUR *(fuki):* The 4-foot-long, ½-inch-diameter stem of this spring vegetable, *Petasites japonicus,* has a flavor resembling that of celery.

CHILIES *(togarashi):* Japanese chilies *(Capsicum annum),* usually sold dried, are 2½ inches long and fiery hot. See also 7-spice chili powder.

CHINESE CABBAGE *(hakusai):* Splendidly tight and crisp heads of *Brassica pekinensis* are as delicious as they are inexpensive.

CHIVES: Popular Japanese varieties include *asatsuki (Allium ledebourianum)* and *nira (Allium tuberosum).*

CHRYSANTHEMUM LEAVES *(shungiku):* The fragrant greens of *Chrysanthemum coronarium* resemble spinach or trefoil.

CLOUD-EAR MUSHROOM *(kikuragé):* A delicate variety with a wavy cap, *Auricularia auricula-judae* grows on trees and has virtually no stem. Solid dried, it is also known as Dried Black Fungus or Wood Ear.

DAIKON: The marvelously versatile Japanese giant white radish *(Raphanus sativus)* is often as thick as a man's arm and 18 to 24 inches long.

EGGPLANT *(nasu):* The Japanese variety *(Solanum melongena),* sweeter and more tender than its American counterpart, averages 4½ inches in length and 1½ inches in diameter, and weighs 2 ounces.

ENOKIDAKÉ: This pale white mushroom *(Flammulina velutipes),* has a 5-inch-long stem and a tiny 3/8-inch-diameter cap. Usually sold fresh.

GINGERROOT *(shoga):* The 4-inch-long knobby tan root of *Zingiber officinale* is peeled and freshly grated. Two parts by volume of powdered ginger may be substituted for 1 part fresh grated gingerroot. Gingerroot shoots *(shin shoga)* are a popular soup garnish and red pickled gingerroot *(beni-shoga)* is thinly sliced and served with Inari-zushi.

GINKGO NUTS *(ginnan):* These tender ½-inch-long delicacies from the giant *Ginkgo bilboa* tree are sold fresh or canned.

GLUTINOUS RICE *(mochigomé):* Used to make mochi and a variety of treats, *Oryzae sativa glutinosa* contains no amylase, and therefore cooks to a sticky, moist consistency. Occasionally known in the West as sweet rice.

GLUTINOUS RICE *(tororo imo):* When rubbed on a fine metal grater, these yams (all of the Genus *Dioscorea)* develop a highly cohesive, glutinous quality. Available fresh in many varieties, including *jinenjo* and *yamanoimo.*

GREEN NORI FLAKES *(aonoriko):* A sea vegetable seasoning made by crumbling the fragrant, bright-green fronds of dried *Enteromorpha prolifera.* Delicious on noodles.

HEMP SEEDS *(asanomi):* The tiny light green seeds of *Cannabis sativa,* about the size of sesame or poppy seeds, are widely used in Japanese deep-fried tofu burgers.

HIJIKI: A stringy black sea vegetable *(Hizikia fusiforme)* sold in pieces about 1½ inches long. Often misspelled "hiziki" in the West.

JUNSAI: A "water shield" *(Brasenia purpurea),* this tiny wild pond plant, surrounded by a slippery gelatinous coating, is used in soups.

KABOCHA: Also called Hokkaido pumpkin, this delectable fall vegetable *(Cucurbita moschata),* with its dark-green edible skin, looks like a 6-to-8-inch-diameter acorn squash. Substitute winter squash or pumpkin.

KAMPYO: Strips shaved from the dried *yugao* gourd or calabash *(Lagenaria siceraria)* are used for tying food into bundles or rolls.

KATAKURIKO: Japan's most popular, low-cost cooking starch. Often synonymous with potato starch.

KINAKO: Roasted soy flour; see Chapter 4.

KINOMÉ: The fragrant, bright green sprigs of the *sansho* tree *(Zanthoxylum piperitum)* are plucked in the spring and used as a garnish.

KOMBU: A sea vegetable *(Laminaria* species) somewhat resembling kelp and sold as leathery olive brown fronds. 3 to 6 inches wide and 2½ to 6 feet long. Used to make soup stocks and in stews.

KONNYAKU: Eight-ounce gray, firm jellylike cakes made from the starch of *Amorphallus konjac*, the devil's tongue plant, a relative of the sweet potato. Konnyaku threads *(ito konnyaku)* and noodles *(shirataki)* are used in one-pot cookery.

KUDZU POWDER *(kuzu-ko):* The white, starchlike powder extracted from the roots of the kudzu vine *(Pueraria lobata),* which grows abundantly in the southeast U.S., is a high quality cooking starch and natural medicine widely used in East Asia. For details see *The Book of Kudzu* by Shurtleff and Aoyagi.

LEEK *(negi):* The Japanese leek *(Allium fistulosum)* or Welsh onion is somewhat sweeter, mellower, and faster cooking than its Western counterpart.

LILLY BULB *(yuriné):* These fresh roots, about the size and shape of a bulb of garlic, have a mild flavor and are used in tofu treasure balls. The bulb of the tiger lily *(oni yuri; Lilium lancifolium)* is most widely used but those of the Maximowicz's lily *(L. maximowiczii)* and star lily *(L. concolor)* are also used.

LOTUS ROOT *(renkon):* The sausage shaped roots of the lotus *(Nelumbo nucifera),* which grow in the mud at the bottom of ponds, are 2 to 3 inches in diameter and 5 to 8 inches long. Prized for their crisp texture, they are best when fresh.

MANDARIN ORANGE *(mikan):* Japan's most popular and least expensive domestic fresh fruit, it is available from November until March. Delicious.

MATCHA: Powdered green tea, widely used in the tea ceremony.

MATSUTAKÉ: The most expensive and most delicious of Japanese mushrooms, *Trichloma matsutaké* grows a cap up to 8 inches in diameter.

MIRIN: Sweet sake used only for cooking. For each tablespoon of mirin called for, you may substitute ½ teaspoon honey or 2 teaspoons sake or pale dry sherry. Or you may substitute 1½ teaspoons honey and 2½ teaspoons water.

MISO: Fermented soybean paste; see Chapter 4.

MIZUAMÉ: A natural grain sugar extracted from rice, millet, or barley, it looks like a solid, pale-amber resin and may be softened by heating. Also sold as Millet Jelly, Amé, or Rice Honey. Close relatives are barley malt syrup and sorghum molasses.

MOCHI: Cakes of steamed, pounded glutinous rice, each about 3 by 2 by ½ inches.

MUSHROOMS: See Cloud-ear mushroom, *enokidaké, matsutaké, nameko, shiitaké,* and *shimeji.*

MYOGA: The pinkish white buds of the *Zingiber mioga* that emerge from the plant's base each August are a popular garnish.

NAMEKO: Tiny yellowish-brown mushrooms with a slippery coating, *pholiota namcko* are sold fresh or canned.

NATTO: Fermented whole soybeans; see Chapter 4.

NIGARI: Bittern or bitterns. The traditional Japanese tofu coagulant extracted from clean seawater. See Chapter 8.

NOODLES *(menrui):* See rice-flour noodles, ramen, soba, somen, and udon.

NORI: A sea vegetable sold in paper-thin purplish-black sheets about 8 inches square and packaged in bundles of ten. The Japanese presently consume about 9 *billion* sheets each year. Other *Porphyra* species are known in the West as laver.

OSMUND FERN *(zenmai):* The slender young fiddlenecks of *Osmunda japonica* are a springtime delicacy.

PICKLES *(tsukemono):* Salt pickled vegetables *(shiozuké),* miso pickles *(misozuke),* and rice-bran pickles *(nukamiso-zuké)* are widely used as seasonings in Japan. Famous varieties include *Narazuké* (Uri melons pickled in sake lees) and *Takuan* (dried daikon pickled in nukamiso).

RAMEN: Crinkly yellowish-white Chinese noodles now widely used in Japan, especially in the form of Instant Ramen.

RICE FLOUR *(joshinko):* Finely ground white rice widely used in the preparation of steamed desserts and dumplings *(dango).*

RICE FLOUR NOODLES: Slender, round, white noodles about 10 inches long; popular in salads.

SAKÉ: Japanese rice wine containing about 15 percent alcohol and widely used in cooking. The lees *(sake-no-kasu)* are used in dressings and soups and for pickling other foods.

SALT PLUM *(umeboshi):* The partially ripe fruit of the *Prunus mumé* (which is actually more like an apricot than a plum), is salt pickled, usually with red beefsteak leaves, and used as both a tart seasoning with rice or in salad dressings, or as a highly alkaline natural medicine.

SANSHO PEPPER *(kona zansho):* A fragrant and spicy brownish-green pepper made from the seedpods of the *sansho* tree *(Zanthoxylum piperitum),* the same tree that bears *kinomé* sprigs.

SEA VEGETABLES *(kaiso):* See agar, green nori flakes, hijiki, kombu, nori, and wakame.

SESAME SEEDS *(goma):* The delicious calcium-rich seeds come in white and black varieties and are usually lightly roasted and ground before use. Substitute one half the amount of sesame butter or tahini.

SEVEN-SPICE CHILI POWDER *(shichimi togarashi):* A zippy blend of ground dried chilies and other spices including sesame, *sansho,* grated dried orange peel, green nori flakes, and white pepper.

SHIITAKÉ: Japan's most popular mushroom, *Lentinus edodes* is sold fresh or dried and widely sauteed or used as a basis for stocks.

SHIMEJI: Small mushrooms with tan caps 1 to 1½ inches in diameter, *Lyophyllum aggregatum* are usually sold fresh.

SHOCHU: A popular and very potent type of inexpensive spirits related to gin and often made from sweet potatoes.

SHOYU: Japanese all-purpose soy sauce; see Chapter 4.

SNOW PEAS *(saya endo):* Also called edible-pod peas, these are the paper-thin type widely associated with Chinese cookery.

SOBA: Japanese buckwheat noodles. A great food.

SOMEN: Very slender wheat-flour noodles, usually served chilled in summertime. Substitute vermicelli.

SPINACH *(horenso):* *Spinacia oleracea* is milder and slightly sweeter than its Western counterpart. Delicious.

SUDARÉ: A bamboo mat about 10 inches square used for rolling sushi and other foods.

SURIBACHI: An earthenware grinding bowl or mortar with a serrated interior surface, the usual suribachi is 10 inches in a diameter and 3½ inches deep, and is accompanied by a wooden pestle *(surikogi).*

SWEET POTATO *(satsuma imo):* One of Japan's most beloved and tastiest foods, *Ipomoea batatas* has no exact counterpart in the West. About 1½ to 2½ inches in diameter and 4 to 8 inches long, it has a pale red skin and a light-yellow, richly-flavored meat.

TAHINI: A smooth creamy paste made from unroasted or very lightly roasted, hulled white sesame seeds. Due to the removal of the calcium-rich hulls, tahini is not as nutritious as sesame butter, and some commercial varieties use caustic soda in the cleaning and dehulling process. Contains 19 percent protein.

TAMARI: A type of soy sauce resembling shoyu; see Chapter 4.

TARO: A 2½-inch-diameter root vegetable also known in the West as dasheen or albi; the most popular of the many Japanese varieties are *sato imo (Colocasia antiquorum), yatsugashira,* and *akame imo.* Rich, creamy, and delicious. Used to make Hawaii's *poi.*

TOGAN: Also known in English as "white gourd," *Benincasa hispida* is a mild flavored vegetable.

TRANSPARENT NOODLES *(harusamé):* This slender vermicelli, made from mung beans or sweet potatoes, is also popular in Chinese cookery.

TREFOIL *(mitsuba):* Prized for its unique pungent aroma and handsome green leaves. *Cryptotaenia japonica* is most widely used as a garnish.

TURNIP *(kabu):* The Japanese *Brassica rapa* is a heart-shaped white root about 3 inches in diameter having a mild, slightly sweet flavor.

UDO: Neither quite celery nor asparagus, *Aralia cordata* is a crisp and tender oddity with a unique hint of lemon flavor that is enjoyed fresh or cooked. The best varieties grow wild.

UDON: Fat, white, wheat-flour noodles similar to a No. 2 spaghetti.

URI MELON *(shirouri):* Also called "white melon," "white gourd melon," or "Oriental pickling melon," *Cucumis melo* var. *conomon* is a pale green fruit shaped like a cucumber about 12 inches long and 3 inches in diameter. Widely pickled in sake lees or miso.

WAKAME: A dark-green sea vegetable *(Undaria pinnatifida)* with fronds about 3 inches wide and 12 to 18 inches long, it is sold both fresh and dried; widely used in soups and salads.

WASABI: A hot green horseradish-like paste made from the grated root of the *wasabi* plant *(Wasabia japonica)* which is cultivated in terraced mountain stream beds. Sold fresh or powdered.

WHEAT GLUTEN *(fu):* Both fresh and dried varieties, sold in a multitude of shapes, are widely used in Japanese cookery.

YUZU: A citrus fruit similar to a citron, lime, or lemon, the fruit of the *yuzu* tree *(Citrus junos)* has a green to yellow, refreshingly fragrant rind which is slivered or grated and widely used in soups, sauces, and tofu or miso preparations.

Note: Monosodium glutamate (MSG), a flavor intensifier also known as Aji-no-moto or Accent, is a highly refined white crystalline powder that differs in structure from natural glutamic acid. When used in more than very small quantities, it is well known to produce in some people the "Chinese Restaurant Syndrome" characterized by headaches, burning sensations, a feeling of pressure in the chest, and other discomforting symptoms. Originally extracted from kombu, it is now produced by fermentation or hydrolysis of molasses or glucose from tapioca, cornstarch, potato starch, etc. We and many others interested in natural healthy foods strictly avoid use of this product.

Index

THE SOYFOODS CENTER, founded in 1976 by William Shurtleff and Akiko Aoyagi, has offices in California. Our basic goals and activities are related to soyfoods and world hunger.

Soyfoods: Our center is, above all, a source of information about soyfoods, especially tofu, soymilk, tempeh, and miso, about which we have done extensive research and written books and recipe pamphlets. Like a growing number of people, we feel that soybeans will be one of the key protein sources of the future on planet Earth, and that both traditional and modern soyfoods from East and West will serve as important sources of delicious, high-quality, low-cost protein in the diets of people everywhere, regardless of their income. We are interested in each of the following soyfoods, listed here in what we consider to be their approximate order of potential worldwide importance: tofu (soybean curd), soy flour, soymilk, tempeh, shoyu (natural soy sauce), textured soy protein (TVP), miso, whole dry soybeans, soy protein isolates and concentrates, roasted soybeans or soy nuts, fresh green soybeans, roasted full-fat soy flour (*kinako*), soy sprouts, yuba, and natto. We have developed hundreds of tasty and nutritious Western-style recipes for the use of these foods and compiled extensive, up-to-date information on their nutritional value, history, and production.

World Hunger: Presently more than 15,000,000 people die each year of starvation and malnutrition-caused diseases; three fourths of these are children. We constantly relate our work to this urgent problem of world hunger by studying and developing creative, low-cost, village-level methods for soyfood production using appropriate technology, by traveling and speaking in less developed countries, and by sending complementary copies of our publications to and communicating with key soyfoods researchers and producers in these countries.

Meatless Diets: Over half of all agricultural land in the United States is now used to grow crops (such as corn, soybeans, oats, and wheat) that are fed to animals. The affluent American diet is emerging as a major cause of world hunger as well as of degenerative diseases such as heart disease and cancer. Soyfoods, which are low in cost, high in protein, low in saturated fats, free of cholesterol, and relatively low in calories, can be used as delicious replacements for meats and dairy products as part of meatless or vegetarian diets. We encourage the adoption of such diets which help to make best use of the planet's precious food resources, are conducive to the development of a healthy body and clear mind, kind to animals, economical, and ecologically sound.

Commercial Soyfood Production: We encourage and aid people throughout the world in starting community or commercial production of soyfoods by providing technical manuals, technical advice, materials, and equipment. We have helped to establish the *Soyfoods Association of North America* (SANA) and its international publication *Soyfoods*, to found *Bean Machines, Inc.* (a company selling tofu and soymilk equipment), and to develop catalogs of large and small scale equipment. We have compiled various technical manuals and presently serve as consultants for a wide variety of companies.

Lecture Demonstrations: We have done more than one hundred programs relating to soyfoods for natural food groups, research scientists, food technologists, nutritionists, commercial producers, university audiences, international symposia, home economists, and cooking schools. We have also done numerous television and radio programs and cooking classes throughout the world. We welcome invitations.

Soyfoods Center Network: Our main Center in California is devoted primarily to research and publication about soyfoods. We have the world's largest library (more than 3,500 documents) on soyfoods. Our growing International Soyfoods Center Network, with branches around the world, is helping to introduce soyfoods around the world.

New Lifestyles: Our work is deeply involved in the development of lifestyles conducive to the welfare and survival of all beings on planet Earth. Thus we encourage voluntary simplicity, self-sufficiency (particularly food self-sufficiency on personal, regional, and national levels), right livelihood, a deeper understanding of selfless service, and of daily life and work as a spiritual practice, ecological awareness, holistic health, appropriate technology, the rapid development and adoption of solar energy, and the phasing out of nuclear energy.

Publications and Catalog: Our Center has published a number of full-sized specialty books on soyfoods including Tofu & Soymilk Production, Miso Production, Tempeh Production, Soyfoods Industry and Market: Directory and Databook, and History of Soybeans and Soyfoods. We also provide a free catalog listing our other widely distributed books on tofu, miso, and tempeh, materials such as pamphlets, tofu kits, and slide shows related to soyfoods, and a list of soyfoods manufacturers in North America and Europe.

Your Financial Support and Help: Our work, now reaching people throughout the world, is not supported by government or corporate funds. We do, however, welcome contributions of any size from individuals and private foundations to aid us in furthering the soyfoods revolution and helping to put an end to world hunger. We have established *Friends of The Center* for supporters willing to contribute $35.00 or more; smaller contributions are also welcomed. If you would like to contribute your time and energy to our work, please contact us.

Bill Shurtleff & Akiko Aoyagi Shurtleff
The Soyfoods Center
P.O. Box 234
Lafayette, CA 94549 USA
Tel. 415-283-2991

ABOUT THE AUTHORS

William Shurtleff and Akiko Aoyagi Shurtleff spent their formative years on opposite sides of the Pacific. Born in California on 28 April 1941, Bill received degrees in engineering, honors humanities, and education from Stanford University. He taught physics for two tyears in Nigeria in the Peace Corps and has lived and traveled extensively in East Asia and Third World countries. He speaks seven languages, four fluently, including Japanese.

Akiko Aoyagi Shurtleff, born in Tokyo on 24 January 1950, received her education there from the Quaker-run Friends' School and the Women's College of Arts. She has worked as an illustrator and designer in Japan's modern fashion industry and America's emerging soyfoods industry.

Since 1972 Bill and Akiko have been working together, doing research and writing books about soyfoods. They have lived for six years in East Asia, mainly in Japan, studying with top soyfoods researchers, manufacturers, nutritionists, historians, and cooks. Over 500,000 copies of their eleven books on soyfoods are now in print. The titles and publishers are listed on the copyright page at the beginning of this book.

In 1976 Bill and Akiko founded The Soyfoods Center, and since that time they have worked to introduce soyfoods, especially traditional low-technology soyfoods, to the Western world. They feel that soyfoods can play a key role in helping to solve the world food crisis while providing high-quality low-cost protein and healthier diets for people everywhere. Their work has led to the establishment of hundreds of soyfoods businesses making tofu,

soymilk, miso, tempeh, and other soyfoods, and to the publication by others of more than 25 books about these foods. Their nationwide tours and many lectures, demonstrations, and media appearances have drawn widespread acclaim.

Their global view and uniquely holistic, interdisciplinary approach are aimed at presenting the best of both traditional lore and modern scientific knowledge about soyfoods in a language accessible to both laymen and professionals.

By constantly addressing the problems of world hunger, the suffering of human beings and animals, and the perennial longing for good health and liberation, they hope to make their work relevant everywhere and a force for planetary renaissance.

If you would like to help in the larger work related to soyfoods and world hunger, if you have questions or suggestions related to this book, or if you would like to receive a free copy of their Soyfoods Center Catalog, the authors invite you to contact them.

THE SOYFOODS CENTER
P.O. Box 234
Lafayette, CA 94549 USA
(Phone: 415-283-2991)

SENDING TOFU TO THE FOUR DIRECTIONS

Many men and women throughout the world today are in search of meaningful work. In industrial and post-industrial societies, "alienated labor" is fast losing its appeal as respect for traditional craftsmanship revives and demand for its products grows steadily. In developing nations, where hunger is often a basic fact of daily life, countless individuals are in need of truly productive labor, labor which serves the fundamental needs of society. Whether in a rural village or bustling megalopolis, the traditional tofu shop could serve as a practical yet revolutionary means toward the satisfaction of all these crucial needs.

In any setting, the tofu shop can be set up and operated with a minimum of capital and technical know-how. To make the very best tofu, after all, requires only the simplest ingredients, tools, and workshop to make: soybeans which are or can be made available in bulk at relatively low prices almost everywhere; tools which can be handmade or purchased inexpensively; and a shop which need be no bigger than 12 by 15 feet and which, situated near or even adjacent to one's home, can be operated as a cottage industry, with the work and income shared by the members of one's family or community. Retailed directly or through secondary outlets, tofu products can be attractively priced anywhere in the world, and demand for these high-quality foods is bound to grow rapidly over the months and years ahead.

In Boulder or Boston, New Delhi or New Guinea, the daily practice of the traditional tofu-making art offers more than just the challenges and benefits of self-employment and independence. In its subtlety and depth, it can be an enriching exercise in concentration, heightened sensitivity, and creative self-expression. And like Gandhi's spinning, it can serve as the center of a regular pattern of daily life conducive to clear-mindedness, meditation, and peaceful living.

The obstacles to learning the tofu-making art are perhaps greatest in areas such as India, Africa, and South America, where tofu could make its most immediate contribution to human welfare. These obstacles can best and perhaps only be met on the national level. The Japanese government is presently taking an increasingly active role in aiding less developed nations. But only very recently have the Japanese themselves begun to recognize the unique treasure they possess in their traditional technologies for utilizing soybeans as food. We would urge the Japanese government to initiate a program whereby Japan's knowledge and experience in this field would be shared with receptive, protein-short countries around the world. A pilot program could be modeled on those the Japanese are now using effectively for other technologies: it might include the invitation of teams of foreign representatives to Japan to learn the tofu-making process in detail; the sponsoring of Japanese craftsmen in setting up schools abroad; and the subsidizing (where necessary) of private entrepreneurs invited to developing nations to open shops operated by host nationals. Similarly, we would urge the governments of developing nations to educate and encourage their citizens to incorporate tofu products into their daily diet.

Since 1976 over 185 new (Caucasian-run) tofu shops and soy dairies have been started throughout North America to bring the present total to 115. In 1978 representatives from these shops plus producers of tempeh, miso, shoyu, and other soyfoods established the Soyfoods Association of North America (SANA), a trade association to serve the burgeoning new industry. To aid in the establishment of tofu shops and soy dairies, we have written *Tofu & Soymilk Production: The Book of Tofu, Volume II* which is now available exclusively from our Soyfoods Center, P.O. Box 234, Lafayette, California, 94549. An easy to follow technical manual, it is based on over five years of research. In cooperation with Takai Tofu & Soymilk Equipment Co., Japan's largest and best known manufacturer, we have developed an illustrated English-language equipment catalog which is now available from The Soyfoods Center.

These developments now make it relatively easy for people everywhere to start their own tofu shops and soy dairies—and to send these fine foods to the four directions.